BU

BUDDHA

LIFE AND WORK OF THE FORERUNNER
IN INDIA

Received in the proximity of Abd-ru-shin
through the special gift of
one Called for the purpose

To
SD Julie
+ Spencer,
may this book be an inspiration of strength
to you all as it has been to me.
With all my love,
Poppy
Christopher

April, 1996

GRAIL · FOUNDATION · PRESS
GAMBIER, OHIO

Original German edition:
Buddha: Leben und Wirken des Wegbereiters in India

Paperback edition, Third edition, 1995.
Only authorized edition.

Cataloging-in-Publication Data

299
BUD

Buddha: life and work of the forerunner in India : received in the proximity of
Abd-ru-shin through the special gift of one called for the purpose.–
Gambier, OH : Grail Foundation Press, ©1995.

278 p.; 23 cm.   (Forerunners)

Summary: Portrays the life and work of the Prophet Buddha
from the spiritual point of view

ISBN 1-57461-010-4

1. Gautama Buddha—Miscellanea 2. Spirit writings
I. Abd-ru-shin, 1875-1941

299 dc20
BP605.B5B83

The complete titles in the *Forerunner Book Series*:

THE SEER OPENS WIDE HIS EYES AND SEES.

BEFORE HIS GAZE ARISES LIFE,

WHICH HAS BEEN INDELIBLY ENGRAVED

IN THE BOOK OF THIS GREAT CREATION:

BRISK activity reigned in the Palace at Kapilavastu. The Prince was expected back from a hunting expedition.

He had already been away ten days, he, the centre of his family, of the court and of the realm. What could have happened to him in that time? Never before had he been absent for so long.

"When is Father coming?" little Rahula had asked countless times throughout the day, nestling now against his mother's knees, now in his ayah's arms.

Neither knew what to answer, and they comforted him with all kinds of tit-bits. But his mother, the beautiful Princess Maya, went ever more frequently to the high apertures from which it was possible to look down into the valley.

"Siddharta, why do you stay away so long?" she lamented.

But her cries and lamentations did not bring her husband back. Just as little did her tears, which flowed ceaselessly as the days passed without news.

Maya had covered her head, with its long shining, blue-black tresses, with white veils, and refused to take any food. But the old ayah scolded her:

"You must not lose heart, my Princess, my flower! Take off the widow's veil. It is not time to wear it yet."

Watha threw herself at the feet of her mistress, whom she had served from birth, and begged her to take some food.

Then joyful cries and the clear sound of horns rang out. Gongs were sounded. The listening women could be in no doubt: The Prince was returning!

Maya rushed eagerly to her look-out, but all she saw was an imposing retinue of horsemen riding into the Palace courtyard. Just then Kapila, the faithful old servant, came running up to his mistress; folding his arms across his breast he bowed low and announced:

9

"The Prince will arrive before the sun has set. He has sent the trophies of the chase and part of the baggage train in advance, because he himself is taking a roundabout way home."

And now the Palace began to bustle with activity. The spoils of the chase were unloaded, examined and discussed. Riding-animals and hunting-birds were put in their stalls. All this did not proceed without chatter. There was so much to tell, after being parted for more than ten days. In addition, everything had to be arranged in the most perfect way for the reception of the Prince. The whole Palace was to be resplendent!

It was beautiful, this Palace, fabulously beautiful, made entirely of white stone. Built on one of the foothills of the rugged, snow-covered range of mountains which they called the Himalayas, it commanded a wide view over the valley, in whose fertile plain the great river carried its waters towards the distant sea.

This white castle, which stood out luminously against the dark, almost gloomy background, could be seen from afar. It lay amidst carefully tended gardens. Large flowers wound themselves round tall trees, climbed from treetop to treetop, forming archways through which one could walk, enveloped in fragrance.

Delicious fruits thrived in these gardens. The vigilance of a large number of servants kept away poisonous snakes and small harmful animals.

From time immemorial the Palace had been the home of the princely line of the Tshakya, who held dominion over the glorious plains of the Ganges, right into the Himalaya mountains. Prosperity and happiness had always attended the Tshakya-princes, who liked to call themselves Gautama. Under the leadership of the present Prince, Siddharta, who was loved by all, prosperity had changed to wealth, happiness to earthly bliss.

The warbling of the birds had faded into a soft singing as the retinue approached. Pages in white fluttering garments rode ahead at full speed on small nimble horses. They wore colourful sashes round their waists, their white turbans were tastefully draped and richly adorned. Even by looking at the servants, it could be seen how wealthy the Prince was.

After that the great elephant, by which Siddharta loved to be carried, approached with mighty strides. Over the magnificent red saddle rose a golden howdah which protected the Prince from the rays of the sun. Now the light of the setting sun played on the golden ornaments, making them flash and sparkle.

Behind the elephant paced the Prince's white steed. It was an animal of rare beauty from distant lands. Its mane and long, full tail shone silvery-white.

Then followed the attendants on horseback, and finally the armour-bearers, who wore green sashes and had green cloth braided into their white turbans.

Nearer and nearer came the retinue. Maya could now discern everything clearly, and she hastened towards her husband. Prince Rahula rushed from the other side, having escaped from his ayah, who followed him breath-lessly.

But in spite of the utmost haste, they all reached the high, gilded portal of the Palace only after the Prince had dismounted from his elephant over the backs of crouching and kneeling servants. Happily he went to meet his dear ones.

He was still a young man, with a figure inclining to fullness, slightly above medium height, with handsome features. His long hair fell in loose curls to his shoulders, and the pallor of his cheeks was accentuated by a dark beard.

He held out long, slender hands to his loved ones, and called out joyful words of greeting and endearment to them.

Servants received him and accompanied him to a room where fragrant water rippled in a depression in the floor, which was inlaid with costly stones. After the bath his body was anointed.

Stretched out on splendid rugs, he took his meal and then made his way into the garden to his wife and child, whom he found on carpets under tall, shady trees.

Only now did he tell them about the hunting expedition, which had brought a lot of game, including a tiger and two big leopards as trophies.

"One of the skins shall adorn Rahula's couch," he promised the little one. But the boy shook his head:

"Rahula does not like anything that others have killed. He will soon carry off a skin for himself."

His father laughed.

11

"The boy's nature is different from mine. At his age I had no thought yet of future exertions, but took what the servants brought me or what my father assigned to me. I am eager to see how he will develop. I believe he does not even attach any importance to all the splendour that surrounds him."

This Maya confirmed, adding:

"He is much more serious than other children of his age. Perhaps he will be a scholar."

The little boy had run across the luxuriant flower-beds to some bushes. Engrossed in their conversation, the parents had paid no further attention to him. Now he slowly returned to them with tears streaming down his little face, threw himself on the ground beside his father, and burst into violent sobbing.

He did not answer his mother's anxious enquiries into the cause of his grief; he only calmed down slowly. Then he lifted up his little head and asked earnestly:

"Why is the big snake allowed to eat a little song-bird? It was singing so sweetly. Then the snake came and....oh...."

Maya leapt up, terrified, and clapped her hands to call the servants.

"A snake! There is a great, poisonous snake in the garden! We cannot remain here!" she cried, as they came running up.

Prince Siddharta calmed her:

"Let the people search, my flower. Nothing will happen to us here."

Then he turned to his little son, who was still looking at him questioningly, and said lightly:

"The snake must have been hungry. It wants to eat and be satisfied."

"Then it should take other animals, mice and rats," said the child emphatically. "Why does it harm human beings and animals at all?"

The Prince reflected a moment. What was he to tell the child?

"The snake is Vishnu's companion. Do you know who Vishnu is?"

"Yes, I know," said Rahula proudly. "Watha told me. Vishnu is an evil, dark god who hates all living things."

"Does my son also know the name of the shining god who loves the whole Creation?" the father asked tenderly, stroking the child's curls from his flushed face.

"The good god is called Shiva. But there is yet another. Watha says he stands above these two and unites them. Can good and evil be united? Is he a little good and a little bad?"

"You want to know a great deal at once. Men say that Brahma stands above Vishnu and Shiva. Perhaps you will hear more about him later."

Rahula was not satisfied with the answer, but he received no other. Watha came and took him into the Palace. Maya, however, took up the child's question in his stead:

"Who is Brahma?" she asked thoughtfully. "You put it so strangely: 'men say'. Do you not say so? Do you not believe in Brahma?"

"No, Maya, I do not believe in him," was the surprising answer. "Brahma is a concept which the wise, the scholars have thought up to enable them to explain to the people what otherwise they would not understand. If the people believe that a supreme god holds the reins of world-rule in his twenty hands, they will no longer ask why one man meets with this fate, and another with that."

With eyes that seemed not to take in their surroundings, he gazed into the distance.

But Maya was alarmed. Hitherto she had believed firmly in Brahma. And now her husband, who seemed to her the highest in wisdom and goodness, cast the image of the god into the dust with a few words. She could not rest content with that.

"Siddharta, do you not believe in Shiva and Vishnu either?"

For a moment the husband hesitated, then he turned to look at his wife. A look of understanding came into his eyes. Suddenly he knew that if he were to speak the truth he would be taking the firm support from the childlike soul:

"Indeed, Maya, I do believe in them, although perhaps rather differently from you."

She uttered a sigh of relief.

"And you really do not believe in Brahma at all?"

"I can only say that I have not found him, but I have never yet sought him either. Are you satisfied now, little flower? Lift up your beautiful head and ponder no more. Sing instead."

Maya acquiesced with a smile, and taking up the small stringed instru-

13

ment by her side she sang a little song to the sound of it. And the Prince, who had stretched himself out and lay looking up into the deep blue of the sky, thought himself the happiest of all men.

A FEW YEARS had passed in undimmed happiness. A second boy, named Suddhodana after his grandfather, played around his happy parents. Rahula loved his little brother, and for his sake tried to join in his wild games; but otherwise he had probably become even more thoughtful.

Whenever he found his father in a mood to tell stories, he besieged him with questions, and begged him to tell him of his youth or of the family's past. Today too he had pressed his father until he consented.

"My little brother is named after Grandfather. That was your father? The people speak with reverence of Prince Suddhodana. But I know nothing about Grandmother. Was she as beautiful as our mother?"

"She too was called Maya, and she was equally beautiful. She came of a royal line from beyond the Himalayas. I never saw her; for she died a few days after I was born."

"Then you no longer had a mother! Who looked after you?"

"The old, faithful servant Kapila – but he was not old then – and his wife Kusi. My father had no time for me, for his neighbours gave him much trouble. They sought to dispute his right to his property, and ever again he had to set forth with his warriors to drive them from the borders. But I lacked nothing. The loyalty of these two surrounded me with all that a child needs."

"Even with love?" interposed Maya.

She could not imagine that a motherless child would really lack nothing.

"Even with love," the Prince repeated emphatically. "The older I grew, the more I learned to treasure this love, which had arisen not from natural ties, but from a loyalty that would lay down its life if need be. Only that is true love. Even animals feel maternal love. Love such as was bestowed on my childhood and youth is found only among high-minded human beings."

"Is Kapila high-minded? Surely he is only a servant?" the boy wanted to know.

The Prince told him that Kapila was of noble descent, but through adverse circumstances had become dependent.

"Is our city really named Kapilavastu after him?" went on the boy persistently.

"Not after him, but certainly after his ancestors, who long ago built this city," replied the father.

"Do names always have a meaning?" was the boy's next question. "Why did you call me Rahula? It sounds almost like 'the one solemnly promised'. To whom have you solemnly promised me?"

"My son, you owe your name to a wise man who came this way and stayed with us on the day you were born. He asked me to give you this name. You would recognise its meaning later. You see, my name is Siddharta, that is one who has reached his goal. Now my name does not fit me yet, but one day in the future I shall reach my goal; then the name will also be fulfilled."

"Why do we call ourselves Gautama? That has no clear meaning at all!"

"This surname stems from ancient times, and is said to have been taken from a bard who was a descendant of our house. That is why we use his name."

Rahula would have asked even more questions, but his father wanted to go riding, and his white steed was waiting at the gate.

Maya gazed after her husband as he rode away at full speed. For weeks now a sadness that she could not explain had weighed on her soul. She scolded herself; after all, she had everything she could possibly wish for. Yet anxious misgivings oppressed her, as though her happiness would not last much longer.

Her trusting, devout nature could not be diverted by her husband's remarks about the gods. She had never asked him about it again, but she had prayed for him the more fervently, and offered her sacrifices. And her intuitive perceptions had streamed upwards beyond Shiva and Vishnu to Brahma, in whose omnipotence and greatness, goodness and love she firmly believed.

How often she had been allowed to experience them! Many a time, when in some outward or inward distress (which was not altogether absent from her life either, blessed though it was with happiness) she had turned in

15

fervent supplication to the deity, she had been answered. Either her petition was fulfilled, or else quiet voices whispered to her to endure, or showed her a way out.

Of late, however, she had a friend, who she was firmly convinced had been sent to her as a helper. Whenever she sat by herself in the garden, a little old gnome, whom she alone could see, came and joined her.

He was dressed like a Brahman, and seemed also to possess the wisdom of one. With him she could discuss all that passed through her mind and soul. She was always sure of receiving friendly counsel and wise instruction. But he had forbidden her to speak of him to anyone. If other people approached her he disappeared. Yet he had no need to do so, for the others did not see him.

Today also, Maya was not alone for long. A soft laugh made her look up from her musing. The old gnome was sitting facing her on the window-sill. He had never appeared in the Palace before. He addressed her kindly, and asked what she was depressed about.

"I do not know myself why I am fearful," she answered. "I am afraid of the future, although I tell myself again and again that we have nothing to fear."

"There is cause for your alarm, Princess," the little creature said earnestly. "Your husband is too careless. He has greatly angered the powerful prince your neighbour, but instead of listening to the warnings of his counsellors he makes light of them. Instead of mustering his warriors and guarding the frontier he rides out into the forests. I have instructions to warn you. Pack your valuables, jewels, ornaments and even your clothes. Make several bundles of them and have them ready, so that you can flee with your sons and Kapila as soon as it becomes necessary."

The Princess was deeply shaken.

"Let me pass on your warning to the Prince," she begged. "Perhaps the fate hanging over us may yet be averted!"

"You may tell him as soon as you see him. But meanwhile make all the preparations. Everything must be ready by this evening. And now come with me. I want to show you a secret passage that leads from the Palace far out into the mountains. It is no longer known to anyone. You and your sons are to make use of it."

"May not Watha come with us? You said nothing about her."

The old fellow shook his hoary head.

"She is too old," he said at last. "She will not have to suffer if you leave her behind."

"And my husband? If the misfortune can no longer be averted, must I leave him? May he not escape with us through the secret passage?"

"You must leave him for the sake of your sons, who need their mother. But life needs your sons. They must be saved. The Prince, however, must learn through want what he does not yet know today: that above him lives an Eternal God. Pray for him, that he may soon find the true wisdom! And now come with me!"

Down countless steps the old gnome led the woman, who followed him as though in a dream. She shuddered as she entered the vaults, which she had never seen.

At last they came to a little room which had neither doors nor windows. Beside a pile of stones that were lying there as if left by accident, the little man pointed to a projection on the wall. Maya grasped it, and with a grating noise a part of the masonry moved sideways, leaving a gap wide enough for a person to slip through. The old one pointed to a bundle of torches stuck on the wall.

"This is the entrance. Do not forget to take a torch with you so that you can light your way. Go in with confidence. The path is safe, and leads so far into the mountains that no enemy will find you. Now take note of the way back, so that you can find this refuge in case of need."

When the Princess had returned to her apartment she implored Brahma to help her to be strong. She now knew quite definitely that disaster was imminent and that it was inevitable. After that she turned to the packing.

When she had finished, she was so consumed with inner restlessness that she looked for something to do. She dragged one bundle after another down the many steps, thus impressing the way ever more on her memory. Then the last bundle had been carried down. But Prince Siddharta had not yet returned home. Could he have lost his way, could something have happened to him?

When it was time to sleep she sent the boys to bed. She herself could not think of sleep. Dressed, she sat down beside the sleeping boys and prayed.

17

But then she must have fallen asleep after all. Indescribable noise made her start up suddenly. It was as light as day in the room, but the light came from outside. The clashing of weapons was heard, cries of pain drowned the shouts of the men. Before she fully realised what had happened, Kapila burst into the room:

"Princess, save yourself and the children! The town and the Palace are in the hands of the enemy!"

"Where is the Prince?"

"We do not know! He has not returned from his ride, nor have his companions. But save yourself. Already they are storming the apartments!"

Maya took the frightened boys by the hand, called to the faithful servant to follow her, and hurried down into the vaults. Heavy footsteps echoing on the stairs made them flee even faster.

They reached the dark room. Quickly she opened the door in the wall, let the boys and Kapila pass through, and carefully closed the opening. A torch was lit, and through a very long, winding passage they reached the open air at noon on the following day.

Where the passage ended, a mountain-spring rippled. Beside it stood a building which perhaps was once the dwelling of a herdsman, but which could now give them shelter even though it was rather dilapidated.

Gratefully they took possession of it without asking where they would find the food they needed. Maya's only clear thought was the concern for her far-off husband.

KAPILAVASTU was in the hands of the enemy. They had ransacked it, scorching and burning, murdering and plundering. For days horror raged through the hitherto so happy city.

The rest of the domain had surrendered without resistance, from fear of suffering the same fate as the capital. The neighbouring prince had united the little realm with his own, and was governing it as the undisputed ruler.

And still Prince Siddharta had not returned! Something terrible must have befallen him, to make him stay away from his country in this great affliction.

Those who thought so were right. On the night that was so fateful for his country, the Prince with his small retinue had been attacked on their homeward way by a well-armed troop of the enemy. They defended themselves valiantly, until a sword-blow felled Siddharta.

He awoke several times in the night, groaning, but each time relapsed immediately into deep unconsciousness, which encompassed his senses for a long time.

At last, when he had passed yet another night in this state, he regained consciousness, weakened by pain, loss of blood and hunger, but with a clear mind. And he saw lying there his companions, who had paid for their loyalty with their lives. But the enemies too lay on the ground. Hardly any could have escaped.

Siddharta tried to struggle to his feet but it was impossible. The wound was too painful, and he was afraid it would bleed afresh. But what was he to do? Die here, alone and miserable? Surely he must have been away from home for a long time now. Why did no one come to look for him? And among all these thoughts that tormented his weary head, one kept recurring:

"What can I do to save my life?"

He found no answer. If he believed in the gods, he would pray now. But to him the gods were only concepts, not realities! Again night fell. Siddharta's torments became unbearable. He could try for once to find help in prayer.

He called on the gods; but since behind his prayer was the thought: "Who knows if it is of any avail?" his pleas lacked the power to swing upwards.

Luminous threads sought him, threads ascending from out of the devout prayers of his wife; but they found no anchorage in his doubting thoughts. Ever again they had to return to her who had unconsciously sent them forth.

Now he began to contend with the gods. He had lowered himself so far as to ask for their help, but they had not listened to his pleas! So there really were no gods. He had been quite right.

The night seemed endless. If only he could die! A thousand times better to leave this earth at once than to be tortured to death. Then new thoughts rushed in on him. Leave the earth, and what then? Where would his way lead after that? If there were no gods, there was no hereafter either. Would he dissolve into nothingness?

When such thoughts came to him in the past he had thrust them aside. There was time enough for them when he was old and frail. But now he had to come to terms with them, and he found no answer!

The sun had risen, and was sending delicate rays into the forest-thicket where the sorely wounded Prince lay. One of these darts of sunlight played on the iridescent back of a beetle, which was making its way along the ground through the plants beside the Prince. As Siddharta's gaze followed it, envy arose in him.

"Why should you live if I have to die?"

He raised his feeble fist to kill the beetle. But he felt his hand held fast. That was not weakness; otherwise it would have dropped down. Some unknown power had put a spell on it. What was it? Now he even heard a voice:

"You shall not harm any creature."

Where did this voice come from? It was as though it had sounded within him. But who was holding his raised fist? So after all there were beings who could not be seen, and who had power? A ray of hope vibrated through the Prince's soul.

"You invisible ones, whoever you may be," he implored with fervour, "help me! Do not let me perish! If you save a little beetle, have pity on me also."

He repeated the petition several times, it sounded ever more heartfelt. Then the breaking of twigs and the rolling of stones announced that some being was approaching.

Before Siddharta could distinguish whether it was an animal or a human being, a man in shabby clothing stood before him. He was a member of the lowest caste, whose touch the Prince would formerly have shunned with abhorrence. But now he saw in him only the saviour.

"Help me," he implored with pale lips. The man looked in his direction.

"There seems to be one still alive," said he in astonishment. "I thought you were all dead. I was hoping to make off with rich spoils, and now I suppose you want to prevent me? The best thing I can do is to put an end to your life."

"You who saved the beetle, help me too!" cried Siddharta with his last strength.

The man laughed coarsely.

"I have saved no beetle; but I will let you live. After all, you cannot stop me taking from the dead what they no longer need."

The Prince shuddered. Robbing corpses! There was a heavy penalty for this crime. But he could not prevent it.

When the man had packed everything that seemed to him of value into one of the coats, he turned to go. But the Prince begged him:

"Do not leave me lying here. Get me something to drink, and all that is on me shall be yours."

Again steps were heard, and the man fled! The new arrival seemed hardly better than the one who had just been plundering here. He looked at the naked corpses, touched them with the tips of his toes to see if there was any life left in them, and then turned to the Prince.

"At least he left one for me, the thief," he muttered to himself, and without further ado began to undress the wounded man.

Suddenly he saw Siddharta's wide-open eyes looking at him imploringly. Terrified, the man dropped his victim. He wanted to flee like the other man, but a ray of sunshine dazzled him and made him reel.

Who knows what went on in his soul at this moment? He turned to the Prince and said:

"I will carry you to a place where you can get food."

He saw the gratitude in the eyes of the wounded man. Then he lifted up the almost unconscious Prince in his strong arms, and carried him through the thicket.

When Siddharta regained consciousness he found himself lying on a hide in a fair-sized cave. Beside him stood a large vessel of tea, and within his reach was a stone, with various kinds of food on it. But the Prince was too weak to take the food and drink that he craved.

Terrible, fresh agony! The man must have robbed him of all his clothing, he was cold. He looked down at himself. He was dressed in rags of the vilest sort.

"Have you saved me from a quick death, only for me now to perish here, you invisible ones?" asked the Prince; but he sounded wretched, and no longer arrogant. "Oh help me again, you whom I see not nor know, but in whom I believe, because I know that you exist."

From the back of the cave, which he could not see, came a child, a little girl. She looked curiously at the man who had been sleeping until then, but was now stirring.

"Do you want a drink, man?" she asked.

She knelt down eagerly and held a little cup, into which she had ladled tea from the big vessel, to the Prince's lips. What a blessing! Then she offered him a bite of bread.

For days this little girl was Siddharta's sole companion. She tended the wounded man as best she could. She brought him food and tea whenever he wanted it. But she said nothing more than what was absolutely necessary. Evidently silence had been enjoined on her.

Slowly the wound healed and strength returned. One day the Prince was able to sit up, and soon after that he tried to walk a few steps. Then he wanted his little nurse to tell him where he was. She shook her head. So he would have to wait until he was strong enough to leave the cave.

And that day came also. He asked the little girl whether he was free to go where he pleased. She nodded. He thanked her with kind words, and wanted to know her name, but even this she withheld.

"I am a Prince, little girl," he told her. "Once I am back in my realm, I shall be able to reward you for your services."

At that she pointed to his rags and laughed outright. He took food with him, and walked out into the forest. Obeying an inner compulsion, he kept to a definite direction.

After some days he perceived that the forest had come to an end. By evening he stood on a hilltop and saw Kapilavastu lying below him.

Breathless with joy, he looked for his Palace. Was he being fooled by a dream? He could not see the white splendour! He decided to wait until morning; then he would be able to recognise everything better. But the morning brought no change in the picture either. Where once his Palace had stood lay a dark heap of rubble.

He rushed down the slope as fast as his strength would allow. The nearer he approached the spot, the more distinctly he perceived that the once white stones were blackened with smoke. A frightful conflagration must have destroyed his home.

Where were his wife and children? Breathing heavily he scrambled up the rocky slope to the citadel. A shepherd was grazing a flock of sheep, long-haired beasts that nibbled reluctantly at the ash-covered herbage.

Siddharta addressed the man, who turned away from the ragged figure with disgust. At last he allowed himself to be moved by the persistent pleading of the beggar and gave him information, even though he did not understand why the pariah wanted to know about the family of the Prince.

He told of the fatal night, and the days of terror that followed. He recounted that the country now had another prince, who was no worse than the former ruler. No one knew what had become of Siddharta and his family. The Princess and her sons had probably perished in the flames. But Prince Siddharta had never returned from a ride on which he had gone just on that ill-fated day.

"It will be as well for him to keep away now, if he is still alive," the shepherd concluded. "The new prince has promised a reward to whoever brings Siddharta before him, dead or alive."

Siddharta staggered on. He could not think. Only to get away from the place of his one-time sheer inexhaustible happiness. Begging, he wandered unrecognised through the country that lay between him and the neighbouring realm to the east.

Even though he could not disclose his identity here either, since he could not tell whether its ruler was friendly with the prince his enemy, he had no need to be afraid of being recognised. Here nobody would have anything to do with him. The gifts for which he begged were thrown at his feet, and he was refused shelter under any roof.

To everyone he seemed a pariah, a member of the lowest caste, which was shunned and accursed. He must not be surprised: his body was covered with the dirt and congealed blood of weeks, his hair was matted, and his beard hung in a wild tangle round his sunken cheeks.

Nothing was left of his former well-groomed and handsome appearance, nothing of his cheerful disposition and carefree nature. A solitary, unhappy man, he skulked on his way, seeking. What he was seeking, he did not seem to know himself. His dear ones were certainly dead, consumed by fire, gone!

Who could say whether they would ever meet him again in some other guise? The boys were still too young to have burdened themselves with any guilt for which they would now have to atone in some other embodiment, and Maya, the delicate flower, had surely passed guiltless into nothingness.

Only he was left. But why? Surely there must be a meaning? Nothing happened in the world without purpose, of that he was certain. Thus he sought the reason for his continued life on earth.

But first he now wanted to find out why men had to live at all. Life, which had formerly seemed to him the most glorious gift from an unseen power, now presented itself as an unending chain of suffering. Wherever he looked he found suffering, nothing but suffering!

His way led him through the lower levels of life. Oppressed humanity, entangled in bonds wherever he looked. He had reached the age of twenty-nine without ever suspecting how much misery there was in this world, which had seemed to him so beautiful.

He had loved the radiant sun; now he observed that it wrung streams of sweat from arduous toilers; that the streets grew dusty under its scorching rays, so that he could hardly lift his weary feet any more.

He had thought it a delight to gallop off on his swift steed, or to be carried by the sure-footed elephant; now he had to swallow the dust whirled up by others, he had to leap aside when a troop of horsemen came roaring past.

How little had he valued a drink of water; now he often went thirsting on his way. Now he also saw how men had to drive the water pumps. Day in, day out they were harnessed to the great wheels, and went round in a circle until they were dizzy. Oh the misery, oh the suffering!

He saw men, women and children lying by the roadside, blue and bloated, with all the symptoms of gravest illness. Festering boils covered their bodies, spreading pestilential stench.

Others again he found with individual limbs snow-white, half their bodies decayed. Leprosy! He too did as the others, and fled when he met such pictures of misery. Not for a moment did it occur to him that he might try to alleviate their suffering.

He had been wandering now for six months, driven by two thoughts: "How can I sustain my life today?" was the one, "Why am I alive at all?" the other.

Then on the road he met with a snake-charmer, who was too weary to walk on to the next town, as well as carrying the baskets with the squirming reptiles.

Snakes had always aroused aversion in Siddharta, but something in the man's face attracted him. He went up to him and offered to carry the baskets. The man gladly accepted.

"Are you not afraid of becoming unclean, for surely you must look upon me as a pariah?" asked Siddharta cautiously.

The man answered in the negative.

"I am not an adherent of Brahma," he said. "I do not concern myself with castes and the like."

Thereupon Siddharta took up the heavy baskets and walked slowly beside the stranger. Towards evening they came to a village where the man seemed to be known. Joyful shouts greeted him, and he was directed to a shed where he could stay with his snakes.

"May my servant also spend the night there?" asked the charmer, and the people, who probably assumed that the servant was of the same stock as his master, agreed.

My servant! The word went through Siddharta like a thunder-bolt. He who was accustomed to commanding countless servants, to having the lazy ones whipped and punished, he himself was now called a "servant". And he had to rejoice at it. Through this service he had earned the first roof over his head in more than half a year.

His "master" Sariputta instructed him to look for mice in the shed.

Siddharta, to whom these little nimble creatures were also loathsome, nevertheless set to work without hesitation, and managed to catch a sufficient number of them.

Then it came to the feeding of the snakes. While it was going on, Sariputta told him this and that about the lives of the animals, which made Siddharta realise that they too had not been created without purpose.

Once he had brought himself to look closely at them, he had to admit that they were beautiful. Each one was differently marked and differently

25

coloured. It was strange that none of the creatures was unfriendly to him. Sariputta was glad of that.

"Never yet have I had an assistant," said he, "whom the snakes would have welcomed. Soon I shall be able to entrust you with the feeding by yourself."

Who would ever have foretold that one day Siddharta would be glad to be able to serve a snake-charmer and not be disagreeable to his snakes. And yet it was so. For the first time since the dreadful calamity, Siddharta knew what he had to do, and could be of some use. That gave him satisfaction.

Before moving on the next day, the snake-charmer had to give a performance with the snakes in the village market-place. The way in which the great bodies swayed to the sound of the pipe, how their heads rose and fell according to whether Sariputta piped softly or loudly, really won Siddharta's admiration.

When Sariputta now finally condescended to perform tricks without the snakes, something like joy penetrated the Prince's heart for the first time.

In the city that Sariputta visited, the first thing he did was to buy his servant decent clothes. That was a great step on the arduous upward path which Siddharta had to tread. Once he had risen out of the most despised of all castes, he would surely succeed in making progress. He thanked Sariputta, but the latter declined his gratitude, saying:

"What I did was done for my own sake. I cannot journey through the country with a servant who is despised. Besides, I clearly perceive that you are no pariah. Perhaps you will tell me later how it came about that you are seeking your way in these rags."

Now there was much work. Sariputta was able to do more than just make snakes dance. He was called upon to heal the sick and exorcise demons. His sole equipment for this was a bundle of colourful peacock-feathers, which he dipped in water in order to sprinkle the sick.

Siddharta only learned this from the talk of others. He himself had to guard the baskets with the precious snakes while his master was away, and he was not allowed to accompany him into any of the houses. But he was no longer despised at every turn. Other servants, even craftsmen, spoke to him. They brought him food and fruit.

After a few days they resumed their wandering. Sariputta had recovered,

26

and was more talkative. He asked Siddharta what it was that occupied his thoughts so continuously, and did not scoff when the latter replied that he was seeking the meaning of his life.

"Do you know then what life is?" he asked the servant.

"Life is suffering," came the latter's prompt reply.

"If you know that, you have already learned much," applauded Sariputta. "Life is suffering, thus we have been given life in order to overcome suffering."

Siddharta was silent. He could not grasp the meaning of the words so quickly. Then he asked:

"What is the use of overcoming suffering? It is always there in any case. Every new life is new suffering. When we have overcome the suffering ordained for us, we shall also have come to the end of our life. What purpose does it serve then?"

"You must find that out for yourself, Siddharta," said Sariputta. "I am only allowed to give you a hint now and then. But you yourself must find the answer to your question. With it you will also find that which makes life worth living."

On another occasion Siddharta asked his master if he believed in the gods, and received the surprising answer:

"What do you understand by gods?"

"I mean Vishnu and Shiva," said the Prince, almost embarrassed.

"I believe in Shiva, the destroyer of all life," replied Sariputta solemnly, but he could not continue because the other interrupted him in alarm:

"You are mistaken; surely Shiva is the good, wise god!"

"You can take that as you please. I believe in him as the destroyer of all life. Is he not good, if he puts an end to what we sometimes think we can no longer endure? Is he not good, if he allows the suffering which we could not overcome of our own strength to end?"

Siddharta was silent, but he was not convinced. Now that he had almost come as far as to be willing to believe in Shiva, he was shown to him from a completely different aspect. Here was a man who called him good, and yet also the destroyer; the priests in Kapilavastu taught that he was the promoter and preserver. Who was right?

27

SIDDHARTA had now been travelling with the man for some months. He had become quite accustomed to the life. Then one day Sariputta told him that they must part.

"I have been commanded to let you go your own way again, so that you may mount a step upwards. As long as you go with me you cannot advance any further. What I was commanded to do for you I have done."

"Who gave you these commands? And who is concerned with me and my ascent?" Siddharta wanted to know.

Sariputta sat down opposite him and began to explain. He told him that he, Sariputta, was a yogi, a man who seeks to raise himself above the mass of humanity through pious exercises.

For this he had a guide, who appeared to him plainly. This guide gave him the exercises he had to practise, and the prayers he had to say. He had not yet reached the highest step, but he had come so far in his development as the "raven", that is as far as the step of helping.

"You must know," he told his attentive listener, "that all steps have names, by which we recognise one another. As raven, one has to help some fellow-man forward on his way. You were led to me so that I should lighten the burden of your life. I have succeeded in that. You have cast off the rags of the pariah, and have gained recognitions that can lead you further. Implore the highest of the gods, whose name I may not utter, to send you a guide also; for when you have found the purpose of your life you will be allowed to work for the blessing of many."

Their farewell was brief. Siddharta was too stunned by what he had heard to be able to ask all that he would still have liked to know. He thanked Sariputta for his help, and once more fed the snakes, which he had come to love. Then their ways parted.

"What recognitions have I gained?" he asked himself. "I know that life is suffering. But I did not feel this suffering so much when I walked and worked with Sariputta. Therefore suffering is increased through idleness, perhaps even called forth by it? It must be so. Idleness comes from the craving for pleasure, for debauchery, it comes from self-love and indolence. Hence suffering is a result of craving. If we kill the cravings within us we shall also overcome the suffering. Is this right? I must prove it first."

28

Joyfully he went his solitary way. Something within told him that what he had discovered was a valuable recognition in any case.

Sariputta had given him some money so that he would not need to beg again, until he had found new work. He helped wherever he saw that help was needed, and as he was of good will, and did not shirk any work, his services were gladly accepted. He did not stay long in any place; everywhere he felt the urge to move on.

Then he encountered on the highway a travelling merchant with many bales of merchandise, especially costly fabrics, who was in great trouble. His draught-ox had broken a leg and had to be killed. Far and wide, there was nobody who was prepared to sell him another.

Siddharta offered to help the merchant pull the cart to the next village. Things went better than either of them had thought at first.

Amuruddba, as the merchant was called, found that the helpful Siddharta was a welcome companion. He asked him whence he came and where he was going, and although the Prince gave only scant information it satisfied the merchant, and he offered to let the helper remain with him until something new should present itself.

Siddharta gladly accepted. He longed for work, and he liked Amuruddba. Would he always find his "masters" on the road?

With the money that Sariputta had given him, he bought himself better clothing, and now had suddenly skipped an entire caste, that of the tradesmen. He had long ago shaved off his beard, and his cheeks were beginning to fill out again.

He was a handsome merchant, who inspired confidence, and Amuruddba found that since this companion had joined him he was selling much more. They had bought a new draught-ox. They sat on the cart in turn, while the other walked beside it. And on the way they conversed.

Amuruddba was a man who had thought much during his long journeys. He too had occupied himself with the "meaning of life", but he had come to conclusions entirely different from those of his new companion.

"I believe," said he, "that we have flowed from the soul of the world, and that we must find our way back there. But because this soul of the world is the epitome of all good, our one endeavour must be to become as perfect as possible. Thus for me the purpose of life lies in attaining the utmost perfec-

29

tion. And it is clear to me that a single life is not enough for this. Therefore I believe also in the transmigration of souls."

That was something new again for Siddharta, but he did not yet know what to make of it. He continued to think along the lines in which he had gained his recognitions. He had found that in order to avoid suffering the cravings have to be destroyed.

Amuruddba wanted to become perfect in order to be able to return again to the starting-point of life. Indeed, if he was right in thinking that all life had flowed from the soul of the world, the merchant's recognition was several steps higher than his own. Yes, if he was right in that! Who could tell him?

Slowly Siddharta began to enter into the merchant's way of thinking, then once again there was a parting. Amuruddba had returned to his native city to buy new merchandise, and had found his younger brother grown to manhood and ready to accompany him on further travels. Therefore Siddharta was no longer needed. The two men, who in spite of all differences had got on well with each other, parted with regret.

But with Siddharta the regret did not last long. He was fully convinced that something new would now present itself again.

"I need only go on to the highway," he said to himself, "and I will find a new master. And each one advances me a little further."

More than two years had now passed since he had lost his good fortune. Sometimes he thought with longing of Maya and his sons, but his whole former life lay behind him as though submerged. He would not have liked to take it up again, had he been offered the opportunity to do so.

"What has become of my suffering?" he asked himself.

"It has been engulfed in active life and movement. I no longer have any time to indulge in gloomy thoughts," was his answer to his own question, only to draw again fresh conclusions from it, in keeping with his nature.

For some days now he had been travelling alone, always intent on what fate would bring him, what aspect the new companion destined for him would have.

Suddenly he was surprised at himself.

"So I really believe that my companion will be led to me? Then I must also admit to the possibility of a guide, of whom Sariputta spoke. I seem to be undergoing all kinds of changes without noticing it!"

He walked on deep in thought, until a loud call roused him from his dreams. He looked up and saw a Brahman who was stooping over a man lying by the wayside.

"If you are the man you appear to be," the Brahman called to him, "come and help me! Here is a human being who needs our help."

Siddharta went up to him and saw a man who had been badly knocked about. He was bleeding from several wounds, and his clothes were in tatters. As he was unconscious he could give no information about what had happened to him.

With Siddharta's help the Brahman bandaged the wounds. Then he asked him to make haste to the next village to get a cart for the wounded man. Siddharta gladly set off, thinking as he went:

"If this Brahman is to be your new master, you will be fortunate. He seems to be a wise and noble person."

The wounded man had not regained consciousness when they lifted him into the ox-cart, and drove carefully to the little town that lay a few miles off. There they consigned him to the care of the priest, to whom the Brahman gave some instructions. Then the wise man turned to Siddharta and asked him whither he was bound.

"I am looking for work," he answered briskly. "If you can make use of me, I will go with you most gladly."

"Judging by your attire you are a merchant," said the Brahman, whose name was Maggalana, "but judging by your speech you belong to a higher caste. Can you read and write?"

Siddharta replied in the affirmative.

"Then I shall be glad to accept you as a companion and pupil," consented Maggalana. "Come with me, and help me as you have done today. You will always have your maintenance, but more than that I shall hardly be able to give you."

"I am content," replied Siddharta joyfully.

Again he had advanced a step further, outwardly and inwardly, and again he had found his master on the highway.

31

This time an arduous journey on foot lay ahead of him. But it was lightened for him by the profound discourse which opened up the whole world of the Brahman faith to the marvelling Siddharta.

He was now thirty-one years old, and had lived among his people to whom this faith was sacred. He had known nothing of it! When he was supposed to study as a boy he had resisted, and opposed the teachings of his old priest with hair-splitting ideas.

His wife Maya had retained her childlike faith as long as he had known her. He had been careful not to destroy it, but had gently smiled at it. What a foolish person he had been!

Maggalana taught him to recognise that Amuruddba was right to believe in a soul of the world, only Maggalana called this soul Brahma.

He taught that Brahma, Shiva and Vishnu formed a trinity which embraced all that could contribute to the blessing of men. Below this triangle stood yet other gods, whom Siddharta would come to recognise later. The main thing was for the pupil to become clear about the trinity of the supreme gods.

Brahma formed the apex of the triangle. He breathed, as it were, the breath of life into all living things, he animated all things, he guided all things. He was goodness and love, from whom flowed every good impulse in man.

Below him, but inseparably linked with him, were Shiva and Vishnu. The former was the dispenser of joy, who carried out Brahma's thoughts; Vishnu on the other hand was the destroyer of everything hostile, of all that sought to oppose the triangle of the gods.

So closely involved were the three with one another that even a wise man often could not distinguish which of the gods was at work at the time. What Brahma had begun, Shiva continued and Vishnu defended.

But opposed to all stood Maro, the evil principle, the tempter of all men. He it was who inflamed evil cravings, he drove men against one another, destroyed peace and happiness, rushing them into war, dissension and perdition. He caused violent death.

Siddharta received these teachings with an alert mind. He could not understand that he had doubted divinity, that Brahma had been for him only a concept. New life grew in him, which made him joyful, gave him

32

new strength, and the certainty that his existence on earth had a purpose and a goal.

He spoke to Maggalana about this also.

"Every life has a purpose and a goal," said the master earnestly. "But I believe this to be true of yours in a higher sense than that of most other men. Will you not tell me the story of your life?"

Siddharta, who hitherto had not spoken of it to anyone, did so. And it was wonderful: as he recounted in simple words what had happened to him from childhood on, all that had come to pass seemed to take on a new and important meaning. What Sariputta had called "guidance" ran through all his experiences like an unbroken thread.

When he had finished, Maggalana too was silent for a long time. Then he rose and laid his right hand on Siddharta's head in blessing.

"Brahma has wonderful things in mind for you," he said solemnly. "You must be one of his favourite creatures. It would be wrong to let you waste your best years on the highway. We have many good schools; the best is in the south of our country. I will take you there, so that you may learn all that priests can teach you. Perhaps you will become a priest yourself, yet you may be destined for other works. I do not know. But whatever it may be, you have still much to learn, and there is no more time to lose."

Siddharta agreed, and even looked forward to the school. Now he had passed through almost every caste from below upwards. The only one still missing was the warrior caste, to which he had once belonged. A strange path!

Maggalana pressed on. He hired an elephant, which carried them comfortably on its broad back in a kind of litter. The Hindu who guided the great animal sat on its neck. The two travellers had no need to concern themselves with anything, and could freely discuss all that came to mind.

Siddharta wanted to learn also about the other gods, in order not to appear too ignorant in the school. Smiling, Maggalana granted his request, well aware that it sprang from ambition rather than from devoutness.

He spoke to him of the world-guardian, who had to see to it that all Brahma's commands were rightly executed, that the wheel that guides all the stars was running accurately at all times. Lokapales was the name of this god, who never showed himself to men, because he was always short of time.

"Can the three supreme gods be seen then?" asked Siddharta in amazement.

"Ordinary mortals do not see them. But among the wise there are some who have been given special inner eyes. These are allowed to see the gods, so that they will be able to tell human beings of them."

"Who is Indra?" asked Siddharta, and added apologetically: "My wife sometimes spoke of him."

"I was just about to tell you of him," replied Maggalana. "We in the south call him Shakra, the mighty. He it is who leads warriors, and strengthens them when they take up arms in a just cause. But he also gives strength and courage to all who are going through inner struggles, so that they may triumph over evil desires, and may find the right way again if they have strayed on to a wrong path through the temptation of Maro."

THE NEARER they came to their destination, the more the landscape changed. Different trees grew here, larger fruits, more colourful flowers.

The people too looked different. Whereas in the north they were more full-bodied, here they seemed to be smaller, and almost parched. The air was oppressive, the sun beat down fiercely. But sometimes at night a refreshing wind blew, bringing relief.

Maggalana explained that the wind came from the sea. The sea! Siddharta had never seen it, but had heard of it. It must be wonderful with its roaring, surging waves, much greater than the sacred River Ganges.

The buildings too were quite different from those in his homeland. The houses of the nobility looked like airy temples, but there did not appear to be many of them. On the other hand the dwellings of the poorer people gave the impression of earth-mounds that had been placed haphazardly together. They had no windows, only openings to slip in by, which were curtained off with mats or thin fabrics. Nor was there any ventilation for the smoke from the hearth.

Siddharta thought about it, but could come to no conclusion. So he asked Maggalana.

"Surely they must suffocate in smoke, for hardly anything can escape by the low covered opening in front," said Siddharta thoughtfully. "We build the flues as high up as possible."

"I can well believe it. For you have to light a fire in your dwellings," was the Brahman's reply. "Our people cook out of doors. If you look carefully you will see beside each hut piled-up stones which serve as a hearth. But mostly there is no cooking. Milk and fruit are taken raw, only bread is baked from time to time."

"Why do your people not build proper houses?" asked Siddharta, whose alertness took in everything.

"It is too hot to live in stone or wooden houses. The earth keeps the room cool, and it is used only at night or during the rainy season. Nor are these mud huts a sign of any particular poverty; for some families have several of them. People avoid living too close together because of the excessive heat. They prefer to build several huts side by side.

"You are surprised that these dwellings lack all adornment? Perhaps that too is because of the heat. People take no pleasure in their dwelling, because it is only makeshift. Most of the time is spent in the open air, in the shade of the trees.

"All need for adornment, all joy in what is beautiful, is lavished on the embellishment of the temples. Once you have seen our places of worship you will no longer think that our people lack the sense of beauty."

They had been travelling for a long time now. Siddharta had lost all count of time. It seemed to him to be many weeks.

Then mountains rose up again to their right, tall verdant mountains, which lacked the wildness of the snow-clad Himalayas. They rode towards these mountains and reached them after a few days. There they had to leave the patient elephant.

They hired shaggy mules, and the Hindu was instructed to wait with the elephant until Maggalana returned. The Brahman wanted to journey north after he had taken Siddharta to his destination.

"Are we taking a Hindu attendant with us?" Siddharta asked, but received the answer:

"There are no Hindus here. The natives are called Dravidians. They are the small dark-skinned people, with a luxuriant growth of hair, at whom you have shown your surprise several times in the past few days. They have their own belief in gods, but are docile and well-behaved in a childlike way. Although they do not like working because of the intense heat, they are extremely obliging and always ready to help."

Siddharta wanted to know what gods they believed in. Pleasantly Maggalana told him.

"They are still in a childlike state, and accordingly so also is their belief in the gods. The more highly a people develops, the higher also are its gods; for it involuntarily seeks them higher than itself. But if a race is still as undeveloped as our Dravidians, it will find the beings which it worships as gods quite close to it, in Nature itself.

"The Dravidians are closely connected with the beings which animate flowers and trees, rivers, winds and flames. They are friends, helpers, teachers and guides to them. In gratitude for all that they receive from them, they bring offerings and worship these beings. They are made happy by this, and I believe that Brahma himself would not wish it otherwise than that they should continue in this state of bliss until they are able to comprehend more. Then the time will have come for them to get acquainted with the real gods."

Siddharta had indeed been listening, but his thoughts had remained at one sentence:

"The more highly a people develops, the higher also are its gods." What a prospect!

"Maggalana, do you think that if we develop further, we too shall come to find even higher gods?"

"I do not know, Siddharta, often as I myself have thought about it. I hope and believe that our peoples too will develop upwards. But how high this development will be, whether it will be high enough for us not to have to return to the earth as a people at all but to be allowed to live on in the beyond, or whether it will still continue step by step on earth, I cannot discern. And even less can I say what the belief in the gods will be like in accordance with this development.

"Brahma seems to me the highest and most perfect, which can be surpassed by nothing else. But perhaps it is not so after all, perhaps above him stands one even higher, whom we shall one day reach. Should it not be enough for us to recognise the gods whom we are permitted to understand, and to serve them and emulate them with all our strength?"

Siddharta tried to be satisfied with that, but this question pursued him throughout his life.

THE UNPREPOSSESSING but useful mounts had climbed steadily upwards. The path was narrow, covered with loose stones, and worse still, was a veritable playground for snakes. If one of them shot out suddenly from behind stones, or wound down from a tree, the mules abruptly sprang aside together with their load, thereby endangering the lives of the riders.

Then the animals trembled so much that no amount of coaxing would induce them to move on until the snake was out of sight. Maggalana told him that countless people fell victim to the bite of these poisonous cobras, for their venom was deadly.

Siddharta distinctly recognised the curious marking on the flat heads. They looked exactly like the largest snakes that he had come to know when he was with Sariputta. He was not afraid for a moment, and he felt that he should try to see whether he was agreeable also to these snakes living in the wild.

Without telling Maggalana of his intention, he dismounted and walked in front of the mules, keeping a sharp look-out on all sides.

There a particularly large cobra lay coiled by the roadside. It seemed to be sleeping off a meal, and thus was harmless. Siddharta approached slowly, his eyes unwaveringly fixed on it, and whistled softly through his teeth.

The snake raised its triangular head and seemed to listen. The mules stood motionless, but Maggalana watched, partly in horror, partly in admiration, what Siddharta was doing.

The latter spoke to the snake in low, curious words; he seemed to be coaxing it in a kindly way. Slowly the splendidly marked body uncoiled, slowly it began to move, and glided into the bushes beside them.

A feeling of bliss which he could not put into words went through Siddharta's soul. It was not self-conceit, or the thought of being able to command the creature, rather was it the inner sensing of closeness that made him happy.

37

The same thing happened three more times. Siddharta spoke to the snakes, begging them to spare men and beasts who wanted to go up the hill, and the snakes obeyed his will. Yes, suddenly he knew that he could now remount his mule, and no more snakes would cross their path.

When he told Maggalana, the latter looked at him, speechless. But the Dravidian approached him and kissed the hem of his garment, with an expression of such delight on his childlike features that his plain face seemed quite transfigured.

Now white spires, high cupolas and flat roofs rose up before them. A city?

Maggalana pointed to it and said: "Utakamand." Joy and pride vibrated through the word, and by this Siddharta, who had never heard the name before, realised that it must be their destination.

The school was magnificently situated on a high plateau, surrounded by rocks. The sunlight flooded the white buildings, making them sparkle and glisten.

A mountain stream rushed down to the valley in countless waterfalls, spraying all around with jets and drops. It was enchantingly beautiful. Where the sun touched the drops they flashed in glorious colours.

But a fine mist lay over the whole, and it seemed to Siddharta as though he saw airy white figures emerging from it, as though he heard delicate notes of great sweetness above the sound of the water. His whole intuitive perceiving was devotion and worship. But he knew not for whom they were intended.

They rode on, and soon passed through the gate of the outermost building. It was only a passage, through which they reached a large court-yard. They gave their animals into the care of some servants, who also appeared to be Dravidians, and entered one of the bright buildings.

Siddharta was amazed: was this supposed to be a school? His own Palace had not been more richly furnished and adorned! Colourful mats, carpets and tapestries wherever he looked!

Golden and bronze images of gods stood everywhere, on pillars of dark, almost black wood. Beside each of these works of art were two bronze vases filled with bright flowers.

They walked through a number of rooms, each of which was similarly

38

decorated. At last they found the Head-Brahman, bent over manuscripts and surrounded by scholars. He was a white-haired, very dignified man, who greeted Maggalana pleasantly. When he heard that Siddharta had come as a scholar, he looked at him penetratingly several times. Then he said slowly:

"We were told that a scholar was coming to us. You, Maggalana, were to bring him. So far it was right. But he bore a different name."

He was silent for a while, and then his face lit up suddenly and he asked more eagerly:

"Tell me, Siddharta, have you another name as well?"

"I am also called Gautama," replied Siddharta, who had almost forgotten this family surname.

At that the Brahman stepped up to him in joyful excitement:

"Then you are the one promised to us! We shall be glad to instruct and help you, to prepare you for your work on earth. May Brahma grant that we teach you in his will."

A few days sufficed for Siddharta, who was now called only Gautama, to become fully accustomed to the community which had accepted him. Maggalana could leave his charge behind with confidence when he set out on his return journey to the colder north.

Life in the school was strictly regulated, but nevertheless adapted to the needs of the students. They rose very early. The first ray of the sun had to find all residents dressed and at prayer.

This morning worship was held in a domed hall intended solely for this purpose, and consisted of a series of prayers. One of the Brahmans prayed to Brahma in his own words, and thanked him for his protection during the night. Then all present responded slowly in a well-trained chorus:

"Brahma, thou source of all good, we thank thee!

"Let our gratitude become joyful activity, so that it may be of value."

After that a Brahman prayed for help and strength for the tasks of the day. The rest of the assembly prayed in chorus:

"Shiva, thou benevolent one who carriest out Brahma's thoughts, give us of thy power that we too may do Brahma's will.

"Vishnu, thou destroyer of all evil, destroy every evil impulse within us."

Afterwards special orders for the day were sometimes given, or attention was drawn to dangers, mainly of a spiritual nature, which threatened individuals or all of them.

From the "morning-hall" they went in well-ordered procession to a terrace where Dravidians served the morning meal, which was eaten amid laughter and fun.

In spite of the merriment which prevailed every day, over-loud talking and laughing were not tolerated. If a newcomer was too noisy, his neighbours gently drew his attention to it. If he would not take their hints, then the Head-Brahman sent a servant to invite the one concerned to sit at his table.

The morning meal was followed by a few hours of instruction in the various lecture-halls. Always only a small number of scholars gathered around a Brahman, who imparted to them of his wisdom.

Gautama had soon discovered that he could choose his teacher during the morning instruction, while the evening instruction was subject to firm rules.

As soon as it began to be oppressively hot, the echoing of a gong announced the end of the "morning". Scholars and teachers retired to airy dormitories protected from the rays of the sun by white curtains, stretched themselves out on couches, read, talked or slept, according to their needs and wishes.

Dravidians incessantly waved large feather-fans hung from the ceiling to cool the air, others sprinkled the floor with water taken from the sparkling, cold mountain stream. In spite of this it was often so hot that any thought of learning was out of the question.

Around midday, servants brought baskets of fruit, which they offered to the resting scholars.

Only when the high mountains caught and warded off the rays of the sun did the gong sound again, inviting them to bathe in large pools. These were fed by the mountain stream, but had absorbed enough warmth from the sun not to be harmful. The open-air baths, taken even when it rained, were among the most refreshing things offered in the course of the day.

The bath was followed by an ample meal in a spacious hall, at which the atmosphere was not quite so lively as in the cool of the morning.

When the meal was over, the scholars went out into the open to play all kinds of games, running-games being the most favoured; after that, all set to work. Brahmans gave lectures, which were expounded by the scholars, and even occasionally debated as well. Other scholars then had to take up the defence. A cheerful, fresh tone vibrated through the whole.

The Brahmans, far surpassing the scholars in age and wisdom, had no wish to be other than older brothers, good companions who were allowed to help the younger ones on the upward way. That characterised all life in the school.

Despite all the cheerfulness, they could not for a moment forget that they were living here in order to find the way which the soul had to follow. Each had to discover his own way, he was not allowed to rest until he believed that he could see it clearly. After that he could advance together with those who had found the same path.

He who walked apart was neither admired nor despised. It was assumed that his path must lead first into solitude. Only he who found nothing, because he would not seek, disappeared quietly from the community.

Gautama embraced this new life with complete enthusiasm. He had ceased to ask what the object and purpose of his existence was. He was satisfied with the present situation, and was content as never before.

One day the Head-Brahman called him aside. He asked him what he had now learnt. Cheerfully Gautama gave him the information, enumerated what knowledge he had acquired, and what was still unclear to him.

The Brahman shook his head.

"You were not led to us to acquire earthly knowledge, Gautama. Brahma has other plans for you. I see that I must take your instruction into my own hands. From tomorrow, leave your companions during the hours of work and come to me."

Somewhat dazed, Gautama returned to the others, none of whom asked him what had been the object of the conversation. When on the following morning he was missing from among the scholars, they were at first dismayed, for some were afraid that he had left the school. They had come to like the cheerful, clever companion, and they would have been sorry to lose him.

41

In particular Ananda, one of the older pupils, was genuinely attached to Gautama. Therefore he did not rest until he had found out the reason for his absence.

He then told the others, and they were all struck with great admiration. It had never happened before that a scholar was instructed quite alone, and moreover by the head of all the Brahmans. Gautama must be a favourite of the gods.

At play they all vied with each other to show him their goodwill.

But now it was only seldom that he joined in the communal games. Since he began to receive his instruction alone, a change had taken place in him. He had always been a deep thinker, who did not simply accept what others told him, but turned it over and over until he had examined it from all angles.

Now, however, the old Brahman showed him something altogether new: Through all kinds of events and institutions he demonstrated to him Brahma's Laws for the upbuilding and maintenance of the Universe, and exhorted him to think about how he could adapt himself to these Laws.

In this way his own life appeared to him in a completely new light. The old man asked him if he had understood why he had fallen from the highest to the lowest caste, only to work his way slowly up again.

Gautama answered truthfully that he did not consider his interpretation to be a complete one. He could only imagine that he was meant to become acquainted with all castes from his own experience.

The Brahman shook his head.

"With this explanation you are still far from the goal," he said kindly. "I shall ask you again in a few months' time."

But in the meantime he instructed his pupil untiringly. He allowed him to participate in the discussions which often arose in the instruction of the younger men. So far as purely earthly matters were concerned, Gautama was always ready with the right judgment and good advice, but when it went deeper he failed.

This failure could only be explained by his continual seeking and pondering about the deity. How often had he already been on the verge of acknowledging a god, whatever his name, over him as a guide and leader, even worshipping this god, giving thanks to him. But ever again something drove him away from this path.

Yet the old man did not lose patience. He did not try to convince him, but held up his own faith to him as an example, in the firm hope that one day the pupil would open himself to it after all.

Beautiful, quiet months had gone by. Then the Brahman again questioned his pupil about the cause of his sudden fall.

Hesitantly he answered:

"Father, I believe that I have very much to learn: humility, helpfulness, the blessing that lies in work, the happiness of connection with one's fellow-creatures. I believe that my 'masters' have taught me all that on my arduous path."

"Now you begin to see more clearly, my son," smiled the wise man. "In a few months' time I shall ask you again."

When the others played, Gautama often strolled up and down near the playground, like all those who did not wish to take part.

In the late afternoon of one particularly hot day, as he was doing so, loud shouts roused him from his deep thoughts. Looking up, he noticed that all the players were fleeing in great haste to the far side of the playground. What could be the reason?

In spite of the agitated cries of the scholars, he reached the deserted place with a few quick strides, and found himself face to face with a huge, excited snake. It was a cobra, with particularly beautiful marking.

Angry and hissing, it reared up, flicking its tongue at him. But he began to whistle softly, meanwhile gazing at it steadfastly. At once the creature's excitement abated. The whistling grew louder, and changed to a tune with a distinct rhythm.

Thereupon the cobra began to sway the upper part of its body to and fro, as dancing snakes do.

The scholars gazed spellbound, but did not dare to move. Again the bliss of being connected with the creature passed through Gautama's soul. He let the tune die away slowly, and spoke softly, lovingly to the poisonous reptile.

The latter sank down, crept a little nearer to him, then swept round in a wide circle, and glided back into the undergrowth from whence it had come.

43

This called forth great rejoicing, louder even than the previous cries of alarm, and bringing all the Brahmans rushing to the scene. All admonitions to calm down were in vain; even the otherwise most thoughtful scholars found it the only way to express their relief and joy over the miracle.

One of the younger Brahmans asked:

"When you had the creature in your power, Gautama, why did you let it go without killing it?"

"Kill an animal whose friendship has just been won!" exclaimed Gautama, quite horrified. "This cobra will never come here again. It has promised me that."

Now the excitement became even greater.

"We did not hear the snake speak!" cried some, while others asked: "What did it say?"

Gautama shrugged his shoulders, went indoors, and left it to the Brahmans to give the necessary explanation. Part of his joy was spoilt by the sensation caused through what to him was a simple happening.

When he came to the Head-Brahman in the evening, the latter spoke with him, and Gautama realised that the event seemed neither wonderful nor mysterious to the old man. It was something else that occupied the sage.

"Tell me, Gautama," said he, thoughtfully, "how is it possible for you to feel yourself connected with the creature to such a high degree, and not to recognise its Creator?"

"I do not know, my father," confessed Gautama. "Give me time. There is nothing I more ardently wish than to reach this goal."

"Perhaps the creature can teach you," suggested the old priest.

This way appealed to Gautama. He began to converse with the birds that came fluttering towards him whenever he walked alone in the garden or forest. He asked them whether they could see the gods, whether there were gods. And he thought he heard their answer:

"Look around you, they are standing beside you!"

But however much he looked, he did not see them.

On one of his solitary walks he came upon a wounded tigress. She lay whining miserably in a thicket, whither her trail of blood had led. She mewed like a big cat.

But he thought he understood her moans, which were not to do with her

44

deep wounds, but with the cubs left behind in the cave, which would starve without her.

"You good mother," said Gautama kindly, "wait a little. I will look for your children."

The great animal's tail beat upon the ground, as though she wished in some way to show him her gratitude and joy. And Gautama set off, led by whispering voices: "You must go this way!" – "Here lies your path!"

He followed the invisible guides, and soon reached the tiger's den, in which two most delightful little cubs were playing. He spoke kindly to them, then picked one up and carried it away with him.

Spitting, the other tried to leap at him, but he comforted it by saying that he would soon fetch it too. Then he heard the whispering voices talking to the little animal, which now became quite docile.

The joy of the old tigress, as the two cubs lay suckling by her, spoke so clearly from her eyes that Gautama could not part from her. When the little ones were satisfied he fetched water, and washed and dressed her wounds. Then he brought her meat, which he had obtained from the school cook.

For some days he looked after the tigress and her young ones; their relationship grew ever closer. Then suddenly he found a magnificent full-grown tiger with his charges, which leapt up with a loud roar as Gautama approached. But the tigress calmed him down, and the cubs brushed around Gautama. That satisfied the tiger. The following day they had all disappeared.

Now Gautama tried to solve the riddle of the little whispering voices. He sat down under one of the tall shady trees and asked softly:

"Who are you, you little beings who are helpful to me when I help the animals? Are you also creatures? Who is your Creator?"

He heard quiet laughter, and seemed to feel someone gently stroking his hand. Yet he saw nothing. But then he heard a soft voice speaking eagerly to him:

"You great foolish man! You think you know so much, and you do not even know the Nature around you. We are the guardians of all beings. There is no animal, great or small, that we do not care for, no plant, no stone, that we do not attend to. We are servants of the gods. More we ourselves do not know."

"Who created you, little ones?" asked Gautama, in whose soul love also for these beings was beginning to stir.

"We were there before human beings existed. Perhaps the gods created us, perhaps we were in the world at the same time as the gods. We do not know. We do not ask about it either. We serve them, and protect the creatures."

"Why can I not see you?" was Gautama's next urgent question.

"That we do not know, man. Open your eyes and you will see us. And if you cannot do so of your own accord, then pray Vishnu to destroy that within you which still prevents you from doing so."

"How clever you are!" cried Gautama in admiration. Renewed tinkles of laughter answered him.

"You are not clever, at least not yet," whispered the little voice. "But you are good, and that is better than being clever. You love the animals. You helped Maina the tigress. You do not fear the snakes. That is why we help you too. You need only call us; we are always around you, but we like to be asked for our help. Only in extreme emergency do we also help without being asked."

Gautama had to return to school, but his soul was filled to bursting with joy and happiness. If he was thus one with the whole of Creation, surely it would reveal all its secrets to him, would help him to find and to recognise the gods.

He did not think of telling his teacher about his experience; but even without words the latter noticed the great change that had taken place in Gautama.

AGAIN MONTHS had passed, and the sage reverted to his question. This time Gautama was prepared for it, and answered promptly:

"Oh father, although I was a prince, I was more ignorant than the poorest pariah. Therefore I had to learn by experiencing, and work my way up through all the castes. I thank my destiny that I was permitted to do it in a few years instead of in many repeated earth-lives."

"This time you have found the right answer, my son," the sage commended him. "But it does not please me that you are grateful to your destiny. What is destiny?"

46

"I do not know, my father," confessed Gautama. "It is the path which I must tread. But I cannot yet see who ordains this path."

"Then pray to Shiva that he may open your eyes!" said the teacher.

The invisible ones had directed him to Vishnu, his teacher to Shiva. Gautama determined that now he would really begin to pray, and turn to Brahma, since after all the two other gods unite in him.

Once he had seriously determined on this, he also began to carry out his decision. He had in fact prayed before with the others, but for him it had been only a formality.

Now that he had consciously turned to Brahma with a request, he realised what blessing lay even in establishing connection in the inner volition with a being from On High. Indeed it was by no means so important for his prayer to be answered, if only he penetrated ever deeper into this connection.

A feeling of happiness flowed unceasingly through him, which could not be compared with what had gone before. The feeling of oneness with the creatures had made him happy; stretching upwards into higher realms filled him with bliss.

Only now did he begin to see the deep meaning behind everything earthly. He recognised how superficial he had hitherto been, even though so many thoughts had moved him. They had not been of the right kind.

He must not think about Brahma, he must stretch upwards to gain connection with him. Then he would experience him within himself, recognise him! Certainly nobody could teach him that.

And Gautama's figure, which was usually stooped because he always held his head bowed towards the ground, straightened and became erect. His features lost their constantly changing expression. They radiated an inner bliss that could not remain hidden from anyone.

His rather sluggish movements became harmonious and smooth. Everything he did seemed to be in harmony with his thoughts.

A few days later he went to his teacher and said, simply but with deep conviction:

"I have found a god. Whether his name is Brahma I do not know. I will call him so, because I have no other name for him. But Vishnu and Shiva are not his equals, not even of like nature, they are his servants. Now I know this for certain."

The Brahman rejoiced with him, and then said firmly:

"Then your time of learning with us is ended. We can teach you nothing more. You had to acquire your best knowledge yourself. Tend and cultivate it, so that it may spread abroad and bear ever new fruit."

"I am to leave you then, my father?" asked Gautama regretfully. "May I not remain here in the school until I know what is Brahma's will for me? I have no idea yet what I am to do in the world, and how I can serve this supreme god."

But the Brahman remained firm.

"When you were announced to us we were instructed to teach you all that we know ourselves. But after that you were to go out into the world. You will find your task, as you have found all else."

"Then I must travel the highway again," said Gautama with a smile. "All good things came to me from there."

"Try it," advised his teacher.

After that they spoke no more of it. But a few days later Gautama departed down the mountain towards the new life.

CONFLICTING thoughts filled him as he proceeded on his way. When he found himself alone on the highway for the first time, he had had to struggle for his daily bread. That was not necessary now: the school had provided amply for him, so that he had enough to live on for some time.

But in this way he was deprived of a certain incentive. For it was quite immaterial which way he turned; quite immaterial whether he journeyed on at all, or lay down in the shade to dream. This gave him a feeling of apathy. He was a burden to himself, because he did not know what to do with himself.

But into this drowsy inactivity there sounded like a battle-cry:

"Up, Gautama! You have to find your task! Enough time has already been lost! Not another day must you be idle!"

And the man who just then, dissatisfied with everything, was about to lose himself in dreaming and brooding, started up, straightened himself, and was conscious that his life had a purpose and a goal.

Not far from a village he found a child crying. He might have been the same age as his little Suddhodana when he saw him last.

48

For the first time in years the thought of his family passed clearly through his soul. He knew indeed that they were dead, perished in those terrible flames. But where might they be now? Who could tell him that!

Kindly he turned to the weeping child, lifted him up, and asked him what the trouble was. Stammering, the boy told him that he could not find his father and mother. He must have wandered away from home without his parents' knowledge.

Gautama spoke kindly to the still sobbing child, and carried him to the village. A wailing mother rushed towards him, and tore the child from his arms; a grateful father invited him into his hut so that he could thank him.

Gautama entered the home of these simple people, and shared their meal. Meanwhile a small spotted dog with long ears attached itself to him. Gautama had never seen such a dog before. He caressed it, even though it was considered unclean to touch a dog. He spoke to it, and the intelligent eyes of the animal seemed to answer:

"Let me stay with you."

"Will you sell me the dog?" he said, turning to the people.

They immediately offered to give it to him as a token of their gratitude, but Gautama would not hear of it. He gave them some money, and took the cheerful little fellow with him. He had asked what the animal's name was, but nobody had thought it worth a name.

"Then I will call you 'Comforter'; for you shall go with me into solitude and lighten my gloomy thoughts."

The dog ran merrily round its new master, who took up his journey once more.

They came to a crossroads. Gautama wanted to take the path to the left; meanwhile the dog bounded to the right, came back again, barked, tugged at Gautama's robe, and indicated as best it could that theirs was the road to the right. Gautama yielded good-naturedly.

"Do you want to be my guide, Comforter?" he asked with a smile.

The words brought to his mind Sariputta's remark that he had a guide. Could not he, Gautama, also be given such a helper, if he asked Brahma for one?

He immediately engrossed himself in prayer and asked fervently for a guide, since he himself did not know how he was to arrive at his task. Then

49

he rose up strengthened, and went on his way with greater courage than before. The guide would now appear at the right time; that he firmly believed.

The whole day passed without a village appearing.

"Comforter, you are leading me into solitude!" he called to the dog, almost reproachfully.

"Solitude," answered a voice within him. "You need solitude now, so that you may become clear about all that you have absorbed within you over the past years. How much of it has become experiencing for you? Sift and look, do not weaken in praying and deepening; only in this way will you be able to recognise your task. First prepare the instrument, then use it. First help yourself, then you will be able to help others."

"Who speaks to me? It is not you, you little invisible ones! Can it be the longed-for guide?" –

Weeks followed during which Gautama seldom saw a human being, and never spent the night under the protection of a roof. Comforter seemed to have the knack of finding lonely roads. Men who considered him unclean had taught him that. He avoided them.

However, Gautama tried to follow the instruction he had received. He let his whole life pass before his mind's eye. His real life had begun only on the highway; he knew that now. Only there had learning and experiencing begun for him, only there had his days been of value.

And his "masters" appeared in spirit before him, each one asking:
"What have I taught you?"

Each had given him exactly what he was able to absorb on that particular step of his development.

"One day, when I lead men, I shall proceed in exactly the same way," he thought, without realising the significance of this thought.

Once conceived, the thought would no longer be dismissed. Ever more often it crept into all his deliberations, never in the same form, but always present in some way or other.

Gautama tried to speak with his guide. He received no answer. On the other hand, whenever he concentrated on bringing this or that before the guide he was filled with greater clarity.

He became clearly aware that this was the best way for him to deal with everything. And the guide did not answer questions. Then if Gautama sought the answer in his inner being he always found it.

In order to be able to listen entirely within, the seeker had even closed himself to the little invisible beings, and ceased to take notice of the animals around him. Comforter had been the only exception.

Slowly he now began to open himself again to the outside world. Rich powers streamed to him from all sides. He heard the whispering voices again, and the animals came to him trustingly. His life became rich and worth living.

A PARTICULARLY beautiful day was drawing to a close. The golden sun had set like a luminous ball. In the blue evening sky star upon star appeared, gleaming like silver, sparkling.

Gautama was resting under a big solitary tree, gazing around him with understanding eyes. How full of wonders everything was! How could he ever have doubted the existence of a God in view of this glorious lawfulness!

Comforter had nestled against his feet. The animal's trusting nature did the man good. Golden threads glided softly through the air, fine, luminous threads such as Gautama had never seen before. Nor did he know whence they came. Now he saw that they alighted on himself.

Just then the little whispering voices began:

"Gautama, listen: the threads have found you. They have sought you for seven years long! For seven whole years they came, they found you but could not link with you, because your cloak repulsed them. Today at last you are so opened to the Light that the threads have been able to lower themselves on to you."

"Where do the luminous threads come from?" Gautama asked the invisible beings.

However they did not reply, but the guide, for the first time, answered Gautama's question:

"They have issued from the devout thoughts and prayers of a human being who prays for your welfare. Do you know who, out of love, has remembered you before Brahma every day for seven whole years?"

51

"Maya, my wife!" cried Gautama with conviction. "She was pious, she was good, and she loved me truly."

"Yes, Gautama, your wife has not ceased to pray for you. It is thanks to her prayers that powers were able to approach you which at first were only a little attracted by you yourself. Send her your gratitude, she deserves it."

It did not occur to Gautama to ask where Maya might be. He sought her in the beyond, and was glad that someone there thought lovingly of him. He thanked her with a full heart, but as a departed spirit, worlds away.

The whole sky was now a glimmering sea of stars; Gautama could not take his eyes off it.

"Stars," he cried, "are you too servants of Brahma?"

But the stars did not reply. Gautama sank into reflection. Everything in the world pursued its ordered course, everything had a purpose and a goal. Therefore he too must adapt himself to fit into the Cosmic Laws, so that his life should not go by without purpose.

And he implored, as never before, that Brahma would at last remove the veil that obscured his way, would grant that his task might be revealed to him. He found ever new words for his plea, which he bore aloft more and more fervently, as though he would storm the heavens.

Exhausted, he fell silent at last. His physical body was shaken by the intensity of the soul's struggle.

Then he heard quite unearthly sounds approaching, following each other like soft, soothing waves. It was as though everything in Nature vibrated in accordance with these sounds, as if trees and flowers bowed, as if the stars were dancing in a shimmering roundelay.

All around him was filled with rosy light, which took the shape of flower-petals. The blossom, in the centre of which he himself was seated, appeared to him like a huge lotus-flower from the sacred River Ganges.

Other sounds were heard, the rosy hue of the flower-petals changed to light blue, then to gold, until finally the flower shone forth in purest white. His soul was overwhelmed. He could not think; in pure intuitive sensing he absorbed what was now revealed to him.

A resonant voice spoke:

"Siddharta, guard the purity which now surrounds you! Let yourself be enfolded by it, as the flower-petals mantle the innermost part of the

52

blossom. As the lotus-flower drifts along the sacred river, so let yourself be guided through the stream of life. As it dispenses fragrance and refreshes the eye of man by its loveliness, so should you also give of the knowledge which Brahma has bestowed upon you, comfort and strengthen those who approach you. And just as it is rooted firmly in the bed of the river, so let your roots also rest in the beyond, from whence Brahma's Grace will grant you ever new knowledge. Do not let yourself be cut off from it."

The voice fell silent, the sounds grew fainter, the pure blossom disappeared. Gautama's soul was opened to take in all glory, like a draught of clearest water.

New sounds came. This time they were not delicate vibrations. Nature was filled with a rushing; it seemed as though the sounds were to proclaim something infinitely high, sublime. Gautama sensed that. He cast himself down on his knees, and touched the ground with his forehead.

Again the voice rang out:

"Look up, man!"

Gautama obeyed the command and raised his eyes. The heavens above him seemed to be opened. A flood of light and radiance poured forth from them. It appeared to the gazing soul like paths of rays. And he followed these paths with the eyes of the spirit, high and ever higher.

Then he saw a Temple shining in purest white. Streams of water seemed to flow from it, pouring out over the Universe and refreshing it.

And then the portals of this Temple opened, luminous beings with pure wings emerged from it, and held aside a golden curtain. Gautama's soul gazed into a sanctuary. And the voice at his side spoke:

"You are blessed among thousands of men in being allowed to behold this. Hold it fast in your soul, Siddharta. Never forget it. It is the Temple of Him Who is Lord over all the Worlds. What you see is still only the lowest of all the Temples. Strive with all your soul, that you may also be shown a higher one."

The sublime picture faded, the sounds died away; but the voice spoke on:

"The Lord of all the Worlds, Who has allowed you to be guided and prepared, calls you to His service! Siddharta, will you devote your life to Him? Will you be His servant, faithful and trustworthy, ready at any hour?"

When the voice ceased, Gautama answered:

"Whoever you may be who summon me in the Name of the Lord, I say to you: I will!"

"Then in the Name of the Lord of all the Worlds, Whose servant I also am, I call you to the service of your own people! Go through the lands which you have traversed during the past seven years, gather disciples around you and teach them. In speaking, you will so remould the knowledge which the Eternal One has allowed to be mediated to you that your people will be able to receive and understand it. Teach them to lead pure lives, teach them to lead active lives. But above all teach them to worship the Eternal One, the Lord of all the Worlds, out of a devout soul!

"Everywhere in the great realm, develop communities of human beings who have recognised Him and wish to serve Him. Show them how to teach others. So the pure doctrine will slowly spread, like the roots of a great tree. This tree, whose seeds the Eternal One allows to sink into you today, will bear rich fruits.

"Siddharta, the Lord of the Worlds expects great things of you! Strive with all your might to be able to fulfil them. One great danger lies on your path: that surrounded by earthly comforts you become idle in well-being. Now that you know, avoid it!"

The voice was silent. Gautama was filled with jubilation, praise and gratitude. He awaited the morning in prayer.

To him who had now found his task at last, the sun seemed to shine in a completely new light. All, all had been told him. He knew how he had to proceed, to be able to carry out the Command of the Lord of all the Worlds.

And while Gautama once more called the words to mind, so that he would never forget them, it struck him that the voice had called him Siddharta. If he was called by this name again, was he no longer Gautama? Siddharta signified: one who has reached his goal!

That was it! He had reached the first goal set him, had found his task. Anyone from the race of the Tshakya could call himself Gautama, Siddharta was his own name!

"I may stand in the lotus-flower amid all purity, if I myself remain pure," he cried exultantly. "Brahma, help me to do so!"

Comforter jumped around him, barking. He bent down to the dog and caressed it, saying:

"We two shall not be alone for long. Now pupils will join us, according to the Command of the Lord of all the Worlds." The animal looked at him attentively.

"You do not know either how that will come about?" Siddharta smiled. "We must wait. The Command was to gather disciples, not to seek disciples. I shall wait, and the disciples will come."

Cheerfully he reached up into the tree under which he had had the wonderful experiences during the night. From its branches hung delicious fruits which refreshed him.

"Thank you, tree, for all that you have given me," cried Siddharta merrily. "I shall call you Brahma's Tree."

As he was about to continue his journey he saw a man coming along the path. A rare occurrence in this lonely region. He gazed towards him curiously. What could this man want here? To what caste did he belong?

Long before he was able to see the features of the approaching man, he could tell by his robe that he was a priest. He wore a robe of rich blue silk, held by a wide, brightly-embroidered sash. The older pupils with whom Siddharta had been living during the last few months were dressed exactly like that. He gazed eagerly at the approaching man. But the latter suddenly uttered a cry of joy and began to run.

"Gautama, Gautama!" he cried happily. "At last I have found you! I have been seeking you for weeks. At times I thought I was quite near you, then again you seemed to be far, far away. Finally last night I distinctly heard the words: 'Today you shall be united with him!'"

It was Ananda who came running towards him, the scholar who had been most attached to Siddharta. The latter was glad to see his former fellow-student, but could not understand why he had been looking for him.

"I would like to become your pupil, your disciple, Gautama," besought Ananda. "Do not send me away! The Head-Brahman told me that it was Brahma's will."

Instead of replying, Siddharta turned to the dog to conceal his deep emotion, and said to it jestingly:

55

"You see, Comforter, we have not had to wait long at all! I was not to *seek* but to *gather*. Where there is one, more will join."

Then he told his friend of his experiences, and gave him permission to accompany him. He imposed only two conditions:

He was not to consider the dog unclean, for nothing created by the Lord of the Worlds is unclean; and he must no longer call him Gautama.

"I have become a Siddharta!" he ended with a touch of pride.

As they conversed they had begun their journey, and without knowing it Siddharta began to teach, by passing on his experiences.

Ananda was an attentive listener, who also knew how to ask at the right time, so that everything which Siddharta had absorbed within him had to be remoulded and come to life, to enable him to pass it on in the right way.

"Do you still think that life is only a chain of suffering?" asked Ananda.

Siddharta reflected for a while and then replied:

"According to Brahma's will it is not so; that is certain. The Lord of the Worlds did not make creatures in order to let them suffer. Nevertheless it is a fact that our path here on earth is full of suffering. Hence it has come into the world against the will of Brahma. We have brought it upon ourselves as the consequence of evil deeds!

"Once we know this, we also have in our hands the means to fight against the suffering: We must change, then life will change for us!"

Ananda interrupted him:

"What do you mean by that: life will change for us?"

"Surely that is clear!" answered Siddharta quickly. "If we change, we shall no longer attract any evil effect. Instead of a chain of suffering, life will become happier."

"But it will not have changed through that, *we* shall have arranged it differently through our improvement," the pupil persisted. "Now I understand it."

"You can also put it like that," admitted Siddharta, and then continued:

"Hence if I want to get rid of the suffering, which has come into the world against Brahma's will, I must seek to improve mankind. That is my task. But since a single human being would not be enough for this, I must gather pupils around me, whom I allow to share my experiences. They must then help to spread among men that which can make them better."

"And what can make them better?" Ananda asked thoughtfully.

"The right knowledge of Brahma, the Lord of the Worlds!"

Siddharta was about to continue, but was interrupted by the disciple, who, as though driven by some strange power, asked:

"Is Brahma really the Lord of the Worlds?"

Siddharta stared at him, speechless.

"How can you doubt, after all I have told you?" he asked in turn. But Ananda did not let himself be intimidated:

"We knew Brahma before you thought you had found him. I believe that He Whom you have found stands far above Brahma."

"I know that He Whom I have found really is the Lord of the Worlds! I do not have a name for Him. I call Him Brahma."

"You must not do so, Siddharta!" said Ananda heatedly. "With that you confuse the concepts. Think of all the people who have known of Brahma up to now. If you tell them that this god is the Lord of the World, they will not be affected by it. It will not speak to their soul, as it does not speak to mine, because .... because .... it is not true!"

Then Siddharta realised that he had been about to treat the sacred knowledge which had been revealed to him thoughtlessly. Now he understood also why, when he spoke of Brahma, nothing in him vibrated and resounded as it did when he used the name "Lord of the Worlds". And he was grateful to Ananda, who had helped him to a better understanding.

But now the pupil walking by his side was irksome to him. He would have liked to speak to his guide, to ask him what he was to call the Lord of the Worlds. Then Comforter leapt up at him and seemed to say:

"See, I don't disturb you either! Let Ananda walk beside you just as I skip round you, as something that belongs to you, but can only distract you from your thoughts if you yourself allow it."

And Siddharta became absorbed in his inner being and spoke with his guide, as he was now accustomed to do. The only answer he received was:

"Wait!"

Towards evening they came to a village, and decided to spend the night there. A lodging was soon found. The people were trusting and cheerful, almost like the Dravidians, but belonged to another tribe. Before he slept,

Siddharta prayed with great fervour for enlightenment. And in the night a wonderful picture was shown to him:

He saw the earth spread out like a vast plain, covered with mountains and streams, towns and villages, inhabited by animals, plants and human beings.

Among them all moved, floated and flowed transparent, luminous figures of various forms and sizes. They seemed in some way or other to be taking care of all living things.

But none of these figures stood by itself alone. They appeared to be suspended from above as though by a chain, of which they were the lowest link. These chains were made up of beings similar to themselves.

Right at the top, they united in a single great, outstanding link. Siddharta saw the one who formed this link, and great awe filled him.

"Was that the Lord of the Worlds?"

A deep, ringing voice called:

"Brahma!"

Then Siddharta awoke, and knew that what he had been allowed to behold was no dream but reality, reality deeper than his day-life. But he also knew that this was not the end of what would be revealed to him. Therefore he did not speak of it to Ananda. The latter however was well aware that something great was taking place in Siddharta's soul, and left him alone until evening.

All day long Siddharta turned over in his soul what he had seen.

"What I have been allowed to see must be the invisible ones," he concluded. "So Brahma is the ruler and leader of the invisible ones. Then he is certainly not the Lord of all the Worlds. Or is he? Then where are Vishnu and Shiva?"

He could hardly wait for the night to come. His prayers assailed the heavens, supplicating for further knowledge.

Another picture rose up before him:

He saw Brahma, from whom the animistic chains descended, standing on the brink of an immeasurable space. His eyes gradually became accustomed to the breadth and height.

He saw glorious, luminous beings, who formed circles in constant joyous movement. These circles sparkled in the most delicate colours, whose lively movement was accompanied by musical tones.

Upwards, the rings narrowed, although the beings who formed them seemed to become ever larger and more majestic. Now Siddharta saw that the centre of all circles was a blue curtain, before which red roses floated downwards.

The beholder knew that this curtain concealed the Holiest Mystery. Only when the living curtain was drawn, only then would the Lord of the Worlds reveal Himself.

"No one can see Him," said the deep voice, which was now quite familiar to Siddharta.

"What can I call Him, Him Who is so exalted that even angels cannot approach Him?"

"Call Him the Eternal One," the voice answered.

As it uttered the Name, streams of most glorious light flowed from behind the curtain. Then strength surged into Siddharta's soul, and the voices of those whom he had unconsciously called "angels" rose in jubilation.

Fervent thanks and great joy filled the blessed one even long after the vision had faded into soft tones. But towards morning he heard the voice of his guide, which sounded quite different from the deep voice in the night:

"Arise, Siddharta! Do not dream over what has been given to you, but transform it into deed. Two days' journey from here will bring you to the kingdom of Magadha. King Bimbisara needs you!"

So ready was Siddharta to obey the command that he awoke Ananda at once and set out immediately, even before the sun had risen behind the mountains. The disciple murmured somewhat at this wandering in the dark, but Siddharta was sure that he had done what was right, and walked on cheerfully.

His soul rejoiced, and now became aware of his surroundings again. And behold: the little beings who had so often helped him no longer remained invisible. Since he had seen them in the night in the vision, he was allowed to see them also now.

They flitted busily around him, as though they really wanted to show him how much they had to do in the service of the Lord.

He watched them as they helped a little bird to build its nest, saw how they straightened the tendrils that were disordered by the wind, how they shook the dew from the flower-buds where there was too much of it.

They did all this joyously, and the joy communicated itself to everything that was open to it.

Siddharta told Ananda about it and tried to awaken happiness about the new seeing in him also. But the disciple neither saw nor sensed anything intuitively and thought that it was better for him to keep only to the gods whom he could understand.

"Understand the gods!" exclaimed Siddharta in horror. "Ananda, how am I to begin to bring you light?"

At which the pupil reminded him that it was he who had drawn Siddharta's attention to his wrong idea of Brahma. The master admitted this, but begged the other not to deduce from it that he knew everything, and could learn nothing more.

"I have come to learn," said Ananda, "but you will understand that I will accept only what I myself can grasp. If I am to believe in the beings of whom you tell me, they will surely reveal themselves to me."

Siddharta contented himself with that, and was sure that Ananda would yet experience the working of the little servants of the Eternal One.

THEY HAD been travelling for two days, from time to time asking in a village for the way to Magadha. Only on the third day did they reach a fortified town.

They found the gate closed, and all calling was in vain. No one appeared. It was a strange gate, made of bronze, which was let into the wall.

Siddharta examined it closely. There were all kinds of symbols on it, partly engraved and partly embossed. Surely they must have a meaning. As he mused, he let his fingers glide over some of these symbols, and suddenly the gate gave way, apparently opening of itself. At the same time armed men came rushing out, shouting in excitement:

"Who is able to open our gate?"

Siddharta confessed that it was he, because no one had answered his calls, and he needed to speak urgently with King Bimbisara.

The men looked at each other in utmost amazement. Then they surrounded Siddharta and Ananda. But before leading them away, they explained that the dog must remain outside the town.

"I will not be parted from Comforter," Siddharta assured them, as he called to the animal and took it up in his arms.

Now the men were satisfied; they had been afraid that the dog might jump on someone and make him unclean.

A large escort took the two travellers to the town-centre, where a palatial building rose up in an open square. One of the leaders entered the building, while a dense circle of curious people gathered round the two strangers.

"They have opened our gate," the armed men declared. "They know our King's name!"

Both statements were received with loud expressions of amazement. Siddharta felt as though he were in a dream; everything seemed quite unreal to him.

At last the portals of the building opened. Servants emerged, crossed their arms over their breast and bowed several times. Then they invited the strangers to enter. Again the dog was to remain outside, but Siddharta took it inside with him. He knew that in doing so he was probably showing a lack of respect to the King, but something stronger than all such considerations urged him to do so.

In a large, dimly lit chamber some men were gathered round the King, who was seated on a golden chair.

Siddharta stood still and awaited his greeting. The King rose. He was a middle-aged man, rather stout, with somewhat weak features and very small but sharp eyes. Now they were directed full on Siddharta, who calmly returned the gaze.

"Did you open our gate, stranger?" the King asked, instead of greeting him.

Siddharta was silent.

"How is it that you know my name?"

Still Siddharta was silent.

"Stranger, I pray you, speak!" the King implored him. "So much depends on it for me, for our country."

"How can I speak when you neglect the simplest courtesy, King of Magadha?" replied Siddharta in a tone of indifference.

"Spare me the ceremony of greeting, O stranger," begged the King. "We

61

have no time to lose. Later I shall make up for all that now I have neglected, but answer me!"

"Very well, I tell you that it was I who opened the gate, and that your name was revealed to me."

Siddharta spoke as though under compulsion. He himself could not understand why he did not say that he had opened the gate by chance. Something prevented him from doing so.

But the King looked at him in delight and asked: "Tell me also, have you been journeying on the highways through the castes?"

"It is as you say," was Siddharta's surprised answer; for the King seemed to know about him.

But Bimbisara rejoiced, and gave every possible expression to this joy.

"Welcome, noble Prince!" he said, bowing. "We have long awaited you. The prince of the great neighbouring realm, to whom we have paid tribute ever since we lost a war under one of my ancestors, is arrogating ever more power over us. Now he demands that all ten-year-old maidens be handed over to him. In a few days' time we are to take them across the border. And my daughter, the Princess of our Realm, is among them."

Siddharta listened in amazement. Why did the people not defend themselves?

The King continued his account:

"It was foretold to us that when the prince's arrogance was at its height a foreign Prince would come to help us. He had journeyed on the highways through all the castes. He would open our locked gate, whose secret is known only to a few trusty men, and he would know the secret name of the King.

"Now you know why I could not wait to find out if you are the promised one. Now help us!"

"Yes, Prince, help us!" also begged the counsellors and servants with him. But Siddharta asked:

"Was nothing else foretold to you about the helper?"

"He would tell us about the heavenly beings, without whose help we would ever again fall into the power of dark princes," said the King after a moment's reflection.

"What do you know of the gods?" asked Siddharta.

"Nothing, my Prince," replied Bimbisara. "No one has told us about them."

"Whom do you worship?" was Siddharta's next question.

"We have found no one who was worthy of it, my Prince," was the answer.

Then Siddharta knew that here was to be the starting-point for his work. The distress of the people was to open their hearts to him. All this he understood quite clearly. Not so Ananda, who had listened speechless with horror.

"Master, let us go," he urged. "Truly this people in their unbelief have fallen to the wrath of the gods. If we stay we must perish with them."

"You are mistaken, Ananda. If we go we shall deserve the punishment of the Eternal One, but if we stay we can lead the people to the Light."

The brief dialogue was conducted quietly. Those around them looked anxiously at the strangers. What would they decide?

Then Siddharta turned to the King and said pleasantly:

"I will help you!"

A sigh of great relief went through the crowd.

"I will help you. But I am not able to do so out of my own strength. I shall implore for help from the Lord of the Worlds, Who has sent me to you. If He gives me strength I am ready to face anyone. Now tell me, O King, about your neighbour. Tell me what has happened."

And the King explained that every two years a heavy tribute was exacted. On the last occasion horses and arms for a hundred warriors had to be taken across the border. This time their daughters were demanded of them.

But the neighbour's arrogance went so far that before receiving the tribute he would fight a duel with one of the foremost warriors of their people. He proclaimed that if the warrior was victorious he would never again demand tribute, and would also return what was brought now.

But no one was able to vanquish the prince, who was helped by evil powers. He fought with snakes and tigers, with jackals and hyenas, which he let loose on his adversaries.

On hearing this, Siddharta's mind was completely at rest. He knew with certainty that he would be the victor. Nor would the Eternal One have commanded him to help Bimbisara if He were not going to assist him.

63

The King equipped his helper with a good weapon and an excellent shield. He wanted also to give him a mount, one that was accustomed to warfare, but Siddharta declined it. He wished to meet his adversary on foot.

When the appointed day came, a mighty procession of armed men, headed by the King, set out to accompany Siddharta. By his command, the maidens who had been demanded were left behind. So strong was the King's trust in the promised helper that he obeyed his will without question.

They crossed the border in good time, and presently found themselves in a wide forest-clearing. Then in the presence of all Siddharta bowed down, and touched the ground three times with his forehead. Thereafter he remained on his knees and prayed:

"Thou the All-Highest, the Eternal One, Thou Who art, though men know naught of Thee! Thou hast sent me to awaken the hearts of this people. Grant me the strength to free these men from the bondage of the Darkness and of evil!"

Amazed, the men heard this prayer, which they interpreted in their own way. Such certainty, but also such reverence, vibrated through the words, that the hearts of those waiting here in fear and grief were deeply touched by them. It was the first seed-grain that fell into their hearts.

Now armed men approached the clearing from the opposite side, led by the giant prince, his weapons sparkling like gold. He carried his head high, his angry eyes flashed searchingly over the assemblage.

"Where are the maidens who are to be ours today?" he shouted at the King.

Instead of the King, Siddharta answered, calmly but in a loud, clear voice:

"We simply did not bring them, because it would only give us the trouble of taking them home again."

The prince had not expected such an answer. He bellowed with rage, and challenged Siddharta to do battle with him. Siddharta stepped forward calmly.

"Before we fight you must tell me that the conditions hold good: if I am victor, this people will be exempt for ever from paying tribute. And you will be my prisoner."

"And if I am victor?" shouted the prince in reply.

"That you will never be again! Now answer my question."

The prince wanted to laugh and jeer, but his tongue seemed to be paralysed. Fear had gripped him in face of so much victorious confidence. But then he thought of his helpers which were hidden behind, and he promised what Siddharta had demanded.

Siddharta drew his sword, clasped his hands round the hilt in prayer, and awaited his adversary. Suddenly he saw before him a little elemental being, who was looking around with a watchful eye.

"Beware!" whispered the little being, and the outstretched finger pointed to the edge of the forest, out of which two gigantic snakes were creeping towards them in great coils.

Siddharta laughed merrily, and began to whistle through his teeth as was his wont. The snakes listened attentively. He spoke to them and ordered them to leave the place, and they obeyed at once.

His adversary foamed with rage, and shouted at the snakes to carry out his commands. They paid no heed to him, but took themselves off.

Then Siddharta said:

"Know, you men, that the animals are creatures of the Eternal One. They would rather obey the Light than the Darkness!"

The enemy let out a cry of encouragement, and two splendid tigers, just released from their chains, bounded towards Siddharta.

He looked at them without speaking. They turned away from him, and were about to rush at King Bimbisara, who stood unprotected before his warriors. A call from Siddharta brought them to a halt.

"You must not harm this man either," said he. "He belongs to me."

Before anyone knew what was happening, the tigers had leapt on the hostile leader and torn him to pieces, making off with their prey. His people fled screaming, as if they were afraid that the same fate might also befall them.

But Siddharta stood with radiant countenance in the centre of the battle-ground. When the enemy had vanished, he called Bimbisara and his warriors to kneel down with him in gratitude to the Eternal One, Who had so visibly given His help here.

Not one held back. From hearts deeply stirred their gratitude rose up to

65

God Who had revealed Himself to them, so that henceforth they should believe in Him.

Siddharta remained at the court of the King, and taught all those who came to him. Ananda travelled through the realm and did likewise. After three years the people of Magadha knew of nothing better than to serve God and to fulfil His Will.

Joy and happiness had come to the country with this knowledge. The people, who even before then had been striving to live rightly, distinguished themselves by their good and pure morals. Bimbisara, however, laid aside his kingship, and became the high priest of God in the realm of Magadha, through which he travelled full of zeal, proclaiming and admonishing.

Although Siddharta had come to love the people among whom he now lived and worked, he felt the urge to move on. Someone else could fill his place here. But he did not yet know which way he should turn.

THEN ONE day a small troop of men from the neighbouring realm came to beg him to bring to their nation also the blessing which the people of Magadha enjoyed.

Bimbisara, whom this request reminded once more of all the wrong that he and his people had suffered through their savage neighbours, warned Siddharta earnestly:

"Do not go to them, Siddharta. Their ways are too coarse, their hearts too hard. We had no gods when you came to us; but they have, and they are terrible. They make human sacrifices to them!"

"That is just why I must go to them, Bimbisara," answered Siddharta with deep conviction. "I shall ask my guide; what he tells me I shall do gladly."

And he sent up the question in prayer, but received only the curt reply: "Do you need to ask?"

"No, indeed!" cried Siddharta, "I knew at once that this would be the next stage of my journey."

He commanded the escort to wait for him. Then he took leave of them, and set out with Ananda. But he had not gone far when he heard someone following him. He looked back and saw one of the lesser priests from Magadha.

Siddharta stopped, and stood waiting patiently until the man, breathless from running, was able to speak. Only then did he ask him what he wanted.

"Master, take me as your pupil!" the priest implored. "A voice within me continually says that I should join you. Take me with you!"

"Then the voice must be right," conceded Siddharta. "What am I to call you?"

"Give me a name which I shall bear henceforth in honour of the Eternal One," begged the priest.

An idea flashed through Siddharta's mind: he would now retrace his steps. His pupils should receive the names of his former "masters"!

"Then I shall call you Maggalana, my friend. The first Maggalana who came into my life was a Brahman like you. Strive to become as pure and clear as he!"

Maggalana thanked the Master and joined Ananda, to whom this reinforcement of their group was welcome. On their departure Bimbisara had given them an armed escort, so that their appearance in the new country could be in keeping with their task. Each member of a higher caste counted as two.

Hardly had they crossed the frontier than they noticed a vast difference in all that met the eye. Mountain-ranges traversed the country; but the valleys nestling between them were not cultivated, although they were made fertile by the brooks and rivers that flowed through them. Herds of cattle, mainly goats, grazed on the mountain-slopes, but they too appeared to be untended and semi-wild.

Sturdy yaks, which were used as draught-animals, were kept in enclosures. They also gave the impression of neglect. And the dwellings! They were miserable huts of clay, straw and wood, on which not the least care had been bestowed.

A roughly-carved, garishly-painted board, depicting a most horribly distorted human figure, was propped against each of the huts. Comforter growled at these grotesques, and Siddharta had to agree with him.

But his guides bowed each time, and on being questioned told him that these were images of the gods.

"How can you make such images?" asked Siddharta, horrified. They replied casually:

"Who is going to stop us?"

Then the Master enquired no further, but resolved to wait until he could speak with the prince himself. This came to pass at sunset of the same day, when the troop rode into the capital of the country, which seemed to consist for the most part of mud huts, as in the rest of the land.

There were no town walls or gates. People rode unchallenged from any of the intersecting roads to the centre of the settlement.

Here stood a few buildings of stone. They were crookedly and incompetently built, but nonetheless demonstrated the attempt to emulate the neighbouring peoples. The "palace" of the prince was even an imitation of Bimbisara's palace.

The new prince received Siddharta with great obsequiousness. He knew that the sage was responsible for the death of his predecessor, and was grateful to him for it. He would have liked to become ruler of the Virudas long before, he even thought he had a greater right to it than the previous prince, who on his own authority, and disregarding all others, had ascended the throne and maintained himself there.

But whereas the last prince had been a born ruler, who knew how to govern all his people with an iron hand, Viruda-Sava, as the new prince was called, was a weakling, under whose rule everything threatened to collapse. He perceived this and looked for a way out. At the same time he had followed with envy the blossoming of the neighbouring people. He attributed everything to the new faith.

Now he wanted the same for the Virudas. This quickly became clear to Siddharta. However much the prince attempted to hide his thoughts, the Master still saw through him. The source from which the desire for knowledge of the Eternal One flowed was impure. Could any blessing arise there? Siddharta answered evasively, but agreed to stay as a guest in the palace for the time being.

Filth and garbage wherever the eye fell!

"See," said Siddharta to his two companions, "the soul creates its environment according to its own state. A pure soul cannot live in such squalor!"

He gave orders that the rooms prepared for him and his companions should be cleaned by his own servants. The palace-servants watched this work with astonished looks.

When the rooms had become somewhat habitable, people gathered round, foremost of all Prince Viruda-Sava. They could not comprehend what had wrought this transformation. It was a long time before the curious were turned away, and Siddharta could retire to rest.

He longed to speak with his guide about his work among this dark people. He was firmly convinced that he would be ordered to move on. But this was not so.

"You must do your very best, Siddharta," his guide said firmly and earnestly. "These people must not continue to exist as a danger to neighbouring tribes."

"Then let the others defend themselves by force of arms!" cried Siddharta. "How can anything pure blossom from such Darkness?"

"It is not for you to decide on the worthiness or unworthiness of those who are sent to you," admonished his guide. "Nor is it a question here of warding off external dangers. As long as this people worship their self-made idols they will send out evil thoughts into their surroundings. The Darkness is untiringly active. It does not rest, it never gives up when it is a question of gaining adherents. You can learn from it in this respect.

"Let yourself be filled anew with strength every day, and work as you have never worked before, so that at least some of this people may still be saved. For it is the Will of the Eternal One that it shall not survive in its present state."

Now that he knew that it was really his task to work here, Siddharta set about it undaunted on the very next morning. A lofty fighting spirit filled him; he felt that here it was not so much a matter of proclaiming as of fighting in the Name of his Lord.

When Viruda-Sava asked him again if he would help the people, he declared himself ready. Delighted, the prince exclaimed that he would be the first to worship the new god! Siddharta should prepare the sacrifice that he would offer.

"What would you sacrifice?" asked the Master, astonished.

"Whatever the new god demands," was the indifferent reply. "You need only say. Not long ago we took ten prisoners. We have looked after them well, they are plump. Shall we slaughter them in honour of the god?"

Shuddering with disgust and horror, Siddharta was unable to speak for some time. But Viruda-Sava considered the silence to be a sign of dissatisfaction with the paltriness of the sacrifice.

Eager to convince the teacher of his good will, he solemnly declared:

"You are right, foreign men are not good enough for the noble god whom you want to bring to us. It must be men from our own people that we sacrifice. I shall see to it that ten of our warriors are made ready."

At this Siddharta burst out vehemently. He refused to utter a single word about the Eternal One so long as Viruda-Sava was capable of expressing such thoughts.

The latter was aghast at the boundless anger that he had unleashed with no evil intent. He wanted to apologise, but Siddharta shouted at him to be silent, and would have gone on venting his displeasure. Suddenly a luminous being stood before him, and placed its finger on its lips. At the same time he heard a gentle voice:

"Siddharta, your anger is not in accord with the Eternal Laws. How can you expect this man to know better, when no one has yet helped him? Show him that the Eternal One is of a different nature from his incompetent idols. But show it to him gently, for how else is he to believe in the Goodness of the Lord of all the Worlds? People judge the master by the servants! Remember that!"

Siddharta was ashamed. He turned kindly to the man who stood trembling before him:

"Viruda-Sava, you do not yet know that the Lord of the Worlds wants no sacrifices. He would rather *preserve* life than have it destroyed for His sake. You may not worship Him yet. First you must get to know Him, and perceive inwardly how exalted He is; then you may try to approach Him in prayer."

Viruda-Sava, indeed, hardly understood the meaning of these words, and yet he felt that there must be something special about this new god. Reverence which he had never known before seized him and made him fall silent.

Siddharta began to teach. But he soon perceived that the concept of a god was completely foreign to the prince. He could not form any idea of it.

70

"What gods have you worshipped up to now?" enquired the teacher, hoping to be able to make a link here.

Instead of answering, Viruda-Sava clapped his hands, and ordered the servants hastening towards him to bring his gods. Two horribly carved and painted wooden boards were brought in. Viruda-Sava explained:

"This one is Hagshr, the other is Shuvi."

Involuntarily he bowed as he spoke, so that Siddharta could see that the prince had a certain reverence even for these abominations. Patiently he asked further:

"Do you pray to the gods?"

"No, I make sacrifices."

"When do you make the sacrifices? Only when you want something from them, or regularly?"

"When it is the time to do so," was the rather unsatisfactory answer.

Then Siddharta asked:

"Please tell me about your gods."

Slowly Viruda-Sava began:

"They are as they look, ugly, cruel and bloodthirsty. If we do not make sacrifices to them they do us mischief. They frighten us at night so that we cannot sleep; they set wild beasts on us. They send disease and death, and make our enterprises miscarry.

"Therefore we have always to offer sacrifices if we want to escape all these things, particularly if we plan some military or plundering expedition. At the same time, however, we are also shrewd: we do not make sacrifices before the military expeditions, but promise the gods to fatten the prisoners if they will grant us victory. Then the gods see to it that we take a good many prisoners."

Breathing a sigh of relief, the man stopped. Probably he had never before made such a long speech. Siddharta was deeply shaken. The Dravidians were a guileless, pure people, whose childlike outlook had preserved them from evil. But the Virudas had fallen into the power of the Darkness with all their thoughts.

He hardly knew how to begin to bring light to these poor souls. Repeating the names of the gods with a shudder, it struck him that they

71

were the ones well known to him, but horribly garbled. Shuvi was quite clearly Vishnu, and Hagshr must stand for Shakra.

"Your gods cannot harm you if you have no fear of them," he said to Viruda-Sava in a firm tone. "They are made by human hands, and human hands can destroy them."

"These are only their images, but we must not do any harm to them either; for the gods would avenge themselves," asserted Viruda-Sava.

"If these are only their images, where are they themselves?" asked Siddharta, glad to have found a point of contact.

"Everywhere," the other assured him nervously. "They are all around us."

"What will happen to me if I destroy one of these images?" the teacher enquired.

"I do not know. You would probably be struck by lightning, or the god himself would strangle you."

"I tell you, Viruda-Sava, nothing of the kind will happen. Look out!"

Before the other could prevent him, Siddharta had seized the prince's sword, which was leaning against the wall, and cut one of the idols in two.

Shrieking with terror, Viruda-Sava covered his face with his hands. There was silence in the room. Nothing happened.

"Look here!" said Siddharta encouragingly, "The idol is destroyed, but no god has appeared. Do you know why? Because there is no god that looks like this monstrosity. There are powers of Darkness which may be similarly shaped, but I do not know them. They dare not approach me, because I am a servant of the Lord of all the Worlds."

Viruda-Sava cast anxious glances at the shavings lying on the ground, then he asked:

"Am I also protected because I am standing beside you?"

"You are protected because you have recognised that your idol is nothing; because you want to be a student of the new faith. Viruda-Sava, just think: if your gods had any power, your predecessor would not have been torn to pieces by the tigers when I allowed them to do so. Who do you suppose has given me the power over the animals?"

Without answering the last question, Viruda-Sava blurted out:

"He deserved no better, brutal tyrant that he was!"

Again it seemed as if the soul was about to slip from him. Siddharta had to take stronger measures. Without hesitation he now destroyed the second idol also. It did him good to be able to vent all his inner displeasure on something. But Viruda-Sava evidently was no longer much afraid. He hardly expected anything dreadful to happen.

"Now let the servants kindle a pile of wood outside," suggested Siddharta. "Then we shall burn the pieces on it."

He had expected opposition, but the other allowed it to be done. When the fire was burning brightly he even helped the Master to throw in the remains of the former idols, and suddenly he called out, half chanting, in a triumphant tone:

"Here burn Shuvi and Hagshr, the false gods. They are too cowardly to avenge the destruction of their images. They are afraid of the strange, great God. Come, you people, and see how they burn!"

And he began to dance around the flames. Others joined him. The tumult became ever greater; for the others had also begun to sing – if this string of discordant sounds could be called a song – and to proclaim that Shuvi and Hagshr were being destroyed here for ever.

When the flames threatened to die down, they brought out all the terrible idols that were leaning against their homes, and threw them into the fire, which flared up brightly each time they did so. All the caricatures were destroyed.

Women and children looked on from a distance, fearing that a sacrifice was being made. When they saw what was being burnt, they began to laugh and clap their hands. Boys started to make an ear-splitting din with little rattling drums.

Hearts pounding with excitement, Siddharta and his two pupils watched the repulsive spectacle, and yet it was clear to them that a great step forward had been taken. But Siddharta was allowed to see still more:

He saw terrible forms rising from the flames: .... all the thoughts that had been attached to the grotesque idols!

These forms tried to settle on the screaming, raving people, and weigh them down. But other figures also emerged from the flames, not forms, but entities. Luminous, colourful, clear beings, who restrained the forms and put them to flight, until they were caught with the smoke by airy beings, and drifted away.

73

"I thank Thee, Eternal One, that I am permitted to behold this!" he prayed, deeply moved. "It is wonderful to know ourselves thus surrounded at every moment by Thy servants, who are our helpers."

At long last, no more fuel could be found for the flames, which died down slowly and expired with a crackle. It seemed almost dark around them. Struggling for breath, the frenzied dancers came to a halt. Then Siddharta called to them to seat themselves around him, and he would tell them stories.

"Tell us stories!"

They shouted with joy like children. They could think of nothing more beautiful. And he began to describe to them how he had seen all the evil shapes rising from the flames, and how the servants of the Eternal One, the Lord of all the Worlds, had repelled them, so that they had to go up in smoke. And the smoke was destroyed by the winds.

Siddharta was a born story-teller. He himself had no idea how grippingly he could paint a picture, how vividly he could narrate. All eyes were glued to his lips: it occurred to no one to question what he said.

Yet none of them reflected on what he had heard. They received it as one listens to stories. When he had finished, they begged him to tell them more stories the next day.

"Shall we light another fire?" they wanted to know.

"But we have burnt all the idols," said Siddharta with relief. However, because of their urgent pleas he determined that if any more idols were found the fire would be lit again.

Exhausted, disgusted, and yet grateful, he went to rest that night. The day had brought immeasurably much.

NEXT MORNING Ananda came to him in great alarm.

"Master, the priests are angry with you. You have burnt the idols with which they worked miracles. They are after your life."

"Do you think, Ananda, that they can harm me?" replied Siddharta calmly. "The Lord of all the Worlds still needs me for His great Work. So long as I am permitted to serve Him, no harm will come to me, even if all the priests of the Virudas were to unite against me. I thank you for warning me. Perhaps this knowledge can help me to break the power of the priests."

About midday Siddharta was called. A large crowd had gathered in the open square, and the fire was already lit. A huge pile of idols of much coarser workmanship than those of the previous day lay waiting to be burnt. Siddharta approached. Visible only to him, a little being in a multi-coloured coat was leaping about on the pile, giggling:

"They are no fools, these Virudas. They made all these in the night and this morning, so that there should be food for the flames."

This was an unpleasant surprise. First Siddharta thanked the lively little being; then he considered what he should do to prevent such things. A cry of distress broke from his inner being:

"Eternal One, we surely do not want to give a show; let me know what I must do!"

Thereupon he became calm. Slowly he took hold of some of the boards, shook his head and addressed those who were watching him, filled with expectation:

"If we burn these boards, a good many evil thoughts will rise up, for these idols have been made by stealth and cunning in the night and this morning; but the servants of God will not dispel the evil spirits because you have attracted them to yourselves."

They stood there with heads hanging, like scolded children.

The flames went out for want of fuel. But Siddharta called the men to come closer and promised to tell them stories again. Relieved, they came and seated themselves in a circle.

This time he spoke of the servants of the Lord of the Worlds. He described how they zealously carry out all tasks assigned to them, how they help men and teach them, if they are pure and open.

Outside, behind the men, a circle of attentive women and children had formed. All of them listened intently. And Siddharta continued his narratives until deep darkness forced the people to seek out their dwellings.

As they dispersed, he asked Viruda-Sava to have the pile of boards taken away and burnt. They had not been images, but no mischief should be done with them either. With that he turned to go.

Suddenly a rough hand seized him from behind, while another sought to take him by the throat.

But Siddharta had turned quickly, and with a strength that no one would have credited him with fended off his assailant, who uttered a curse and escaped. Nobody had noticed the attack, and Siddharta kept silence about it.

During the days that followed he continued to teach and narrate. As long as he only related, people readily accepted everything. But when he spoke of the Lord of all the Worlds, when he proclaimed that he who would serve Him must be pure and without fault, his listeners became wearied. They began to whisper quietly, to snigger, and finally they went away.

Only a small circle gathered more closely round him. These were men whose faces looked less brutish than those of most of the others. Their eyes lit up when he spoke of the Eternal One; sometimes they interrupted his talk with shouts of joy. Viruda-Sava, however, was not among them!

Then Siddharta decided to proceed differently. He invited the men who had remained with him to the end to come into the courtyard of the palace the following day, but not to tell the others. Now he would no longer tell tales regularly in the great square.

His directives were carried out. Every day the same men came to him, and the longer he taught them, the more eagerly they listened. Now they even had questions of their own, and sometimes they would bring with them a new man, whom Siddharta welcomed kindly to the circle.

He had been teaching in the capital for months now, and he felt that the time had come for him to work in the rest of the country as well. He invited the men who had become his pupils to accompany him, which they were happy to do.

And so one day he set out. He had wanted to send back his armed escort, but both Ananda and Maggalana had earnestly warned him not to. So he took them with him as well.

They passed through fertile but neglected country. Wherever they came upon a village, Siddharta spoke to the inhabitants, and the Virudas who accompanied him fetched the idols from the huts and burnt them.

But they made sure that there should be no commotion while they did so. Siddharta had told them how terrible the wild dance was.

If then the Master found a soul that seemed to long for the Eternal One, he would stay for some time. But mostly after two or three days he moved on disheartened.

Sometimes people would join their band. They were then included among the others, and instructed by them.

IN THIS WAY time seemed to fly. Siddharta no longer knew how many months he had been travelling. Was it not years now? None could tell. He had wandered through the country of the Virudas in every direction with his band of pupils, which had increased to about a hundred.

Then one day he stood at the foot of a fairly high mountain-range, which formed the boundary of the realm. Though all of them were tired, he felt urged to climb the mountains. Briskly he began to lead the way up the narrow path made by the goats. It was easier than he expected, and his companions followed him without a murmur.

Well before sunset they stood at the summit and looked down. The fertile plain lay like a carpet between the great and small mountain-ranges. The waters of the River Krishna rolled to the sea, which was to be seen like a blue line in the distance.

"The land of the Virudas is beautiful," said Siddharta to his followers, "but the people have not been grateful; they have paid no heed to the great gift bestowed on them with it. Nor have they recognised the Grace which the Eternal One showed in allowing Himself to be proclaimed to them. Therefore the people will be destroyed, save for the few who are standing here with me. They will have to perish in all their sins, so that no trace of them will remain."

He had spoken like a seer, an inner power drove him; he himself was not conscious of what he had just said. But his companions stared at him. Surely that could not be true! How was it to come about?

Maggalana went up to the Master and addressed him. Siddharta awakened as if from a dream; but when the disciple told him what he had just announced, deep sadness overspread his features.

"To tell you the truth, I did not know what I was saying to you," he explained, "but he who spoke through me knew. It is time for the judgment of the Eternal One to fall on the people of the Viruda. It is not right that these people of the Darkness should become the ruin of all the neighbouring countries. But you who are with me, fear nothing; you will be saved, for you have become servants of the Eternal One. You will have to look on with me at the destruction of your people, so that you will bear witness of it to others."

The night was spent under a radiant starlit sky, the early dawn broke. Then a tremendous roaring and rumbling was heard from the bowels of the earth.

"These are the servants of the Eternal One who work in the rocks," explained Siddharta.

A violent gale set in. It came from the sea, howling and wailing, it raged round the rocks on which Siddharta's flock huddled closely together.

"Throw yourselves on the ground," commanded the Master, "otherwise the storm will carry us away."

A violent storm broke, rain rattled down, it grew quite dark. Only now and again came vivid flashes of lightning. This went on for hours. At last the heavy downpour abated, the raging in Nature fell slowly silent, the rolling and swaying of the earth ceased.

Siddharta was the first to rise, but hardly had he cast a glance over his surroundings than a cry of utmost horror burst from his breast. The others leapt up, looked about them, and cried out as well.

Where a few hours ago had still been fertile land now surged the waves of the sea, from which the mountain peaks stood out like tiny islands. The country of the Virudas was no more!

Deeply shaken, the survivors looked down. No one could speak. At length Siddharta began to pray from the bottom of his heart. He thanked the Eternal One for delivering them from the judgment that had overtaken the dark people. Then, however, he invited his followers to make their way down the other side of the mountains. And again they willingly followed him.

In the terrible experience that had affected every one, they had become useful instruments of the Eternal One. Their wives and children, all that they had possessed, lay buried under the waves of the sea.

Now these human beings knew how lowly the creature is, and how high and sublime above him the Lord of the World is enthroned. One word from Him is enough to make all the works of man crumble away.

At first the deeply-shaken men remained with Siddharta. They helped him as before. The people whom they now sought out had not all fallen to the Darkness like the Virudas. Most of them opened themselves readily and gladly to the tidings which Siddharta and his companions brought them.

Then the Master began to assign his pupils in groups to all parts of the country. They took the knowledge about the Lord of the Worlds, and with it the striving for a more worthy life, everywhere.

But Siddharta decided to extend his teaching now, if possible to deepen it, and to this end to take up a permanent residence in the centre of the country. He had been wandering restlessly about for too long already. Many a recognition had dawned on him during this period, but now it seemed that the time had come to let others do the travelling.

He had arranged with the pupils whom he sent out that they should present themselves to him at regular intervals, and hear what new and better things he would have to convey to them. They in turn were to report on their activities, and the progress that the knowledge of the Eternal One was making among men.

Naturally they would also find pupils and followers; that could not fail to come about if their teaching was right. They were to bring these new pupils with them each time they came. He would then have them instructed.

The picture of a school like the one at Utakamand floated before his mind's eye. It was only a matter of finding the place for it, which had been shown to him in spirit.

On his ride north he had come to the region between the two mighty rivers, the sacred Ganges and the Indus, which the original inhabitants of these regions considered to be their father.

They believed that they had been formed out of the mud of this river, after which Brahma had breathed life into them through the rays of the sun. Therefore this river was sacred to them; they felt an inner relationship with it.

A great desert called Thar extended between these two rivers. On the advice of his little elemental friends, Siddharta and his followers rode round the desert.

"In this region you will find only sand wherever you look. It is a dismal piece of land. Keep away from it. But at the same time, when you turn further north, you will find a fertile, rich region. Build your city there.

"Do not let yourself be tempted to settle in a town already built. You know that if you do so you may come into a sphere of impure radiations, of evil thoughts. But the city which you are to establish is to be built in honour of the Lord of the Worlds, and is to radiate in purity and in thoughts of the Eternal One from the beginning. Bear that in mind!"

Siddharta was filled with great joy at being allowed to build a city in honour of the Lord of the Worlds. He would not be short of labour, for everywhere pupils from many castes joined him. Among them were skilled workers of all kinds.

He told some of them of his plans. They too were happy that they were found worthy to be instrumental in the work.

As he rode along, Siddharta often wondered how it was possible for such a great desert to extend in the middle of the country, immediately beside such a particularly fertile region. As this thought left him no peace, he asked his little friends. Perhaps they could explain to him how the two different kinds of soil had come into existence.

They knew why, and gladly communicated their knowledge to him:

"Long, long ago, when this part of the earth was still uninhabited by men, everything was formed quite differently. The sea, which now extends over vast distances on either side of the lands of the Sons of Indus, was then a single body of water. From the Vindhya mountains over which you rode with such difficulty some months ago, right up to the great Himalayas, which of course you know, surged the mighty sea. The land to the south rose out of the sea like a great island."

"I do not understand," said Siddharta, confused. "Where were the Indus and the Ganges?"

The little narrators laughed.

"The sacred Ganges did not yet exist! The Indus, your father, came down from the Himalayas, even as it does today, but it poured its rushing waters straight into the sea; for there was no land for it to flow through first."

"Were you already here at that time?" asked Siddharta. "Did you see all this yourselves?"

"No, there were stronger beings here before us, who could join in rebuilding the mountains and valleys, in changing the course of the rivers and seas. The mermaids have sung to us of how they had to leave the lands at

80

the foot of the snow-capped mountains at the behest of the Lord of the Worlds. There were rumblings in the bowels of the earth, rocks forced their way upwards, the land rose out of the waves, the sea had to flow away on both sides. But it left behind sand, vast tracts of barren sand.

"That also came to pass at the behest of the Lord of the Worlds, Whom we all serve. He knows why He has ordered it so. But where the sea left the fertile land behind, where the plants and animal-remains were decaying in the ground, arose the fertile region to which we are now leading you.

"The Indus was able to expand, many rivers rushed to meet it from all sides. The Ganges, which flows through the whole wide plain, also came into being then."

"Shall I be allowed to build the City of the Lord on its banks?" asked Siddharta, who had followed the account of the little beings with eager expectation.

"No, you must not build it too near its waters; for it tends to overflow its banks and flood the surrounding country. That is a blessing for the fields, but it would damage the city."

A sharp wind had sprung up, bringing with it fine grains of sand from the west, a greeting from the Thar desert. Now Siddharta knew why the little beings had warned him against this region. The grains of sand stung painfully. Noses swelled up, eyes became inflamed, and the ears began to ache.

And yet this lasted only a few hours! What would they have had to endure, if the little ones had not been their guides? Ever anew Siddharta, deeply grateful, felt himself connected with them.

The further north he went with his steadily growing band, the more glorious the country became. Its fertility was indescribable. Field after field of trees extended, bearing all kinds of fruit, and linked to each other by creepers of sweet-smelling blossoms. Birds with magnificent plumage enlivened the region, in which there were no towns, but only small villages and isolated settlements.

"Whoever wants to work the land will have to live alone," Siddharta advised his enquiring pupils.

The further they advanced in this plain, the more evident became the monkeys. At times almost unbearable jabbering rent the silence, which to the learning travellers had become a necessity.

81

The long-tailed, agile creatures also kept on pestering the travellers. They fearlessly stole items of food, and even articles of clothing that caught their attention. They poked their nimble fingers into everything, destroying it or using it for their own purposes.

The men were not unfamiliar with monkeys, of every size and kind, but they had never encountered so many before. Whole packs of them lived in the forests, strictly segregated from each other.

They were not peaceable. Whenever members of one kind approached another pack, there was fighting. This always trebled the already abominable noise, so that the pupils said sadly:

"How are we to build a city for the Lord of the Worlds here? The monkeys will disturb all peace, all harmony."

Siddharta comforted the disheartened men. At the right time a remedy would be found for this too. He knew that he only needed to communicate with the monkeys, and he would be able to induce them to respect the City of the Eternal One.

But he did not wish to do this yet. His companions could learn so infinitely much from these animals. If only they could realise how terrible meaningless chatter is, how senseless continual squabbling.

ONE DAY the little beings led Siddharta to an eminence from which an enchanting view opened over the vast plain. The fertile land extended on either side, with the waters of the sacred river flowing through it. Southwards the golden desert shimmered in the distance, while to the rear the view was obstructed by high snow-clad peaks.

Siddharta's heart beat faster: the Himalayas! Although nothing could be distinguished clearly, he could yet sense that here towered the gigantic mountains among which his homeland lay.

Home! Such a long time since Siddharta had thought about it. To him the period of earthly happiness was as though submerged in all the great experiencing. It lay behind him like a fairy-tale. But today something still stirred, like a longing for what had once been his.

Then the long-missed voice of his guide sounded in his inner ear:

"Siddharta, this is the place where you will be allowed to build a city for the Lord of the Worlds, the Eternal and Supreme! It is to be a city of wisdom and learning, a city of purity and of striving towards the Light. Therefore it must be built entirely of white stone, so that you will always be reminded of its purpose. The name of the city is to be Indraprastha."

The guide was silent.

Siddharta told his followers that they would remain here and build the city. To this end they should all leave the Mountain, and build dwellings for themselves at the foot of it, or half-way up. After that they would be allowed to help on the Mountain itself.

Filled with joy that the long journey had come to an end, the men hastened to their allotted task, and dwellings of the most varied kinds sprang up, according to the national character of the builders. But on the Mountain the animistic beings also helped.

First the school was built. The plan for it was shown to Siddharta in the night, so that during the day he could always state exactly and without thought how everything was to be arranged.

On the first morning the Master found an enormous pack of monkeys occupied with the white stones. The animistic beings stood by, evidently enjoying the eager curiosity with which the animals touched and sniffed at everything.

But to Siddharta it seemed a desecration. He asked for inner help.

"What we are about to build here is to stand in honour of the Lord of all the Worlds, and bear witness to Him."

Turning to the monkeys, he said:

"We human beings have yet to learn how best to serve the Lord. For this we need uninterrupted quiet. I ask you to stay away from this Mountain in future, so that you do not divert us from our worship."

Siddharta had spoken quite seriously, and had almost forgotten that he was speaking to animals. Indeed they seemed to have let his words pass them by like a torrent, but they had grasped their meaning: To please the Lord of all the Worlds, they were to keep away from this Mountain!

That seemed to them very hard! For they wanted to see what was going on there!

Siddharta suddenly understood this. He had to laugh against his will, won over by so much original curiosity. He wondered to what extent he might meet them. Then one of the great animistic beings began to speak:

"Now you see why we stopped working and let the nimble ones have their way. When you came up to us just then, you did not understand. You must not keep the nimble ones away altogether, it would make them sad. Let them come and go: they will keep quiet, we know."

Siddharta bowed to the wisdom of the animistic being, and acquiesced. But the nimble ones, as they had just been called, were so happy that they immediately began to chatter. However, a sharp sound from their leader silenced them.

The building progressed without hindrance. When the school and all adjoining buildings were completed, a spacious house for about a hundred people was built.

Siddharta did not yet know what purpose it was to serve, but having received the plan and the commission for it from his guide, he was little concerned about the rest. This house had unusually small rooms, as well as two large, long halls.

These first two buildings lay in close proximity to each other. A little further away a guest-house was built, in which visitors were to be received. Here every room was spacious and airy, and a large garden surrounded the whole. In addition farm buildings arose.

When the houses were ready, Siddharta gathered all the scholars and disciples in a large open square, which lay a little apart among tall palm trees, and thanked the Lord of the Worlds for all the help which they had experienced. He prayed that blessing might be bestowed on the new city, so that all that was taught, thought and done in it should be in His Honour, and he promised that they would always be of one mind.

He then selected from among his followers those who would be the first to enter the school. There were about seventy older and younger men, who approached the fountain-head of knowledge with great joy.

Afterwards Siddharta chose all those whom he wished to entrust with a task. He had reserved the management of the school to himself, but he still needed teachers, whom he found among his disciples.

Now he was on the lookout for a merchant who could take over the business affairs of the city. For this an older student was found, who expressed his willingness to remain permanently with Siddharta.

Then the Master called him Amuruddba, in memory of his former master, the merchant. Amuruddba was entrusted with the management of external affairs. Together with Siddharta, he had to decide on the accommodation of the students and guests, as well as to ensure that there was always enough fresh food available.

He eagerly took charge of the duties entrusted to him. Thus he considered it worth while to acquire fields in the valley to grow corn and fruit. There were enough farmers from this region among his present followers, happy to be employed in this way. Craftsmen, gardeners, labourers and cattle-farmers were also chosen.

This left a small group of twenty older men for whom there was no work. They all came from the caste of scholars, and fervently begged to be allowed to spend their lives on the Mountain.

Siddharta accepted them as guests for the time being. He would no doubt receive further instructions. And behold: one night he suddenly knew what purpose the large house with the small rooms was to serve. He was allowed to offer accommodation to those who would devote their lives wholly to the worship and service of the Eternal One. They must be tested, and submit to certain statutes.

But until these statutes were established, he calmly left the men in uncertainty about their future.

He felt urged, however, to get all external matters settled quickly, so that he could give his undivided attention to consolidating the teaching. He had pondered over so many things, discovered much that was new, created better expressions, greater clarity for many old things. All this the others were now to share with him.

The pupils moved in when the furnishing of the school was completed. Thus the dwellings on the mountain-slope fell vacant. They were to serve as quarters for newcomers.

A great Festival for everyone was to mark the beginning of the teaching in the school. On the same day Ananda and Maggalana arrived unexpectedly with a group of companions.

There was great joy all round. While the new arrivals marvelled at the settlement on the Mountain, Siddharta asked them for an account of their experiences and achievements. Good work had been done, and now they had come just at the right time to be able to bring new ideas with them.

ON A RADIANTLY beautiful morning, they all assembled in the great open square. Siddharta prayed the Lord of the Worlds for His blessing on the school, and laid down some laws that were to be binding:

"The Lord of the Worlds is the only God. School and settlement are dedicated to Him.

"No one may be compared with Him in any way, not even in thought.

"But all creatures of the Eternal One are equal. There are no distinctions in caste.

"All creatures, be they humans, animals or plants, are to be considered equal. No one may offend against them."

These laws were to apply to all adherents. For the school he laid down particularly:

"Take no intoxicating drinks. They dull your faculties, and tempt you to sin.

"Let your lives be chaste and disciplined. Bathe every day, and care for your body out of gratitude to Him Who gave it to you.

"Do not tell lies. That is contemptible, and degrades you as well as him to whom you lie. It is the duty of all to speak only the truth. Do not lie in your deeds either, by acting differently from your thoughts and intuitive perceptions.

"Let no man take from another what is his."

When Siddharta had given these laws, he asked them all whether they would acknowledge them. A joyful avowal was his answer.

Actually it had been arranged that the pupils and their teachers should then go into one of the large school-halls to hear what Siddharta had to say to them. But because so many guests had come, and moreover all the other followers had begged to be allowed to be present also, they remained in the open square, especially as the sun was not yet too fierce.

Siddharta began to speak:

86

"My friends, pupils, guests, and also you animistic beings who are assembled with us, I greet you all!

"This is the first address that I give to you on the teaching of the Eternal One. Heed it well, and take it to heart! I hope that many another will yet follow, but this first one is particularly important.

"When we spoke about life, I told you that it is a chain of suffering even if it does not yet appear so to the younger ones among you. This suffering has been brought upon us by ourselves, mainly through wrong desires. Therefore we must overcome the desires, and then suffering will no longer be able to approach us to the same extent.

"Now comes the new, which I have not yet told you. Listen carefully!

"If we wish to conquer the desires, we must change. How can we do this, especially we older ones, we who already have the greater part of our lives behind us?

"I reflected upon this for a long time, and then help came to me from above. I found the way to the total transformation of man. It consists of eight stages, each of which must be experienced completely before we can then enter upon the next one. Nor can we omit any, for one arises from the other.

"If you wish to tread this path with me, you will first enter upon the stage above whose portal are inscribed the words:

"*Right Belief.*

"You must stress both words equally; for the belief is the main thing, but then it must also be the right one. Without belief you are helpless. But you must also believe what is right. You must cling unshakeably to the belief that the Eternal One is the Lord of all Worlds. All others, like Shakra, Vishnu, Shiva and Lokapales are His servants, who can only help you if you serve the Eternal One with them. Maro is the evil one; turn away from him. If you believe all this in the right way, with your whole soul, you will come to the second stage, above whose portal is engraved the word:

"*Resolution.*

"The belief in the Lord of the Worlds must be so strong in you that you form the resolution to serve Him alone, to regard yourself as nothing, and to leave all former things behind. You must begin a new life, as most of

87

you have already done. Away with the old! Away with all that would bind you to the past. Then you will move almost imperceptibly into the new stage, which is called:

"*The Word.*

"The Eternal One does not want loquacious servants. You should be sparing with words, but you should weigh every word you speak to see whether it is valid. This includes the commandment: Do not lie! Think about this. It is easy to sin with words, but to make amends for it again is hard. But out of the words arises:

"*The Deed.*

"This is the next stage. It is all the same in the end whether your words lead you or others into deed. If they were good words they will produce the good deed, but if you did not pay attention to your words, evil deeds will arise, bringing harm to you and others; so beware! Instead, strive with all your might to let no day pass without doing at least one good deed. Conquer yourselves. Force yourselves to do things that are hard for you. All the more easily will you master this stage.

"When I now announce the next stage, some among you will smile. It is called:

"*Life.*

"Indeed, you will think, we do all live! If that has to be mentioned at all, it should have come first. No, my friends, you do not yet live! To live does not mean merely satisfying the natural requirements, like animals or plants. It means bestirring oneself and moving, to show that one is alive. It means using every moment to the full, be it in work or in thought. Such a life carries us out of earthly life into true life in the beyond, when our time for it has come.

"Therefore the next stage is called:

"*Striving.*

"You should strive to live in such a way that you will find your starting-point again. We have come from the beyond, and we must seek the beyond. You know that we cannot achieve this with *one* life. We must be born into this world many times.

"But I will explain to you: we come back as human beings, not as animals or plants. They are of a different species from ours. The two can never be

88

intermingled. The Brahmans teach that an ill-tempered man becomes a tiger, a timid man becomes a mouse. I ask you: what help is that to him? Can he make any progress by it? No!

"We come again, but as human beings. We shall continue to return until we are able to reach our starting-point. That comes about through working ourselves a little higher with each life. It means striving.

"But once we have succeeded in making our whole life a striving in the right way, then it becomes

"*Gratitude*

"to Him Who gave it. Gratitude should fill us, it will make us glad and happy. He who gives thanks has no time to complain; he who gives thanks, gives thanks in the right way, will let this gratitude become deed. He will help others as he has been helped.

"The last stage is open only to those who have faithfully passed through, lived through, all the others. It is called:

"*Inner Absorption.*

"When you have reached this point, you will be given the ability to listen within yourselves. Great things will be revealed to you there. Nothing that *you* think, but such things as the Eternal One allows to be proclaimed to you! He lets His servants speak to us in the stillness. He who can become absorbed, be it in contemplation or in prayer, will hear the voices, and will know that here he is already linked with the beyond.

"But with that he has become a new man. With that he has overcome all desires, all suffering!

"I would like to tell you one thing more: In the beginning I pointed out that you have to pass through one stage after the other. That you may not enter upon any one stage until you have really fulfilled the foregoing one. But by this I do not mean that the old is then disposed of for ever. You must not infer that from my words. On the contrary, what you have gained during one stage must have become so much your own that it goes with you into the ensuing stages as your inalienable property!"

They had all listened deeply moved. There was not one who failed to understand the Master's words, not one who would have departed without resolving to tread the eightfold path.

BRISK ACTIVITY followed the Festival. But Siddharta had to devote himself more to the visitors than to the others. Ananda in particular had many questions.

He was concerned that in the City of the Eternal One there was no Temple.

"I have not been commanded to build one," said Siddharta. "There is a Hall of Worship in the school, as in Utakamand. That suffices for the scholars. In the large house which I should like to call the monastery, there is also a Place of Worship. But let the others assemble in the open air to pray. Besides, each one can pray wherever he feels the urge to do so. I am reluctant to assign a place for it.

"We must first free ourselves inwardly from the temples of the gods. Then perhaps the Eternal One will permit us to build a Temple to Him."

Maggalana came to him. He had been thinking over the whole arrangement of the settlement. He was anxious to speak with Siddharta.

"Master," he began hesitantly, "please allow me to ask: what do you live on?"

"You must ask Amuruddba, that is not my concern," was the calm reply.

"I have asked him, Master, and his answer startled me. Do not think me presumptuous if I warn you that your money is running out. What will you do then?"

"We have bought fields, on whose produce we can live."

"Master, what the fields produce you consume. If still more people come, you will need to buy more. Then you will have to obtain materials of various kinds, parchment and dyes and much more besides. How will you pay for these?"

"I do not know, Maggalana," said Siddharta, who was not in the least perturbed by what the disciple was trying to put before him. "When the time comes, the Eternal One will let us know His Will in this matter also."

"Do you think, Master, that the Lord of the Worlds will have us advised in these earthly matters for ever? We ourselves must look around and find solutions."

"Do you know any such solution, Maggalana?"

"Yes, Master. I believe that the people whom you want to take into the monastery, and feed and maintain without payment, could provide the necessary funds. Let them wander through the region with alms-bowls, and they will bring in just as rich a harvest as the Brahmans do.

"Everyone will gladly give to them if at the same time they also proclaim the teaching, as far as they are able. After all, there is no disgrace in begging for alms," added Maggalana almost apologetically.

The plan met with great approval, not only from Siddharta, who saw in it the answer to the burdensome question of money, but also from the others, especially Amuruddba.

It was decided that alms-bowls similar to those of the Brahmans should be provided. Ananda volunteered to attend to this; he also wished to buy the material needed for clothing the alms brothers, or "Begging Brothers", as they were to be called.

Siddharta ordained that these Brothers should wear yellow outer garments, as a sign that they were prepared to carry the Light into the Darkness. Underneath they were to wear blue loin-cloths, one fold of which was to be made deep enough to hold all their possessions.

Since they were to bathe once a day, they could wash their loin-cloth at the same time. The sun would dry it quickly enough. Wherever they were they should sleep on the floor, not on a bed.

That is why their rooms in the "monastery" were so very small – because there was not to be a single item of furniture inside. A mat covered the floor. That was all.

These Begging Brothers were kept almost in poverty, in spite of which Siddharta insisted that they were to be distinguished by their cleanliness, as well as by the flawless condition of their clothing, from the beggars who were clad in rags.

He would not tolerate any rents or spots on their yellow garments. Everything had to be mended immediately. If this was no longer possible, the wearer received a new outer garment.

Nor were they allowed to swarm out to collect alms all at the same time. They took turns, according to a very definite plan, so that they always had more time to become absorbed in spiritual things at home than for wandering about. Siddharta wanted to prevent the Brothers from growing accustomed to a life on the highways, and to begging.

When all things had been arranged, and the regular life could now really begin, monkeys again appeared here and there. But they behaved with the utmost discretion, and seemed to be awaiting the moment when they could attract Siddharta's attention.

The opportunity presented itself. Siddharta was pacing up and down in the garden, musing. He was so engrossed in thought that he had missed the main meal. Now hunger asserted itself, and the Master looked around him for a ripe fruit.

Suddenly a hairy little arm was stretched out from the dark green foliage of a tree, and the little hand offered him a splendid ripe mango.

Gratefully he took the fruit, and at the same time seized the donor by the paw, pulling it from the tree. He had to laugh at the quaint expression of the little monkey, which looked up at him with a mixture of trust and bashfulness. But at the same time he realised what this little labour of love was to signify.

"You wish to be allowed to look about here?" he asked kindly. "Come along, then."

For a long time the inhabitants of the Mountain still looked back on the long-tailed visitors with joy.

New groups had arrived, asking to be admitted. Because Siddharta spoke with each one before allocating him to the school, the monastery or the dwelling-houses, he was very much occupied.

At this time the demand for the monastery was almost greater than for the school. Siddharta was surprised, and he asked one of the older men why he so wished to become a Begging Brother.

"Because one can do so much good in this way," was the reply.

Questioned more closely, the man said that the Brothers were always greeted with joy in the plain below. They were helpful, and did not shirk any work; they knew many things that were of benefit to cattle and men, and also they were wonderful story-tellers.

Everyone was happy when a Yellow Brother came, everyone gave gladly; for what he received in return was worth more than his small gift.

This was news to Siddharta. He questioned his Yellow Ones, and learned that in fact they had decided out of gratitude for the gifts to help people not only in spiritual but also in earthly ways. Nothing could be said against this.

Among the newcomers there were some who clung so firmly to the concept of sacrifice that they thought their service to the Lord of the Worlds would be incomplete if they did not make offerings to Him.

Vainly Siddharta tried to make clear to them that the shattering of the ego was the greatest and also the only sacrifice that a human being can make to the Eternal One. They wanted to do something that could be seen.

"Do not be so rigid," admonished Siddharta's guide when he perceived the Master's lack of comprehension, and he continued:

"Give them something to do that will be hard for them. That will satisfy them, will injure no one, and will help their souls to advance."

Then Siddharta suggested to the people that twice in every month, from one sunrise to the next, they should abstain from eating any food. The idea delighted them. That really was a sacrifice!

They always fasted at the change of the moon, and were in particularly high spirits on these days. But their doings created a precedent. Others wanted to do likewise. They begged Siddharta to introduce fasting as a commandment. This he rejected:

"The men fast because they want to sacrifice something to God. But sacrifices must be made voluntarily out of an inner urge, if they are to have any value. If you wish to fast, you must do so without a commandment."

That suited them all. Fasting at full moon and new moon became the established custom. If, however, anyone wished to break the fast, it was his affair.

In eager activity, in zealous endeavour, month followed month. Years went by thus. No one heeded it. Fast-days and visits were definite landmarks in the passage of time for all who did not have to work directly in Nature. There the passing of yet another year manifested clearly in the coming-into-being and decaying.

One day Siddharta was sitting in his room. From a trader in the valley, Amuruddba had bought a manuscript which seemed to him to be of value.

He had brought it to the Master, and the latter was struggling to decipher it.

Suddenly shrill sounds, such as he had heard long ago, reached his ear. He listened. There was no doubt about it, a snake-charmer must have made his way up here. He had to see him.

He hastened into the garden, where he found a circle of scholars and teachers gathered round an old man who was making three beautiful snakes dance to the sound of his pipe. The man as well as the animals attracted him. He crossed the circle of onlookers. The old man looked up, their eyes met, and almost shouting with joy the Master called:

"Sariputta!"

It was indeed his first master on the arduous journey in the dust of the highway. It was Sariputta, who had taught him to understand the animals. Now he could thank him for all that had made his life rich.

But Sariputta had also recognised him, although there was an immense outward difference between the despised pariah and the richly-clad Master. It did not surprise him to find his former servant here in splendour and magnificence.

"I well knew, Siddharta, that you would rise, otherwise I would not have been commanded to teach you," he said simply.

Speaking in turn, the two then told the listening scholars of the time when they had met each other, and journeyed together with the snakes.

"These are no longer the same snakes," Sariputta explained.

Nevertheless the Master wanted to see whether he would still be able to control the beautiful creatures at his will. He took the pipe and began to play. But the sounds which he drew from the wood had nothing in common with Sariputta's shrill sounds.

For a moment the snakes hesitated, and then they half raised their bodies, making the onlookers fall back, and stood swaying, intertwining in such a way as no one had ever seen before.

After a while Siddharta lowered the pipe, and began to speak to the snakes. They appeared to listen attentively, then slowly they crept closer to him and stretched up their triangular heads against his robe. He stroked their heads gently.

Then they ventured further, crept cautiously upwards and coiled round

94

him, but so gently that he hardly felt the heavy bodies. As before, supreme happiness filled his soul.

"Now go back to your baskets," Siddharta said kindly. "You have made me very happy indeed with your trust."

The snakes obeyed. And the scholars broke into cheers. What wonderful things the Master could do! The Eternal One had truly given him power over man and beast!

Sariputta, who at first had been rendered speechless with admiration, now at last brought out the reason for his presence. He had observed the Yellow Brothers in the valley, and had heard that they knew more about the gods than he did. He had come to ask the sage to accept him as a scholar and to teach him.

Gladly Siddharta agreed to impart of his knowledge to *him* who had laid the first foundation for it.

"You shall not go to the school, Sariputta," he said warmly, "but shall learn from me whenever you wish. Nor shall you be given a new name; for I have conferred the names of all my former masters here, and only Sariputta was still missing. Remain Sariputta."

But what was to become of the snakes? Sariputta did not know. However Siddharta said quite simply:

"They shall decide for themselves what they wish to do." And he went over to them and spoke to them:

"Your master Sariputta wants to remain on the Mountain of the Eternal One. Choose for yourselves which way you will take. Yonder lies the forest. You are free to go there, or you can remain near the Mountain, but you may not kill anything in the vicinity except the destructive mice."

The snakes seemed to listen attentively. One of them crept up to Sariputta as if to say farewell, and then slipped into the low undergrowth where it was soon lost to sight. The other two did not follow its example. They crept here and there and finally chose a tool-shed, which they regarded as their future home.

Because Siddharta feared that there might be harm from an accidental bite, he had the snakes' poison-fangs extracted.

For years the snakes remained the well-liked companions of the people on the Mountain. A great friendship united them with Comforter. They helped him to keep away unwelcome visitors. After about two months the third snake had returned as well, and its poison-fangs were also removed.

In the course of years the school and monastery had become too small for the greater number of people who asked for admission. At the request of his disciples, and in agreement with his guide, Siddharta decided to build monasteries and schools in different parts of the country, and to appoint his disciples as their principals.

Wherever possible, he chose a mountain on which to build a monastery or school. The outer structure was always exactly like the one on the Mountain of the Eternal One, but Siddharta did not allow the use of white stones. There were red monasteries and grey monasteries, and similar schools. The school of which Ananda was principal was built entirely of soft yellowish-brown stone, and was called the yellow monastery.

Siddharta himself consecrated each of these buildings to the Eternal One, even if they were far away from the Mountain. Afterwards he maintained regular contact with them. Messengers went to and fro, visitors came from the monasteries to the Mountain, but above all it was the elemental beings who brought news.

One day Maggalana rode in with a larger group. Among his companions was one who towered above the others, and also stood out through the expression of his face. It was impossible not to notice him.

"Siddharta!" called some of the permanent dwellers on the Mountain.

Maggalana smiled.

"Does it strike you too?" he asked, sure of the answer. "Even on the first day that he entered our monastery, I saw that he bears the features of our Master. That is why I have brought him here, so that the Master himself may look into the circumstances."

Siddharta came to greet them, and when the two men stood face to face the resemblance was still more striking. Siddharta himself noticed it. It was as though he were seeing himself at the time when he was still Prince of Kapilavastu.

Strangely moved, he beckoned the guest to come with him into his room. There he asked him his name, and whence he had come.

"My name is Rahula," answered the stranger, who was no less moved than Siddharta.

"Rahula!" cried the former, struck almost speechless with joy. "Then you are my son, my child whom I mourned as dead! Where is Maya your mother, where is your brother Suddhodana?"

The other stared at him.

"You know my mother, my brother? Who are you?"

"I am your father, Rahula, your father who lost you when you were just a little boy!"

Only then did Rahula understand that he had found his father, whom he had deeply mourned as dead. Questions that left scarcely time for answers followed in quick succession. Slowly the excitement of the two men subsided, slowly order came into their thoughts.

Siddharta learned of the wonderful rescue of his dear ones and of their life afterwards. For a long time Maya had remained in the mountains with her two boys and the faithful Kapila. Rahula could not say how long it was. They had lived on the fruits of the forest.

Sometimes they also caught birds, which they were able to roast. Their elemental friend, whom the boys had learned to see and love, was often with them.

One day holy men came from the other side of the mountains. They said that God had sent them to fetch and care for the lonely human beings. They led the mother and Kapila safely on mules. Suddhodana and he had also been allowed to ride them sometimes.

After a journey lasting many days, they came to a beautiful valley in which there was a monastery. The mother, with Suddhodana and Kapila, found shelter in a small hut in the monastery gardens. They also gave her work to do. She had to care for the garden of healing herbs and keep it in good order, with the help of Kapila.

The holy men had taken him, Rahula, into the monastery school and taught him. There he had received the tidings of the Supreme Being, and vowed to dedicate his whole life to His service. When Suddhodana was older he too had been admitted to the school.

Only a few years ago, first Kapila and then the mother had died. She was glad to be allowed to pass into eternity, for she believed that there she would find again the husband whom fate had snatched from her. She could never be convinced that it might have been the Will of Brahma that had taken the Prince from his loved ones.

"Brahma cannot demand anything unnatural of men," she used to say. "And it is not natural for a Prince to forsake his country and family."

The holy men had told Rahula not to torment his mother with knowing-better. She was happy in her faith, which flowed out of true piety. That was enough for the Eternal One.

The news of his wife's passing was a painful blow to Siddharta. Since seeing his son, the longing for Maya had awakened in him.

Strange! He had long thought her dead. Now when he heard that she had been alive until just recently, he lost her a second time.

"What became of you then, Rahula?" Siddharta asked his son.

"Long ago the holy men took Suddhodana to the court of a prince, where he could learn all that he needed as a future ruler. A short time before our mother's death he returned. After that, on the advice of the brothers, he rode to Kapilavastu, where the people joyfully received him as your successor, Father. They had long since grown weary of the rule of the conqueror.

"The Supreme Being, Whose wish it was that Suddhodana should take over the realm, stood by him. My brother succeeded in driving out the usurper and making himself sovereign."

The name "father" sounded wonderful to Siddharta. Severed ties began to entwine him anew.

"Why did not you, the elder, become my successor?" he then asked.

"You forget, Father, that I had pledged myself to the Supreme Being. To serve Him seems more glorious to me than anything else. I wish to be a servant and not a ruler."

After that Siddharta told his son briefly all that he had experienced, and they marvelled at the wonderful guidance that had directed their lives.

"Let me enter one of your monasteries, Father," the son begged. "I had gone to Maggalana before I knew about you. If you so wish I will return to him. But I would much prefer to be near you, and to learn from you."

"We will not decide on that today," said the father. "We must leave it to the Will of the Eternal One to decide where you are to serve Him."

But in the night Siddharta became aware of the sweetly alluring ties that sought to weave themselves around him every time the word "father" was uttered – indeed even at the very sight of his son.

Had the Eternal One loosed him from all earthly ties, only so that at the first opportunity which offered itself he should rejoin that which had been severed? He wrestled bravely with every impulse that sought to entice him. In the morning he was free, and assured his son that it would be best for him to return with Maggalana to his monastery.

Rahula understood his father, and bowed before his greatness. A few days later he rode away, and life on the Mountain went on as usual.

Not for long, however, was it to remain so. News came from Utakamand that the Head-Brahman had died, and that he had named Siddharta as his successor. The Brahmans entreated him to come, even if only for a year; they too were prepared to go more deeply into the new doctrine. It would be his duty, since he had found the first beginnings of it in their school.

Utakamand was one of the Master's dearest memories. Gladly he answered their call, although it was hard for him to leave the Mountain and Indraprastha. He felt the inducement to bear the tidings of the Eternal One to the place where the people were so very near to understanding. It would be wonderful to work, to think and to keep silence with them there.

But he left everything to the Eternal One, and prayed his guide to tell him the Will of the Lord of all the Worlds.

"You have chosen aright, Siddharta," came the answer. "On the long journey to Utakamand you will be able to visit the schools and monasteries that have been built in the meantime. In doing so you will uncover many wrong things, and will be able to make good many a deficiency. But above all you will learn much that will be of benefit to you and to the others."

As Ananda had arrived a few days earlier, Siddharta entrusted him with the charge of Indraprastha, and rode off to the south, accompanied only by a few faithful followers.

ALTHOUGH he did not stay long anywhere, his journey lasted for weeks. He was driven onwards. The nearer he came to his destination, the greater was his longing. Much had changed; new villages had arisen, small settlements had become towns.

Everywhere he found Brahmanism co-existing peacefully with the teaching of the Lord of all the Worlds. So long as the adherents of Siddharta, as the others called them, built no temples, they were considered harmless.

But it seemed to Siddharta that the worshippers of Brahma were only a step away from the true teaching. He was convinced that the covering veil would easily fall away.

One evening the region seemed very definitely familiar to him. He looked about him again and again; suddenly he knew where he was. He told his companions to encamp for the night; but he himself rode away from them until he came to the giant mango tree under which he had once before spent a night.

Here he had found his task, here he had become certain of his faith! He dismounted, and let his horse graze. It was his habit never to tether animals which were kept for his special use and were accustomed to him. He spoke to them, and advised them not to stray too far, and it had never happened that such an animal lost its way or came to any harm.

Now once more he lay under the tree, the shimmering, starry sky above him. He listened deep within himself, and found only gratitude to the Lord of the Worlds, Who had guided his life so wonderfully, Who had succoured him every single day.

Out of this gratitude arose a new pledge, and the supplication:

"Let me recognise Thee ever more clearly, O Eternal One!"

Again, as at that other time, ringing sounds swelled around him, and out of them a shape took form, softly tinted, like a lotus-flower. But it was not he who stood in the centre. A Sign never before seen shone golden out of the radiant white flower-petals.

And this Sign spoke to his soul; he perceived It intuitively with absolute clarity. It spoke of a world which was infinitely far above him, to which nevertheless his soul was bound with golden threads of gossamer.

He listened to the sounds, he heard what they were saying to him; he absorbed the continually changing colours. He was no longer conscious of himself. He was only a vessel into which the Eternal One poured His Grace, that he might use it, and pass it on to others. Streams of Holy Power flowed through him.

As a creature of the Eternal One, he felt himself one with the whole world around him, into which the Power flowed as it passed through him. But he also felt himself drawn upwards in the Power by the golden threads.

Suddenly he was aware of the circular swinging in which he was permitted to be a minute part. Astounded, overwhelmed, he prayed.

Then the pencil of rays which he had once before been permitted to see shot down from above, surged round him and bore his soul aloft. Again he beheld the Temple of the Eternal One, "the lowest", the voice had said at that time. But now he was allowed to enter, not just to see it from afar. He was able to enter the Sanctuary, and found himself in a community of souls to whom his own called joyfully: "Brothers!"

He worshipped with them before the shrine, then he bowed his forehead to the ground and saw nothing more. The eyes of his soul were too dazzled.

After that he found himself once again in a sea of sounds under the tree. Before him shone in lovely purity the lotus-flower with the wonderful Sign. Longingly he stretched forth his hands.

And it seemed to him as though the flower was laid on his heart, and then on his forehead. He had the inner sensation that it was sinking deep down within him in both of these places, releasing undreamed-of things.

And the voice of the messenger from above spoke melodiously and vibrantly:

"Bear the Sign of your Lord upon you. Keep It pure and radiant. It will keep your soul and thoughts luminous, if you yourself do not dim It."

After this Siddharta was no longer conscious of himself until the rays of the sun awoke him in the morning.

Siddharta was filled with joy.

"The Sign of my Lord, thus of the Lord of all the Worlds? Am I allowed to bear It? Has He thereby chosen me to be His servant? Why was I not inside the lotus-flower this night? Because something else stood there! I had to make way for this something. Now I understand what it means: At one time I thought myself so important that everything had to revolve round me; now I am learning to stand back. Now at last I know that everything revolves around the Lord of the Worlds. I am filled with bliss that I have been allowed to discover this."

AT LAST he beheld Utakamand, as he had once seen it with Maggalana. But he hesitated to ride in; for he wanted first to engrave all the impressions deeply within him, so that they should become indelibly and eternally his own.

He spent this night too in the open, and then he rode up vigorously with his faithful followers. The road had been widened, and they could ride their horses without trouble right to the top.

His approach had been observed; teachers, scholars and Brahmans ran to meet him. He was received with the greatest joy.

He was no longer used to such a noisy bustle. At Indraprastha scarcely less work was done, but things moved in a more sedate, more dignified way. Was it because the Mountain-dwellers had the knowledge of the Lord of the Worlds?

A few days passed in taking over the management and attending to all kinds of other formalities, and then Siddharta began each day by telling the assembled inmates of the school about the Eternal One.

After that, everyone was free to come to his room and ask questions. Only then did he perceive that after all it was not so easy to make a Brahman into a believer in God. Far too many thoughts intervened.

The believers in Brahma clung fast to their doctrine of reincarnation; according to which every human being has to live on this earth at least once as a stone, a plant, or an animal. But only his existence as a human being can release him from the eternal cycle of births.

Siddharta cogitated and prayed over how to find the right words to expose this false belief in all its untenability. At last he had it:

He asked the Brahmans what purpose reincarnation was to serve. The answer was shattering:

"Master, we are not able to say. In many cases it will be punishment, in others the inevitable consequence of what we have brought on ourselves."

"What purpose will it have if I come next time as a flower?"

Again they wanted to plead ignorance, but he pressed them to answer him, as they would an enquiring student. At last one of them said:

"Master, I imagine that if I were to return as a flower, it would be meant to refine me."

"Do you know whether you have already been a flower in former lives?

102

Have you any idea what you once were? No? Well then, of what use are the frequent rebirths to you?"

Then he began to show them that rebirth is a Grace from the Lord of all the Worlds, Who gives men the opportunity to work their way upwards. But there can only be ascent in a direct line. A to-ing and fro-ing, now man, now animal, then again stone or plant, leads not further on but away from the straight path. Once human being .... always human being! But with a firm volition to do better each time – that leads upwards, to the origin.

"Where is our origin?" they wanted to know.

"In the beyond," was the reply. "I cannot give you a better answer. I know that we come from above, and that our way, if it be the right one, leads upwards again. Is not that enough?"

On another occasion they asked him about the concept of sin.

"You speak of sin and guilt, Master, when hitherto we have found only faults. Is there a difference?"

"Faults are what entangle us in sin," replied Siddharta, after briefly reflecting on his answer. "But sin is all that separates us from the Eternal One through ourselves."

"Can sin be forgiven?"

Siddharta's answer was a short, sharp "No!"

They were startled.

"Master, if a man does you wrong, you will not hold it against him for ever. If he confesses his fault, repents and seeks to make amends, surely you will forgive him. Is the Eternal One not better than any man? Why will He not forgive?"

"He does forgive, for He is Goodness and Grace, but He is also Justice! He indeed forgives, but we may not forgive ourselves. We must redeem ourselves, loose ourselves from the bonds that seek to entangle us, from the sin that reaches out for us. No other can do it for us."

They did not understand that. To them there was a contradiction in the words of their Master. Siddharta felt this, and was aware that he had only partly succeeded in expressing that which he carried so clearly within him. If he told them that there could be forgiveness for sins, they would make no more effort to improve their lives; he knew that.

Better, a thousand times better to let them sigh over their sins. That kept

103

them awake. It became ever clearer to him that his people were a race of dreamers, who would rather indulge in easy contemplation than discipline themselves through hard work. Out of this had also arisen the concept of Nirvana, of the great nothingness into which the perfected soul was finally allowed to dissolve, to rest from its earthly wanderings.

He must combat this with all his might. How could he ever have judged the Brahmans so wrongly? Because he had found the true faith in passing through theirs, he had assumed that it must be the same with everyone. Truly these gentle, visionary worshippers of Brahma did not make it easy for him to grasp their souls.

"Lord of the Worlds, Thou the Eternal One, help me! I want no honour for myself, I want men to recognise and serve Thee!" so did he often pray.

The one year which he had set aside for Utakamand had flown by as if on wings. He had not yet accomplished the half of what he considered to be necessary before he could leave the school. After that he wanted Maggalana to take his place. He who reminded him so much of the first Maggalana who had brought him here, he was to lead Utakamand.

But first the soil had to be prepared. And Siddharta worked untiringly. They were all attached to him, old as well as young; they also listened to his words in complete devotion and repeated them among themselves. But it was a fruitless listening; the souls were not gripped.

Siddharta tried to show the people here his own path, to let them experience each single step of development with him. But this did not advance them either. They listened as they would to a teller of tales.

Then one night he had a vision. He saw a boy who had made a stockyard for himself with coloured stones. Each stone was a yak-ox or a buffalo, a goat or a sheep. He played happily with them, and wished for nothing better.

Then a man came and took the stones from him.

"Worthless stuff," he said, "look, here I have carved animals of wood for you, play with them."

But the boy cried for his stones, and rejected the wooden animals.

"How foolish of the man," said Siddharta on awaking, "he should have played with the boy and the stones, and only then shown him the wooden animals. Then the boy would have asked for them himself."

And a voice within Siddharta said:

104

"And you?"

It was as though scales fell from his eyes. He saw what he had done wrong. All wrong, despite the best volition! If only he had not done too much damage already!

From this day on he spoke with the Brahmans about Brahma and Shiva, Vishnu and Maro, Shakra and Lokapales. They listened joyfully, and enthusiastically accepted it when he was able to tell them more about the activity of these gods than they had known before.

He told them of the working of the animistic beings, whom he referred to as "lesser gods" in order to come nearer to their understanding. And behold, their souls, which previously had closed themselves convulsively, fearing for their sacred possessions, now opened up.

Now they realised that he did not want to take anything from them, but on the contrary to give them something more. Now they gladly reached out for what was offered. In an unbelievably short time he was able to tell them again about the Lord of all the Worlds, Who is also the Lord of the gods.

This they now understood. It was a joyful giving and taking, a happy learning together, that filled the school at Utakamand, so that it often seemed to all of them as though the power would almost shatter the old walls.

The second year drew to its close; what earlier had seemed impossible had been accomplished. Now Siddharta sent a message to Maggalana. Weeks passed before the faithful one arrived, and with him Rahula. It was a joyful reunion of father and son, who were becoming ever more alike.

"Let Rahula be your representative here," Maggalana begged. "He deserves it, he is more advanced than I. He has a special gift for teaching and for understanding others. I feel drawn back to my own sphere of activity.

"Leave Rahula here, Master. He is so much like you. When he speaks to us it will be as though we were listening to you," pleaded the Brahmans.

Rahula gladly agreed to undertake the task when his father offered it to him. Father and son taught side by side for a while yet; then Siddharta took leave of the school, which was now twice as dear to him. He saw that a spirit of vigorous activity and resolute thinking would move in with Rahula, so that unrest and confusion could no longer find a place here.

105

NOW SIDDHARTA rode again over the familiar roads. Once again he spent a night under the mango tree. But this time he was not allowed to see anything. Nor did he brood over the "why", but reflected all the more deeply on the treasure of his earlier experiences.

He visited all the schools and monasteries which lay on his way. This time he travelled leisurely, for Maggalana had brought good news from Indraprastha. His experiences in Utakamand helped him everywhere. He had become kinder and more tolerant.

Only a few days' journey from the Mountain he came to a monastery where, to his horror, he found also female inmates. They were clad outwardly like the Brothers, wearing a yellow robe over a blue underskirt. They had wrapped a white cloth round their head and shoulders, which almost completely veiled their faces.

At first Siddharta said nothing at all, but let all the impressions work on him. Greater comfort prevailed here than in other monasteries; for the Sisters saw to cleanliness and beauty. He found flowers in the rooms. Could this be allowed?

"How did you come to admit women?" he asked the principal.

"Master, they begged to be admitted. I know that women are considered inferior. But you yourself have done away with the castes, and said that all human beings are equal. So I thought that man and woman must also be equal."

"You are mixing right and wrong, my friend," said Siddharta thoughtfully. "It is true that before the Eternal One only the condition of the soul counts, whether it be of a woman or a man. Perhaps women stand even higher, because theirs is the finer intuitive faculty. What is certain however is that they have different radiations from men, and that wherever they are they seek to bring beauty and refinement into life.

"But we have no use for that in our monasteries. Not for nothing is the greatest simplicity, indeed deprivation of all comfort, stipulated. It is impossible for men and women to live in the same monastery."

Siddharta paced the room with long strides. He had to collect his thoughts. What did he really know about women? The only woman ever close to him had been Maya, who was to him the epitome of everything precious on earth. Could he imagine Maya in a monastery?

106

The more he pondered over it, the more clearly he had to answer "yes". Maya's deep piety would adapt to every rule, she would joyfully take upon herself any deprivation, but – – and now his thoughts became clearer – – she would have refused to live together with strange men in the confines of a monastery.

That was it! If women wanted to lead a monastic life, they must be by themselves. Then the rules for this way of life could be adapted to their particular nature; for it was not right for women to sleep on the floor. Their bodies were too delicate for that.

The Eternal One did not want the physical vessels to be destroyed. He only wanted the men to be hard with themselves, in order to become all the more useful instruments.

Emerging from these reflections, Siddharta suddenly turned again to the principal:

"Can you tell me, my friend, how the women whom you have admitted occupy themselves? Are they also sent out to collect alms?"

"They are not sent, they go voluntarily; but they have no alms-bowls. Nevertheless they often bring home gifts. The best thing is for you to ask Anaga, whom I have made the leader of the women. I do not understand them very well," he concluded, somewhat embarrassed.

"Then send for Anaga."

The leader was glad not to have to give any further account. He certainly should have asked before introducing something so completely new, but Siddharta had been in Utakamand. That was how he justified himself.

A fragile, not very tall woman came to Siddharta, and bowed. He was so little used to dealing with women that at first he did not even know how he should speak to her. Then his innate chivalry triumphed over the oppressive silence.

"Your name is Anaga?" he asked kindly.

"Yes, Master."

A musical voice timidly whispered the short answer.

"Come nearer, and tell me what drove you and the other women to enter the monastery. Why are you not with your families? Why do you start new things not done by anyone before?"

107

With each question, his voice had grown louder and more indignant. The women should keep to themselves! After all, they could not be used as servants of the Eternal One!

"Really not, Siddharta?" a gentle voice within him asked.

But he would not listen. The woman should speak!

"Speak!" he said imperiously, not considering that he was completely depriving the timid being of her courage.

A glowing blush crossed the delicate countenance, out of which the eyes shone like blue gems. Blue eyes? He had never seen such eyes before. Siddharta looked at her again, and the lustre of these stars pierced his heart. He who had learned to understand dumb animals suddenly understood the soul that spoke to him out of these eyes.

He now addressed the trembling woman, standing before him like a lovely flower, in quite a different tone, kind and gentle.

"Anaga, sit down here on this mat and try to answer my questions."

The woman sat down, her hands lightly folded in her lap, her eyes fixed on them. The silken shawl that covered her head and shoulders was dazzlingly white.

"You women had heard of the Eternal One, had you not?"

Anaga nodded, then she whispered:

"Yes, Master. My husband had learned to serve the Eternal One. He shared everything with me, even the knowledge of the Lord of all the Worlds, which was more important to him than all else. Through him I learned to worship the Eternal One. My husband told me that I too could serve the Lord, if I did everything in His honour. Then my husband died quite suddenly, he was drowned while trying to rescue a child from the river...."

She could not continue, perhaps the memory was too painful. Siddharta was careful not to interrupt the flow of her thoughts with even a word. What spoke to him out of this woman was so new, but also so overwhelming, that he was eager to hear it all.

After a few minutes Anaga continued:

"We were childless. I was completely alone. I am not of a high caste, in which widows can let themselves be burned, so that the soul of the husband can take hers with him into the beyond. We poorer folk must see for ourselves how we get on. But you know that, Master," she sighed.

Again there was a pause, during which many voices spoke within Siddharta.

"Why have you never thought of the sister-souls? Because you are a man, only the men were of importance to you! Do you think that the Eternal One makes distinctions?"

Anaga interrupted these voices by continuing:

"An ardent love for the Lord of all the Worlds had awakened within me even while my husband was alive. He had awakened it. Now it became so strong that it sought to express itself.

"I saw the Yellow Brothers journeying through the villages, and I felt it would be good if there were Yellow Sisters, who would visit the women whom the Brothers passed by as they would something unclean.

"I began to call on the women whom I knew to be in some need or other. There was a mother whose children were sick. I helped her care for the little ones. There was a woman in destitution, she did not have enough to live on. I shared my possessions with her.

"And all to whom I went I told of the Eternal One, and of His great Goodness and Love. They all wanted to be His servants! Then I told those who had husband and children that they should do as I had done when my Amaru was still with me. They should do all things in honour of the Eternal One, and their homes would prosper.

"But those who were alone like me I gathered around me. I taught them to understand the Eternal One aright; I showed them how they could help others. They did as I did, and were happy as I am. Then came the great experience."

Again the woman was silent, lost in thought.

"Master, I have never spoken a word of it to anyone. If I tell you about it, I do so in the hope that you will not turn us out of the monastery afterwards. Listen:

"I was sitting at the bedside of a woman who was sick unto death, and I prayed. It was deepest night, a lantern burned dimly at the far end of the room. I prayed for right recognition of the Will of my Lord.

"Then suddenly wonderful rose-coloured light filled the whole room, a fragrance as of the most glorious blossoms filled the air, sounds such as no earthly instrument could produce surged around me. I thought that I had

109

passed into the beyond without realising it. I felt very, very light. Then that too ceased; I was no longer conscious of myself, I forgot myself completely. Do you understand, Master?" she asked, endeavouring to make everything clear to him.

"Just go on, Anaga, I understand you very well," Siddharta, deeply moved, encouraged her.

This woman, whom he had held in low regard, had been found worthy to receive tidings from On High!

"When I had completely surrendered myself, a delicate figure suddenly stood before me. She was the most glorious woman imaginable. Luminous veils covered her; in her hands she held fragrant white blossoms. And she spoke to me, the poor Anaga, whose father and husband had been only merchants. O Master, the bliss!

"She knew my name! 'Anaga,' she said, 'the Lord of the Worlds accepts your services. Pure has been your life, pure your intuitive perception. Keep it thus. In purity you shall go before the women of your people. You shall teach them, you shall awaken their sleeping souls, and make them too servants of the Eternal One. There will be helpers around you, so that you may always know what the Lord of the Worlds, Who is also your Lord, desires of you and your sisters.

"'Make Helping Sisters of those whom you have gathered around you, and who like you wish to serve the Lord. Enter a monastery, forget yourselves, and live only in service of the Eternal One!'

"Master, I cannot repeat all the glorious words quite as they were spoken, but this is definitely their meaning.

"The luminous figure vanished, and with her the sounds and the rays, the fragrance and the blissful joy that had filled me. Instead I felt within me strength such as I had never known before. And in this power I did my work on the sick woman, who was allowed to recover; then I looked for my helpers and entered the monastery with them.

"How difficult it was to win over the principal! How I had to beg and plead before he would relent and admit us! At last he yielded, and we have been here ever since.

"And now, Master, I implore you, you who know what I have experienced: do not send us away. Permit the Sisters to help the women. Let us learn and advance further in the recognition of the Most High!"

Anaga had raised her delicate hands imploringly. Heavenly radiance of more than earthly purity seemed to surround her.

Siddharta did not hesitate over his decision for a moment.

"Anaga, hear me: I have learned from your words that it was wrong to forget the women in our upward-striving. I rejoice that you have opened my eyes. Accept my gratitude!

"Far be it from me to turn you away, when the Eternal One Himself allowed you to be led to the monastery. But it is not seemly for you to share the life with men. I will have your own convent built in the vicinity. You shall lead it. Together with you I will draw up the rules and statutes, which for you women must naturally be quite different from those for the men.

"Meantime continue to live as before. The blessing of the Lord of all the Worlds is clearly with you!"

Happy, Anaga withdrew. Siddharta, however, called on the principal to order a home for the serving women to be built as soon as possible. The little rooms were to be twice the size of those in the monasteries. A simple but comfortable couch was to be placed in each.

The principal was surprised; but Siddharta explained:

"Just consider, day and night they nurse the sick. When they are at home they must be able to rest and refresh their bodies. Their earthly forms are different from ours."

He had learned much this morning. With the promise to return to bless the convent, he mounted his steed and now rode without a break towards the Mountain of the Eternal One. He allowed himself only a few hours' rest at night.

He had not announced his coming, but the cavalcade had nevertheless been espied, and joyful activity spread over the whole Mountain. One of the snakes was lying across the road to guard it. Siddharta greeted it and praised its vigilance.

Ananda ran to meet him, happy that the Master was in their midst again. Nothing unusual had taken place during his long absence, only Comforter had died. Siddharta missed the dog, but he could not be persuaded to get another. The disciples did not understand him in this, but he thought:

111

"I no longer wish to let my heart become attached to anything of my own, even if it be only a dog."

Ananda had returned to his own work. Life on the Mountain resumed its daily course.

After careful sifting and examining, Siddharta tried to write down such of his teaching as he considered worthy to be preserved.

Then a message came from Srinar that the convent of the Sisters had been completed. Siddharta was not anxious to ride out again so soon, nevertheless he wished to see and consecrate the convent. He also looked forward to seeing Anaga again.

The house, outwardly built exactly like the monastery, made a very pleasing impression within. Instead of doors, Anaga and the women had made silk curtains for each of the rooms. The couches too had colourful covers, and flowers stood in pretty vases by every window.

"Do not be angry, Master," begged Anaga. "If we would carry joy into the lives of others, we women must have beauty around us. It will help us to be more receptive if we do not cut ourselves off from what is beautiful."

Twenty women had gathered around Anaga. They were all dressed alike. Common to all was the radiance in their eyes, which spoke of an active inner life and a great joyousness in service.

Quite spontaneously, groups had formed. Some of the women were skilled in nursing the sick, and knew about healing herbs, and how to prepare ointments and teas. Others cared very lovingly for lonely, neglected or sick children.

They looked after them, taught them, and sought to bring them up to become useful human beings. Others again helped overworked women in their households. But all were diligently active. They accepted no reward for their work; if food was given to them, they handed it over to the monastery.

Now Siddharta wanted to know who attended to the feeding of the Sisters. It transpired that no one had thought that the women, too, had to eat.

Anaga said: "After all we are out-of-doors most of the time, and there we get what we need."

But Siddharta was alarmed at how little his adherents were used to thinking about others. He arranged that Anaga should have meals prepared for the Sisters in their convent. They were not to be fed sumptuously, but adequately. In future they were to be allowed to keep for themselves whatever gifts of food were offered to them in gratitude for their work.

After seeing to the outer requirements, the Master turned his attention to the spiritual needs. Who was to instruct the Sisters? Anaga could teach them, but who was to speak to them, to pray with them?

It seemed to Siddharta that this must be done by a man, and he directed that on every seventh day the principal of the monastery should give an address to the women in the great hall, which all the Sisters were to attend.

Thus everything was now wisely ordered, and the Master set out on his homeward journey.

JUST BEFORE his little band reached the Mountain they encountered a stately cavalcade, whose colourful garments awakened memories in Siddharta. Where had he seen such soldiers before?

The men were obviously about to ride up to the Mountain. Siddharta urged his horse forward to reach the top before them. Swift as an arrow he flew past, with so firm a seat that the strangers broke into shouts of admiration.

On the way he met one of the guardian-snakes, and told it to withdraw, because the arrivals certainly intended no harm. It crept obediently to the side of the road, rolled itself into a ball, and waited.

On the Mountain he found everything prepared to welcome him and the strangers, who had already been espied as well. Siddharta had barely time to exchange his short riding tunic for the usual long silk robe before it was announced that messengers from Kapilavastu wished to speak to him.

That was why the colours were familiar to him!

He went out joyfully to greet the guests. They had been allowed to dismount. They stood close together, and gazed at the former Prince.

Then one of the older men who stood in the front rank could contain himself no longer. With the cry: "Siddharta, my Prince," he fell on his knees before his Master, and raised the hem of his garment to his lips.

Siddharta recognised him. He had been one of his counsellors and companions, who because of a fall from his horse had had to remain at home at the time of the fateful ride. It was a joyful greeting. After that, Siddharta turned to the others with the words:

"I bid you also welcome. Perhaps I still know one or two among you."

He made them come up to him one by one. With some he was struck by a resemblance that reminded him of the man's father; others were quite strange to him.

The last man but one to step before him was more simply dressed than all the others. His face was finely chiselled, and lighter than that of his companions.

"Maya," cried Siddharta, not knowing what he was doing.

The stranger bowed low. He did not wish to show the emotion that overcame him. But Siddharta had pulled himself together. He grasped the hand of the man who stood before him, and said:

"Suddhodana, my son! I would recognise you even if you were to stand before me in rags. The resemblance to your mother is too great. Welcome! I was carrying you in my arms when you were snatched from me ...."

But his son, not wanting to let any tender feelings arise in front of the others, interrupted him cheerfully:

"And you shall carry your own image in your arms, Father! Little Siddharta has come with me to greet his grandfather."

At a sign from the young Prince, a servant hastened out and brought in a little boy, who though still very small already walked sturdily. The resemblance to his grandfather was unmistakable.

When the guests had been accommodated and the little boy also placed in kindly hands, father and son sat together. They did not know each other yet, but still they were so close.

Suddhodana said that Rahula had told him about their father. He had been wanting to come for a long time, but had decided to bring the little Siddharta to meet the big one.

"So I had to wait until he had outgrown his ayah; for to ride with women-folk – no, Father; that I did not wish to do, not even to be able to see you before now," he concluded, laughing.

This sunny laughter, the way he threw back his head at the same time, everything reminded him of Maya.

Again Siddharta felt how sweet bonds were seeking to ensnare him. That

114

must not be. He must restrain himself, but his son and grandson should not suffer through it.

After the meal, Siddharta suggested that the Prince should look round the buildings and gardens. From one of the gardens rang out cries of joy which contrasted with the usual quiet. They went there first, and found the little boy blissfully happy between two great snakes. The Prince's heart missed a beat. His child with the poisonous reptiles!

But before Siddharta could explain about the snakes, the little one called out:

"They are such dear, beautiful animals; I can understand very well what they tell me. They like me because I am like Grandfather, and I understand them!"

Impetuously he pressed one of the flat triangular heads against him.

His father was still struggling with an inner unease; but Siddharta gazed happily on the picture at his feet.

"Can you really understand the animals, little one?" he asked, and was delighted to hear that the child spoke to every animal, and that every animal trusted him.

"Then, my child, tell people that they should never wantonly or even maliciously harm any animal. Tell them so whenever you have the opportunity to do so," begged the Master. Then however he promised the little one a special treat. He was to see the monkeys.

Prince Suddhodana assailed his father with requests to visit his realm, to show himself to his people, among whom many a one still knew him. But Siddharta stood firm. He demonstrated to his son that he was needed here in his work, that he had given up all thought of ruling and of princehood.

Instead he began to speak of the Lord of all the Worlds.

Suddhodana had not grown up in Tibet in vain. He was well instructed. Even though he called the Eternal One the Sublime One, what did a name signify?

"Do you teach your people, my son?" Siddharta enquired earnestly.

"Certainly, Father! I sent for priests from Tibet, who lead us in divine services in the temple. Many of our people pray with us to the only true God. Where is your temple?"

Siddharta explained to his son why he had built none. Suddhodana shook his head.

"That would not be right with us," he said modestly. "Our people need visible signs for their worship. It is bad enough that we cannot show them a picture of God; but on this point I stand firm. Whoever is not willing to pray to the Invisible One should keep to his old faith. But I really could not imagine our country without temples."

This however was the only thing which the son could not quite understand. He openly admired everything else, and resolved to imitate many things.

Evening fell. And the monkeys arrived in droves, curious as ever. Little Siddharta broke out in jubilation when he saw so many animals.

He did not rest until his grandfather released him, so that he could run to join them as fast as his feet would carry him. Here he took a little monkey's hand, there he slipped a long tail admiringly through his fingers. To the monkeys the child was something quite new. They admired him greatly, and began to chatter quietly with him. The little one clapped his hands:

"Father, they can understand me, just as I can understand them. They are dear little men!"

The Prince did not feel quite at ease. He did not like his child being among these wild bands. The monkeys sensed it and avoided him, whereas they approached Siddharta trustingly.

But the latter was revolving deep thoughts in his soul. To him the child's confidence in the monkeys was more than mere play. He felt that the younger Siddharta would one day also approach the souls of the people in this way.

But he said aloud: "He who is closely connected with the creatures of the Eternal One stands aright in the cycle of all happenings. He will always be able to fill his place, because he understands and loves the world around him, and by doing so he cares for it."

When the monkeys had departed, not without first raiding the mango-grove, the old man drew his grandchild to him and said:

"I will pray the Eternal One that you may keep this understanding, my child. Whether you then become a prince or a teacher, this closeness will help you in your ascent."

The little one did not understand him yet, but he held his grandfather's words in his soul, and later they bore fruit.

The days which Prince Suddhodana was able to devote to his father passed all too quickly. Promising to come again, the cavalcade departed. Little Siddharta sat on his father's horse.

IT WAS OBVIOUS to some extent that the strange guests had brought unrest with them. Even though every pupil, every worker had gone about his duties at Siddharta's explicit behest, nevertheless opportunities had not been lacking for people to exchange opinions and tell one another various things.

What excited them all most was the fact that Siddharta had been a prince. They had not known this: they rejoiced over it. Eventually their thoughts could not remain hidden from the Master. He sought at once to guide them on to the right course. He summoned everyone to the great square and spoke to them.

Their behaviour during the guests' visit had shown that they were still far from being so inwardly secure that anything pressing in from without could not take hold of them. It was not good that they had yielded so unreservedly to the influence of those whose nature and schooling was so different. But above all, it was not good that even now they were pervaded by thoughts which should have no room within them, much less on the Mountain of the Eternal One.

Was it anything special, that he had once been a prince? They had all been something else before they became servants of the Eternal One. Was it not better to be a servant of the Lord of all the Worlds than prince of a small realm?

He spoke to them in this way for a long time, until he perceived that they were ashamed. Then he dismissed them, with the exhortation to be doubly zealous now and make up for lost time.

Again Siddharta tried to engross himself in his manuscripts. But a fresh interruption came. Maggalana appeared, and a few days after that Ananda. Both brought the same complaint: a sage who called himself Djinna had appeared in the country, and was preaching that the gods could only be appeased by mortification, self-mutilation and the like.

Exasperated, Siddharta shook his head, but then said:

"Are we to be upset by the teaching of a blockhead? Whoever would believe him deserves no better."

"But he is leading people astray," persisted Ananda. "Master, it would be a good thing if you were to confront him!"

"What are you thinking of, Ananda?" asked Siddharta earnestly. "Are you trying to advise me to seek out this heretic and argue with him in public? Or am I to follow his trail and say to people: Do not believe what this man teaches, it is not the truth?"

Ananda was dismayed. He had expected Siddharta to hurl himself at the spiritual opponent and render him harmless. Instead the Master seemed quite indifferent to whether anyone was spreading false teachings.

"Does the man deny the Lord of all the Worlds?" asked Siddharta.

"No," was the answer of both disciples. "He does not speak of Him at all. He speaks only of the old gods whom you know."

"Then his teaching cannot affect us," Siddharta decided. "If he were to attack the Eternal One, we should have to oppose that with all our might. But it means nothing whatever to us if people mutilate themselves for the sake of those who cannot help them in any case. He who has recognised the Eternal One will take care not to fall into such a delusion. And the others may do what they please."

The disciples realised that there was no way to influence Siddharta. In the evening they spoke together in the garden. Maggalana said:

"Actually I am ashamed that I have approached the Master with this demand."

"Ashamed? Why?" exclaimed Ananda angrily. "I find it unwise of Siddharta to be so little concerned about it. If Djinna finds a following, we shall lose adherents!"

"Ananda, bethink you," exhorted Maggalana. "The Master is not concerned about having a large number of adherents, but rather that men should recognise the Lord of the Worlds, and thereby become free again from the bonds of sin. That is why he does not trouble himself over those who refuse to know anything about the Eternal One. It is just that which makes me so ashamed of having been unable to distinguish between seeking to drag down the Lord of the Worlds, and debasing men."

"You are now talking almost as learnedly as the Master," said Ananda in surprise. "Sometimes I cannot understand you."

"And yet he is right," another voice joined in the conversation. "Do not be alarmed that I overheard your difference of opinion. He who would converse privately should not speak so loudly."

The disciples had now recognised Sariputta who joined them.

The yogi had grown old, very old, but his spirit still retained a wonderful freshness.

They all loved him, and even now both men were prepared to let him resolve their difference of opinion harmoniously.

Calmly he explained to them how pointless it would be if the Master were to emerge from his dignified seclusion to confront a Djinna in the streets and public places.

After all, what did the new sage teach that was so terrible? He knew nothing of the Lord of the Worlds. Well, many Brahmans did not know either. He believed in the old gods. That was better than proclaiming new ones, or introducing idol-worship.

He wanted to redeem sins through self-inflicted punishment? Nothing could be done about that. Still it was something if men felt remorse over their sins.

"He only says so, Sariputta!" burst out Ananda, who did not willingly allow others to speak. "He says that the mutilations are for the forgiveness of sins. But afterwards he also says that through them a better place in the beyond can be attained. He is even reputed to have said: Arm off, silver chair; arm and leg off, golden chair; starving to death, throne in the beyond. But anyone who manages to make his limbs crooked and twisted becomes one of the minor gods himself."

Sariputta laughed.

"If people believe such nonsense they deserve nothing better. But put aside your disagreement, you two. We must not come before the Master in disharmony."

Pleasantly Maggalana held out his hand to Ananda, who willingly grasped it. As they walked on, Sariputta said:

"There is indeed something beautiful about the Master's command to keep peace at all cost!"

119

ON THE WAY to the Mountain Maggalana had spent a night at Srinar, and had brought a request from there to Siddharta.

Anaga, the principal of the convent, asked whether the Master could not come to visit them again soon, as she had many things to discuss and decide.

"I advised her," said Maggalana, "to travel with me and visit the Master. But she was quite alarmed at the suggestion. 'Women,' she said, 'may not approach the Mountain of the Eternal One; only men are there.' So I promised her that I would speak to the Master, and bring back his answer on my homeward journey."

At first Siddharta said nothing, but he re-opened the conversation on the following day.

"Do you know what Anaga wants to ask, Maggalana?" he enquired.

"No, Master, she said very little to me."

"Then I shall ride with you when you shortly leave us again," Siddharta decided.

He much regretted that something always came to prevent him from writing, but ever again he told himself that he had been appointed to the service of the Lord for those who were alive today and only through them for those to come. Therefore he now rode to Srinar in a happy frame of mind.

He looked forward to the talk with Anaga, from whom he had already learned so much. But when she stood before him, he was surprised.

She was the same, and yet a completely different person. Her blue eyes had become even more radiant. This radiance had now imparted itself to her whole countenance. Although the white silk scarf concealed her brow, the radiance, which was not of this earth, shone through. Her figure had become erect, her bearing and her movements were still graceful, but they were more purposeful.

"Truly," Siddharta had to reflect, "through her calling to the service of the Eternal One she has been raised above all the women of our people."

Modestly she waited for him to address her. When he asked her what her wishes were, she answered him calmly.

"Master, we must build many more convents," she said emphatically. "Our house is so full that there are always two women sharing a room, and even then it is not enough. I have now arranged for four women to use the same room: while two are carrying out their duties down below, the other two are in the house. But we cannot continue in this way for much longer."

"Why have you not had the house enlarged, Anaga?" asked Siddharta, but he knew the answer before she gave it.

"That would have been no real solution, Master. If there is such a great need for a convent among us, in this little part of our huge country, what must it be like in the other principalities? Everywhere the women fare in the same way. The men receive the teaching from the Eternal One, but rarely is there one among them who will communicate it to his wife.

"Master, we must build convents all over the country! It is necessary! Many women have become so mature here that they would be suitable principals of these convents. Let a convent be built wherever there is a monastery. We do not disturb the Brothers. Our life runs its course, well-ordered and completely apart. Master, grant this for the sake of the many souls of women who cannot find the way to the Light unaided."

Siddharta heard the imploring note in these words. Anaga raised her hands in supplication. And voices sounded in the Master's soul:

"Have you not yet learned to respect the soul of woman? It is purer than the soul of man, lighter and more luminous. Honour it, lest one day it indict you before the Throne of the Eternal One!"

Siddharta had become very serious, so serious that Anaga feared for the fulfilment of her request. And oh, she had an even greater one to make!

At last the Master spoke:

"You are right, Anaga. We must help the women. It is your sacred task, which the Eternal One has given you. But I am to help you, so that the earthly way may be smoothed for you. Just warn me, call me, and I will stand by you. You shall not ask in vain!

"I shall instruct all the monastery leaders to build houses for women near their own, according to the design of this one. And you shall choose and train women leaders, so that they will be ready when the convents are built."

"I think," said Anaga, after joyfully thanking him, "that we should let every woman leader be accompanied by a few Sisters from here, so that a right beginning will be made everywhere. At the same time this would empty our convent, so that there would be no need for us to enlarge it."

"That is a very good idea," commended Siddharta. "You too, Anaga, must select helpers for the time when you leave this convent."

"Does the Master want me to superintend one of the new convents? I am ready."

Anaga said it, but some hesitation was perceptible in her voice. Where would the Master's will call her?

"Obviously you cannot remain here, if we acquire at least twenty new convents. You must preside over them all, just as I control the management of the monasteries. But to this end, it is necessary for you to preside over the convent that we shall build on the Mountain in honour of the Eternal One!"

"Master!" Anaga rejoiced. "So women will also be allowed to come to the Mountain of the Eternal One! Are we not too lowly for that? Will He bestow this high grace on us? O, Eternal One, All-Highest, Thou Lord of all the Worlds, I thank Thee, I thank Thee in the name of all the anxious souls of women whom Thou wilt draw upwards to Thee!"

Siddharta was deeply moved by the woman's rapturous gratitude. The men who had been allowed to come to the Mountain had indeed been happy, but they had taken it for granted, as a reward, so to speak, for their intention to serve. But the women had served quite simply out of an inner-most urge, without expecting anything in return. What an example!

He turned again kindly to Anaga:

"So in future we shall work side by side and together for the good of our whole people, Anaga. I look forward to that. Have you any more plans for us to deal with?"

"Master," the woman confessed. "I have one more great thought, which leaves me no peace. And I know that the luminous woman, the messenger of the Eternal One, has awakened it in my soul; therefore it must be right. But you must help to carry it out.

"You see I am grieved for the children of our people. So many grow up without knowledge of the Eternal One, indeed even without knowledge of the gods. I have seen children in whom the inner urge – unknown to them-selves – to worship something is so strong that they make gods out of wood and rags, before which they kneel. Where will this lead? These children will grow up, and be the people. If we do not take care of the children, the

122

people will perish even before it has grown up. I cannot put it into words as it lives within me," she apologised.

"I understand you very well, Anaga," Siddharta assured her. "If we wish also to help the people for the future, we must look after the children. You are right. Have you considered yet how this is to be done?"

"Yes, Master," exclaimed Anaga, who was happy that the great petition met with no opposition. "I think we should establish schools that will instruct children whose parents have found their way to the Eternal One...."

Siddharta interrupted her.

"Schools?" he asked. "You know that we have only schools for adults. What should children learn in schools? There are no schools for children in the whole country. How do you picture that?"

"I do not mean such schools as we have," said Anaga, who could not help smiling.

She had been pondering these thoughts for a long time, they were quite familiar to her. She could not understand why the Master did not know at once how she pictured the schools.

"I thought that we should gather together small children, and encourage them to be clean, well-mannered and peace-loving. We would teach them to worship and understand the Eternal One, so far as a child's spirit is able. In addition, depending on their aptitude, we can teach the girls how to sew, embroider, gather herbs and look after the sick. The boys would leave us in any case as soon as they reach the age of six."

"Why do you want to turn the boys out so soon?" asked the Master.

"They must pass into the hands of men. Usually they do help in the workshops from this age, or make themselves useful in other ways. Things are better for boys than for girls," she added with a sigh.

"Do you not think, Anaga, that perhaps we must separate the sexes even earlier? You women will teach the very little ones, place in their young souls the first concepts of the Lord of the Worlds. After that you will continue to look after the girls, while the boys enter a school run by Brothers."

Again Anaga was overjoyed.

"If that were possible, all my most beautiful dreams would come true! That is just how I have pictured it, but I did not dare to tell you so much at once."

"Always tell me everything you think, Anaga. By doing so you will help both us and the people. You have clear, good thoughts."

For days they planned, considered and rejected. But eventually things were settled according to the outcome of their first discussion.

Eager building now began all over the country. The schools, simple houses with airy halls, were built in the valleys, so that even the smallest children could reach them. The convents, however, stood halfway up the slopes, between the schools and the monasteries. Thus they were protected and yet independent.

Siddharta himself rode from monastery to monastery, to discuss all that was necessary with the principals. Everywhere he found only joy, no opposition as he had feared. The time had come for this fruit to ripen. Now it was happening. How wonderfully the Will of the Eternal One took effect at all times and in all places, if only people listened to It.

The convent on the Mountain of the Eternal One was also built. Like all the others, it was to be not quite on the Mountain, yet high enough for the Sisters not to feel excluded. The school, a light but very simple structure, was built in the valley.

Then came the time when all was completed. Siddharta set out for Srinar. He had a plan for the best way to organise the new places. And this plan gave him pleasure.

On the appointed day, Siddharta arrived in Srinar with a number of elephants. All admired the animals, which were a familiar sight to them, but which they had never seen before in such numbers.

At Anaga's request the convent, from which so many women were now setting out to take up their work in the service of the Eternal One, was to be blessed first.

Siddharta had not believed that so many women were gathered together here. Therefore it was certainly high time for them to spread into the other convents.

"Does nothing strike you about these women?" he asked the principal of the monastery, with whom he was strolling round the buildings.

"I cannot say, Master; I am used to them. But I think they are happier than other women. They are all beautiful," he added. "I wonder if Anaga deliberately selects particularly beautiful women?"

124

"I do not think so," said Siddharta, smiling. "The women of our people are beautiful. If they look otherwise, then we are to blame, we who have held them in such low esteem and oppressed them for so long. But these Sisters are free from all ties. Their souls can unfold. That permeates their bodies and makes them beautiful."

The Festival, which was held on the great assembly square, was a wonderful event. Siddharta blessed the women, and promised them strength from above, so long as they stood pure in the service of the Eternal One.

Afterwards he visited the newly-built school, with some of the women and Brothers. Cheerful voices greeted him. At Anaga's invitation, a throng of small children had arrived.

They marvelled at the people, they were delighted with the things the school Sisters had given them to play with. They were pathetic figures, these first children of the Sisters' schools, emaciated, and bearing marks of gross neglect, even maltreatment. But that would improve.

On the following day it became apparent why the many elephants had come with Siddharta's retinue. They were to make the arduous journey easier for the women.

The Master decreed that all the women were to go with him to Utakamand. There he would leave behind those allocated to that school and the convent; but he would move on with the others from convent to convent, until finally there remained only those who, besides Anaga, would be allowed to live on the Mountain of the Eternal One.

But things did not go so smoothly as Siddharta had imagined. Most of the women were afraid of the great animals, and only by dint of severity could they be induced to settle into the comfortable seats. Once there, they simply collapsed.

Anaga, who had quickly overcome her initial fear, comforted the women, and assured Siddharta that their anxiety would soon subside.

Nevertheless it was several days before the women travellers would take their seats in the morning without continual persuasion. They looked forward to Utakamand, because they would be able to rest there for a few days, and they envied the companions who could remain there.

Siddharta too was happy to see the beloved school again. He rejoiced over his son Rahula, who had only good news for him. The school and monastery were thriving. They welcomed the arrival of the Sisters; for all had become conscious of the women's need, as they looked more deeply into human life.

"Are you happy in your office, my son?" asked his father, whose eyes rested with pleasure on the slender, muscular frame.

"I am blissfully happy; I could not imagine any work more beautiful. I feel sorry for Suddhodana, who has to trouble himself about people of all kinds of faiths. Look how splendidly everything here is developing, because we are of one mind, and feel ourselves to be servants of *one* Lord."

"I believe Suddhodana would not care to change places with you. He is the born ruler. His whole nature is different from yours. Outwardly he resembles your mother in every detail; inwardly he has the nature of my father, after whom he was named."

"And Siddharta, the little one? Does he resemble you because he bears your name?" asked Rahula, smiling.

"Outwardly and inwardly, so far as it can be said of such a small child," confirmed Siddharta.

But Rahula was thoughtful.

"He can no longer be so small, Father. Think how many years have passed since you saw him. He must be about ten years old."

"Time always seems to me much shorter," the father confessed. "Every day is so full that we have no time to count. Is it really so long since the little boy played with snakes and monkeys?"

"Just think how much has happened since then!" his son reminded him. "Many convents and schools have been built. That has taken time!"

Only reluctantly did Siddharta tear himself away from this so dearly loved plot of earth, and from those whom he was leaving behind. Then he moved on from convent to convent, seeing that all things were in order, and appointing the women to their work.

They rode past Srinar. The delicate women had been too long already on the road. Siddharta had not rightly considered this, but he saw it now. When the realisation came to him, he discussed it with Anaga during their next halt.

126

"Why did you not call my attention to this mistake, Anaga?" he asked reproachfully.

She looked up at him kindly.

"It does not matter if we are tired, Master. We have had much joy in return, we have seen beautiful things, and above all we have learned much. Also, I am now able to have a clear picture of the leaders at work everywhere. That is surely necessary."

"Do not make excuses for me," protested the Master. "I did not think of all these benefits, but have taken you with me as if you were goods to be delivered along the way. I perceive again and again that I am not used to associating with women."

AND NOW they arrived in Indraprastha. Anaga's heart beat violently. She was to behold the Mountain of the Eternal One, she was to be permitted to tread upon it! On the last morning before their arrival, she asked of Siddharta to be allowed to make her way on foot with her three women.

So it came about that Siddharta and his retinue were jubilantly received up above without the women as witnesses of the welcome.

The men felt it a relief. The Master was again fully in demand at once, so that he forgot about the women.

But the women ascended the Mountain slowly, silently, step by step. Holy thoughts filled them, worship vibrated in them. Now at a turning of the road they could suddenly see the white buildings.

Anaga felt giddy. How glorious it was! She let her companions walk on, and sat down by the roadside. None of them noticed the great snake slipping sideways into the bushes.

Anaga became deeply absorbed within herself. She wanted to listen to the voices that would speak to her from above, as they often did. Nor did she wait in vain now. The luminous sublime figure seemed to descend from out of the blue firmament, and stood in loveliness before her.

"You are now entering on your real service, Anaga," said the light-being graciously. "Hitherto you were being prepared; now your great sacred task begins. You are to become the guide and helper of all womanhood among your people. Through you, through your example, but also through your

127

strictness and education, they shall awaken, they shall abandon their flower-like existence and learn to live. No longer must you care only for those in need, for those who are troubled, oppressed, sick and dying. You must leave that to your helpers. You are to seek out those who are spiritually asleep.

"Great strength will be given to you. Light helpers will show you the way to the sleeping souls of your sisters. Awaken them. Show them what it means to be a true woman. Will you do that, with your eyes raised to the Eternal One as His handmaiden?"

And from its innermost depth Anaga's soul replied, simply but fervently: "Yes, I will."

"Then be thou blessed!"

The figure disappeared. For a long time Anaga continued in prayer, then she stepped out briskly towards her destination. And by her side walked a luminous helper. Was it a female one?

The three approaching women had been sighted from above. Siddharta was told, and now it occurred to him again that he had intended to await Anaga at the convent. He hastened there, and was in time to meet the three women arriving ahead of her. They were gazing towards Anaga, who was looking about her as though transfigured.

"Anaga grows ever lighter," said one of the women.

"Do you know the reason why?" asked Siddharta. The women looked at one another, then one of them replied:

"Because her soul is blossoming."

Now BEGAN a time rich in activity for the Helping Sisters. Sariputta was able to direct them to quite a number of huts where their help was welcome. They were received warmly everywhere. They had not expected the beginning to be so easy.

"That is because we are dwelling on the Mountain of the Eternal One," explained Sisana, the youngest of the four. "The people are grateful for everything that comes to them from there."

But the Yellow Brothers perceived it in a different way. Filled with astonishment, they saw what the delicate women accomplished in willing devotion. With a perseverance which none of the men would have brought to it, they undertook when necessary the hardest work, always with a cheerful mien, always untiring.

"Master," said Amuruddba one day, "it is a blessing for us too that you have called the Sisters to the Mountain. The Brothers work much more willingly in the gardens and stables, now that they observe the women at work. And the men in the valley listen to us far more readily, since the helpfulness of the women has paved a way for us into their houses and to their hearts."

But Anaga, mindful of her task, kept away from all such work. To begin with she had to look after the school, but soon one of her assistants proved sufficiently competent for Anaga to be able to entrust the children to her. With the help of a young widow who lived nearby, and whose soul belonged to the Eternal One, this helper kept the little group in splendid order.

Now Anaga was free for her specific task. How was she to set about it? However much she prayed and asked for direction, she heard nothing. She was probably meant to find the way by herself.

If only one of the Brothers would show her one such sleeping female soul! But she hesitated to ask, because she cherished the tidings which she had received as something sacred.

One day as she went down into the valley, she took a path that led between flowering gardens. Magnificent flowers covered two trees in one of these gardens. Involuntarily Anaga checked her steps. All flowers had an irresistible attraction for her.

Then she saw a young woman lying under one of the trees on a couch made of fine, soft rugs. A veil was laid over the whole figure, probably to keep the insects away, because the rays of the sun were caught in the foliage of the trees.

The woman lay motionless. Was she asleep? As this question arose in Anaga, she knew immediately:

"This is one of the sleeping souls. You must go to her."

She entered the garden quietly, she who was so shy that in the past she had fled from people. She softly approached the couch. The woman was not asleep. She was staring up into the sky with open eyes, but now she turned towards the intruding stranger.

"What do you want here?" she asked in a drawling tone, from which it was impossible to tell whether the question was prompted by indignation or surprise.

"Pardon me, friend," replied Anaga gently, "I have never before seen such beautiful flowers. May I look at them closely?"

Vouchsafing no reply, the woman turned away from the stranger. There was so much contempt in the gesture that another woman would surely have been discouraged. But Anaga only exclaimed in an undertone:

"You poor soul!"

What had the stranger said? What made her exclaim this? Was not Vasissa the wealthiest woman in the whole district? And what Anaga's kindness had been unable to accomplish, her exclamation did. The woman half raised herself from her couch, glared at the stranger and asked furiously:

"How dare you call me poor? Do you not see that I am surrounded by wealth?"

"Are you not poor?" replied Anaga with a winning smile, "if you answer a friendly request with unspoken contempt? Are you not poor when you can lie here under the most glorious flowers without noticing them? You must be poor, if you stretch your limbs lazily instead of bestirring them in joyous activity. Your heart must be empty, that is why I pity you."

Vasissa had listened with increasing astonishment. No one had ever spoken to her in this way.

"Did you come into my garden to tell me this?" she asked scornfully.

"I believe I did. I came into the garden to look at the flowers. But what I am looking for is sleeping souls; indeed that is why I was led here."

"What is a sleeping soul? Who led you to me?"

"That calls for a full reply. May I sit down with you?"

Without waiting for an answer, Anaga sat down on a moss-covered stone, fixed her wonderful blue eyes on the woman, and said:

"You want to know what a sleeping soul is? Think of a sleeping person. He continues to breathe, because his body does it for him. But he knows nothing of himself. He is alive, but he gains nothing from this life. Do you understand what I mean?"

Anaga had only intended to make a comparison with the soul, but there was no need. The words burst out of the woman irresistibly, breaking down all barriers:

"Don't talk of people who are asleep! What else is our whole life but an everlasting sleep! Do we women do anything other than eat, drink, sleep and breathe? And why do we do so? Because we have to live! It would be a thousand times better if we had never been born. It would be a thousand times better if we were allowed to die! To die, to dissolve into Nirvana. To be one with the great nothingness that weaves above us."

The woman had spoken ever more passionately, her voice finally choked by tears. Anaga had risen, she went to the weeping woman and gently placed her hand on her brow.

"I have been led to you at the right moment, sister," she said, and infinite compassion vibrated in her words. "You see, you do know what a sleeping soul is. Let yourself awaken, sister-soul. Let me show you that life is a gift from the gods, a gift from the Eternal One. We have only to learn to use it."

Anaga went on speaking to Vasissa, whose tears dried up. She remained with her for a long time, until servants appeared in the distance. Then Anaga took her leave, promising to return on the morrow.

As she walked towards the garden the next morning, she saw the woman standing expectantly by the road. Together they strolled through the splendour of the blossoming trees and flowers.

Anaga was able to prove to the poor rich woman that she could derive untold joys from this unused wealth. Together they filled a basket with flowers, and Anaga persuaded Vasissa to go with her to the school, to visit some women who would surely be made happy by a single flower.

Vasissa's soul had been very near to awakening. It only required loving firmness on Anaga's part to bring it to life. Once awakened, it unfolded swiftly and to unexpected beauty. She became closely attached to Anaga, to whom she gave constant support in the way of gifts for the poor, the sick and the feeble.

Seeing the rich woman so often in the company of the Yellow Sister caused a sensation in the neighbourhood. Soon first one, then another of the idle women came out of curiosity to ask Vasissa for the reason. Most of them did not understand it. Others were deeply moved, and tried to make their visits coincide with those of Anaga. They listened when the Sister spoke of the Lord of all the Worlds. They enquired further, and it was not long before they too began to awaken.

And Anaga saw what a wonderful task had been assigned to her. She was grateful for it. Her own soul blossomed to ever greater wealth and beauty. Each time she gave, she herself received without knowing it.

But Siddharta looked at her in astonishment every time he met her. Just what was it that so inspired the fragile Sister? She hardly seemed to walk any longer, she almost floated as she moved.

When she went to people, streams of peace seemed to flow over to the others. Even the Brothers often sought her out in order to have differences of opinion settled by her.

Gradually the convent received new residents, who were immediately given work.

During this time Siddharta was able to devote himself more to his writing again. It gave him pleasure to collect and round off his thoughts as he wrote. Many a thing that he had said in the past now seemed to him no longer appropriate in its previous form.

In particular, the idea of the forgiveness of sins occupied him greatly. With the best of intentions, he had not been prepared to admit that sins could be forgiven. Could he maintain that? Were not the people now more mature than they had been years ago? Could he not now expect them to hear the truth?

He decided to discuss it with Rahula. His son had such a calm, clear judgment, such a modest and yet direct way of expressing it. He would learn best from him what was the right thing.

He had sent a message to his son to come and give an account of Utakamand. For it was already more than two years since he was last there. How time flew!

And while his thoughts often wandered to his elder son, those of the younger travelled to him, even taking on tangible form.

ONE DAY a youth stepped across the threshold of his room, looked at him with bright eyes and said:

132

"Do you know me?"

Siddharta knew at a glance who stood before him.

He saw his own image, as though he were looking into a rejuvenating mirror.

"Siddharta," he cried.

The youth was delighted that he had managed to surprise him. He had crept up the Mountain as stealthily as possible, leaving his companions behind at its foot. He had then begged the servants not to announce him. There was no need to tell anyone who he was. His name was written on his face.

"Grandfather, I come to learn from you! I am now twelve years old. Father and I think I cannot do better than enter your school."

"I am happy with your decision, Siddharta," the Master assured him. "Did your mother let you go willingly?"

"Mother?" laughed the youth. "I have outgrown Mother. Besides, she has enough little ones to spoil. After me comes a little Rahula, who is almost eight years old. Then follows a little Suddhodana, after him a little Arusa, who is named after Mother's father. Finally last year came a little Maya.

"You see, Grandfather, Mother does not really need me. It was with difficulty that Father let me go," said Siddharta seriously, "but he knows that it will only be for a few years, and that only with you can I learn what I need for our people."

When the lad, who was the image of Siddharta, was brought to the school, he was joyfully received; however, the teacher pointed out that it would be advisable to call him by another name.

"Call him Gautama," said Siddharta. "He has a right to that name, because it belongs to our race. Besides, I myself was called by it throughout my time at school."

All were in agreement, and Gautama joined the others, who were much older than he, as a pupil. However, his intuition was so pure and light that he grasped things better than all the rest.

Best of all he loved to sit with Siddharta and question him about everything that passed through his mind.

A few months went by in this way, and then Rahula appeared. The disciples burst into loud shouts when they saw the three together. Rahula and

Gautama both resembled Siddharta so closely that it was like seeing the Master simultaneously at three different periods in his life, as a youth, as a mature man, and in old age.

It could not be denied that the Master had aged. How old would he be? He himself did not know. They calculated that he was certainly close on seventy. Nevertheless he still showed himself to be one of the most active. His spirit was undimmed, his eyes shone youthfully.

At the first opportunity, Siddharta put to his son the question that occupied him so powerfully. He had first to explain to him what had earlier given rise to the wrong statement. Rahula shook his head.

"I do not believe that it was necessary to tell the people something that you yourself did not think right. In any case, Father, I consider it unworthy of you to uphold it even now."

Suddenly the voice of the youngest, who they had thought was in the garden, rang out:

"I quite understand why Grandfather spoke in that way. Just think, Rahula, my father, what people were like before they knew of the Eternal One. If Grandfather had told them that God, the Lord of the Worlds, forgives sins, their minds would have been completely at ease. You are in Utakamand, where all the people believe in the Eternal One. In Kapilavastu you too would think differently. Our people, who are able to work so hard if it is necessary, do not like to make spiritual efforts. They would rather go to soothsayers or magicians."

"What are you saying, Gautama?" asked Rahula, horrified. "What kind of people are those of whom you speak?"

"They are bad people, who spread darkness around them. They capture the souls of men by saying that they are able to appease and pacify the gods. They dance, and chant all kinds of absurd incantations, for which they take money, and the people do not realise that they are being deceived. For it is so much more convenient to get rid of sins in that way than through personal effort, through self-conquest or through penance. Father says that our people are afflicted by this, that large sections of them never really come awake. Many even fall asleep again after they have been aroused."

"Just listen to the lad," Rahula tried to joke, so that Gautama should not see how proud of him his two relatives were. "He talks like a grown-up!"

Gautama did not know whether to take offence, or to pretend not to have heard the banter. He decided on the latter; for now that he had begun to speak, there were still many things that weighed heavily on him.

"That is also why I wish, when I am older, to leave the government to our Rahula, and live like you two, solely for others. I want to serve, not to rule."

The two looked at each other. How all was repeated in these three, feature by feature! In them all, the glowing love for the people, which expressed itself in the wish not to rule but to serve.

"You little Gautama, would you not like to go with me to Utakamand, where your grandfather was so happy?" asked Rahula, who would have loved to mould this wonderfully open soul.

But Gautama declined.

"Perhaps I shall be allowed to go with Grandfather when he visits you, that will be soon enough for me. I cannot miss a day on which I may learn from him."

Then they spoke of Anaga. Rahula asked about the Sisters' work and the progress of the convent. Siddharta could give him information about everything; only that which was done by Anaga, who indeed worked tirelessly, baffled him.

"You don't know that, Grandfather?" asked Gautama in surprise. "She awakens sleeping souls. The other day I heard a woman called Vasissa say to another: 'Anaga snatches the women out of a meaningless day-to-day existence, so that they unfold all the more richly.' That is her work."

"I should indeed like to speak with her," requested Rahula.

Siddharta was glad to allow it, provided it was agreeable to Anaga.

Rahula went to look for her in the convent, but did not find her at home. On the following day Siddharta was asked to go to her. He thought Anaga had misunderstood the message left by Rahula, and believed that the Master had asked for her.

For a moment he was uncertain whether to act on the request or to send Rahula, then Gautama put an end to all doubts:

"Let the three Gautamas go together; that will please her!"

Siddharta assented, and the three walked the short distance downhill to the convent.

135

There they found hushed but intense agitation.

"Master, our Mother is about to leave us!" cried some of the Sisters, who were standing before the house weeping.

Siddharta was profoundly shocked. Surely that could not be! Anaga was still so young, and so needed here. In her quiet, unassuming way she had become the centre for all the convents, the principal of all the schools. Whatever she took in hand prospered. And now was she to leave them?

"Where is she?" asked Siddharta.

He was taken to an airy apartment where Anaga was resting. She paid no heed to the other two who had entered behind the Master. She looked only at Siddharta. A happy smile flitted over her pale face, which had become unspeakably small.

"Master, I thank you for coming. I have to bid you farewell. I have been called by luminous messengers from the Eternal One. I am to be allowed to ascend and continue to serve Him above. I no longer have sufficient strength for this earth. I have trained Patna, so that she can take my place down here. She will be able to do so; for her volition is pure, her strength still unspent."

Anaga fell silent. Siddharta tried to speak, but she prevented him.

"I have much to say to you, Master: You have allowed me to work, and let me have my own way, and I thank you for it. You have never called me to account for what I was doing. You knew that my work was assigned to me by luminous messengers of the Eternal One. To awaken sleeping souls was my true calling. Now Vasissa will do that in my stead. She will fill my place completely, for she is aglow with love for her sister-souls. I thank you, Master, for all that you have given to me, to us and to our people."

Anaga's eyes opened wide, she raised herself slightly, and although her eyes rested on those around her, she appeared to be gazing far beyond them.

"Hear what the messenger of the Eternal One says:

"Siddharta, you man of pure volition, of stout heart and high recognition, take care that you serve the Eternal One more than your people.

"Rahula, you who are greater than Siddharta, see to it that the inner fire does not consume you before your time. You are called to do great things; but do not burn your candle at both ends, or it will be extinguished before you have completed your task.

136

"Gautama, you who are to become the greatest, remain pure, remain humble and chaste, and the Eternal One will call you to be His servant in Eternity."

Gentle sounds filled the room. Deeply moved, the three listened; it seemed as though they saw light figures taking their place around Anaga. Suddenly she began to speak again, but her words were no longer addressed to men:

"O Light-Being, to Whom my life belongs, let me continue to serve Thee wherever it may be!"

Siddharta was blessed to see the luminous figure that bent over Anaga, and bore her soul aloft.

When the radiance and the sounds had passed away, Anaga's lifeless form lay on the couch, the countenance transfigured by supernal bliss.

GREAT SORROW prevailed on the Mountain of the Eternal One, because the beloved Sister had gone from them. Everyone had felt close to her, although outwardly she had held equally aloof from all.

Vasissa and Patna bewailed that they would not be able to take the place of her who was gone. With the best will in the world, they lacked the strength that had filled Anaga.

When Rahula heard this, he asked his father to allow him to speak to them. He felt that Siddharta took the same view as the lamenting women: no one could replace Anaga. Had *he* addressed the two, his words would have lacked any conviction.

Rahula, on the other hand, thought differently. He had revered Anaga and admired her working, but he had not been part of the community which had always surrounded her. Thus he had retained a clearer view.

He knew that if a person was called to fill some post or other in the service of the Eternal One, it was entirely his own fault if he did not receive all the strength he needed for it.

Instead of complaining, the two women should quite simply open themselves and look upwards in supplication. The help would not fail to come. He told them so, forcefully and plainly.

His words made a deep impression on Vasissa. She rose and thanked him:

"You have helped me greatly, Rahula. I shall pray for help every day, and then do all that lies in my power. I am not to be compared with Anaga, nor shall I brood over whether she could do some things better."

"That is right, Vasissa," commended Rahula warmly. "The Eternal One demands no more than that each should give of his best. Whatever then is still lacking, He will add."

But Patna was not to be satisfied.

Rahula allowed her to go on complaining until her stock of words and ideas was exhausted. When he then remained silent she looked at him expectantly. He who had found such encouraging words for Vasissa must surely acknowledge the modesty with which she had voluntarily held back.

But to him, who lived wholly in others and in doing so completely forgot himself, to him it was given as to hardly any other to see through the souls of men. He also saw this pretended modesty as it really was.

In answer to her enquiring gaze he began to speak:

"You are right, Patna, to doubt that you could fill Anaga's place adequately. It calls for much more than you are capable of summoning up."

Hastily she interrupted him:

"Anaga herself called me to her place. I shall do as Vasissa does, then surely things will work out well. Why should not the Eternal One grant me the necessary strength?"

"Because you are lacking in humility," sounded Rahula's grave and stern reply. "Patna, with all your lamenting you only wanted to make me contradict you and praise you.

"You yourself are inwardly convinced that you can do the work just as well as Anaga did, but you have not convinced me of that. I shall ask my father to assign you some other work."

Patna's eyes widened with horror. She had not expected the interview with Rahula to be like this. How unfeeling he was!

But before she had become clear about what she ought to reply he had left the convent, and was walking up the Mountain with calm, sure strides. To see Rahula walking always gave people an impression of inner certainty, which had a calming effect on those around him.

Siddharta was startled when Rahula told him the outcome of his interview.

"Were you not too harsh with Patna, my son? Women have these small weaknesses, which must be taken into account."

"I think, Father, that if women serve the Eternal One they must conquer their weaknesses, just as we do ours. But what you call a small weakness in this case seems to me like the inner rottenness of an outwardly beautiful fruit. And such fruit must be removed before it infects others. Will you let me take Patna away with me, so that she may really learn to serve in the convent at Utakamand?"

Siddharta was not to be so quickly convinced, and Rahula would probably have had to go on speaking for a long time, if at that moment Patna had not suddenly entered the apartment unannounced.

How the woman had changed in a short time! Her features had coarsened, there were ugly lines round her mouth, which was pouting sulkily.

"What do you want up here, Patna?" Siddharta asked with kind reproach.

"I am well aware that it is unusual for me to enter the men's houses, although we women are certainly no less than they in the eyes of the Eternal One," said Patna in a defiant tone, "but I had to come! I thought that this one," and she pointed to Rahula, who had left his seat as she entered the room, and gone over to the window, "would seek to prejudice you against me.

"I was exaggerating when I so belittled myself in his eyes. I hoped for comfort from him. When it was not forthcoming, I allowed myself to be carried away. Therefore if my words did not please him it is his own fault. Rest assured, Master, that I am capable of taking Anaga's place, and guiding all the convents in the country with a sure hand."

Even more than those of his son, Patna's words proved how right Rahula was. This woman would be damaging to the whole cause. And a voice within him whispered another name to Siddharta. Now he knew what he had to do.

"It does not lie in your hands or in mine, Patna," he said firmly, "to appoint the successor to Anaga. That is for the Eternal One Himself to decide. I have just now received word that Sisana has been chosen for the task. So this question is settled, and harmony can once more dwell among us."

Patna turned as white as a sheet.

139

"Anaga named me as she lay dying," she said. "Anaga was the principal of the convents, not you, Master. We women are guided by what she said."

"Every word that you speak condemns you, Patna," came the very calm reply. "It grieves me that you should allow yourself to be so carried away. Go to your room, and seek to regain the composure of your soul in prayer."

Sobbing, Patna left the Master's room. She could not even summon up enough self-control to hide her feelings from the others.

But so great was the self-discipline that not one of the men spoke to another about the woman. They had no wish to know what her trouble was. They were not called upon to help her, therefore they did not send out their thoughts in her direction.

In the course of the day, Siddharta summoned the women to the great open square, and told them that henceforth Vasissa would take sole charge of the work on the sleeping souls of the sisters, in which she had already given much help to Anaga. Sisana was appointed successor to Anaga as superintendent of the convents.

Patna was not present at this meeting. But on the days that followed there was no sign of her either, so that the Master had to send for her. His messenger returned unsuccessful. Patna was nowhere to be found.

Thereupon Siddharta went himself in search of her. But his enquiries in the convent were fruitless, until at last Vasissa came up from the valley, where she had been working for some days.

She told him that she had met Patna down below, wearing the clothes that she had worn in the past. Patna told her that she had to journey far across the land in the service of the Eternal One, to win souls. That was the last that was heard of her.

AFTER RAHULA had gone home, Siddharta once more became absorbed in his records. But in addition he reflected unceasingly on the last words of Anaga. What had she meant by her warning? Surely in serving his people he was at the same time serving the Eternal One? How could he possibly forget the Lord of the Worlds in doing so?

140

The warning, however, had come not from Anaga's soul, but from above. He must heed it. Indeed he wished to do so, but he did not understand it.

Nor did he understand the meaning of the words addressed to Rahula. How could he use up his strength prematurely? He well understood the metaphor of the light burning at both ends. But was Rahula such a light? Probably both warnings were meant for possible events to come, and did not yet apply. With that he finally reassured himself.

Gautama too pondered over Anaga's last words. He had scarcely heard those that concerned himself; he was too preoccupied with the other two warnings.

Could it be that Rahula was greater than Siddharta, whom they called the Master? In what then did the greatness consist? The young Gautama thought and pondered, compared the two men who were an example to him, and did not find the solution.

One day, as he was strolling through the garden deep in thought, his eyes fell on a tall cedar growing towards heaven. It was rare in this region, and therefore had been allowed to grow free; nothing was planted around it.

Far and wide it extended its branches, which gave out a delicate, aromatic scent in the sunlight. Gautama had often seen the cedar as he walked by; today he paid attention to it.

He had to think: Rahula is like a cedar! He strives unswervingly upwards, nothing can divert him. And as the cedar provides shade and scent for others, so he thinks of others and lives his life only for service. Then the youth suddenly knew why Rahula was greater than Siddharta. And he also understood the significance of his consuming his flame too rapidly.

Once Gautama had placed the wick in an oil-bowl in such a way that both ends stood out, while the middle part fed the ends. Then he lit both ends and enjoyed the flames, until suddenly everything went out in an incredibly short time.

Rahula worked beyond his strength. Wherever there was physical work to be done and not enough help available, Rahula would tackle it. Gautama had noticed this himself.

And his companions had told him how Rahula concerned himself untiringly with those under him, teaching, comforting, inspiring and admonishing them. And he even wrote during the night. No wonder, thought Gautama, that the Eternal One Himself had sent a warning.

Siddharta was different. He did not devote himself wholly to one task, but while he was doing it was already thinking of new ones. Yet he could at times spend a whole day lying under a tree, musing. Gautama could not imagine Rahula doing that.

Still he thought it right that the Master should spare himself, for he was old. It would be sad if he were to pass away like Anaga, and that there should be dissension over his succession. It was to be hoped that Rahula would succeed him. At present Ananda often represented Siddharta when he was absent, or wanted to rest. But Ananda was neither so wise nor so refined as the other two.

While he was thinking thus, one of his little friends stood before him.

"Come with me, Gautama," he beckoned him.

The youth followed immediately. The little beings frequently drew his attention to something beautiful or unusual.

Now the elemental being led him into the forest. Making their way through undergrowth of all kinds, they came to a sunny, solitary spot. There lay one of the great guardian snakes, looking about it with lifeless eyes.

"Are you about to leave the earth, beautiful one?" asked Gautama, crouching beside it.

He understood that it wished to see him once more, as he had always had a kind word for it. Gently he stroked its beautifully-marked back, but the snake wanted something more. Gautama understood the name "Sariputta".

"What is the matter with Sariputta?" he asked affectionately. "Shall I call him? No? What is it that you wish then?"

The little being intervened:

"It would like to ask you to take care of Sariputta; he will be very lonely. This is the last of the three snakes. They visited the old man every day. That was his secret joy. Sariputta is very old. Be good to him."

Gautama promised to do so. He was touched that an animal had such great fidelity that it would not leave the earth without providing for the human being. He spoke softly to the snake, and thanked it for all the faithful service that it and its sisters had given to the Mountain.

"We shall miss you all," he assured it.

The snake crawled painfully into the undergrowth. Gautama begged it to stay, but it no longer heeded his words. However, the little friend said:

"Let it be. Are you not aware that no animal wants to die with a human being looking on? If you men knew that, you would not torment dying animals that you love with your solicitude. They pull themselves together and prolong their expired life-span, just to be able to die alone."

Pensive, Gautama returned to the school. How much he had learned. He went to see Siddharta, and told him of the death of the last snake.

"We shall have to get another guard," he said.

"The snakes came unbidden," replied Siddharta. "Perhaps some other creature will appear."

After that Gautama arranged it so that he had to meet the old Yogi as he was walking in the sunshine. He addressed him with diffidence. The almost withered old man seemed to him very venerable. He gave him greetings from the snake, and was afraid that Sariputta would be sad. But the aged man said almost cheerfully:

"I am very relieved that it has been allowed to go before me. Who else would have cared for it?"

And Gautama was amazed at the closeness of the connection between man and animal; each had been concerned about the other.

But Sariputta began to speak of the great task that lay before Gautama.

"You will have to guide and lead our whole great people, Gautama. This I know. See that you learn to understand them. Do not stay here all the time. Go out to the other regions.

"Believe me! I have travelled with my snakes from the lofty mountains right to the blue ocean, from the cool to the scorching regions. Everywhere the people are different, according to descent, physical body, customs and inner quality. No two principalities are alike. And our country comprises many of them. Learn to know them, for otherwise you cannot rule them."

"But I do not wish to be a ruler, I want to serve, Sariputta," said Gautama decidedly. His eyes shone.

"Whom would you serve, son of a Prince?" asked Sariputta in return. "Do you know what it means to serve?"

"To serve means to devote oneself whole-heartedly to the task which has been recognised as one's own."

"And whom do you wish to serve thus?"

Sariputta asked the question urgently. Without thinking, Gautama answered:

"I wish to serve the Eternal One!"

"Not your people?" Long-drawn-out and painfully came the words from Sariputta's lips. He looked at the youth imploringly.

"Of course I want to serve my people, that is to say I want to serve the Eternal One in my people. That is probably the right way to express it," replied Gautama.

He did not understand the old man's sorrow. But the latter began to speak, slowly and deliberately at first, in the manner of very old people, then ever faster and more unrestrainedly:

"Gautama, hear me. Our people must be closer to our hearts than all else on earth. The Eternal One has countless servants down here and up there in the beyond. You know that as well as I do. You can even see them. Do you not think that he has enough? But our people will have only you to help them.

"Gautama, scion of the Tshakyas, do not throw away your princely heritage. If the Eternal One had wished to make you a servant, He could have let you enter your body in a hut.

"Gautama, I see the time coming, it is not far off, when our people will stray on to wrong paths. What the Master has brought them they will mingle with other teachings. The precious wisdom will be lost in sophistries and false thinking. I see a time, perhaps far off, perhaps near – for the Light there is no long and no short time – when our whole people will have to be subject to foreign rulers. We shall be pariahs, all, all of us!

"Gautama, darling of the gods, only you can prevent it. Devote yourself to your people with your whole soul. Grasp the sceptre of your realm with a firm hand! There are adherents of Siddharta in all principalities. Gather them, take possession of the realms through them, unite with their rulers or resist them. It does not matter how you do it, so long as you forge a strong whole out of the many individual parts. Then for a long time to come the people will be strong enough to resist foreign invaders. Then they will blossom, to the joy of men and of the Eternal One.

144

"Gautama, consider: What I reveal to you here is worthy of one blessed by the Eternal One, as you are! You will be greater than Siddharta. The people will love you, the people whom you have saved from misery and bondage!"

Breathing heavily, Sariputta had to stop, but his eyes, those piercing, sharp eyes, still begged and implored.

Gautama stood before him, looking at him kindly. But his eyes were as though turned inwards; for his whole thinking was an ardent prayer:

"Eternal One, let me know whether this is a temptation, or Thy Call to me!"

"Neither the one nor the other, Gautama," sounded within him. "You had to hear this, so that you could choose your way from a free decision. The Eternal One will have no servants under compulsion."

And again the soul of the youth rose up in prayer:

"I wish to be Thy servant, O Lord of all the Worlds! Wherever Thou dost place me I will work. But I wish to be a servant, not a ruler!"

After this, great peace entered Gautama's soul, and he turned lovingly to the old yogi, in whose words he now recognised and honoured the great, selfless love for his people.

"Sariputta, I promise you that as servant of the Lord of all the Worlds I shall never forget my people. Whether He makes of me a ruler, a sage or a helper, I will embrace my people in love."

"Then let Siddharta be called, for I would fain take my leave of him," whispered Sariputta.

It was not long before the Master came, deeply moved that his first "master" was about to go from him.

"Let me depart freely, Siddharta," the old man begged feebly. "I can no longer be of use to my people. But I know that one will come after me who will help them."

Whether the yogi had meant Gautama, whether he saw another, no one dared to decide.

Sariputta's eyes closed to this world, but his other eyes opened. Wonderful pictures must be passing before them, for the old, hitherto so weary voice rang out jubilantly.

"I see my people in affliction and misery. Strangers enslave it, strangers

145

enjoy the beautiful things which our glorious country produces. But I see One coming Who is strong and mighty, just and gracious; He will set the people free! He will teach them to walk on the right path, He will awaken the sleeping souls.

"Lord, Thou Eternal One, I beseech Thee: Grant that when the Ruler comes I may live again among my people, to prepare them for His Rule! O Eternal One, my whole life has belonged to my people. Let it be so again!"

Deeply moved, the two visitors looked at the old man, whose features seemed almost transfigured. Once more he began to speak, this time more quietly:

"O Eternal One, I thank Thee that Thou wilt hear my prayer! Yes, I will renounce for the sake of my people. I will wait somewhere in the beyond until the time comes when I may return to the earth to lead my people to the Ruler. I thank Thee!"

His body stiffened. Siddharta placed his hand on the faithful heart; it had stopped beating.

"Sariputta, in the love for our people we were one. May the Eternal One grant that I be permitted to help you at the time when you prepare our people for the Ruler!"

After a silent prayer, the two went to tell the Brothers of Sariputta's departure.

SARIPUTTA, like Anaga before him, had been laid to rest in the way that was usual on the other side of the Himalayas.

Hitherto it had been the practice here to burn the lifeless bodies of nobly born men on pyres. The higher the rank of the dead man, the finer the wood used.

If he had died childless, or if the sons were already grown men and no longer needed the mother, the widow allowed herself to be burned with him, so that her soul would pass over into the beyond with that of her husband.

All other corpses were wrapped in cloths and carried out into the forest, where the animals would dispose of them. Because, according to the belief

146

of the Brahmans, the soul had already set out on its journey, what happened to the body was of no consequence.

Since the people as a whole believed in the Eternal One, Siddharta had put an end to this horrible practice. But he had only fought against the burning of widows, and the depositing of mortal remains in the forests, without yet offering anything better.

He had left it to the people to decide whether they wanted to burn the dead bodies. This had been done in most cases, but some carried their dead to the sacred Ganges.

Then one day Rahula had told him about the form of burial that was customary in the monasteries of Tibet. That made a deep impression on Siddharta, and he decided to adopt this practice. Thereupon he had both Anaga and Sariputta buried in small caves in the Mountain of the Eternal One.

The caves were walled up, and in front of them were placed tablets with a few words on them. The one before Anaga's tomb read:

"Anaga, our sister in spirit."

Her grave was in such a position that the women could easily walk past it. They always brought flowers with them, which they placed on the tablet or laid on the ground.

When Sariputta's tablet was to be prepared, Siddharta reflected for a long time over the kind of words that would be appropriate. He found none which expressed briefly what he wanted to say.

He had already written down some things, but whenever he was about to give the order to the Brother who was working on the tablet, he destroyed what he had written. So also today.

Then Gautama came to him. Since Sariputta's death the youth had become very serious. Siddharta did not know what might be going on in this soul. As the grandson did not speak about it of his own accord, the grandfather respected his silence.

"Siddharta, have you given instructions yet for the epitaph on Sariputta's tomb?" asked the youth diffidently. The other replied that he had not.

"Then may I ask you to have inscribed: Sariputta, our brother, was with us. He will come again as the Helping Brother of our whole people."

"That is good, Gautama; tell the Brother he is to write these words!"

That was all Siddharta could say. He was deeply moved that the youth had found that which he had been struggling to find for days.

Anaga was right: Gautama was the greatest of them.

Gautama was about to leave to carry out the Master's command, but he turned back once more and said, apparently out of a serious resolution:

"Siddharta, have you time for me to ask you a question afterwards?"

The Master nodded assent. The other went away. It was obvious to Siddharta that he was now about to learn what was stirring in the young man's pure soul. He also noticed that Gautama had suddenly called him Siddharta. He would ask him the reason why.

The youth very soon returned, and sat down on a tiger-skin at Siddharta's feet. Siddharta gazed at his pure features, which though they looked serious showed no trace of excitement. The young face looked calm and composed.

"Siddharta, you know that I am happy to be here...."

The old man's heart contracted; surely the youth was not going to leave him? Something of this must have been reflected in his features.

Gautama laid his hand on that of his grandfather with a gesture of supplication.

"But I must move on," the young voice continued unwaveringly. "I must get to know all the monasteries in the country, and at the same time the people as a whole. Sariputta told me so in his last hour. I did not understand his words immediately, but I knew that they contained a command from the Eternal One.

"Now I have recognised, and Sariputta is helping me. He is still quite near us, but he now understands many things better than before. He sees them differently.

"He has told me that here below he was not able to believe that I could fulfil what the Eternal One expects of me other than as a ruler. Now he knows that I can serve in any outward form. But whatever may become of me, I must help the whole race of the Sons of Indus, not only a part of it. That is also why I must become acquainted with them all.

"Indeed you yourself were led through the whole vast country in your youth. You will understand me."

148

"But you are younger than I was at that time," objected Siddharta, who was pained by the youth's words.

"You were led to it very late, owing to the special nature of your life, Siddharta. I am allowed to have it easier and to learn earlier. You will let me go, won't you? Savi wishes to ride home with his companions tomorrow. Let me ride with them."

"Tomorrow? So soon?" asked Siddharta in dismay.

But then he pulled himself together. It was a sign of old age that he clung to this child. That must not be.

"Go forth and learn, my child," he said tenderly. "I see that it is the Will of the Lord of all the Worlds. If you wish to be His servant He will have you guided and prepared. It is not for us human beings to try to interfere."

Gautama thanked him warmly, and his face, which had been so serious, was transfigured with joy.

The preparations for this ride were so quickly completed that Siddharta was not wrong in assuming that Gautama had made his arrangements long before.

"Would you not like to ride first to Rahula?" Siddharta asked the youth in the evening. "He will welcome you lovingly, and will understand you; he is one of our kind."

"It is for that very reason that I do not wish to go to him yet," said Gautama firmly. "I must become free of all earthly ties, all influences that stem from the same kind. I must no longer know father or mother, so that the Eternal One can mould me to His requirements. I must stand free in His Creation! All His servants, all the powers and forces that issue from Him, may mould me, but never again people who love me."

"Is that why you call me Siddharta?" asked the latter, with growing understanding.

"Yes, that is the reason. It came unsought. I revere you as the Master that you are to me and to all. In this way I can maintain the connection with you which I had to sever with the grandfather."

In the presence of the Brothers, the farewell next morning was heartfelt but very brief. The Brothers were sorry that Gautama wanted to leave. Countless were the good wishes that they called to him, but even more so the prayers for an early return.

149

They all missed the bright presence of the youth. He had not been noisy, seldom had he drawn attention to himself; but streams of joyfulness had passed from him to the others, which for most of them had now dried up.

Others again felt them still flowing, and sensed that Gautama was often still with them in spirit, and that the connection could outlive the separation.

Siddharta also belonged to these. His longing for Gautama's presence had lasted barely a day, then he found abundant compensation in the spiritual flow between them. He recalled the golden threads which Maya's devout prayers had once woven around him. How could he so completely forget that!

These threads too had sought to teach him something. They showed so clearly that prayers are not in vain when they flow from a pure heart. They attach themselves to the other person, strengthen him, bring about a connection. To what end? Is it enough if the connection between the two persons has been made? Siddharta mused further.

No, prayers must rise to the Throne of the Eternal One; only then could they have any effect. Then why the golden threads that stretch from one to the other?

Siddharta was interrupted in his reflections. It was announced that strangers had been sighted. Now that the snakes no longer lay on the roads the people were doubly watchful. As yet nothing evil had ever approached the Mountain of the Eternal One, but Amuruddba was very cautious.

He too had grown old. His passing would one day be a great blow to the Mountain. The Master decided to speak to him soon, so that he would train someone in good time to take his place. Who else was to do all the things which Amuruddba's loyalty had silently and unobtrusively undertaken?

He was about to become absorbed anew in contemplation when shouts rang out, announcing the arrival of the guests. Quick steps approached the room; Prince Suddhodana stepped over the threshold. This was an unexpected joy, and father and son greeted one another affectionately.

When the Prince had quietly seated himself, he asked:

"Where is Siddharta the younger? I have come to discuss important matters with him."

The Master gave a start. Almost hesitatingly he reported that Gautama was no longer with them; there was no holding him back.

"So he is gone?" said the father, and a sunny smile lit up his features. "That is just what I wanted to bring about! I have learned that my eldest son has decided to devote himself wholly to the service of the Eternal One, and to renounce all claim to the principality. So I knew that he must now get to know all our peoples; because one day he is to help the whole people."

"You, and also Gautama, speak of 'our people'. What do you mean by that? I did not want to ask the lad about it; but please explain to me how far you extend this concept."

Suddhodana answered without much reflection.

"I call our people all those who have developed from the Indus-stock, whether they have then become Dravidians, Virudas or Vastus. According to ancient tradition, the Indus is father to them all. They dwell between the Himalayas and the ocean. It is an immeasurably vast land, which is washed round on all sides by turbulent seas. On one side only, the gigantic snow-peaks rear up, like sentinels guarding our frontiers.

"Within these frontiers, mountain-chains and individual mountains divide the land into many small sections, over which we princes rule. That is a good thing. Indeed we are meant to care first of all for our subjects.

"But in addition there must be men who are like you, Father, and as the young Siddharta is to become, who over and above all the small realms regard the great whole as their people, unite them in one faith, and help them to grow strong inwardly and outwardly."

Suddhodana was silent for a moment.

"Father," he then continued lovingly, "I have been thinking about everything for so long that I was almost ready to give up my realm to enter the service of the Eternal One. But little Rahula is still too young. I would have to wait until he is wise enough to govern a realm.

"In the meantime however a luminous messenger came to me. He showed me that I can also serve God if I fulfil my task as a prince rightly. He showed me that I must persuade Siddharta to go on learning; and

151

finally he entrusted me with a task which I am allowed to perform quite specifically in the service of the Eternal One.

"Hence I have left my country for a time, to journey from one principality to the next and speak with their rulers. I am to make them aware of the danger that threatens our people if we do not unite closely. I am to try to conclude a treaty with them all for mutual help in times of danger and need.

"If I succeed in this, Siddharta's path will also be easier."

Siddharta the elder had followed these explanations closely. He sighed a little as he said:

"I perceive that I am growing old by the joy which fills me at the thought that I do not have to deal with either your task or that of Gautama. But I understand that you are both inspired by the thought of uniting all tribes. And now tell me about your dear ones."

The Prince did this so eloquently that Siddharta felt a wish to see them all.

"Perhaps I shall yet return to my old realm once more," he said good-humouredly, "even if only to see my descendants who are growing up in the Palace."

"You should also see the Temple which we have built, Father, I cannot understand how you can be content without one. There is such joyful solemnity when we pray to the Lord of the Worlds in the beautifully-adorned hall."

"What hall can be more beautiful than the one that He Himself had built, my son? When we see the vast expanse of the blue sky above us, when the fragrance of flowers caresses us or the wind sings to our words, we feel that we are standing in the midst of what has been created by the Eternal One. We are linked with His works, we feel at one with His servants, and therefore we have connection also with Him in spite of all our imperfection."

"That is how *you* feel and inwardly sense it, Father," said Suddhodana, not yet convinced. "Believe me, only a very few people will think like you in this matter. And subconsciously they will miss something, if you deny them the Temple of the Eternal One."

Siddharta promised to discuss it with his faithful adherents, but then he thought:

"Even if I decide to build the Temple, Gautama will be the one to carry it out. I pray the Lord of the Worlds to leave me in my office until Gautama is mature enough to receive it from my hands. Of course he is relying on me to call my eldest son; but Rahula is closely linked with Utakamand. Fresh vigour is required for the Mountain of the Eternal One."

After that he related what Anaga had said as she lay dying, and also reported what Sariputta had said, so far as he knew. The yogi had already said most of it before Siddharta joined them.

Later Suddhodana asked whether his father still understood the language of the animals. Siddharta answered that he did, but added at once:

"In this too Gautama surpasses me. It is wonderful how he converses with all created things. He even speaks to flowers and trees."

"Would you not like to test your talent again?" the son asked. "I have brought you a new pair of guardians for the Mountain."

He clapped his hands. Servants who seemed to have been waiting only for this signal entered, and placed two very young lion-cubs at the Master's feet. The little animals nestled trustingly against him. He bent down and stroked them.

"Do you really think, Suddhodana, that we can allow these little creatures to run about freely? What are we going to feed them on as they grow older? We should have to let them kill other animals. And we do not want any bloodshed on the Mountain of the Eternal One."

The Master looked doubtfully at these most delightful but uninvited guests.

"Keep them until I go, Father," the Prince said. "Then we shall know what to do."

The little lions would not leave Siddharta. They went with him everywhere like dogs. If they had to be locked up, to prevent them from following him to the place of worship, they raised a doleful outcry, until the Master reassured them that he would soon return.

They caught mice eagerly, which was thoroughly useful; for the increase of this pest made the absence of the snakes obvious.

Siddharta looked forward with suspense to the monkeys' next visit, but the agile creatures liked the tawny cubs and played with them. It seemed as though the animals also observed the commandment that peace should reign on the Mountain of the Eternal One.

After some weeks Suddhodana continued his journey. He left the lions

153

behind! When Siddharta realised this, his son was already too far away to be able to turn back. Now they simply had to wait and see what would happen next.

In the meantime, the Master enjoyed the affectionate, amusing little animals.

VASISSA and Sisana had entered into the spirit of their work. All the women discharged their various, often not easy, duties so naturally and quietly that they were not noticed at all.

The two seldom went to see the Master. It had to be a very special reason that took them to the Mountain. And so also was it this time. They had a request to make, and as it was close to both their hearts they wished to present it together.

Siddharta listened with delight to what they had to say. Vasissa had been successful in her work of arousing souls. Many women's souls had awakened, and exchanged idle existence for an active life.

Now both found that the work must not be limited to a single principality. Quietly Vasissa had trained women who had come to an understanding out of personal experience. Now it was a question of sending these women all over the country.

"If only you had come earlier," said Siddharta. "Prince Suddhodana could so easily have taken the women with him. I am too old to undertake such long journeys now."

"Forgive us, Master, we were not thinking of it in that way. We do not want the women to be publicly appointed to their office with all due honour. Those Sisters who have not yet awakened would regard them with distrust from the outset. They are to journey quite quietly and inconspicuously through the realms on foot, visit the convents and attach themselves to them. We should be grateful if you would give the women a letter to take to the principals of the convents."

Siddharta understood their motive, but he was alarmed at the extent of self-sacrifice that drove these delicate, pampered women on to the highway.

"You do not realise what that means," he warned them. "The women will

154

have to suffer privations of all kinds during many weeks of travelling. Their feet will swell and pain them. I know from experience; and I was a strong man when I journeyed on dusty highways. If they would at least ride on elephants!"

Vasissa laughed.

"Better go on foot than mount such an animal! The others have told us enough about that. No, Master, the women are willing to undergo any hardships they may encounter, if only they are permitted to serve. It is just because they are grateful to have found the way to the Lord of the Worlds that they wish to lead others to Him. But if they were to arrive riding on elephants it would attract attention."

Siddharta tried once more to make the two women change their mind. So they asked him to come to the convent as soon as possible to ask the chosen Sisters themselves.

The following day he accepted the invitation. He found a group of twenty women of noblest birth. They were still young, and were looking forward to the work. They were of delicate build. But when Siddharta expressed his misgivings, the women laughed:

"We may be delicate, but we have stamina. We can endure more than people think. The Master can let us go with confidence, if he has no other reason to disapprove of our plan."

And it happened as the women had planned: the twenty set out, but not all together. They went in twos and threes, on different roads. But the protection of the Eternal One was with them; for there was not one among them who had undertaken the journey for her own sake.

GOOD TIDINGS came from Gautama, who by now was already far away. His father had found him vigorous and eager to learn, in a monastery beyond the Vindhya Mountains, and marvelled at the change that had taken place in the young man.

"He is no longer a boy, almost no longer a youth either," wrote the Prince. "Out of his eyes, which can radiate such happiness, looks the mature man. We shall experience good things with him."

The messenger who brought this letter supplemented it with verbal infor-

155

mation. The Prince had told Gautama about the lions. The latter was horrified at the thought that because of the Commandment on the Mountain the animals might have to feed for the rest of their lives on things alien to their nature. If the Master was willing, he, the messenger, would take the two animals to Gautama. There were extensive forests near the monastery, where they could hunt.

The suggestion pleased Siddharta. He spoke kindly to the lions, and they willingly allowed themselves to be stowed in baskets and lifted on to the back of the elephant that was to carry them.

The elephant was less docile. The smell of the beasts of prey was offensive to it. It trumpeted so that all the men came rushing to it.

The attendant wanted to beat it, but Siddharta, who had also come, forbade this. He laid his hand gently on the elephant's flank and spoke to it in a low voice. The animal grew calmer, only its trunk still lashed to and fro.

The Master explained that it was the only one that could take the two lions to Gautama. But the animals were quite harmless, quite tame.

He had them taken out of their baskets and handed to him. Then he carried them about in his arms, showing them again and again with kindly words to the elephant, which finally stroked the little creatures with its trunk. Now they could risk putting the lions on the back of the beast of burden.

But to the Hindu Siddharta said:

"You see that love conquers in every case. Of what use would it have been if you had beaten the elephant? You would have lost its confidence and affection for good; because the animal was quite right. It has an innate aversion to beasts of prey, through which it is able to protect itself from them. If you do not overcome this aversion by persuasion, you will never subdue it with the stick."

The Hindu, who loved his elephant, could understand that.

WHEN MONTHS had again passed, Ananda and Maggalana came on a visit. Both had aged visibly, and they declared that they had chosen successors to take charge of the monasteries and schools in their stead. They were no longer sure that they could do everything as the Eternal One demanded.

Times had changed. It was necessary for young people to take over the leadership.

"And what would you like to do?" asked Siddharta, who was well aware that he could no longer expect them to remain in office.

"We thought that we would rest near our Master, and wait until the Eternal One calls us home."

"Then let us build a home, as beautiful as possible, where, with other older people who are yet to come, you can pass the rest of your life," decreed Siddharta.

The idea pleased them, and they besieged the Master with requests to have apartments in this rest-house prepared for himself also.

But he shook his head and declined:

"I cannot lay down my work yet; for Siddharta-Gautama is still too young to be my successor. And it is not the Will of the Eternal One that the administration of the Mountain be taken over temporarily by someone else, who would then have to relinquish it again. But I have enough helpers of whom I can make use, and there will often be times which I may happily spend in your company, my friends."

Maggalana felt the urge to make himself useful in some way still. He offered to write for Siddharta. If the Master would indicate to him what he had in mind to record, then perhaps Maggalana could put it into shape and write it down.

"We can at least try, Maggalana," said Siddharta gladly. "There is many a thing that I would like to say, but whenever I look for words, it has flown."

"Was it then sufficiently mature to be recorded?" asked Maggalana thoughtfully.

Siddharta did not understand him.

"Why not?" he asked lightly, not expecting an answer.

One day as they were working together, Siddharta remembered his thoughts about the golden threads. He told Maggalana about them, and the latter was happy.

"I have always felt, Master," he said with animation, "that thoughts sent forth in prayer seek out those for whose sake they have arisen in us. How wonderful it is that they become golden threads, which take hold of the others and draw them along."

157

"Where do they draw to, Maggalana? Surely only to the one who prays. You see, that is the point beyond which I cannot go, often as I have pondered over it. Surely the main thing is not just for us human beings to be linked with one another!"

"Stop, Master," interrupted Maggalana animatedly. "Your thoughts are on a wrong course. Just consider: where are all our prayers trying to go, if they are really in earnest? They are meant to rise up to the Eternal One, to cast themselves down before the steps of His Throne."

Now it was Siddharta who interrupted the other:

"Yes, I know and believe that, Maggalana. But then, how do the golden threads come to me?"

"When your son Rahula prays for you, his thoughts are occupied with you in love, you are the object of his prayer. Thus his thoughts travel to you like golden threads, and seek to discover if you are in such a state that they can take you with them.

"If you are also praying, or if your soul is filled in some other way with the Eternal One, then Rahula's prayerful thoughts receive strength. United with yours, they rise upwards, and through this their supplication is strengthened. It is really so simple, Master."

"Yes," admitted Siddharta, "it is so simple; a child could understand it, but that is just what I no longer am in my seeking and pondering. It is good that you have come to help me, Maggalana."

But Maggalana went into the garden under the tall, shady trees and mused. Kindly thoughts played around him, and grew into luminous, bright forms, which went forth in search of similar kinds.

And something awoke in Maggalana, which he had not known before. It became ever stronger. He felt the urge to write. He hastened to the room which had been allocated to him for this purpose, and wrote without ceasing. The words poured from him like a gushing spring.

He told the story of a pious maiden who has given her whole heart to the Eternal One, but who then meets a man who wishes to marry her. The maiden's parents give their consent, the maiden herself, Kalisadha, loves the man; but she will not marry him, because he refuses to hear about the Lord of all the Worlds.

He leaves the district in anger. Kalisadha's prayers seek and find him, they woo and beseech. And in his last hour they finally gain dominion over him. They lead him upwards, so that recognition comes to him.

This tale was rendered so simply but expressed in such heartfelt words, adorned with so much beauty, that the souls of the listeners were gripped by it. In the evening Maggalana read out his story in the circle of Siddharta and his faithful followers.

"Where did you get the story from?" Amuruddba wanted to know. "You have expressed it perfectly."

"Where from? I do not know. It came to me as I was sitting in the garden."

"How could it come to you?" laughed Ananda.

"That I do not know either. I suddenly seemed to see Kalisadha, her parents, the man she loved, and all that they did, clearly before me. They also went with me as I entered the house and began to write."

No one else laughed any more. It seemed great to them. It was an art that Maggalana was practising. There were indeed story-tellers in the country, but none had ever written down anything of this kind; the story-tellers had never dealt with such tales. It had always been battles, adventures and gruesome events that they described.

And Maggalana now wrote down his tales every day; they could all hardly wait for him to present them at night.

In this way something completely new had come into their lives. But Siddharta no longer had a scribe to assist him. It was as though everything conspired to prevent his teaching from being recorded.

AGAIN GUESTS came to the Mountain of the Eternal One. A train of stately elephants, led by men on horseback, was sighted. Who could they be? It looked like the cavalcade of a prince.

Siddharta went to meet the new arrivals at the gate of the school. He watched with surprise as a kind of ladder was let down from the saddle of the first great elephant, which the rider descended, slowly and deliberately. He himself had always used the backs of his servants for that.

The person descending was a portly man of medium height, in rich silk attire. Meanwhile the rest of the riders had dismounted from the other animals, and come to the assistance of their lord.

159

The latter now stood before the Master. Siddharta saw an old man with snow-white hair, surrounding a once chubby but now wrinkled face. His figure, too, inclined to corpulence. The eyes had a very special look and expression. Now where had Siddharta seen these eyes before?

He greeted the guest, and asked what he wanted. Without disclosing his name, the latter asked to be allowed to enter the house. He had a very long journey behind him, and would be glad to rest for a while on a soft couch instead of the elephant's back.

Not until the guest and the nobles of his retinue had been accommodated in one of the reception rooms did he begin his account, though still he did not reveal his identity. And his voice too awakened distant, long-forgotten memories in Siddharta, who could not identify them.

So he listened intently, as the guest now narrated:

"Until a few months ago, I had no thought of undertaking this long journey. It was a glorious evening after a particularly hot day. Some of my friends and I were on a sequestered place on the banks of our wide river. We were tired, and did not talk.

"Suddenly the breaking and crackling of branches drew our attention to the approach of some large animal. Some of us seemed to be paralysed, others sprang up. We had no weapons with us. And already it was emerging from the undergrowth – a magnificent Bengal tiger, which was on its way to the watering-place.

"The wind was certainly in our favour, for the animal had not scented us, and was just as surprised as we were. It hesitated a moment; then one of the men made an awkward movement, and the tiger leapt – in my direction. I could not move a limb, and gave myself up for lost. Suddenly a bright voice rang out:

"'Friend, do not touch the man! He did not attack you, he has no weapon. It is not the Will of the Eternal One that His creatures should kill one another out of bloodthirstiness!'

"As if by a miracle, the magnificent animal obeyed. It turned in mid-air, and landed on the ground not far from me.

"Then it raised his head, and like us looked in the direction of the speaker. He was a young man, who now went up to the tiger, praised it, and then invited it to quench its thirst. Nobody would prevent it from doing so.

160

And again the animal obeyed; it drank, and then with great dignity returned to the forest.

"We now had time to look at our rescuer.

"'Siddharta,' the name escaped my lips, and the young man asked, smiling:

"'Do you know me, O King?'

"'So you too are called Siddharta, like him who once delivered us from a terrible fate,' I called to him...."

The speaker got no further, for Siddharta cried, deeply moved:

"King of Magadha, so you have seen my grandson?"

"Gautama!" cried Siddharta's faithful friends, and all the voices began to buzz together.

It was indeed Bimbisara, who, prompted by Gautama's accounts, had come to visit his former rescuer. They had much to tell each other. Gautama had entered the principal monastery of Magadha in order to study there. On a lonely walk through the forest he had met the king with his retinue, just in time to save his life.

"But when I left you, had you not renounced your kingship, Bimbisara?" asked Siddharta in astonishment.

"My successor died shortly afterwards, leaving no descendants. So at the urging of my people I relinquished the priesthood to others, and took up the reins of government once more. I can serve the Eternal One also as a king. But now I had a longing to see you again.

"Because the principals of the monasteries speak of you as 'The Master', I had never thought of looking for you behind this Master. It was your grandson who told me about you, about your life, and the Mountain of the Eternal One. As my son is grown up, I was able to leave my country. Now I am here, and I shall not soon leave you again."

When Bimbisara had been staying on the Mountain for some time, he liked the nearly completed rest-house so much that he asked to be admitted to it.

He sent his retinue back to Magadha, retaining only one attendant. Bimbisara was a faithful servant of the Eternal One, from whom they could all still learn, as could he from them.

He came from the hot region, where peoples and customs are quite differ-

161

ent from those in the region of the Himalayas. Again and again the men discovered differences that partly amused them, and partly awakened serious thoughts in them.

"It is good that Siddharta, whom you call Gautama, is becoming acquainted with all the sons of Indus," acknowledged Bimbisara. "Only so will he one day be in a position to understand them all, and in that way to govern them. He is the born ruler, Siddharta. As he stood in quiet dignity before us and the tiger, the sharp words of command tempered by the ray of love in his eyes, we all felt as though we must pay homage to him."

"But I do not think that he will become a ruler," said Siddharta almost regretfully. "He wishes to be a servant of the Eternal One, as I am. So we may not elect to rule a country and care for subjects."

"That is not how I mean it, Siddharta," Bimbisara retorted. "He is not to become a prince, but ruler in the realm of the spirit. He is to make souls subject to him, and thus to the Eternal One."

They often spoke on this subject, especially when the rest-house was completed and occupied. Then Siddharta often felt drawn to the circle of his old friends. He got into the habit of taking his meals with them, and prolonged the conversations that followed ever more.

Then came an interruption to this quiet life. Suddhodana came once more to visit his father.

"I have brought you something young again," he said in his cheerful way. "But this time it is not a young beast of prey."

As he had done the last time when he brought the lions, he clapped his hands. However, no servants appeared at this signal; instead a youth, not much more than a child, stepped before Siddharta with a low bow.

"This is our young Suddhodana. Apart from his name he has not much in common with me, even in appearance," jested the Prince. "Outwardly and inwardly, he resembles the Siddhartas. That is why he too wants to learn here on the Mountain of the Eternal One. His aim is one day to help his brother Gautama."

So the young Suddhodana entered the school on the Mountain as a pupil. He lived in the same rooms as his elder brother. He enjoyed the same privileges as the latter once had. He studied with even greater zeal and understanding, but .... he was completely different from Gautama.

What in Gautama was instant illumination from within, Suddhodana gained only through arduous pondering. He was serious far beyond his years. Some thought he could never have been a child. Generally he had neither eyes nor ears for his surroundings.

He did not trouble the servants, but he took no notice of the people either. Gautama had had a pleasant word for every service, however small. This youth took it for granted that others should render him service. Each one had his task to fulfil, for which in his opinion he merited neither thanks nor acknowledgement.

Towards his grandfather and his old friends he had a natural deference; however this did not prevent him from expressing his opinion, which nearly always differed from their own, without the slightest hesitation.

"Suddhodana," sighed Siddharta one day, "what do you want to learn here? After all, you know everything better than we do."

"Forgive me, Grandfather," said the youth, with a dignity which would have appeared absurd in any other person. "I only know it in a different way from you. Whether or not I know it better is yet to be seen."

He always had the last word, but he said it in such a way that no one ever had any cause to rebuke him.

Once Siddharta asked him whether he too had a connection with the beings and the animals. The youth laughed, but as yet he lacked the sunny cheerfulness of his father.

"No, Grandfather, I leave that to childlike minds. Animals stand so far below me, the human being, that I consider it unnecessary to treat them otherwise than as their master. I do not see the 'beings', as you call them, by which you probably mean gnomes and their like; so it would serve no purpose if I were to concern myself with them."

"Perhaps one day you will be glad to have them come to your assistance," answered Siddharta somewhat impatiently.

The nature of this grandson was completely incomprehensible to him. After all he was of the same stock as Gautama; moreover he sincerely aspired to Truth, and yet the brothers were so totally different.

He pondered a great deal over this. He did not wish to discuss it with his faithful followers; it would have seemed like disparaging his grandson.

Then one day he asked the youth himself:

"Can you tell me, Suddhodana, how it is that you are so different from Gautama? Surely you both want to attain to the same goal: to be servants of the Lord of all the Worlds!"

"And would you consider it right for us to strive for this goal in the same way, one trying to outdo the other, in order to keep to your image? Grandfather, do not brood over me. I believe that I have to be as I am in order to provide the intended complement to Gautama.

"I am of a totally different disposition from him, whom I admire. I should like to resemble him. But something within tells me: remain as you are, so long as your nature does not drive you on to a wrong course.

"You see, Grandfather, I know that Gautama is going to be a very great man. Then people will crowd round him, they will flatter him and court his favour. Others will live in awe of him and will not dare to tell him what they think, and what is perhaps quite right.

"Then I must be there to warn him against the flatterers, and to encourage the timid. That is also why I always deliberately reject at first everything that comes from you or from him.

"That has nothing to do with my reverence for you and my love for him. I have to tread the arduous path, to achieve everything myself, so that I shall hold it quite firmly and securely when I am permitted to be with Gautama as his chief servant."

Never before had his grandson spoken so much, never before had he been so close to Siddharta's heart. It was indeed a splendid kernel which lay hidden in the rough shell!

While he was speaking, the lad had unconsciously taken Gautama's place on the tiger-skin. The grandfather gently stroked the flowing blue-black hair, and let his right hand rest for a moment on his grandson's head as if in blessing.

The latter looked up at him. His clear blue eyes mirrored inner calm and truth.

"That I should be so blind!" Siddharta sighed to himself. "For if Suddhodana were not good his father would not have brought him to the Mountain of the Eternal One!"

For a long time this was the only occasion when the two spoke so intimately to each other. But a ray of understanding often passed between them, and whatever Suddhodana might say, never again did Siddharta lose his equilibrium because of it.

His teachers were satisfied with Suddhodana. He made great progress, but this was due more to his diligence and perseverence than to his natural ability.

What he did in his free time no one could discover. Apparently he had no special interest at all, he read only what his teachers gave him, he did not associate with the servants and was not to be found in the stables. He disappeared as soon as the lesson ended, and returned only when the school timetable required it.

Siddharta would have liked to know what the youth was doing during this time, but he was prepared to wait until Suddhodana found enough confidence to tell him unasked.

Then again a day came when the younger one's soul opened quite easily.

"Grandfather," he said out of deep reflection, "I have been reading what you said about suffering and the eightfold path. It is very beautiful, but it is not all that we human beings need for the closing of the cycle of our existence. You put so much stress on the deed. But so long as we still do something out of volition, we are not yet completely open for the guidance. Our life must reach the point where we allow the power from above to work in us, through which we do only what then breaks forth from within us."

"So you want to do something after all, Suddhodana," interposed Siddharta. "We must not be inactive, especially since our people tend only too readily to forget the reality in dreaming."

"Certainly we must all do something, but it must not be a willed action! It is not given to me to put into words what I intuitively perceive," the youth complained. "Gautama will say it one day, and then all will understand."

After a short pause, the grandson asked another question, but this time his thoughts had taken quite a different course:

"You said recently that one day perhaps I would need the help of the invisible beings. Do you remember? How were you thinking of that?"

"In the way that your grandmother was permitted to experience it when the elemental servant of the Eternal One saved her and her two sons. But you know what happened then, do you not?"

His grandson replied that he did not. Incomprehensible as it seemed, for some reason the father must have refrained from telling his children of the miraculous rescue. Now Siddharta told the story as well as he could, and the youth listened breathlessly.

"Why was I not told of this sooner?" he burst out. "I would have judged many things quite differently, and thought far more naturally about many things!"

"Well, it is not too late for that yet," the Master consoled him. "Besides, you did want to experience everything yourself. Perhaps that is why your father has remained silent."

"That must be so. This account overturns the whole picture that I had formed of God's servants. But I am glad that I have been able to hear it now."

From that day forth the young man underwent a change which all were aware of. He could sometimes be seen standing before a flower or a bird's nest, deep in thought. He became more friendly, and his features lost their hitherto closed look.

Suddenly he declared that he had now learned enough here, and he wished to go in search of Gautama. Siddharta suggested that a messenger should first be sent to the hot region to discover Gautama's whereabouts.

But before this plan could be carried out, Suddhodana had ridden away on his small white horse, accompanied by his two servants. They had to be content to know what he intended to do.

AMURUDDBA had found a successor, and worked with him. Thereafter he had handed over his duties to him, and now the ever-active man sat idly under the wide-spreading trees, thinking.

He had never been known to do that before, and he himself found no pleasure in this inactive life. His health began to fail, and before many months had elapsed he passed away.

No one was with him in his last hours. When he retired to rest in the evening he had said to Ananda:

"In the past I looked forward every evening to rising the next morning. There is no point in it now."

After that he rose no more. When his friends went to look for him he had passed over.

When they had buried him in a cave near Sariputta, and the plaque: "The faithful Amuruddba" stood before it, Siddharta said one evening:

"It was a good thing that I insisted on Amuruddba's placing his duties in younger hands. What should we have done now, if he had not listened?"

Maggalana replied, quite calmly and naturally:

"Then he would still be here."

"What do you mean by that?" the Master asked in surprise.

"He died from weariness of a life that no longer offered him any work," was the reply.

They then spoke at length about activity and leisure. Siddharta also told them what his grandson had said on the subject. Each one held a different opinion.

Bimbisara found it glorious to be allowed to rest after a life full of trouble and toil.

"I believe that it was out of this sensing that the belief in Nirvana once arose among the Brahmans. Weary people welcomed with joy the thought of dissolution into nothingness," he said.

But Maggalana contradicted him:

"When I am allowed to enter the beyond, I would like also to be allowed to work there," he said slowly. "A life without activity, wherever it may be, has no value for me."

"Why these opposing views?" asked Ananda. "Unite your wishes, and the happy middle course will emerge. I think that in the beyond we shall find all kinds of joys which will occupy us without straining us."

"And what does the Master think?" they asked Siddharta.

"I think that we shall be allowed to go on learning up there. We shall see everything differently, understand many things better. That will lead us further and further. Perhaps we may also become guides for those among our people who seek the Eternal One."

Then they went back to the beginning of the discourse, and Siddharta begged his friends just to live in whatever way suited them. He did not want to lose yet another loyal follower through weariness of life.

But he could not hide from himself that his days were numbered. Secretly he sent messengers to his sons, and to Gautama, who had informed him that he was now in Utakamand, the last school that he wished to visit. He sent word to them that they should make haste, if they wanted to see him again.

After that he began to sift his manuscripts, to make notes, to inspect all institutions; but everything was desultory, unlike his usual self.

His loyal followers became aware of this, and asked themselves if it was a bad sign. They dared not speak to him about it. And yet he would have been glad to speak with them, if they had asked him. If only at least Suddhodana the elder would come. But the son was far away.

Gradually the restlessness gave way to a state of continual dreaming. He loved the solitude, he who during the last years had been happiest in the circle of his disciples. He withdrew, often not leaving his apartment for days, and became absorbed in deep thoughts.

Figures whom he had not seen for a long time came to him. Luminous messengers approached and reminded him of this and that. With them he associated, with them he spoke. He seemed no longer to think of the people around him, of his task in their midst.

At last both his sons arrived, almost at the same time. Rahula was accompanied by Gautama. They could not imagine that the once ever-lively Siddharta had withdrawn so completely from all things.

Together they entered his room, where they found him deeply absorbed. He did not hear them addressing him, and they were afraid that he had already left the world. But his breath still stirred his breast. They waited a long time, then one of the sons would have spoken to him, but Gautama raised his hand in warning.

"Do you not see," he whispered, "that a messenger from the Eternal One is speaking with him?"

When the luminous figure, which was visible only to Gautama, had gone, Siddharta opened his eyes. Great was his joy to see the three men standing by him.

His first question, however, did not concern them, but the youth who had set out to look for his brother. Nobody had seen or heard anything of him. This disturbed the old man. But they urged him to trust in the help which would be extended to this grandson.

Siddharta now began to ask about all that had occupied him of late. But before they could answer properly he was already asking a new question.

So they decided that at all times only one of them should be with the man whose life was drawing to a close. That made it easier for him. He began to collect his thoughts, and became cheerful again.

He solemnly appointed Gautama as his successor. When the latter asked Siddharta to tell him how he had pictured this or that, he said:

"That is not necessary, Gautama. My time has passed, and with it my thoughts. Everything must now be done not as I have planned it, but as you see it with the help of your guide. A new time dawns. The old is passing away with me, the new approaches. The Kingdom of the Lord of all the Worlds will develop gloriously among our people.

"You, Gautama, are called to build up anew what I have only begun. All strength from above will be with you. I see so much that should be improved. I can no longer change anything, but I know that you will do so."

On one of the following days he asked to be carried to the great open square. While the men were assembling he remained on the couch which had been put up for him under the great tree, but then he rose and went to his usual place in the centre.

In a clear voice he took leave of them all. He told them that at the behest of the Lord of all the Worlds he had chosen Gautama as his successor. With that he was the chief of all servants of the Eternal One among their whole people.

"It does not depend on age, my friends, but on the wisdom bestowed by the Eternal One. But I beg you, Gautama, to keep that name. Let the name Siddharta go into oblivion with me. I have reached my goal, soon I shall awake in the beyond."

He found kind words for each of them, then he raised his hand in farewell, and allowed himself to be carried back to the school. He no longer spoke with any of his family; all his thoughts had already gone from this earth.

His lips moved gently. They were still trying to say something. At last those who stood around him clearly heard him utter a name that was not known to them. Then he called:

"My Lord Whom I sought to serve, forsake me not in this hour, which shows me how small I was!"

Luminous figures seemed to float around him, his countenance became transfigured. After that he called once more:

"Yes, I will be a helper to my people when Thou comest to judge them!"

These were his last words on earth.

THE DAYS that followed passed like a dream for all. They mourned Siddharta, but his death had come as no surprise. With his last address they had all intuitively sensed that with him something "old" was departing from them, and the "new" must now come.

It was good that the new Master had already been appointed, that they did not have to look for him.

But Gautama himself drew back. He left it to the others to make the usual preparations for Siddharta's funeral; but from small, almost imperceptible changes it could indeed be felt that he was directing everything.

Maggalana had asked to be allowed to keep watch by the Master's lifeless body. Gautama had looked at him penetratingly. Maggalana had begun to fear that his request would meet with a brusque refusal, when the young Master's eyes lit up radiantly:

"Yes, Maggalana, ever-faithful one; if to any one among you, it is to you that his soul will draw near once more. Stay with him as long as the soul remains near the body."

How did Gautama know the other's most secret thoughts? Amazed, the old man bowed before such greatness. Thanking him, he departed, and went to the room where Siddharta's earthly cloak lay ready for embalming. He as a former priest knew best how to do this, and therefore the task had already been assigned to him by the others.

Praying, he approached the couch. He did not pray to Siddharta. He called on the Eternal One to permit the Master, who now undoubtedly saw more than while on earth, to tell them something which could help them to advance. Then he set about his work with loving hands.

Meanwhile the other disciples were sitting together, discussing the preparations.

170

"We must send messengers all over the country to announce Siddharta's death," cried one of them, happy that this great thought had come to him first.

The others agreed with him.

"We shall have to hold back the funeral until the messengers have returned," said Bimbisara.

But then it was felt that nothing like that should be done without consulting Gautama.

Ananda undertook to go to him. But when he spoke of the need to send messengers to the schools and monasteries, he received the calm and friendly answer:

"That has already been attended to."

Startled, Ananda returned to his friends. They all knew that nobody had ridden out during these days!

"You must have misunderstood; Gautama said that the measure seemed to him unnecessary," suggested Bimbisara.

But it caused a stir among them. And now they did not know whether they should wait for news from the monasteries. This time Bimbisara went to ask Gautama.

"Those principals who are worthy to attend our Master's funeral will surely arrive in time," declared Gautama confidently. "Since Maggalana has embalmed the body, we can wait until the tablet is also ready."

"Has a decision been made on the inscription?" asked Bimbisara, and was told that the artist was already working on it.

Bimbisara too now returned to the rest-house, no less startled than Ananda before him.

"Gautama is not lacking in respect for old age," Bimbisara assured them, "but one hardly dares to ask him anything. His gaze goes right through the questioner. But his answer is always such as to make one think that he considers the question completely unnecessary."

"The new is beginning already," said Ananda, with an attempt at a joke. "We shall have to get used to it."

Gautama's upright figure seemed to have grown even taller. A luminous current emanated from it, surrounding it with a mantle of aloofness. Awe kept the others away from him who, after all, had grown up in their midst,

171

together with all those who were living on the Mountain at that time. But he seemed to have become a completely different person.

And while they all pondered, discussing their thoughts until they became shallow and scattered, Maggalana sat day after day in the quiet room, which only Gautama entered regularly in the morning and in the evening.

His earnest prayer had found fulfilment: after the first days of waiting, he suddenly perceived Siddharta's soul. At least he thought that this was what he saw.

It was a luminous entity, bearing Siddharta's form and features, but it was nebulous, transparent, now striving upwards like flames, now undulating like a mist. It did not always manifest, and did not speak. It appeared and disappeared unexpectedly.

It was Gautama who prompted it to speak. He was standing in prayer beside Maggalana when the figure appeared again. He looked at it kindly, not in the least surprised.

"Siddharta, can you not yet detach yourself from your earthly cloak? We shall delay the funeral until you are able to begin your ascent. Then it will be easier for you."

A voice sounded faintly across the room. Maggalana could not have told whence it came:

"I thank you, Gautama, you blessed of the Eternal One. To be allowed to place in your hands all that I left unfinished will make my ascent possible. Otherwise I would still be bound to my half-finished work for a long, long time to come."

Maggalana was shaken. How could the great Master speak thus of his work on earth, to which he had devoted all his strength! He did not utter this, but his thoughts could be understood not only by Siddharta's spirit-being but also by Gautama.

Again the voice sounded, faint as a breath:

"Even while I still walked the earth in my body, I knew that I had become slack in the latter years. I thought that my advanced age justified me. Now I see that there is no time in our life which exempts us from doing our utmost in service to the Eternal One. Tell this to the others in the rest-house. There must be no rest-house, Maggalana. Even for one who has grown old, there are still tasks if he looks around for them."

"Are you still brooding, Siddharta?" asked Gautama lovingly. "Do you not see, where you now are, that persisting in thoughts of what we have done wrong does not advance us? Turn away from the earth and 'your work', as you call it. You have nothing more to do with it. Direct your spirit upwards, and begin the ascent."

How great Gautama must be, to rebuke a Siddharta! Marvelling, almost worshipping, Maggalana gazed at the still so young Master, over whose features heavenly peace had spread.

The figure disappeared, and for some days it did not appear again. Maggalana was just about to report this to Gautama when Siddharta's soul suddenly stood in the room again. It had become finer, more transparent, the voice speaking to Maggalana sounded even fainter:

"You faithful one, take care of the old ones. They are not to rest from activity! Even as you are tirelessly active, so shall they also work, each according to the powers bestowed on him.

"Gautama will lead you in the right way. He will make amends for many of my mistakes. Where I have taught wrongly, he will bring about what is right. Believe him, trust him."

Before Maggalana could reply, the figure had vanished, and did not appear again.

And now the disciples of the departed one, and those who were closely connected with them, were arriving on the Mountain. Tents had to be pitched to accommodate them, there were so many.

The principals of the monasteries and convents came, men and women, from the whole wide land. They arrived as fast as they could ride.

Bimbisara and Ananda asked one and another of them:

"Who gave you the news of the Master's death?" Every time the reply was:

"Messengers came!"

This reply was given with such finality that they did not feel inclined to enquire further.

And now Gautama appointed the day of the funeral. He arranged everything quite differently from how it had hitherto been done. On the evening before the festival, as he called it, Siddharta's body was carried into the wonderfully-decorated cave.

173

It had been prepared with greater care than the earlier ones. Inside, it was completely panelled in white stone, such as had been used for building the school.

The white stones gleamed, flowers stood before them. That was all. No costly materials, nothing of silver or gold embellished the grave. A bowl of frankincense was placed at the foot of the couch; beside it sat Maggalana, who wished to keep also the last vigil.

Next morning when the sun had risen, they all, men and women, assembled in the open square. Until now women had never been allowed to participate in a festival. If for some specific reason they were obliged to attend an address by Siddharta, they had had to be content to stand behind the men.

This time it was different. Gautama himself had arranged for them to be summoned, and now he led them into the centre of the square, where they were allowed to form the inner ring around a high stone.

The stone was white, of the same kind as that used for the building. It shimmered pure and bright. On it stood an exquisitely-shaped bowl containing frankincense, from which bluish veils floated upwards.

Beside the stone stood Gautama and Rahula. Behind the women stood the men, in ever-widening circles. And behind them squatted the monkeys, silent, motionless, on the ground, on tree-branches. No movement betrayed their presence, and they never showed themselves on the Mountain of the Eternal One again.

Anyone whose inner eye was opened could also discern innumerable beings, great and small.

And Gautama began to speak. His voice rang clear over the wide square, completely filling it:

"Faithful ones! We have had to bid farewell to our Master, who brought into all our lives the best that we possess: the tidings of the Lord of all the Worlds!

"We commit his body to the earth, with which it was linked in love. His soul has begun the ascent into Luminous Heights. It will be arduous, but there are helpers at hand. If any among us feels that he owes him gratitude, he should render this gratitude through prayers, which may lovingly support the one who is on his upward way.

"The words for his grave-stone were received by me from above: 'He who achieved his goal on earth – Siddharta – has become the one who awakened in the beyond – Buddha.'

"Whatever he still lacks to enable him to return to the home of his soul he will now gain in his ascent.

"Rejoice that he has closed the cycle of his earth-lives, rejoice that he was permitted to live among us, that he was our teacher, our Master!"

Gautama uttered a fervent prayer, and then Rahula began to speak:

"I stand before you, my friends, at the behest of the Eternal One. He Himself has chosen Gautama, and had him prepared to be our leader.

"Siddharta told you that something new is to begin. He knew that Gautama is of our kind. But the Lord of all the Worlds has called him and blessed him especially. He is to communicate to all of us the knowledge that lives within him, so that it may become easier for us to tread consciously the path which the Eternal One has marked out for us.

"Hearken to our leader! Follow him, for he wishes to lead upwards all those who are of good volition. Do not cling to the old, which was right for its time as a transition to something better, but must now disappear to make room for what is better still. Open your souls in prayer at all times, in this way shall you too partake of the Power from above, so that you may pass it on to those who come to you.

"Never weary in your working!"

Silence reigned for a long time after these words. Each one sought to retain as much of it as possible. All felt that something absolutely great had entered their lives. They looked in awe at the youthful leader who stood so simply before them.

Then he gave the signal for them to disperse. Following his instructions, they walked in small groups to the cave, looked inside, and bade farewell to the departed.

Maggalana had attended the festival in the square, and did not enter the cave again. As the last one stepped back, the tablet, on which were inscribed the words that Gautama had already made known to them, was brought at a signal.

Pure gleamed the white stone, golden sparkled the letters. A low whisper went through the crowd:

"Siddharta has become Buddha!"

All stood motionless as the tablet was put in place; then Gautama left the square with Rahula, followed by the others.

EVERYDAY life resumed its course. At first all the guests were still on the Mountain, and Gautama let it be known that they should remain until he had spoken with them.

Some of them immersed themselves in the manuscripts; nowhere but on the Mountain of the Eternal One were there so many of them. Others discussed questions which occupied them, thoughts which moved them. In spite of the number of people, there was no noise or disturbance anywhere.

Then again came a day when women and men were summoned to the great square. This time the men stepped back entirely of their own accord, to let the women enter the innermost circle.

Gautama was already standing beside the incense bowl, while Rahula, with Suddhodana his brother, had joined the group of men.

"Faithful ones, I have summoned you here because we have no room large enough to hold us all. However, I do not want to make a speech, but to discuss with you what is to be done in the near future. After I have mentioned a few things that now seem important to me, each may fearlessly speak his mind. Let us take counsel together. The voice of every one who has something to say shall be heard.

"Friends, ever since I came to this Mountain it has troubled me that you have no Place of Worship, and no regular Hours of Worship. Siddharta had well-considered reasons for this, which I understood. But now these reasons no longer apply. Times have changed, and we can think of building a House for the Eternal One. Let him who thinks differently raise his hand."

He looked around searchingly; many hands went up.

"Will you tell me, friends, what makes you think otherwise?" he asked encouragingly.

Many answers rang out together. But Gautama smiled, and this smile so transfigured his countenance that it seemed no longer of this earth.

"We cannot understand you unless you speak one by one. Let us begin

176

here, then each shall speak in turn," he decided, at the same time pointing to Bimbisara, who was standing near.

"I think that what was right in Siddharta's time should not be changed so soon after his death," the old man said grudgingly.

"Your loyalty does you credit, Bimbisara," replied Gautama, "but remember that he himself referred to the new which has to come."

"A Temple might well be possible here on the Mountain," the next person said. "If we were to build down below we should come into conflict with the Brahmans."

"That is why to begin with we shall only build a Temple up here. Then we shall see what happens next," was Gautama's prompt reply.

Many hands dropped. These were the two objections that had worried most of the men. There were still various remarks, such as: "There is no money for building," or "A Temple of the Eternal One must be outwardly different from all others. Who is going to produce the plans for it?"

But these points were quickly disposed of, so that in the end it was agreed that a Temple should be built on the Mountain of the Eternal One.

"We shall soon begin to build," promised Gautama. "I shall summon you all again for the consecration. That will be a great sacred Festival, for which you should begin to prepare even now."

They were all delighted, and gave expression to their joy. Thereafter Gautama discussed various other things that had struck him when he visited the different schools, monasteries and convents.

"It is quite right," he said, "that you should keep mainly to the way things are done here on the Mountain. Siddharta was directed to it by his luminous guide, so we know that it is in accordance with the Will of the Eternal One.

"But you must not simply imitate everything without thought. The people are completely different in the north and south, in the east and west. Above all you must adapt to the inner and outer needs of these people. For you are here for the people, not they for you."

"What do you mean by that, Gautama?" asked an old man.

"Well, I think that, in regions where there are frequent outbreaks of disease, much more attention should be paid to the care of the body, even among the ordinary folk. Up here on the Mountain, where we scarcely

177

come in contact with others, our daily baths and ablutions are enough. In other places beggars, and those whom you visit in their huts, pass on all kinds of infections to you. Then you have to cleanse yourselves after coming in contact with them. You must also try to educate people to practise greater cleanliness.

"We here on the Mountain have horses and small shaggy mules as beasts of burden. You in the regions of Utakamand and Magadha have to make use of elephants, while camels are well adapted to the west. But you cling to the horses, because Siddharta used them. Just think of the advantages which two elephants would bring to the monastery!"

Now they understood what he meant, and promised to stop imitating others.

After that day the general exodus began. They rode off in groups. The tents were taken down, and the inhabitants of the Mountain were alone once more. A feeling of emptiness would have crept in, but Gautama did not allow it to arise.

Maggalana had delivered Siddharta's message to the friends. He expected them to abandon the rest-house, but that did not occur to any of them, although of course they saw that Maggalana had moved with his writings into a tiny room in the monastery.

He was untiring in the writing down of tales, which came easily to him when he was resting in the garden. But in between he undertook to look after a section of the large flower-garden. In dry weather he carried water, but in the rainy season he tied up tendrils, dug round the plants and attended to his charges.

But the others did nothing at all! That was not to his liking. At least he would warn them once more.

Ananda had invited him to the rest-house one evening so that they could talk together. He went, because it seemed to him that he could find no better opportunity.

He found ten old men, comfortably stretched out, awaiting him. They greeted him happily, and asked if he was not yet tired of his little room.

"Your old room is waiting for you!" cried one of them, while another said rather derisively: "Maggalana is afraid of losing the good ideas for his stories through associating with us."

178

"That is not so, my friends, for you can see that I have come to you," began Maggalana hesitantly. "Since Siddharta has charged me with the abolition of the rest-house, I can no longer live in it. I should be so happy if you too would leave it.

"Siddharta said that there was a task for each one of you, a task which he can perform even when his strength is diminishing. Ask Gautama for work if you do not know yourselves how you can be usefully employed."

"Siddharta himself arranged this well-earned rest for us," retorted Ananda. "You must have misunderstood him in what you thought you heard him say. Had he not wished us to enjoy the reward of our labours, he would not have said that we should be allowed to live as we like. No one was to die any more from weariness of life."

"O Siddharta," thought Maggalana, "how bitter the harvest of what you have sown without thinking must be for you now!" But he said aloud:

"Do believe me, my friends, when the Master surveyed his life from a higher standpoint he recognised these very utterances to be wrong. It is because he wishes to save you from hardships that he makes this known to you. But if you do not listen to him you will make his ascent difficult. Your wrongdoing will burden him, because he was the cause of it."

Even these words, which were hard for Maggalana, made no impression on the old men, who had already become too used to the comfort to give it up again.

For a moment the thought came to Maggalana that he must turn to Gautama. But he abandoned the idea because it seemed as though he were putting himself above the others, as though he were accusing them. So he only prayed the more deeply for his friends.

MEANWHILE Gautama had drawn up plans for the Temple, which were shown to him from above. He had the great open assembly-square prepared for the Temple building. That gave work for everyone; and suddenly the old men in the rest-house were invited to take over the tasks of those whose energies could be used for the building work.

They did not like this at all, and conferred among themselves, only to find that it was impossible to decline the invitation. They had to accept the

179

work, but only for a short time. After that they would certainly see to it that they returned to their quiet life.

The tasks allotted to them were not arduous, but they had to be executed punctually at the specified time, and just that came hard to the old men. As they were resting from their labours one evening, and talking about the work they had done that day, Gautama joined them.

He thanked them for helping so willingly when there was a shortage of manpower. There would be ever more work to do, so it was good for them to become gradually used to working again.

But he had yet another proposal. The rest-house had to be demolished. Enough rooms were available in the monastery to accommodate them all. It would be best for them to go with him at once, in order to move into their new rooms.

He left them no time at all to air their views on this new measure. Warmly welcoming, he took them with him and gave them accommodation in the monastery, one here, another there. All as far apart as possible.

"You will be thankful to be able to enjoy the absolute quiet of the monastery when you come home tired from work in the evening," he said kindly. "Since talking is not permitted after the evening meal, each one of you will be able to immerse himself in thoughts of the Eternal One until he falls asleep."

The rule of silence was new. When they enquired next day they were told that Gautama had only recently introduced it. But the Brothers were very happy about it; for the evenings were the only time when they could concentrate undisturbed.

"We need it," said one of the older Brothers, "but the newcomers do not know that yet, and have often disturbed us with foolish, idle chatter."

The old men were not at all pleased to be subject to discipline again, but they complied. Their rest-house was pulled down. At first nothing new was put in its place, so that Ananda felt that surely such extreme haste had been unnecessary.

But the building of the Temple went on apace. They worked at it from morning till night. Gautama was always there. No one could tell when he found peace for other work.

Nevertheless he was fresh and able to help even with the hardest physical

180

tasks. Nothing was too small for him. Where a man was needed he stepped into the breach, giving to all a living example of his words, that work is never demeaning.

He had assigned tasks even to the women. They had to provide the mats which were to cover the floor of the Temple.

Although the floor, like the walls, was laid with white stone, it was slippery underfoot, and the pure white became soiled during the rainy season. Therefore the floor-stone was to be covered with coloured mats.

In some districts the women were particularly skilled in weaving. Gautama had asked there for materials that could be used for curtains. Around Utakamand the women made beautiful basketwork from raffia; such could also be used in the new Temple.

As Gautama stood on the building-site one day, taking pleasure in the curve of the walls, a young man came up to him, also viewing the building with great joy.

It was the younger Suddhodana who had appeared again, lean and sun-tanned. He looked at his brother with clear eyes.

"I have come to be your servant, Gautama! Do not send me away from you," he pleaded humbly.

Gautama smiled.

"And yet I am going to send you away!"

The younger man was startled; however, the elder went on:

"I have just been wishing that I had someone whom I could entrust with a journey. And so you have come exactly at the right time. In the Himalayan region where our father was brought up there are workshops where they make sheets of transparent, coloured glass. You must go to these places and bring me back some of this glass."

Suddhodana was happy with the commission, and asked for further details. Then he rode away, accompanied by a few servants with pack-animals.

Gautama had advised him to let his father tell him the way. He could certainly have done so himself, for his guide had told him exactly where the right sheets were to be found; but it was important to him that the youth should visit his parents, after being away for so long.

As the Temple grew, many thoughts went through Gautama's soul. It

181

seemed to him that in addition to this visible Temple a spiritual edifice must also be built on earth, whose supporting pillars should stand firmly rooted in all the principalities of the people.

"These pillars are the monasteries, convents and schools," he thought. "That is right. They can always be added to as the need arises. But just as our Temple supports the domed, transparent vault above, so must the spiritual edifice likewise unite upwards with all its pillars.

"This is to be the Mountain of the Eternal One, this central point for everything! Is it indeed so? And if it is, must it not then be accessible to every one? Must not the principals of the schools, monasteries and convents have a much better connection with the Mountain?

"Siddharta allowed the men to come to him whenever they had anything on their mind. It would be better if they came regularly for longer periods. That would also remove the danger of the principal of a school, monastery or convent making a personal imprint on the whole."

Gautama's thoughts were unending. He consulted with his guide, and enquired into the Will of the Eternal One. By the time the earthly Temple was completed, he had also laid down his guidelines for the arrangement of the spiritual Temple.

He felt an urge to visit the monasteries and convents in the country, but first the Temple had to be completed. No one apart from himself knew how the building was to be arranged, no one understood the plans he had drawn up.

The building of the Temple had taken three years; then at last the invitations could finally be sent round the country. Again no messengers rode out, and yet Gautama said he had notified the principals. Then one of the disciples ventured to ask whom he had sent.

"Do you not know?" smiled Gautama. "The little servants of God gladly undertake such tasks. They pass it on by word of mouth, and in an incredibly short time the message reaches its destination, where it is transmitted to one of the persons who can understand the elemental beings."

To think that it had never occurred to them! Now they found the explanation so simple.

In the days which preceded the consecration, many preparations for the arrangement of the Festival were still being made. The women wove

182

wreaths and garlands; the maidens practised a solemn measure, in which they moved with great reverence.

Then some of the younger Mountain-dwellers went to Gautama.

"Will you not also choose some disciples from our ranks?" they asked.

Gautama shook his head. But they did not give up.

"Siddharta had disciples, like all wise men. We revere you as our Master; let us be your disciples. Our loyalty shall be our gratitude to you."

"There is no need for that between us," said Gautama. "Only he who is truly Master can have disciples. I am not a Master. I am a servant of the Eternal One, as you also wish to be. Thus I am your Brother and not your Master. Let your loyalty merge in one with mine, but offer it to the Lord of all the Worlds, not to me. To Him we owe all that we are and know. Let us never forget that." –

Again, as after Siddharta's departure, tents were pitched. A wooden building to accommodate the women was erected on the site of the former rest-house. Everything was done in a practical, simple and beautiful way.

The guests arrived. The Mountain was filled with active life. Suddhodana the father and Rahula the son were also among those invited.

Gautama had called them, not because they were his kinsmen, but because he regarded them also as pillars of the spiritual Temple. They were well aware of this.

In spite of all his kindness and friendliness, Gautama was remote from them, as from all other human beings. He seemed to have an equal love for all that was created, having concern for all.

The day for the consecration of the Temple was ordained from above. The co-operation of the elemental beings was clearly discernible: the sky, out of which the golden sun beamed down, had never been so radiantly blue. Gentle and cool winds brought with them the sweet scent of flowers. At the same time it seemed as though they also brought chords of lovely and melodious music.

The people had assembled silently in front of the school. At the head of the procession walked the older ones, followed by the women, and lastly the almost endless train of men.

Sisana stood with the group of maidens at the Temple door, and awaited the procession. On each of the broad steps stood two children dressed in white, holding garlands of flowers.

The long procession mounted the steps between them. Now the first of them had reached the door, which opened at Sisana's gentle touch.

A flood of light dazzled the eyes of those coming in from the sunlight. How was it possible? They dared not raise their eyes yet, but followed Sisana with bowed heads. Inside they were received by younger men, who led them to the seats which Gautama had assigned to them.

Then solemn chords, which bore the souls aloft, surged through the hall.

The bowed heads were raised, and wherever they looked the eyes beheld beauty. The sunlight streamed colourfully through the glass panes of the dome, and was refracted in the cut gems which were mounted in abundance.

In the centre of the circular chamber stood the white stone. Upon it glowed the precious chalice, wonderfully fashioned of gold, with crimson gems.

Gautama approached the stone, raised his arms, and invoked the blessing of the Lord of all the Worlds upon this Temple which had been built in His honour. Then the maidens trod their solemn measure to the sound of the instruments. They placed the garlands of flowers around the stone, and withdrew.

And now Gautama began to speak. His voice sounded quite different from how it was out-of-doors. All raised their heads as they listened, as though to make sure that it really was the young Master who spoke to them.

"As you mounted the steps to the Temple – there are twenty-one of them – maidenly figures stood on either side with garlands of flowers. They were to symbolise the steps in the beyond for you. Step by step in ardent toil must your souls climb them. But luminous beings stand ready to help you upwards.

"That it was Sisana, a woman, who opened the door of the Temple to you was also intentional. The Lord of the Worlds created woman more luminous and lighter, so that she may go before us men. She is to smooth the paths for us. We have forgotten this in the course of our earth-lives. Now I must remind you of it:

184

"Men, honour women, who help you to maintain purer morals, who form the link with the Luminous Heights!

"Women, so conduct yourselves that in this way you are also fulfilling the Will of the Eternal One! Teach your sisters to recognise the purpose of their existence on earth.

"Our country has neglected much in this respect; here too everything has to become new. Help me to bring this about, all you who would be servants of the Eternal One!"

After that Gautama spoke of the spiritual Temple which was to be built; of the pillars and the dome which was also to form a spiritual vault over the whole people.

"Hear now what the Eternal One decrees through me:

"Each principal is to spend every third year here on the Mountain of the Eternal One. He must see to it that one of the Brothers is able to take over the management during that year. When he then returns to his monastery or school after twelve months, the Brother who has deputised for him must in turn live up here for a year. The Sisters shall do likewise.

"Thus a lively exchange of all thoughts, plans and arrangements will constantly take place, but first and foremost we shall all grow spiritually through it.

"I however shall not remain on the Mountain. Every year a different one of the Brothers, who will be appointed each time, will represent me. I shall travel from school to school, and above all bear witness to and proclaim the Eternal One in all parts of the country where as yet there are no schools.

"Our whole people shall be ablaze, shall awaken out of their spiritual sleep. Brahma himself, who is a servant of the Eternal One, does not wish the worship of the greater part of our people to come to a standstill with him. We must convince the Brahmans how incomplete their faith is.

"But hear me, friends: We, you and I, are to convince them through our lives, through the strength of our faith, through the joyfulness of our working, so that they have to ask us: 'What helps you, Brothers?' Only then may we speak.

"Before that it would not be right. He who cannot convince through himself should be silent. He is of no use, can only do harm. Above all, however, we must avoid any discord. Do you think we should be serving the Eternal One if we were to carry strife and discord into the countries for His sake?

"Let this Temple always remind you of what I have been allowed to tell you today. Hold your Temple in honour, for it has been built for the Lord of the Worlds. Let us assemble here every seventh day to worship Him and hear of Him. Afterwards no work shall be done, so that you may reflect in the stillness on what you have been allowed to receive in the Temple. That again is something new which the Eternal One bestows on you. Receive it in the right way!"

Prayer and blessing concluded the Festival, which remained an unforgettable experience to all.

A few days later the guests had departed again. Gautama too made ready for a journey that was to keep him away for a long time. He allotted the tasks, but did not say who was to speak in the Temple in his stead. He seemed to hesitate; they all noticed it, but could not explain the reason. Of course, on reflection, they could find no one who would be able to replace him in this particular respect.

Then one day a man came to the Mountain whose attire showed that he was a priest. He wore a loose, soft white woollen robe. A simple belt of the same material held the folds together. Although he arrived unannounced, Gautama went to meet him and greeted him warmly.

"I have been expecting you, Brother," he said, in a voice that all the bystanders could hear. "You have come at the right time."

The two disappeared into Gautama's apartments. After that they were to be seen together now here, now there; and it was observed that Gautama was explaining everything to the guest.

But at the next Hour of Worship in the Temple Gautama announced that Brother Te-Yang from Tibet, whose acquaintance he had made during his stay in Utakamand, was willing to act on his behalf here on the Mountain. He would conduct the Hours of Worship, and undertake the management in Gautama's place. The Brothers should have confidence in him; he was a learned man, and a faithful servant of the Eternal One.

A few days later Gautama rode away, with two companions and two servants.

186

"I shall keep in touch with you!" he called as he left, to those who felt sad at his departure.

ALL HAD assumed that he would ride south as usual. But he rode in an easterly direction, along the Ganges. The fertile plains delighted his eye, he was enchanted by the ever-widening river.

Now why had the Brothers never come this way before?

He thought he remembered Siddharta once saying that the people who lived in these parts belonged to a tribe who had immigrated here, and believed in completely different gods. Their souls could not be approached with Brahma and Shiva; and if anyone were to speak about the Lord of all the Worlds without transition, the people's reaction would be hostile.

That was now a long time ago. Moreover, Gautama wanted to see for himself what he could accomplish. He rode joyously through all the beauty and fruitfulness, avoided small settlements, and slept at night in the open air.

It was towards the end of the fifth day that he came to the first town. Actually it seemed to be only a very extensive village; for the buildings were not much better than huts. Dirt prevailed everywhere, even though the sacred river, the Ganges, carried its waters past not far away.

Gautama shuddered at the thought of entering the place but – if he was to make contact with the people, he must make a start sooner or later.

Not far from the town he came upon men who seemed to be returning from a hunting expedition. He spoke to them in order to find out the name of the place.

They did not understand his question. But their question in reply reminded him of the Tibetan language, which he knew. Thus he finally succeeded in communicating with the people. They explained that their town was called Bhutan-Ara, and that today a great festival in honour of their god Bhuta was to be celebrated.

They did not understand him when he asked whether he might attend it. Why should he not be allowed to do so? He had dismounted, and was walking with them towards the huts.

A throbbing sound came to his ear, becoming clearer as they approached

187

Bhutan-Ara. It sounded like the booming of exceptionally large drums, and through it sounded the jarring tones of some small shrill instruments in which no trace of any rhythm could be discovered, although the beat of the drums could easily have provided it.

Now came a mingling of human voices, high and low, apparently joining in haphazardly anywhere, to express their joy or their devotion. If this was the outward form of the worship, what must the god for whom it was intended be like?

Gautama had to force himself to go on. He saw ghastly forms rising upwards, floating like mists, then sinking down again.

As he and his companions drew near to the festival ground, the forms began to hover around him. They sought to connect with him, but did not succeed. All within him was vigilant defence.

He glanced round at his four companions. Like him they were walking unmolested through the horror, but they were unaware of any of it. Their defence lay in their pure attitude, and came about unconsciously.

Women, children and young men rushed to meet the hunters, and took the game from them with much clamour. It consisted of a kind of gazelle and some water-fowl, the latter being particularly welcome.

While the women were clad in what had once been colourful rags but had now become drab, the men and children were completely naked.

All, however, were more than lavishly adorned with chains and metal rings. Around their legs they wore narrow bands of gold and silver, which were clumsily wrought, and jangled noisily at every step. Round their necks they wore broader rings, varying in number.

Gautama soon observed that the higher the rank of a man, the greater the number of rings round his neck. All had their blue-black, slightly curly hair piled up as high as possible on their heads, securing it with metal pins or little wooden pegs.

Gautama thought it safer to leave their mounts outside the village. He told his companions and servants to find a resting-place on the banks of the Ganges. He too would probably go there to spend the night in the open. They should keep a fire going, to make it easier for him to locate them.

His companions begged him to take at least one of them with him for

188

protection; but he thought it more important that they should watch over the animals. He knew that he was under the best protection of all.

The Bhutanese had viewed the departure of the animals with suspicion. Were they thinking that they would make a good sacrifice if they could get hold of them? In any case it was these covetous looks that prompted Gautama to take this precaution.

Meanwhile, with the ever-growing crowd of strange companions, he had arrived at the square where the festival was being celebrated. Evil-smelling, smouldering flames burned in open pans mounted on posts. They appeared to serve the twofold purpose of lighting up the square and acting as sacrificial flame. In the dense smoke that rose up from these flames, Gautama saw the forms of human thoughts and lusts.

He called inwardly for help in all this horror. He would try to approach the souls of these savages, who could hardly still be called human beings. But he needed Light-forces to stand by him. They came instantly. Luminous beings pressed round him, cut him off from the Darkness, and created space for him to breathe.

On the square men, women and children were dancing in wild unrestraint. They circled the image of their deity, which was carved out of wood and gaily painted, and towered high above the people. Bhuta's features resembled those of a pig, because of the great tusks and broad, short snout.

Those who had just accompanied Gautama joined the hunters in the wild dance, while the women busied themselves at a fireplace to one side. They were roasting the game, but without skinning or plucking it. A horrible stench drifted across.

Meanwhile the festival seemed to be approaching its climax: two of the idol's priests pushed through the crowd and placed themselves beside Bhuta. One was completely wrapped in various furs. He carried a huge sword, on which he leaned. It was a real weapon and seemed to be very sharp.

The other was dressed in feathers, and wore an enormous, elaborately constructed cock's tail; his headdress too was evidently meant to represent the cockscomb. From time to time he moved his arms, to which short wings were attached, and uttered a most improbable crowing sound.

189

Even though Gautama felt disgust, he was nevertheless fascinated by this savage spectacle; for he kept asking himself what it could all mean.

Suddenly the "cock" leapt on to the idol from behind by way of a kind of ladder, and shouted loudly.

Immediately the musicians were silent, the dancers stood as though rooted to the spot.

A band of men stormed in from the background, and fell on the men and women standing nearest to Bhuta. They tried to escape, but were swiftly caught, bound and led before the priest with the sword, who beheaded each with a well-aimed blow.

Gautama counted twenty victims. The others pushed forward screaming, in order to be bespattered with as much blood as possible.

When the unfortunate victims lay dead on the ground they were packed on to biers, stacked one on top of the other, and then the whole horde trooped off by torchlight to the Ganges.

For a moment Gautama was afraid that they would discover his people's encampment, but nobody troubled about it. Evidently there was a particular spot which they were looking for.

A long stretch of the river-bank, which they were now approaching, was muddy. And hordes of gavials lived in this mud; animals which Gautama had encountered before. These crocodile-like creatures, with their thick tails and very long, tapering snouts, had always filled him with horror.

The victims' bodies were thrown to these brutes for food. The jaws snapped greedily at them, cracking, smacking noises were heard. Some of the creatures left their mud-bed and waddled closer to the men, who retreated screaming.

Now the victims had been devoured, but the animals were not satisfied. The greediest of them gave chase, faster than Gautama would have thought possible. Shrieking, the savages fled.

Gautama hung back deliberately. A great feast would now take place, at which the participants would probably imbibe intoxicating drinks made from rice or roots. So he certainly would not be able to speak to these dehumanised people.

He walked slowly along the river-bank until he saw the glimmer of his people's fire. The gavials did not come near him.

190

His companions were happy when he returned to them safely, and sooner than they had expected. But he would neither speak nor eat. Deep in thought he sat by the fire, pondering how best he could grip the souls of these creatures.

When his people had gone to rest, he besought his guide for help and counsel. His prayer was urgent. It was so important to him that these brutalised men should be torn away from the horror.

Then his guide appeared to him. Only in very special cases did that happen. As a rule Gautama only sensed him, and heard his voice. Now his guide was accompanied by another figure, a naked savage with rings on his neck and feet. But Gautama saw that it must be a spirit-being. Then the guide began to speak:

"This is the first king of the Bhutanese, who ruled this country about a hundred years ago. He loved his people, and although he knew nothing of the Eternal One he introduced worthy forms of worship for Bhuta. He is deeply distressed that the people have sunk to this level in the course of time. If anyone can show you the way to their hearts, it is he. Speak, Bhutani!"

And the king spoke, hesitantly and awkwardly; but Gautama could understand him. He thanked the sage for seeking to uplift his people.

He said that Gautama should tell them that he had seen him, Bhutani. That would make an impression; for the memory of him was still alive. And it was prophesied that if Bhutani should appear happiness would come for the people.

The two priests were skilled in sorcery; Gautama must beware of them.

"I have no fear, Bhutani," said Gautama calmly. "I have come in the Name of the Lord of the Worlds. He will protect His servant."

THE FOLLOWING noon, when the sun was at its height, and Gautama assumed that the people would have slept off the effects of the festival, he set out for Bhutan-Ara. He took the same route as on the previous day, avoiding the banks of the Ganges.

Deathly quiet reigned in the village, everything seemed to be still asleep. The festival-ground was red with the blood of the victims; the Bhuta-column had been removed.

Gautama looked about him searchingly; at last he discovered, beside a hut, a boy whose bright eyes regarded him with admiration and curiosity. In a friendly voice he enquired for the king's house, using the Tibetan language. But the child did not understand him. He called shrilly into the hut, upon which a man came out, surveying Gautama morosely. Gautama repeated his question. Then the man in turn asked:

"What do you want of him, if I tell you where to find him?"

"That I shall tell only to him," was Gautama's calm reply.

The man hesitated for a moment, then curiosity prevailed.

"Come then!" he bade the stranger, and walked ahead of him among the huts until they came to a larger one, outside which stood a small image of Bhuta.

Beside this idol hung a drum, which the man immediately began to beat vigorously with his fists.

Things came to life about the house. Women and children came running, and finally a man appeared, who differed from the others only by the incredibly large number of rings round his neck. Surely he could no longer bow his head because of his high rank.

So this was the king of a comparatively large country. He was furious at being so abruptly aroused from his sleep, and asked angrily what the stranger wanted.

"I am to give you a message from Bhutani," he said.

At the mention of this name, all present raised an ear-splitting clamour. Gautama had to be silent, no one would have heard him. At last the excitement subsided, and the king made a sign for the guest to continue.

"Would it not be better for you to hear the message alone?" Gautama suggested, but the king decided:

"All shall hear what you have to say! Speak clearly: where did you see Bhutani?"

"He came to me last night."

"I ask you: *where* did you see him; that is the important thing," came the unfriendly question.

"On the banks of the Ganges, about sixty men's lengths from here." Again the blood-curdling clamour arose, then came the next question:

"What did he look like?"

192

How was Gautama to describe him? He looked around in perplexity, and saw him standing there. Gautama pointed in his direction and said:

"There he is, can you see him? He looks like you, king."

All eyes turned in the direction indicated, but apparently no one could perceive anything. However the answer must have been the right one; for the king's angry features relaxed and he asked:

"And what had Bhutani to say?"

"Eternal One, grant me the right words!" implored the sage; and then he said slowly and impressively:

"He is sad because his people have forgotten what he once taught them. He would like his people to find the promised happiness! But so long as they sacrifice human beings, and worship Bhuta in such a way that Bhutani must feel ashamed, he cannot help the people to find happiness either."

This time the expected outcry failed to materialise. The men looked at one another in silence, and said not a word. Encouraged by this, Gautama continued:

"Bhutani came to ask me to take charge of his people. I am to teach you better customs, I am to help you to become good again, as you once were. Then through me you will find the promised happiness."

Now there was shouting again. But whereas the first uproar had expressed surprise and amazement, this one demonstrated joy. They crowded round the stranger, tried to touch him and to show him their confidence. When there was silence, the king said:

"The place where Bhutani appeared to you was foretold to us. We believe you, stranger, and beg you to teach us and help us! If you can see Bhutani, he will tell you what you are to show us. We shall obey you."

"Bhutani is pleased with his people, because he sees by your words, O king, that you have not yet become altogether base. He will help you and me."

More and more listeners had arrived. The newcomers were told by the others what had taken place. Suddenly a stocky man, who looked particularly brutish, forced his way through the crowd.

"O king, do not allow strangers to influence our people! They only want to take possession of the land. If Bhutani wants to show himself, let him do so to us, the priests!"

193

"So that is the sword-man," thought Gautama. Aloud he said:

"I have come to you alone, quite unarmed. How then am I to conquer your land?"

"Yes, he means well by us!" shouted most of the men.

But the priest raised his hand for silence. Then he turned to Gautama:

"If Bhutani has appeared to you, he will have told you why Bhuta has to have a pig's snout."

It seemed to Gautama as though he heard the answer, so that he had only to repeat it.

"You have been grubbing after buried treasures for so long that the lips of the god have become longer and longer. It does you no credit, you Bhutanese."

"That is the right answer," said the priest, astonished. "But I do not believe you yet. First you must pass one more test."

But it was not to come to that. Holy strength so filled Gautama that it broke forth from him overwhelmingly. Dazzled, the priest shut his eyes. But Gautama, usually so gentle, cried in a thundering voice:

"It is not for you, bad leader of a deluded people, to put to the test him whom the Lord of all the Worlds Himself sends to you! You people do not deserve to be helped by Him, but for the sake of your king who grieves over you I will try to change your souls. But you, priest, conduct yourself with moderation, and do not cross my path again!"

Step by step the sword-man fell back, overawed by the words, and still more so by the radiance that shone around the stranger.

Gautama announced that he would tell stories. Anyone who liked to come would be allowed to listen. And they all came like children, seated themselves round him, and listened to what he had to say.

And it flowed to him. Was Bhutani telling him of things long past, or was another whispering the words which he was to speak? He did not question, but recounted what came to life within him.

"Long, long ago, before any of us were born, and when our great-great-grandfathers lived here, the valley between the two great rivers was inhabited by a contented, happy people. All that they needed they had in abundance. The fertile plain gave them plenty of corn and fruit, the rivers gave them fish, the thick forests provided game.

194

"Their god, whom they called Bhuta, treated them kindly. He sent out his little servants to help men also. And the little beings showed them how to make use of water and fire. They brought them metals and precious stones.

"But an evil urge awoke in the people: the lust for blood! When they killed an animal they drank of its warm blood, and often they killed for blood, and not because they needed the meat for food.

"Bhuta was angry, and forbade more killing than was absolutely necessary. For a short time the people obeyed; then they fell back into their sin.

"But then they once had a wise king . . . ."

"Bhutani, Bhutani!" shouts interrupted the narrator, proving that the people were listening with undivided attention.

"Yes, Bhutani was the name of the king," continued Gautama, who was greatly enthralled by his own account. "He heard of Bhuta's anger, and implored his people to desist from their evil habits, which had become vices. But at that time there also lived a priest, who knew just as much as the king, but who was not so good. He was in touch with forces of the Darkness, and the lord of these forces helped him to make the people forsake Bhuta and belong to him.

"This priest, whose name was Vutra, secretly told the men that drinking blood would make them strong. No one could withstand a person who drank warm blood every day. With his help, they began once more to kill as much as they could. But Bhutani appealed for Bhuta's help and was stronger than Vutra, for the Light is always stronger than the Darkness.

"To cure the people of the lust for blood, he forbade sacrifices altogether. Henceforth they prayed in purity to Bhuta. Vutra had fled, because he was afraid that they would kill him. Now the people had become better again, and Bhuta was pleased.

"Then one day he promised that the Bhutanese would find a great treasure, a sublime happiness. When Bhutani died, he would be allowed to appear once more, to tell the people that the time of fulfilment had come. A stranger to the land would help the people.

"They rejoiced, and lived in constant expectation of the time of happiness. But instead of striving to become ever purer and lighter, they sank

195

ever deeper into guilt and sin. For a long time now, Bhuta has been unable to reveal himself to any of them; for the people horrified him. They had returned to their blood-sacrifices again, even slaughtering human beings.

"Since they could no longer see Bhuta, they made images of him. These images became more and more bestial. Just look at them! The whole people were almost engulfed in filth and darkness.

"Although men do not deserve it, the Light fulfils Its promises. And so a stranger to the land has now been sent to bring to the people of Bhutan-Ara the salvation, the happiness. Look at me!"

Gautama had risen, and stood before the people with outstretched arms.

"I have come to help you! I am allowed to bring you good tidings, you poor souls."

Only a few had understood the deep significance of his words, but all had grasped that they were the depraved people for whom the time of happiness was now about to dawn. They pressed confidingly around the stranger, whom yesterday they would have gladly sacrificed.

When would he show them the buried treasure? For they were convinced that it must be a question of such a treasure. But they did not dare to urge him yet.

In the days that followed, he told them more and more about Bhuta. It was quite clear to him that this god was none other than Brahma, the merciful. For they called their great river the Brahma-Bhuta.

It was pointless to speak to the king about it, for he was just as dull-witted as his subjects. But Bhutani answered. He pointed out that the Bhutanese had come in from the east and driven out the original inhabitants, who believed in Brahma. These dispossessed people had called their river the son of Brahma, Brahmaputra. The conquerors had wanted to replace Brahma with their god, and for that reason had called the river Brahma-Bhuta.

Gautama told this to the people, who were happy to hear something so remarkable. They thought no further. Everything had to be shown to them down to the minutest detail, with explanations to try to make it clear to them. But at last they understood that Bhuta was a god of helpfulness, who expected the same from men.

But now came the difficult part: to show people that Bhuta was only a servant of an even higher God. Here, where the whole population without exception were subject only to the king, and did not know service, Gautama would find no understanding. He must clothe it in different words; this was becoming clear to him. He prayed for help, and it was given to him.

A violent storm, such as the people had never before experienced, broke out unexpectedly. And then, when the lightning had struck in various places, the king in sheer terror cried to Bhuta:

"O god, let the storm cease!"

But the tempest raged more fiercely, the lightning struck more devastatingly. Then Gautama knew that he could venture forth. He mounted a rock, so that all could see him, raised his arms and implored:

"O Eternal One, Lord of all the Worlds, reveal Thy Power to the people! Let the raging of the storm cease, deprive the lightning of its power."

Hardly had he finished than the storm abated, the thunder-claps died away. There was peace in Nature.

But the frightened people cried:

"Have you another god? He is stronger than Bhuta. We will make him our god!"

Now it was easier to speak of the Eternal One, to Whom even Bhuta was subject. Since the people were unable to grasp the concept "eternal", Gautama coined a new name: King-God.

All understood this. The King-God ruled over the gods, as Bhutani had once ruled over his people. Bhuta was one of these gods who were subject to the King-God. But they, the Bhutanese, were subject to Bhuta, from whom they took their name.

Now they understood, and rejoiced in the new recognition. Only the king was in a difficulty.

"Master," said he plaintively, "where do *I* stand? Now the men regard Bhuta as their ruler, and think they no longer need an earthly leader."

With this complaint, however, the king himself had put into Gautama's mouth the words with which he could enlighten the people. At the next opportunity he re-stated:

"At the very highest is enthroned the King-God, Who rules over the other gods. After Him comes Bhuta, who is the invisible king of the Bhutanese, and has his visible representative here in your king."

They understood that.

Then Gautama did away with the terrible idols, as well as the sacrificial festivals. He himself prayed with the people to Bhuta and to the King-God. One thing, however, caused him concern: The treasure which they should have found was the knowledge of the Eternal One; but they were expecting an earthly treasure, and in view of their spiritual limitation he could not even blame them for that.

Again he bore all his problems aloft, and left it to the Eternal One to find a way here.

He had already been a long time with the Bhutanese; for he did not wish to leave them until their hope had been fulfilled, or until they understood the spiritual fulfilment.

He had walked with some of the people as far as the mighty Brahma-Bhuta, which came rushing and thundering down from the high mountains. He had told them about servants of the King-God who invisibly guide these masses of water, but who also build up the mountains.

They had listened devoutly. They had helped him to carry the tidings of the King-God to other sections of their people. They had behaved in a more civilised way since they felt themselves to be connected with the higher realms.

One day the conversation turned to buildings. Gautama explained to them how houses were built in other countries. The king expressed the desire to own such a house, and Gautama promised to give the necessary instructions. The men, however, must undertake to burn down the old, dirty huts as soon as the new ones were built; for as soon as one house was built others would quickly follow.

First of all Gautama had an excavation made, to allow of a firm foundation for the building. And in the course of this excavation the men came upon the "treasure".

It consisted of artefacts of gold and silver, ornamented with precious stones. Apparently the original inhabitants who were driven away by the invaders had entrusted all their belongings to the earth. The men were jubilant. Gautama thanked the Eternal One, Who had thus rendered help beyond all understanding.

He then proposed that the most beautiful articles should be presented to

198

the King-God. They would build Him a temple and place the vessels in it. That made everyone happy. To begin with, a small temple was built instead of the house.

Gautama had spent two years here, but he did not regret it. With the help of the Eternal One he had been able to accomplish much. The completely brutalised people had learned to seek God, and to live as well as they could in His Laws. Gautama promised that he would send them a priest of the King-God in his stead, and then set out on the homeward journey, in spite of the fervent entreaties of the people that he stay awhile with them yet.

HIS COMPANIONS, whom he had sent home long ago, appeared punctually at the time indicated to them by the elementals. On the way they recounted what had taken place on the Mountain in the meantime, and were surprised that Gautama was aware of everything already. He smiled:

"But I told you that I would remain in contact with you. The invisible ones brought me news, and always carried back my instructions as well."

Thus he also knew that at their earnest petition the Tibetan had remained for another year, but was now about to return home. He was only awaiting Gautama's homecoming.

And Gautama rejoiced when he saw the Mountain of the Eternal One from afar. There, he felt, was his earthly home.

He was tumultuously received by his people who, although under Te-Yang they had been in the best of hands, had missed him sorely. They really sensed a difference, even though they imagined it to be due to the Tibetan's foreign origin.

Ananda had died, and been buried in a cave. A tablet stood before it, but they had waited for Gautama's return before proceeding with the inscription.

They told him that the disciple had not been willing to submit to Te-Yang's leadership. He was always grumbling that things were different in Siddharta's time. So the Lama released him from all obligation to work. With great delight Ananda had embarked on a life of ease, but a few days later he was found dead on his couch.

They expected Gautama to say:

"You see! An example of why I advised you to work!"

But he said nothing. Why should he say what they all knew?

When he was asked about the inscription, he decided that the tablet should bear the words:

"Ananda, the first disciple of Siddharta."

Suddhodana the younger begged to be allowed to accompany his brother on his journeys in future.

"To be your servant seems to me the highest earthly vocation. Let me be with you, Gautama."

And his brother promised. The youth had become a firm, upright man whose company the sage enjoyed.

Rahula had come to the Mountain to spend his year there. He was happy with the new arrangement, which would allow him to hear and see entirely new things for once, and to become completely absorbed in his thoughts. But things turned out quite differently. Gautama asked him to undertake the administration and Hours of Worship on the Mountain during these months. He himself was planning to ride out again soon, and would accompany Te-Yang part of the way.

Just now he usually called the men to the hall of the school in the evening, and told them about the savage people whom he had met. They had many questions to ask. Most of them could not imagine such brutalisation at all.

Those who had come from other places also had to report. There was a lively exchange of thoughts. Then suddenly Gautama announced that he had been commanded to leave on the following day. This time he took with him no one but Suddhodana. Te-Yang rode with them.

Again they travelled north, towards the source of the sacred river. Te-Yang and Gautama carried on learned discussions, in which the younger man took no part. But it could be seen by the sparkle in his eyes how much he joined them in thought.

Then Te-Yang had to ride on to Amritsar in accordance with the instructions sent to him, and cross the mountain-stream Salech, while the brothers turned east towards the mountains.

Now Suddhodana suddenly knew where they were going first: Kapilavastu was their destination! He had not thought that Gautama would visit his parents, he who had freed himself of all earthly ties. He voiced this, and his brother said:

"I am not going there to visit our family. I have to make decisions; what their nature will be I cannot yet say. At the right time I will come to know it. But you should enjoy the homeland, for it is probably the last time you will see it."

THEY RODE in one day unannounced, but they could not remain unrecognised. Their features betrayed their lineage. There was tremendous excitement when the royal son became known.

The news of his coming sped before him to the Palace on the hill. Lovingly he greeted his parents and his brothers and sisters, who hastened to meet him, and told them that he intended to stay with them for some time.

Little had changed in the Palace and the city. Gautama saw that his father and brother ruled the country absolutely in accordance with the teaching of the Eternal One, that they exercised a good influence on the people, and even further afield on the neighbours.

The Prince spoke about these neighbours, and Gautama soon realised that it was because of them that he had had to come.

The father of the present ruler had been able to unite three smaller principalities with a firm hand, and then called himself king. This title, together with the flourishing kingdom, had passed to his son, the present king.

The country and the people prospered, their wealth increased, their morals were pure. Everything was in as good a state as any prince could wish for. Only one thing was missing to make his happiness complete: he had no son to inherit the realm after him.

A beautiful daughter had grown up at the court of Khatmandu, and the sole wish of the ageing king was to arrange such a marriage for this daughter that blessing should arise from it for the country.

Princess Yananda, however, had the gift of sometimes seeing in her dreams things which later came true. Thus she had already seen her husband when she was quite a young girl, and she refused to marry any other prince. She described him so clearly that those who knew Siddharta-Gautama were in no doubt that he was the chosen one.

King Khat had spoken with Suddhodana. He would have been very happy if a son of that race were to take over his realm. But the Prince, who was convinced that Gautama would not give up his service for anything in the world, refused to send for his son.

Events had come thus far when Gautama arrived, unexpected and uninvited. Now the Prince thought he really saw the Hand of the Eternal One.

"Can you not be a servant of the Lord of all the Worlds even though you marry?" his father asked.

But Gautama said no, although the Prince pointed out to him how important it would be if good sons came from the marriage, who in turn would become servants of the Eternal One.

"The realm is vast and powerful, Gautama. You must remember that also. If you become king of Khatmandu you will have immense power. You will then be able to work in a completely different way to spread the teaching. You will have riches and armies behind you."

"Stop, Father," cried Gautama, with more animation than was his wont. "If the Lord of all the Worlds needs riches and power on earth, He can so arrange it. He can create a kingdom for me, so immeasurably great that we cannot envisage it .... if He so wills! But that I should break the vow I have given Him, that I should bind myself with earthly ties, is not His Will."

"Why then should He have sent you here now? Tell me that. You yourself say that you have come at the behest of the Lord!"

"Could it not be to put my steadfastness to the test?"

With this the discussion was closed for the time being, but Gautama was well aware that he had not convinced his father. And he knew that he must not leave until this matter had been finally settled.

A few days later the Prince began afresh:

"Hear me, Gautama. I have received news that King Khat wishes to see you. He will agree to anything you may demand. You can be absent from the country for months at a time, during which Yananda will rule; but do not refuse him. He would never get over it.

"He would think of us with ill-will, even become our enemy. Thus you would endanger the continuance of our realm, for he has more warriors than we. It is surely not the Will of the Lord of all the Worlds that you should stubbornly bring down such a fate upon your homeland."

Gautama was silent. He did not wish to go on giving the same answer, and yet he knew that he could never consent.

Gautama spent this night in ardent prayer. He sought a way to convince the Prince, but did not find one. Instead, some helpful being whispered a plan in his ear, a plan so daring that at first Gautama shrank from it. But the more he thought about it the more he liked it.

The following morning he went to see the Prince and asked him for a few days' leave of absence. He wanted to make his decision in solitude.

Suddhodana was glad that his son found his wish worthy of consideration. With that, he thought, the resistance was already broken.

But with the help of a faithful old servant Gautama obtained the clothes of a hunter, and went out into the forest. The elemental beings showed him the way.

On the second day Gautama came to the banks of a wonderful blue mountain lake, which mirrored the white peaks. He was completely absorbed in thought when he felt a slight tug at his clothing. He looked up and perceived a little elemental being, who signalled him to follow quietly.

A few steps brought them to an open summer-house, of which there were many in the mountains. On a couch lay a beautiful maiden, sleeping peacefully.

Gautama thought that he had never seen anything so lovely. He advanced softly. Her rich attire proclaimed the king's daughter. This must be Yananda!

What bliss to be able to call this woman one's own! What happiness to be allowed to reign over a great, well-ordered realm by her side!

Only for a moment did these thoughts awaken in Gautama. He cast them forcibly from him. Bliss? Delight? Was there any greater happiness than to be a servant of the Lord of all the Worlds? Was there any greater bliss than to know that he was allowed to bring the Truth to the people?

Away with the temptation! The temptation, which had stretched out its tentacles even towards this pure one, had to give way.

Gautama was about to withdraw as quietly as he had come. It was certainly part of his plan to meet the Princess, who had come to the lake with her attendants to enjoy the cool air; but he did not wish to come upon her unexpectedly.

Before he had reached the gate, however, she awoke. Her alarm at finding herself not alone gave way to the greatest joy. There he stood before her, he whom she had beheld in her dream!

"My husband!" she cried, still only half-awake.

Then she realised that she had betrayed herself, and did not know how to hide her embarrassment.

But Gautama, who was strengthened by the inner battle he had just fought, approached her again and spoke to her. He begged her to trust him. Very much depended on a complete understanding between them.

"Yananda," he asked earnestly. "do you believe in the Lord of the Worlds?"

"With my whole soul," was the reply.

"Do you wish to serve Him in loyalty?"

"I can think of nothing more beautiful!"

Question and answer had followed in quick succession. Then Gautama took the maiden's slender hand in his, as she stood before him in all her appealing loveliness.

"Yananda, the Eternal One calls you to service now, now! You can serve Him and our whole great people by forgetting me. Forget your dream, renounce your wishes! Earthly happiness is not for me; my life is dedicated to the highest service. Help me to leave you without thoughts of regret."

With his whole heart he besought her.

They stood in silence, face to face, each seeking to read in the soul of the other. Then Gautama began to implore the Eternal One to give Yananda power and strength. It was as though Gautama's glowing volition flowed across to the maiden. She was no longer faint-hearted.

"I will, Gautama. Tell me what I am to do."

Together they discussed the plan for the sake of which Gautama had come here. Yananda was prepared to sacrifice her whole life if it was the Will of the Eternal One. Gautama had already sacrificed his, but he did not tell her that.

They parted as friends. Never had two such pure human beings found one another in loyalty, only to give up all claim to each other in service to the Eternal One.

Not until long after Gautama had disappeared into the forest did Yananda call her women.

A few days later Gautama told his father that he would take the Princess in marriage if he were really the man whom she had seen in her dream. He would do this solely to protect his people from the enmity of King Khat.

Filled with joy, the Prince sent invitations to the King's Palace. Soon afterwards the guests appeared.

It was a solemn moment when Yananda, on her father's arm, entered the great hall, where all the nobles of the two peoples were assembled to hear her announcement. She looked indescribably lovely, although her countenance was very pale.

"See, Yananda," the King addressed his child, "here stand the noble sons of a princely race to await your choice. Look at them, and tell me, which is he who was shown to you in your dream."

All looked in suspense at the maiden, whose pale cheeks began to tinge with a rosy hue. She did not speak. Slowly her great dark eyes moved from one to the other.

"Is your future husband here?" her father wanted to know.

"Yes, Father."

Softly as a breath of air, the words fell from the beautiful lips. A joyful movement passed through the ranks, for they all knew that if the choice fell on Gautama he would no longer refuse.

"Who is it?" her father asked more urgently.

Suddhodana, who felt sorry for the embarrassed maiden in her shyness, directed that one by one the princes should bend the knee before Yananda. She could then point to the chosen one.

The first to pass before her was the future Prince Rahula, but he had to rise from his knees without Yananda having looked at him properly. Then it was Gautama's turn, but he managed to arrange it so that Suddhodana the younger went before him.

The young man gazed ecstatically into the countenance that bent graciously over him.

"This is he, Father," whispered the maiden.

Endless jubilation surged through the hall. Even though no one had imagined that the younger brother would supplant the elder, it now seemed credible to all. Suddhodana was very like Gautama, but not so unapproachable as his brother.

There was a babble of voices, and no one noticed that in this moment two human hearts had to suffer the bitterest renunciation for the sake of their loyalty.

Feast followed on feast, in which Gautama took little part. Everyone understood that he now wished to return to his work. But Suddhodana approached his brother and asked:

"Will you release me, Gautama? I wanted to serve you with my whole life!"

"You will do that, brother, only in a different way from how you understand it now."

For the first time, Gautama had called him brother. And Suddhodana found it harder than he had thought to tear himself away from the young Master.

But Gautama rode south, solitary and alone.

YEARS HAD passed in which the stream of happenings flowed evenly on. It had carried away the old and cast ashore the new. And then years had rushed past in which events swept by as if in a roaring whirlwind.

It was as though the Eternal One had wished to show men what affliction is, so that in their misery they might learn to stretch up their hands in longing.

The sacred river had to forget that it symbolised a source of fertility for those who lived near it. Irresistibly it overflowed its banks, flooding fields and villages, so that death and destruction followed the retreating waves in place of flowering life.

Mud covered the land, mud in which the loathsome gavials wallowed far inland, up to the dwellings of men. After that the ardently prayed-for rain failed to appear. Rivers and ditches dried up, many thousands of waterwheels stood still, the harvests withered, and grim famine tormented man and beast.

A great plague stalked the land; severe epidemics followed, again bringing with them death in the most terrible form.

Then tormented mankind cried out, but only a very small part stretched beseeching hands upwards. Many, very many groaned and lamented in dull despair, without seeking deliverance anywhere.

For their faith had taught them that what comes cannot be altered. It had to be accepted, death would bring release. The poor souls would find rest in Nirvana.

And the others clenched their fists and learned to curse. Destruction to those who did not think of helping! Vengeance to the powers which inexorably pursued their appointed course! How they pictured vengeance they did not know. But cursing relieved their minds, and made them feel that they were still something.

Weeping with those who wept, powerless and despondent, the Brahmans tried at least to console the people. They referred to Brahma, who would not be angry for ever. One day he would have to let the sun of his grace shine again. Whoever could endure until then would be doubly helped. The more they realised that they could do nothing to relieve this affliction and suffering, the more eagerly they pointed to the future. They became ingenious in painting pictures of all the good that one day would come again to mankind.

They gave no account of how they pictured the fulfilment of their utterances, which sounded like soothsaying. Probably they thought as little about what they said as did those who were cursing. All that mattered to them was to silence everything with words.

But Gautama and his followers had become silent amid the happenings, in which they clearly sensed the Hand of the Lord of all the Worlds. They were careful not to lead the faint-hearted on to wrong courses through empty consolation. The Eternal One wanted to rouse the people from their sleep! They must not sing lullabies to them.

All that the people had brought upon themselves must work itself out, but it must do so in the right way if it was to become a blessing. Hundreds were perishing, not because of a destructive rage, but because they would not listen at the right time.

Where despairing ones came with questions, they received as good an answer as the servants of the Eternal One could give. Where in awakening a soul grasped the outstretched hand, it was held fast, and drawn up out of destruction and ruin.

The Brothers and Sisters worked tirelessly in the service of others, in the service of their Lord. But Gautama performed superhuman feats. He was always to be found where things were at their worst. His helpers showed him the most threatened places.

When he appeared, the tormented people breathed a sigh of relief. The cursing ones lowered their fists for a short time, and looked to him who towered above them all like a rock of salvation. Many a one learned to recognise his salvation, and let himself be guided.

Gautama often said to the Brothers that it was much easier to come to grips with those reviling in despair than with those who were sinking away in dull submission. Only very few of these could be pulled up, in spite of the most loving efforts. They would not let themselves be saved.

While some principalities and kingdoms had escaped lightly, others had been terribly ravaged by death and destruction. The south of the country had been spared the worst. The River Krishna had dispensed its waters steadily, so that the failure of the rain could do less harm than elsewhere.

Good news also came from the united kingdoms of Suddhodana and Khat. On the other hand, things were bad in the plain of the Bhutanese. The river had swallowed up most of their homes, it had even carried away the temple. Fields and herds of cattle were destroyed. The soil was untilled, because there were no men to cultivate it.

But greedy hordes invaded from the north-east, and took possession of the deserted estates. Their ravaging was worse even than that of the Bhutan people at one time. They brought with them horrible graven images, their idols demanded bloody sacrifices. And they took these sacrifices from the inhabitants of the country. They were a much bigger and stronger race than the Indus people, whom they easily subdued.

And then the tormented neighbours sent word to Gautama on the Mountain of the Eternal One. But he knew about it already, and had considered what was to be done. To him personally, bloodshed in any form was abhorrent; and yet he realised that here armed force must be used in good time to put a stop to it, lest the harm should penetrate even further into the realms.

Evil emanated from this eastern corner. Had the Eternal One allowed the Bhutanese, who were lapsing once more into their old state of

208

depravity, to perish so that now others who were even worse, real devils in human form, should murderously attack the neighbouring countries?

Here he could produce no remedy with words. And day after day, night after night, he prayed and begged for clarity. And before he had gained this clarity the cry for help came from the plain.

But it seemed as though the cry had rent the last veils that hung before clear recognition. Suddenly Gautama knew what had to be done.

Those who were affected must pull themselves together. Trusting in the help from above, they must resist the enemies from the Darkness valiantly and resolutely. Suddhodana must lead them, he who had led so many trained soldiers to battle!

Gautama himself rode to the afflicted ones, and put fresh heart into them with his words. He showed them that even this distress was a means employed by the Eternal One to awaken the people and make them strong.

"You must fight for yourselves, then the Lord of the Worlds will help you," he called to the faint-hearted.

And they pulled themselves together.

Gautama had sent messengers to Kapilavastu and Khatmandu. He knew that the Princes would do what was right without the need for his presence, and he was not mistaken. Even before the soldiers from the mountains arrived, Gautama had returned to his task, which enjoined works of peace upon him.

The affliction that had come upon the lands had called forth completely new thoughts in many a one. Many souls had to be strengthened; others, wavering ones, had to be won. But often there came Brothers who, quite independent of one another, suggested that a bridge should be made between the belief in the Eternal One and the teaching of the Brahmans.

Gautama could not understand this request. Again and again he pointed out that the Brahmans only needed to open their eyes to be able to see that they had stopped half-way.

No bridge was needed here. They only had to move on from the gods to God. It was so simple and self-evident.

Gautama understood that the Brahmans, who in developing their doctrine had become entangled in a web of human thoughts, could not recognise this simplicity because they just did not want to. But that the Brothers, who had the Truth, should consider such a bridge necessary was beyond his understanding.

He did not send them away when they approached him with these questions. He listened to them patiently, and tried to show them what was wrong in their thinking. But in their view the fact that so many of them wanted the same thing was an indication of the need for it. Gautama shook his head uncomprehendingly.

"And if we really could and should build such a bridge, what benefit do you expect from it?"

"We should live in brotherly harmony with the followers of the Brahmans, all peoples would unite in resistance to diverse teachings, which so-called wise men like Djinna bring into the country."

"Do you not live in brotherly harmony with the others?" asked Gautama in surprise. "Surely you have been forbidden any discord on matters of faith."

Then they had to admit that nowhere had the harmony been disturbed. Nevertheless, they considered it better to proceed together.

Now Gautama no longer answered them, but laid all these thoughts in prayer before the Eternal One. He knew that he must stand firm for the purity of the faith; but how was he to convince the others?

A few days later he sent a message through the whole country. All Brothers and Sisters who were in favour of fraternising with the Brahmans and their teaching were to be on the Mountain of the Eternal One on a certain day. But only they should come; meanwhile the others should carry on their work.

He had been afraid that he had expressed his own thinking too clearly in the tone of his message, and perhaps thereby prevented some of the waverers from coming, but this was not the case.

The Brothers came in large numbers, glad that in this way many a one would be given the opportunity to be on the Mountain. But the Sisters were absent. Not a single one had joined them.

Not far from the convent, Gautama had had a large space prepared to receive the people. The Temple hall would not have contained the crowd.

But also it was repugnant to Gautama to discuss such things in the Temple of the Eternal One. He, otherwise so imperturbable, found it difficult not to be overcome by indignation; again and again he prayed for calm and equanimity.

Now the hour had come in which Gautama was to speak to the Brothers, who surrounded him in a semi-circle.

Searchingly he let his gaze wander over the assembly, and was glad to see that those whom he had always considered the best were absent on this occasion. So he was not quite alone in his thinking.

After first invoking the Blessing of the Lord of all the Worlds in a loud, fervent prayer, he began to speak slowly. In a few words he put before them the wish of those present: to make a bridge between the teaching of the Brahmans and the teaching of the Eternal One.

Then he was silent. Surely they must see how impossible their demand was! But they did not see it. They gazed at the speaker with eager expectation.

So he continued. His voice, low at first, rose higher; it swelled to a hurricane which roared over them all. He began by showing them that water was a wonderful drink, intended to revive the thirsty. Milk too was a restorative for many. But if milk and water are mixed, water ceases to be a refreshment, milk loses its power to strengthen the weak.

"You understand that. But why will you not understand that it would be unpardonable weakness to mix the richly-bubbling spring of the knowledge of the Eternal One with a teaching which in itself is not wrong, but came to a standstill in its early stages?

"There is no bridge between the Brahmans and us! *They* must take the step to recognition of the Lord of all the Worlds. For that we offer them a helping hand. But we must not go to meet them, because in doing so we should be going backwards."

He was silent for a few moments, and let his eyes rove searchingly over the assembly, to see by the lighting-up of individual faces whether his words had struck home. Disappointed, he continued:

"Imagine a deep ditch. After endless efforts we have got across, and are now standing safely on the firm ground. But the Brahmans are toiling on the other side, not daring to take the decisive step which would bring them over.

"We stretch out our hands to help them. But they do not grasp these

211

hands. Should we then go down to them in the ditch, into which perhaps they would leap from their side, only to be together with them? How could we benefit them by that? But it would harm us.

"I believe you have understood me now, dear friends. I feel the barriers which have surrounded you falling away. Give thanks with me to the Eternal One for His Grace in allowing us to recognise Him! But this Grace imposes obligations on us. Not one step may we deviate from the path that leads us to Him. Not a single detour may we make."

When he had finished he sent them into the gardens. They were to reflect on his speech without discussing it among themselves. When he called them again, those who still had doubts should express them freely.

He dared not hope that none would raise objections; and indeed several of the younger and even some of the older Brothers were anxious to speak.

One of them wanted to know why they had given up the teaching of the Brahmans, and yet still spoke to people about Shiva, Vishnu and the others. His objection was applauded.

Again Gautama was confronted with a problem.

"Dear friends," he said, forcing himself to appear calm. "I told you that the teaching of the Brahmans, as it was in the beginning, was right. It has simply remained in the bud. But if it was right, why should we not make use of it in order to speak more intelligibly to people? You yourselves know that Vishnu, Shiva and the others really exist. Yet they are not gods, but servants of the Eternal One!"

"We have no need to go down into the ditch to the Brahmans," objected another. "We must stretch a plank over to them, on which they can come to us."

"How do you picture this plank?" asked Gautama kindly.

"I do not know. If we are prepared to extend this help across to them, surely we shall find it."

"Those are empty words," cried another of the Brothers, irritated. "I understand now what Gautama means. We may not deviate one step from our teaching. If others wish to have it, *they* must take the steps that lead to it. A plank cannot be placed over the ditch, there is no such plank."

Another Brother suggested that they should try to win the Brahmans over by promising that if they believed in the Eternal One they would be allowed to continue as priests. This suggestion met with the indignation it deserved.

After many hours, Gautama was able to let the Brothers go, in the firm conviction that now they were all of one mind, and had given up their strange ideas.

This day had wearied him, he who usually knew no fatigue. With slow steps he walked up to the monastery, seeking out a small cell that lay a little apart.

There by the window, in the last ray of the setting sun, sat a very old man, who joyfully turned his face with its weatherbeaten features to the visitor.

When he recognised Gautama, childlike happiness beamed from his eyes. These eyes had remained young, young too was the soul of which they spoke.

"Maggalana, Father, I come to you because I am weary," Gautama greeted the old man.

As he spoke he went to him, and sat down on a fur rug at his feet. It was his accustomed place. Gently the old man's hand stroked the brow of the man looking up at him.

"I see that you are tired, and the day has not satisfied you. Have you not been able to convince the foolish ones?"

"I have, Father. In the end they understood what was at issue. But that they could come with such suggestions at all proves to me that they no longer know what the treasure which they possess is. That saddens me. Instead of letting the knowledge of the Eternal One grow ever deeper – how little do we really know of Him – they want to adulterate and corrupt it with human thoughts!

"And now that they have understood at last how wrong what they had in mind is, their thoughts will not rest until they have discovered something else, perhaps even more foolish.

"Then I shall have to confront that. But how long shall I still be here to do so? Is the teaching to fall apart after my death, as though it originated from human beings?"

"Gautama, I do not know you in this despondency," Maggalana reproved him gently. "From Whom does the teaching come? Who revealed Himself to Siddharta? Why did the Eternal One do so? Surely not to let His

213

Truth dwell among men but a short time. When you are called away, my son, other hands will be there to take up the threads which you must leave behind. It is the concern of the Lord of all the Worlds, do not forget that!"

"You are right, my father. I am ashamed of my weakness. Nor is it right to allow myself to be so wearied by people."

It grew dark in the little room, but it suited the two who sat there. An intimate trust, which made both happy, had blossomed between them in the course of years.

Gautama had become used to speaking to Maggalana of things which occupied him deeply. The old man never thrust any advice on him. It was just as though Gautama found an echo in the soul of the other, through which things became clear to him more quickly.

Today for the first time he had let him see his grief over mankind, which often stole silently upon him.

Then they spoke peacefully of other things. Maggalana told him what he had written during the day. And then Gautama asked him about the early days of the Mountain. The old man particularly loved speaking of that, and Gautama always learned from it.

"I shall soon have to set forth again," he declared suddenly. "Perhaps I shall join the Brothers who will be returning to Magadha. Maggalana, would you not like to see your old homeland again?"

"My home is here, Gautama, nowhere else," the old man replied. "But my days are numbered. See to it that you do not stay away too long, for I should like you to help me to depart."

"Our elemental friends will bring me tidings when you are about to leave this cloak, my father," Gautama assured him. Then he left him.

A FEW DAYS later he rode away from the Mountain with the last of the Brothers. He had still been waiting for news from the east. Although the fighting was not quite over, Suddhodana and his allies had nevertheless succeeded in driving the intruders out across the frontiers of the realm.

Impassable conditions in the mountains and unfamiliarity with the country prevented them from pursuing the intruders there. Instead, Sud-

214

dhodana wanted to build a fortified wall between the mountains, to keep hostile neighbours away.

Gautama agreed with that. He could calmly leave all these cares in the hands of King Suddhodana. His brother understood him absolutely, and strove at all times to act in accordance with the Eternal Laws.

Had he understood what a sacrifice he too had had to make, Gautama wondered? Or was he untroubled in his happiness? Gautama never dared to ask. News of the family life of his dear ones never penetrated to him.

He was still convinced that he could not have acted in any other way. And whenever he thought of Yananda, he strove to see in her the Queen of Khatmandu.

The little band was on the road for days; daily its members dwindled. Ever again Brothers whose path branched off departed. Finally he remained alone with two very young people from Magadha.

They were so filled with awe that they did not dare to speak. Gautama did not notice. He was completely engrossed in thought. Nor had he paid any attention to the sky, where the clouds were massing ominously. His little friends tried in vain to warn him. He did not heed them.

Then suddenly the storm broke out with tremendous violence. It was impossible to ride on. He turned to ask the Brothers if they knew of any village nearby.

"There is no village near or far," said one of the two diffidently. "But behind yonder hill is a large Brahman monastery. We could reach it quickly. But you may not wish to ask for shelter there."

"Why not?" Gautama wondered. "Surely they will not turn us away."

They rode quickly on the road indicated, and soon found themselves at the gates of the imposing monastery. Gautama had never entered one like it before. He looked forward with interest to what he would find there.

The drenched travellers were warmly received, and provided with dry clothing. In the darkness, which was only lit up occasionally by lightning, the Brahman who received them had paid no attention to what they were wearing.

Thus it was that when they came to the meal in the simple clothing that had been given to them they were taken for ordinary travellers.

The violent storm had now abated, but the rain was still coming down in torrents, so that there was no question of travelling further until the next day.

No one asked for their names. They were treated kindly, and the residents were happy that the travellers joined in the prayer to Shiva. After they had eaten rice and fruit, the monks remained in the great hall, and invited the guests to do likewise.

Gradually a conversation developed, which however was restricted at first to the most commonplace superficialities. Gautama asked about the hardships of the past years, and learned that in Magadha also they had been bearable.

"That is because we in this realm have remained for the most part loyal to the old faith. The gods have obviously rewarded us for our loyalty," said one of the Brahmans sagely.

"But in the region of Utakamand there was no damage whatever," objected Gautama. "And yet all the people there believe not only in the gods but also in the Lord of the Worlds."

"Who has told you that the adherents of the new faith have remained faithful to our gods?" an old Brahman wanted to know. "Surely there is only Either – Or. Either they believe in the gods as we do and as all our forefathers did, or they adhere to the new god and spurn the old."

"Why should they spurn the old ones?" Gautama, who was enjoying this conversation, wanted to know. "They believed in them also. If they have now found the One Who stands above the gods, surely they have only taken a further step upwards, which should make you rejoice."

The Brahmans looked at the speaker in astonishment.

"Are you also perhaps one of those who have taken this step?" they asked.

Gautama answered in the affirmative. They looked at him suspiciously. They had heard that the adherents of the new teaching were easily recognisable by their suspicious looks and their conceit. Here they found nothing of either. On the contrary, the more closely they looked at the guest the more they liked him.

"You seem to be sincere. Tell us about your teaching," they invited him.

No one could speak as he did. It was as though golden veils were woven

216

around them, golden veils which covered something holy, and which the speaker drew off one by one.

He spoke of their gods as no one had ever spoken before. They had become something commonplace to them, now they had meaning.

Gautama presented them in their work, in their service, to which the Lord of all the Worlds had appointed them. But he spoke also of the little servants, who carry out the commands of the Eternal One everywhere. All this stood before their spiritual eye like a building that has been well planned.

It had grown dark, they had not noticed it. Serving brothers now came with little lamps and food. Gautama had to break off, and one of the Brahmans expressed what they all felt:

"Whoever you are, stranger, you have been blessed above thousands! You have built a glorious temple in our hearts. Stay with us until you have placed in it the image of the One for Whom the temple was built."

Gautama could think of nothing better. He gladly agreed, and only sent home the two Brothers, who were completely filled by the great something which they had been allowed to experience. He did not wish to ask for hospitality for them also.

Day after day he proclaimed the Lord of all the Worlds, and in the hearts of these upright people he kindled a longing to become His servants also. They were allowed to put forward all their objections and questions, and received satisfactory answers.

Then they wanted to know what they must do to obtain the new faith. Gautama pointed out that they already had it, because they were convinced of the Invisible, Eternal God.

"Do we not need to renounce the old faith?" one of the Brahmans enquired.

"No, certainly not; for you have kept the old teaching pure, without human thoughts and additions. So you can keep what you had, and you have received something new as well."

"How shall we show that we now wish to be servants of the Eternal One?"

"Quite simply by your life! Believe in Him, proclaim Him, and keep to His paths. But I shall ask the Brothers in Magadha to visit you from time to time, and advise you. Perhaps one of you will also come to the Mountain of the Eternal One some day. To do so you need only join the Brothers."

Then they ventured the question that had long been on their minds: "What are we to call you, Master?"

Calmly Gautama told them his name, which was unknown to them. He preferred this to having them now revere him on account of it. He stayed with them a few days longer, and then rode away.

If only all the Brothers who had wanted to build a bridge could have shared this experience with him! How simple it had been to induce these Brahmans to take the last step. They had done so without any persuasion, entirely of their own accord, after they had come to recognition. That was how it must be! Moreover, these Brahman Brothers would continue to speak of it among their fellows. A beginning had been made.

Gautama was joyfully received at the school in Magadha, which had become one of the most important in the whole country. The young Brothers had described the conversations on the Mountain.

Now all wanted to know what Gautama had achieved among the Brahmans. His success was irrefutable proof of the rightness of his thinking. At the same time it was an example and guide-line for them.

The Master did not stay here long. He felt drawn to Utakamand, the only school which had not sent any Brothers to the meeting. Rahula's influence on the Brothers was strong, and his views always coincided with those of Gautama. They never needed to confer together, and yet they enjoyed doing so.

Deep in thought, Gautama rode thither. He had refused any escort. He remembered Siddharta, who had often travelled this way. He thought of the mango tree under which his grandfather had received such high revelations.

An ardent wish to be worthy of similar grace arose in him. And – without his being conscious of it – this wish became a prayer which, borne by the purest intuitive perceiving, mounted aloft.

Engrossed in thought, he had paid no heed to the road. Now night fell, and he did not know where he was. Fortunately it was a starlit night, no storm threatened.

The elementals would keep snakes and other dangerous creatures from him, so he had no need to light a fire. There was plenty to feed his horse; it made no difference to him if he had nothing to eat.

So he decided to spend the night here, not far from a little watercourse, rather than ride on and perhaps lose his way.

Tired, he dismounted, and stretched himself on the soft grass. How big and sparkling the stars were! Wondrous works of Creation, like all else. He gazed at them with ever-growing admiration.

Then it seemed to him that they were coming nearer. At the same time he felt a lightness, as though he were being loosened from his body. Then he noticed that the stars were not coming nearer; but that he was moving towards them. Was he already far away from the earth, he wondered.

He looked down curiously and saw himself stretched out on the grass asleep. Then he realised that his soul was being allowed to wander, and great joy filled him.

But now he no longer noticed where he was going. He felt himself gliding into a world of sounds and light, the details of which he was unable to grasp.

Enchanting beauty surrounded him; but then the sounds grew fainter, the colourful rays faded, the floating ceased.

He found himself in a meadow, in which stood some isolated trees. Everything looked unreal, and yet he was able to walk on the ground, softly and lightly, as though he were weightless. No animal, no human being was near, no spirit being. All was dead and still. But where was he?

Slowly his eyes became accustomed to his surroundings, and then he saw a well made of stone in the middle of the wide plain. He walked towards it.

Now he saw a man bending over the side of the well, apparently to look down into the depths. Then the man stood back, took a few steps in a certain direction, but – as though drawn by force – he returned to the well.

Now Gautama had reached him. It was Siddharta!

What could there be for him to see? Gautama's soul sought to address him, but it could not. Siddharta did not even notice him. He was completely engrossed in what he saw. Then he pulled himself together and walked a little further. Gautama made use of the moment to look for himself over the edge of the well.

It went deep, deep down. But there was no water below, only a landscape, in which people were moving about. It was the Mountain of the

219

Eternal One. Just as he had recognised this, Siddharta approached again, pushed the gazing soul aside with an unconscious movement of the hand, and leaned over the wall again.

Gautama stood, deeply moved. Sounds and colours, rays and beauty, but with them also warmth came back. Suddenly he found himself lying once more in the grass by the watercourse. His horse had nudged him with its nose.

What was the significance of this experience? It was meant to tell him something, he was convinced. Why did Siddharta gaze unceasingly down this deep shaft? Was something unusual taking place on the Mountain? Was it threatened?

Now Gautama became anxious, and earnestly besought his guide to come to his aid. Then he felt his helper near him. And his voice rang out:

"Siddharta clung with his soul to people and country! True, he served the Eternal One, but only in his people. He is still firmly linked with that part of the earth on which he lived. He cannot release his soul from it.

"A long time must pass before he gains the strength, in recognition and then in volition, to continue his upward journey, which has only just begun. He will be allowed to ascend, but only when all these bonds and fetters fall away from him, severed by himself.

"But you, Gautama, have been allowed to see!"

The voice was silent. The reclining man fell into a deep, refreshing sleep. But when he awoke, the vision and the words of his guide remained in his mind.

Now he knew why just this had been shown to him: he too had begun to feel anxiety about the fate of his people, to become despondent at the thought that he must leave them!

Did he want to fall into the same error as Siddharta? Chilling dread passed through him. Anything but that!

"Eternal One, I thank Thee. Henceforth I will serve Thee better!"

After a bathe in the little cold stream had revived him, he rode on, found the right way, and arrived in Utakamand before evening.

Utakamand had grown, new buildings had had to be erected. Besides the schools and monasteries there were now workshops, where objects of beauty were fashioned.

220

Besides the production of silk in the extensive mulberry-groves, the women were engaged in spinning and weaving. They dyed the materials that they made in subtle, unusual colours.

"What do you do with such quantities of material, Rahula?" asked Gautama.

"What we do not need ourselves we take to the cities on the coast. Often ships call there, which offer precious things in return for these fabrics. Thus we get elephants' tusks in exchange, from which we carve bowls and dishes, vases and ornamental pins. You must come and see our carved work, Gautama."

And Rahula led his guest into extensive halls in which young people were busily at work. Under their skilled fingers arose masterpieces of carving, which as Rahula explained would later be taken away by ships. They received other things in exchange for them.

"Why do you do this, Rahula?" Gautama wanted to know. "Until now our schools have been the sources from which man was permitted to draw the knowledge of the Eternal One. Now they seem to me like workshops and trading centres."

He did not say this with disapproval, but his question showed that he did not understand it at all.

Rahula smiled.

"Our schools can still be likened to the clear fount. But the number of pupils had grown too large. How were we to feed them? Besides, they easily got used to idleness and daydreaming, to which our people have a tendency in any case.

"Then one night this way was shown to me. Now the pupils, men and women, have to work to earn their livelihood. Certain hours of the day are devoted to instruction, others to absorbing.

"Everything is exactly regulated, and we believe that no one loses anything through it. When the young people leave us, in addition to the best, the knowledge of the Eternal One, they have other things that they have learned, which will let them continue to earn their bread. But we retain the most skilled ones as teachers in the workshops, and they are happy to stay."

This pleased Gautama, especially when, after repeated visits to the

221

schools, he had convinced himself that teachers as well as pupils stood on a very high spiritual level.

"Have you completely given up the work on the sick and needy, Rahula?" he asked one day.

"No, the Yellow Brothers still carry it on," was the reply. "But what they receive for it is just sufficient for the monasteries and convents. We have to help ourselves."

Rahula had something more to show his guest. He led him into a workshop in which chalices were made of precious metal. They were cast in various sizes, and took the form of a lotus-flower. Then the young people used sharp instruments to etch on them the fine veins that run through the leaves. Glorious effects of light and shade were achieved by these etchings.

Gautama took one of the little works of art in his hand and examined it closely.

"It is very beautiful," he then said, "but it is almost a pity to sell it. What will you do with it?"

"We wish to present one such chalice to every Temple of the Eternal One," said Rahula joyfully. "We have been saving for a long time to be able to buy the silver and gold. We have instituted a third fast day in the month so that we may all contribute. Sometimes too we have received more than we expected for our work. The surplus was also handed to me. Now the chalices are almost finished, and we can take them to the Temples. That will be a great Festival for us all."

Gautama saw ever more clearly that, as before, Utakamand was the model for all other schools, monasteries and convents. Nowhere else was the high spiritual knowledge interwoven so simply and naturally with hardworking daily life.

"I had meant to ask you, Rahula, to return with me to the Mountain, to take over the management there for another year. But now I dare not call you away before the chalices are finished."

"I shall be glad to go with you, Gautama," was the friendly reply. "It will be more than a year before the great number of chalices are ready. And there are several Brothers here who can act on my behalf."

Gautama recounted his experience in the Brahman monastery, and asked whether Rahula had had any similar experiences.

222

"We live in peace with the few Brahmans who are still in our district," said Rahula. "From time to time one of them comes to us to ask about our teaching. We always sense whether he is prompted by curiosity or longing. We answer accordingly.

"Some old Brahmans have recognised the Lord of all the Worlds, and teach about Him. Generally their pupils then also come to us for some months or years. The others, who are afraid to go forward, do not trouble us."

Then Rahula enquired which of Siddharta's disciples were still alive.

"Only the two from Magadha," answered Gautama. "And they are very, very old. But whereas Maggalana is still amazingly active, 'King' Bimbisara, as he likes to be called again, is happy to do nothing.

"We have lodged him in a small, uncomfortable cell in the monastery, to force him into helping with the work in some way or other; but he knows how to make himself a comfortable couch in the open, or to sleep in a corner of the school hall. He grows more and more spiritually indolent, whereas Maggalana has remained young and fresh."

"Does he still write stories?"

"Very seldom. He says that the source has run dry. Instead he makes transcripts of valuable documents, which we are then able to pass on to other schools. He has also tried to record the life-story of Siddharta, but it did not get past the beginning."

"And yet that particular life would be worth recording. How wonderfully the Master was guided. You and I experience nothing in comparison to him."

"Would you change places?" asked Gautama, through whose soul passed the memory of his nocturnal experience.

"Certainly not."

It seemed as though Rahula was about to add something more, but he refrained.

A FEW DAYS after that, they rode northwards, accompanied by a servant. Rahula wanted to go westwards to the ocean, to show Gautama the beauty of the rocky coast.

They rode round a fairly high mountain-range, on whose slopes grew plants that were new to them. They looked like little trees, with branches spreading from the roots. Heart-shaped leaves, fresh and green, swayed on slender stalks.

While Rahula, after the first look of admiration, paid no further attention to the shrubs, Gautama could not take his eyes or his thoughts from them. He deliberately chose his resting-place so that he would have the strange plants within sight.

"Little guardians of the plants, show me their qualities," he begged.

For some time now he had seemed to see the elementals flitting among the strange little stems. They came willingly at his call. They showed him how these stems seemed to consist almost entirely of fibres like raffia, which were brownish and strong. Gautama twisted them in his fingers, and the little beings said happily:

"That's right!"

Gautama had taken some longer fibres and was beginning to fasten them to a branch and twist them into long cords, which seemed to be very strong. Certainly these cords could be put to many uses. Could the fibres also be intertwined, or interwoven?

Rahula awoke and looked in amazement at his companion, who instead of sleeping was busily at work.

"See what I have found, Rahula," cried Gautama joyfully. "The elemental beings have shown me the fibres of those shrubs. These cords will be more durable than the threads which we spin from cotton. They are also stronger than the raffia with which the women weave their mats. Thank you, little ones!"

A few days later, when they had journeyed right round the foot-hills of the mountain-range, they found fertile plains with wide fields of rice and millet. And in the distance, as they turned more to the west, shimmered the blue sea.

One day they stood on the edge of one of the numerous cliffs along the coast, and gazed in wonder at the majestic waves rolling towards them. Now they washed over the beach, then again they were dashed to pieces, and dissolved in a spray of white foam.

224

"Do you see the beings riding on the waves?" asked Gautama. Smiling, Rahula shook his head.

"I can only imagine them. As a child I sometimes saw friendly little beings; now they elude me. But I am glad that you can see them. Are they like the little manikins who showed you the raffia the other day?"

"No, they are quite different. Gossamer bodies nestle to the movements of the waves, fluttering light hair mingles with the foam. Delicate hands bear shells and seaweeds, or catch fish and other creatures further out. They are the ones which seem to me to be feminine.

"Others, sturdier in build, though still transparent and delicate, drive the waves. They stretch their arms aloft in jubilant delight. If a wave drives them on to the cliffs, they swing themselves up as high as they can, and plunge back into their watery element with cries of joy.

"It is all beautiful; the longer one looks, the more one is able to see!

"If only I could show that to men!" resumed Gautama, after a thoughtful pause. "If only they would grasp it aright! It would so link them with all parts of Creation that it would become impossible for them to live against the Laws. Surely men must once have been thus intimately connected with Nature. What drove them on to other courses?"

"That wretched, obstinate would-be-knowledge, Gautama," replied Rahula solemnly. "Tell men something, and they will immediately weave their own thoughts around it, dim their view of the simple and natural, and boast about their self-discovered knowledge, severing all connection with what is not human like themselves. Believe me, he who would slay the intellect in men would be doing a good deed."

"And yet even the intellect is a gift of the Eternal One," replied Gautama. "You could just as well say that because fire often causes harm if man does not guard it, all fires should be extinguished. No, Rahula, we must not say 'slay', but rather, 'use aright'."

In the days that followed, the mountains came ever nearer to the sea. A time came when the riders had to look for a passage, so that they should not be impeded in their journey north. They both found it hard to leave the blue waves, which extended westwards into vast distances.

Now they were rapidly approaching familiar regions, occasionally encountering monasteries, convents and schools, as well as villages, in the

225

centre of which stood a small Temple of the Eternal One. They were joyfully received everywhere, and urged to stay. There were many questions to be answered.

In the region through which they rode first, prolonged drought had destroyed the entire cotton harvest.

So Gautama directed the people to fetch from the mountains the plants which the elementals had shown to him. He asked Rahula to ride on ahead and take charge of the administration on the Mountain of the Eternal One. He himself went with a party into the mountainous country to find the plant, which the helpers had called "yuta".

He showed them that they must not take the freshly-sprouting little stems, but the dry ones. They gathered whole bales of them, and returned with heavily-laden pack-horses.

Now began brisk activity. Under Gautama's direction the fibres were extracted, and then twisted together. The more successful they were, the greater was the people's joy. The women tried interlacing and interweaving the fibres, and both methods produced durable coarse materials which were suitable for mats and things of that kind.

"We can also use these strong pieces to wrap goods in," declared one of the men. "I do not think any rain will penetrate."

They tried it and found that he was right. Unless rain poured on to it virtually for days on end, not a drop would penetrate the fabric.

But then some of the women had not woven the material so closely; the fibres were loosely spaced.

"What are we to do with that?" they complained.

And the principal of the nearby convent knew what to do.

"Let us try to use such fabrics for collecting salt," she suggested. "Just as we now let sea-water wash over branched saplings, and dry them in the sun, so it must be possible to make use of this loosely-woven fabric."

This too was good advice. Gautama told the happy, and thus receptive people about the little beings who had taught him how to use the fibres. They all listened gladly, but only in a few cases was a connection possible between man and the helping servants of the Eternal One.

A few weeks later Gautama followed Rahula, and arrived on the Mountain without further delay. There he was met with the news of Bimbisara's death. Only after hard struggles had his soul broken away from his body. It seemed as though he had been determined to remain on earth.

When he was alone with Gautama, Maggalana described how Bimbisara had come to him on the last day of his life and complained of declining physical strength.

"Perhaps I should not have drifted so in the last years," he had said. "Indeed I can tell from your appearance how work keeps you fresh, and yet you are older than myself. If there is a beyond, as Gautama tries to show us, then I hope to be allowed to make good my negligence over there. For believe me, Maggalana, in spite of my love of ease, I am a true servant of the Lord of all the Worlds."

Gautama looked earnestly at the speaker.

"He has recognised his failing, Maggalana, but only on the other side will he have to feel the full weight of it," he said. "I am sorry that I did not after all force the old man to bestir himself. Perhaps in that way I could have spared him some of the things he now has to answer for."

"What inscription will be put on his tablet?" Maggalana wanted to know.

"King Bimbisara of Magadha," replied Gautama. "He attached so much importance to his title that because of it he finally forgot to be a servant of the Eternal One."

ONCE MORE Gautama rode forth. This time his way was to lead him to the east, from whence the invaders had now been driven. He wanted to see the wall that had been built; moreover he longed to know in what state the once ravaged country now was.

He did not wish to go to Kapilavastu or Khatmandu. But involuntarily his thoughts often turned there, and faint tidings came to him. Suddhodana the elder had been allowed to depart this life, as also had King Khat, who had already handed over the government to the younger Suddhodana some time ago.

Rahula reigned in Kapilavastu, and was the happy father of a healthy son, whereas the marriage of Yananda and Suddhodana had so far been denied the heir. Several lovely girls played around their parents, but their wish for a son had remained unfulfilled.

227

Could Yananda have made the sacrifice in vain? Suddenly as it had arisen, with equal haste did Gautama push this thought from him. Best not to think! What had happened could no longer be changed. And it had been done in purest volition.

The country of the Bhutanese still showed all the traces of the great battle which had raged there. As yet not a single temple had been rebuilt, hardly a field was cultivated, even though the region was fertile. Great expanses of forest seemed to have gone up in flames.

People whom he asked about this confirmed that the savages had set fire to the forests in order to set up a barrier between themselves and the advancing soldiers. There had been a lack of rain and the trees were dry and parched. It had taken immense efforts to bring the fire under control.

"But Suddhodana was able to command the fire-spirits," said an old man. "He begged them to consume no more than was absolutely necessary. And the fire died out after a few days."

But the fire-spirits had told them that they should leave the ashes on the ground. Thereby the soil would become twice as fertile after the next rain.

That was also why no stumps had been cleared yet, so that the soil would have time to absorb the strengthening. Only then would they be able to grow in accordance with the directions of the invisible beings.

Again Gautama found an opportunity to draw the attention of the people to the wonderful help of the little servants. Here also he found open ears and willing souls. They had all experienced this help themselves.

Gautama was surprised not to see the Bhutanese people anywhere; he wondered whether they could all have perished. He learned that those who had survived the great happening had joined the invaders and been driven out of the country with them.

Afterwards Suddhodana had divided the realm among people from all the tribes who had taken part in the fighting.

"Do you live in peace with each other?" asked Gautama, and received the answer:

"We all pray to the Lord of the Worlds, so there can be no discord."

"And who rules over you?"

"The son of one of the neighbouring princes. Suddhodana allowed us to

228

choose the ruler we wanted. He had selected three sons of princes. We asked for this one because we know that he is just and good."

So all was in order here, and Gautama could go on his way. He felt drawn to the mountains, and he yielded to the longing. However different they were from the ever-roaring, ever-turbulent ocean, the two had something in common: both spoke with eternal voices of the Creative Power of the Lord of all the Worlds!

"One would think that you stood unshakeably firm, you giants," cried Gautama, filled with admiration, as he raised his eyes to the icy crests.

"They have already undergone many transformations, and have yet to go through many more before the Earth has run its course," echoed back the answer to him.

Between two rocky summits, a weathered countenance regarded him. Its white beard flowed down like a mountain-stream thundering into the valley. The head was large, but it aroused no fear.

"Guardian of the mountains, I greet you!" Gautama called to him.

"I greet you, servant of the Eternal One!" came the echo in reply.

"Do you cause the mountains to move?" Gautama wanted to know.

"When our Lord commands it, we push within the bowels of the earth. We loosen the foundation on which the mountains rest, we hollow out and fill up. We contract and expand."

The face disappeared; Gautama looked about him.

He had ridden higher up than he intended. It was not possible to return to an inhabited region that same day. But not far away he found a spacious cave in which horse and rider could spend the night, as it was not cold. So they both settled down there.

Gautama occupied himself with what he had just seen. How great these servants of God were, how tiny the little elemental beings who brought the precious stones from the interior of the mountains out to the light of day!

All were adapted to and merged wonderfully with one another. It seemed as though he saw such little gnomes flitting about, but before he could discern them clearly he had fallen asleep.

In the night he awoke. The cave was lit up, but he could not recognise the source of the light. He sat up on his bed of moss and looked about him. Then a delicate female figure, clad in white, approached.

"Yananda!" he cried, leaping up. "How is it that you come to me?"

"I have asked to be allowed to come and speak with you, Gautama," sounded Yananda's voice faintly, as though from far away.

He wanted to question her, but the graceful white hand motioned him to be silent.

"Ask me nothing now, Gautama. Hear what I have to tell you. I cannot begin my ascent until your eyes have been opened to what we have done wrong. We acted with the best of intentions, but we sinned against God's Eternal Laws."

"You say you cannot begin your ascent – Yananda, are you no longer among us, the living?"

"No, Gautama. The Eternal One has called me away because I was not needed here. But let me speak. Brief is the time that has been given to me:

"We both had a wrong concept of that which men call 'duty'. Duty is unconditional fulfilment of the Will of God within the task assigned to us. It was my duty to present the realm with an heir and to educate him in worship of the All-Highest. I have not been able to fulfil this task, because the one to whom I was to bear the son withdrew from me.

"He gave me up to another. The other is a good man. He loved me. But I could not forget the one who was shown to me in my dream. I considered that to be a sin. I was a good wife to the other, and yet often I wept all night through, because it was becoming ever clearer to me that the Eternal One is not served by a lie.

"If you thought that your duty required you to live alone, we ought both to have accepted this. We should not have resorted to falsehood to uphold the peace of the realm.

"That we have done this is our sin. But Gautama, that which down here I only faintly divined has now become certainty to me:

"Our sacrifice was unnecessary! Do you think your picture would have been shown to me in a dream if we had not been destined for each other? You and I together would have been able to present the country with the heir who would guide the realm and the faith with a sure hand after your death. Who will take your place when you are called away?"

"That is my concern also," cried Gautama vehemently. "But I believe that I do not have to ask about that. The Eternal One will ordain it."

230

"The Eternal One had ordained it, Gautama! But we wanted to be wiser than He. We did not ask whether what we did was His Will. Some well-meaning but short-sighted helper suggested the plan to you, because you could not rid yourself of the concept of duty as you understood it.

"Had we listened to the Eternal One, we should not have needed to make the sacrifice of renunciation. You could have been His servant, and we should have proved through our life that you served Him in the right way.

"Thus we could have set the people a living example of how, resting in the Eternal One, true marriage must be. It was easier to renounce each other from the outset than to make the daily sacrifice of not-binding-oneself.

"Do you understand me, Gautama?" asked Yananda urgently.

A groan was the answer. A veil was torn from before Gautama's spiritual eye. Glaringly before him lay his mistake, into which he had also dragged Yananda. Could he ever be forgiven?

Yananda resumed:

"When I began to sense faintly where I had gone wrong, I begged the Eternal One for forgiveness from the depths of my heart. I prayed fervently that at least Suddhodana should not have to suffer. And I was heard. The Lord of the Worlds has taken me away, and has led a woman to my husband who is worthy of love, a woman who will give him the heir.

"For this I give thanks to the Eternal One! Ever more clearly I see my guilt, which was forgiven me before I had atoned for it. I shall be able to atone in another life for what I did wrong. I shall be allowed to ascend a little way so that my recognition may deepen. But I cannot begin the ascent until I have awakened you.

"Recognise your sin, Gautama, and make atonement for it even now, so that it will not hinder you in your ascent in the beyond!

"Thanks be to the Eternal One that I have been allowed to speak with you. Farewell."

Quietly as it had come, the figure of Yananda disappeared. But Gautama lay weeping on his bed. What had he done! Out of a pure volition, he had thought that he must deny himself.

It had been wrong! Then can even pure volition be wrong? If so, man could no longer trust himself. Then all that he did and thought could indeed be wrong. By what standard was he to judge?

231

How had Yananda expressed it?

"We did not ask whether what we did was the Will of the Eternal One!"

Yes, that was it! He had rushed ahead in blind zeal, and had forgotten to ask. After all, he usually placed everything in the Hands of the Eternal One before he carried it out! And this time he had been so sure of his ground, because it had cost him the hardest self-conquest. And the Lord of the Worlds did not want this sacrifice!

If now after his, Gautama's death, there was no one to keep alive the knowledge of the Eternal One, then he, he alone was to blame for it. Frightful thought!

The Eternal One chose and trained a Truth-bringer, had him prepared and guided, and then – this servant failed!

Gautama's despair became ever greater.

"You could have known, must have known!" something whispered in him.

Why then had not the helper warned him? Because he alone had to make the decision!

The night passed in agonising self-reproaches, in accusations and remorse. In the morning a broken man lay on the bed of moss. He would most gladly have prayed:

"Take me hence, Eternal One! I am not worthy to be Thy servant."

When he vaguely perceived this, and struggled for words to form it into a prayer, a luminous figure again stood before him. This time it was his guide, who so seldom appeared to him.

"Do not unintentionally add sacrilege to sin, Gautama!" he warned earnestly. "It is for the Lord alone to decide whether you still seem worthy to Him as a servant. Pull yourself together! Bethink you: has He ever forsaken you when you prayed to Him? Which of your enterprises has He not allowed to succeed?

"If He were angry with you, He would long ago have withdrawn His Holy Hand from you. You asked whether a pure volition can also go wrong. You see that for yourself. You have erred out of the purest volition. Why? Because through intellectual thinking you have created a concept of duty for yourself.

"This rigid concept does not hold good before the Eternal One. Learn in

232

all things to ask what is His Will, and fulfil It; thereby you will fulfil your duty to the best of your ability.

"Do not sin through false grief, Gautama! Recognise the immeasurable Goodness and Mercy of the Eternal One which lies in His letting you be warned. You can still make some amends by teaching others to put God's Will before all else. Only in this way will you be able to atone.

"What you have drawn to yourself in the happening you can no longer change. You will die without an heir, without a successor. Try to train one of the younger Brothers to be able to take your place when you are called away."

The guide disappeared. Like a man stunned, Gautama remained sitting on the bed for a long time afterwards. He would have dearly liked to spend the next few days in the cave, but the thought of his horse, which needed food, drove him to his feet.

Never again should any creature suffer because of him. He rode to the valley, a stricken, well-nigh broken man.

The beauty and grandeur of the mountains no longer spoke to him. He saw no little helpers on his way, he heard no voices. His soul was filled with the great indictment against himself.

And again his guide came to him. This time he was even more demanding than before:

"You must pull yourself together, Gautama! Because you made a mistake, of which you did not even become conscious for many years, you have no right to paralyse and incapacitate the servant of the Eternal One that you still are! Let what you have done be a lesson to you. Save yourself and others from similar happenings. But let that be enough!

"When the Lord of all the Worlds sees true recognition of faults, and at the same time a sincere volition to lay aside these faults for ever, He is no longer angry. That does not mean that He will intervene in the wheel of the happening to avert the consequences of what you have brought upon yourself and your people. That He will never do! But He forgives you, and grants that you continue to serve Him. Thank Him for His Grace."

Gautama rode for a long time, turning these words over in his soul. He had sought shelter from a storm which had raged by. Now that it had passed, a little bird began to sing again here and there.

"Listen to us," twittered the sweet voices. "When the storm is over we

233

thank the Eternal One Who has protected us, and we sing as before. You do likewise. Serve the Lord even better than you have done hitherto."

"You are right, little ones," cried Gautama earnestly. "Let what is past be past, until the inexorable finger of Him Who comes to redeem the debt raps on the door of the soul. That I shall not evade!"

But in spite of this earnest volition, Gautama did not know where to direct his steps. He felt completely empty. No special work awaited him anywhere.

Then Gautama implored the Eternal One to give him tasks. These tasks should be hard, so that he could become completely absorbed in them. He had dismounted in order to pray. Now he went back to his horse, which gazed at him questioningly with large eyes.

"You would like to know where we are going, old fellow," he said, stroking the animal. "Yes, if only I knew myself!"

"You are going to the Mountain of the Eternal One," sounded quite firmly. "Maggalana sends a message. He needs Gautama's loving help."

So the time had come for Maggalana, the faithful one, to be allowed to depart.

Gautama rode as fast as he could back to the Mountain, where nobody was expecting him. He asked Rahula to continue to act on his behalf as though he were not there.

The latter saw at once that a deeply incisive experience must have raged over Gautama's soul. He found the sage completely changed. A wistful earnestness was reflected in the formerly so sunny eyes, even greater calm and restraint spoke out of his every movement.

As soon as possible, Gautama went to see Maggalana. He found him in his usual place by the window, but the once busy hand was stilled. The old man's eyes wandered musingly into the distance. When Gautama entered, a glimmer of great joy lit up the tranquil features.

"Have you really come as you promised, Gautama?" he cried. "I believe it is time for me to make ready to leave the earth. I was longing for you to come!"

"I was glad to come when I received your message, my father," Gautama assured him. "But you will hardly need me. As a faithful servant of the Eternal One, you will be able to pass over with ease."

234

"I too think, Gautama, that the parting will be easy for me. I go filled with longing. Death has no terror for me. But I wanted to speak to you once more, because I have a message for you. Sit down beside me so that I can tell it to you. It will take time, I am old, and my thoughts often recede as though they were shadows."

Gautama sat down at the feet of him in whom he had always seen the most perfect human being. Maggalana began:

"Some weeks ago, luminous figures from other realms began to visit me, as though they wanted to prepare my soul for the glory which awaits it over there. Thereby they loosened the ties that still sought to hold me. Eventually all that remained was my love for you, Gautama.

"Better perhaps than yourself, I know how to read in your soul. Without speaking of it to you, I have shared your inner struggles. You have never told me of the sacrifice which you wrung from yourself with the best of volitions, for the sake of your task.

"My son! My heart bled for you, that by that very act you burdened yourself with guilt."

A deep sigh from Gautama interrupted the old man.

"I know it now, my father. I have recognised, and repent from the bottom of my heart."

"When I thought of the moment which must bring you recognition, I suffered deeply, Gautama. I could not help you, I could only send up ever fresh prayers. This concern for you was the only thing that still kept me on earth. Now I prayed that the Eternal One might let you recognise before I went, now I begged to be allowed to go, in order to be near you when this hardest time of your life should break over you."

"So I have made you suffer too, my father!" said Gautama impetuously, but a movement from Maggalana restrained him.

"My anxiety for you was blessing, Gautama. But hear me further: A few days ago a wonderfully luminous figure brought me tidings that Yananda herself had been allowed to show you where you had failed. 'He is suffering intensely,' said the spirit-being, 'but it will serve to mature him. If he has recognised in the right way, he will yet be permitted to come to you. Then tell him....'"

Maggalana's voice became solemn, his eyes began to shine in a radiance not of this earth.

"'Then tell him that he is not to lose heart! This experience will release him from himself. The smaller he becomes through it, the greater can the Eternal One become in him and through him.

"'Ultimate recognition will be granted to him!'"

Both fell silent. Something of the peace which filled Maggalana entered Gautama's soul.

Then, however, Gautama opened himself completely. He needed to speak to the old man about everything that moved him. As he did so the agonies which tormented him were eased. When he spoke of Yananda's appearance, of her words, he realised ever more the infinite grace that lay in his being allowed to receive this message.

On one of the following days, it became shamefully clear to Gautama what an impression he must have made, seen from the Light, when he begged the Eternal One over and over again to awaken someone who would be allowed to continue after him what had been begun! Was it not as though he, the erring human being, would exhort the Eternal One? And yet it was his fault alone that the successor was now lacking! How much patience the Lord of the Worlds must have with His servants!

Maggalana's gentle words of comfort succeeded in calming these stormy waves also.

When Gautama was not sitting with the old man, he was strolling in the gardens and woods with Rahula. These two had much to discuss with regard to the great work.

In Utakamand, as well as on the Mountain, there were a few young men who could be trained to become future principals.

Rahula suggested that Gautama should take a personal interest in them, so that through close association they could grow into their future tasks.

This was just what the Master had hitherto resisted doing. Now he saw it to be a part of his atonement that he must forgo his solitude for the sake of a successor. But first he asked his guide if this sacrifice was right.

When he received assent, he asked Rahula to send for the three youths from Utakamand. He called the three whom he had chosen from among the Mountain inhabitants to come to him at once. He did not accept them as "disciples", henceforth they were to accompany him as "pupils".

Maggalana was happy with this decision.

"That was the last thing that I wished for," he confessed.

Gautama asked him why he had not voiced it, but the old man shook his head. He no longer spoke much at all, but preferred to sit quietly with Gautama. Then when they were together in silence, it could happen that luminous beings, visible to them both, would join them. Sounds and colours from other planes surged around them and uplifted them.

Once Gautama heard Maggalana speaking with one of the messengers. He asked him a question, and the luminous one answered audibly:

"Siddharta is having a hard time. He still does not recognise where his fault lay. He still does not want to see. His soul continues to live down here, and yet it would be allowed to ascend! If he were to detach himself there would be no obstacle for it!"

"Can you not help him?" Maggalana asked gently.

"No, Maggalana, all help is at hand, but he must ask for it himself, it could not come to him before. When he recognises his fault and despairs of himself we will intervene, but not sooner."

So Gautama knew that Siddharta was still standing at the unfathomable deep well, looking and looking. When the luminous beings had gone, Gautama told the old man of his experience.

"It will probably be a long time yet before his soul feels the fetters that hold it down," was Maggalana's opinion. "Let us remember him in our interceding prayers."

Again a few days passed.

Gautama had been at another school with his pupils, to let them see how the principal had been obliged deliberately to introduce outward changes, in keeping with the conditions there. They then spoke about it on their way home. One of the young men had asserted that in any case it was safer not to forsake the path already marked out, for then no mistakes could be made.

Gautama proved to him that it was just in that way that the worst mistake would be made. Man must remain alive, and never lapse into rigid forms.

As they talked, they had stopped several times on the way, and it was late when they reached home. It was long past the hour when Gautama usually visited Maggalana. He hastened to his cell, and found him completely absorbed, so that he did not notice Gautama's entrance.

237

There was a wonderful radiance in the small room, which was filled with sounds of infinite harmony.

"What overwhelming grace," breathed the lips of the old man. "Hast Thou truly a task for me in Thine eternal Realms, O Supreme Lord of all Worlds? May my feeble strength serve Thee in Luminous Heights? Lord, I thank Thee!"

Gautama thought that life had already ebbed away, but Maggalana began to speak once more:

"Gautama, my son, wherever you may be, hear me. The Eternal One has forgiven you! Thank Him by no longer brooding. He will reveal great things to you. Prepare yourself!"

Then sounded softly through the room:

"Eternal One, Lord Most High, Who hast called me to be Thy servant, I am ready!"

Praying, Gautama knelt beside the cloak, from which the soul set free was borne aloft by luminous hands.

The cave for Maggalana, in which the mortal remains of this faithful man were laid to rest, was made ready next to that of Sariputta. With sincere mourning his last abode was prepared, much love laid him to rest. But before the closed burial chamber Gautama had a white tablet placed with the words:

"He serves in the Light."

A few days after the burial, the young men from Utakamand arrived, and Gautama set out with his six pupils to show them the realm. They were to become acquainted with the various races that made up the great community.

Enough opportunities to instruct them arose on the way, especially since they were lively spirits, who knew how to add depth to any conversation through their questions.

Gautama himself, however, found it irksome to be surrounded by the pupils. He missed the quiet hours of self-communion during the day. How much he had usually experienced on his rides! Now he had to devote himself completely to the others.

But whenever he was inclined to complain about it inwardly, he remembered the reason why he had undertaken this onerous task. Then it became bearable again.

Now he had to compensate for the quiet time that eluded him. He found it in the night. Of his own accord he made it his habit to rise from his couch at a certain hour, so that he could become inwardly absorbed under the starry vault of heaven.

Quietly recognition upon recognition opened up to him. He thought he could see into the workshops of Nature. All that was created was animated. Everything spoke to him through the little beings who moved at God's behest.

When he met his pupils in the morning, he told them of what he had received during the night. One of them, Nagardshuna, listened with special joy.

It soon emerged that he too was able to see the invisible beings, although not as clearly as Gautama, and not at all times. But he could not understand them. Again and again he asked what he must do to achieve this also.

Gautama reflected.

"You must love them, Nagardshuna," he answered. "You must lovingly seek to grasp their nature, then they will communicate with you. I can give you no other advice."

It was inevitable that when Gautama and his pupils came to other schools they were gazed at in wonder, as though they were something superior to all others. For hitherto the Master had always refused to be accompanied. These six youths must be specially close to him.

Not only were they marvelled at and admired, but people honoured them and sought to win their favour.

At first the Master silently observed how the young men behaved. Only two of them seemed not to notice the eager approach of the people. They went their way quietly, unmoved by praise or acclaim.

Nagardshuna noticed it, and these proceedings repelled him. Whenever they came to a school or a monastery he drew back. This had earned him the nickname of Muno, the hermit.

But the other three revelled in all that was offered them. They were happy that people regarded them as something special. They themselves

239

finally came to believe that Gautama would certainly not have chosen them if they had not deserved it.

Then one day the Master spoke seriously to them all. He explained what great danger to the right, direct development of the soul lay in yielding to the praise and homage of people. Only he who was also able to free himself from it, only he was so detached as to be able to receive recognitions.

Nor was it right for them to withdraw from men in annoyance or disgust. They had all been chosen to help mankind. This they could do only through constant association with them. A hermit fails in his duty through selfishness.

Irrespective of praise or blame, man must learn to find the centre of all his own circling within himself. Once this point had been discovered, he would perceive that it rested in absolute stillness. But from there the connecting threads went upwards. The more often he concentrated on this one point, the more firmly the threads were woven and joined. He who thus gathered strength could be a helper and guide to others.

"Have you also found the lotus-flowers which were bestowed on Siddharta?" asked one of the pupils. "Rahula says that anyone who earnestly strives for them can attain to them."

"I must confess that I have not sought lotus-flowers," said Gautama. "I always try to open myself, and then I receive the strength in the form in which I need it at that time. I think it varies with every human being."

To his joy, Gautama was able to see that his admonition bore fruit. The young men paid less attention to the favour of others. Where they encountered it in an obtrusive form they thrust it from them.

One day in the course of their journey they came to a village south of the Vindhya mountains, where as yet there was no Temple of the Eternal One. There they spent the night. While Gautama, as was his wont, passed the night in the open, the others were received here and there in the huts.

In the morning they told him that they had heard of a great sage who was preaching in the surrounding district, and proclaiming that there was no God at all. They begged Gautama to go and see the man.

Although he would have preferred the sage to come to him, Gautama yielded to his pupils' plea. They knew exactly how to reach him. He lived in a remote region among the mountains.

Indeed, after a fairly short journey they came to a well-built hut. It stood on a flat ledge. Two goats were grazing before it. Beside the entrance was a large stone covered with a goatskin, and on it sat a man in a brown hairshirt. His beard and locks were neatly trimmed.

He shaded his eyes with his hand, and looked at them as they approached. They had expected him to ask what they wanted, as was usual, but he did not stir, and seemed to be waiting for them to address him.

"Are you Vindhya-Muno?" asked one of the young men. The man laughed.

"Can't you see that, questioner?"

Gautama had walked to the edge of the precipice and was gazing out over the country. His pupils had wanted to see the man; let them try to deal with him. For himself the first glance had been enough.

But the six young men stood embarrassed before the seated man, and did not know how they should begin to speak.

Vindhya-Muno seemed to be enjoying himself. He laughed again, and made a grimace.

Nagardshuna was annoyed.

"I can understand that you do not believe in a God," he called.

This so surprised the man that he asked:

"Why do you think so?"

"One who like you idles away his time in doing nothing, and although he is healthy lives on people's alms, giving nothing in return, cannot believe in God, otherwise he must fear the punishment which God will impose on him."

The man was taken aback, but did not wish to give himself away. Gautama was eager to see how things would proceed.

"Do you believe in a god then?" the Muno asked. It was meant to sound derisive. Nagardshuna answered briefly:

"Yes."

"Listen, friend," said the man to that, "it is inconvenient to believe in a god. One has to pray to him, one has to make sacrifices to him. One is not allowed to do this or that. It is much easier to go through life without this belief, free and unburdened."

Then Gautama turned round.

241

"And where does your life lead you, Muno?" he asked earnestly. The latter was startled.

"Who are you? Do not look at me! Your eyes go right through me."

"Where does your life lead you?" repeated Gautama relentlessly, fixing his radiant eyes on the Muno.

"I do not know, nor do I want to know! I am content to arrange my life as comfortably as possible. If there is really anything after it, I must try to be ready for that also."

"Man, I tell you there is something after this, which will be too hard for you!" exclaimed Gautama.

The man cowered, but said nothing.

Steps could be heard. Along a mountain-path came two men with bundles. It could be seen that the Muno felt awkward on account of the seven strangers standing before him.

Gautama motioned to his pupils to draw back a little. Nevertheless they could hear every word that was spoken.

The men opened their bundles, and laid all kinds of provisions on the ground at the Muno's feet.

He thanked them, obviously embarrassed. Apparently they were not used to that. After a brief silence they began to encourage him:

"We wish to hear words of wisdom from you, father," they said. "Teach us how to counter the emissaries of the new teaching. They say that there is a god who rules over all the worlds. If there is such a god we must obey him."

"You must do as you wish," said the hermit evasively.

The men looked at him in astonishment.

"You have never spoken to us like that before. You have taught us that we human beings are the highest that Creation has produced, and therefore we can make everything subject to us. But when we say this to the Brothers from the monasteries, they answer: 'You cannot even control yourselves.' What are we to reply to that?"

"That is splitting hairs," said the man sullenly. "The best thing is not to reply at all."

His eyes wandered warily to the strangers, who just then caught the attention of the men.

"Is it because of them, Muno, that you are so upset?" one of them asked. "Are they also adherents of the teaching? Then you could answer for us immediately. We would learn from it."

The hermit was silent and stared at the ground. But Gautama drew nearer.

"Why do you want to reject the teaching about God?" he asked kindly. "Look, this man cannot tell you anything; for there is really no proof that there is no God. But all Nature speaks clearly of Him. Everything that you see around you bears witness to the fact *that He is!*"

"This man has told us that belief in a god will turn life into bondage and prison. But we want to enjoy our life."

"That is sensible," Gautama commended him. "Are you succeeding then?"

The men looked at one another. Then the older one answered:

"No matter what I do, I cannot get away from cares and need. It is no different with my neighbour here."

"But if you can make all Creation subject to you, then command cares and need to depart from you."

"Sire, no man can do that," said the younger man. "We must endure what is laid upon us."

"Who has laid it upon you? How did it come to you?"

"We do not know. Perhaps after all there is a god who plagues and torments us."

"No, men," cried Gautama loudly. "There is no such god!"

"So you say the same as he," shouted the elder man joyfully. "Tell us then how we can be certain of our knowledge."

"There is no god who torments men," repeated Gautama. "But there is a benevolent, merciful God Who helps men. He gives no one more to bear than he has incurred for himself.

"What do you think: If a man recklessly throws a fire-brand into his homestead so that flames shoot up, who has set the dwelling ablaze?"

"None other than himself!" answered the younger man.

"And it serves him right if all he has is burned," added the older one.

"So you do not say: a god who torments men has set the house on fire?"

They both said no to that. Then he explained to them how everything

243

that comes to them is the harvest that springs from their deeds. They understood that.

Then the Muno opened his mouth again for the first time and said with a mocking laugh:

"You have succeeded well, wise one, in showing that man does everything himself, that there is no god."

Gautama countered by asking:

"And who created man? Did he do that also himself?"

At which the elder of the two men said frankly:

"Indeed I myself have sometimes wondered who made the mountains and rivers, the plants and the animals."

"Yes," said Gautama kindly, "and when you have thought about these things you clearly sensed that there must be a Being Who is above us all. No man could do that. But we call this Being God. And when we recognise how wonderful are His works, we fall silent in awe of Him, we worship Him."

Cursing, the Muno flew into a rage.

"Have you come here, stranger, to deprive me of my harvest? What have we to do with you?"

"It would be better if you were to listen to what we have to tell," was Gautama's calm retort.

But the hermit quickly picked up a stone from the ground and hurled it at Gautama. The stone missed the Master's head by a hair's breadth.

The pupils would have rushed at the Muno, but a sharp call from Gautama stopped them.

"Let him be, he cannot harm me. God Himself protects me!" said Gautama loudly and clearly.

Then however he turned to go, and the two strangers joined him and his pupils. They begged Gautama to go with them and tell their neighbours about God.

He did so gladly.

It was as though all the souls from whom the Muno had taken the gods, without putting God in their place, had hitherto groaned under chains and fetters, which now began to fall away as Gautama taught them.

People thronged to them from the other villages, so that Gautama divided his pupils, and sent them across the country as far as the Muno's influence had reached.

That took some weeks. Then one day, just as he was proclaiming God in a small square, Gautama found himself face to face with the Muno.

"I had a wish to hear you speak for once," said the hermit arrogantly.

Gautama did not deign to answer him, but calmly went on with what he was saying. Then the Muno interrupted him, and called out to the people:

"Do not believe him; he is a fraud, who seeks only his own advantage."

A man called back:

"He is not! You demanded payment from us for your blasphemy. We had to clothe and feed you. This man takes nothing from us, but teaches us what makes us happy."

"Let me ask him just one question," said the Muno insistently. "If he can answer me that, I will go away and disturb you no more."

The men nodded.

"Tell me, wise man, what is the soul?"

"The soul, Muno, is that which weeps within you day and night, because you allow it to starve, because you mishandle it. The soul is the best in us, which stems from above, and rests not until we bear it up again. But if we do not do this the soul weeps, as yours does."

And at that the man covered his face with his hands and wept bitterly. The bystanders looked at him in astonishment, but Gautama made them a sign not to disturb him.

When the worst pain was over, Gautama put his arm round the man's shoulders:

"You poor man, what you must have suffered! How your soul must have starved, that you could find no other way than to try to destroy it. But friend, the soul cannot be destroyed. It is stronger than anything else; for it comes from above. It knows about God, but it can only speak to you of Him if you listen to it."

And Gautama went on talking to the man, who went with him like a child. He was at every meeting. He had many questions to ask. At last he pleaded:

"Wise one, take me with you."

But Gautama showed him that his task lay here.

245

"Here where you have spread your false teachings, here you must stay to testify to God! In that way you will atone for your guilt."

THE YEAR that Rahula had intended to spend on the Mountain had expired. He had appointed another leader, and returned to Utakamand. Gautama went there with his pupils in the course of the next few months.

He was glad to be able to discuss the question of his successor with Rahula. The only one who could be considered for this was Nagardshuna, but Gautama was afraid that he would not learn to master his easily inflammable nature sufficiently. He who was to manage the schools, now nearly fifty in number, and the thirty monasteries and convents, must be inwardly firm and imperturbably calm.

"Leave Nagardshuna here, Gautama," Rahula suggested. "I too must think about the choice of my successor, for I shall not continue much longer in my work. I have a feeling that I shall be allowed to enter on the upward path. Perhaps the youth can be trained to the work here. Then his strength will not lie dormant. But I would like to give you two other youths to take with you. They are particularly talented young men, I will tell you no more than that."

This suited Gautama, but he asked Rahula also to take back the least capable of the six, who in any case had come from Utakamand.

"I should not like to have more than six pupils with me," he said.

Soon after that he set out on his journey again. Rahula took leave of him for this life.

"I shall not send for you, Gautama, when I am permitted to depart this life. You have greater things to do. I should like to be buried here, where I have worked. After all it is only the cloak that remains here. You will know when I am allowed to go. Then think of me, with the wish that nothing may tie me to this earth any more."

It was hard for Gautama to part from Rahula, the last one to whom he was linked by implicit trust. He knew that from now onwards he must go his way entirely alone. But he also sensed that it was right, for the way was to lead upwards.

The new pupils kept him very occupied. They were alert spirits, completely different from each other, alike only in the absolute volition to serve.

246

The elder, Vanadha, had studied much. He could repeat, explain and expound many writings. At the same time he had retained a childlike faith, which protected him from any danger that might otherwise have arisen out of his erudition. He looked up to Gautama in reverence, and took upon himself as a matter of course all those tasks that were less agreeable to the others.

The younger man, Siddha, was like sunshine personified. It was as though a spring of light and joy bubbled within him, which nothing could check. Even when he walked in silence with the others, a wave of cheerfulness passed over to them.

They once asked Gautama about it. It was not clear to them by what means Siddha produced this effect. Gautama told them that Siddha's luminous thoughts were so strong that they flowed over to them.

"You know of course that base intuitions create demons which, if they are sufficiently nurtured by us, can even become independent and attack others."

They knew that. Some of them had even seen it.

"Well," continued Gautama, "now visualise this same process in the Light. Good, happy, beautiful thoughts and intuitions bring forth light beings which, according to their indwelling strength, make their way to wherever they find homogeneous species. Simply absorb them, for a cheerful human being is able to achieve more than a downhearted one."

They all loved the youth, who was not only cheerful, but also truly good.

Although he could not see the elemental beings, he nevertheless felt himself linked with them in his great love and regard for all created things. He was receptive to all that Gautama told his pupils, and knew like none other how to pass it on in the right way.

Very soon it became clear to Gautama that here he had found his successor. His guide confirmed this, and advised him to return to the Mountain of the Eternal One, resume the leadership, and let Siddha work under him.

Gautama had been absent for more than three years. He was happy to be able to give up the nomadic life. The Brothers were glad to have him in their midst again. But soon they sensed that Gautama had gone far beyond them. Over his being lay serenity such as only high maturity of spirit bestows.

His words were few, but each one made an impression, because it hit exactly on what it was meant to convey. Although he was now very grey-haired his bearing was upright, his step springy, and his eyes once more had the sunny radiance which they had all missed for so long.

Among his own people, and yet separated from them by a touch of unapproachability, Gautama's life was one of abundant work. None spoke to him unasked, but everyone who was called to see him was happy.

While he allowed Siddha to participate in all that he did with regard to the management and teaching, he had instructed Vanadha to draw up a list of all the schools, monasteries and convents that had been built in the vast realm, and to add to each name a description of its situation.

At the same time, he was to recount all that he knew about every single school and every monastery. One of the other pupils was allowed to help him in this. It grew into a comprehensive work, which promised to be of great benefit.

Brisk activity reigned on the Mountain. Spurred on by the presence of the Master, each strove to do his best. And stimulated by a few words from Gautama, who would not tolerate standstill anywhere, new plans for improvements, extensions, or innovations came into being.

He took a special delight in attending to the women's sphere of activity. Sisana had had the prudence to train successors; she complained however that none of the male principals on the Mountain, not even Rahula, would listen to her concerns.

"We do not know the first thing about women; that is your business, Sisana," was the answer which she had generally received.

Nevertheless her guidance was so strong that she had regulated the women's work, and extended their field of activity, even without the help of the Brothers in charge. Besides the schools for the little ones and the girls, homes for very small motherless children had arisen, as well as work-places for women where, according to the region, cotton or silk was produced.

Gautama had seen some of these places with satisfaction. The women who worked in them attracted attention everywhere because of their cheerful, unaffected way of living.

"Since we relieve the harassed women to some extent of anxiety about their children, motherhood is no longer regarded as a burden," explained Sisana. "We hope that a happier, freer generation will emerge."

248

Wherever Gautama looked, he found prosperity and progress of the most beautiful kind. The Eternal One had bestowed rich blessing on his work. Again and again he thanked Him for it, well aware that without the power from above, without the guidance, he could not have achieved anything.

He now found time again for absorption and self-communion, and with it contact with the sources of power. These were his most treasured and best hours, which never failed to bear rich fruit.

ONCE AGAIN Gautama was sitting alone. Something from the beyond, of which from time to time he had already been allowed to see or divine certain things, was about to be revealed to his spirit.

Suddenly Rahula came to him. This fitted in so naturally with his thinking that at first he did not fully realise that the presence could not be physical.

He greeted him warmly, but the greeting was returned as though from far away. Now he saw that the figure was of an almost transparent delicacy.

"So you have been allowed to pass on, Rahula?" he cried, greatly moved. "Have I bound you to the earth through wrong doings, that you have not yet been able to begin your ascent?"

"No, Gautama," Rahula answered. "I have been allowed to begin my ascent, and I see that it will lead me upwards to Luminous Realms. But I am permitted to give you a message: Bring your work to a conclusion, so that you will be prepared at any time to lay it aside at the call from On High. Let others work under your supervision. The Lord will appoint you to a new task."

And Gautama was happy; for this message was fresh proof that the Lord of all the Worlds had forgiven him. It was also the confirmation that at present it was right for him to become absorbed, to see and to receive, in order to be able still to bear witness.

From this day on it was as though special power descended into him every time he retired into silence. Sacred knowledge permeated him, connections became clear to him, a wide view opened up to him.

Beings approached him, and drew his attention to the differences in their realms. They indicated to him that they differed not only in their form and work, but also in their origin.

As he absorbed this within him, he always seemed to see coloured circles moving round a centre. The nearer they swung to the centre, the finer, lighter, and also more radiant they appeared to him.

"Where are the human beings?" he asked involuntarily during one such experience.

"Look," was the answer, and a hand pointed to the very outermost, the heaviest and densest ring, which nevertheless was striving to swing and radiate. "These are the ones of good will."

"Who is He around Whom they all revolve? Is it God?" he asked, almost trembling.

"It is not the Lord of all the Worlds, it is a Part of Him, His Holy Will! You cannot see Him now, Gautama. But you will yet be permitted to behold Him."

Most deeply did Gautama feel that a great revelation had come to him. Yet ever again he had to meditate and think: the Will of God, a Part of God!

Was the Will not God Himself? At any rate It must be the strongest out of God. After all it is the will of man which drives him, which brings forth his actions. And the Will of God? Was it the Will of God Who created the worlds? It must be so. And Gautama knew in his heart that he had been granted the right recognition.

What was he to call this Part of God when he told men about Him? He had not received this knowledge to keep it to himself. He must proclaim it so long as it was still possible for him to do so. But by what name should he speak of this radiant Centre?

"The Will of God, the Holy Will," the voice had said.

But men would not understand that. Surely it meant that God had severed a Part of Himself, a Part Which then stood alone by Itself. Was he allowed to say: "The Son of God?"

Ever again his thoughts came back to this. The more he reflected on it, the more he was filled with the intuitive sensing that he had touched upon something quite Holy.

250

He must speak of it to the others, but he could not do so until he himself had everything quite clear before his spiritual eye. Otherwise he would be proclaiming only half-Truth to men.

"Eternal One," he implored, "let not my thoughts go astray! Let me see Thy Glory ever more clearly. Show me if my intuitions are right! Let me discover the Name of the Holy Will!"

Often he implored thus, always he was filled with great strength, but the Name he did not hear.

However, he was allowed to see the picture of the swinging circles ever more clearly. They began to ring harmoniously, their rays were interwoven, and yet they were distinctly separate.

But often from the apparently veiled Centre broke forth cones of flames, bright rays, which shot across all circles, illuminating and uniting them all in their light. It was wonderful! It told him so much!

"Perhaps I can tell men about it, without giving the Centre a name," he pondered. "Although I cannot yet bring them the best, why should I withhold it all from them?"

And he began to tell the pupils how wisely everything in the Creations is ordered.

"Why do you see circles?" asked one of the youths. "I have always envisaged steps."

Siddha rebuked him.

"There are steps as well. We must all climb them, work our way up, if we wish to arrive at the place from which we came.

"But see, Brother: everything that moves in Creation describes a circle. We come from above, and wish to return there. The seed becomes a tree, the tree again drops seed into the earth for the cycle to begin anew.

"Look where you may, you will encounter the circling everywhere. Hence I should like to say: Moving in the spiritual way is rotation. Is it not so, Gautama?" he added enquiringly.

The Master nodded.

"You can also mention, Siddha, that all our thoughts, words and deeds return to us when they have described a circle, bringing harm or blessing. But," and now his spirit seemed to be far away, as slowly, and with ever growing enthusiasm, he said, "Every circle has to have a centre, which must

251

not be ourselves. Now it is veiled, it is Will, Holy Will! But later we shall receive another name for it. Then our happiness will be complete."

Deeply moved, the pupils looked at one another. It was too high for them, they did not understand him. But *how* he said it gripped them, and showed them that they were standing on the threshold of a holy shrine.

Again Gautama withdrew from them for a few days. His soul was occupied with the Holiness that was about to be revealed to him.

He pondered over the origin of man. He had been created, like every living thing; that was what he had thought hitherto. But man returned to the earth, to atone, to learn. No other living thing did that.

Within man was that which yearned upwards, that which he called soul. The soul must be immortal. Not in one poor human lifetime did it complete the cycle from above and back again; many lives were needed for that. Why had he not known it before?

He could have told men much, much more!

"Whence does it now come to me?" he wondered, and gave the answer himself: "God allows it to be revealed to me!"

If God only now allowed him to know, then only now had the time come for it. He would rest content with that, and rather strive to absorb everything of which God deemed him worthy.

The soul is immortal, it comes from above, he reflected. But it is not Divine, otherwise it would be able faintly to sense, perhaps even to behold God. Hence it is created through the Will of God, the Holy Centre, around Whom the Creations revolve.

Vanadha entered with a document. He wanted to be told what to write about a monastery which he did not know.

Gautama gladly gave him the information, and then, as Vanadha had already turned to go, the Master asked in a clear voice:

"Vanadha, where does the human soul come from?"

The question came as a total surprise to Vanadha, who had been completely engrossed in his work. He considered for a moment, then he said:

"I think it grows in us like our heart."

"But our heart does not ascend with us when we leave the body," Gautama replied.

252

Vanadha reflected again.

"Master, I do not know. Let us ask Siddha, here he comes."

And, glad to escape the question, before Gautama could agree he called to Siddha: "Siddha, where does the human soul come from?"

"From above, Vanadha," was the swift reply.

Then Gautama asked further:

"So you think that it is of Divine origin?"

"No, Master, I do not mean that. All the beings who surround us, our small and great helpers, also come from above, and are not of Divine origin. Our souls must also come from wherever they originate."

"And how do you picture the soul?" asked Gautama, who was enjoying Siddha's replies.

"I picture it as a luminous, delicate angel, a light-being which is imprisoned within us and awaits liberation. It must be a living being; for it can rejoice and weep, sing and mourn."

They could not continue their conversation, because one of the young men who wrought exquisite golden ornaments for the Temple brought in something special, which all three inspected with the utmost joy.

It was a lotus-flower on a long upright stem. Leaves were swathed round the stem in such a way that the flower was carried freely. Fragrant oils could be poured into a slight depression at the top, and lighted. That looked very beautiful, as though a sacrificial flame were rising up from the flower.

"Behold our soul," said Vanadha, but then he became quite embarrassed. He much preferred to conceal his intuitive perceptions from everyone.

Gautama praised the artist, who told them that for three days the little helpers had shown him lotus-flowers in this arrangement, for there were no such flowers up here.

"So it was easy to work accordingly. I do not merit your praise, Gautama."

Then the Master went over to the workshop with the young man, to inspect the other works of art. One of the youngest had fashioned a small figure in silver. The long garment seemed to flow down the little body like gossamer. And on its shoulders the little being had wings wrought of silver net, inset with coloured gems.

Gautama was enchanted.

"Where did you see the figure, Brother?" he asked the young artist. The latter blushed.

"I always see such beings among the flowers, Master."

"That makes me happy," said Gautama.

He was always glad to perceive that the Brothers' eyes were opened to what existed outside physical substance. In this way they became connected with finer spheres.

Stimulated, Gautama returned to his apartment.

Joyful activity, pervaded by the spiritual, animated the people. The souls were firmly linked with their Luminous Home. A solidarity that went beyond the borders of the principalities bound the Brothers together, and united them all in one striving.

Among those who believed in the Eternal One, there certainly were isolated Brahman settlements or monasteries, like spots on a panther's coat, but Gautama regarded them as a kind of preliminary step to right recognition, and hence left them alone.

Nor indeed were they hostile, but their attitude was quiet and withdrawn. Any other emerging teachers and sages had been unable to assert themselves or their views. The knowledge of the Lord of the Worlds dwelt too strongly in the people, they did not let it go.

"O Eternal One," prayed Gautama with fervour, "how wisely Thou hast guided the people, enkindled in us all the flame of true faith. Thou hast established a Kingdom for Thyself among us, who have been a people of dreamers. I thank Thee!"

What he did not express, although it vibrated deep within him, was the wish to be allowed now to entrust the task completely to younger workers, to withdraw into solitude and quiet inner absorption. It was the wish that had filled him all through his life.

But the Lord knew the wishes of His faithful servant and sent him a messenger, who was permitted to tell him that his longing was to find fulfilment.

"Gautama," spoke the messenger solemnly, "you have faithfully served the Lord of the Worlds. He will grant you the ending of your earth-life in the solitude that you long for. Take one pupil and a servant with you, and as

254

soon as the moon is full, ride north towards the mountains. The way will be shown to you."

Only a few days were left before this time; the moon was already waxing. Without telling them of his intentions, Gautama once more allocated their tasks to Siddha and the others.

Siddha sensed that the journey, of which the Master only spoke so casually, must be of great importance. Gautama's eyes shone, his movements quickened, as though fresh youth were about to enfold the old man.

Neither by word nor by look did Siddha betray that he had knowledge of what the Master wished to keep secret. But the others perceived nothing. They tried to dissuade Gautama from undertaking the journey, which at his age – he was nearly eighty – could become too much of a strain. But as he grew ever more vigorous the warnings ceased.

Lidandha, one of the youngest pupils, and Vada, the servant who had attended Gautama for a long time, joyfully made ready to accompany the Master. They were filled with pride that they were the ones he had chosen.

"Let us take two pack-horses, with tents and provisions," decreed Gautama on the day before their departure. "To begin with, I would like to seek out some lonely region, where we may have to manage as best we can."

ON THE MORNING that followed the night of the full moon they rode forth, accompanied on a long stretch of the way by pupils and Brothers. The farewell, which was to be the last on earth, was joyous. Even Siddha forced himself to appear cheerful.

At first Gautama, contrary to his usual habit, talked with his companions. He drew their attention to the brilliant colours in Nature, and described how the little servants were adapted to these colours and to their surroundings in a practical way.

"It shows us," he said, "that the Eternal One wills that all things should blend without abrupt transitions. We human beings must adapt ourselves much more to what is created around us than we have hitherto been wont to do."

They rode north towards the mountains. For quite some time Gautama

255

had seen that a great, luminous animistic being was leading his horse. He entrusted himself completely to this guidance.

When they broke their journey at night the being disappeared, to take up its task again in the morning as they set out.

Gautama began to communicate inaudibly with it, but did not enquire where they were going. He asked for information about a number of things that caught his attention on the way.

The animistic being willingly answered his questions. Because of this Gautama unintentionally became silent towards his companions. They were immersed in their own thoughts, and enjoyed the silence.

After ten days the riders had reached a green meadow encircled by high mountains, where they found a dwelling, built against a rock. It was a solid, well-built hut of stone and wood, inside which there were even seats and a wide couch.

"We have reached our destination," the animistic being told Gautama. "Let this hut be put in order for you. A little further on there is another, larger one, which can make a home for your companions. Over there lies a fair-sized village, where they can obtain food. Be happy here."

The guide disappeared, and Gautama looked around him, enraptured. It was glorious here, between mountains and sky. A mountain stream plunged noisily into the valley, flowers grew in the green grass, and not far away there stood a group of shady conifers.

While Vada spread covers on the couch and soft mats on the floor, Gautama walked on with Lidandha in the direction indicated by the animistic guide, and within a short time they had come on a second, larger hut.

Although this one was somewhat dilapidated, it could easily be put in order, and would serve as a homestead for the two companions. Beside it was also a stable; goats had probably been kept here at one time.

"We shall do that too, if Gautama intends to stay here for some time," Lidandha decided.

When they had inspected everything carefully, Gautama made his way back to his own hut.

"It is glorious here," he cried in delight. "The only thing I lack is a large stone in the centre of this green space, where we can hold Hours of Worship. I have brought a lotus-chalice with me!"

256

The very next morning, a stone for worship stood on the spot indicated by Gautama. His two companions were awaiting him there with happily smiling faces.

"My thanks to you!" he called to them. At once he felt linked to this new home.

Lidandha and Vada repaired their hut, and afterwards went out to explore the surrounding countryside. In the direction opposite to that from which they had come they saw a large village, and decided to visit it soon.

But they were somewhat dismayed at the thought that probably they would not have enough money, if their stay was to last for some time.

To ride back was not to be thought of. The distance was too great, and they had not been able to commit the route accurately to memory. Nor had they thought of such a possibility.

Subdued, they went to Gautama, who good-humouredly asked them what the trouble was. When they told him he laughed.

"What do you think we are going to do with five horses here?"

Then they suddenly saw a way of getting what they needed.

"Do not sell them all at once," advised Gautama. "There is enough grass up here for a few animals to feed on. Take two horses to begin with. Then we shall find further ways and means."

On the following day the two men went on their exploratory ride, taking the horses with them to sell. Filled with all that they had seen and heard, they returned at sunset. They had sold the two pack-horses at a profit.

"They asked us whether a hermit had come again to live on the mountain. We said yes. There was great joy among the people, all of whom believe in the Eternal One."

"Did you mention my name?" asked Gautama, somewhat concerned. He would not have agreed to that, as he did not wish to be in contact with people.

"I wanted to," Vada admitted, "but Lidandha forestalled me, saying that you were a hermit from the race of Tshakya. Hence your name was Tshaky-amuno."

Slowly Gautama repeated:

"Tshakyamuno, a beautiful name! Henceforth I shall use it. You see,

257

only as a child have I had a name of my own. At the wish of the Eternal One, I later took our family name, Gautama. Now I shall become even more involved in my family, from which inwardly I had actually freed myself completely."

Lidandha, relieved that the Master was not angry at his arbitrary decision, continued his lively account.

"The town is called Kusinara, and is the capital of the principality of Kusinara, which borders on the kingdom of Khatmandu."

He said this without knowing that a brother of Gautama was the king of the neighbouring country. And Gautama kept silent about it.

Before the next full moon, the three had settled down completely. They began each day with an Hour of Worship by the stone, at which were also present countless invisible beings, whom Gautama clearly perceived and was glad to have there.

Then the Master walked a little further up into the mountains, where he became engrossed in thought.

Vada attended to their maintenance and to the horses, which had been joined by several goats. But Lidandha tried to write down what the Master had taught on the previous day.

Towards evening Gautama returned, and shared with his companions what he had experienced inwardly. It was a simple, inwardly rich life that they led.

One evening Gautama found his companions somewhat uncertain of themselves, as though they were afraid to tell him of some experience. What could have happened?

He asked them, and Lidandha explained that two women had arrived, wishing to speak with the Tshakyamuno. But he would not disturb Gautama.

So he told them that the Muno was not available to see ordinary people. He was now conversing with the Eternal One. But if the women would be content with the pupil, he would be glad to answer their questions. And they had been satisfied, had asked various questions, and then in gratitude had left these delicious fruits.

Gautama smiled.

"You are still extremely young for a sage, Lidandha," he said, "but if the

258

women were satisfied, I will be also. I should not have liked you to come for me. But tell me, would it not have been better for you to send the women away unanswered? Now more people will come!" he added with a sigh.

"No, Master," replied the pupil. "I could not send the women away, because the Muno who lived here before gave advice to everyone. That is part of it. But I told them that they had been fortunate, that information is given here only every seven days. People are to adjust to that."

Gautama was amused by the young man's wise circumspection. But he still wanted to know what the women had asked.

"First they asked whether we believed in the Lord of all the Worlds. When I said that we did, one of them wanted to know whether it was true that the great Master, Gautama, put women before men. To this also I was able to say yes.

"But then came a difficult question: why was there not a Divine Being Who took women under Her care? Surely in the proximity of God there must also be a woman! She and her friends had intuitively perceived that this was a certainty. Also one of the women had once been permitted to behold a heavenly female figure."

"And what did you say to her about that?" asked Gautama, who was rather perplexed by this question of the women.

"What was I to tell her? I know nothing about it. I told her that I was only the Muno's pupil. I would ask him, and if they would return in seven days' time I would convey his answer to them."

Vada laughed.

"How wise our little one is," he cried in amusement. "What he cannot answer he passes on to the Master!"

"Surely that is better than giving the wrong answer," Lidandha defended himself.

Gautama agreed with him. But then he said earnestly:

"The women have asked about something which all of us have always overlooked. It is quite right:

"If the Eternal One wills that the women should stand above us, then up in the Heavenly Gardens there must be a female being who guides the women here on earth. To think that I never concerned myself with this!"

259

Hereupon Gautama fell silent, and did not speak another word throughout the evening.

His companions knew this about him, and at such times dared not break the silence except in very urgent cases.

When Gautama was alone in his hut he became absorbed in prayer. Then he went out into the open air. He thought it would be easier to find what he was seeking under the wide expanse of the starry firmament.

Luminous figures were floating in the moonbeams, which fell upon the earth as gently as if they were veils that enveloped it.

"Look at us, Gautama," sounded the little voices. "We are female beings. You have often seen us, but you have never reflected that we stand beside the male beings."

"Is this twofold division everywhere then?" asked Gautama.

"It exists as far as we can see," fluted the gentle voices. "Everywhere the woman stands beside or even above the man."

"Everywhere?" Gautama asked himself. Then he cried:

"No, not everywhere! God the Eternal One, the Lord of all the Worlds, stands alone!"

"You are right, Gautama," sounded the voice of his guide. "God the Lord is unimaginable. He embraces everything. With Him there is no division into male and female, because He is All in All. But under Him are high beings, far higher than Brahma and Shiva. In them the division is already to be found. There are female and male beings. But one female being is the highest."

"What shall I call her to the women? How am I to announce her to them?" Gautama asked urgently.

"You will be allowed to divine her. Then you yourself will find the name for her which will best help your people. She has many names, for her nature is many-sided. She is the most perfect woman. Blessed is he who is permitted to behold her."

"When, when shall I be allowed to behold her?" implored Gautama.

"I do not know. Pray, and wait!"

As he had been instructed, Gautama spent the following days in expectant prayer. He became deeply engrossed in the thought of this highest of all women, without being able to form a picture of her for

260

himself. But each night he went out under the sparkling deep-blue sky, and prayed.

It came to pass on one such night that it seemed to Gautama as though Nature stood still. Not a leaf stirred.

Everything was so reverent that holy expectation also gripped Gautama's soul. He went to the worship-stone and placed his hands on it, to support himself and at the same time to seek connection.

Quite quietly, quite imperceptibly, the descending rays reddened. Was the moon changing her light? Gautama looked up. Directly above him the finest little rose-coloured light-clouds hung in the deep blue.

They moved, slipped aside effortlessly, making way for wide golden rays which broke forth in more-than-earthly beauty. In the light of these rays the small clouds looked like lovely little children.

But Gautama heeded them no more. The miracle which was taking place in their midst held him spellbound.

Something was gliding down along the golden rays, roseate, shimmering and glowing. At first this also looked like a great cloud, but then it changed, took on form, and above the beholder floated the fairest image of woman that a human eye ever beheld.

A dark-blue mantle, the colour of the sky at night, seemed to envelop the graceful Figure, which was encircled by long, silver-shimmering hair as though by a second mantle.

Before Her face, whose loveliness could only be guessed at, hung a luminous veil, through which the eyes shone like suns. On Her head the womanly Figure bore a golden crown with seven coloured gems, from which rays of light emanated upwards.

Gautama had dropped to his knees.

"Lady of all the Heavens!" he exulted, worshipping. And "Lady of all the Heavens" resounded around him like soft music from a thousand voices.

His arms stretched upwards. Deep longing seized him.

"Highest of women! I thank Thee that I am permitted to behold Thee, I thank Thee that I am permitted to proclaim Thee to mankind!"

The sounds ringing out around him grew stronger. Streams of power seemed to emanate from the Luminous Figure, and permeate him.

261

And he thought that he heard in the sounds a voice of ineffable, melodious timbre:

"Tell womanhood on earth that in the Divine Gardens there is a Garden of Purity! They shall strive to ascend to it."

The colours grew paler, the sounds fainter. Quietly as it had come, the wonderful picture disappeared. And Gautama thanked the Eternal One. Jubilation filled his soul.

TWO DAYS later it was time for the women to return. Gautama wished to speak to them himself, but he had arranged for his companions to remain near him, and listen.

The women arrived even before it had become hot. This time there were three women to receive the answer to the question.

"Tshakyamuno!" they exclaimed joyfully when they saw him. "Now we shall be allowed to hear the right answer!"

He invited them to rest, and they were glad to do so; for the ascent had been tiring for them.

Then they repeated their question, and Gautama told them that they had divined rightly. In one of the Holy Gardens, which however lay far below the Dwelling of the Eternal One, reigned a wonderful, holy woman, the Lady of all the Heavens.

She was so radiant that no human being could bear the sight of Her, so She wore delicate veils over Her countenance. She thought lovingly about earthly womanhood, and exhorted them to become pure and remain pure, so that one day they could seek and find the Holy Garden of Purity.

The words poured spontaneously from his lips, borne by the devotion alive within him. He himself knew that his grasp of all this was still too slight to allow him to proclaim more about it.

Perhaps not even all that he did say was right. But the women had to have an answer, and the Lady of the Heavens stood so clearly before his spiritual eye that he only needed to describe what he saw.

The women however were delighted. They were deeply grateful for what they had learned.

"Now we know for certain that there is a Woman in the Heavens Who takes care of us. She must have influenced the great Master Gautama to deliver the women from contempt, and set them before the men. Why then did he not tell us about the Lady of all the Heavens?"

"He might not have known about her," said Gautama cautiously, but he met with fierce contradiction.

"I know why," said the youngest of the women, "he had to wait until we ourselves asked about it. Not until then could we receive the answer. Do you think, Tshakyamuno, that we may be allowed to go to the convents and tell them about the Queen of all the Heavens?"

"Yes, go," cried Gautama joyfully. "That is the right spirit of sisterhood: if one has received something glorious herself, she passes it on! Your thinking is right, I am happy about it! But," he added thoughtfully, "they will not believe you. They do not know the Tshakyamuno."

At that the youngest of the women looked at him with understanding eyes.

"If you permit it, we shall not call you Tshakyamuno in the convents, but will use your real name. Then they will believe us. But you need have no fear that we shall disclose your whereabouts. We clearly perceive that you have chosen this solitude. We respect that."

"How do you know who I am?" asked Gautama, astonished.

"I have often seen you at night, when I was moved by thoughts of the Eternal One. When I saw you just now I recognised you again."

At that Gautama gave them permission to take these tidings to all the women, in his name. They asked for his blessing on their plan, and he invoked the Power of the Eternal One upon them.

That was a great experience for them all.

When the women had gone, Lidandha said regretfully:

"We did not even ask for their names!"

But Gautama thought that the name was unnecessary. The women who had received the holy revelation for their sisters on earth were known in the Light above. That was enough.

Gautama immersed himself deeply, ever more deeply in the new knowledge. The Lady of all the Heavens became a concept which seemed familiar to him from time immemorial, and yet only now had the Light One appeared to him.

263

He did not want to puzzle over it, but his thoughts kept returning to this point. Then he recalled the gracious Figure, the lovely voice, and from the depths of his soul arose a name which he was not able to keep to himself.

This name filled him with infinite happiness. And linked with it was a second name, whose power filled him completely.

All this was glorious, even though it was in vain that he tried to grasp the names aright. He knew that it would be possible for him one day, even if it were only in the hour of his departure from this earth.

MONTHS PASSED. The first year had come to an end. The three did not notice it in their solitude. Sometimes people came from the lowlands with all kinds of requests.

Once they had carried up a sick child for the Muno to bless. He felt compassion for the boy. In fervent prayer to the Eternal One he laid his hand on the burning forehead, and the fever subsided, the boy recovered. But Gautama forbade the people to speak of it, lest a throng of supplicants should come up to the mountain.

They indeed promised, but in view of the child's sudden recovery they could not keep silence. So then Gautama withdrew into the mountains every seventh day, very early in the morning, leaving it to Lidandha to give answers. He was not able to heal. After that the stream ebbed of its own accord.

In return, people always brought food with them, which was very welcome; for the proceeds of the sale of the horses were melting away.

Vada asked anxiously:

"Master, what shall we do? If we sell our horses, we shall never be able to ride abroad."

"Keep your horses and sell mine," was the answer, which alarmed them. "I shall have no further need of it."

That saddened his companions; to them it was a sign that Gautama would like to end his life up here, perhaps feeling his death to be near.

They gave a great deal of thought to how they could avoid selling the horse. Then they distinctly heard a little voice. However hard Vada looked about him, he could not see where it came from.

But Lidandha saw a little manikin standing before him. It led him to a place where stones of different colours were lying.

"Take, Lidandha," the little being encouraged him. "You will need them. If the Master is in want, call us. We will help."

Involuntarily Lidandha had taken the stones, whereupon the helper disappeared. Vada had heard everything, but had seen no one. But both were filled with their experience, and gave thanks to the Eternal One.

Lidandha took the stones to Gautama, who found among them one which he had never seen before. It was a yellow crystal of brilliant fire. The other two, of a rich blue and glorious red, were known to him. The elemental beings had often shown them to the seeking Brothers in the mountains. But this yellow stone delighted him.

"Where did you find it?" he asked, quite animated.

Then Lidandha told how the little being had shown them the stones, and for what purpose.

Gautama was pleased, and at once began to consider how he could send the stone, which seemed to him particularly precious, to the Mountain of the Eternal One.

When his pupil had left him, Gautama called for the little helper, who came immediately.

"I knew that you would be happy about the stone," said the little being animatedly. "You ought to wear a circlet set with these precious stones."

"I no longer need a circlet," protested the Master. "But I should like to know where such stones are to be found."

"They are embedded in the sand of our rivers. Those who know how to look for them often find very beautiful ones."

"I should so like to have such stones set in a consecrated chalice in the Temple on the Mountain of the Eternal One. But I do not know how I can send the message there. Would you be my messenger, little one?"

"Master, have you never called to Siddha's soul?" the elemental asked. "It often seeks you. Call it, and tell Siddha about the stones. Then we can help the Brothers to discover them. Our people know places in the sacred river where these yellow beauties are to be found."

The helper disappeared. Gautama mused. He should call Siddha's soul?

265

Then he would make contact with people again, would hear again about the Mountain. He had wanted to avoid that.

But the thought of having these particular gems set in a vessel in the Holy Temple was too tempting. Again and again the Master pondered what he should do.

But with these continual thoughts he had already unconsciously thrown out a bridge, on which Siddha's soul was able to reach him. In the night it stood before him, clear and sunny, as it had always shone through Siddha.

Great was Gautama's joy. All doubts were forgotten. How wonderful to know that this youth was to be his successor! Siddha himself was overjoyed that after fourteen months he had found the Master at last.

"I have often been near you, Gautama," he said, "but you had cut yourself off. I could not reach you."

Gautama showed Siddha the yellow stone, and then told him how it was to be used in the Temple.

Not a word was said about the experiences of the Master, or of the Brothers. Siddha was as reticent as ever, and waited for a question from the Master. But the latter no longer wished to know anything that could divert his thoughts from the inner absorption.

Pleasantly he bade farewell to the luminous, happy soul. But Siddha asked:

"May I come to you, Master, when you are about to leave this life? Let me be near you."

It was a great experience for Gautama to know that it was possible to summon a human soul, or to let his own soul go out to find another. Indeed he had heard that great sages had been able to do this, but he had never thought of trying to do it himself.

Actually it was obvious. If the soul could journey to distant, higher-lying spheres, why should it not be able to go consciously to some other spot in the surroundings familiar to it? Why had his guide never pointed this out to him?

Because he himself had to experience it out of some great need. Siddha's loyalty had found the way to him. Out of his purity he would yet discover many a thing which could help men upwards.

He should have told him about the Lady of all the Heavens! Why had he not thought of it? But perhaps the women were meant to receive tidings of it first. This was probably so, for the sublime female Being Whom he had been permitted to behold was the Heavenly Helper of womanhood.

Now She stood again clearly before his spiritual eyes. He thought he heard the glorious sounds, saw the luminous little roseate clouds. Again a name rose up in him, a name which he had never heard on earth, and yet it was so familiar to him. And then the other, the Power-dispensing one.

Gautama was on his knees, praying, supplicating:

"Eternal One, let me hold fast the Names Which fill all my inner being! Am I to blame that a thin veil still separates me from the revelation of that which alone is Life?"

Then a picture was shown to him: Vast luminous halls extended into immeasurable distances; rays of light streamed through them from above, then returned to the centre, where they converged in one point, and rose upwards again from there. A continuous cycle of the most glorious kind.

Gautama was allowed to gaze at this picture for a long, long time. More he did not see, but it sank deep into his soul, and there awakened resonant memories.

When had he seen these halls before? When had he experienced this flowing radiance? He did not know yet, but from out of his soul arose the memory of a Chalice, exquisite beyond compare, in which surged radiant Power. And One raised this Chalice!

At this moment it seemed as though a veil were drawn before his memory. And yet he knew that this One was the Centre of all the circles which he had seen. He must find this One.

The picture did not leave him after this. The light-halls greeted him whenever he became absorbed in prayer. The radiating seemed to pervade him glowingly, filling him with ever new power.

One day he found a connection: If this One Who raised the Chalice was the Centre of all the circles, then He was the Holy Will of God.

Holy revelation, which caused the human soul to vibrate in worship! Now there could be only *one* more step to the recognition of this One, of Whom suddenly he was certain that he knew Him.

Soul, *recognise* Him also, so that you may find the true life!

His outward life changed very much. Often he slept the whole day. He was wrapt in a light slumber, which then passed into a half-waking state, in which he dwelt with the invisible ones.

The little elementals led him to the source of the springs, into their workshops and their treasure-chambers. He then told his companions about it at the only meal which he took.

In vain Vada brought him fruit, which he usually enjoyed so much. Gautama ignored it. He only kept regularly to the evening meal and, contrary to his usual habit, he was communicative whenever he saw anything special.

"Bear it in mind, you must tell the others about it," he then used to exhort them.

But when the two had gone to their hut for the night his true life began. He spent the nights in prayer and absorption. His soul made long journeys. It never did so at random. Here too Gautama let himself be guided.

He had been allowed to see Siddharta once more. He no longer looked down in such a spell-bound way, although he was still not able to detach himself from the well. But a faint recognition seemed to be dawning on this earthbound soul that it must, and could, sever itself from the connection with its people.

An ardent wish arose in Gautama that this servant of the Eternal One might wrench himself free. The wish became a prayer, which was endowed with strength to shake the other's soul. Siddharta perceived this influence. Astonished, he looked about him, questioningly his gaze penetrated into the distance.

"O Lord of all the Worlds, let him find!" implored Gautama.

LIDANDHA and Vada had once more ridden together to Kusinara to make some purchases. Latterly they had always arranged that one of them remained with Gautama, but this time the Master had laughingly insisted that they should both go.

"What is likely to happen to me here?" he asked. "And if I need help there are countless elementals at my disposal."

And when they objected again he said:

"It is much more likely that something might happen to one of you, if you ride alone down the steep rocks. It is a comfort to me to know that you are together."

So they had parted. They would not be away for long. They had spread a cloth beside the altar-stone, which cast shade on the one who was resting there. Of late that had been Gautama's favourite resting-place.

Today he had made himself a comfortable seat with rugs, and arranged the cloth in such a way that he could see the sky through a gap.

Then Gautama sat leaning back against the stone with his hands clasped, and looked up through the gap, yearning, longing.

Gently, imperceptibly, luminous figures came up behind him. He did not see them. Instead he saw rays like pure gold coming from above. At first there were only three rays, which seemed to be seeking a way to him, then there were more, ever more.

Now came sounds also, sweet, soft notes and thunderous, jubilant peals, which made his heart beat as though it would burst. And now streams of colour flowed down from above, as harbingers of high revelations.

. The picture which he had already seen once appeared to him again, but this time it did not seem to be a picture. The hall was alive with all kinds of currents. Glowing, luminous, the Chalice stood on an Altar. Beings pressed round it.

Gautama's soul intuitively perceived a connection with all this. It longed impetuously to be among the others. Gently, unconscious of it, the soul was lifted up. And it stammered in the richness of intuitive perceiving, stammered words, names, which it knew, but of which Gautama had known nothing in the earthly body.

Above, a golden curtain appeared to move aside. Glorious chords sounded, solemn and festive, and from out of the folds of the curtain One stepped forth and took hold of the Chalice. White was the robe, silver were the locks, like rays of fire the eyes of this One.

"Parsifal, my Lord and King!" exulted the soul of Gautama. "Thee it was that I served unknowingly. Thou, Thou art the Centre of all circling, of all happening. Thou art the Holy Will of God, Thine Eternal Father."

The whole great Revelation was granted to him as the last gift of the Grace of his God. Jubilating, his soul received it, freed from all seeking, assured of the Eternal, Everlasting Truth.

But his body could not bear this excess of power. Luminous hands gently released it from the upward-floating soul, which hastened to where its King called it. Luminous beings received it and helped it.

The heavenly light went out, Gautama's body lay beneath the protecting cloth. Infinite peace transfigured its features.

Beside it stood two souls, which had journeyed here out of human bodies to be near him in these minutes of highest experiencing.

It was Grace from the Eternal One, that He granted them this. They knew it, and they thanked Him for it. They had been allowed to witness everything, everything in order to proclaim it, to help in paving the way to the Light for mankind.

They were Suddhodana, the King, and Siddha, the first Brother. These two, who were the lightest and purest of all those still alive on earth whom Gautama had loved, had been led by their loyalty to find their way to him in his last moments.

Filled with gratitude, they returned to their earthly cloaks, and announced Gautama's homegoing.

"Now he too has become Buddha. He has awakened in other fields. Gautama Buddha is greater than Siddharta Buddha!"

The tidings resounded through the peoples of the Indus, from the mountain-peaks of the Himalayas down to the shores of the surging sea.

When the two souls had gone, the invisible ones stepped to the lifeless cloak of their friend. Little elemental beings brought the promised circlet with the precious yellow stones.

"It is his due, for he has been permitted to behold the King!" they whispered, and placed it round the cold brow.

But on his breast they placed a strange jewel, whose like no human eye in this country had yet seen. It was a cross with arms of equal length, whose centre was formed by a white stone.

"He has served the Eternal Cross of Truth," they said among themselves, "therefore he may bear this image when his earthly form is laid to rest!"

When the two companions returned to the mountain just before sunset, they found that their Master had closed his eyes to this world. Lidandha saw the guard which the little helpers and the great luminous beings had formed around the body of their Master. Opened by the shock of the loss of their Master, they both saw with amazement the ornaments which were invisible to earthly eyes.

"As servant of the Supreme King, he is allowed to wear them," one of the little men whispered to Lidandha.

"If only we had stayed with him," Vada lamented. "He had to die all alone!"

"Was allowed to go home!" corrected Lidandha, but his heart, too, was heavy with sorrow.

They spent the night in prayer beside the cloak of Gautama. When morning came, they discussed the need to convey the news to the Brothers, so that the lifeless body could be taken to the Mountain of the Eternal One.

Lidandha decided to ask the helpers. Their answer was:

"Wait! Everything is already prepared."

And so absolute was Lidandha's trust in them that he convinced Vada too that they could abandon all anxieties.

When the sun was at its zenith, a magnificent procession of horsemen approached. In the rays of the sun, resplendent figures on richly-caparisoned horses appeared; at their head rode one who looked like Gautama restored to youth.

Amazed, and as though stupefied, the two solitary men gazed at the approaching cavalcade. Who could be coming?

The riders sprang from their steeds, and reverently approached the worship-stone, at the foot of which Gautama's body still lay, covered with a length of embroidered silk.

Had someone already known of his demise? It must be so. The men placed themselves in a circle around the worship-stone. Their leader, however, stepped up to the lifeless body, lifted the cover, and gazed with wistful love into the beautiful, still countenance.

"Men of Khatmandu," he then began, in a voice which pierced Gautama's companions, so strongly did it remind them of his, "Gautama has become Buddha! He was chosen before thousands to serve the Lord of all the Worlds. He did so, devoting his whole life. What drove him was nothing but the loyalty which he owed his Lord. Men will never know how much he sacrificed in order to be able to proclaim the Eternal One to them. But he lacked nothing. He felt richly rewarded in being allowed to serve.

271

"We all owe him gratitude. Let us give it to him through never departing from what he has taught us!"

Now Suddhodana asked where Gautama's companions were. They came forward, and told him all they knew.

Then the King began to speak once more and told the deeply affected listeners about the death of the great Buddha. Although he did not understand all the connections, they nevertheless heard a revelation which lifted their lives above the commonplace. None forgot this hour beside the dead Buddha.

Afterwards King Suddhodana brought the bier on which the body of his brother was to be carried to the foot of the mountain. There a carriage with gilded carving and four noble horses awaited the precious remains.

At that Lidandha took heart and asked:

"King, where are you taking him?"

Suddhodana hesitated a moment, then he mastered himself and said:

"I should have liked to take him to Kapilavastu, but you are right: he belongs on the Mountain of the Eternal One. You have shown by your question that my thinking was selfish.

"But first we must embalm him in Khatmandu, lest the body should decay before we reach our destination."

So it was done. Gautama's companions joined the train which took the lifeless cloak to Khatmandu, and from there to the Mountain of the Eternal One.

As the cavalcade reached the plain of the sacred river a second, less magnificent procession came to meet it: Siddha, with some of the Brothers who had come to fetch the dead Master.

On the Mountain of the Eternal One they found a multitude of people, Brothers and Sisters from all parts of the realm. Wherever the messengers on horseback had not yet been, elemental beings had taken the tidings.

The burial chamber was lined with the precious white stone, and at the head of the couch which was to receive the dead Master stood a golden vessel with seven yellow stones, a masterpiece without equal.

Clearly visible to all who could see, and to so many whose eyes were opened on this day, were many beings, great and small, who took part in the funeral.

Siddha gave the farewell address at the worship-stone, and as Suddhodana had done in the seclusion of the mountains, so he told here of the passing of the Master.

Better than the King, he knew how to clothe the experience in words that all could grasp. In humility they experienced the Grace of the Lord of all the Worlds, Who had granted to the departing servant, and with him to them all, such a high revelation.

Siddha had had a tablet prepared, with golden arabesques on the white background. The only words in the centre were:

Gautama – Buddha

To the astonished question of some of the Brothers, Siddha answered very simply:

"It was his own wish."

Whatever else the Master had said to his successor was to remain locked in his soul.

Abd-ru-shin

In The Light Of Truth: The Grail Message

The Author was born in 1875 in Bischofswerda, Germany. His given name was Oskar Ernst Bernhardt. After being educated and trained in business, he established himself in Dresden and became financially successful. In the years that followed, he made many journeys abroad, and wrote successful travel books, stories, and plays.

After residing for some time in New York, Mr. Bernhardt journeyed to London, England. There, the outbreak of World War I took him unawares, and in 1914 he was interned on the Isle of Man.

The seclusion of internment brought with it an inner deepening. He reflected continuously over questions connected with the meaning of life, birth and death, responsibility and free will, God and Creation. More and more the desire awakened within him to help humanity. He was released in the Spring of 1919 and returned to Germany.

He began to write the first lectures for *In the Light of Truth: The Grail Message* in 1923. His explanation of the Knowledge of Creation resounded among his hearers.

In 1928, Abd-ru-shin settled in Austria, Tyrol on a mountain plateau called Vomperberg, where he continued writing *The Grail Message*. The seizure of power in Austria by the Nazis in 1938 ended his work there. He was arrested, and his land and property were appropriated without compensation. Abd-ru-shin was exiled to Kipsdorf in the Erzgebirge, where he was under surveillance by the Gestapo. He was forbidden any further work for making *The Grail Message* known publicly.

On December 6, 1941, Abd-ru-shin died from the effects of these measures. After the war his family returned to Vomperberg, and carried on his work.

If you have questions about the content of this Work,
please contact Reader Services at:

Grail Foundation Press
P.O. Box 45
Gambier, Ohio 43022
Telephone: 614.427-9410
Fax: 614.427-4954

IN THE LIGHT OF TRUTH: THE GRAIL MESSAGE
by Abd-ru-shin

Linen edition, three volumes combined
ISBN 1-57461-006-6
5.5" x 8.5"
1,062 pages
Paper edition, three-volume box set
ISBN 1-57461-003-1
6" x 9"
1,096 pages

Original edition: German
Translations available in:
Czech, Dutch, English, Estonian, French, Hungarian,
Italian, Portuguese, Rumanian, Russian,
Slovak, Spanish

Available at your local bookstore
or directly through the publisher.

Grail Foundation Press
P.O. Box 45
Gambier, Ohio 43022
1-800-427-9217

Publisher's catalog available on request

Further Writings by Abd-ru-shin:

THE TEN COMMANDMENTS OF GOD
THE LORD'S PRAYER
72 pages
Linen clothbound
ISBN 1-57461-007-4
Paperback
ISBN 1-57461-004-X

QUESTIONS AND ANSWERS
232 pages
Clothbound
ISBN 3-87860-145-X

PRAYERS
16 pages
Paperback
ISBN 3-87860-138-7

Available at your local bookstore
or directly through the publisher.

Grail Foundation Press
P.O. Box 45
Gambier, Ohio 43022
1-800-427-9217

Publisher's catalog available on request

excursions

Duke University Press   Durham & London   2007

Excursions *michael jackson*

© 2007 Duke University Press

All rights reserved

Printed in the United States of America on

acid-free paper ∞

Designed by C. H. Westmoreland

Typeset in Warnock Pro by Keystone

Typesetting, Inc.

Library of Congress Cataloging-in-

Publication Data appear on the last printed

page of this book.

Contents

Acknowledgments

For generous support during my fieldwork or critical feedback on draft versions of the chapters in this book, I wish to thank Brian Boyd, Susanne Bregnbaek, Mark Edwards, Ann-Kristin Ekman, Lisa Guenther, Ghassan Hage, Manuka Henare, Isata Jah, Sewa M. Koroma, Gerard Macdonald, Bronwen Nicholson, Hans Lucht, Vincent O'Sullivan, Michael Puett, Jennifer Shennan, Cris Shore, Jonathan Skinner, Donald Swearer, Allan Thomas, Henrik Vigh, and Rebecca Williams. My excursions would have been impossible were it not for travel and research grants from the Institute of Anthropology, University of Copenhagen, and from Harvard Divinity School.

To think with an enlarged mentality one trains one's imagination to go visiting.—HANNAH ARENDT, *Lectures on Kant's Political Philosophy*

Preface

theme and variations

I imagine myself on a long road. Behind me, the road disappears into darkness, and I think of those who traveled this way before me—precursors and pathfinders. Looking ahead, I am aware that the new day will dawn on others who will walk stretches of this road that I will not live to see. Now I take in the landscape around me: a seemingly boundless plain under skies that go on forever—filled with the blazing sun in summer, rain clouds in winter, and at night the stars. Other roads there are, to be sure, with strangers walking on them, strangers whose preoccupations are very different from my own, and I do not know when and how my road will intersect with theirs. But how small and transitory is my place in this vastness! How quickly the earth, the road, the sky outrun me in every direction! And yet I do not live as though my life were without signifi-

cance. I feel as I have always felt, that I am going somewhere despite the
difficult terrain, the adverse weather, the times I lose my way. And I have
a strong sense that my own life is connected to the lives of those behind,
around, and ahead of me. It may be illusory, but without this sense that I
am vitally a part of this world in which I move, without the possibility of
conversations and interactions with others, including people in societies
remote from the one in which I was born and raised, I would not press on.

Conversations

Following Michael Oakeshott, I like to think of the intellectual life as a series of conversations involving different voices and idioms, including those of poetry and science, rather than as a project that might deliver us from the curse of Babel, imposing "a single character upon signifi-cant human speech" (1991:488–89). Conversation is open-ended. One might say it is aporetic, because difference is accepted as grist to the mill rather than argued away, and reason is "neither sovereign nor alone" (489).

My own work has its origins in three kinds of conversation. First comes the ongoing dialogue with the authors who have captured my intellectual imagination, and to whom my own projects pay homage. A second set of conversations has sprung from ethnographic fieldwork in Sierra Leone, Aboriginal Australia, and New Zealand. Third are those conversations with close friends, students, and colleagues that also shape the way I think and write. But because it is impossible to divine in retrospect from where or from whom one's ideas have come, conversa-tion admits neither one authentic voice nor any final conclusion. In-deed, this is the humanizing effect of conversation—that it refuses to prioritize the voice of reason over voices that may, at first hearing, seem less reasonable, and that it carries us so far beyond what any one person says that we can honestly say that whatever new understand-ings are born of it, they belong to us all. So, of any text we read or of any interlocutor in the marginal worlds in which we sojourn we can say that there is no one reading, no one truth, and that, moreover, the "identity or plurality of the [persons] involved is unimportant" since every thinker "*creates* [his or her] own precursors" (Borges 1970:236; emphasis original). What we call knowledge is thus inescapably a stepchild of intersubjectivity, and its value lies less in the abstract claims it makes than in its function as a "tool for conviviality" (Illich 1973)—a means whereby we bring our intellectual forebears back to life in relation to the questions with which we grapple now, a way in which we do justice to those whose voices have been muted because they allegedly exist outside the modern world, and a process by which we attest to the fact that meaning emerges not from isolated contemplation of the world but from active engagement in it.

This book is also concerned with the disconnectedness of our being-in-the-world—one might almost say its incoherence. The world cannot be put into words, and the ultimate questions of being cannot be answered. But in so far as we have no option but to speak, think, and act, we are bound to struggle for the kind of language, the kind of thought, and the kind of action that does greatest justice to life as it is lived. In the *Bhagavad Gita*, Arjuna finds himself between two armies, each of which includes kinsmen, teachers, companions, and friends, and he despairs at the impossibility of reconciling the idea of victory with the taking of life. However, his charioteer, Krishna, offers him exhaustive philosophical arguments for seeing beyond his immediate predicament, so that finally Arjuna overcomes his doubts and yields to a higher and eternal truth. But why should Arjuna's dilemma be dismissed as illusory? Why should human beings kill one other in order to live? Given the carnage and desolation across the Indo-Gangetic plain, described toward the end of the Mahabharata, Arjuna's doubts seem vindicated (Sen 2005:5).

Although, in this book, I focus on the quandaries of everyday life, I do not conclude that life is absurd; only that it is necessary to constantly remind ourselves of the limits to which existence can be subject to reason, and to open ourselves up continually to that which lies beyond our grasp (see Jaspers 1955), embracing a tragic view of life that refuses the idea of implicate orders or intelligible design but also recognizes that life would be insufferable without such illusions.[1] T. S. Eliot observed that "humankind cannot bear very much reality" (1948:14) and Robert Graves spoke of the "cool web of language" with which we spell away "the overhanging night," dull "the rose's cruel scent," and "retreat from too much joy or too much fear" (1965:47) But the ways in which we define meaning, whether in the stories we tell or the theoret-

Knowledge is the stepchild of intersubjectivity.

ical models we build, are not descriptions of how we live, and there is always far more to be said than we can possibly encompass with the concepts, cognitive schemes, and vernacular expressions that we customarily have at our disposal. The phenomenological epoché is one way of addressing this problem of overcoming conventional mindsets, for by emphasizing the need to continually see the world afresh or from another vantage point, the epoché inspires the kind of "disciplined naïveté" (MacLeod 1958:34) that we usually associate with poetry.

Thinking Poetically

What does it mean to think poetically, and what is the place of such thought in the academy? Of Walter Benjamin, Hannah Arendt wrote that "he thought poetically, but he was neither a poet nor a philosopher" (1973:154). Taking Benjamin's work as a point of departure, let me outline the place of the poetic in the excursionary essays that make up this book.

In the first place, to think poetically does not necessarily mean writing in the highly condensed, allusive manner one associates with poetry; rather, it is a way of keeping alive a sense of what it means to live in the world one struggles to understand, rather than treat that world as a text or abstract object of contemplation. Theodor Adorno notes that the rebus was the model of Benjamin's philosophy (1981:230), a way of seeing ideas through pictures. *Non verbis sed rebus*—not by words but by things. Though sometimes recondite and dense, poetic writing gives us pictures of the world that are sometimes organized as a shocking montage rather than a consoling narrative. Sometimes images are juxtaposed that do not conventionally or logically belong together. Sometimes these pictures imitate the forms that the world itself appears to assume—journeys, epiphanies, and critical events that bear comparison with waves gradually swelling and forming out of the sea, then moving inshore before collapsing and expending themselves on a shelving beach.

In the second place, poetical thinking is neither focused on one's own subjectivity nor on the objectivity of the world, but on what emerges in the space between. It thus refuses to create an illusion of impartiality and authority by excluding from its picture of the world the author's

Poetics & phenomenology.

Space bet- objectivity & subjectivity

relationship with others, and the particular circumstances in which his or her understanding was reached.

In the third place, the poetical abhors the didactic. It has no axe to grind, no moral to draw, no knowledge to possess. What occurs and appears to us is explained in terms of neither antecedent events nor unconscious processes; rather, its meaning is consummated in the newness with which we see the world and the new ways that become available to us to act in it: the foreign suddenly familiar and the familiar strange.

Finally, the poetical is not to be confused with the rhetorical, for in so far as metaphor and allegory reduce the particular to a mere sign or embodiment of a general idea, or depend on distinctions between surface and depth, they go against the grain of our intent, which is to give everything its due and place every domain of experience on the same footing. Here I part company from Walter Benjamin, for whereas he embraces Plato's view that ideas and phenomena are "fundamentally different" and goes on to proclaim the task of the philosopher as one of practicing "the kind of description of the world of ideas which automatically includes and absorbs the empirical world" (1998:32), assuming "the act of naming" as the way in which "ideas are displayed," I take the view that what is most fascinating about human consciousness is the way in which intelligibility and sensibility arise together, often in surprising and illuminating combinations. Words, ideas, emotions, impressions, and imaginings are all entailed in the events of which we form a part, and no one should be privileged in our accounts of them.

Excursions

In the mythology of the Bosavi, who live in the rain-forested Southern Highlands of Papua New Guinea, people turn into birds when they die. Birds are *ane mama*, the "gone reflections" of the dead who have passed on to the treetops and there constitute "a metaphoric human society" (Feld 1982:30, 31; 2001:54). Birdsong is thought to be "talk from the dead," and the sonic patternings of sadness and weeping among the bereaved are echoed in the calls of different species of birds. As Steven Feld notes, "poetic language is bird language" (1982:34) and " 'becoming a bird' is the passage from life to death" (218). At the same time, the

Preface xiii

semantic field of Bosavi song overlaps, mimics, and merges with the sound of water falling and flowing through a landscape of places that themselves give form to song (Feld 1996). In the conventional wisdom of the West, birds are not persons, and the anthropomorphic equation of them is a sign of primitive thought—beautiful perhaps; mistaken certainly. But if we consider the effects of this conceit in Bosavi life— the way this equation enables people to live with loss, to express their grief, to connect meaningfully and intimately with the forest environment in which they live and work—we may be persuaded to be less judgmental about its reasonableness.

In the fall of 2004, Steve Feld came to Copenhagen to give some lectures and workshops at the university. Because this was his first visit to the city, we spent much of our time together, walking the streets, taking in the sights, and catching up on what we had been doing since we last saw each other in Sydney seven years before. As I listened to him talk about his sound recordings of bells in various parts of Europe, I began to recognize an uncanny parallelism between his current work and my own. I had also been making excursions to various places and writing around the themes these happened to inspire. To some extent, I told my companion, this way of doing ethnography had been born of necessity: I had failed to get grants for more extended fieldwork and, besides, the constraints of family life made it difficult for me to travel abroad for more than a few weeks at a time. Perhaps, too, the rigors of living and working in places like Central Australia and Sierra Leone had begun to tell, and I thought of the way my mentors had reinvented themselves—George Devereux turning his attention to Periclean Athens and dreams in classical tragedy, Edmund Leach bringing his brilliance to bear on Old Testament mythology, and Jack Goody researching the symbolic meaning of flowers in various societies around the world. But my excursionary ethnography also sprang from my interest in events, and in finding new ways of practicing an empirically based writing, much as Steve was experimenting with sonic bricolages that mixed such things as birdsong, bells, and bicycles. After describing my recent trips to Lebanon, Sweden, New Zealand, and the south of France, I confessed to my colleague that it nonetheless seemed presumptuous to write about places in which one had passed no more than a few days, and any self-respecting anthropologist would undoubtedly find this way of

"excursionary ethnography"

going about one's business both shallow and suspect. Fortunately, Steve was more confident about this itinerant and ad hoc way of pursuing one's intellectual and aesthetic interests, and he recounted anecdotes from his own recent fieldwork that quickly confirmed my view that many valuable insights and illuminations are ephemeral and come to us, as it were, unbidden. Though we both had ample experience of the rewards of long sojourns and systematic research in remote regions of the world, there were, we agreed, in the contemplation of objects—or in the adventitious juxtaposition of sounds, colors, ideas, words, and images—equally interesting possibilities for seeing the world in a new light. One spring day in Finland, Steve said, as he was preparing to record the bells of the seven-hundred-year-old Lutheran cathedral at Turku, a flock of chaffinches (*peipponen*) began clamoring around him as if in anticipation and then in response to the swelling and enveloping clangor of the bells, and this reminded him of the "sonic resemblance" between birds and bells—the rainforest birdsong in Papua New Guinea "sounding as quotidian clocks and spirit voices" and European bells heralding and marking "religious and civil time" (Feld 2004). Yet though this perceived resemblance between birds and percussive sounds, and between the ways both mediate between earth and ether, enhances our experience, it explains nothing. Still, this was also something we found congenial, for we clearly shared a fascination with forms of writing or sound recording that had recourse to notions of epiphany and event, in which purely contingent overlappings, fusions, and juxtapositions suggest new ways of thinking about phenomena, even though these may entail no causal explanation or certain knowledge. One excursion I had planned to make was to Oslo, I told Steve. I had wanted for some time to see Edvard Munch's paintings, and also visit the city in which Knut Hamsun had lived.[2] Hamsun's skepticism—which Isaac Bashevis Singer calls his Pyrrhonism (1976:10)—had always struck a chord in me. And it appealed to me that these two great Norwegians were born within four years of each other (Hamsun in 1859, Munch in 1863). Given my interest in the interface of art and philosophy, I hoped to gather experiences that would occasion a meditation on the tension between showing and telling. Steve had spent a lot of time in Oslo, and he had twice visited the Munch Museum. He described how, after one of these visits, a Norwegian colleague and friend took him along the path above the asylum where Munch had painted *The Scream*. "The painter would no doubt have heard the demented or despairing cries of the inmates as he worked at his easel on the path," Steve said. "And in the distance he would have seen the inlet and the low hills, flowing together, just as he painted them, except today the view is marred by construction work going on in that area." This was precisely the kind of insight I had imagined I might have, and it was both unsettling and heartening to realize how kindred spirits happen onto the same path. One night, over dinner, we discovered that we both had a low threshold of tolerance for artificially fermented, chemically doctored wines, and this led to a discussion of how one could identify and buy "natural" wines in which the vagaries of weather, soil, and winemaker were not clinically "corrected" with synthetic yeasts, enzymes, sweeteners, and migraine-causing sulfites. This in turn prompted me to think how the elusive concept of *terroir* might be used as a metaphor for what Steve and I were striving for in our work—the mysterious triune of earth, climate, and the vintner's art translating into a threefold combination of good field-work, a convivial environment, and a sense of craft and ancestry.

One misty morning, I was waiting outside Sankt Johannes church in Nørrebro while Steve, standing under a chestnut tree a few yards away, recorded the stroke of eight, followed by the angelus on the church bells, allowing this sound to mingle with the soft clicking of bicycles passing along the street, as well as footsteps and traffic, and the distant chiming of another set of bells across the lakes. As I watched my colleague, concentrated on his work and carefully monitoring the tape recorder in his hand, I began to experience this familiar location not through my eyes and skin, but through my hearing. The distant bells, for instance, I had never noticed before, nor the subtle interleaving of the sounds of cycles, the cold breeze now stirring, and the pedestrians passing on the sidewalk. Our habitual accounts of the world depend not only on what we see, but on solid and linear geometry, on time-tables, graphs, and classificatory diagrams. In a soundscape, however, one was wholly in between, caught up in the crosscurrents, layerings, blurrings, and metamorphoses of things that have no fixed definition of their own, but come into being solely within these changing fields of mixed emotions, associations, and auditory flows. This brought to mind how attuned intersubjectivity is to the senses. To emphasize one

terroir

area of the sensorium—sight over sound, smell over hearing, touch over all—is to subtly alter one's experience of self and other, something which in different people and different societies is used to both devastating and therapeutic effect. Steve's inspired sound compositions also brought home to me how surprising juxtapositions can spark off associations, memories, and ideas that neither are intrinsic properties of the things or words momentarily combined nor reflect the personality of the sound engineer. And so it was—as Steve finished his recording and we strolled on toward the lake, looking for a café where we might buy a coffee before his lecture that morning—that our conversation turned to the uncanny similarities between the mood of unrequited longing and loss that pervades the guitar songs of Bosavi youth (just as it pervaded the dirges of their forebears), Māori *waiata*, and the songs my wife Francine and I used to hear as we lay awake at night in our caravan at Lajamanu, listening to the Warlpiri Tanami Band practicing on the other side of the football oval. This tone of grieving and loss could not signify nostalgia for a time or place these people knew firsthand (the traditional life of their grandparents was long gone); rather, it articulated a longing for a choice they had never had since, like adopted kids, they had never inhabited the world whose passing they now lamented, and had therefore never had the freedom to embrace or repudiate it as their fathers had. This was their loss: The inability to exercise control over their lives. The discovery that one was chaff blown in the wind of history, a creature of forces that had swept one's own world away, and that had carried one into another world where one had no place.

In these somewhat disconnected thoughts is the suggestion of a picture. Echoing William James's description of radical empiricism as a "mosaic philosophy," the essays in this book attempt to preserve the ways in which, in both body and mind, the author experienced, dwelt on, and made sense of certain events. Three references may capture something of what I have hoped to achieve. The first is Joseph Needham's account of taoism, a philosophy that enjoins us not to try to possess the world as an object that may be known, but, instead, to fully enter into it as an aspect of ourselves not yet fully realized. As Needham notes, all manner of scientific discoveries were accidentally made in the course of these disinterested immersions in nature (Ronan 1978:

103). Second is Albert Camus's comment, that "for the absurd man it is not a matter of explaining and solving, but of experiencing and describing. Everything begins with lucid indifference" (1955:78). And finally I take a remark by Michael Kimmelman concerning Shomei Tomatsu's photographs: "Declining to preach, the art maintains an attitude of remote skepticism, which, as the photographer Leo Rubenstein notes in a remarkably perceptive essay for the show's catalog, is how an honest man necessarily regards his times" (2004:44).

Existential Aporias

Opening any newspaper any day of the week, one confronts problems that seem to admit of no solution. In the case of a severely brain-damaged woman kept alive by medical machines, who has the right to decide whether or not to prolong her life? The state or her family (and who in her family)? How can we reconcile our respect for life and the taking of life in cases of abortion, capital punishment, and war? How can we speak of *universal* human rights when in practice these are so often made to serve partisan interests? In the case of circumcision or the wearing of the *hijab* in Europe, should the laws of the secular state take precedence over Qur'anic injunctions—and how are those injunctions to be read? Are indigenous or migrant peoples' cultural rights compatible with universal human rights? And how will peace be secured in the Middle East? While this book touches on quandaries and questions like these, my concern is not with political, ethical, or legal issues per se, but with what Theodor Adorno referred to in his "reflections from damaged life" (1978) as "gaps," or what I shall call existential aporias.

In a previous book, *In Sierra Leone*, I described my reunion with an old friend who had survived the horrors of a ten-year-long civil war only to find himself destitute and marginalized. Shocked by the stories Noah told me, I was moved to ask if he was still *sunike*—a Kuranko word that Noah translated as "free thinker," though it meant specifically one who was neither a Muslim nor a Christian. Noah replied, "I have never embraced any moral system, and I hope I never will." Sometime later, when we were talking about the options open to those who lost limbs, loved ones, and livelihoods in the war, Noah again surprised me

lucid indifference.

gaps or existential aporias

with his acceptance of how little one can do to redress wrongs or explain the events that befall us.

> Say a hawk came out of the blue and seized one of your chickens. What can you do? You can't get it back. The hawk has flown away. You have no means of hunting it down or killing it. All you can do is accept, and go on with your life.[3] Look at me. I have no way of taking revenge on the rebels who took away my livelihood, but at least I can rid myself of them. I can shut them out of my mind. I can expel them from my life. (Jackson 2004:68)

Comments such as these inspired me to ponder what drives some of us to believe that there is some overarching or implicate order in the world that rewards virtue, punishes evil, reveals meaning, or rescues us from nothingness, while others, like Noah, seem less anxious about divining the hidden workings of cause and effect, or of destiny, and focus instead on steadying themselves in the midst of life's flux, struggling day by day to embrace the rough and the smooth with equanimity. Perhaps there is an echo here of Voltaire's experience of the Lisbon earthquake in 1755, which cured him of the theodicy of G. W. Leibniz, or of Adorno, who observed that after Auschwitz "we cannot say any more that the immutable is truth, and that the mobile, transitory is appearance" (1973:361).

In the passage in *Minima Moralia* entitled "Gaps," Adorno begins aphoristically: "The injunction to practise intellectual honesty usually amounts to sabotage of thought" (1978:80). Adorno refuses to make distance from experience an acceptable price for rendering experience intelligible. He is critical of the academic conceit that words mirror the world, or that one can disclose all the steps whereby one reached some understanding or, for that matter, became the person one now is. One may contrive the appearance of such a movement from cause to effect, one thing leading inexorably to another, but this is simply an intellectual sleight of hand that produces systematic understanding at the cost of describing life in all its wavering, confusing, deviant, and contradictory detail. "If life fulfilled its vocation directly," Adorno concludes,

> it would miss it. Anyone who died old and in the consciousness of seemingly blameless success, would secretly be the model schoolboy who reels

Causality as intellectual sleight of hand.

off all life's stages without gaps or omissions, an invisible satchel on his back. Every thought which is not idle, however, bears branded on it the impossibility of its full legitimation, as we know in dreams that there are mathematical lessons, missed for the sake of a blissful morning in bed, which can never be made up. Thought waits to be woken one day by the memory of what has been missed, and to be transformed into teaching. (1978:81)

What we miss, gloss over, censor out, or artificially fill in when we impose narrative or intellectual order on our experience is what we might attempt, were we trained otherwise, simply to describe and accept. This would mean acknowledging the gap between precept and practice, the engrained habits that contradict our fantasies of freedom, the gulf between my reality and the reality of others, the difference between what can and cannot be said, the lived particulars that defy our generalizations, and the contradictions that point to "the untruth of identity" and "the fact that the concept does not exhaust the thing conceived" (Adorno 1973:5). Anticipating a changed philosophy that gives up persuading itself and others "that it has the infinite at its disposal," and that scorns "solidification in a body of enumerable theorems," Adorno makes a case for a way of thinking and writing whose substance lies "in the diversity of objects that impinge upon it and of the objects it seeks, a diversity not wrought by any scheme." To these objects, he writes, "philosophy would truly give itself rather than use them as a mirror in which to reread itself, mistaking its own image for concretion" (1973:13).

Adorno's gaps are reminiscent of what the Greeks called *aporiai*. *Aporia* literally means "lacking a path" (*a-poros*), a path that is impassable. But unlike *odos*, *poros* connotes a sea lane or river road—passages that leave no permanent trace, surfaces "widowed of routes," where there are no stable landmarks and every trail must be blazed anew (Kofman 1988:10). An aporia is where we find ourselves out of our depth, in difficulties, all at sea. "The sea is . . . the aporetic space *par excellence*," writes Sarah Kofman, "and it is still the best metaphor for the aporia of discourse" (12). More generally, an aporia is a "puzzle," a "question for discussion" or "state of perplexity," and the aporetic method for broaching problems without offering immediate solutions

acknowledging the gap bet. precept + practice.

Aporia = "lacking a path"

is exemplified by the Socratic method and the philosophical skepticism of thinkers such as Pyrrho, Timon, Arcesilaus, Diogenes, and Sextus Empiricus. Sextus was quite explicit about the connection between skepticism and the aporetic method (1996:89), arguing that the skeptic way be embraced as a way of life (*agoge*) or disposition (*dunamis*), and that the suspension of judgment (*epoché*) helps us achieve inner tranquility or peace of mind (*ataraxia*). Also influenced by Pyrrho, Michel de Montaigne advocated that we accept both good and ill since both "are one substance with our life"—a life that is "composed, like the harmony of the world, of discords as well as of different tones, sweet and harsh, sharp and flat, soft and loud" (2004:394). More recently, the aporia, defined as "an antinomy arising through the simultaneous existence of mutually exclusive entities, each irreducible to the terms of the other" (Ackerly and Gontarski 2004:16) has become a key postmodern trope, as in the writings of Samuel Beckett where logical absurdity and existential impasses combine to create overpowering images of human absurdity and indecisiveness. The last lines of *The Unnameable*, for example—"I can't go on, I'll go on," may serve as an example, or the following from his *Three Dialogues with Georges Duthuit*: "The expression that there is nothing to express, nothing with which to express, no power to express, no desire to express, together with the obligation to express" (Beckett 1987:103). Such ironic and aporetic situations also fascinated Jacques Derrida who wrote, for example, of the impossibility of experiencing the one event that most singularly and intimately concerns oneself—one's own death (1993).

The classical Greek aporia was primarily a *logical* conundrum that may be resolved through rational ingenuity—as in Zeno's paradoxes where motion seems to be both possible and impossible. As Immanuel Kant observed, such aporias are artifacts of the way we *think* about the world and are not inherent in reality. In this book, my focus is, however, less on the aporias that arise from intellectual contemplation than on the enigmas, gaps, and double binds that seem to inhere in the human condition itself, such as the fact that every individual is unique yet shares most of his or her phylogenetic traits with every other member of his or her species; or the fact that every human being needs to act in relation to others and the world, yet is to the same extent acted on; or the vexing gap between experience and expression that makes mutual

Beckett & "logical absurdity"

Zeno's paradox

understanding so fraught with difficulty. By describing how such perplexities are lived, I hope to paint a more compelling picture than if I simply analyzed the historical or social circumstances under which they made their appearance, or suggested how they might be resolved.

Some of the best examples of the limits of rational thought may be found at the beginning of the Sung dynasty in China (ca. 960 BCE) when the "paradoxical words and strange deeds" of the Zen masters of the T'ang period were developed into the classic form of the koan (Dumoulin 1994:245). Although the Chinese term *kung-an* signifies "public announcement," the koan's announcement takes the form of puzzle that mystifies the listener or reader, inspiring him or her to abandon rational or habitual ways of responding to doubt and become open to new forms of understanding, such as we might call lateral thinking, poetical thinking, or negative dialectics. Heinrich Dumoulin aptly refers to the koan as "a kind of spoof on the human intellect" (253) and notes that its aim is to foster a sense of reality devoid of any sense of contending dualisms. As one Zen master put it: "We have not to avoid contradiction, but to live it" (qtd. in Benoit 1984:97). Accordingly, Zen is "not speculation at all but immediate experience of what, as the bottomless ground of Being, cannot be apprehended by intellectual means, and cannot be conceived or interpreted even after the most unequivocal and uncontestable experiences: one knows it by not knowing it" (Herrigel 1972:17). Consider the following from 1036 BCE, when the Rinzai school of Zen was entering its golden age. The koan takes the form of a play of question and answer.

Q: "All people have their own native place owing to the causal nexus. Where is your native place?"
A: "Early in the morning I ate white rice gruel; now I feel hungry."
Q: "In what way do my hands resemble the Buddha's hands?"
A: "Playing the lute in the moonlight."
Q: "In what way do my feet resemble the feet of a donkey?"
A: "When the heron stands in the snow, its color is not the same"
(Dumoulin 1994:247)

One finds echoes of this oblique and disconcerting technique in many traditions and many places.[4] Like many ethnographers, the renowned Danish explorer and ethnologist Knud Rasmussen plied his Iglulik Eskimo informants with endless questions, expecting to get a coherent and consistent account of their worldview. But despite the fact that Rasmussen was fluent in Iglulik, his inquiries were met with "long and circumstantial statement[s] of all that was permitted and all that was forbidden" and his "why" questions were regarded as unreasonable and impertinent. One evening, as the light was fading and snow-filled wind gusts blew across the ground, one of Rasmussen's Iglulik informants, a man called Aua, impulsively invited the ethnographer to accompany him across the frozen landscape. First, Aua pointed to a group of bowed and exhausted men returning from their long vigils over blowholes on the ice. They had not killed a single seal, and their entire day of "painful effort and endurance had been in vain" (Rasmussen 1929:55). Aua asked Rasmussen why this should be so. Aua then led Rasmussen to Kublo's house where a couple of children crouched, shivering, under a skin rug on the bench, the blubber lamp turned down low to conserve fuel. Why should the house not be warm and bright, the children enjoying life, Aua asked. He then led Rasmussen to a small snow hut where his sister Natseq lived alone; she was suffering from a malignant cough and had not long to live. "Why must people be ill and suffer pain?" Aua asked. "We are all afraid of illness. Here is this old sister of mine: as far as anyone can see, she has done no evil; she has lived through a long life and given birth to healthy children, and now she must suffer before her days end. Why? Why?" "You see," Aua went on, "you are equally unable to give any reason when we ask you why life is as it is. And so it must be. All our customs come from life and turn towards life; we explain nothing, we believe nothing, but in what I have just told you lies our answer to all you ask" (55–56). Aua then listed for Rasmussen the things they feared—the capricious weather spirits, sickness, hunger and death, the old woman of the sea, and the vengeful souls of the dead, including the spirits of slaughtered animals. Against these perils, Aua said, they relied on the old rules of life which are based on the experience and wisdom of generations.

> We do not know how, we cannot say why, but we keep those rules in order that we may live untroubled. And so ignorant are we in spite of all our shamans, that we fear all the invisible things that are likewise about us, all that we have heard of in our forefathers' stories and myths. Therefore we have our customs, which are not the same as those of the white men, the white men who live in another land and have need of other ways. (56)

For intellectuals, explaining rather than simply enduring life seems not only necessary but natural. Yet the kind of stoic acceptance of the limits of human understanding evident in Aua's conversations with Rasmussen should not be dismissed as an outmoded way of thinking that has no value in our modern world. Though we expand our scientific grasp of life, there are always limits beyond which we, too, are faced with the invisible things that Aua alludes to, and for which we require wit and wisdom rather than reason to address.

Throughout Africa there is a spirited tradition of riddles (Hamnet 1967) and dilemma tales (Bascom 1975) that play up ambiguity as a way of inspiring debate on the recurring dilemmas of everyday life. In one such Kuranko story that I collected in northern Sierra Leone in 1970, three brothers with the same father but different mothers, all of whom were born on the same day and initiated at the same time, claim the right to succeed their father as chief when the old man dies. Because the only way of evaluating the competing claims of the three brothers is in terms of their mothers' behavior, the storyteller appeals to his audience to remember how, in the early part of the story, each of these women saved the life of her husband when he was a young man traveling the world in search of fame and fortune. The first woman saved the future chief from the murderous wrath of her father. The second woman sacrificed her only daughter to the djinni safeguarding a river crossing, so that the future chief could traverse it. The third woman told the future chief the answer to a conundrum that her father set every young man who came to his village. After considerable debate, the storyteller presented his own view by approving the argument of the first brother for why he should become chief in his father's stead. "A man's fortune in life depends on his mother, and a man should never forget from whom he got his start in life, and with whom his life began. The brothers were all equal, in age and ability. But the brother whose mother first saved the life of the chief had the prior claim. If a person trips over a stone and falls down, he should not think first of the place he fell but of the place he tripped" (Jackson 1982:38).[5]

I concur with both Louis-Vincent Thomas, who writes that the whole point of such dilemma tales is to foster a "multiplicity of points of view and the sharpening of a critical sense" (1958–1959:579), and Jack Berry, who notes of Adangme tales that "no solution is suggested.

+ not everything can or should be explained.

Each of the audience must give his views and an *ad hoc* solution is accepted at each telling depending on the consensus of the opinion of those present and the weight of the arguments advanced" (1961:10).

There are resonances here of James's radical empiricism, where incompleteness and tentativeness are given the same analytical weight as the finished and the fixed. It is a philosophy that urges us not to subjugate the complexities and aporias of lived experience to the tyranny of reason or the consolation of order, but to cultivate that quality that John Keats called negative capability, the capability of "being uncertainties, Mysteries, doubts, without any irritable reaching after fact & reason" (1958:193). This view finds expression in Georg Groddeck's declaration, in a letter to his friend and colleague Sándor Ferenczi, that "the difference between us is that you are compelled to want to understand things, whilst I am compelled not to want to understand . . . I am happy to remain in the dark, in the imago of the womb, which you wish to escape" (Fortune 2002:35). It bears a family resemblance to Michel Foucault's view that any "discursive formation" is not "an ideal, continuous, smooth text that runs beneath the multiplicity of contradictions, and resolves them in the calm unity of coherent thought"; nor is it "the surface in which, in a thousand different aspects, a contradiction is reflected that is always in retreat, but everywhere dominant. It is rather a space of multiple dissensions; a set of different oppositions whose levels and roles must be described" (1972:155). It is present throughout Derrida's work, which moves from the impasse of age-old problems that admit of no solution to exploring the possibility of writing and living as if these problems were simply thresholds one has to cross, curtains one has to draw back, in order to enter a more edifying domain of existence (1993:12–13). And it is a view that finds expression in our idea of tragedy, as David Mamet so lucidly explains in his obituary for Arthur Miller. Plays such as *Death of a Salesman* and *The Crucible* make us "feel fear," he writes, "because we recognise, in them, our own dilemmas . . . . We are freed, at the end of these two dramas, not because the playwright has arrived at a solution, but because he has reconciled us to the notion that there is no solution—that it is the human lot to try and fail, and that no one is immune from self-deception" (2005).

I am not advocating a lapse into fatalism or nihilism. Rather, I want

why not?

James' radical empiricism
- incompleteness & tentativeness are valued

a space of multiple dissensions + oppositions

I agree

to suggest that the intellectual rage for systematicity and totalization constitutes a magical compensation for our failed attempts to control the world or calm our anguish at the world's disorder.[6] This does not necessarily mean that we give up on our attempts to change the way things are, or uncritically embrace any point of view; it is a case for a more sober sense of the limits of thought, and a reminder that we inherit, culturally and biogenetically, not an adapted or seamless nature but a set of incompatible and conflicted potentialities. Accordingly, no movement toward greater openness is without its gestures for closure. African dilemma tales, for all their tolerance of multiple points of view, foster a quest for ethically viable understanding. Zen practice, while dismissive of the idolatry of salvation, has its own agendas for deliverance from illusion. And despite his stoic resignation, my friend Noah sought social justice as well as an improvement in his personal lot. The case is, then, for recognizing the oscillations in everyday experience between quite contradictory tendencies—for acceptance and for change, for conceptual and nonconceptual realities, for the transitive and the intransitive—and respecting these juxtapositions in our discursive commentaries. As Adorno cautions, "Necessity compels philosophy to operate with concepts, but this necessity must not be turned into the virtue of their priority—no more than, conversely, criticism of that virtue can be turned into a summary verdict against philosophy" (1973:11).

I call these essays "excursions" not only because each emerged from a sojourn in a place away from home, away from settled routines and certainties, but because the image of a journey suggests that thought is always on the way, is always a struggle, and the thinker a journeyman whose attitudes are perpetually unsettled and tested by his or her engagement in the world.

The existential aporias with which I am concerned in this book include the tension between our need for ontological security in systems of social relations or shared ideas that effectively insulate us from chaos and uncertainty, and the antinomian impulse toward openness, variability, and growth that gives us a sense of living in a world that we decide. I am fascinated by the paradox that while every human being belongs to the same species, everyone is irreducibly himself or herself. I address the tragic irony that the same powers that enable us to bring

xxvi preface

"a case for a more sober sense of the limits of thoughts"

life into being enable us to destroy it, that revenge and reconciliation are always options for those who have suffered at the hands of others, and that while we have the capacity to dominate the world as though it were an object to exploit, know, or tame, we also submit to the world as though we were its subjects. I explore the gap between being born into a lineage that defines one's identity or foreshadows one's destiny, and being born to oneself in a world far removed from anything one's forebears knew. I consider at length the struggle to strike a balance between the things over which we have some control and the things over which we have none, and I address the intellectual pathos of striving to change the world for the better through the application of "true" knowledge only to find that knowledge without power cannot even save the life of the sage who possesses it. And I return continually to the gap between direct and indirect experience, lifeworld and world-view, real and abstract relationships, alluding to the paradox of human evolution that has adapted us to life in small groups only to confront us with large-scale, impersonal, or virtual worlds in which we must work out a modus vivendi with strangers, exploring the split between labor and capital in which, as Karl Marx observed, "the process disappears in the product" (1906:201), and asking how we can overcome the gap that opens up between ourselves and others as we talk past each other, missing each others' meanings, and interpreting each other's worlds solely in the light of our own interests and preunderstandings.

The perfidious reproach of being "too intelligent"
haunted him throughout his life.

—THEODOR W. ADORNO,

A Portrait of Walter Benjamin

1 In the Footsteps of Walter Benjamin

It was late in the evening when I arrived, and the town was being buffeted by a stiff wind off the sea and squalls of rain. After checking into my hotel, I had dinner in the hotel restaurant and then turned in early, halyards slapping against aluminum masts in the harbor and a lighthouse flashing in the darkness. My last thoughts before falling asleep were of a photograph I had seen that morning in a Danish newspaper of a listing wooden boat with splintered upper strakes being towed behind an Italian coast-guard cutter on whose cramped fore-deck huddled thirty or forty bewildered African asylum seekers, and of a report in another paper of a proposal by several European governments to create "holding centers" in North Africa for these clandestine immigrants who every night risked their lives[1] crossing the Mediterranean in unseaworthy boats, hoping to find work and a livelihood in Europe.

If migrants are sustained by their hope in the future, refugees are afflicted by their loss of the past. Of no one was this truer than Walter Benjamin. I had come to Banyuls-sur-Mer on the French Catalonian coast with the intention of crossing the Pyrenees on the anniversary of Benjamin's own fateful journey on 26 September 1940. But though I had contemplated making this trip for at least a year, I had never fully fathomed my motives. I only knew that one must sometimes abandon any conception of what one is doing in order to do it, accepting that reasons and meanings cannot be imposed on events but should be allowed to surface in their own good time. Still, I was mindful of Benjamin's notion of translation "as a mode" that requires one to "go back to the original, for that contains the law governing the translation, its translatability" (1969:70). Could shadowing a writer through a landscape, or repeating a journey precisely sixty-four years after the original had taken place, enable one to know that writer's frame of mind or translate his thought? And what kind of translation is it, anyway, that seeks parallels and echoes, not between languages but between experiences and, as Benjamin himself suggested, between the lines?

Walter Benjamin was born in Berlin in 1892, and reborn twenty-one years later in Paris. But while Paris was where he came to feel most at home, it would be truer to say that it was the Paris of the nineteenth century that captivated him and later became not only a refuge but the subject of his monumental though unfinished *Passagenarbeit* (*The Arcades Project*). Hannah Arendt suggests that the allure, for Benjamin, of this fabulous city had something to do with the "unparalleled naturalness" with which it had, from the middle of the nineteenth century onward, "offered itself to all homeless people as a second home" (Arendt 1973:170); for Benjamin, however, it was more immediately the "physical shelter" afforded by its arcades, the ghostly presence of a perimeter connected by medieval gates, the villagelike intimacy of its old neighborhoods, and the homeliness of the boulevard cafés that invited one to live in Paris as one lives within an apartment or a house. Besides, Paris could easily be covered on foot, making it an ideal city for strollers, idlers, and browsers—that is to say, flaneurs. And Benjamin, who had never been successful at getting an academic job and was obliged to lead a freelance existence that involved "the precarious, errant practices of a critic, translator, reviewer and script-writer for radio" (Steiner 1998:11), living under his parent's roof until he was in his late thirties and always dependent on the support of friends, was in many ways a man who had missed his time, a would-be man of letters and leisure with old-fashioned manners, a passion for antiquarian books, and little practical sense, someone whose idea of history never completely encompassed the unfolding tragedy of his own epoch. As he wrote in his essay on Marcel Proust, with whom he undoubtedly identified: "He is filled with the insight that none of us has time to live the true dramas of the life that we are destined for. This is what ages us—this and nothing else. The wrinkles and creases on our faces are the registrations of the great passions, vices, insights that called on us; but we, the masters, were not at home" (1969:211–12). Did he ever feel at home in twentieth-century Germany? "One has reason to doubt it," writes Arendt. "In 1913, when he first visited France as a very young man . . . the trip from Berlin to Paris was tantamount to a trip in time . . . from the twentieth century back to the nineteenth" (1973:170).

When the Nazis seized power in January 1933, Benjamin could no longer count on an income from writing, and his attempts to write under pseudonyms such as K. A. Stampflinger and Detlef Holz proved fruitless. In March he left Germany and stayed with friends on Ibiza for six months before settling in Paris, supported by stipends from the Frankfurt Institut für Sozialforschung, where Max Horkeimer, Friedrich Pollock, and Theodor Adorno were his staunch allies. Though often isolated, and with Europe moving ineluctably toward war, Benjamin worked patiently at his projects, declining the offers and urgings of friends such as Gershom Scholem, Arendt, and Adorno to move to Palestine, England, or the United States. He was, he explained to them, no longer capable of adapting (Scholem 1982:213). Yet Benjamin was well aware of the fate of Jews in Germany after *Kristallnacht*—the mass arrests, the new edicts, the concentration camps, the panicked exodus. And even as Scholem tried to find funds to bring the reluctant Benjamin to Palestine in the spring of 1939, the Gestapo was ordering the German embassy in Paris to expedite his repatriation, probably because of a "Paris Letter" he had published in 1936, in which he made no bones about his antifascist views, observing for instance that "culture under the Swastika is nothing but the playground of unqualified minds and subaltern characters" and "fascist art is one of propaganda" (Brodersen 1996:24). Though he continued to seek naturalization in France, Benjamin's efforts in the summer of 1939 seemed to have been devoted mainly to his essay on Baudelaire, and he passed up an invitation to Sweden in order to finish it.

When war was declared on 1 September 1939, all Germans, Austrians, Czechs, Slovaks, and Hungarians aged between seventeen and fifty and living in France were subject to internment. Men rounded up in Paris were first taken to football stadiums—the Stade Colombe and the Stadion Buffalo—where they remained for ten days and nights, sleeping in the bleachers, killing time playing cards, strolling around the track, or planning how they might gain their release (women were assembled for screening in an ice-skating stadium, the Vélodrome d'Hiver). The internees were then trucked to the Gare d'Austerlitz under military escort, thence in sealed railway carriages to various hastily prepared camps throughout France. Benjamin was interned first at Nevers, where empty châteaus, vacant factories, and farms had been converted into concentration camps for *ressortissants* (enemy aliens) including *ressortisants allemands* (aliens from Germany), and then at Vernuche, where three hundred prisoners were crammed into a disused furniture factory. In November 1939, thanks to the intervention of friends in Paris, notably the French poet and diplomat Saint-John Perse, Benjamin was released and seemed finally reconciled to leaving France (Horkeimer had managed to secure for him an emergency visa to the United States). But once again, like an ostrich burying its head in the sand, Benjamin took refuge in intellectual labor, unable to break his long-standing habit of seeking security in an interiorized existence, in libraries, and in the collecting of rare books. After renewing his reader's card for the Bibliotèque Nationale, he attempted to begin researching and writing his sequel to his Baudelaire piece.[2]

In a letter to Gretel Adorno, dated 17 January 1940, he wrote of this tension between the exigencies of his own survival and the work that was his life:

> The fear of having to abandon the Baudelaire once I have begun writing the sequel is what makes me hesitate [to leave Paris]. This sequel will be work of monumental breadth and it would be a delicate matter to have to

start and stop again and again. This is, however, the risk I would have to take. I am constantly reminded of it by the gas mask in my small room—the mask looks to me like a disconcerting replica of the skulls with which studious monks decorated their cells. This is why I have not yet really dared to begin the sequel to the Baudelaire. I definitely hold this work more dear to my heart than any other. It would consequently not suffer being neglected even to ensure the survival of its author.

In May 1940, Hitler's armies overran the French forces, and in June they entered Paris. That same month, the Franco-German armistice was signed, with its ominous Article XIX requiring the French government to "surrender on demand" anyone the Third Reich wanted extradited to Germany—an edict that effectively ended the issuing of exit visas to German refugees like Benjamin, whether in the occupied or unoccupied zones.

After entrusting his precious manuscripts to friends, Benjamin and his sister Dora joined the 2 million or more refugees trudging *en pagaille* toward the unoccupied zone. After spending most of that summer in Lourdes in the Lower Pyrenees, he traveled to Marseilles in August to ratify his emergency visa to the United States. There, he briefly met Arthur Koestler, to whom he confided (as he had to Arendt in Paris) that he carried with him fifteen tablets of a morphine compound—"enough to kill a horse." From Marseilles, Benjamin and two other refugees (Henny Gurmand and her sixteen-year-old son José) traveled to Port Vendres, where they met Lisa Fittko and her husband Hans, who were in the process of reconnoitering, with the help of the socialist mayor of Banyuls, a new escape route across the Pyrenees. During the previous few months, refugees had fled France by taking a train to Cerbère, the last town before the Catalan frontier, and then walking to Portbou in Spain through the railway tunnel or over the steep ridge along which the border ran. Only a week or ten days before Benjamin tried to reach Spain, several other Jewish refugees—among them Lion and Marta Feuchtwanger, Alma Mahler Werfel, Franz Werfel, Heinrich Mann, and Golo Mann—had successfully used the route via Cerbère, traveling on to neutral Portugal, where they found ships to America. But with increasing Gestapo pressure on the Spanish government, and the French police obliged to collaborate under Article XIX of the armistice agreement, French exit visas were impossible to procure, and Cerbère was, in any event, too carefully watched by the *gardes mobiles* (military police). After a five-minute train journey from Port Vendre to Banyuls (though, in her memoirs, Lisa Fittko thinks they may have taken the coastal path), Lisa Fittko led Benjamin and his party on an afternoon reconnaissance of the route they would take the following day. After walking for almost three hours, they reached a clearing at which Benjamin announced he intended to sleep for the night and wait for the others to rejoin him in the morning. Fearing for his safety, Fittko tried to persuade him against this plan, but *der alte Benjamin* (that old Benjamin), as she called him (though he was only forty-eight, and she thirty-one) prevailed, and she had no option but to leave him, without provisions or a blanket, clutching the heavy black leather briefcase he had brought with him and that he claimed to be "more important than I am, more important than myself" (Fittko 1991:106). Well before first light on the next day, the others again left Banyuls-sur-Mer. Passing through the village of Puig del Mas, and making themselves inconspicuous among the vineyard workers, they climbed to their rendezvous with Benjamin, and on across the Col de Cerbère toward Spain.[3] After a grueling twelve-hour journey, they arrived in Portbou only to find that their transit visas, which would have taken them through Spain to Lisbon, had been cancelled on orders from Madrid.[4]

That night the exhausted and dispirited travelers were placed under guard in a local hotel; in the morning they were to be escorted back to France. At ten o'clock that night, unable to see any way out, Benjamin swallowed some of the morphine tablets he carried with him. He died at seven the following morning.[5] Ironically, had the refugees attempted the border crossing one day earlier or one day later, they would have made it, for the embargo on visas was lifted—possibly on compassionate grounds, possibly for some unspecified bureaucratic reason—the same day Benjamin died.

The last thing Benjamin wrote was a postcard. As Henny Gurland remembered it many months later in the United States, the five lines on the postcard read: "In a situation with no way out, I have no choice but to end it. My life will finish in a little village in the Pyrenees where no one knows me. Please pass on my thoughts to my friend Adorno and explain to him the situation in which I find myself. There is not enough time to write all the letters I had wanted to write" (Brodersen 1996:245).

These were the details I had gleaned from my reading. But as with so many written sources, it is often impossible to get a sense of the life that lies behind the language, or to lift the veil with which memory screens out landscapes, faces, voices, not to mention the physical and emotional experiences that might tell us what it was like to undergo the events that are so summarily recounted. So it was that with a faxed copy of an old map I had been given at the tourist information office at Banyuls (I was evidently not the first foreigner to ask about the route that Walter Benjamin had taken across the Pyrenees) and a hastily packed lunch in my rucksack, I set out at first light along the road that led up into the hills behind the town.

Once past Puig del Mas, and climbing the narrow winding road that was marked on my map simply as "Vers Mas Guillaume" (Toward Guillaume's Farmstead), I began to feel less and less certain that I was on the right track. The steep slopes above and below the road were covered in gnarled and stunted Grenache vines that miraculously found some purchase in the dark brown schist, and whose tendrils and leaves were splayed, unsupported, over the seemingly barren ground. All this was undoubtedly the same as it had been in 1940. The workers, for example, bent over the vines, snipping bunches of grapes and placing them in panniers on their backs, which they upended from time to time into rectangular plastic bins along the roadside. But whereas in 1940 these *vigneroles* had walked up to the vineyards, today they came in cars or small trucks. And back then the men carried spades over their shoulders, from which hung *cabecs*—baskets for toting the stones for repairing terrace walls and storm-water ditches. Moreover, the narrow, tortuous road was probably not tar sealed. So when I stopped to scan the slopes above me for signs of a "clearing" or for "the seven pines on the plateau" that according to Fittko always indicated the right direction (1991:124), I was lost. Well past Puig del Mas now, I asked an old man, working alone among his vines, if I could get to Spain if I continued walking up this road. He thought I was crazy. "You get to Spain along the coast road," he said. "This road goes nowhere." I explained that I was looking for the smugglers' track that Jewish refugees used in 1940 to avoid the frontier posts. Could he perhaps take a look at my map and set me straight? The old man appeared to have considerable trouble reading the map, or making sense of the penciled line that marked the *ruta realitzada per Walter Benjamin en el seu èxode*, and kept insisting that one could only reach Portbou via the coast road. From the way he turned the map this way and that, I concluded that he was trying to see the map as a picture that bore some natural resemblance to the landscape with which he was so familiar, and was baffled by the abstractions of cartography. "This road goes nowhere," he repeated. "It goes up the valley; then it comes to a dead end."

I decided to retrace my steps to Puig del Mas. There, I asked another old man, walking his labrador dog along a narrow street, if he could decipher my map and tell me how I could find the old route over the mountains. "In 1940 it was called *la route Lister*," I explained (General Enrique Lister, a commander in the Republican Army, had used it when escaping into France with his troops in 1939, after the fall of Barcelona). But though the dog owner had a dim memory of such a path, he had no knowledge of it and knew of no one I might ask for information. So I returned, reluctantly, to the *syndicat des initiatives* in Banyuls, only to be assured that I had been on the right road after all. "Just keep on going," I was told. "You have to climb to the Col de Cerbère. Spain is beyond."

Two hours later I trudged past the old man who had told me that the road led nowhere. He was lugging a pail of grapes down through his vines to the roadside. On seeing me, he shrugged his shoulders in disbelief: "Ah non!"

It was windy now—the tramontane blustering out of a clear blue sky. Behind me, in full sunlight, were the terracotta roofs and pale ochre walls of Puig del Mas, and ahead, in the distance, was the sea, scoured and flecked by the unrelenting wind. In the lee of a roadside wall, and shaded by cedars, I sat down, drank from the bottle of water I had brought with me, and scribbled some notes. I could hear men's voices in the vineyards below me, borne on the wind, and I caught a whiff of burning cigarettes and the stale fermented smell of grapes. Looking up at the range, I could see where the highest and steepest vineyards gave way to a wilderness of pinewoods, evergreen oaks, and scrub. I wondered where Benjamin had passed the night, and whether he might have found sanctuary in one of the many small, conical huts made of schist—called *boris*—where vineyard workers took shelter from the wind, prepared coffee or food, and sometimes slept overnight. I also found myself reflecting on his unbroken resolve to press on. Not to retrace a single step. Certainly, as he told Fittko, his weak heart and lack of fitness made it impossible for him to even contemplate the effort of making this journey more than once, and he must have been haunted not only by the degradation of internment and the disorienting weeks of flight but by the realization that he had long passed the point of no return and that his whole life—apart from those remnants contained in the briefcase he would not be parted from—was irretrievably lost. As Arendt observed, this was a man who could not imagine living without his library or his vast collection of quotations, and for whom America offered no other prospect, as he confided to her in Paris, than of being carted up and down the country and exhibited as the "last European" (Arendt 1973:168). As I threw my rucksack across my shoulder and prepared to set off again, I recalled those lines of Malcolm Lowry's about the "great ruin that brings upon you this migraine of alienation" so that "behind you, thousands of miles away, it is as if you could hear your own real life plunging to its doom" (1969:177).

By mid-morning I had reached a fork in the road—perhaps the "junction" that Fittko refers to in her memoir. The road to my left appeared to lead toward the head of a deep valley, directly under the steep and overgrown slopes of the mountain. The other road led straight on, going east and inland; a sign indicated that it was one of the *circuits du vignoble de Banyuls*, one of the drives through the vineyards of Banyuls. I asked a man and a woman, hard at work among the vines, if they could tell me which route would take me up to the col. They pointed to a stony track that began where the road divided and quickly disappeared into the broom, grass, and scrub.

It was hard going. Within minutes my heart was pounding, and I was out of breath, but I was confident now that this track would lead along the spur and thence to the col. But the track soon petered out, and I found myself standing on the terrace of a vineyard, trying to figure out where I had gone wrong. Rather than turn back, I decided to take a shortcut down through the vineyard to the road below in the hope that it would take me toward the head of the valley from where I might find a path up onto the range. But all my efforts to find a path or force my way through the dense scrub were unavailing, and realizing that the sealed road I had taken simply looped back toward Banyuls, I asked a man who was dumping grapes in his truck by the roadside whether he could point out to me the path that led up to the col. Without hesitation he directed my attention back to the spur I had first followed, and the highest vineyard on the western side where a white truck was parked beneath some pines. That was the way.

Confident now of my direction, I walked quickly back along the valley road, then took a dirt track up through a stand of parasol pines, resinous in the wind, until I was once more on the path along the spur. Now, rather than forge straight ahead as I had done before, I took a turning to my right that I had ignored earlier because it seemed to be bearing west rather than south toward Spain. This path, I now discovered, turned sharply left and led along the spur toward the summit road that was now visible, cut into the side of the mountain, and headed toward the col.

With my goal in sight, I decided to stop for lunch, enjoy the view, and write some notes. From Fittko's descriptions, I could well have been sitting where Benjamin and the others rested from their exertions four or five hours into their ascent. She describes how they had to clamber up through a vineyard to the ridge, and how this climb defeated Benjamin who had to be half carried up the steep rubble slope, one arm around José's shoulder, the other around Fittko's, the black briefcase presumably in Gurmand's hands. When they stopped, Fittko ate a piece of bread she had bought with bogus food stamps and offered some tomatoes to the famished Benjamin who, with his inimitable courtesy, said, "By your leave, *gnädige Frau*, may I serve myself?" I sat under a gnarled cork oak, out of the wind, and laid out my own lunch: some sachets of honey, bread rolls, and an apple that I had taken from the breakfast buffet at my hotel, plus a couple of bananas, a bottle of Evian water, and a cellophane bag of walnuts I had bought at a *tabac* on my second trip from Banyuls. In the distance, the Pyrenees were lost in a blue haze. Below me, the wind riffled and battered the scrub. Grasshoppers flickered among the stones.

Half an hour later, as I was hoisting myself up over the limestone boulders that interrupted the upward path, I marveled at the determination and patience that had enabled Benjamin to accomplish what would have been ordinarily inconceivable and impossible. Fittko was struck by what she called his "crystal-clear thinking and unfaltering inner strength," and she recalls how, during his night alone on the mountainside, he had worked out a plan of action in which he would harbor his resources by walking for ten minutes and resting for one. Hans Fittko, who had met Benjamin during their internment at Vernuche, remembered how the older man had quit smoking the better to survive his ordeal. Yet it was not because this might improve his physical fitness, nor even because tobacco was hard to come by; it was, Benjamin explained, because concentrating his mind on not smoking helped him distract himself from the hardships of the camp—evidence, perhaps, of his Taoist commitment to that eternal patience whereby running water finally "gets the better of granite and porphyry," wearing away stone.[6]

The track passed under a pylon, and a few minutes later I was on the old unpaved road that zigzagged up toward the crest. I stopped only to eat some wild blackberries and get my bearings for the return trip. Then I was on the col, and looking down over windswept rocky slopes to the marshaling yards at Cerbère. Portbou, I guessed, lay just over the ridge from there.

The road toward Spain, cut into the side of a hill, descended gradually above a valley in which I could make out farmhouses among plantations of pines and cedars. I sat in the long grass and watched the wind raking the heather and brushwood on the exposed upper slopes of the range. The only sounds were the distant barking of a dog and the wind howling in the girders of a nearby watchtower. How could one not remark the grim irony of this place—named for the three-headed dog that guards the opposite shore of the Styx, "ready to devour living intruders or ghostly fugitives"? (Graves 1955:120). Far beyond Cerbère lay the wind-whipped sea, with cape after cape vanishing into the haze of Spanish Catalonia. I felt exhilarated to have made it, for last night I had slept badly, filled with trepidation about setting off into an unknown region without a guide, and all that morning, as I stumbled along paths that led nowhere, missed critical turnoffs, and failed to reconcile my map with the terrain around me, I had felt tense with anxiety and doubt. There was, of course, no more certainty that I had taken exactly the same route Benjamin took than that my experiences bore any relationship with his, let alone afforded me any insights into his work. But perhaps such certainties are beside the point since our relationships with even those closest to us are not necessarily founded on knowledge in the intellectual sense of the word, but rather on a sense of a natural affinity or fellow feeling that cannot be explained.

Perhaps this is why I had mistakenly made my trip a day earlier than the actual anniversary of his own, as if I had unconsciously, magically, and belatedly sought to prevent his fate, much as some people—including Heinrich Mann's wife Nelly, when the day came for her to cross the frontier from Cerbère to Portbou—did everything in their power to avoid traveling on Friday the thirteenth. In any event, I returned to Banyuls, where I had left my things at the hotel, and the following morning packed my rucksack, paid my bill, and set out for Portbou. My plan was to take the morning train and spend the day exploring the town where Benjamin had died, but at Banyuls railway station I checked the timetable only to discover that the 9:10 a.m. train to Portbou had stopped running a week ago, and since it was Sunday, I would have to wait until 2:20 p.m. for the only train that day. It did not take me more than a few seconds to decide that I would sooner be on the move than stuck in Banyuls and waiting for a train that might never come. So I retraced my steps through the old town and back along the seafront road, heading south. There was no footpath and scarcely any grassy verge along the narrow highway, and after hitching for an hour without success, I yielded to the road, resolved to walk the whole distance. Apart from the belligerence of the wind and the cars that often passed uncomfortably close, I was elated to be on the open road with the sea beside me, wearing its fingers to the bone on the jagged foreshore, and further out its surface annealed by the harsh light and smeared by the same incessant wind that shoved at my back. It is sometimes uncanny the way unforeseen events turn out to be a blessing in disguise, though this seems never to have been true of Walter Benjamin. His remarks on Marcel Proust could well have been reflections on his own character—a man in whom "weakness and genius coincide"; a man who "died of the same inexperience which permitted him to write his works. He died of ignorance of the world and because he did not know how to change the conditions of his life which had begun to crush him. He died because he did not know how to make a fire or open a window" (Benjamin 1969:213). Even his dear friend Arendt confessed that he seemed destined, "with a precision suggesting a sleepwalker," to stumble into catastrophe after catastrophe (1973: 157), and she recalls a succession of Kafkaesque episodes in which, for example, the young literary critic, counting on a promised stipend for reading a manuscript, received nothing because the publisher went bankrupt and, much later, in the winter of 1939–40, when the danger of bombing made him leave Paris for a safer place, Benjamin sought refuge in Meaux, a troop center and probably one of the few places that *was* in serious danger during this period of the *drôle de guerre*. Undoubtedly Arendt also had in mind the tragic irony of 26 September 1940 when Benjamin and his party arrived in Portbou only to be told that Spain had closed its borders that day, and that visas issued in Marseilles would not, in any case, be accepted. Had he attempted the crossing a day earlier, all would have been well; a few weeks later, his visa would have been accepted: "Only on that particular day was the catastrophe possible" (Arendt 1973:169).

In the three days Lisa Fittko spent with Walter Benjamin she formed an impression of a man whose intellectuality gave him a certain inner strength but made him "hopelessly awkward and clumsy" (1991:109). From her teenage years on, Fittko had been a political activist. A gutsy, no-nonsense young woman who had quit her university studies to fight fascism, she would have been left cold by Benjamin's mystical Marxism. "Faut se débrouiller!" she exclaimed. "One must know how to help oneself, to clear a way out of the debacle," which in France in 1940 meant knowing how to "buy counterfeit food stamps, scrounge milk for the children, obtain some—any—kind of permit—in short manage to do or obtain what didn't officially exist" (1991:113). Above all, it meant committing oneself to action, taking initiatives, seizing opportunities, living on one's wits, and never allowing oneself to panic or lapse into passivity and complaint. Fittko was not alone in her exasperation with people who asked only "What will happen to us?" rather than "What can we do?" The leader of the Emergency Rescue Committee in Marseilles, Varian Fry, found the intellectuals "particularly difficult" and noted that "they were jittery with fear at the thought of staying, and paralyzed by fear at the thought of leaving. You would get them prepared with their passports and all their visas in order, and a month later they would still be sitting in the Marseilles cafés, waiting for the police to come and get them" (1945:16).

Between May and June 1940, Fittko was in the concentration camp at Gurs, in the foothills of the Pyrenees. The camp had been built in April 1939 to accommodate Republican refugees and members of the International Brigades fleeing Spain after the civil war—rows of barracks in a sea of mud, each barracks containing sixty sleeping pads with palliasses, twenty-five barracks to each *îlot* or section, each îlot separated from the others by barbed wire. At the end of the camp was the *îlot des indésirables*, the section for the unwanted ones, known for their opposition to the Nazis and kept under strict surveillance. Among the indésirables at Gurs was Arendt, and it was through an audacious ruse, in which Fittko was actively involved (the distraught *commissaire spécial de police du Camp de Gurs*, panicked by the German advance, agreed in a drunken moment to allow Fittko and others to sort the indésirables into dangerous and less dangerous categories),[7] that Arendt was released from the îlot des indésirables and able to make good her escape from the camp.[8]

The light on the sea was like fish scales. The wind-combed grass on the hillside and a grove of cork oaks brought back memories of the East Coast of New Zealand. How strange it is, the way one's thoughts are set free by walking. I felt that I was writing a poem with my body, not my mind, by moving rather than using words. The poem was I on the road. The *terroir* of a piece of writing, I said to myself—the way words soak up the earth and the light.

At Cerbère, footsore and weary, I bought an espresso and sat in a seafront cafe, watching the traffic wend its way slowly up the steep road that presumably led to the border. Again, I found it difficult to imagine how some of the émigrés who passed this way in 1940 managed to climb the hill. In his memoir of this time, Varian Fry speaks of his concern for the physical resources of many of the political and intellectual refugees he helped. In Marseilles, Alma Mahler Werfel and Franz Werfel "never went around the block without taking a taxi, if they could help it," and when they did walk anywhere, "it was always on the level, never uphill" (1945:57). It was therefore touch and go whether the fifty-year-old Franz Werfel, who was "large, dumpy and pallid, like a half-filled sack of flour" (5–6) and had a heart ailment, or the seventy-year-old Heinrich Mann, who escaped with his nephew Golo and the Werfels, would be able to make it over the hill. Enervated by the midsummer heat, and often having to crawl up the "sheer slippery terrain . . . bounded by precipices" (Werfel 1959:244), they nevertheless crossed the mountain, and after bribing the soldiers at the Spanish frontier with packets of cigarettes, they were waved through. I could not help but compare the fate of Walter Benjamin, who a week later would attempt a much longer and more arduous trip across the Pyrenees, clinging to his briefcase full of notes as if it were a lifeline, and the fate of Alma Mahler Werfel, who held on to the scores of Gustav Mahler's symphonies and Anton Bruckner's Third with similar tenacity, and whose twelve suitcases were brought by Fry and Dick Ball on the train from Cerbère to Portbou, with the fate of her husband, whose period of limbo in Lourdes had inspired him to write what would become one the most celebrated pieces of émigré writing in the wartime United States, *The Song of Bernadette*. In her memoirs, Alma Mahler Werfel would also recall the terrible arbitrariness of those times. "When I think how many killed themselves up there in the hill or landed in Spanish jails, I see how lucky we were to have our American scraps of paper honoured by the officials at Portbou" (1959:246).

And so I began the hardest part of my journey. The wind was now so strong that at times I was almost knocked off my feet or could make little headway walking into it. I chose to hug the rock face rather than walk along the outer edge of the road, even though there were few places where I could safely step aside while cars passed. But as I approached the ridge, I could see that the road doubled back, presumably descending from that point on into Spain. I passed a sign warning of *paravent violent*, violent winds, cut across the corner of the road, and was immediately in sight of the *douane*, customs—a narrow building around which the downhill road flowed like a stream. Its offices were devoid of furniture; there was no indication that it was still in use; and I felt a momentary pang of disappointment that I could simply walk past this point where the fate of so many desperate travelers had been decided by the caprice or greed of a frontier guard, a cable from Madrid, or even the hour of the day. Perhaps nothing defines the plight of the refugee more than this overwhelming sense of a life no longer in one's own hands, of that total dependence on the goodwill of others, and yet of an utter ignorance about the future. I therefore found it poignant to recall that one of Benjamin's last published essays had been a commentary on Bertolt Brecht's great poem, "Legend of the Origin of the Book Tao Te Ching on Lao Tzu's Way into Exile,"[9] in which he pointed out that an act of pure friendship between a customs officer and the seventy-year-old sage, going into exile on an ox, was the only reason that Lao Tzu's inimitable work survived to be passed down through the centuries to us. It thus stands as a reminder of the one hope we have that compassion will triumph over indifference.

As I walked quickly down the winding road, I could see Portbou below me—dominated by the great barn of its railway station and its church, but with a white-walled cemetery and cypresses conspicuous above the bay. I reached the town at 11:45 p.m., having covered the eighteen kilometers from Banyuls in under four hours. But before exploring the town, I decided to make sure I could get a train to Perpignan that afternoon and thereby catch my flight to Paris early the next morning. After buying a ticket for the 13:56 p.m. train I stowed my rucksack in a station locker, grateful to be rid of its weight on my back, and descended a flight of stone steps into the town. I did not have to hunt about for my destination; the W. Benjamin Memorial was clearly marked, and within minutes I had located the cemetery where, among the tiered white tombs, some of which had hinged windows to protect the flowers and photographs that had been placed in front of the niches, I found myself standing in front of the brown schist boulder that commemorated Benjamin's death in Portbou on 27 September 1940. Where he was actually buried no one had yet discovered. Although Henny Gurland had supposedly paid the town authorities to have Benjamin buried in the cemetery, Arendt passed through Portbou in January 1941 and found no trace of his grave. "It was not to be found," she wrote Gershom Scholem; "his name was not written anywhere." And she described the cemetery above the blue waters of the bay as "one of the most fantastic and beautiful spots I have seen in my life" (Scholem 1982:226).

Someone had inserted a rock rose between the boulder and the marble plaque in front of it, and on the boulder various visitors had placed small stones or white polished pebbles from the nearby path. I sat against a concrete wall, out of the wind, and copied into my notebook the words on the plaque.

Walter Benjamin
Berlin, 1892—Portbou, 1940
"Es ist niemals ein Dokument der Kultur,
ohne zugleich ein solches der Baberi zu sein"
Geschichtsphilosophische Thesen, VII

The German phrase had also been translated into Spanish.

But if I had been able to choose, from Benjamin's work, an epitaph, it would have been the lines that preface his eighth thesis on history: "The tradition of the oppressed teaches us that the 'state of emergency' in which we live is not the exception but the rule." For as I sat there, my journey at an end, I was thinking how, as Benjamin observed so often, the presence of the now (*Jetztheit*) makes it inevitable that thoughts of any one tragic death give rise to thoughts of all wrongful death. And so I thought of the nameless individuals who at that very moment were held in limbo and incommunicado, stripped of their rights, subject to torture or the degradation of interminable waiting in places as far afield as Guantánamo Bay in Cuba, the Abu Ghraib prison near Baghdad, and the numerous "immigration camps" and "detention centers" around the world in which asylum seekers, driven from their homelands by persecution or want, were not only excluded from the protection of our laws but also ostracized from our definition of humanity.

For a moment, as I gazed at the boulder and the plaque bearing Benjamin's name, I was fighting back tears. Then, bending down, I took a white stone from the path and placed it on the boulder, taking superstitious care not to dislodge any of the others that had been put there—possibly fifty, possibly a hundred—one for each of the pilgrims who had found his or her way to this place, half hoping, perhaps, for a moment of truth, or even a sign of redemption. I then broke off a leaf from the small, variegated coprosma bush growing by the boulder and put it in my wallet.

Why was I so moved by this place? Cemeteries are for families. The living come to cemeteries to reconnect with kith and kin, to keep alive—with flowers, prayers, thoughts, and the small rituals of cleaning or tending a grave—the presence of those who have passed away. But what kinship brought me here? What affinity drew me to Walter Benjamin?

And then it occurred to me that this affinity had less to do with the inspiration I had drawn from Benjamin's ideas of allegory and narratively coherent experience (*Erfahrung*), or from the notion that the form of our writing may imitate the "natural" or spontaneous forms in which the world appears to us; it came mostly from the way I had taken heart, for many years, from his example and come to see that the maverick life of a thinker, arcane and obsolete though it is nowadays seen to be, is as legitimate as any other vocation. Though our backgrounds and upbringing were utterly unlike, and he died the year I was born, had I not, from the beginning, been attracted to the life of the mind only to find that such an existence had little value in the country in which I was raised? But in contrast to Benjamin, I did not aspire to intellectual greatness. This was not because I embraced the anti-intellectualism of my native culture or, like Pierre Bourdieu, felt ashamed of thought;[10] it was because I had always been convinced that thought and language were profoundly inadequate to the world, and could neither save nor redeem us. It may not have been Benjamin's intellectuality that made him so maladroit. But it did offer him a kind of magical bolthole where he could avoid taking action and console himself that the world was safe and secure as long as he could make it appear so in what he thought and wrote.

Perhaps we should learn to judge the intellectual life not in terms of its practical capacity to improve the material conditions of our lives but in terms of whether it enlarges our capacity of seeing the world in new ways. In his *Prison Notebooks*, Antonio Gramsci asked: "Are intellectuals an autonomous and independent group, or does every social group have its own particular specialised category of intellectuals?" (1971:5). Experience has taught me not to think of intellectuals as groups, but to celebrate originality of thought, wherever and whenever it occurs, for it is as likely to make its appearance in an African village (I am thinking here of my friend Noah Marah and the storyteller Keti Ferenke Koroma, of whom I have written at length) as in a European university. And this faculty of seeing the world in a new way, of seeing through customary jargons and received opinions, has a lot to do with living in what Karl Jaspers called "border" or "limit" situations (grenz-situationen) (1985:229–80) or "training one's imagination to go visiting" (Arendt 1982:43), which is to say, making a conscious virtue out of the pariah status that, for example, Jews had thrust on them in Nazi Germany and Vichy France (Arendt 1978).

Yet for all the insights they might yield, such indeterminate situations, in which one's very identity is in doubt, are at once nightmarish and farcical. Writing in 1943, Arendt observed of "we refugees" that "the less we are free to decide who we are or to live as we like, the more we try to put up a front, to hide the facts, and to play roles" (1978:61).

We were expelled from Germany because we were Jews. But having hardly crossed the French borderline, we were changed into "boches." We

Gramsci

were even told that we had to accept this designation if we were really against Hitler's racial theories. During seven years we played the ridiculous role of trying to be Frenchmen—at least, prospective citizens; but at the beginning of the war we were interned as "boches" all the same. In the meantime, however, most of us had indeed become such loyal Frenchmen that we could not even criticize a French governmental order; thus we declared it was all right to be interned. We were the first "prisonniers volontaires" history has ever seen. After the Germans invaded the country, the French government had only to change the name of the firm; having been jailed because we were Germans, we were not freed because we were Jews. (61)

Hannah Arendt was an optimist, albeit an ironic one, aware that the intellectual advantages of not being at home in the world were offset by the subterfuge and pretence to which the pariah must have recourse in order to survive. Every attempt to reinvent oneself, learn a new language, respect the advice of one's saviors, and pretend to forget that one ever had another life, or that one dreams nightly of those that perished, poems known by heart, places one called home, was in part a carefully managed performance, calculated to appease those in whose homeland one had no option but to make a new beginning and to fool oneself into thinking that new beginnings were possible. That Benjamin was not alone, among these refugees, in refusing the illusion of another life, and in deciding to end his life rather than endure further humiliation and loss, is something for which Arendt felt the greatest sympathy, for behind the compliant and optimistic facade of the grateful migrant is a constant struggle with despair of themselves—since deep down they do not believe that their misfortune is a result of political events outside their control, but the result of some mysterious shortcoming in themselves, a defect in their personalities, an inability to maintain the social appearances to which they have for so long been accustomed. And so they kill themselves, not, as Albert Camus might have said, as a declaration that life is absurd and that the game is not worth the candle, but because, as Arendt puts it, "of a kind of selfishness" (1975:60).

With Benjamin there was, I think, an inability to embrace the illusion of a future. Yet without an investment in what might be, one is doomed to dwell solely on what has been, and, in the case of those in extremis, to see the hardships one is presently forced to endure as the only reality. I have always shared Adorno's and Horkheimer's view that Benjamin's social criticism was compromised by his religious idealism, and I have, in particular, never accepted the idea that the present is simply a site of eternal return for all that has gone before, and that the possibility of renewal lies in meditating on a dismembered past.[11] In this view, entropy is inescapable (the debris piling up at our feet as the storm of progress hurls us away from Paradise), and redemption depends on the appearance of a savior. But perhaps it was Benjamin's unworldliness I found so unsettling—the accusation that the intellectual is by definition maladapted to real life, to practical tasks, to marriage, to human relationships, his head in the clouds, his life in an ivory tower, his ideas of no earthly use. Yet I shared the view of Arendt and Adorno that the thinker does not owe it to society to demonstrate how it might be changed for the better. Though Marx had taken exception to the notion that the task of the philosopher was simply to understand the world, not change it, I had a deep aversion to prescriptions and exhortations as to how one should lead one's life and was drawn to Anna Akhmatova's desire to describe, before all else, and to stand as witness to the common lot. And I was mindful, as I left the Portbou cemetery and descended the hill toward the bay, that at the same time Walter Benjamin was being hounded from pillar to post through Vichy France, Akhmatova was waiting in line, as she had done for seventeen months, outside the Leningrad prison where her son Lev Gumilev was held without trial, and where, one freezing day a woman recognized her and asked in a hoarse whisper whether she could describe their terrible vigil. "I said, 'I can.' And something like a smile passed fleetingly over what had been her face" (Akhmatova 1974:99).

After lunch in a seafront café, I returned to the station and retrieved my rucksack. The train took me to Cerbère within minutes, and with an hour and a half to kill before my connection to Perpignan, I wrote up my notes in the station waiting room before going for a stroll through the streets from where I could see, high on the col, the tower where I had rested the day before after my walk from Banyuls.

On the train to Perpignan, I found myself in a carriage with only two or three other passengers—a young deaf-mute woman who was sitting across the aisle and sending text messages on her cell phone. Each time she hit a key the phone beeped loudly, until a young man, perhaps a student, who had kicked his shoes off and had been lounging sideways in his seat and reading a paperback novel, got up and asked her to turn the phone off. She pointed to her ears, miming that she could not hear him.

I turned to look out my window, peering through my own reflection at the ruined towers of thirteenth-century Cathar castles on the conical hills, relics of yet another epoch of intolerance and violence, and beyond, in the blue sky, a curiously distorted hogsback cloud that resembled a teased-out inverted comma—a portent, perhaps, of a change in the weather; I did not really know. And I fell to wondering why we expend so much effort on interpreting signs—reading the sky, the sea, the faces of those we love—for insights into some inner and normally invisible state, or set such great store in trying to divine or alter the course of the future.

o to describe rather than prescribe.

For the great unknown in history, that has baffled
the philosophy of history in the modern age, arises ·
not only when one considers history as a whole and
finds that its subject, mankind, is an abstraction
which never can become an active agent; the same
unknown has baffled political philosophy from
its beginning in antiquity and contributes to the
general contempt in which philosophers since Plato
have held the realm of human affairs.

—HANNAH ARENDT, *The Human Condition*

2 Of Time and the River
the interface of history and human lives

At Nahr Al-Kalb, on the northern outskirts of Beirut, the so-called
River of the Dog flows from a gorge of serrated limestone cliffs and
moves swiftly across stony shoals before vanishing beneath a built-up
littoral and into the wind-whipped sea. Here, inscribed on roadside
rocks, are the cuneiform characters of Nebuchadnezzar, as well as the
corroded bas-relief of this sixth-century Babylonian king. Nearby are
hieroglyphs left by the pharaoh Ramses II. And there are plaques commemorating Napoléon's incursions into the region and British and
Anzac successes against the Ottoman Empire in 1918, as well as Latin
eulogies that the Syrian-born Roman emperor Septimius Severus addressed to his victorious Gallic legionnaires. Visiting this tourist site in
the company of my friend Ghassan Hage, I had the impression that
each conquering army, while aware of the repetitiveness of history,

remained convinced that it was making it. Yet as Karl Marx famously observed, "men make their history, but they do not make it just as they please; they do not make it under circumstances chosen by themselves, but under circumstances directly encountered, given and transmitted from the past (1934:10). Even more radically, Hannah Arendt has argued against the idea of "making" altogether. Although we recount our histories as we recount our lives—as narratives of visionary, outstanding, and self-sacrificing individuals—"the real story in which we are engaged as long as we live has no visible or invisible maker because it is not made" (1958:186). In every historical narrative there are heroes, to be sure, like Nebuchadnezzar and Napoléon at Nahr Al-Kalb, but, Arendt reminds us, these individuals were not the authors of the events we associate with their names. Although stories require agents who make things happen and to whom things happen, in reality we act and speak without ever being the sole authors of our destinies or lives, and history is "an endless new chain of happenings whose eventual outcome the actor is utterly incapable of knowing or controlling beforehand" (Arendt 1977:59–60).

But in what sense can we speak of action (praxis) without an actor? In precisely the same way that it is possible to speak of subjectivity or intersubjectivity without a subject. For human existence makes its appearance in the indeterminate or potential space *between* actors, confounding our original intentions, eclipsing our supposed identities, leading us to do things we did not think we had it in us to do, and obliging us to constantly rethink the very notion of who we are. At the same time, all human action is conditioned by a plethora of often competing influences, interests, and persuasions that are the outcome of previous experience and that have ramifications going far beyond what any actor knows, desires, imagines, says, or does. The "simple fact," Arendt observes, is that "we don't know what we are doing when we are acting," and we can neither grasp, practically or intellectually, the manifold influences that bear on us or the future implications of what we do (2000:180). This is not to reduce human existence to contingency, for our lives would be unthinkable without at least the *ideas* of agency and design. What Arendt wants to emphasize is the fact that human action always involves more than a singular subject; it occurs within fields of *inter*action that she calls the "subjective in-between."

Accordingly, whatever anyone does or says is immediately outstripped by what others do or say in return. Every action calls out a reaction that "strikes out on its own and affects others" (1958:190). This is the force field that Michel Foucault speaks of as "governmentality," where power is not an intrinsic property of persons or institutions but finds expression between interacting subjects (1983:221). Obvious ethical questions are entailed by this view since if one can never know exactly the extent to which one's actions make a difference to the ways things are, or the extent to which one is responsible for what one does, it becomes difficult to decide, for example, if or when one should be condemned for one's failings or praised for one's good deeds.

Though it may be impossible to understand every antecedent cause or contingent factor that bears on our actions, Arendt does not take the view that we are thereby in thrall to the past, for we may, through *forgiveness*, find release from the consequences of our past actions or the effect of the actions of others on us, and through the *promise* we make to ourselves and others, we may find redemption from "the chaotic uncertainty of the future" (1958:237). These strategies, she says, reflect the fact of natality—the power of action to bring the new into being. Thus when we recount a story about any event that has befallen us, we play down the boundless field of influences and consequences that impinge on us and create the impression that our lives and histories lie, at least to some extent, within our ken and control.

While forgiveness and the promise, like storytelling and redressive rituals, offer the perennial possibility of redemption, suggesting that we are responsible for our actions and can change our course and put the past behind us, Arendt avoids the question of whether such strategies are merely magical means of transforming our *experience* of the world —in which case the world is simply made to *appear* other than it is—or real means of changing the way things are. I will return to this question shortly because in the light of Lebanon's recent tragic history, it would be depressing to admit that Plato was right and that we are the playthings of the gods (we might now say our history or our genes), for this would seem to imply the fatalistic conclusion that nothing we say or do can help us escape the mimetic and repetitive cycles of violence that have bedeviled us in the past and that all our piety and wit cannot err the moving finger of history back to cancel half a line.

However, Arendt is not denying human freedom; she is simply pointing out that freedom is exercised in some domains, but not in other and that it is important not to delude ourselves about the extent which we are the authors and arbiters of our own lives. The problem, she observes, is our tendency to conflate acting (praxis) and making (*poesis*). Poesis, which is synonymous with what is nowadays called agency, suggests the sustained, self-conscious, goal-oriented way a person or persons work at making or producing something—researching a book, combating terrorism, building a house, having a family, treating a disease. Praxis, by contrast, denotes a field of human action and interaction that is largely beyond our comprehension and control, and which we simply suffer.[1] While Foucault stripped history clean of heroic movers and shakers by reimagining it as a succession of different discursive fields (episteme), Arendt succeeds in getting rid of the notion of an agentive subject without, however, reducing history to anything as abstract as discourse. For her, the *vita activa* consists less in our intellectual conception of who we are, of what things mean, or the knowledge and moral precepts we espouse than in our decisive interactions with others in a world that nonetheless exceeds our understanding and eludes our grasp. While our retrospective accounts and interpretations of these interactions in the *vita contemplativa* will almost certainly involve the ascription of intention and the allocation of blame, we *act*, for the most part, habitually and unreflectively, moved by deeply embedded dispositions that have far more to do with the struggle for being than the striving for meaning.[2]

One might cite, for example, in defence of this view, the way in which a war quickly outstrips the sociocultural conditions that brought it about or the political ideologies that gave it justification, running its course like a storm or a fever, possessing a life and logic of its own. In this vein, Lebanese refer to the civil war as "the events" (*al hawadith*), a "mild and faintly contemptuous understatement" that bears a close relation to the Arabic word for "accident" (Makdisi 1990:65). Or one might remark the ways in which, despite our rational planning, our good intentions, and our care of self, markets pass through cycles of boom or bust, marriages go on the rocks, friends fall out, luck deserts or favors us, and "the best laid schemes o' mice an' men / Gang aft a-gley, / An' lea'e us nought but grief an' pain, / For promised joy." In mundane rituals and stories, we seek to repair the damage to our shattered illusions of omnipotence. Monuments to the war dead, with their lists of specific names and battles, or truth and reconciliation hearings, with their stories of individual suffering, bear testimony to our human unwillingness to resign ourselves "to the brutal fact that the agent of the war was actually Nobody" (Arendt 2000:179). Similarly, our perennial hope of enlightened leaders, and our search for gurus and saviors, testifies to our inability to live without the illusion that we have, within our own hands and minds, the power not only to create history but to create it as nature or God or reason determined it should be.

Sectarianism is perhaps the most ubiquitous and problematic example of this conviction that history, and not just the myths with which we make it intelligible, is largely a product of human agency and human will, for which we may be judged righteous or wrongheaded, heroic or villainous. Arendt's contrary view—that history has a life of its own that is beyond our complete control and comprehension—entails a non-judgmental attitude. For if human beings commonly "know not what they do," our intellectual task becomes less a matter of determining the causes of human action, or of deciding who is responsible for the way things turn out in this world, than of exploring the ways in which people struggle against the disadvantages of their circumstances and recover from the adversities of their histories. Knowing why things happen, or judging people for the errors of their ways, is thus less important than trying to understand how, in the face of hardship, human beings still find life worth living, and endure. But such research requires a method not of standing aloof and seeing the world from a disinterested, superior standpoint, but of actively engaging with others in their place, on their own terms. "Training one's imagination to go visiting," as Arendt (1982:43) called this method of intellectual displacement, does not entail agreeing or even empathizing with the other, as her famous study of Adolf Eichmann makes clear. And though it repudiates Archimedean detachment, it does not imply the kind of suspension of ethical concern that would lead us to exonerate a person of a crime on the grounds that we understand what drove him or her to commit the offence. Rather, it simply asks that we do not invoke cultural, religious, or intellectual superiority in privileging received opinions or our own particular point of view.

One morning in late April, Ghassan and I drove into the Shuf mountains. We passed through Druze villages in a vast landscape of great stone bluffs, terraced valleys, and abandoned silk mills before coming to Beit ed Dîne where we spent an hour strolling through Emir Bechir's palace, designed in Mamluk style by Italian architects and built in the early nineteenth century. According to the tourist material I read, this had been a benign age:

> In all the reception halls and the rooms of the harem area are inscriptions on the walls, most of them gentle reminders of the true values. "An hour of justice is worth a thousand hours of prayer," says one. "Fear God, and you will begin to be wise," declares another. Emir Bechir was known far and wide for his just dealings with all men, regardless of their station. Bechir, in fact, was a remarkable man—as the man who built Beit ed Dîne would have to be. A contemporary traveller, who knew him well and stayed here a good deal, wrote of him: "Bechir was baptized a Christian; he lives like Turk; and he will die like a Druze." This was quite a compliment, for it meant that Bechir had managed to combine in himself the interests of all members of the community at the time. Stories about his personal courage and strength of character are legion. He managed to include at Beit ed Dîne, incidentally, a church, a mosque, and a place of worship for the third great Lebanese religious community, the Druze.

As if to counter these images of civility and multicultural tolerance, Ghassan pointed out to me the defaced photographs of the Druze leader Kamal Jumblatt, assassinated on 16 March 1977, two years after the start of the civil war. In photo after photo, Jumblatt's eyes had been gouged out with a ballpoint pen.

As we drove on into the mountains, Ghassan drew my attention to the mulberry trees along the roadside and at the edge of the cultivated fields. He was presently writing a paper, he said, about the increasing fetishization of religious identity in Mount Lebanon during the nineteenth century, and he reminded me how yesterday we had observed, on the campus of the American University of Beirut, several young women with plasters across the bridge of their noses. This was on a par, Ghassan said, with Asian women having recourse to cosmetic surgery to achieve more European-looking eyes; the Lebanese students wanted to Europeanize their appearance by having their noses straightened. And this desire to acquire the symbolic capital of Europeanness could be traced to the rise of sericulture in the Shuf in the nineteenth century.

After migrating into the southern Shuf mountains in the seventeenth century, the Maronites lived as landless serfs or peasant farmers under Druze overlords in a quasi-feudal system known all over Mount Lebanon as *iqta*. Gradually, however, the Maronites came to monopolize the commercial and craft activities that the Druze considered beneath their dignity—and so were uniquely situated, in the early nineteenth century, to embrace sericulture and profit from the rising demand for raw silk, first on the Egyptian market and then in France. As the Christians increased their landholdings and wealth, they began to challenge the political supremacy of the Druze, who were profiting from the Maronite enterprises by taxing silk mills, local trade, crafts, and the weighing of silk. Communal tension led to open conflict in 1841 "when a series of small incidents" precipitated a civil war that was played out, Ghassan said, not as a struggle between "two socio-economic sets of relations" but "in the form of a religious conflict" (Hage 2004:189). In 1860 violent conflict again flared between the Maronites and Druze, with sectarian divisions even more firmly entrenched. Yet for centuries, the Maronites on Mount Lebanon had regarded themselves as an integral part of Arab culture, Ghassan noted, and it was only with their growing economic dominance in the nineteenth century that they began to cultivate a specifically European persona, projecting images of their own superior way of life and counterimages of the allegedly inferior, socially backward, lazy, and illiterate Druze. These contrasted essentializations became, within a generation, "second nature," obscuring the historical circumstances that had produced them and taking on an intractable life of their own so that the internecine violence between Maronites and Druze in the 1980s was, whatever its many immediate causes, systematically explained and justified in religious terms.

From time to time, during our conversation, Ghassan pulled the car over to the side of the road the better to hear my questions and collect his thoughts; the noise of the tires on the asphalt, and the wind rushing past the car, simply drowned my voice. Finally, we decided to stop and buy some lunch, and in a deserted café we ordered grilled chicken pieces in Lebanese bread and two beers before sitting down at a table and continuing our conversation.

Ghassan's talk had put me in mind of Arendt's notion of plurality as the human condition of being at once identical with *and* different from everyone else "who ever lived, lives, or will live" (1958:8). In other words, our humanity is both shared and singular, and our identity

plurality.

consists in being both the same (idem) as others and uniquely ourselves in contrast to them (ipse) (Ricoeur 1992:2–3, 116). For Arendt, however, human distinction does not automatically imply otherness. Although all human beings are distinctive, she argues, none is absolutely other, for we share the same capacity for interacting and communicating with one another based on vague perceptions of our common humanity (1958:175–76). To make a person other, one arrogates being entirely to oneself and makes of the other a mere object of one's actions, one's judgment, one's compassion, or one's hate. Sameness is played down—sacrificed we might say—and difference played up until an absolute opposition is made between self and not-self, as Ghassan's chronicle of the Shuf had shown. But violence is not inspired by otherness as such; it is a desperate expression of the desire to make other through the systematic suppression of everything that is manifestly shared or the same. So it was that as the Maronites forgot that their emergent sense of identity as Europeans was "a product of the capitalist relations of dependency established by France and the class relations underlying it" (Hage 2004:202), they remained "haunted," as Ghassan put it, by images of dirty, smelly, brutish, peasant being, which they attempted to exorcize by fantasies and strategies of being European and white—cultivating European tastes and manners, speaking perfect French, getting a European education, and so on—and seeking to ethnically cleanse Mount Lebanon of "Arabs" who carried the stigma of, and were the scapegoats for, all that they abhorred in themselves and their own past.[3] As the custodian of Maronite identity, the church naturally aided and abetted this identity fetishism, while the Druze, fearing disempowerment, fought back with their own fetishized notions of identity, ethnic superiority, and divine right. A situation not only of alienated thinking came to prevail but of schizmogenesis—an ever-widening gap brought on by separation, by lack of reality testing, and by the mistaken conviction that one's ideas about self and other were both historically and divinely sanctioned.

However, I dissented from Ghassan's tendency to see sectarianism chiefly as a product of politico-economic changes, and I reminded him of something about which we both had written at length (Hage 1999; Jackson 2002), namely, the way sectarianism provides not only a way of justifying political and economic supremacy but offers to the disempowered a magical means of reclaiming some sense of having value,

Otherng

hope, social standing, and power. Predicated on a Manichaean logic that sees the world in terms of good and evil, black and white, sectarianism's attraction is first and foremost its simplicity. There is no complexity to understand, merely a threat to identify and a defensive position to take up. Its second attraction lies in its appeal to a logic of reversal that presumes to set the world to right according to the rationale "the first shall be the last and the last shall be the first." A white supremacist, members of a terrorist cell, and a beleaguered ethnic minority may all have very different claims on our sympathies, but all seek through sectarian reason to bolster their sense of rightness, presence, and value in the face of a world in which, from their point of view at least, they have been robbed of their humanity or birthright. Though such persons may create great mayhem, they are, as Arendt so perceptively noted, without power, for power is consolidated in numbers and mass consensus (1970: 44). But where the terrorists make up for their numerical weakness in weaponry, achieving in explosions, fire, and chaos the recognition, presence, and voice they could not otherwise find, others will have recourse to forms of community, real and imagined, or cosmological identifications that effectively fuse or merge their individual being with a more stable, extensive, and durable domain of collective belonging. As Ghassan observed, one of the most satisfying powers of

> the collective "we" lies precisely in its capacity to make an "I" experience what the "I" itself cannot possibly experience. "I" can be uneducated and yet confidently claim that "we are highly educated compared to the Muslims." "I" can be a peasant but can proudly boast that "we are a very sophisticated people." "I" can speak only in Arabic but can proudly claim "we have always spoken French." Likewise "I" can be poor but note that "we are a rich community." (2004:203)

Though the racist will evoke some generalized idea of the civilization to which he or she belongs, and which he or she will struggle to the death to defend, people far more deserving of our sympathy will utilize the same magical strategy to gain our attention, to enlarge their sense of presence, support their political claims, and bolster their sense of self.

Our journey had now taken us high into the mountains, and the mist made it difficult to see far ahead. We found ourselves beyond villages now: the last people we saw were a goatherd sitting on a rock, his kids playing nearby, his wife gathering wild thyme. As we approached Jabal el-Barouk, I was still turning over in my mind what Ghassan had been saying earlier about the way cultural or class distinctions come to be expressed, and essentialized, as religious differences, and I wondered what appeal we can have to higher moral authority to help us reconcile our differences, to heal the wounds of sectarian conflict, when each side has arrogated the divine to itself, convinced the gods are on its side, and the other an infidel or heretic.

Curiously enough, I would find one answer to this question among the cedars. At the edge of the forest, we were flagged down by two uniformed men who informed us we would have to pay a fee before going on and be accompanied by a guide. So a young Druze man, a horticulture student at the Arab University of Beirut, clambered into the backseat of the car and immediately began regaling us in French with information about *cedrus libani*, the national icon of the country. Ghassan was clearly bored, but I was entranced by the mythical and biblical references the man was reeling off, not to mention the details about the cedar's ecology and history and about its value in the ancient world—the pitch to ease toothache, the sawdust to keep snakes at bay, the resin to aid in the mummification of the dead, the timber to build temples, palaces, and ships. But what held my attention most were allusions to Lebanon's cedars in the book of Ezekiel and the Epic of Gilgamesh. In Ezekiel (31:1–18), the Assyrians are compared to the cedars, standing higher than any other tree, all great nations dwelling in their shadows. But hubris and God's hand brought the Assyrians low, breaking their branches and destroying their power. Thus the awful conclusion to the chapter: "To whom art thou like in glory and in greatness among the trees of Eden? Yet shalt thou be brought down with the trees of Eden unto the nether parts of the earth." Hubris also figures as a theme in the Mesopotamian Epic of Gilgamesh, versions of which, on clay tablets, date to between 1700 and the 700 BCE (Foster 2001:xi-xii). Gilgamesh, the ruler of Uruk, exalted for his physical perfection and strength, is also "a wild bull," headstrong, rampaging, and arrogant: abusing his subjects, abducting young women, "harrying the young men of Uruk beyond reason." To counter his unbridled powers, the gods create a wild man out of clay named Enkidu. Rather than compete with Enkidu, Gilgamesh takes his mother's advice and makes his rival a boon companion and counselor. With Enkidu tamed and humanized, Gilgamesh proposes a journey to the cedar forests of Lebanon since felling these great trees is a traditional Mesopotamian way of demonstrating kingly power. Though Enkidu is appalled at the prospect of two mere mortals venturing into the wild country of Humbaba, the monster whom Enlil, the high God, has appointed to protect the cedar groves, Gilgamesh dismisses his appeals, declaring, "You make me ill; I must set [my hand to felling] a cedar tree, I must establish eternal fame." As for the advice of the elders of Uruk, who tell Gilgamesh that his feelings have carried him away and that Enlil himself has set Humbaba to guard the cedars, Gilgamesh is unheeding.

On reaching Mount Lebanon, Gilgamesh does battle with Humbaba, a battle so formidable that the rift valley of Lebanon is formed by their circling feet. Defeated, the monstrous Humbaba begs for his life, but Enkidu exhorts Gilgamesh to finish him off. This Gilgamesh does, though not before Humbaba has cursed the heroes with the words "May the pair of them never reach old age!" After severing Humbaba's head, Gilgamesh fells the cedars, from which Enkidu makes a great door for the sanctuary of Enlil at Nippur. On returning in triumph to Uruk, the city goddess Ishtar becomes so enamoured of Gilgamesh that she proposes marriage. Gilgamesh not only refuses her; he insults her. In retaliation she has her father Anu unleash the bull of heaven, but Gilgamesh, with Enkidu's help, kills the animal. It is at this point, however, that Gilgamesh's world begins to fall apart. Enraged by Gilgamesh's killing of Humbaba, Enlil takes the life of Enkidu. Gilgamesh, grief-stricken and oppressed by thoughts of his own mortality, never fully recovers: "No man can usurp the power of the gods. He may build his monuments and cities, but death will always be his journey's end."

Ghassan and I had now come as far as we could go. Deep snowdrifts blocked the road. And so we climbed out of the car and, for respite from our guide's unrelenting commentaries, trudged into the mist-swathed forest of cedars, some of which were between one and two thousand years old. Here, in the presence of these great trees, whose lower boughs touched the ground, whose bifurcating trunks were living images of human plurality, and whose longevity and deep rootedness made them natural icons of tenacity and renewal, one could, for a moment, feel free of history, though not of religion. These are God's trees, our guide remarked, after we had rejoined him. When they are about to die they split open, so that they are like hands brought together in prayer, symmetrical and accepting, in the face of God's decision to end their life.

Driving back to Beirut that afternoon, Ghassan and I were wrapped in our separate thoughts. I had experienced the powerful and moving way in which human beings collapse their singular biographies into collective histories, and how these histories are then metamorphosed into mythology—the I merging with the we, the we merging with the thou, the thou merging with nature or with being itself. Sometimes the transcendent category is a totemic creature, a tutelary spirit, a high God; sometimes it is a community or nation, real or imaginary—a pure land, a redeeming idea, a defining moment in history. But if such identifications unify, they simultaneously divide, for the we seldom encompasses all humankind; rather, it defines us against a counter category of them who are typically supposed to lack humanity. Is it realistic to hope for a world in which this is not the case? And can transcendent values, centred on notions such as the equality of all in the eyes of God, or human rights, or the psychic unity of humankind, or the power of love to rise above sectarianism reinforce this hope, or do they inevitably become, despite their rhetorical claims to universality, masks for particularistic interests?

A couple of days after visiting Jabal el-Barouk, I made a second journey to Mount Lebanon. After a breakfast of *maroushi* bread, yoghurt, and vegetables, followed by Turkish coffee, I drove with Ghassan, his wife Caroline, and their two daughters to a point along the coast road north of Beirut where we met up with a couple of Ghassan's old school friends, both now living and working abroad. George Estephan was an architect, just back from West Africa, and Abass El-Zein was an engineer and writer, based like Ghassan at the University of Sydney, and now on sabbatical at the American University of Beirut.

Abass and I were in the back seat of Ghassan's car; George drove ahead in a second vehicle with his daughter, Ghassan's daughters, and his Nigerian bush dog. As we passed through the Maronite Christian suburbs and into the hills, Abass told me how much of Lebanese life is ruled by sectarian divisions. "They have a long history," he said. "If I apply for a new passport or a driver's license, I have to go to my grandparents' village in northern Lebanon for a birth certificate, even though I have no living relatives there and no personal connection with the place." And he went on to explain the so-called confessional basis of political power in the country, with each of seventeen religious sects and ethnic groups represented in proportion to its number in the total population—but numbers based on the last official census, which was in 1932.[4] At that time, the Maronite Christians were in the majority; now the Muslims undoubtedly are, particularly the Shiites. Like other intellectuals I had spoken to, Abass lamented the simplistic labels that were a legacy of civil war—the ways in which terms such as Sunni and Shi'a, Christian and Muslim, West Beirut and East Beirut, left-wing and right-wing glossed over the numerous ideological, class, regional, and personal differences between people and erased memories of the antebellum cosmopolitanism and social intermingling that characterized so much of everyday Lebanese life, at least in West Beirut. His view was pretty much the same as many expatriate intellectuals espoused, and reminded me of Edward Said's commencement address to the American University of Beirut graduating class of 2000, in which he declared, "There is no such thing as an entirely Western, or Islamic, or Arab idea. All ideas are mixed both in origin and use. Similarly, everyone of us today is a composite person," before exhorting his audience to resist, as he had done all his life, "the labels, stereotypes, myths imposed by the more powerful on the weaker as a method of conquest" and to enter into "dialogue and coexistence with others" (2000). But, for all its universalising rhetoric, such a view belongs to a particular class and masks the privileged position that allows this class the luxury of its liberalism.

After driving through several Maronite villages, with their familiar roadside shrines to Saint Maron, we descended a vertiginous and narrow road into a valley of jagged rocks, pines, and evergreen oaks. Far below lay Nahr Ibrahim, the river of Adonis, the river of love and redemption. This was Shi'a country now, and after parking the cars near the village of Janneh, we set off down a track beside tilled fields and orchards, willows, mulberry trees, and aromatic sycamores toward the river. A loudspeaker atop the local mosque was calling people to prayers, and a Hezbollah flag fluttered on a pole stuck in the front bumper of a derelict Land Rover.

The river was swift running, as if fed by snowmelt, but George said its source was actually a spring high in the mountains. We crossed the river on felled trees to which someone had nailed pieces of broken wood to provide footing—some of us crawling on all fours, as the torrent rushed past beneath, others crossing quickly, confident of their balance. George was the last to cross, carrying his terrified dog in his arms as we watched from the safety of the other bank, fearing what would happen if he lost his footing and fell.

The river was now on our left. To our right, the steep slopes beneath the bluffs had been stripped of trees. We soon discovered why—a charcoal burner's makeshift tent, coffee pot, and scattered belongings, and two nearby mounds of fire-blackened earth, releasing wisps of smoke from the smoldering wood beneath. Again I fell into step with Abass, who had told me earlier that he had grown up in Beirut and had been twelve when the civil war began in 1975. His parent's house was less than a hundred meters from the demarcation line. After graduating from the American University of Beirut in 1986, he went to England to do his PhD in engineering and after many travels wound up in Australia, where he married. He had published a novel about the war, he said. It was a kind of Romeo and Juliet story. The two main protagonists are young lovers, Kareem Kader (a Muslim) and Raawya Naoum (a Christian), who meet in the Beirut Conservatory of Music before the war. When war breaks out, Kareem becomes a sniper, Raawya a volunteer nurse, and it is his fate to accidentally kill his beloved, significantly as she is crossing the green line, the no-man's-land that divided East from West Beirut.

But is not love, I asked Abass, like coexistence and dialogue, or the invocation of transcendent powers, natural or divine, just another liberal-romantic cliché, a dream? Can one realistically found a civil society on love? Abass neither agreed nor disagreed. But he said that in Lebanon sectarianism ran so deep that Maronite, Druze, Sunni, and Shi'a leaders alike had vehemently refused to allow a civil marriage bill to pass into law, arguing that this would lead to everything from moral degeneration among the young to the destruction of family and country.

To whom or what, then, can we appeal if we are to coexist peacefully in this world? Do we lift up our eyes unto the hills or walk among cedars? Do we escape into academies and monasteries, leaving the world behind? Do we take heart from the healing power of love? And are there invisible hands, omnipotent gods, capricious spirits, natural laws, or historical dynamics that define the limits of our freedom and our responsibility and may help us define our path?

Perhaps modernism makes us assume too much: responsibility for our own lives; the discovery of life's meaning; the salvation of others; the punishment of those who do wrong. On the one hand, those on the left encourage us in the belief that protest and righteous indignation can change the world—not only the world as it appears to us but also our forms of government. On the other hand, the president of the United States broadcasts his vision of an "ownership society" based on an ethic of what C. B. McPherson called "possessive individualism" (1962). "By making every citizen an agent of his or her own destiny," George W. Bush declared in his combative 2005 inauguration speech, "we will give our fellow Americans greater freedom from want and make our society more prosperous and just and equal."

My sojourn in Beirut, like my visits to Sierra Leone after the war, brought me to a very different view of the human condition—roughly the Homeric vision of human beings as fettered and frail, despite their vitality, cunning, and will. At every turn victims of demonic or Dionysian forces beyond their understanding and control, they are prone to emotions and ambitions that get the better of them, are blind to the implications of their actions, and exceed their own measure in their visions of what they might know or attain (Onians 1951:303). This view has analogues in the Taoist image of a human being in a small boat on a wild river between towering cliffs. This person has an oar with which to steer, but the river's force places a limit on the oarsman's ability to navigate. Such a view finds expression in the Kuranko pragmatism that accepts that forgiving and forgetting may not be possible when one has lost loved ones and one's livelihood in war, yet sees that coexistence is imperative since those who did you wrong can neither be destroyed nor avoided. You have to live with them, as you have to live with hardship. These things cannot be wished away. So coexistence has to be built, not on love or even liking, but on an attitude of live and let live; not on dialogue but distance, accepting that there is much in this life that is beyond us, that we are out of our depths, not waving but drowning, though some things are within our reach, for which we may be praised

Homeric vision of human beings as fettered & frail despite their cunning & will or blamed. It is all very good, accruing moral credit for ourselves by exhorting humankind not to be cruel, to enter into dialogue, to settle its differences by peaceful means, to rise up against tyrants. But this is the voice of modernity, predicated on the assumption that we can make history the way we want it to be and through knowledge, democracy, and foreign aid bring humanity from the dark ages of sectarian hatred and civil strife and, by remembering Auschwitz, prevent it returning again. But the contrary view, which should also be heard, is that we can never legislate away intolerance, or through scientific innovation bring an end to suffering, or through punishment prevent crime, or through remembering history alter its course. And so, for we who reflect on the human condition, there is a need not to judge, not even to seek to know what conditions create human violence, but to bear witness to how people endure their lot, affirming life in the face of death.

Not long after writing these lines, I read in the *New York Times* the terrible story of Nidal Abu Snaineh. Nidal's family happened to be waiting in their car at a checkpoint in northern Jerusalem when a suicide bomber, sitting in an adjacent vehicle, panicked as Israeli police officers approached him and detonated shrapnel-filled explosives. Nidal's father was killed instantly, his daughter and mother severely injured, and Nidal's six-year-old son, Mahdi, was hospitalized with multiple shrapnel wounds. "What happened changed our lives," Nidal explained. "We can't understand what happened, but it changed our lives. I don't know how to explain such a thing, just destiny. I believe in destiny. This is our destiny." His wife reiterated Nidal's remarks. "This is our fate. They went to the checkpoint and there was an explosion. I don't know more than that. What can I say? I can't blame anyone" (Erlanger 2004:2). What struck me in the comments of this devastated couple, as they kept vigil at the bedside of their gravely wounded son, was that for all their despair, they expressed neither a desire for revenge nor any judgment—on others or on themselves. The modernist project of identifying causes, finding fault, seeking justice, and commemorating the past may seem natural, even necessary, to us, but it may help us endure calamities less effectively than the fatalism that freely admits that comprehension and control are often beyond our grasp. My argument is not for the kind of fatalism that the West so often ascribes to the East—an attitude of submission and abnegation in the face of life, our destinies already written. It is for a stoic or defiant acceptance of fate, *after the fact*. So when I rail against the modernist project, I am not seeking to make a case against fighting injustice and creating a world of greater equality; I am speaking against the hubris that attends us when we see ourselves as omnipotent actors in whose hands rests the destiny of all humankind, and arguing for a greater acceptance of what we cannot do and cannot understand. Resignation this may be, but by playing down the extent to which we, or others, know what we are doing, it may imply a less judgmental, more forgiving, attitude toward ourselves and others and be more conducive to the birth of new life in the face of history's calamities. This may be why the devastation of a natural catastrophe such as an earthquake or tsunami may be easier to survive psychologically than the atrocities of war, though sometimes war is experienced *as if* it were a natural disaster. In Sierra Leone, for instance, many amputees I spoke to were very aware that the violence was arbitrary—an expression of an "evil" that had, with the aid of drugs, taken possession of the perpetrators. If the amputees were victims, it was simply because the rebels classified everyone who was not for them as against them, and because they happened to be in the wrong place at the wrong time. It was not that they had been singled out on account of their specific identity. This refusal to make a public spectacle out of allocating blame and punishing the instigators of the violence also had a lot to do with the exigencies of life in the aftermath of war.[5] A similar pragmatism seems to have prevailed in Lebanon. In August 1991, the Lebanese government pardoned most of those who committed crimes during the civil war. And the sole monument to the war, though originally meant to stand in the city center, ended up in a Beirut suburb. Yet the state cannot be held solely responsible for this amnesia, for in the face of Lebanon's sectarianism, most people saw that unity could only ever be apparent, and that remembering the past would not effect reconciliation but simply revive old divisions (Young 2004:9). Coexistence, here, is less a matter of achieving *communitas* than of respecting a state of truce, in which the various parties consider it in their own interests to keep the peace, agreeing to disagree, maintaining a guarded distance from one another, attending to the business of life. Coexistence is not a matter of reconciliation, dialogue, or even mutual regard; it is simply the absence of violence (Sampson 2003:180). Yet in late

February and early March 2005, demands for the withdrawal of Syrian troops from Lebanon after the killing of the former prime minister Rafik Hariri, and the resignation of the government, suggested a transcendental turn that revived the spirit of independence. Lebanese of all ages, from all walks of life, and from various religious and civil groups took to the streets chanting "freedom" and "sovereignty." "The feeling was exhilarating," remarked one protester at Martyrs Square broadcast on the BBC news. "The crowd started the protest with different banners of various Lebanese parties, but at the request of opposition leaders, these banners were dropped and everyone was united by the Lebanese flag. I think this was the single most important detail. I would not have been comfortable around other flags, *because after a civil war not a single faction, not a single party or politician is innocent*" (2 March 2005; emphasis added). Ironically, however, six days after the anti-Syrian protest marches, a pro-Syrian march organized by the Shi'a organization Hezbollah filled another downtown square (Riad al-Solh), also waving Lebanese flags and chanting "freedom" and "sovereignty."[6]

It is impossible to predict the efficacy or outcome of such agentive action because, as I have argued earlier, it is impossible to anticipate the outcome of *interactions* between opposed forces. This is the gloss I give to the notion of fatalism, arguing that in analysis if not in life we avoid extolling one mode of action over another on a priori grounds and accept that though we can neither know with any certainty the causes or outcomes of any human action, we may describe its effects in depth and detail and so appreciate the irresolvable complexity of every human situation. Thus fatalism, so long the foil of the West—an Orientalist tactic for writing off the reasoning of the non-Western world—may be placed on par with any other worldview as one way of reckoning with adversity, one way of avoiding the judgmentalism that so often perpetuates violence, one way of accepting the forces over which one cannot prevail, one way of enabling life to be reborn from the ashes of history, one way of giving ourselves another chance, and even, dare I say it, one way of understanding the world.

prediction is hard.

• but we can still explore details & depths of
" the irresolvable complexity of

every human situation."

National polities both encapsulate local and
familistic forms of identity and yet also draw their
primary imagery from these.
—MICHAEL HERZFELD, "Intimating Culture"

3 Imagining the Powers That Be
society versus the state

In the course of visits to Sierra Leone in the years after the war, I
was struck by the extraordinary expectations people had of their
government and by the impatience displayed when these expectations
were not met. It was as if the demise of the corrupt and autocratic
regimes, both civil and military, that had governed Sierra Leone for
almost forty years after the ending of colonial rule had reawakened
in people the same exaggerated euphoria they felt at independence,
leading them now to anticipate an immediate change for the better,
with education, jobs, wealth, and medical care freely available for
all. In May 2004, for example, an article appeared in the Freetown
newspaper, the *Independent*, concerning the plight of ordinary Sierra
Leoneans in the postwar period and concluding with a direct appeal to
the president.

Mr President, you promised the people that come the year 2007, no one in Sierra Leone will go to bed hungry, but since you said those words, things have been going down the hill at an alarming speed. There is a Creole saying that goes thus, "Marade wae geh for sweet, na de bachelor's eve you go know" [A happy stag party presages a happy marriage]. Our own bachelor's eve is getting grimmer by the day. In your Independence Day speech, you tried to say that the battle is always tougher when about to end. OK, it may be true. It is also true that it is the time when the casualties are most. If you survive, then you survive for good. But there are times if you survived, it would have been better if you had died because you would be worse than an invalid. So what use will it be come 2007, the year of "plenty," to 90% of the citizens of this country majority of whom might be suffering from stomach ulcers and faulty liver by then? As far as I am concerned and so are millions of others, the war ended in 2000 and the slide toward doom should have ended then. The president and his Sierra Leonean People's Party have all the apparatus including a super majority in parliament to have raised our standards of living, but why? why? why? Remember, what you sow is what you will surely reap. If you have ears to hear, better hear and if you have eyes to see, better see!!! (Collier 2004)[1]

I was intrigued by the impassioned plea with which the author began, and the minatory note on which he or she ended—a combination of complaint and threat that is not uncharacteristic of human addresses to higher authorities, be they presidents, parents, ancestors, or God. And though some might see this newspaper article as evidence that patrimonialism still governs the lives of most Sierra Leoneans, leaving the poor no option but to petition men of wealth and influence for work, school fees, or the means of making a livelihood, I prefer to see in it resonances of a universal and all-too-human search for recognition or rescue, wherein respectful appeals to higher powers go hand in hand with anger and resentment when the help is not forthcoming or goes to someone felt to be less deserving. And so in downtown Freetown, the streets were noisy with hi-life songs that pilloried politicians as selfish, greedy, corrupt, and incompetent, holding them responsible for the country's ills. In one song called "Swegbe" (from *swear*, meaning "to curse"), the singer recounted how fed up people were with listening to the president's long weekly speeches on TV when so many had no food in their bellies, and went on to complain about inflation, the bribes one had to pay to see a doctor, the foreigners who were profiting from the nation's wealth, and the traffic officers who fined people even when they had done nothing wrong.

Another popular song, "Borbor bele," ("Fat Cats") by Emmerson Bockarie mined the same vein:

> The money we get from aid
> all disappears,
> we never see a cent,
> all they do is steal
> (I said "steal," but mentioned no names;
> we won't mention names,
> we don't want trouble,
> but they know who they are). . . .
> The youth are all suffering,
> we're under stress,
> though we're young we look old . . .
> We have diamonds in Sierra Leone
> but we're still in debt.
> Electricity one hour out of thirty,
> yet those fat cats have cars that cost 500 million leones . . .
> Until corruption [*yoki yoki*] is stopped
> we'll keep on singing this song;
> why do you, *borbor bele*,
> pretend to be nice
> when you're more wicked than the RUF
> If they die
> we'll go to their funeral,
> drink rum and coffee and celebrate
> and we'll pass a message to everyone in Salone
> about the thieves

Coming back to Europe and reading the daily papers, I was struck not by people's relative contentment with their governments but by the same pervasive dissatisfaction I had seen in Sierra Leone. While it is true that the social imaginary of the popular songs I had heard in

Freetown was an expression of extreme social inequalities and a burning sense of injustice,[2] it is necessary to remind oneself that even in wealthy nations, where jobs and education *are* readily available, and most peoples' material needs *are* met, well-being and security remain, for many, frustratingly out of reach. Thus in the immediate aftermath of the tsunami that devastated the coasts of South Asia in December 2004, many Swedish people, accustomed to being protected from the vagaries of war and of natural disaster by their welfare state, found it difficult to accept the tragic deaths of so many of their compatriots. As the Swedish prime minister Göran Persson observed, "we have no experience at all" (qtd. in Cowell 2005:1). In Denmark, many people publicly expressed outrage and anger that their government was not doing more to rescue and repatriate those Danes who had escaped with their lives in the coastal resorts of Sri Lanka, Thailand, and the Maldives. Offers of free plane tickets home and the Danish prime minister Anders Fogh Rasmussen's attempt, in his New Year's speech, to be seen as a benevolent father figure were regarded as opportunistic and belated attempts to make good a profound and widespread loss of faith in the powers that be: it was as if people felt that governments, like gods, should not allow such catastrophes to happen in the first place.

Human beings tend, as a matter of course, to be more or less dissatisfied with their lot. It is rare to meet a person in any society who does not want more of something and less of something else and who imagines that things could be a whole lot better, even while admitting that things could be a whole lot worse. This is not necessarily because that person's circumstances are unendurably harsh; it simply shows that human existence is never a stable state. Not only is it subject to unforeseen vicissitudes such as sickness, loss, war, and economic collapse; it is in its very nature a projective affair in which we strive, both in practice and in the imagination, for what we do not yet have or to recover that which we once possessed, while all the time comparing ourselves with others. Being is thus, as Karl Jaspers put it, "potential being" (1967:63–66) and lived in perpetual uncertainty, which is why the central question of existence is never to be or not to be, but rather how much being one can reasonably hope to possess given one's inner resources and capacities and given the world in which one finds oneself. In effect, being and our reasons for being, are, as Pierre Bourdieu puts it, "unequally distributed"

human beings & unequal genies

(2000:240). One result of this inequality, which refers as much to differences in personal abilities as it does to the scarcity of natural resources and entrenched social divisions, is that people may readily interpret their losses as someone else's gain and imagine that they might get what they lack, and often feel that they are owed from some higher or supernatural source—God, society, or what Bourdieu calls "the central bank of symbolic capital": the state (2000:240).

Kinship, Kindness, and Public Culture

In October 2004, a well-known Danish bank ran an advertising campaign around the slogan: "En bank skal vaere der når jeg har brug for den" (a bank should be there when you have need of it). This slogan brought home to me the extent to which people imagine that such polities as the clan, the nation, and the state, or institutions like banks, schools, hospitals, churches, mosques, and corporations may possess and dispense the same benefits that family life ideally provides—love, protection, trust, and recognition. That is to say that the state is imagined, as God is often imagined, as a protoparent. But as psychoanalysis has shown, parents tend to be regarded ambivalently, as providers as well as withholders of care. And Melanie Klein captures this succinctly in her image of the mother as both the "good breast" and the "bad breast" (1989).

Although we expect rulers to be just, and governments to be responsive to the needs and voices of the governed, even elected leaders are often deaf to public opinion, while dictators and divine kings, for all their talk of paternalism or of the nation as a motherland, fatherland, or family, deliberately distance themselves from the populace. Yet people continue to hope that the polis will function along the same lines as the *domus*, the home, and they feel confused and angry when this hope is dashed, railing against the indifference of state bureaucracies, the corruption of politicians, discrimination in the workplace, the lack of human contact or sympathy in clinics or retirement homes and villages, and the oppressiveness of the state to which they pay taxes and pledge their allegiance.[3] Moreover, while rulers may have little regard for the commonweal, they recognize the pervasive expectation that a state or ruling house will show compassion, provide security, and foster well-

the state: the central bank of symbolic capital

being in the way they opportunistically manipulate icons of familial life—the politician kissing a baby or espousing so-called family values, the monarch visiting hospitals and charitable institutions, the tyrant casting himself in the role of the paterfamilias.

But critical questions arise from this politics of display, these "metaphors of collective intimacy" (Özyürek 2004:104), these ersatz expressions of familiarity.[4] Despite the fact that, as Jürgen Habermas has pointed out, the rise of the "rational-critical public sphere" in early modern Europe was initially seen as an extension and completion of the intimate sphere of family life (1989:50), one wonders whether the polis can *really* be founded on the values of the domus? Can a leader really be a father to the nation, or citizens children of the state? Can a school teacher really act *in loci parentis*? Can psychologically distressed individuals ever feel safe and secure in a state institution? Can refugees reasonably expect hospitality in a country of asylum or have their cultural preferences and religious practices fully accepted? Can the motherland mother us?[5] Is it indeed desirable that impersonal institutions take on the character of family or private life when this so often entails nepotism, cronyism, and patrimonialism or, as ethnographers have observed among many indigenous peoples in South America, the "continuous looting" of leaders on the assumption that a leader is supposed to be generous to a fault (Clastres 1977:22)? In most human societies, the fiduciary rights and obligations, duties and contractual agreements that define the public sphere certainly bear a family resemblance to the vows, promises, and covenants that characterize much of what we call domestic life—the life we lead with trusted friends and close family. And many people would find it hard to conceive of the body politic without imagining that it at least held the potentiality to care for them in crisis, to accord them recognition and respect—in other words, to obey the same principle of reciprocity that obtains in their most immediate lifeworlds. But is it realistic to hope that a state can be modeled on the morality of the family?

If by morality of the family we mean love, then Hannah Arendt says no, it is not possible. "Love, by its very nature, is unworldly, and it is for this reason rather than its rarity that it is not only apolitical but antipolitical, perhaps the most powerful of all antipolitical forces" (1958: 242). But the equivalent of love in the "larger domain of human affairs,"

Arendt argues, is respect—"a kind of 'friendship' without intimacy and without closeness . . . a regard for the person from the distance which the space of the world puts between us" (243). Respect is made manifest in the actions of forgiving and promising, and for Arendt these actions are essential to the binding together of people in larger polities, including the sovereign state (245). While the faculty of forgiving helps "undo the deeds of the past, whose 'sins' hang like Damocles' sword over every new generation," the binding power of promises makes it possible for a community to reaffirm its determination to live together and renew its faith in the future (237). All these actions—respecting others, forgiving ourselves and others for the mistakes of the past, making promises that affirm the possibility of some future compact— are *public* commitments that effectively transcend the immediate desires, interests, and identifications of private life.

But can respect, forgiveness, and the promise, any more than love and religious belief, be made into effective *political* instruments for the creation of a viable public morality? I have my doubts. First, as Ghassan Hage has pointed out (1996:472–77), the family conjures images of *both* maternal care *and* patriarchal control, and this ambiguity is carried over into images of the state. Thus if the state is to imitate any aspect of the domestic domain, it is likely to be the unequal power relations of patriarchal dominance rather than the forgiving, loving, caring attributes of the maternal domus. Second, one might note that in multicultural societies, where there are many *different* family values, the values of the majority tend to determine both legal and moral codes—for example, in France, where it is now illegal to wear religious head coverings in public or to practice cliterodectomy, or in Scandinavia, where so-called forced marriages and honor killings in Muslim communities are considered violations of human rights (see, e.g., Wikan 2002; Kurkiala 2003). In other words, in constructing the migrant as a guest who should respect the values of the host society, and even express gratitude to that society for admitting her or him as a citizen and giving equal access to its social services, the moral majority effectively delegitimates the migrant's own values and makes her or him feel like a second-class citizen, ashamed of her or his own habitus and doomed to fight a losing battle to survive in the society of adoption. Third, whenever people have sought social renewal through pub-

respect — friendship w/o intimacy,

lic actions of expiation, forgiveness, and the promise—as in the truth and reconciliation commissions in South Africa, Rwanda, and Sierra Leone—the gestures toward social justice and unity have been overshadowed by the specters of vengeance that, in Arendt's words, constitute "the exact opposite" of forgiveness, or punishment, to which we have recourse when forgiveness is inconceivable (1958:241). Fourth, it may be true, as Arendt notes, that the power to forgive underwrote both the Roman principle of sparing the lives of the vanquished (*parcere subiectis*) and the right of most Western heads of state to commute the death sentence, but how often, in reality, is this power exercised? For while one can think of examples of public figures making promises and initiating acts of reconciliation—for example, Prime Minister Gough Whitlam's inauguration of land rights in Australia as a way of redressing the wrongs of the past and creating a new covenant between Aboriginal people and the state—one can just as readily think of examples of public figures repudiating such acts on the grounds that it is not in the power of the state to forgive the deeds of the past—for example, Prime Minister John Howard's refusal to apologize on behalf of the Australian state to Aboriginal people who were forcibly taken from their birth parents and communities, the so-called stolen generation, and placed in state homes in which they were often abused and traumatized. Indeed, if the modern bureaucratic state is, in Arendt's words, ruled, like Kafka's castle, by nobody—with "nobody left with whom one can argue" or "to whom one could present one's grievances" (1969), how can we realistically expect the state to listen and apologize to those it has harmed or disappointed, let alone compensate them for what it has taken from them? And given that the bureaucratic state, as Max Weber observed, "does not establish a relationship with a person . . . but rather is devoted to impersonal and functional purposes" (1978: 959), how can its utterances ever avoid bad faith? It is thus possible to argue that failed states are not just places like Sierra Leone and the Sudan; the state fails people everywhere. Yet this is not exactly the argument I want to pursue here. Rather, I want to assume that the existential viability of any human society requires *both* a separation of the public and private domains—the former characterized by imposed duties and obligations, the latter by personal dispositions and aspirations—*and* imaginative and artistic strategies that create the sem-

the state fails people everywhere
public/private

blance, and sustain the illusion, that these domains may be integrated or fused. Though some scholars have claimed that supposedly primitive societies are by definition stateless (Clastres 1977:159) and lack the concept of citizens with individual rights (Chabal and Daloz 1999:157), or have posited profound differences between modern and premodern social imaginaries (Taylor 2004), I want to bracket such assumptions in order to see to what extent the ethnographic study of "other" societies may illuminate processes not readily apparent to us when we reflect on our own. Let me then refer back to Sierra Leone, specifically the Kuranko area in the northeast of the country where I have carried out intermittent fieldwork since 1969.

Hare and Hyena

One of my first ethnographic forays into Kuranko country was a day trip to the village of Dankawali in the section chiefdom of Kamadugu in November 1969. As with many first experiences, details of this field trip, which I made with my research assistant Noah Marah, remain vivid in my mind, and I can remember as though it were yesterday stopping my Land Rover at the top of a steep forest track and waiting while a troop of olive baboons moved slowly into the bush from the stream at the foot of the hill. There were two or three females in the group, each with several young, and the alpha male stood his ground until they were safely off the track. When we drove on, leaving the bush behind us and entering open savanna, we glimpsed other baboons patrolling the granite ledges of a nearby inselberg, and Noah explained how this entire mountainous area was the haunt of djinni; indeed, the first road across the mountain, which was made in 1961–62, proved impassable until a red sheep was sacrificed to them.

I was to hear much more about the djinni (*nyenne*) later that day. But first there were introductions to be made to the village chief and his big men, and reasons given for our visit. All went well, and I received gifts of kola, and a lengthy explanation as to its meaning. It was the first food in the world—the kola was the tree of life in the Garden of Eden. It is therefore the first food a child is given—masticated and placed in the newborn's mouth. And it is kola that seals a betrothal. This is why kola is given to strangers; to incorporate them into the community, to signify a desire for their well-being and respect for their life. He who neither gives nor receives kola is "not a person."

After a meal of rice and chicken, the elders took me to a grove of trees along the Milimili stream where they explained, through Noah, that the first chief of Upper Kamadugu became powerful and prosperous through the help of a djinni. But since Moré Musa Kargbo's time,[6] no chief has enjoyed its favor, though all have waited for it to reappear and grant its boon or blessing. Every year a sacrifice of a cow or sheep is made to the djinni. At this time, village women catch large quantities of fish and cook them, together with rice, and give the food to the men before withdrawing. To ensure that there is no ill-will or unresolved grievances among the men—for this would spoil the sacrifice and offend the djinni—kola is split and cast on the ground. If the two cotyledons are odd, then something is amiss ("woman palaver" or adultery is most commonly cited) and confessions are enjoined to cool and purify the relationships darkened by mistrust. If all is well, the Sisay, who are joking partners to the Kargbo rulers, proceed to utter incantations (*haye*) or chant suras to the djinni, before the men eat half the food under a large lenké tree that stands in the streamside grove; the rest of the food is left for the djinni who, I was told, invariably eat it that same night.

Still in the forest glade, the elders pointed out a spot downstream known as Mansa Milimili ("Chief Milimili"), where there lived twin djinni known as Nyenkinanké who assume the form of a long snake. Upstream, they said, was an even deeper pool where twin crocodile djinni lived in a stone box beneath the water. When a chief, or big men, was near death, passersby might hear the creaking of the lid as the stone box opened to receive the spirit.

These commentaries on the meaning of gift giving and kola, together with the elders' remarks on the *social* relations that obtained between rulers and the world of powerful bush spirits, provide insights into the ethic of reciprocity that pervades every sphere of Kuranko life—political, jural, and domestic. Parents, chiefs, ancestors, and djinni all figure in the same social imaginary, for all protect and nourish those under them to the same extent that these lesser mortals feed and respect their superiors. Thus of anyone in a superior position Kuranko say "mal in bolo" (we are in his hands).

"ethic of reciprocity"

But what if a parent is negligible or withholds care? What if a chief or big man ignores or exploits those that look to him for protection? What if an ancestor or djinni is indifferent to the sacrifices offered? And I wondered how long and how patiently the chiefs of Upper Kamadugu were prepared to wait for the reappearance of the djinni who helped Moré Musa in his campaigns against the Kissi and the Sofas in Upper Guinea. And how, I asked myself, did people deal with everyday breakdowns in the reciprocity that ideally governed relations between superiors and subordinates?

That night, as if in response to this question, an elderly man called Nonkowa Kargbo recounted a story that, had I then been fully aware of the ominous effects of President Siaka Steven's shadow state in Sierra Leone, I might have seen as an allegory that applied equally to local and national political spheres. Nonkowa began:

> Once upon a time, Hare got himself a yam to plant. He showed it to Hyena and asked him how to plant the yam. Hyena said, "First boil it, then peel it, then plant it." Hare did as he was told, but that night Hyena came and unearthed the yam and ate it. So the yam never grew.
>
> It wasn't long before Hare realized he'd been tricked. He decided to have his revenge. Hare pounded some rice flour (*dege*), mixed it with honey, and smeared it over his body. Then he lit a fire and lay down beside it. Then he sent word to Hyena, his elder brother, to say that he was ill and that Hyena should come and examine him and tell him if he was going to live or die.
>
> Hyena came. He said, "What is this stuff all over your body?" Hare said, "It is my sickness. Will you taste it and tell me whether I will live or die?" Hyena licked Hare's body. "Eh, younger brother, this sickness of yours is very sweet!" He kept licking the rice flour and honey from Hare's body and saying, "Young brother, this sickness of yours is very sweet!" Finally he said, "Young brother, could you show me how you became so sick?"
>
> Hare said, "All right. But you must go home now, and return in the morning. Then I will show you how I contracted this illness. But before you go, elder brother, can you tell me whether I will live or die?" Hyena said, "You will live, and I will come and visit you again in the morning."
>
> That night, Hare washed the rice flour and honey from his body, but kept it within reach, so that when Hyena came in the morning, Hare told

him that it was the residue of his sickness. Hyena ate it up without a word. Hare then said, "Now, come back again tomorrow and I will tell you how I contracted this illness."

When Hyena returned next day, Hare said, "Elder brother, I will now show you how I became so ill." Hyena listened attentively. Hare told Hyena to call his sons. Hyena did so. Hare then told Hyena to have his sons collect some firewood. They did so. Hare said, "Elder brother, do you think you will be able to endure it?" Hyena said, "Yes, I will." Hare said, "Well, have each of your sons bring a long pole." This was done.

Hare ordered Hyena to light a big fire, and then jump into the flames. "When you cry, 'Get me out, get me out!' your sons should use their long poles to push you further into the fire. But when you cry, 'Push me in, push me in!' then it will be time to pull you out. Do you understand?"

Hyena said, "Yes," and immediately jumped into the fire. When he cried, "Get me out, get me out!" his sons pushed him further into the flames. Finally, when he was good and roasted, he cried, "Push me in, push me in!" whereupon his sons pulled him out. They took him to his house and laid him down there. Hare said he would come and see him in a couple of days.

When Hare came to visit Hyena there were flies everywhere. Hyena had begun to putrefy. Hare said, "Something stinks around here!" People said, "It is Hyena, your elder brother. He is very ill." Hare then said, "Well this sickness is just like the boiled yam. My elder brother told me to boil and peel it before planting it in the ground. I did what he told me to do, but he came in the night, dug it up and ate it. Now, if a boiled yam can grow, then my roasted elder brother will live!" And with that he jumped through the window and was gone. Soon after, his elder brother died. */ Cruel.*

After giving me a rough and ready translation of the story, Noah told Nonkowa that I was curious to know whether elder and younger brother often found themselves at odds in everyday life. Nonkowa's response was edifying:

> The elder brother is sometimes inclined to abuse his authority and neglect the welfare of his younger brothers. The younger brother is often made to run errands, fetch water, and summon friends for his elder brothers. But the younger brother may also seek the support, protection, and friendship of one elder brother if another fails him, and younger brothers

may sometimes outsmart the elders by playing them off against one another. The elders fear the possibility that a younger brother may cause rifts or quarrels among them by telling one that another insulted him or refused him help. By enlisting the support of a sympathetic brother he can cause dissensions among his elder brothers. That is why the elder should not underestimate the younger and why elders look after the younger ones.

As Nonkowa implies, those in positions of authority do not always exercise that authority wisely or well, and underlings are sometimes driven to redress situations of inequity or injustice by means of cunning and even lawlessness. Such underhand tactics make their appearance *both* in mundane life *and* in fantasy, dream, ritual, and myth, as the ubiquitous stories of Hare-Hyena vividly illustrate.[7] But what appear to be simple tales of sibling rivalry have allegorical depths that lead us far beyond the experience and concerns of Kuranko villagers and invite comparison with worldwide strategies, both real and imaginary, for closing the gap between the sphere of one's mundane humanity and the sphere of higher powers. Not only are there close parallels between trickster stories, rituals of rebellion, and forms of resistance in everyday life; narratives themselves have recourse, in all human societies, to similar structural devices for annulling the lines that ordinarily divide superordinate and subordinate, private and public, divine and mundane spheres in order that a transfer of powers or exchange of properties may occur between them. It is, however, important to emphasize that one cannot explain the ways in which people imagine higher powers simply by reducing such imaginaries to the mundane domain of parental authority or familial relationships—something Meyer Fortes does, for example, when he writes that "all the [Tallensi] ancestors are projections of the parents" (1949:176). Unlike Durkheimian and psychoanalytic models that tend to reduce intersubjective relations between groups and categories (community, nation, ancestors, gods) to intersubjective relations between persons, I prefer to place domestic and politico-jural domains on the same footing and to explore the artifice whereby images of both are constructed and circulated and the strategies whereby the image of one is adjusted to the image of the other.[8]

Kuranko narratives typically begin with a situation that conforms to

"similar structural devices"

putting domestic & politico-jural domains on the same footing & how each is constructed

Gregory Bateson's description of complementary schismogenesis: a chief alienated from his people, a husband at loggerheads with his wife, cowives unable to live together in harmony, a younger son taken advantage of by an overbearing elder brother. At the same time, the narrative exaggerates the differences between these formal social positions and various informal dispositions such as intelligence, beauty, courage, and wisdom. The initial situation is thus:

Polarized positions	Polarized dispositions
senior	stupid, unjust, gluttonous
junior	intelligent, good, restrained

As the story unfolds, a change of positions and dispositions occurs, effectively reversing the initial situation (this chiasmus, or crossing over, is indicated by the dotted lines). The result is an ideal congruence or fit between role and character, position and disposition, that is, the most intelligent and morally upright person now has the upper hand, while the stupid, gluttonous, and unjust other dies or disappears from the scene. Clearly, such fictional displays are a kind of legerdemain that involves a switching between ordinarily separate spheres of existence— senior/junior, male/female, human/extrahuman, public/private—and creates the *appearance* of an equitable relationship between them. Although everyday social life may provide limited opportunities for real reciprocity between commoners and rulers or people and politicians, the *imaginative space* of ritual and story opens up the possibility of just such exchanges taking place.

Duty, Dispensations, and the Division of Powers

Among the Kuranko practically every domain of social life, from the exercise of chiefly power to the workaday world of families, farming, and marriage is ideally governed by the constraints of duty and obligation. The Kuranko word *wale* denotes not only the traditional duties of an office or the requirements of a role; it covers the proper actions, demeanor, and work of being a wife, mother, father, elder, chief, praise-singer, blacksmith, farmer, or neighbor. Thus the phrase, *i'n wale* (literally, "you and work")—used as a greeting, in acknowledgment of a gift,

Bateson – Complementary schismogenesis

Imagining the Powers That Be 53

Seems very Levi-Straussian

and in approval of work well done or words well spoken—suggests that social existence itself is a matter of people conforming to ancestral precedents, fulfilling their obligations and doing what they are supposed to do. It is this seemingly slavish conformity to one's appropriate role or place in the scheme of things that undoubtedly gives Westerners the impression that in Africa "individual rationality is essentially based on communal logic" (Chabal and Daloz 1999:156). But the social order is not sustained simply by people passively playing their roles and mindlessly doing their duty; rather, as Kuranko themselves insist, its viability depends on the intelligence, energy, and skill that they bring to their everyday tasks and, most important, their ability to cooperate with others, to work well together. In Kuranko terms, the town—which stands symbolically for the established socio-moral order of things—must be perennially reinvigorated by energies drawn from the bush—the antinomian realm of passions and wild powers. To put it succinctly, social positions depend on personal dispositions, and it is the integration of these complementary but very different dimensions of social reality that effectively determines the quality of life and the viability of a community.

But first let us consider to what lengths Kuranko go in order to create a social order founded on formality and the control of personal feelings. Initiation is perhaps the best place to begin this exploration, for almost every lesson learned during this intense transitional period of a person's life is concerned with acquiring restraint, forethought, and self-discipline. Without this ability to bring one's emotions under control, to withstand hardship, to keep one's own counsel, and to concentrate one's energies on one's appropriate work, one cannot expect to be considered an adult. It is thus that in every aspect of Kuranko life the respect (gbiliye) on which both good neighborliness and family life depend finds expression in circumspection and reserve. Wives greet their husbands with bowed heads and lowered eyes, and many men aver that only a disinterested attitude can guarantee fairness and harmony in a polygynous household. As for chiefs, they do not address their subjects except through a speaker, and they expect both deference and distance from all but their equals. In public, a man never displays affection or familiarity toward his eldest son and heir, and the youngster maintains the utmost decorum in his father's company, sitting apart, eyes downcast, never speaking unless spoken to. Among in-laws similar constraints apply. A man never addresses his mother-in-law by her personal name and avoids any behavior that might appear to presume intimacy, such as sitting on her bed or using a chair she has just vacated. Similar avoidance behaviors exist between brother and sister. A man must not touch his sister's waist or neck, enter her room unbidden, sit on her bed, or use language in her presence that contains sexual terms or innuendo. Brothers maintain the most respectful and cautious attitudes toward their sisters, to whom they are deeply indebted. The least offence may affect the bridewealth received from a sister's marriage, with which the brother marries. In sum, interpersonal relations in a Kuranko community are based on a semblance of amity, constantly cultivated in the protocols of greeting and exchange that foster mutual respect, rather than on the expression of personal feeling.

Yet despite all the formal protocols and prescriptions that define the socio-moral order, this order would not exist except for influences, passions, energies, and dispositions that have their sources outside it. First, the dutiful performance of one's role brings ancestral and divine blessings (*duwe*) to oneself and one's family, and these blessings find expression in spiritual, physical, and material well-being (*baraka*). In fact, patrimonialism has its origin in this relationship, for in apprenticing and pledging oneself to a powerful benefactor (a medicine master, a successful entrepreneur, a man of power) and dutifully and patiently accepting the hardships of service, one stands eventually to improve one's lot. Second, though the fields of custom (*namui*) and law (*ton*) are based on notions of ownership (*tigiye*) and status superiority (*fisa mantiye*), inborn traits such as intelligence, strength, beauty, and temperament are unequally distributed. Thus, although elders are *ideally* superior to juniors, men to women, adults to children, wife-givers to wife-receivers, rulers to commoners, agnatic kin to uterine kin, and persons to animals, this does not mean that the status superior will, in reality, be a morally better or more socially adroit person than his or her status inferior. And while passion, love, and choice are allegedly inimical to social order, they figure conspicuously in the way things actually work. While most marriages are arranged, many quickly end in divorce, with the woman first eloping with and later marrying her lover. While the law lays down strict punishments for most demeanors, many cases will end with pleas for compassion (*hinantei*), an elder declaring "it did not lay on his hand," meaning "he did not know what he was doing." And while kinspeople are supposedly one's primary source of assistance and prosperity, relations with friends, mentors, and benefactors often offer the best prospects for improving one's chances in life. Evoking the image of town and bush, Kuranko readily admit that when the local community provides few possibilities for a person, the outside world is always open to anyone brave enough to venture out into it and tap its powers.

Yet Kuranko life involves a perpetual struggle to strike a balance between these domains, such that the domains of duty and desire reinforce rather than subvert each other. Thus the bereaved are sequestered and emotions kept under strict control at funerals lest the formal business of separating the spirit from the world of the living and the ensuing business of succession and inheritance be jeopardized. And the same reasoning lies behind attitudes to the marital alliances on which the integrity of the community depends. If marriages are left to the whims and passions of the young, then the social order, based on ancestral fiat and the judgment of older men, is imperiled, just as divisive quarrels among cowives arise from a husband's favored treatment of a preferred wife, or resentment follows the misuse of chiefly power.

What this summary account of Kuranko social reality suggests is that while any socio-moral system—state or stateless—must create at least a semblance of formality, neutrality, and distance from private passions and individual dispositions (something often accomplished by merging human authority with the extrahuman, the transcendent, the divine), human existence would be empty and meaningless within such a system unless people could at least imagine ways in which the formal order was open to informal influence, and the world of individualized passions could find expression in public life. In brief, we need social systems to be both transcendent *and* accessible. Just as every divine king, dictator, or parental imago will be fantasized as above and beyond us, he will also be subject to fantasies of abasement and deposition in which he appears to share the same mortal flaws and frailties as his subjects. We need, as it were, to feel a part of the system *as well as* accept that the system is beyond the powers of any individual to manipulate or abuse it. And this is cognate with the need to imagine that

any socio-moral sys. must have some distance from private passions + indiv. dispositions

otherwise human existence would be meaningless — no way to exert personal influence in public.

there are ways in which the formal protocols of public office are susceptible to the influence of personal emotion, hence our search for strong and inspired leaders who can nonetheless touch us and care for us, for public figures who show sensitivity toward our personal petitions, and for remote or otiose Gods who are, however, complemented by "border figures" such as saints and angels that bring the divine within human reach and make it both familiar and accessible. As Robert Orsi observes in his study of Jude, the patron saint of hopeless causes, Jude "moved back and forth between the satisfactions and comforts of childhood and the challenges of adulthood, between the mentalities and values of the enclaves and those of the 'America' outside, allowing women to draw deep from one to confront the other" (1996: 203). This same thesis may be applied to celebrities and stars who are at once regarded as superior beings *and* brought down, in tabloid stories, to our own earthly level (Jackson 2002:281–82).

The Paradox of Pastoral Power

What compels these social imaginaries in which the gap between the authority or aura of higher powers and the experiences of ordinary people is made to seem less absolute than it is? One answer to this question may be our human need for a compatibility of scale between our own immediate, personal world and the world that surrounds, precedes, and outlasts us—some kind of connectiveness, continuity, or reciprocity between what phenomenologists call *Eigenwelt* (one's own world), *Mitwelt* (the world of others),[9] and *Umwelt* (our biological and physical environment). For if the forces that govern our destinies—be they divine, biogenetic, or governmental—are omnipotent, how does our place in the scheme of things differ from that of rocks and stones? At the same time that human beings acknowledge that they belong to global, transnational, and cosmic force fields that extend far beyond themselves and lie largely outside their comprehension and control, they seek some rapprochement with those external powers, so that the relationship is felt to be one of homely belonging rather than alienation, one of mutuality rather than tyranny. Yet, paradoxically, those in authority can rarely meet the demands or fulfill the expectations of those who look to them for succor, protection, and support, while

Imagining the Powers That Be   57

those who seek such benefits from those in power are rarely satisfied. This disjunction between what is expected and what is received becomes acutely problematic under conditions of scarcity, a product both of limited resources and of the number of people dependent on those who control these resources.

When I was researching S. B. Marah's life story in Freetown in 2002 and 2003, S. B. sometimes alluded to the problem of patrimonial power. Although, in his view, there was nothing intrinsically wrong with patrimonialism, a nation-state could not be based on it. In S. B.'s view, a person's circle of family and friends in contemporary Sierra Leone is very much wider than it was in the past, which increases the likelihood that a power-holder's actions will be misconstrued, his words misinterpreted, and his good fortune begrudged. At the same time, the absence of state institutions for the welfare and protection of citizens means that most people are wholly dependent on family and friends for security and support. Accordingly, personal connections and loyalties take precedence over abstract principles—whether these are enshrined in the law, the constitution, or in religious doctrine. To many Westerners, the resulting plethora of personal and familial claims leads inevitably to corruption. But honoring obligations to kin, friends, and clanspeople is not corruption, S. B. observed. Corruption is, as he put it, stealing public money, or using someone else's money without his permission for one's own profit.

When I pointed out that that it must be very difficult for any politician to satisfy all the personal demands made on him, S. B. agreed. "This is why I don't believe in numbers," he said. He continued:

> If we have too many police, or too many soldiers in the military, it is impossible to provide good conditions for them all, and they grow restless. You never know what they will be thinking or planning. This is why I believe that the military should be very small and very efficient. Make them few, pay them well, and make them take care of the civilian population in case of emergencies. But don't let them go to war. Let the UN peacekeepers handle that. (Jackson 2004:194)

But if African polities were reduced in size, so that politicians were not placed in the impossible situation of making promises they cannot keep, or became the target of demands they do not have the resources to meet, how could the nation-state ever emerge in Africa, where there are often simply too few resources to go around (for instance, universal education to age twelve in Sierra Leone would cost more than the entire national budget)?

For most of human evolution, our species lived in small, mobile groups. We functioned best in families or temporary communities. Perhaps this is why all attempts to press people into wider polities such as states, nations, and empires are doomed, and why so many of the empires of the past fragmented and fell apart as people sought to recover long-suppressed local identities, lands, and languages. All human beings seem to need to feel that there is a compatibility of scale between themselves and the wider world, such that this Umvelt may be interacted with as though it were another person, rather than encountered as a minatory and monstrously foreign form of life. George Devereux (1980) has argued that as the specialized complexity and sheer volume of information increases in any lifeworld, people become progressively disoriented and overwhelmed. One reaction is to try to reduce the scale of this impinging information and activity: to withdraw into one's own local backyard, to focus on a microcosm that one can manipulate and master. Thus the failure of Western attempts to impose centralized and democratic forms of government on African nations should not be automatically attributed to the native incapacity or corruptibility of African leaders, but seen in the light of a preference for the politics of familiarity over the impersonality and hegemony of the bureaucratic state, and a realistic reckoning with a degree of scarcity not conducive to equality and social justice. Despite these difficulties, traditional forms of government in Africa often provide us with enviable models.

Riffling through my field notes written in northern Sierra Leone thirty-four years ago, I catch glimpses of how the people of Firawa, then a village of no more than a thousand souls, and well beyond the reach of roads, regarded governmental power, both local and national. Even though, in the late 1960s, serious criminal cases had to be tried by the district court (located in Kabala, some thirty miles away), most infringements of the law were dealt with in the local court (*gbaré*) of the section chief, Mansa Tala Sewa, and his council of elders (*morgo bannu*; literally, "big men"). Tala Sewa was not averse to petitioning the gov-

o prefereace for the politics of familarity

ernment in Freetown for help in developing his chiefdom—specifically a bridge over the Seli River and a road that would connect Firawa with the markets in Kabala. But he never seemed comfortable in the role of negotiating with the outside world, and even with me—the first European to have ever made his home in Firawa—he sometimes appeared uneasy and baffled, as when I pleaded that I had neither the contacts nor the resources to help with the building of the bridge and the road. Still, he approved my efforts to understand the lifeworld of Firawa, and I admired the dedication and care he showed in his chieftaincy (*man-saye*). Some days he was in the court gbaré from early morning until late afternoon; at other times he moved around the village, dispensing advice, expressing concern, settling minor disputes. Once, for example, a local hunter broke both his legs when a felled tree pinned him beneath its branches. A local medicine master made splints and advised the hunter about what to do to help the healing of the bones. When the hunter failed to pay the fee, the medicine master sought Tala Sewa's help. Tala Sewa then "begged" the hunter and contributed to the fee from his own pocket. "A lesser chief would not have dared do such a potentially humiliating thing," the hunter told me. "But Tala Sewa has such great humanity [*morgoye*], that he can do such things and lose nothing of his authority [*miran*]." Here then was a man who commanded respect rather than demanded it, who worked as hard on his farm as any of his subjects, and whose modesty stood in stark contrast to the autocratic or corrupt ways in which chieftaincy was allegedly exercised in some other Kuranko chiefdoms at that time. But most of all, here was an example in which an ethos of care permeated the sphere of administrative authority, effectively integrating the morality of kinship and the exercise of chiefly power.

Can a modern state preserve *communitas*? Can we actually find in families and local moral worlds the care that our stories and fantasies lead us to believe we may find in states, in divinities, and in higher powers? One is tempted to say that if we cannot, then modernity is a sordid boon and democracy a dubious possession.

More than anyone else, perhaps, the miner can
stand as the type of the manual worker, not only
because his work is so exaggeratedly awful, but
also because it is so vitally necessary and yet so
remote from our experience, so invisible, as it
were, that we are capable of forgetting it as we
forget the blood in our veins.

—GEORGE ORWELL, "Down the Mine"

4 On the Work
of Human Hands

A few years ago I took the opportunity to visit the great copper mine at
Falun in western Sweden, now a World Heritage Site. The first thing
you see as you approach the mine are various eighteenth-century
buildings clustered around the open-cast pit: the old mine entrance,
the dressing plant, the machine director's house, the miner's lodge, the
shaft heads, hoists, and waterwheels. Then you come to the edge of the
great pit itself, 325 feet deep and between 1,000 and 3,000 feet across,
its present shape the result of a massive cave-in on 25 June 1677 when
underground galleries and chambers collapsed down to a depth of
1,000 feet, together with the rock walls dividing what were at that time
three separate open pits. Time did not allow me to tour the old buildings, some of which were now museums, but after putting on a water-

proof cape and gum boots, I joined a tour party that was making the first descent of the day.

I remember being aware of how different this was from George Orwell's experiences of going down a mine. Where Orwell had been obliged to walk hunched over or to crawl on hands and knees along dark tunnels for hours on end to reach the coalface, a modern elevator carried our party comfortably and quickly 180 feet underground, from where we walked along a newly driven drift to the oldest sections of the mine. And while Orwell visited a working mine, and saw firsthand the hellish conditions under which miners toiled far beneath the landscapes of Yorkshire, we found ourselves in a place of ghosts. A working mine, as Orwell so vividly describes, is a place of infernal noise and suffocating dust, of backbreaking work in a dark, confined space. But at Falun, the galleries were as vacant and silent as a graveyard, and the artificial lighting imparted a gray and ghostly pallor to the stone. Dwarfed by the gigantic chamber in which I found myself, its jagged vaults reminding me of a decayed tooth, I had to imagine the labor that had created the underground passages, the explosions that had brought down the ore, the men who had hewn and hacked at the solid rock, carrying the spoil away in wooden barrows and shoring up the shafts with stacked pine logs. When people die, houses are abandoned, wars end, or mines are shut down, these moribund lifeworlds live on for a time in the memories of those who knew them at first hand. Recounted as stories, these memories may be passed on to the next generation, but thereafter all direct experience of the past is lost. Yet we remain haunted by the historic past, as if the labor of those who lived long ago had seeped into the earth, continuing to speak to us in ghostly whispers, their presence felt in the dank air that is like their dying breath. What is it in us that lends credence to the idea of ghosts? That draws us back to the past, sifting through surviving documents, rummaging in archives, visiting industrial museums? Is it the same impulse that compels us to explore lifeworlds remote from our own, as if in comparing ourselves with others we stand to gain a better sense of who *we* are? Or is it less curiosity than compassion for those whose lives must, we imagine, have been so much more arduous than ours and sacrificed to the pitiless demands of capital? Do we seek in these excursions into the past to magically compensate the dead for something we feel was wrongly denied them?

Moribund lifeworlds

These were my thoughts as I followed our guide down old wooden staircases where the only sound was dripping water or the amazed murmurings of some of our party as they spied wooden wheelbarrows and implements lying in the rubble, perfectly preserved for hundreds of years.

We now entered the vast chamber adjacent to the Creuz shaft which plunges 680 feet into the bowels of the earth on the fringe of the central ore body. The shaft, bisected by an enormous wooden wall built between 1833 and 1836, was perhaps the world's tallest wooden structure. Behind the wall were pathways and pumps; in front hung an immense wooden bucket with iron hoops in which, our guide explained, workers and equipment were lowered into the mine and the ore hauled to the surface. At every shift change, the bucket was packed with men, some standing on the rim and clinging to the leather cable. Those coming on shift would move their collective weight to and fro in order to swing the bucket close to the edge of the chamber, whereupon they would jump out.

The copper mountain at Falun was worked from late Viking times (possible as early as the eighth century) until well into the nineteenth century (it officially closed on 8 December 1992). In the seventeenth century—the heyday of Sweden's power—the mine was the source of the nation's wealth, and Falun was the country's second city. At this time, Swedish copper accounted for 70 percent of world production, and many of Europe's great buildings, including the Palace of Versailles, were roofed with Falun copper. One thousand Swedish miners worked below, though most of the engineers and explosive experts were German. Our guide also reminded us that the red paint with which houses were treated throughout Sweden derived from the rock from which the copper ore was extracted. Rich in iron ochers and silicic acid, this waste rock was allowed to oxidize in the open air before being slurried, dried, and calcined. The ruddle was then ground into *Falu rödfärg*, or red pigment.

After a short walk through damp passages, we assembled in yet another chamber where the guide drew our attention to the signatures of visiting dignitaries and members of the Swedish royal family who, for centuries, owned the wealth from the mine. In 1677, our guide continued, a major cave-in occurred. Miraculously it happened on the one day of the year—Midsummer—when the mine was deserted, and there were, it was thought, no casualties. But forty-two years later, a young man who had mysteriously gone missing on Midsummer Eve was found in a disused section of the mine. The copper sulphate in the water had perfectly preserved his body, and when he was brought to the surface, the locals recognized him as Mads Israelsson. He had been due to marry on that long ago Midsummer day, and the bride-to-be, now a woman in her sixties, found herself face to face with the still youthful man who had unaccountably disappeared on the eve of their wedding. It was conjectured that he had gone down the mine on a drunken dare, fallen asleep, and been entombed by the cataclysm. Our guide invited us to imagine this aging woman, who had never married, finally meeting her ageless paramour and discovering his fate. However, Fed Mads was not to rest in peace, even now. His body was placed in a glass casket. And even though it was reclaimed by the elements from which it had been protected for so many years and began to decay, the legend of the "petrified miner" spread throughout Europe and inspired Richard Wagner to sketch the outline of an opera about him, while Johann Peter Hebel (1760–1826) wrote his famous story, "The Unexpected Reunion," about the event.

That night in my hotel room at Dalarna, I could not sleep. I was haunted by the Piranesi-like images of those underground chambers with their gigantic stacks of pine logs caulked with gangue, supporting the roughly hewn vaults and rock walls. I went to the window and looked out at the dark pinewoods and the snow, trying to figure out what it was that had so troubled me about my visit to the Falun mine. Was it the gap between the way the Falun mine was now advertised to the visitor and the way it had been experienced as a workplace in the past—a gap between representation and reality? Or was it the thought of the tens of thousands of men who had toiled in that mountain over the centuries and were now unknown to us? At times one finds it impossible, when confronted by a past that has been evacuated of the lives that charged it with meaning, to accept that it is eternally beyond reach. And it occurred to me that there is an impulse in many of us to refuse the estranging effects of time, to countermand the narratives and statistics that render the meaning of human toil in terms of the conversion of raw material into monumental buildings, human dwellings, and fleets of battleships. They spoke of Fed

Mads as "the petrified man." Perhaps, however, the people of Elsborg saw in his miraculous reappearance the possibility of redeeming their lives from the thankless labor that made the nation great but left their own existence unchanged. For though the names of kings and bishops are still inscribed on the rock faces of the mine, Fed Mads is the only worker whose name survives and who, as it were, has not been buried in the adyta of time and the darkness of the mountain.

Among the fascinating books and essays I read in the weeks after my visit to Dalarna and Falun was a work by Thomas W. Knox, published in San Francisco in 1878, and entitled *The Underground World: A Mirror of Life below the Surface*. Knox's "interesting sketches" included an account of his descent into the Wieliczka salt mines near Kraków in Poland. Then the most productive and largest salt mine in the world, the Galicia mines employed fourteen to fifteen hundred men who worked twelve-hour shifts for a wage of thirty to forty cents a day, though the mine generated a revenue of 6 million dollars per annum. In Knox's eyes, these Polish and Austrian miners were submen who, being "densely ignorant," were "not tortured by brighter memories, nor haunted by pictures of the possible" (1878:934). The Poles in particular, he noted in passing, possessed "a certain kind of stupid contentment" and had "no ambition, and no future." All bore "the marks of un-development, all the traces of an animal and undisciplined nature. Mind, in the strict sense, is omitted in their composition. They are merely machines of flesh and blood, obeying physical instincts, and impelled by the law of self-preservation" (943). Knox makes no bones about the extent to which such views were shared by his guides, and undoubtedly these benighted attitudes were shared by those who prof-ited most from these men's subterranean toil, for it is always comfort-ing to tell oneself that "undeveloped" persons are paying the price of one's own and one's nation's development, though these days we prob-ably rely as much on external as internal censorship to blind us to the true costs of generating wealth and fuelling an urban-industrial state. As I write, yet another explosion in a Chinese colliery, this time at the Chenjiashan mine in Miaowan (Sha'anxi Province), has claimed the lives of 166 men. It is estimated than more than 5,000 Chinese miners die each year, 75 percent of the world's total, even though the country

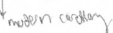

modern corollary

produces only a third of the world's coal. "It's said there is blood on every piece of coal in China," said one miner's widow. "My husband used to talk about the danger all the time. But we are very poor. We have children. What else could we do?" (qtd. in Watts 2005:1–2). Like most miner's widows, Mrs. Wang received 51,000 yuan—the state-estimated value of a miner's life—plus 20,000 as a widow's allowance and a further 20,000 for an unrecovered body.[1] Because this hard-won coal generates energy for the production of cheap commodities that are sold in the wealthier regions of the world, it might have occurred to Mrs. Wang that there is blood on every consumer item that reaches the supermarket shelves of the West.

The theme of the degradation of labor has a long history. The back-breaking and soul-destroying character of manual labor often leaves one feeling that one's hands have become like the stone on which one toils, one's body as hard and one's mind as unfeeling as the materials on which one works. Nowhere is this image of petrification and mineral-ization more vividly conveyed than in the photographs of Sebastião Salgado that document the Brazilian gold prospectors or *garimpeiros* of the Amazon. Here is Enrique Rodriguez Larreta's brilliant descrip-tion of these photographs:

> The bodies appear grey and uniform under the sacks of earth, which they transport up and down the rudimentary staircases of the mine. The dark skin is covered with mud. The photographs transfer a motionless expres-sion. It is as if the strong bodies have become an appendix of that violated and disturbed Nature. The dirt partially hides the trademarks on the T-shirts and shorts—Coca-Cola, Harvard, Princeton University—so common in the shantytowns of Brazil. Dirt provides the uniform grey colour of the gold diggers just as it did that of the slaves in Fritz Lang's film *Metropolis*. All the associations of contemporary critical social the-ory from Theodor Adorno to Michel Foucault seem to be confirmed by these images: the anonymity of the bodies transformed into productive tools, the febrile agitation produced by the bewitched fetishism of gold. (2002:4).

Larreta observes, however, that "every image simultaneously obscures and reveals," and in his own remarkable study of the garimpeiros, he brings to light the experience of the workers and their lifeworlds—the gold diggers who dream of striking it rich; their dread of losing everything; their sense of being adventurers, explorers, and frontiersmen, staking their lives on a lucky break or a change in their fortunes; the system of debt servitude that binds them to local entrepreneurs; the camaraderie that binds them to one another; the violence and illness that threatens their lives at every turn; the accursed world of local nightclubs in which the garimpeiro converts his meager gains into moments of masculine triumph and *communitas*. In reminding us that life is salvaged and celebrated under even the most degrading conditions, Larreta takes our focus from the appearance to the experience of labor.

Though we may be estranged from the world of manual work, and even regard workers as animals or serfs whose lives are mere grist for some industrial mill, it is a singular irony that the laborers who toil underground in dangerous and unhealthy conditions often pay more respect to the earth and to one another than we pay to them. Thankfully, there exist several salutary ethnographies that explore the world of labor with such sensitivity and insight that we are able to make educated guesses about the human experience of underground work in such places as Wieliczka, Serra Palada, and Falun. In June Nash's classic study of Bolivian tin miners, she speaks of the miners' "cannibalistic" relationship to the mine. As one man put it, "We eat the mines and the mines eat us. For that reason, we have to give these rituals to the spirit of the hills so that he will continue to reveal the veins of metal to us and so that we can live" (1979:ix). Clearly, the miners relate to the earth not as subject to object but as to another living subject. In Nash's own words, "Miners talk of the mine as though it were a living organism" (ix).

This is not a survival of animism, but a poetic metaphor that strikes anyone approaching the entrance. The pulsating thump of the *chancador*, or compressor, that breaks up the rock is like a heartbeat, and the hum of the pumps that draw out water from the lower levels and feed water into the lines for the drills is like the respiratory system of a giant mammal. As one nears the mouth of the mine, the odors of hydrogen sulfide are expelled like the gases from an overtaxed digestive system. The reddish-brown *copajira*, or cuprous liquid, drains from the interior like pus-filled blood from suppurating wounds. The miners often refer to the interior of the mine as "the bowels of the earth," and they jokingly say that one of the reasons Bolivia does not have earthquakes is because all the explosive gases that build up inside the earth are released through its mineshafts. (170)

These anthropomorphic metaphors are not simply figures of speech or artifacts of thought. They disclose a vital and reciprocal relationship felt to exist between human subjects and the earth. Alison Leitch's ethnography of the marble mines at Carrara, Tuscany, help us elucidate this relationship further. From the beginning of her fieldwork, Leitch was struck by the ways in which the Carrara quarry workers spoke of the mines as *agri marmiferi*, or marble fields, that grow and renew themselves like cultivated plots or farms. In his *Natural History*, Pliny made similar observations, of scars on the mountainside that underwent natural healing and of marble that reproduced itself, and even today, anthropomorphic metaphors permeate the miners' vernacular: "Marble which breaks easily like 'glass' is thought of as being more 'alive' or as having greater *vivezza*. Marble 'sings' and has 'nerves' which make it strong. It 'sleeps' and 'wakes' and is sometimes described as containing an *anima* or 'soul'" (Leitch 1996:242). Mining is also sexualized, so that the rock chisel (*punciotto*) is likened to a penis and drilling to sexual intercourse, while mining itself is seen as a source of masculine pride. Moreover, the mountain is a living body. As one worker observed, "You see the mountain moves. It recreates itself. Some quarries however move while others grow. You can see the way they grow by how much the marble is broken at the bottom. It gets more solid at the top. So it must be growing from the bottom to the top. If you lighten the load at the top some quarries solidify at the bottom" (242). Moreover, it is thought that while quarrymen can to some extent protect themselves against the dangers that come with using heavy machinery, they can do little to defend themselves from the mountain itself, which is said to be capable of vengeful retaliation for the miners' daily attacks on it. Thus flaws in a block of marble are known as *peli nemici*, or enemy faults. "The mountain reacts!" said one man. "It makes a noise like a living person. The mountain wants its share" (244). Yet men talk to the mountain, cajoling it, "looking after it," appeasing it, paying it respect, in the hope that the mountain will reciprocate.

What is it about the lived relationship between miners and marble that gives rise to these anthropomorphic images, both minatory and sympathetic? To answer this question we need to clear the ground. First, the vital relationship supposed to exist between person and earth is not a product of abstract thought or contemplation, but of immediate, unreflective experience. Though one may learn to think or speak of the earth as human, such forms of knowledge not only have their origins in the ways in which we interact with the earth; they tend to become redundant and die when unsupported by direct experience. Second, it is important to fully recognize that work is often experienced not as a relationship between an acting subject and an inert field, but as an intersubjective and reciprocal relationship, and that this relationship is dynamic. This point has been made with considerable skill by Anthony Redmond in his ethnographic account of Ngarinyin experiences of landscape in the Kimberley region of northwest Australia. Rather than assume a relationship between timeless or static landscapes and transitory or mobile human beings, Redmond shows that the Ngarinyin people experience the landscape as in "a permanent state of unstable equilibrium" (2001:121). Like the human body, the body of the land is said to sleep, wake, dream, pass away, return to life, give birth, and move in response to others. Speaking of a hill on the central Kimberley plateau known as Winjagin, Redmond describes a visit to the site with its traditional clan owners and seeing it through their eyes.

As we approached the hill across the plateau, great ribbons of smoke could be seen wrapping themselves around Winjagin, following the contours of the sandstone "terracing" that winds around the mountain. It was the end of the dry season, and the old grass was burning, much to the delight of the older people, who fear long grass for snakes. The blackened, smoldering stubble left by the fires was pointed out as the burnt hair of the widow-python. Later that evening a band of cloud circling the full moon was pointed out as the python wrapped around the mountain, reflected in the sky for us as a sign of acknowledgement of our presence. From all the signs in the country, it was clear to everybody that Winjagin was "opening" her *liyan* (gut feeling) to us. After all, they pointed out, couldn't I see that as we got up closer to this long unvisited place, the mountain moved toward us, evidenced in the fact that it grew bigger as

- reln bet person + earth as immediate, unreflected thought
- work as intersubjective + reciprocal.
- parallels bet hum. body + body of the land.

we got up close rather than "stay little" as it was when we first sighted it across the plain? (133)

Most of us have experienced a landscape appearing to move or change form as we travel through it. Sometimes a mountain will seem to move toward us, just as Winjagin did in Redmond's account; but it may also appear to recede as one approaches it—an experience I have had many times walking toward Sinekonke ("gold mountain"), the domed inselberg associated with the Marah ruling clan in Barawa, northern Sierra Leone, or driving south across the Hauraki plains in New Zealand toward Mount Te Aroha. Though such phenomena will be interpreted according to preferred cultural or personal schemata, there is always a tension, a gap, between percept and concept, between one's immediate and one's mediated experience of the object. One may think of this relationship on an analogy with a distorting mirror. Our preconceptions dispose us to see the world in particular ways (for the Ngarinyin, the looming mountain was said to be "welcoming" its kinsmen; for me, Sinkekonke "receded" as I approached it because, or so I conjectured, I was moving from lower to higher ground). But the important point is that it is sometimes difficult to perceive whether we ourselves or the world are in motion, as when, for instance, one finds oneself sitting in a stationary train as a second train on a parallel track begins to move out. For a moment one is uncertain as to which train is moving and which is still. At such moments the normal distinction between subjective and objective reality is destabilized or elided.

These kinds of experiences help us understand the anthropomorphic notion that the ground on which we walk, through which we move, or on which we work is not inert, but animated by the same will, consciousness, and life that flows through us. For many Westerners, however, animism is symptomatic of a primitive or infantile mode of thinking that typically confuses movement with will, self with other, and subject with object (Freud 1961b:75−78; Tylor 1891:425), or reflects a "protoplasmic consciousness" that is unable to distinguish between the self and things (Piaget 1973:266). But by fetishizing animism as a developmental stage, a primitive weltanschauung or a logical (pathetic) fallacy that is incompatible with scientific rationality, we readily fall into thinking of anthropomorphic thought as an innate and inescap-

Always a gap bet percept + concept — bet one's immediate + mediated experience

animism is often considered backward, tho.

able trait of human beings allegedly less evolved than ourselves, and so avoid the challenge of inquiring into the conditions under which such a mode of experience occurs in *all* human societies and, most important, into the kinds of experiences and human interests that sustain and affirm the belief that things and persons share common properties.

George Devereux was one of the first ethnographers to attempt a deconstruction of the so-called belief that physical matter may, under certain circumstances,[2] be animated by consciousness and will. His argument was that all human beings tend to react "with panic to the unresponsiveness of matter" (1968:32). The prototype of this panic arises from a mother's temporary unresponsiveness to her infant, an experience that leads to such fantasized compensations as the belief that a comforting object or imaginary friend can respond to the infant's needs. Thus, writes Devereux, "the infant's tendency to compensate for . . . missing responses by means of hallucinated responses may . . . be at the root of the primitive tendency to view matter animistically and to 'detect' in material phenomena a non-existent transcendental responsiveness" (34). While Piaget (1973) saw animism simply as an early stage of childhood development (ages five to seven), Devereux sees it as a magical stratagem for imputing meanings to nature that may then be experienced as responses to our need to relate to the world around us (*Umwelt*) as though it were informed by the same rules of reciprocity and mutuality that obtain in our most familiar and intimate lifeworld (*Eigenwelt*).

This interplay between persons and things preoccupied Karl Marx in his early essays on the nature of ownership, since it is through labor-action that a person not only produces a livelihood but produces and reproduces a mode of life, a sense of identity, and a sense of communal belonging.[3] In agricultural labor, for example, the soil becomes not only "the objective condition" of the worker's own reproduction; it is experienced as "the objective body of his subjectivity" (1964:81), "a prolongation of his body" (89, 92). In other words, labor is experienced not simply as the action of an individual subject on inert matter but as an intersubjective relationship that simultaneously transforms both the object worked on and the worker himself (90–91).

It is important to remind ourselves that in traditional societies "work" includes a range of actions that we in the West would designate as ritual, magical, or even social action,[4] as though these were second-

George Devereux

On the Work of Human Hands 71

ary or surplus to the supposedly primary activities of gardening, herding, farming, hunting, or gathering. But the phenomenology of labor that I have outlined here suggests that identical elements appear in all intersubjective action. Among the Warlpiri of Central Australia, the ceremony associated with sacred sites involves the collaborative effort of patrilineal owners (*kirda*) and their uterine kin (*kurdungurlu*) who supervise or police the body painting and decoration of those who will perform the ancestral dances said to draw out, reawaken, or bring back into embodied presence the primordial forms of life (*kuruwarri*) that reside in the earth at that site and along the ancestral song lines that connect the site with others. In ceremonial labor, then, one reproduces a social past whose reappearance is linked to the burgeoning of desert plants and the increase of game animals after rain or the growing up of a child in one's care, a process that is metaphorically likened to the action of waking from sleep or dawn breaking after a long night. In short, Warlpiri notions of labor as a form of begetting or procreation echo Marx's and Engels's view (1976:43): at the same time that one increases animal and plant life, one reproduces the social relations most crucial to one's identity—with patrikin, matrikin and affiliated compatriots (*warlalja*) and affines (*jurdalja*). And one also reproduces one's own sense of kinship with the site that, depending on one's relationship with it, will be called father (*kirda*), father's father (*warringiyi*), mother's brother (*ngamirni*), mother's father (*jamirdi*), and so on.

Dancing vigorously on the land may be likened to carving an ancestral mask, giving birth, or making a farm. In common parlance, one puts one's sweat and blood into the task at hand.[5] The intense labor of the dancer, carver, mother, or farmer is felt to flow into the object or other, which then becomes endowed with subjectivity. *It* then appears to speak to the human subject in response to the human subject's action on it. The distinctive stomping of Aboriginal men's dance sends vibrations into the ground that are taken as evidence of the stirring into life of the ancestral essences that steep the earth underfoot. Among the Bamana of Mali, the "energy of action" (Bird 1974) is reified as *nyama*— a vibrant force that animates all living things and whose strength is correlated with the stress or intensity of the effort put into vital activity. Thus, the "arduous labour," skill, concentration, and effort involved in ironworking entails the "release" of nyama, as does the work of formal speech, hunting, and circumcision (McNaughton 1988:16). Indeed, so overwhelming is the nyama released from such practices that an unskilled worker may be blinded or killed by the force (69–70). This notion that inept labor may create a negative force in the object worked on is similar to the Māori notion that the vital force (*hau*) carried by every fabricated object may be "turned aside" (*whitia*) and cause illness and misfortune if the object received in exchange is not passed on or reciprocated (Salmond 2000:40).[6]

In so far as labor transfers vitality and spirituality from the laboring subject to the object worked on, labor creates an intersubjective relationship between people and things. This is why artists in many societies experience themselves as channels through which divine inspiration flows into the object. The author of *Tristram Shandy*, when questioned about the design of his book, said, "Ask my pen; it governs me; I govern not it" (Sterne 1980:292). When working on *Under the Volcano*, Malcolm Lowry confessed, "I do not so much feel as if I am writing this book as that I am myself being written (qtd. in Costa 1972:23). And Gola mask carvers in Liberia believe they are inspired by djinni who appear to them in dreams (d'Azevedo 1973:140). Throughout Africa, the notion that some inner force finds expression in the object carved leads to elaborate precautions being taken to ensure that the carver is in the right frame of mind when sculpting a figurine or mask, or in a good relationship with his spirit allies. Among the Anang of southeast Nigeria, the carver relinquishes other commitments, avoids working to the point of exhaustion or in the heat of the day, and abstains from sexual intercourse lest he create an imperfect work or risk injury to himself in the course of the carving (Messenger 1973: 109). Yoruba carvers are equally sensitive to the ways in which an art object may imitate its creator's personality. One master carver, Owoeye Oluwuro, told William Bascom "that a traditional Èfòn sculptor, before he initiated any important commission involving the carving of human eyes, mouth, and nose, had to make a sacrifice of sugarcane, dried maize with red palm oil, and pigeons to prevent the entrance of ugliness into his carving." These sweetening, smoothing, and uplifting images help guarantee that no clumsy adzing will despoil the carved face or create ugly features that might then be transmitted to the face of the sculptor's next-born child (1973:33).

Explaining how he transforms logs into art, the Tanzanian wood-carver Lugwani observes, "I do not impose my own ideas on the wood —it tells me what to do; it helps me to think creatively." And in commenting on the carving of one particular abstract sculpture, Lugwani noted that at first the log seemed resistant, but after two week's work he was able to say, "I am no longer fighting the wood; it has revealed itself to me and we are working together" (Lugwani 2005). Similar reflections may be found in Henry Glassie's study of Turkish traditional art and artisans. "In things they do not see things, but people," he writes (1993: 103); "the artist's gift suffuses an object with spirit" (4).

Clearly, then, the labor expended on an object is gradually felt to inhere in the object itself, investing it with social value. When, as among the Warlpiri, ritual labor demands the collaboration of many different people, the actual place where the ceremonial work is carried out accumulates a value that affirms the intersubjective bonds between both owners and ancestors and kirda and kurdungurlu. That the process of working on an object comes to be experienced as an inherent property of the object itself also helps us understand why religious ideas are so often entailed by labor-action. Sustained, intensive, and collective labor not only creates a binding intersubjective relationship or covenant between self and other, or subject and object; it produces a sense of value and of the sacred that is felt to inhere in the site where that labor takes place. Thus landscape becomes storied, as though the earth itself contained the narratives and scripts that human beings have created as moral constraints and guidelines for their lives (see Basso 1996).

We may now ask under what conditions the reverse process occurs. How does a valued object, embodying the vitality of those who have worked to produce or reproduce it, come to lose value and die? Is this loss of value also a function of the kind of relationship obtaining between a human subject and the thing that is the object of his or her labor?

In West Africa, masks can sicken and die when not worn in ceremony or when out of circulation, and they may even be mourned and given burial rites like a deceased person. In Aotearoa New Zealand there is a Māori saying that for as long as a person lives on the land or returns regularly to it, a fire burns there (*ahi ka*). But if one goes away and does not return, the fire goes out (*ahi mataotao*). And in Aboriginal Australia a sacred site unvisited for several generations—like grassland left unburned or kinspeople who have gone away for a long time—is figuratively dead, and as such it may be mourned and is felt to be haunted by dangerous spirits. But in Warlpiri thought, death and life are functions of relationship rather than absolute and final states. A neglected site, a forgotten ancestor, a primordial event may all be, so to speak, out of sight and out of mind, but none is necessarily lost to the world; it may be brought back into being whenever the living return to it, remember it, dream of it, or perform a ceremony that gives it presence. Any landscape is filled with marks, signs, and vestiges of the dreaming that people notice and discuss as they walk around. But such attention is strictly speaking not a form of remembering, a bringing of the past back to mind; it is an interaction that actually discloses the incipient vitality in the place, quickening it into life and making it present. *Walku* is thus best translated not as death, but as loss,[7] absence, or potentiality, and its opposite *palka* not as life, but as embodied presence.

Death is thus a form of temporary estrangement rather than a permanent state of nonbeing. It occurs whenever any object, place, or person whose being depends on a vital relationship with other beings loses that life-sustaining link. The link may be borne in mind, to be sure, but a mere memory or disembodied conception of a person or place is artificial. It is map, not territory.

Estrangement may also be *deliberately* created as a way of expressing power, for paradoxically it is only when one masks the context in which an object is produced that it attains a reified form that cannot be subject to questioning, and therefore imposes itself on our consciousness, as it were, not through any memory of the work that went into it or the lives that were sacrificed to create it, but simply from its presence as sheer facticity.

The more I thought about the Falun mine and remembered its vast underground caverns, hewn by human hand, shored up by pine logs, and now as empty as a great cathedral, the more I began to wonder why it was that monumental architecture left me cold. Is it because such structures as the Pyramids at Giza, the city of Petra, Saint Peter's in Rome, or the skyscrapers of Manhattan appear to be the work of ma-

loss, death, devalue, etc

On the Work of Human Hands 75

temporary estrangement : loss of a link

chines or even gods rather than toiling human beings? Is it because they bespeak the dominating power of capital rather than the generative power of human labor? Sometimes I think that the giganticism of modernity is intended to affront us. A domineering manner, a monolithic work of art, or architectural grandiosity suggest an impulse to gain a sense of power over others by making them feel small and insignificant. In Philadelphia some years ago, I remember being overawed by the massive stones on which the earliest public buildings rested, so out of proportion with the people who thronged the sidewalks. The great City Hall is the largest masonry building in the world, surpassing the cathedrals of Europe in height and hubris. Lacking any steel frame, its first floor walls, which support the eight floors above, are twenty-two feet thick. Yet massive steel and glass skyscrapers now surround William Penn's Center Square, and his statue, though weighing twenty-seven tons and standing thirty-seven feet high, is dwarfed by these twentieth-century monuments to commercial enterprise and progress. Is there not a contradiction between the ideals of democracy and the inequality of scale, the intimidating power, that we experience in the shadows of these great structures?

It is not my intention to criticize capitalism by sentimentalizing labor, for this would be to ignore the ignominy of unremitting toil and the readiness with which people will escape it if given half a chance. In this context, I recall how rapidly and unregretfully Warlpiri abandoned the hardships of desert foraging for the comparative luxury of work on cattle stations, where they received regular handouts of tea, sugar, and flour. Or how schoolboys in northern Sierra Leone signified their liberation from farmwork by growing their fingernails long, painting them red, or wearing white kid gloves. But the modernist fetishization of the hand that does not get dirty, of the body that shows no signs of wear and tear, and the celebration of machines that do our menial work for us are forms of ritualized forgetting that all too easily blind us to the degrading conditions under which millions of our contemporaries still labor to produce the commodities on which we have come to depend. The passing of the industrial mode of production in the West has seen the rise of a knowledge society, based on electronic media and the processing of information that, for all its immediate benefits, has deluded us into thinking that what makes or unmakes us is what the head

no longer working hands
but rather head
knowledge

rather than the hands may hold, while giving new currency to a Cartesianism that makes mind (either in the form of human brain power or artificial intelligence) the measure of all things. If the phenomenology of labor that I have outlined here has any value, it is not in fostering a nostalgia for physical toil, but in reminding us that human minds are seamlessly and intractably linked to human bodies and emotions, that thought can never save us from ourselves, and that the price of one person's freedom is all too often another person's servitude. Labor is our way back from the enchantment of things and the allure of abstraction to the transfiguring immediacy of the real.

A Footnote on Falun and Fife

In his famous essay "The Storyteller," Walter Benjamin observes that "death is the sanction of everything that the storyteller can tell" and that the storyteller borrows his authority from death (1969:94). Compressed into these two statements are a series of axioms: that storytelling springs from our direct experience of the world and that, in the course of the twentieth century, the value of such experience has been increasingly eroded; that, unlike novels and treatises, which tend toward didacticism and moralizing, stories are open ended and allow us to draw our own conclusions from them; that storytelling requires a community and is an ongoing process in which many share, and in which everyone finds his or her own meaning. To illustrate his assertions, Benjamin refers to a story called "The Unexpected Reunion," by Johann Peter Hebel, that builds on the events surrounding the mysterious death of Mads Israelsson at the Falun mine in 1677. Benjamin is particularly fascinated by the way in which Hebel embeds his story in natural history, so that the devastating loss suffered by the young woman whose fiancé vanished without a trace on the eve of the Midsummer day she was to be married reminds us of the historical calamities and countless deaths that occurred in Europe in the forty-two years before the fateful day when, as it were, Israelsson returned from the dead, his body so steeped in iron vitriol that it had escaped decay.

Perhaps, in salvaging a sense of the reality of labor from the monumental products that both outlast the laborer and extinguish his identity, we may also recover a sense of the lives that history has consumed or left in its wake and that still linger on the ghostly horizons of our consciousness as names on untended graves or cenotaphs, or as photographs that give us a brief glimpse into the actual existence—so uncannily like our own—of our predecessors.

Not long after my trip to Falun I traveled to Saint Andrews in Scotland to visit my old friend Nigel Rapport. On a gray September day, Nigel and I walked from Saint Monans to Elie along the Fifeshire coast. The Firth of Forth lay under a sullen sky, the rain clouds edged with silver when the sun broke through, and it was dead low water, the sea slumped, withdrawn and hushed as if it had drained away. Despite our animated conversation, the grayness and silence cast a pall over the fishing villages through which we passed and the sandy wastelands or links where marram, bracken, dock, gorse, and blackberry lined the path. It did not surprise me, therefore, when Nigel told me that Fife had been, for five hundred years, one of Europe's great coal mining areas and that after the invention of the chimney in 1550, the boggy coastal farms from which it was so difficult to scratch a living began to yield coal in abundance. As we tramped on, Nigel told me of the great coal-fired lime kilns that produced fertilizer for the fields and pointed out to me the vestiges of old slag heaps or bings and, nearer the sea, the foundations of the old saltwater-evaporating pans, also heated by coal. For some reason, the thought of all these vanished industries haunted me, and after returning to Denmark, I endeavored, via the Internet, to find out something about the communities that for so many centuries flourished where now there are only golf courses, grazing sheep, and villages built of stone. From an essay by Emily Johnson I discovered that the last walk-in mine in Fifeshire closed in 1989, putting fifteen hundred men out of work. The miner Alex Robertson left the mine ten years earlier after the mine roof collapsed on his back, pinning his legs and killing one of his workmates. "You just take it in stride," he said of the accident. "It's your job. There are lots of other ways to die. You could work all day in the mine, go up and get hit by a bus."

There are no more men underground in Fife. The mines have been closed: Dunfermline Splint, Bannockburn Steam, Manor Powis Main, Alloa Cherry, Coalsnughton Main, the Stink, the Crow, the Rough, the Ell, the Humph, the Baugh, the Drossm the Tourha, the Creepie, the Siller Willie, the Kailblades, the Corbie, the Stairhead, the Hauchlien. Unlike the millions of years it took for the Carboniferous swamplands to pass, for Pangea to form and dissolve, for the United Kingdom to shift across the globe, the Fife coal industry lasted a mere thousand. It took twenty years for the industry to go from booming to nonexistent. In ten years more perhaps even the names will be eroded away. (Johnson n.d.)

Here are not two worlds—the world of past
happenings and the world of our present
knowledge of those past events—there is
only one world, and it is the world of present
experience.—MICHAEL OAKESHOTT,
Experience and Its Modes

5 Storytelling Events, Violence, and the Appearance of the Past

In summoning the past to reach an understanding of the present, it is
all too tempting to see history as a series of defining moments and
critical events—the Atlantic slave trade, the Holocaust, the colonization of the New World, the crucifixion of Christ, the killing of Imam
Hussein, or, for that matter, 9/11—whose force continues to be felt in
the here and now, shaping the way we live and our worldviews. The
same is true of war, which so utterly transforms maps, polities, and
opinions that we often declare in its aftermath that nothing will ever be
the same again. But this view of history and war often downplays the
ways in which past events are continually being transmuted into myth,
and the ways in which the present, replete with its own preoccupations,
struggles, and interests, appropriates the past, and in doing so revises

the way the past *appears* to us. Although, from an objectivist stand-point, the past has a causal effect on the present simply because it is prior, from a phenomenological standpoint effects may precede causes and, to all intents and purposes, "bring about the past" (Dummett 1978:319–50). Thus, when a resentful younger brother in Sierra Leone complains about being "a slave" to his elder brother's will, or an unhappy wife refers to herself as "a slave" in her husband's house, or a sixteen-year-old schoolgirl expresses the opinion that "anyone who does not try to be educated will be just like a slave," we glimpse not only how the historical past (in this case, domestic slavery) is strategically and rhetorically deployed to explain quite different social and biographical circumstances but also how these contemporary allusions to slavery effectively bring the phenomenon into being.[1] This may be compared with the way we in the urban-industrial West still deploy metaphors from our agrarian past—of herding, shepherding, sowing, reaping, and cultivating—to express experiences that have nothing to do with farming, or deploy the imagery of war to describe domestic altercations, academic arguments, sports competitions, and corporate takeovers (Lakhoff and Johnson 1980:4–5). It is for this reason that we need to draw a distinction between *memory* and *invocation*, reserving the notion of memory for the *biographical* past and using the term *invocation* for the ways in which people refer to events in the *historical* past of which they have no direct personal knowledge in order to find legitimating precedents or explanations for their actions—as in the case of repressed memory syndrome or the phenomenon that Norman Finkelstein calls "the Holocaust industry" (2000). The past, we might say, is thus never one thing but *many* and characterized less by necessity than by *potentiality*.

This point of view echoes D. W. Winnicott's understanding of cultural experience as neither inner nor outer, but as an emergent property of the interplay between the two—something occurring "in the potential space between the individual and the environment" (1974: 118). The "potential space" is the place of play and of art in which every individual negotiates, albeit unwittingly, his or her own particular compromise between what is given and what he or she effectively brings into being. The historian who overlooks this perennial interplay between what has been and what is in the making tends to commit the

Storytelling Events, Violence, and the Past 81

same epistemological error as many of those whose past he or she is studying, that is, privileging antecedent events over present-day praxis, reducing what is now possible to what happened long ago, and attributing to the spectral appearance of the past in the present an abiding ontological presence and identity. Moreover, by explaining the present solely in terms of the past, such a historian not only risks attributing to the ancestors greater power than the living possess; he or she comes dangerously close to bad faith, for by invoking the determinative power of an allegedly pristine past, he or she runs the risk of absolving people from their responsibility for ensuring that the worst of the past never happens again and that the best of it is salvaged and retained. To put it more theoretically, we need to explore how the dead weight of past generations, Jean-Paul Sartre's "practico-inert," is transformed by the human faculty for initiating something new, the faculty that Hannah Arendt calls "natality." At the same time, a phenomenological critique of objectivism is suggested here—for when Karl Marx speaks of the "tradition of all the dead generations [weighing] like a nightmare on the brain of the living" (1934:10), or Arendt writes that the new is that "which cannot be expected from whatever may have happened before" (1958:178), we should construe these statements not as referring primarily to some external reality but rather to our *experience* of reality. It is for this reason that Claude Lévi-Strauss's well-known distinction between cold and hot societies, the first of which deny or countermand the future, the second of which admit and celebrate it, is spurious, for human beings everywhere participate actively, though not always equally, in the creation of the future, whether that future appears to repeat the past or not.

There are also methodological pitfalls in our appeal to the past, such as the implicitly Lamarkian notion that traumatic experiences in previous generations, or during wartime, leave permanent psychic scars whose repercussions continue to be felt, like original sin, unto the seventh generation. Perhaps we should explore more carefully and empirically the questions of what it is that we call "the past," and to what uses this past is put by the living. My working hypothesis is that the "past" has much the same symbolic status as the many other abstractions that we invoke in explaining our circumstances to ourselves —"the ancestors," "the gods," "providence," "luck," "fate" and "tradition."

Such terms tend to be reified and treated as transcendent. And in so far as they are seen as objective—which is to say, outside the field of our immediate comprehension and control—people all too readily declare that they can neither govern nor change them. Causative forces and transcendent entities thus acquire the power to explain and legitimate social practices and worldviews, but at the expense of absolving people of responsibility for their present situation. To treat people as victims of circumstance, without showing how they actively work on these circumstances, is to share in this bad faith.

Since the historical past is not transmitted genetically, it must be transmitted exogenetically, which is to say culturally. But in what form? This question is especially imperative in preliterate societies. One obvious answer is in anecdote, myth, and folktale. But I hope to show that, as stories, the past is not imposed on the present but, rather, offers itself up, so to speak, to the living as a basis for creatively comprehending their present situation and making informed choices about how it is to be addressed and lived. In what follows, I will be mainly concerned with choices between retaliation and reconciliation. For though the past contains the germs of antipathy, defensiveness, and violence, it also contains the possibilities of trust, openness, and reconciliation. Using a Kuranko narrative, collected in the course of fieldwork in Koinadugu District in northeastern Sierra Leone in 1970, I will show that both options are presented by the past and that it is for those in the present to decide which option will be preferred, and how the past will be interpreted.

A Storytelling Session

When we speak of oral traditions, it should not be assumed that *tradition* designates a finite repertoire of stories, circulating ad infinitum and affirming entrenched moral values, for as a performed *event*, any story is like Heraclitus's river—differently realized each time it is told and variously signified in the minds of individual listeners. Hence M. M. Bakhtin's argument that any narrative participates in the "open event-ness of Being" (1993:1) and simultaneously refers back to "the objective unity of a domain of culture" and forward "at the never-repeatable uniqueness of actually lived and experienced life" (2). That

anecdote
myth
folktale

Storytelling Events, Violence, and the Past 83
-retaliation
-reconciliation

present events are always characterized by a degree of hermeneutic openness is immediately evident in any Kuranko storytelling session. Let me therefore review briefly a night session in Kondembaia in February 1970 at which three gifted narrators were present—Keti Ferenke Koroma, Kenya Fina Mara,[2] and Sulimani Koroma—together with a sizeable audience of men, women, and children. Since I have described this session in detail elsewhere (1982:64–66), I recall it now only to reemphasize the significance of the theatrical or performative dimension of Kuranko storytelling, particularly the dialogical interplay of different storytellers. Not only did the three storytellers take turns to tell their stories, but each elected to tell stories that ironically counterpointed the story that had preceded his or her own. At the same time, each gave enthusiastic support to the stories that the others told, interjecting stock exclamations such as *ha, heh, eh, oho,* or *fiu,* or murmuring approval, astonishment, and emphasis. Indeed, in two stories about beguiling women, Keti Ferenke and Kenya Fina actually shared the narration and played the male and female roles. And when stories included songs, Kenya Fina taught the audience the lyrics of the songs and encouraged and enhanced the singing with her mellifluous voice.

This subtle alternation of voices and of various points of view means that Kuranko storytelling events play with rather than slavishly assert social dogmas. Moreover, this play maximizes audience participation, both in the telling and singing of the story and in the elucidation of its ethical implications. For in counterpointing different standpoints, stories place in abeyance predetermined, conventional attitudes based on gender, age, and estate and open up the possibility of dialogue and reflection on decisive questions of judgment and action. But, as I say, Kuranko tales (*tileinu*) not only critique the rigid worldviews associated with established centers of chiefly power and male authority; they play and comment ironically on each other. Thus while individual stories, such as Keti Ferenke's "The Two Momoris," which I have analyzed elsewhere (2002:142–52), may take a dim view of women, such bias will seldom go unchallenged, either by other storytellers or by the audience. A pluralistic spirit prevails, encompassing both stories and persons, for, as Kuranko see it, stories are no more the same than people are. It is the adjustment and reconciliation of differences that storytelling attempts, rather than the strict imposition of unitary identifications. In this sense a storytelling event epitomizes the ideal of social intelligence (*hankili*) and conforms to a model of civility and conversability recognized in all cultures. Crucial to this ideal is the notion of a complementary relationship between different voices and different points of view, a complementarity, moreover, that implies that anyone may, in the event of an unjust use of privilege or power, take action to realign and reaffirm the social order. This is not to say that storytelling works toward unanimity or consensus, and still less that it denies intrinsic and inherited differences in rank, gender, estate, and ethnicity; rather, it is to emphasize the ways in which storytelling, simply by virtue of its being a shared action of speaking, singing, sitting together, and voicing various viewpoints, makes possible the momentary semblance of a fusion of disparate and often undisclosed private experiences. It is, therefore, not so much the substance of what is said or suggested in a story that affirms the ethic of openness and "whiteness" that Kuranko encapsulate in the notion of *morgoye* (personhood), but the very act of participating in a shared event and referring separate experiences to a common source. Keti Ferenke once spelled this out to me by saying that dogmatic declarations about what is right and wrong will have less effect on young listeners than the telling of a story that enables them to see for themselves the implications of certain actions, and thus reach their own conclusions as to what behaviors are most conducive to communal existence.

On the night in question, the room into which we were crowded was shuttered against the tropical night. I was barely able to find a niche for my microphone. Children clambered over one another trying to get nearer the storyteller. Babies slept, oblivious, on their mothers' backs. Old men, chewing kola, unmoved by the commotion, sat in the shadows of hurricane lamps. Young men's faces lost their brashness. And women smiled without inhibition, anticipating another of Keti Ferenke's irreverent and hilarious performances. Having boasted to me more than once that he could tell more stories than I would ever have patience to record, he began apace, partly to impress me, I think, and rattled off ten stories that immediately had everyone in stitches. Though all touched on familiar themes—the vaunting of self, the denigration of others, taking unfair advantage of others, failing to keep promises, not heeding the advice of elders—they exploited ludicrous situations and played for laughs. Even when he broached his own obsessions—the wiles and wickedness of women—he used burlesque and grotesque to avoid too much gravity.

Then Kenya Fina signaled that she wanted to tell a story. Though it picked up on Keti Ferenke's themes of not lording it over others and not using one's superior position to take advantage of those under one's care and protection, Kenya Fina's story focused on the relationship between junior and senior cowives and the unjust ways in which older women sometimes use their privileged position to abuse and exploit younger cowives. "If you are the senior wife (*baramusu*), you should not look down on the ones under you, blaming them for whatever goes wrong in the house."

Now it was Keti Ferenke's turn again. Taking his cue from Kenya Fina, he also told a story about cowives, but he turned it into an indictment of the fickleness of women. Tricked and cuckolded by his wife, the chief in the story ends up ruefully observing that men should try to endure the wanton ways of women, just as the hardy leaf of the *kuron* tree endures high winds and driving rain.

It was at this point that Kenya Fina told what would become, for me, one of the most compelling stories I ever heard in Sierra Leone. But before relating it, I want to quickly comment on the six stories that followed and brought the evening to a close, for this will help make clear the extent to which stories must be understood not separately as a disconnected set of entertainments, but as a strategic series that plays off points of view, one against the other, creating a polyphony of voices and enlarging one's understanding of how the recurring dilemmas of everyday life are experienced by different individuals. As we shall see, Kenya Fina's story of Na Nyale is a plea for compassion and reconciliation, rather than harsh judgment. It was immediately followed by a story in a similar vein by Tina Kuyate, concerning the origins of ingratitude. A male ancestor, given great gifts by a magical bird, fails to give anything back to the bird when it is in need and, as a consequence, loses the bounty he had earlier gained. Keti Ferenke then told a story that pressed his point that women cannot be trusted. In a lighter vein now, Kenya Fina told a comic story about a seductress, showing that men can be as readily swayed by their emotions as women. The session ended with Keti Ferenke telling three more stories, the last of which affirmed the value of friendship. By reiterating the point of "The Two Momoris," though this time without any reference to women, it seemed to sum up all that he and Kenya Fina shared, a poignant demonstration that friendship may transcend lines of age and gender, not only in art but in life.

The Story of Na Nyale

There was once a very jealous chief. He allowed no man to see his wives. So the wives decided on a ruse. They wove several large raffia baskets that could be hung from the walls of the house. Whenever the women made ready to go from the town to the farm, each hid her lover in one of the baskets. The women also prepared food and put it in the baskets. Then they would set off to the farm to do the weeding, and in the evening return to the town, carrying their lovers in the baskets on their backs.

This went on for some time. Then one day, one of the wives, whose name was Na Nyale, decided to leave her lover in the farmhouse when she went out weeding because he was too heavy to carry. What none of the wives knew was that the chief was going to visit them that day. Na Nyale had killed a chicken, prepared it well, and left it for her lover. But while all the other wives took their lovers with them to the place where they were weeding that day, Na Nyale left her lover in the farmhouse.

No sooner had the women left the farmhouse than the chief arrived. As he entered the house, he saw that big basket hanging there. He touched it and said, "Eh, these women are amazing. What have they got in this big basket? I am going to have a look inside." When the chief said that he was going to look inside the basket, it started shaking, shaking, shaking. The chief said, "Eh, the basket is shaking! I must look into this." The basket shook twice. Then the chief took his machete and cut the rope. With the rope cut, the basket fell from the wall—*din*. The basket said, "Mm hmm." The basket hummed. The chief said, "Ah! So the basket can speak. I am going to open it this very day and see what is inside." He took a knife and cut the rope that held the mouth of the basket closed. And what did he see? Fara Mara. Then the chief said, "Who is in this basket?" The man said, "I am." The chief said, "Who are you." "I am Fara Mara," said the man. Then the chief said, "What did you come here for?" The man said, "Allah has destined that this should happen." The chief said, "Well, Allah has indeed destined that something should happen between us today. Now get out so that I may kill you." The man begged, "Oh chief, why don't you simply fine me. Whatever the amount is, I will pay it." The chief said, "No, I must kill you." Fara Mara got out of the basket and the chief seized him. He put one foot on Fara Mara's legs, the other foot on Fara Mara's hands, then he took out his knife and cut Fara Mara's throat. When his throat was slit, Fara Mara's blood splashed onto a cassava plant. The blood splashed over the leaves. The cassava leaf then changed into a little Senegalese fire finch.[3] The fire finch flew to the part of the farm where the women were weeding to tell them what had happened. The bird found that the women had partitioned the area. Standing a little way in front of Na Nyale, whose lover had been killed, it sang: "Na Nyale, oh Na Nyale, Na Nyale, oh Na Nyale / Ni i wara sole to mansa, ni i wara sole to mansa / Wara kemine ye m'bi yo, oh Na Nyale" (Na Nyale, oh Na Nyale. . . . If you have left the basket, then the chief has seen a man today, oh Na Nyale). Na Nyale said to her companions, "Nnn, the bird is crying. I am not going to finish weeding my piece of ground. I am gone, I am gone, oh. The bird is saying something to us." The others said, "All right, go. We will see you later." She hurried quickly down the hill and arrived at the farmhouse. But what did she see? She saw the basket on the floor, all the ropes cut from its mouth. Then she saw the chief. She said, "Chief, what happened here?" The chief said, "Are you the owner of this?" She said, "Yes. But there is no need to be afraid. What did you do with it?" The chief said, "Well, I have not left any man in my farmhouse. If I found a man in the basket with the bones of a chicken and a pan with traces of palm oil on it, then it means that the food he eats is sweeter than the food I eat,[4] and I killed him." The woman said, "After you killed him, what did you do with him?" The chief said, "After I killed him, I burnt his body and threw the ashes in the river." The woman said, "Into what river?" The chief said, "The Seli."[5]

The woman went to the town and got some money. She said, "If I do not see this man today, then no matter what happens, I will not rest. I must find him." The woman then set off, following the river downstream. For two years she followed the river. She said she had to find her lover. Wherever she stopped, she would find palm birds in their nests. She would tell the birds to be quiet, that love was in the air and on the ground and under the water. She would say, "I am searching for my lover." "I ya l moina, Fara Mara, I ya l moina? Dondo / I ya l moi dondo? I ya saya soron n'de le fe / Dondooooo. Don"(Do you hear me, Fara Mara, do you hear me? All is quiet / Do you hear quietness? You died because of me / All is quietttt. Quiet). She heard nothing but the sound of her own voice. She would continue on her way. Wherever she stopped by the riverside she sang the same song. For two years she followed the river, searching for her lover.

Then all the living things of the river met together and said, "That man who was killed and burnt, and whose ashes were thrown in the river . . . whoever ate some should bring it forth now. There is someone searching for him, so desperate she cannot rest. All those who ate the bones should spit them out. All those who ate the flesh should regurgitate it. Those who ate the eyes should give them up. We should put all these parts back together again and make the man as he was." So everyone brought forth the different parts. All those who were able to reassemble the skeleton did so. All those who were able to put flesh on the bones did so. They put all the parts together again. Then they asked who had taken the life. The one who had taken it said, "I took the life." They said, "Well, go and get it." He went for the life. They told him to put the life back in the body. He did so.

Then they told the man that someone was looking for him, someone desperate to find him. At that moment, Na Nyale arrived at that spot. It was a place so fear-inspiring that no one ever ventured there. But so desperate was this woman that she cared nothing for her own safety. She stood there. There was dense forest all around. She heard the palm birds chattering. She scattered some coins in the forest and said, "All you djinni who live here, this is my gift to you. I am looking for someone, for the man who was killed on account of me. If I do not find him I prefer to die by this river. I cannot live without him." Then she scattered some coins along the riverbank and said, "All living things in the water and on the land, listen to me." But silence surrounded her. She stood and sang (as before). Then the man sang in reply: "Ah, n'de Fara Mara; n'ya saya keni i le l le fe dondo" (Ah, I am Fara Mara; I preferred death because of you . . . all is quiet). The woman leapt into the river— gbogbon. She said, "He is here. No one knows my song except Fara Mara. He must be here." Then she saw him.

The creatures that dwelt under the water took care of them for two years. They were well fed and provided for. In the third year they were given a xylophonist.[6] A horse was given to the lover, and the woman was given two boxes of dresses. Then they were carried to the surface. The water creatures said, "Well, we have to tell you that when you return, you should immediately find the man who killed you and take your revenge. If you don't do this, we will kill you. Here is what to do: when you return, ask for him, and spend a night lodged in his house. Next morning, tell him you want to dance. Invite him to dance with you. Sit on your horse and let him sit on his. Then, as you dance, take your sword and cut off his head, thus paying him back in his own kind.[7] By cutting off his head you will satisfy us." The man and the woman said, "All right," and set off.

In every town they came to, they asked, "Is that chief still there?" People said, "What chief?" "That chief who killed a man that year, the man who was hidden in a raffia basket on the farm." Then people said, "He is there." Finally the couple reached the town where that chief lived. But they did not recognize the compound (*luiye*). They asked, "Is that chief still here?" People said, "What chief?" "The chief that killed a man on his farm on account of his wife." They said, "Yes, he is here." Then the man said, "Well, he raised me, so I have come to thank him." People said, "He is here." The man said, "Well, can you show me the way to his *luiye*?" They led him right into the chief's house. Everyone was looking at the two strangers. Then one of the chief's wives said, "Eh! This man's wife resembles Na Nyale, the one whose lover was killed by the chief. She looks like her." The woman went and greeted Na Nyale. But Na Nyale said, "I am not Na Nyale." The other woman said, "Well, people really can look alike!" She went away. But then she said, "But the man looks like Fara Mara." The talk went on, but the strangers said nothing.

Then the man took £15 and gave it to the chief. He said, "You raised me. You have forgotten, but you did." (The chief had no idea that a plot was being hatched against him, to make him do what the strangers wanted.) The woman then gave two skirts (*lapas*) and two head ties to each of the chief's wives. Then they retired for the night.

In the morning the man told the chief that he was going to offer a sacrifice because it was a long time since he had done so. He said, "I did not know that I would find my big man here." Then the chief mounted his horse. The man mounted his. The old women crowded around them, clapping, and the *jeleba*s played their xylophones, singing the praises of the chief. The man scattered coins on the ground. People scrambled to get them. Even Fara Mara's mother did not recognize him. But he did not go to her place. The jelebas were playing. Everyone was happy. But Fara Mara had a sword hidden under his gown. He put his hand under his gown and grasped the sword. He said, "Oh God, I did not start this. This man killed me. My body was burnt and my ashes strewn in the river. If this all happened, oh God, help me take my revenge." As the chief passed him, he drew his sword and with one blow cut off the chief's head. His head fell there. His body fell there. There was a great commotion among the people. Everyone was crying. Fara Mara said, "Heh, heh, heh, heh, everybody be quiet. Everyone can tell me soon why he or she is crying." (A killer's word is always feared.)[8] Then everyone fell silent.

The next day Fara Mara sacrificed two cows, one for himself and the other for the dead chief. He became chief in that town. All the chief's wives became his wives. Therefore, be you a chief or a nobody,[9] if you should find your wife with another man, fine him but do not kill him. To kill is not our custom. That is not how our ancestors did things. Since these events occurred, a stop was put to killing. No one does it now.

The Social Logic of Violence

To understand violence intersubjectively it is necessary to stress that the principle of reciprocity operates both at the level of being and of having, for being is in all societies cathected onto and distributed among the *things* which people call their own and with which they identify. What one *has* objectifies who one *is*. The Kuranko notion of *miran* helps make this clear. The plural *mirannu* refers both to material possessions—particularly those that contain and protect, such as a house, clothing, water vessels, and cooking pots—as well as to personal attributes that give one a sense of self-possession, presence, and substantiality of being, such as forceful speech, physical skill, and social adroitness. But miran, in both senses of the term, material possession and personal disposition, is never a fixed property or attribute. In practice, a person's miran may be bolstered by fetishes that symbolically enclose, contain, and protect (*ka kandan*) the vital spaces that define his or her being—body, house, village, chiefdom—in exactly the same way that in a consumer society material possessions bolster and define a person's sense of well-being, substantiality, and standing. But self-possession may be undermined, sapped, or lost. Just as a person's property can be stolen, a pot broken, and a house fall into disrepair, so a person can lose self-possession and confidence. Moreover, a person's miran can be taken away by more powerful others (such as autocratic parents, forceful public speakers, and powerful bush spirits) whose voice and power press down with great weight, diminishing the miran of those in their presence. Ideally, a balance is struck in which everyone's voice, presence, and property is accorded due recognition in relation to his or her role, age, and gender. But some people assert themselves beyond their due station—as in the case of a chief who exploits his position to take advantage of people, a senior cowife who abuses her junior partners, a man whose jealousy overrules his better judgment, or a woman whose emotions are not held in check. A kind of intersubjective logic then comes into play, one based on the principle of reciprocity, according to which one has the right to counter in kind any action that has the effect of directly nullifying, diminishing, belittling, or erasing one's own being, or of indirectly doing so by taking away properties that one regards as essential to and as extensions of one's being. The phrase "ke manni a nyorgo manni" (something happened; its counterpoint happened in turn) reveals the kinship between the social logic of partnership and the abstract calculus of retaliation. But in the case of *lex talionis*, when the party that feels that its being has been violated takes identical counteraction against the violator, can we call such action violent?

According to Kuranko reasoning, no. If one is innocent, one has every right to avenge oneself against anyone who seeks to do harm. This is why, before avenging himself, Fara Mara declares before God that since he had done nothing to justify the violence of the chief, he now has every right to do to the chief what had been done to him. Not only is this not, in the Kuranko view, a violent act; it is a necessary and honorable one, rewarded by Fara Mara inheriting all that the chief had once possessed. Violating the being of someone who is believed to be responsible for violating one's own is not violence but retributive justice. Which is, on the evidence, what the RUF rebels believed when they severed the hands of several people in Kondembaia in April 1998—for were they not part and parcel of the being of *ferensola*, of the party and people that had robbed them of their power?

However, Kenya Fina's story juxtaposes this retaliative attitude (associated with the djinni, the beings of the wild) with another, based on the notion of personhood as magnanimity. These two ethics are also co-present in the previous story in which Gbeyekan Momori's goodwill and generosity of spirit breaks the cycle of vendetta and payback by focusing not on the immediate situation that has caused grief and pain but by invoking a more abstract point of view. In this same vein, Kenya Fina makes a case for indemnification without death—a form of redemption in which something of comparable value is given to replace what was taken, but without the taking of a life: "Fine him but do not kill him." And it is in a similar vein that an elder at a court hearing will sometimes show empathy (*hinantei*) and plead on behalf of a remorseful wrongdoer: "A sa seria tinyan, koni ma kinikini a ma" (He has spoiled the law, but let us take pity on him). For in the Kuranko view, certain people are innately incorrigible, and therefore unable to stop themselves breaking the law; hence the comments one sometimes hears in a court hearing: "A ka tala, a soron ta la bolo" (He is blameless, he was born with it); or, "a danye le wo la" (that is how he is made).

I have argued that Kuranko stories open up discussion of varying points of view and help restore faith in common sense and conciliation in a world plagued by division. Folktales and historical memory both preserve, I suspect, traces of two quite different strategies of coping with violence—vengeance and forgiveness—and so leave open, at all times, the possibility of choosing how one will react to evil. But at the same time, they reveal the irreconcilable differences and contradictory potentialities that inhere in every being and in every human situation—as when the spirits of the wild demonstrate *morgoye* (humanity) in empathizing with Na Nyale and assisting her on her quest, only to later demand the death of the chief as the price of their goodwill. In dramatizing extreme possibilities, stories may all too easily deceive us into thinking that the world is quintessentially and categorically divided into good and evil, the deserving and the undeserving, the human and the nonhuman, and that we—exemplars of the good and the just—will win out in the end. But in exchanging one standpoint for another, and testifying to the way life is actually lived rather than merely thought, stories also cross and blur such boundary lines, revealing, as in the story of Na Nyale, the potentiality of amity and enmity, love and hate, selfishness and generosity, vengefulness and forgiveness inherent in all relationships, an ambiguity that Primo Levi, writing of the paradigmatically most black-and-white situation of our times, calls "the gray zone" —"indecipherable because it did not conform to any model; the enemy was all around but also inside, the 'we' lost its limits, the contenders were not two, one could not discern a single frontier but rather many confused, perhaps innumerable frontiers, which stretched between each of us" (1989:38).

Avenging and Forgiving

What we call "choices" are often habitual, unpremeditated actions that we only retrospectively dignify with the notion of free will. But there are moments at which we are faced with a dilemma and hesitate and reflect, weighing our options, considering our position, and reckoning what we stand to gain or lose. In my book *In Sierra Leone* (2004), I explore the ways in which ordinary Sierra Leoneans, having suffered grievous losses during the war, addressed the peace. For many people vengeance was not an option. Reconciliation was the only reasonable choice. But it was less a choice based on abstract moral principles or intellectual reasoning than a pragmatic assessment of what was most expedient if one was to salvage one's life and livelihood—a matter of what one could and could not do under the circumstances in which one found oneself. A matter of whether one had the power to see that justice was done, and whether one could endure replaying the horrors one had endured, raking over the coals, stirring up old hatreds and hurts.

My friend Noah Marah and I sometimes talked about the phrase I heard often in the refugee camps of Freetown, "m'bara hake to an ye" (I can forgive, but I cannot forget).[10] Was forgetting possible, and how deep down did the forgiving go? Noah emphasized the powerless of those who had lost limbs, loved ones, and livelihoods in the war, which is why revenge was not an option for them. The best they could do was put the past behind them and move on. Noah's point of view reminded me of a passage in Hannah Arendt's *The Human Condition* (1958:237). Forgiveness implies neither loving those who hate you, nor absolving them from their crime, nor even understanding them; rather, it is a form of redemption in which one reclaims one's own life, tearing it free from the oppressor's grasp and releasing oneself from those thoughts of revenge and those memories of one's loss that might otherwise keep one in thrall to one's persecutor forever. Noah said,

> If I say *i hake a to nye* (I renounce ill-will), I am freeing myself of the effects of your hatred. I am refusing to hate back. But this doesn't mean that justice will not be done. Most of us here feel that God sees everything, and that God will mete out punishment in His own good time. That's why we say, God will take out my anger on him. So I might say, I have left it up to God. Same as they say in Krio, *I don lef mi yon to God.* No one forgives the RUF; they are simply leaving it up to God to see that justice is done. Because how can you ever be reconciled to someone who has killed your father or cut off your hand? Reconciliation, forgiveness, forgetting . . . these are all relative terms. In Sierra Leone right now, we are letting sleeping dogs lie. You understand? We are fed with the war. Fed up with atrocities. If we talk about the war, it is not because we are plotting revenge or want to prolong the suffering. We simply do not want it to happen again.

Grief and Grievance

Noah's observations make it clear that our opinions and beliefs bear an oblique relationship to what is "really" on our minds. This is not only because a plethora of inchoate desires, frustrations, and grievances find expression in one's espoused point of view; it is because opinions do not mirror so much as justify our experience, and offer ways of creating and securing certain effects. In brief, they are performative and pragmatic in character—stratagems for making things happen that are in one's own best interests or that are consonant with what one's significant others deem to be imperative. I had seen this very clearly in the past when talking to Kuranko villagers about why they had, despite a traditional antipathy to Islam, embraced the new religion. Consider the following conversation I had with an elderly man, Fore Kande, in early 1979 about the time the first mosque was built in Firawa. In his youth, Fore had been a renowned wrestler, but he had suffered bouts of serious illness in his old age, so when he told me that it was through Allah that he got well, I asked him to explain. Fore described an herbal concoction given to him by a native healer (*besetigi*). But though this had cured him, "Allah had shown the leaves to the besetigi." He then added, "Koe ba Altal' lon" (Everything comes from Allah). But what was the nature of this belief for Fore? Had he come to it through intellectual reflection, through a conversion experience, or otherwise?

Fore had embraced Islam only two years before. Most of his life he had been *sunike* (neither a Muslim nor a Christian), though for several years he had worked for some American missionaries in Guinea. There had been times in his life when he had prayed, but now he prayed every day. "So what was it that made you a Muslim?" I asked. Because everyone was moving in that direction, Fore said, just as everyone had become involved in the ferensola movement—the campaign to get political representation in the national government. "Be minto i le ti i ban wo ma?" (If everybody is where you are not, would you remain apart from them?) he asked. "What if someone did stand apart from the crowd?" I retorted. "Ke i ma gboiya" (You would be the subject of ill-feeling), Fore replied.

This tendency to be swayed by the spirit of the times, to go with the social flow, may help explain why it is not belief or religious commitment per se that informs people's judgments, but considerations of belonging and solidarity. Although many Sierra Leoneans are critical of the work of the Western-funded and -fostered truth and reconciliation commission—seeing it as a foreign imposition that will revive bad memories, open up old wounds, and perhaps entail further acts of violence and revenge—this does not exclude the possibility that some will see the Western emphasis on talking through one's grievances, of publicly confronting one's oppressor, and of punishing those who perpetrated human rights abuses as a more effective way of securing benefits than silence and resignation. But it is never possible to predict which path will be taken, which one will appear most reasonable or promising.

The relationship between the truths of direct personal experience and the truths of tradition or convention is always indeterminate. In her compelling study of history, identity, and depression among the Flathead Indians of western Montana, Theresa DeLeane O'Nell shows that depression has its origins in personal experiences of bereavement, loneliness, and loss, *as well as* in a deep awareness that as a people, the Salish and Pend d'Oreilles "have been at the receiving end of a history of brute oppression that involved legislated confinement and relocation, bureaucratic delay and fraud, and the systematic and planned eradication of the economic, social, and religious practices of precontact life" (1998:35). Cultural conceptions of emotions, history, and individual biography all flow together to constitute depression. *Personal* grief and *political* grievances are thus deeply entangled in any collective representation.

In Sierra Leone, some people have elected to go public with their stories of personal loss as a way of strengthening their case for government compensation in the postwar period. For example, many women who were sexually abused in the course of the war marched in the streets of Freetown in 2003, demanding justice and reparations. Rather than hide their "shame," they made it the basis of their appeal for social justice. In the same vein, many displaced people have adopted the language of human rights and learned to speak of their suffering as post-traumatic stress disorder in order to gain sympathy and assistance from NGOs. But at the same time, many others have sought reconciliation through a public forgetting of the past, rather than through parading or replaying their war experiences.

Yet private agendas are always implicated in public representations, and action in the public sphere is often simply a pretext for the prosecution of personal vendettas or the pursuit of selfish ends. Though history or culture is invoked to justify and explain one's actions, the primary motivation is often biographical. Such was the case with Foday Saybana Sankoh, an army corporal, cashiered and sentenced to seven years in Pademba Road prison for his alleged role in the 1971 conspiracy to overthrow then president Siaka Stevens. For years, Sankoh nursed an abiding hatred for Joseph Saidu Momoh, the successor to Stevens, and in his embitterment and resolve to see the All People's Congress (APC) destroyed, enthusiastically led the armed wing of the RUF during the civil war. Here was a man who reminds one of Fyodor

Dostoevsky's abject hero in *Notes from Underground*—someone who feels himself so downtrodden, thwarted, and humiliated that he becomes consumed by a cold, poisonous craving for revenge. Indeed, he is so in thrall to his ressentiment that nothing can cure him of it. More imperative even than power was this self-defeating need to keep his hatred alive, which was why, when Sankoh had an opportunity to realize his revolutionary ideals in government, he argued that the RUF had not fought a war to secure posts; its sole objective had been a kind of cleansing or purging, to remove a corrupt regime from power.

While the language of political grievance conjures up the experience of bereavement, it is a language that all too easily takes on a life of its own. It suggests a bereavement that has never been worked through, a loss to which one has never become reconciled, a wound that has not healed. In bereavement proper, anger, protest, withdrawal, and grieving are ways of working through the trauma of separation and loss. But the rhetoric of grievance can, under certain circumstances, become a habitual way of addressing the world and, as such, feed fantasies of revenge, encourage the idealization of the lost object, and, by holding a person in thrall to the past, prevent creative reengagement with the world. The same can be said for acceptance. While acceptance may imply a sober assessment of the limits of one's freedom, it may just as readily lead to fatalism, inertia, and depression, in which external action is supplanted by libidinal "work" on one's own emotions and fantasies of occult power—a kind of "fatalistic submission to the forces of the world" (Bourdieu 2000:223).

I sometimes wonder whether a new fatalism has been born of the Sierra Leonean war. I have spoken to Sierra Leoneans who doubt that "Africans" have the capacity to govern themselves and who see no local answer to the problem of endemic corruption and cronyism among ruling elites. Some have embraced Islam and Pentecostalism, hoping to find in occult exhilaration the hope and direction they have been unable to find in everyday life. And all the while the influx of foreign aid and foreign goods, of the Western agendas for truth and reconciliation, and of NGOs create new forms of dependency and recreate the stigmatized and marginalized situation in which people lived under colonial rule.

But all manner of potentialities, some born of the past, some to be conjured out of the volatile circumstances of a globalized world, combine and permute constantly in the creation of what we call history, and it is the interplay between past and future at the level of events that should be the focus of our ethnographic labors. I have suggested that storytelling events exemplify the hermeneutic openness and indeterminacy of culture as "potential space," while confirming Winnicott's great insight that this is also the space of play. And it is because this cultural space contains many voices, many points of view, and many symbolic possibilities that storytelling events may constitute, for us, a model of how we should approach an understanding of the present.

To emphasize the indeterminate relation between past and future is to emphasize the ethical ambiguity of the present. Thus arguments to the effect that violence in Sierra Leone is an expression of primitive irrationality, of the circumstances of colonial history, or of gerontocratic forms of social organization all carry the risk of assigning such causal weight to enduring primeval, historical, or structural essences that both the capacity and the responsibility of the living to choose their future is downplayed. As a result, the living are regarded as victims of their own history, or of their own African essence, and Europe made, inevitably, the source not only of Africa's salvation but also of the meaning of Africa itself.

Ethical Ambiguity and the Anthropology of Events

The course of history, like the course of any human life, comprises a succession of turbulent events interrupted by periods of comparative calm. It is in these lulls that we take stock of our situation, come to terms with what has occurred, and begin anew. Accordingly, these are also the moments when we foreshadow—in the ways we speak, think, and act—the shape of things to come, which is why ethics must be concerned with a person's relationship with others, and with both the past and future. Thus to express one's immediate grievances solely in terms of the past—colonization, slavery, or the Holocaust, for example —may be, to use a Bambara image, a case of fire giving birth to ash, for one makes of oneself a victim, virtuous by dint of ancestral suffering, while condemning others, who had no hand in the historic injustice, to the role of persecutors and demanding of them the solution to one's

plight. George Santayana once observed that those who cannot remember the past are condemned to repeat it (1953). But what is the
point of remembering the past unless this helps us get beyond it? For
free men and women to claim that they are still slaves, or that they are
still victims of colonization, is a way of expressing all manner of grievances, but it is also a way of blinding themselves to the more immediate
causes of injustice in one's life, of denying the all-too-human injustices
perpetuated by one's own forebears, and of shifting the burden of responsibility from oneself onto others.

Sartre defines human freedom as our capacity to make ourselves out
of what we are made (1969:45). Arendt refers to this generative or
initiatory aspect of human action as natality: "Since action acts upon
beings who are capable of their own actions, reaction, apart from being
a response, is always a new action that strikes out on its own and affects
others" (1958:190). It is this capacity for rebirth, occurring "against the
overwhelming odds of statistical laws and their probability" and appearing "in the guise of a miracle," that redeems us, not simply by
freeing us from our thralldom to the past but by connecting us with
others as cocreators of a viable social world (178). Those of us who have
spent time in Sierra Leone since the end of the war have been struck by
the extraordinary capacity of ordinary people to rebuild their broken

lives, and it is this experience that has led me to argue for Arendt's
notion of natality as a counterweight to Bourdieu's notion of habitus—
with its emphasis on engrained habits of thought and action that effectively bind us to the past, even as the meanings we give to past events in
our imaginings, rationalizations, and narratives eclipse and compromise our memory of those events (Jackson 2005). Important ethical,
social, and political issues arise here, for in so far as we are slaves to the
past, we are not entirely responsible for our own actions, yet in so far as
our responses to the events in which we find ourselves embroiled influence events as yet unborn, we are, to some degree, responsible for the
world in which we live. This is the ethical burden of Akira Kurasawa's
great film *Roshomon*—not just that the truth of any event is relative to
our vantage point and interests but that the outcome of any event
hinges on how successfully we claim final truth for our own view, and
how we relate our own interests to others. In the wake of a violent act,
does one decide on revenge or reconciliation? To what extent can

parents justifiably plead that they are so shaped by the circumstances of their own childhoods that they are powerless not to repeat past patterns in their relationship with their own children? Can history absolve us? Can new technologies relieve us of the burden of choosing our own fate? Can culture be invoked to explain or excuse our actions? My argument echoes Sartre's point: that the onus is *always* on us to accept responsibility for what we are made, even if it is only to assume this responsibility. As Sartre puts it, freedom may be understood therefore as the "small movement which makes a totally conditioned social being someone who does not render back completely what his conditioning has given him" (1969:45). To understand the situations in which this drama plays out, we need not only ethnographies of events but analytical strategies that explore the interplay of history and biography.

Arendt's notion of natality as
counterweight to Bourdieu's habitus

Past generations + capacity for cruelty
& the new.

habitus - binds us to the past

interplay of history + biography

All his life, I forgot to mention, Max has been fighting
to be *en règle*.—HENRY MILLER, "Max"

Migrant Imaginaries

with sewa koroma in southeast london

Whenever I travel to Sierra Leone and exchange my dollars for leones,
receiving what always seems an astronomical sum in the local currency, I am mindful of the bounty this country has given me and of how
little, by contrast, it affords its own citizens. How many times during
the past thirty five years have I walked the laterite path from the Seli
River to Firawa, returning to the village that has inspired so much of my
writing, only to pass young men heading in the other direction, hoping
to make their fortune in the diamond fields of Kono or Kamakwie, or
improve their lot in Freetown by finding a job or benefactor. They risk
everything, these young men, only to come home, often as not, with
empty hands and seek the advice of a diviner or contemplate further
forays into a world whose doors are closed to them and whose ways are
as fickle as they are unfathomable. As for me, I risk very little. A bout of

malaria, a few days of boredom and lassitude, weeks of unappetizing food, and separation from my family—no hardship at all considering what I stand to gain. And then I leave the country, notebooks filled, plans for yet another book forming in my mind, climbing aboard an aircraft in the hot, clammy African night with dozens of young Sierra Leoneans—some anxious, some excited, some nonplussed—as they begin their journey to Europe in the expectation that they will find there what they could not find at home.

In July 2005, I went to Britain to look up several Sierra Leonean friends who had found refuge there during the war. I had known many of these young men and women from when they were children; their parents had been close friends. But I would spend most of my time with a young man I had gotten to know in Freetown only three and a half years ago when I was researching my biography of S. B. Marah. "Small S. B.," as Sewa was known at that time, was S. B.'s sister's son and was working as his uncle's chauffeur and general factotum—work he regarded as menial and ignominious. For many years, it had been his dream to become an automotive engineer, and he was hopeful that sooner rather than later his uncle would provide him with the means to embark on his chosen career. In May 2003, with his plane ticket paid by S. B., Sewa came to London on a student visa to study accountancy— the only subject that the British High Commission in Freetown would approve—and corented a room in his sister Aisha's council flat in Peckham, the predominantly African area of southeast London that was also the heartland of the Sierra Leonean diaspora in Britain.

I arrived at Waterloo Station from Paris on 20 July, thirteen days after the 7 July terrorist bombings in London and at almost exactly the same moment that four unexploded bombs were found in rucksacks abandoned by would-be suicide bombers on three Tube trains and a bus. The city was in turmoil: railway stations were being evacuated, police cars with sirens wailing were speeding through the streets, and rumors were spreading like wildfire. That evening, the papers and TV news were full of talk about the identity of the bombers, as if there was a causal link between the cultural vacuum these second-generation Muslim youths experienced growing up in Britain and the allure of militant sects with their fanatical sense of certainty, their withdrawal from the world, and their fantasies of miraculous and vengeful rebirth. It put one in mind of the Hitler Youth that so successfully harnessed the energy of youthful rebelliousness, replacing filial bonds with blood brotherhood and loyalty to an absolute leader: an abstracted form of belonging—focused on symbols like the flag, the folk, and the nation—that brooked neither dissent nor diversity and united young people in a cause that made them feel they mattered. Was this not also what happened in Sierra Leone when the Revolutionary United Front (RUF) licensed disaffected youth to seize what they felt was owed them and take their revenge on those they believed had done them wrong?

I had not seen Sewa for two years and was anxious I might not recognize him in the crowds in and around Paddington Station where we had agreed to meet. But then I saw him coming toward me, his familiar jaunty walk and inimitable smile, and as we shook hands and declared how bizarre it was to be meeting up in London of all places, I found myself again astonished at the kinship we shared despite the differences in our age, backgrounds, and circumstances. After exchanging customary greetings in Kuranko, I plied him with questions about his family. Was his mother Tina still in Freetown? Was she well? Was Dondo (her twin sister) also there? Was she well? And what of his brother Sheku in Kondembaia? Was he still chief? And how was he faring?

In Edgware Road I suggested we repair to a Lebanese coffee bar so that we could talk without distraction. There, I pressed Sewa for news of the Kuranko villages in which I had worked and lived before the war, including his own hometown of Kondembaia. According to Sewa, nothing had changed in the three and a half years since the end of the war. The villages were practically deserted. No one had the money to buy cement or roofing iron to rebuild their houses, and few could find the time and labor anyway. Most people were still living on their farms. "What of Kabala?" I asked. "Everyone is there," Sewa said.

Sewa had been taken captive during a RUF raid on Kabala in November 1994. Though he eventually eluded his captors and made his way back home to Kondembaia, his cousin Sheku was killed in front of him by a rebel soldier called Kujé. "What of the boys that shot Sheku?" I asked. "What happened to them?" "Kujé was killed in the war. Abu disappeared without a trace."

Sewa could not care less for these individuals. But hardly a day passed, he said, that he did not remember his cousin or think how easily it could have been his life that was lost on that fateful day. "What of the rebels that survived?" I asked. "What kind of reception do they get when they return to their villages?" "Well, some go back. Most do not. They go to the other end of the country and get new names, find wives, and settle down. Now the country is all mixed up, Mende living in Kuranko, Temne living in Kono . . . ." "And you living here, in London!" I said.

After finishing our coffee we walked south—passing Marble Arch and moving on to Victoria, then turning east past Westminster Abbey and the Houses of Parliament, where throngs of tourists were snapping pictures and being lectured on the sights. Sewa had brought a camera with him, and once or twice he asked if we could stop so I could take his photo in front of one of these famous landmarks. He wanted to send the photos home to his mother. He also interrupted our conversation from time to time to call his girlfriend Ade on his mobile phone, telling her where we were and what we were doing and assuring her we would meet her at the Angel in a couple of hours' time.

Halfway across Westminster Bridge we stopped to take in the view. Tourist boats were moving up and down the river whose muddy banks had been exposed by the ebbing tide. Ahead of us lay County Hall, where I had been interviewed for a job as a welfare worker with the homeless in the winter of 1963. A lifetime ago, it seemed, before the London Eye, the Gherkin and Millennium Bridges were built, before Sewa had been born.

Then, as if he was also struggling with similar distances and incongruities, Sewa exclaimed, "You know, Mr Mike, I am thinking that right now my brothers and cousins are all working on their farms back home in Kondembaia, working hard, but I am here in London, walking these streets, living this life here, this different life . . . ."

"Which is harder, life in Kondembaia or London?"

"I have to be grateful to God, tell God thanks for what he's done for me. Because I couldn't imagine me now on the farm doing that hard, hard, hard labor. It's a blessing for me to find myself here, even though it's hard. It's better, you know . . . ."

"Why is it better here? What makes it better?"

"Well, here, as long as you're hardworking, the job is there. You just have to go out and look for it. But back home the jobs are not there."

"What's wrong with farming?"

"Well, you know farming. Overseas, the richest people are the farmers. But back home things are different; the poorest people are the farmers. They don't have the equipment, the things to do the farming; they make their farms with their bare hands, no machines, nothing. So that's like life and death. It's really hard back home."

Though I pressed Sewa to spell out more clearly the differences between the hardships of village life and those of being a migrant he could not. Was farming *really* more arduous than the menial and minimally paid jobs he had been doing in London as a security guard, a cleaner, a night watchman, and a factory worker, or did the difference lie in the fact that farming condemned one to the repetition of time-old patterns while London offered a sense of possibility and new departures? One thing was sure, and this was true to a greater or lesser extent with all the Sierra Leoneans I spoke to in London: although one might rail against many things about life back home—the endemic corruption, the lack of jobs, the electricity outages, and the food shortages— one missed other things with a passion that could not be assuaged.

Sewa was often "seized" by homesickness. It "took hold" of him and would not let him go. He would become preoccupied by tensions within the family—between S. B.'s sons and sisters' sons over the division of the estate, or the lack of "communication" among his cousins. This was why he phoned them all on his mobile every day. Moreover, he was anxious not to lose touch with Sierra Leone or with his family and was determined to return home as soon as he had completed his studies to work as a motor mechanic (he preferred the term *automotive engineer*) and pursue a career in politics. His father, the late paramount chief Sheku Magba 11, was his role model. As a small boy, Sewa had been nicknamed "walking stick" because of the way he followed his father everywhere, dogging his heels, head down, concentrating on placing his feet exactly where his father placed his, literally walking in his father's footsteps. This was the "kingly way of walking" that his uncle S. B. had often upbraided him for, thinking it impertinent that a small boy should comport himself like a chief. But Sewa had inherited more than his father's way of walking; he had the right to rule and wanted to emulate the political evenhandedness and incorruptibility for which his father was known during forty years as paramount chief of Diang. By contrast, the present incumbent, Sewa's brother Sheku, was at odds with the older section and town chiefs, and increasingly embattled and unpopular. "If Sheku gave up the chieftaincy," Sewa told me, "and I was called upon to go home tomorrow and contest, I would do so, even though I am only twenty nine."

That Sewa was sustained emotionally in exile by the "belief" he had inherited from his father (by which he meant both Islam and a sense of what in Kuranko is known as *bimba che*—ancestral legacy or birthright) was made very clear in the way he responded to my question of whether he thought of himself as a Muslim: "I am a Muslim. I was raised in a Muslim home. My father was a Muslim, just as I told you, and my mother too. And I believe in the Muslim religion because . . . ," Sewa hesitated, as if searching for the right word. "A lot of the time I get bad dreams. The only thing that saves me when I get those bad dreams, every month or two weeks, the thing that comes up straight in my mind is *la illaha il Allah. Allahu Akbar, Allahu Akbar*, God is great, God is great. Then I am relieved of that bad dream. Because sometimes I am struggling in my dream, fighting in my dream, not able to shake it off. But that is the first thing that comes into my mind. *La illah il Allah*. I say it for a minute or so, and my fear goes and I am fine."

"What kind of dreams are these?"

"Mostly they are fighting dreams, people trying to stab me."

"In England here?"

"Back home. Most of the dreams I get, I find myself back home. Someone is trying to give me food, you know. Some bad dreams like that. But the one that bothers me the most is I'm fighting with people, you know. It might be like someone I know, maybe one of my brothers or cousins or friends will always appear in my dreams fighting me. That really bothers me, pains me."

I was moved by Sewa's confession and found it difficult to reconcile these dark images with the cavalier optimism he usually projected. "How are they fighting you?" I asked.

"Physically, sometimes, with a knife. Trying to stab me. I have to fight, you know."

I continued, "Are you afraid that when you go back to Sierra Leone people will try to stop you becoming chief?"

My question was off the mark, and Sewa laughed. But he knew what I was driving at, and how it related to what he had been saying moments before about the troubled chieftaincy in Diang. So he addressed the issue, even though it had no bearing on his dreams, assuring me that he would never let the malice or machinations of competitors shake the belief he inherited from his father or prevent him returning home to claim his birthright.

"Your brothers fighting you, is this *fadenye*?" I asked, alluding to the vexed relationship between half siblings in Mande societies that is particularly acrimonious when wealth or high office is at stake. "Well, of course," Sewa said patiently. "Fadenye is there. When you're from a ruling house everyone dreams of becoming chief, so . . . . But no one has shown that to me yet. Because of the way I was raised, I don't think that fadenye thing is a threat to me. It's not. It doesn't bother me."

"Then why are your brothers attacking you in your dream?"

"That's what I don't understand. The last time I phoned my mother I told her about the dreams I always get; I explained everything to her. I also phoned my blood brother Abu, told him about my dreams, the dreams about my stepbrothers, my friends, or different people fighting me. They said, 'All you need to do is pray,' so I am doing that prayer, you know."[1]

We had now reached the London Eye, and I was finding it more and more difficult to absorb or jot down everything Sewa was telling me. So after Sewa had persuaded a tourist to take a photo of us standing under the great wheel on Millennium Pier, I suggested we find a bench further along the Embankment and that I record some of his story on tape. I particularly wanted to understand the guilt that seemed to inform his dreams. Did Sewa, like so many migrants, feel uneasy about the fact that he had been lucky enough to find his way to England while his peers, no less deserving, were obliged to farm or languished in Freetown with no hope of employment and no real future? Was this distress compounded by his guilt at not having been able to return home for his uncle's funeral, and even the terrible arbitrariness of the war that he had survived and his cousin and companion Sheku had not? And then there were all the debts he had incurred in London and would never be able to repay.

The tide was turning, the Thames riding high on a brown flood tide, and as Sewa spoke into the microphone of my tape recorder I could not help but recall my own hardships during the winter of 1963 when I worked across the river in the London County Council Office for the Homeless under Hungerford Bridge (the old footbridge now replaced by the Golden Jubilee Bridge and no trace remaining of the Nissan Hut, where I interviewed so many lost souls). Like Sewa, I endured penury and homesickness. But while I led a much more solitary existence, I never experienced the extreme cultural disorientation that Sewa was at that very moment beginning to describe. Some of his recollections made us both laugh, like the new routines of courtship and seduction he had had to learn. "You got to make friends with the girls before you sleep with them," Sewa said, implying a comparison with Sierra Leone where gifts often secured sexual favors. By the time he met Ade he had changed his ways. He was working as a security guard at Pound Stretcher in Kentish Town, where Ade was a regular customer.

> So I remember one day she walked into the shop, and I said hello to her, and she said "Hi" [Sewa mimicked Ade's guarded tone of voice], you know. I asked her if she lived around there. I said, "Do you live locally?" She said, "No, I live at Angel." But she worked in Kentish Town [where she was a welfare worker in a seniors' home]. I said, "Oh, that's good." You know, I tried to "friend" her [Sewa laughed at the memory of self-consciously following local custom]. I said, "I'm Sewa, but I call myself S. B." She said, "S. B., what does that mean?" I tried to trick her. I said, "S. B. means so many things. S. B. means Sweet Boy!" Heh, heh, heh! She said, "Are you sure?" I said, "That's what it means—Sweet Boy. The S is for sweet or sugar, the B is for boy." So I tried to smooth her, to get her attention, you know. She was smiling. So I was quick to try to get her number. She said, "Oh sorry, I don't give out my number." I said, "That's fair enough; I'll give you my number." She said "No, I don't want your number. I'm not going to phone you. What's the point of me getting your number?" I said, "Well, fair enough, no problem." So I said, "All right, if you don't want to give me your number, that's fine, that's fair enough." She said, "But I'll be seeing you; I come to this shop all the time." Then she said, "I'm going on holiday in a week's time." I said, "How long are you going for?" She said she was going for a month or so. I said, "All right." So she went for the holiday for one month, two months, and during that time

I was sent to another shop, then back to the one in Kentish Town. When she came back from her holiday, I said "Oh, welcome, how was your holiday?" You know, I tried to give her some *nice* smooth talk, you know. "Did your holiday go well?" She said, "Yes, it was all right." So I asked her for her number again. She said to me, I remember, she asked me, "How old are you?" I said to her, "I am twenty-eight." She said, "Oh, a young boy!" I said, "Why?" She said, "I'm two or three years older than you." I said, "Two or three?" She said, "Three, I'm three years older than you." So I joked with her. I said, "No matter how big a truck or train, the driver will always drive it." We have a saying in Krio, you know. *However cow big nar soup.* You know what that means? No matter how big the cow, it'll fit into the pot [Sewa laughed]. Because they will chop it up and boil it down [laughter again]! So I said, "That's no problem, age is just a number, you know." So she gave me her telephone number. Heh, heh, heh!

Sewa went on to describe how he would phone Ade, chatting with her every day, wooing her with sweet words culled from some book on dating that he had picked up. "She didn't know I had this book. I was sending her these sweet words, these nice sweet texts, some lovely, lovely words, you know, and she kept asking me 'Where are you getting all those words?'" One day, Ade invited Sewa to her apartment. He arrived at the door, only to be reprimanded by Ade for having come empty handed. "That's their culture," Sewa explained. "You have to bring wine or something to drink. But I did not know. Back home, we don't have this system, the woman inviting you to her place. It was my first visit, so I was a bit quiet. She said, 'I can't believe that with all the texts and sweet talk you say over the phone, now you have nothing to say!' So I said, 'It's not like I'm quiet; it's my first time, you know.'"

I knew of Sewa's reputation as a philanderer, so I was not surprised that he had found his bearings in London by relying on his good looks, his gift of gab, and his winning ways with women. But though Ade was both a source of security and a guide on whom he could rely to steer a course through a bewildering world, Sewa's future seemed to me very uncertain.

After finishing our recording, we caught a bus to the Angel, met up with Ade and her sister Sarah, and walked to Ade's apartment where Sewa had been living for several months. As Sewa prepared a meal of rice with okra, chili, and sardines, he told me that he was teaching Ade how to cook African food. Though Ade's parents were from Nigeria, she had never visited Africa, and she harbored many typically European prejudices and misconceptions about African life. Sewa was determined to strike some sort of compromise. While willing to do "woman's work" in Britain, he did not want to take his wife back home and suffer the indignity of having to cook and wait on her in front of his family. Or have her eat with her left hand, or appear too forward and outspoken in the company of "Big Men." "When in Rome," I said with a laugh, and told Ade that such adjustments were something every anthropologist had to make if he or she was to find acceptance as a stranger in an African society. "You have to become a silent listener rather than an active participant," I said, "until you get your bearings." "I have a mind of my own," Ade said decisively. "I have no intention of living in the shadow of my husband."

As for Sewa, he had no intention of becoming British. And as the day went on, it became very clear to me that he was determined to return to Sierra Leone as soon as he could, and that Ade would go with him. In the meantime he would do what he had to do to survive in Britain. But the country remained alien to him, by turns baffling, irksome, and sinister.

As Sewa and I left Ade's house after lunch I noticed Ade's English neighbor and his son leaning on their gate and observing us intently. No words were exchanged, and it was only when we were out of earshot that Sewa asked irritably, "Why do they stare at us like that? Back home, I would confront them, I would tell them to stop. If they did not stop I would beat them. But here, you're in another man's land; they just stare at you like that and you can do nothing about it." Sewa was alluding to a Kuranko form of witchcraft called *ya yugo mé* (literally, "evil eye"): to stare at a pregnant woman would cause her pain in childbirth or prolong her labor. And it was widely thought that staring could destroy a person's prosperity.

Later that day, as I strolled back to my hotel, I found myself comparing Sewa's comments on the unflinching and minatory gaze of Ade's white neighbors with the intense preoccupation among the peoples of the Upper Guinea Coast with what Mariane Ferme has called "the underneath of things" and "a hermeneutic of suspicion" (2001:1–8)—

the hidden evil in the world around you that finds dramatic expression in the clandestine activities of witches and the conspiracies of enemies, as well as the oneiric images of black hearts behind white teeth, impenetrable forests and swamps, blocked paths and murky waters.[2] And I remembered how I felt when I first went to live in Firawa, with little grasp of the language and ignorant of local protocols—the disorientation that made me so wary and anxious, not knowing what people were saying about me or when some slight misjudgment on my part would jeopardize my already tenuous situation in the village or oblige me to leave. Is it always true that when we feel powerless and vulnerable we tend to take everything personally, as if others had nothing else on their minds but our foibles and failings?

The following morning I walked from my hotel near Paddington to Speakers' Corner and into Hyde Park. Rain had cleared the air, and I sat for a while under some plane trees writing up notes from the day before and listening to the muted roar of traffic along Park Lane, crows quarreling on the grass, and cyclists ticking by on their way to the West End. But my thoughts were of Sewa's precarious situation. Whenever I had spoken to him on the phone from Copenhagen, he would say how hard it was making ends meet in London, but he never suggested that I might help him financially or admitted to feeling beleaguered or lost. Rather, he would enthusiastically look forward to seeing me and telling me his stories. But I had not bargained for the kind of story he had had in mind.

After meeting Sewa at the Victoria bus station, we boarded a bus to Peckham and immediately resumed the conversation we had begun yesterday. It was almost like being back in Kondembaia, listening to a Kuranko storyteller: the same narrative verve and ludic skill, the same stoic bemusement in the face of life's adversity.

"When I was in Sierra Leone," Sewa began, "I was just thinking when you get to Europe or overseas that's it!" and he laughed at the absurdity of his assumption that everything would be easy, that everything would fall into place.

I had completely the wrong idea. To get my visa back home, that was one step. But when you get into the place you really understand what it is, you know. When I went to the British High Commission in Freetown for my interview, I met this consul called John. He says to me, "Mr. Koroma, you'll get your visa, but make sure that after six months you go and renew the visa." I said, "All right" and traveled to London, where I had to enroll at the London College of Accountancy. I had wanted to study automotive engineering, but accountancy was the only thing they would give me a visa for. So I went there, and that's when my troubles began. They said to me, "Mr. Koroma, before you start your course you have to pay another nine hundred pounds." Do you know what nine hundred pounds means? —what it means to raise nine hundred pounds? I went to my sister Aminatta. She found the money for me. I will never be able to pay my sister back. Only God will bless her. Up to now I feel guilty that I have not been able to help my sister. I feel bad about it. I know how hard it was for her to raise that nine hundred pounds. So I paid that money and started classes.

Sewa found work cleaning toilets in the Mandarin Oriental Hotel in Knightsbridge for four pounds an hour. But his Nigerian supervisor exploited the newcomer's powerlessness and inexperience, ordering him to do extra work that included cleaning the supervisor's own room. Mystified by the fastidious and, to Sewa, obsessive standards of cleanliness demanded by the Mandarin Oriental, as well as confused as to whose orders he should follow, he soon found himself doing the wrong job at the wrong time (polishing the brass nameplate outside the hotel) and was sacked. He then found work as a security guard at Tescos in Kennington, exchanging a "dirty" job for a "boring" one. But whatever employment he found, there was a limit set by the Home Office as to how much a migrant with a student visa could earn, and Sewa was desperately short of money. That December, six months after arriving in Britain, he had to apply to the Home Office for an extension to his visa. The cost was 250 pounds. Moreover, he had to pay half of his college fees (another 500 pounds) and come up with 200 pounds for the rent of the shared room in his sister's flat. Once again he borrowed from friends, including his girlfriend at the time, Stephanie. But money was only part of his worries. His uncle and sponsor, S. B. Marah, had died a few weeks before. "Doubt was in my mind," Sewa said. "I wasn't able to see my uncle. I wasn't able to go to the burial [in Freetown]. Sad, you know. I was having all these problems in my head." Without a letter and bank statement from a sponsor, he could not hope to get an extension on his visa.

I had to go out, find people, go out, beg people, beg people. I was lucky to meet C. D., my cousin Aisetta's boyfriend. He gave me his bank statement. So I took this to the Home Office with all my documents, my results from college, the letter from my college, receipts, everything. I went to the counter and this West Indian man called Fidel Castro [Sewa laughed as he remembered the nickname he had given the official], he's called Fidel . . . so I hand over my papers, you know, and then the man looks at my sponsorship letter, the bank statement . . . the balance is twenty pounds. The man looks at me. He says, "Mr. Koroma, did you check all your documents before you came to this place?" I said "Yes." He said, "Are you sure?" I said, "Yeah." He said, "Mr. Koroma, are you sure? I'm sorry, but I don't think so." And he brings out this statement. He says the minimum they will accept is two thousand pounds. "If your sponsor has a balance of ten pounds, how could that man support you and support himself?" I was in tears. I said to the man, I said, "Really, this man is only trying to help me. My sponsor was my uncle, but he passed away a month ago. I used his bank statement when I got my visa, but now he has passed away, I could not get his bank statement." The man said, "OK, your excuse is valid." So they extended my visa. But I tell you, Mr. Michael, it was hard, it was really hard. Living in London without having the correct stay papers, you're in trouble. This is what makes England hard, overseas hard, this paperwork. That's why I'm working hard, doing my studies, doing the right thing, trying to sort myself out. I don't want to get into trouble, because I am thinking all the time, if you're living here illegally, as an illegal immigrant, and your mum or a relative passes away there's no way you can travel. They don't check you when you're going out, no one checks you then, no one cares. The only thing is your ticket, not your passport. But here, living here as an illegal immigrant you are living in fear, fear of no life. These are the things that make this place really hard for people, I mean people living underground.

What struck me was that although Sewa *had* a valid visa, he experienced himself as someone whose validity was constantly in question, constantly under suspicion. He could never take his residency for granted. He seemed to live in imminent danger of being found out, of making some inadvertent yet irreversible mistake, of being picked up by the police and deported. There was something dreadfully nonnegotiable about his situation. In Sierra Leone, one's destiny was determined by a network of face-to-face relationships with people to whom one was obliged or who were under obligation to oneself, people who in local parlance one could "beg" or from whom one could borrow money, expect a meal, or a roof over one's head. But in London, Sewa discovered that he had passed from a patrimonial to a bureaucratic regime in which power seemed to reside less in people to whom one could appeal than in an impersonal force field that found expression in a stranger's stare, a policeperson's orders, a supervisor's demands, or the letter of the law. In this inscrutable and Kafkaesque world of bureaucratic protocols, indecipherable documents, abstract rules, and official forms of validation, Sewa came up against what Michael Herzfeld has called "a politics of indifference." Or, as Arendt puts it, the "living spirit" of community had given ground to the "dead letter" of a system that recognized no one because it was nobody (Arendt 1958:95, 169).

Even Sewa's relationship with Ade became entangled in red tape and Home Office regulations. On Ade's initiative, they had approached the Home Office to find out what was required if Ade, a British citizen, was to marry a foreigner. "They asked where the foreigner was from," Sewa said.

> She told them, "Sierra Leone." "What kind of visa does he have?" She told them, "A student visa." They said, "We'll send you the form." We filled it out. I had to have a visa that was valid for at least six months. I was lucky; I had nine months left on my visa. So we put the form and the fee of 150 pounds in an envelope and posted it to the Home Office. They told us that if they did not approve the marriage, the money would not be refunded. I said, "All right." Three weeks later—no, one week—they wrote to say they had received our form. They had to do some cross-checking; in three weeks' time they would get back to us. So in three weeks they wrote to say that they had approved the marriage, but the marriage would have to take place before a certain date. But how can they choose the date you get married? They just gave us a date; we had to be married within that time or else it would not be valid. They gave us one month and two weeks to get married. So when we received the form, I had already proposed to Ade, got the rings, the wedding ring, the engagement ring. And, you, Mr. Michael, are the one who is going to do this *namfule* thing for us now [I had agreed to pay the "bridewealth" that a young man's father would traditionally pay the bride's family to seal the marriage].

Perhaps the worst fate that can befall any human being is to be stripped of the power to play any part in deciding the course of his or her life, to be rendered passive before impersonal forces he or she cannot comprehend and with which he or she cannot negotiate. Under such circumstances, some people fight desperately to regain some sense of being in control, while others submit fatalistically to the situation that has overwhelmed them—having recourse to flight, camouflage, or avoidance. Whatever one's response—action or inaction, confrontation or avoidance—one's *experience* of one's situation will tend to be intensified and exaggerated. To put it simply, one becomes in one's own eyes a hero or victim. As Sewa and I traveled across London, I was struck by the heroic imagery in the press. Londoners would not be intimidated by terrorists. As it was in the blitz, so it was now: people would not allow the bombers to bring their city to a standstill. But this defiance and "stubborn resilience" was easy for those who had not suffered or lost loved ones in the terrorist attacks, and I could not help but observe that Sewa, who knew only too well the terror of war, showed no bravado but only a desire to avoid and appease.

By now, the police hunt for the would-be suicide bombers was being described in the papers as "the greatest operational challenge" in the history of Scotland Yard. Six thousand officers, half of them armed with MP5 submachine guns and Glock 17 pistols were patrolling Tube and railways stations and city squares. All this only intensified Sewa's anxieties. "It makes me remember the war," he said. He then told me about the only occasion he had gone to the cinema. An action movie was playing, and his girlfriend at the time insisted they see it. But Sewa could not stand the noise of explosions, gunfire, and car crashes, and he had had to leave the cinema. As for the police presence on the streets, it rattled him rather than made him feel secure. As our bus slowly made its way south, Sewa pointed out a red police car to me. "That's the city police," he said, "they really lay on you, no mercy." And as another police car worked its way through the stalled traffic, its siren wail sounding to my ears like "We You We You We You," Sewa informed me that in southeast London, Sierra Leoneans interpret the siren sound as "Where dem? Where dem? Where dem?" since the police are constantly on the lookout for illegal immigrants. The police also went by a variety of names, Sewa explained. They were known as

"Routine Check" for a while, but as soon as the police got wise to this nickname, it was replaced by the allegedly "Nigerian" word *orobo*. "You have to avoid them," Sewa said, though it was not always possible to avoid eye contact. "Sometimes you don't know where to look. You look at them, they'll get angry and do a routine check on you; you look away and try to move away from them, they'll think you've got something to hide, that you're running away, and they'll make you stand there while they run a check on you again."

I did not know what Sewa had to be afraid of. After all, he had a valid student visa and took great pains to stay on the right side of the law. "Why," I asked, "do the police make you so nervous?" It was not always possible to remain within the law and earn enough money to survive, Sewa explained, and he described one of his most harrowing run-ins with the Metropolitan Police. He was in a car with his half brother Junisa and his cousin Ibrahim. Junisa was driving, even though his license had been suspended after three speeding offences and for using an illegal speed camera detector. They were stopped by police. A routine check. Junisa lost no time in leaping into the backseat with Ibrahim and Sewa, Sewa having taken Junisa's infant daughter onto his knee to make more room. When the police officers approached and asked them to identify the driver and owner of the vehicle, Junisa told them that the driver had run off. The police then demanded to know their names and dates of birth. Sewa was by now perspiring and trembling with fear. In his pocket was a payroll stub showing that he had worked for more than the legally permitted twenty hours that week. The police searched his bag. On finding his security guard uniform in the bag, one of the police officers informed Sewa that it was illegal to work on a student visa. Sewa explained that he was permitted to work up to twenty hours a week, to which the police officer replied, "We will check with your college and the Home Office." At the police station, Sewa and the others were obliged to watch CCTV footage that showed no evidence of a driver leaving the car and fleeing the scene. Junisa was subsequently convicted and sent to prison. Ibrahim was fined for obstructing justice. Sewa got off with a reprimand, but felt he was lucky not to have been deported.

"You seem to be able to elude the police, just like you eluded the RUF," I said. "They call me Slippery," Sewa said, and laughed before telling me a story to prove his point. He had been working at a Pound Saver store at the time. One morning he was folding clothes on a display table when two policemen approached and asked if he worked there. Fearing complications if he said yes, he told them they should ask at reception, giving the impression he was just an innocent customer.

We had now reached Camberwell Green, and as I followed Sewa off the bus and through the crowd, Sewa was telling me that the "bendy buses" only operated on routes into the largely black neighborhoods of the southeast, the reason being that the relative openness of these buses allowed people to enter or exit the rear doors without a valid ticket. The police checked these buses frequently on the pretext that they were looking for fare-dodgers. But they were really looking for illegal immigrants, Sewa said; the "bendy buses" were "traps to catch illegals," and he mentioned two Sierra Leoneans who had been caught the previous week and sent home.

Our immediate destination was Bockarie's shop on Camberwell Road. Bockarie was my late friend S. B.'s half brother, and he sold African music, clothing, books, and magazines, as well as access to Internet services. When we entered the shop the only customers were a couple of Sierra Leonean girls on one of the PCs. Bockarie's son Junisa was behind the counter doing some paperwork, and after Sewa had introduced us, Junisa showed me the copies of some of my Sierra Leonean books that were for sale in the shop. I signed a couple of copies of *Barawa* at Junisa's request, and he asked me if it was easy to write a book and get it published. He had a diploma in business management but was keen to write about the reckless life he had led as a teenager, hoping this would be an example to younger people of what not to do. After exchanging e-mail addresses, I asked Junisa if he had any recent music from Freetown; Sewa had been telling me about a couple of bands, and I would have liked to hear them. It turned out that Junisa did not have these particular CDs in stock, but Elvis could take us to a place where we could buy them.

"Elvis" was the sobriquet of a man in his late forties or early fifties who had, moments before, appeared from the back of the shop. His trousers were frayed, his teeth broken, and his breath stank of rum. His real name was Mohammed. He had fetched up in London fifteen years ago and had no intention of returning home. As he led Sewa and me along Camberwell Road, he poured scorn on his homeland and excoriated Britain with equal contempt. We soon came to a block of Council flats, where Elvis took us to a locked grill door. "Sisay!" he shouted. A man wearing a white singlet came to the door and peered at us suspiciously. "What do you want?" he asked. Elvis explained our business, but Cedric was not satisfied, and it took a lot more explaining from Elvis before Cedric unlocked the door and ushered us into a narrow corridor where we edged past a large Sierra Leonean woman sitting on a bag of rice before arriving at Cedric's room. The room was filled from floor to ceiling with shelves of CDs and all manner of electronic gear—video and DVD players, fax machines, copiers, microphones, CD burners, and boxes of imported CDs from various West African countries. It was now obvious why Cedric had been so cagey about admitting us: he produced pirated copies of videos and CDs for sale to African immigrants in London.

After Cedric had brought cold Pepsis for Sewa and me and a can of Guinness for Elvis, I explained what I was looking for—copies of some of the latest reggae, rap, and hi-life music from Freetown. It turned out that Cedric had several selections. I could buy three for ten pounds. And he immediately began playing me some tracks, his face beaming with pleasure and his gold teeth glinting as he turned up the volume. Indeed, he was so stirred by the beat that he kept rising from his dilapidated office chair and dancing on the floor space that was covered with half-opened cartons and recording equipment. When I had chosen three CDs, Cedric inserted the first in his burner and started the copying process. With the music switched off, I asked him to tell me how long he had been in London. It was a sad story that corroborated some of the things Sewa had been telling me about the difficulty of living within the law when work was so hard to find and racial prejudice endemic in every workplace.

"Never ask Africans what job they do," Cedric began.

It is too embarrassing for them to say what kind of work they do. You just don't ask. People say, "I di go work now," but they don't mention what kind of work they're going to. We do all the dirty work. The work no one else wants to do. It's a waste of time looking for anything better. If you go try, they look at your visa, they look at your black face, they hear your accent, and they turn you away. You know, we have that saying in Krio? You eyes don take load. You know what that means? Your eyes don't carry a load, but they can see if a load is too heavy to carry. So if you're from Africa, you quickly see what you can do here and what you can't do. Let me show you.

Cedric rummaged in one of his desk drawers and brought out a sheaf of papers, among them several diplomas from various courses in maintenance and engineering that he had successfully completed. "At first, they would say I had to have qualifications. Now they say I am over-qualified or too old."

As I examined Cedric's impressive cv, he recounted how he was attacked by shoplifters several years ago and his back broken. This made it additionally difficult for him to find work.

I am not prejudiced, but I will tell you a story. I was working at Tescos as a security guard. The alarm broke down. Three times it broke down and three times a specialist electrician was called to fix it. The fourth time I told the electrician what he should do to get it working again. Because I had a diploma; I knew electrics. So the electrician took my advice and left. Said nothing. No thanks, nothing. You see, it makes you angry. It makes you upset. But you can do nothing about it. You just have to keep trying.

And Cedric showed me a printed e-mail he had received that morning. It gave the time and address where he should go for an interview tomorrow morning. "I will go," Cedric said. "But as soon as the employer sees that I am not only black but an African, with an African accent, he will tell me I am overqualified and too old for the job." "Would you have any prospects if you went back home?" I asked. Cedric laughed: "What is there there?"

Later, after we left Cedric's flat and said good-bye to Elvis, Sewa said he did not want to risk ever winding up like these two men. "You have to get out of here," he said, "or else you will die. You will be just like Mohammed. They don't go back. They don't keep in touch. But one day, when he's no good, even as Bockarie's errand boy or Cedric's errand boy, they'll put him on a plane and send him home. He'll have nothing. No one will know him. He'll go crazy. That's what lies ahead of you if you stay here, if you never get out."

At the end of the day, after writing up my scribbled notes and recollections in the quiet of my hotel room, I struggled to find the right words for Sewa's sense of unease, uncertainty, and wariness. Some of his anxieties seemed to relate to his war experiences, as if the unreal and labyrinthine city through which he moved was like the nightmarish landscapes through which he had traveled after his capture by the rebels. "You're in another man's land," he had explained to me. "You never know when they [the police] are going to grab you. They'll offer you a free ticket home. You're gone. Just like that." In this city of pitfalls, ambushes, and hidden dangers there was, however, one place where one could let one's guard down and find some sense of security and homeliness. Of Peckham—with its Money Transfer shops, with its stores in which one could rent African videos, with its green grocers selling palm oil and cassava leaf and speaking Krio—Sewa had said, "This place full na we; we govern this place." Sierra Leoneans referred to Peckham as Kru Town Road after an old quarter of Freetown, and a well-known night spot was called Pardi's, after Paddy's Beach Bar on Freetown's Aberdeen Road.[3] "That's our ground," Sewa said. "That's the place we not scared. The southeast is our stronghold." But outside this neighborhood one had to be vigilant. Just as Sierra Leoneans had evolved their own argot—referring to a Sierra Leonean passport as "potato leaf" (because of its dark green color) and to a residence permit or stay as "leather" (because it is harder to get and more valuable than a passport) —so they disguised their appearance to avoid becoming targets of local gangs or the police. In Freetown, young men wear American-style basketball trainers; in London, they prefer the trainers, hooded jackets, and baggy trousers that young black Londoners wear. "You have to be in the system or else . . . ," Sewa told me, explaining that local black gangs often picked on newcomers from West Africa, aggressively demanding, "Wot ya got on ya?" and expecting immediate payment.[4] Sewa's tactic was to mimic the cockney "Wot?" and use it repeatedly in response to the locals, hoping they would be fooled into thinking he was one of them and leave him alone.

No doubt many of these tactics of changing one's appearance, hiding one's identity, keeping a low profile, and using a secret language with those one knows and trusts are defense ruses that have a phylogenetic basis. But this tells us very little about the experiential context in which they are deployed—what it feels like to be constantly on the defensive, or how real external dangers become translated into imagined fears. Anyone who has moved from a familiar lifeworld and gone to live in a place where he or she is a complete stranger, linguistically inept, economically insecure, and socially stigmatized will immediately identify with Sewa's intense self-consciousness—the suspicion that people were staring at him, that he was under surveillance, that he was somehow in the wrong, without rights or any legitimate identity—though not everyone would share his preoccupation with the power of the police to send him back to his country of origin with no possibility of return, so ending once and for all his dream of improving his lot in life. It was not that Sewa was seeking validation; rather, he was doing everything in his power to avoid the people, situations, and incidents that made him feel as though he was a worthless nobody. In a recent book I have argued that human existence plays out as a constant struggle to maximize one's inner recourses or capacities, on the one hand, and to avail oneself of the external affordances of one's environment, on the other (2005:xiv–xv). What I admired about Sewa was his capacity for making the most of an environment that not only offered limited opportunities but also constantly crossed and humiliated him. That his inner strength had been derived from his mother and father was very clear to him. They were, as put it, his very life ("ni le wola"). To speak of someone as "being my life" or "being the world to me" is to imply that one's own destiny is never simply in one's own hands; it is determined by one's relationships with significant others and by the ways in which they reflect and care for one, even after they have passed away. In sending his mother photos of himself against the backdrop of the Houses of Parliament, Sewa hoped to inspire in her a validating response, in the same way that enunciating Qur'anic suras, learned from his father, would end his nightmares and assuage his fears.

At such moments, I was mindful of René Devisch's powerful ethnographic accounts of the Yaka (southwest Congo) conceptions of health (*-kola*) and wellbeing (*-syaamuna*) as flowing from a person's vital relationship with a web of forces (*mooyi*) that includes kinship and community, as well as the ancestral realm. Though this realm is largely beyond ordinary understanding, Yaka aver that the source of life is ultimately maternal and that the most critical relationships in any person's life are with uterine kin. Blockages and disruptions in this flow of

— anyone would expect the similar emotions under same circumstances.

forces cause sickness and insanity. So does displacement—and as Devisch shows, maternal images figure as points of anchorage and consolation for migrant youth in the disorienting world of the city, offering them the hope of spiritual connectiveness and renewal (Devisch 1995).

In many ways, Sewa's situation resembled the situation of these young Yaka men in Kinshasa, for whom matrixial images and sexual attachments were imagined as ways out of the wilderness in which they found themselves adrift. Among strangers, who Sewa simply called "those people" ("dem people"), one could expect nothing but indifference, disparagement, or outright menace. "They shame me" (An ya na moliya), Sewa would say; "they make me feel small" (an ya na dogoye). Thus constant exposure to a negative social environment will easily lead one to feel under attack, fearful of ostracism or deportation, and prey to a nagging guilt that the price of one's own improved chances in life is the loss of one's homeland, of one's kith and kin, and of one's heritage. At the same time, the impossibility of being accepted into the society in which one has sought asylum translates into a sense that one is worthless, that one is good for nothing, that one is doomed.

Sewa's experiences made him unusually sensitive to the plight of other migrants. One day on Oxford Street, for example, he observed a young African girl appealing, with obvious desperation, to passers-by for help. Repeating one word, *phone*, she could not make herself understood, and people were ignoring or avoiding her. Sewa asked her what she wanted. Quickly realizing that she could not speak English, he tried every other language he knew, including Mandingo. Unbelievably, the girl was a Mandingo from Guinea. Incredulous and overjoyed, she explained that she and her sister had student visas but were penniless and knew no English. Sewa phoned his sister Aisha, arranged for the Guineans to stay there for a while, and helped them find the kind of cleaning jobs he had done a year before. Another time, when working as a security guard at a Wandsworth department store, he noticed that a certain man came to the store every day and spent some time browsing and trying on clothing before leaving without having made a purchase. His suspicions aroused, Sewa carefully monitored the CCTV and observed that the man appeared to have gained a great deal of weight since entering the store. Sewa confronted him at the checkout counter and asked the man, who was from the Congo, why he was sweating

› helping each other out

profusely when the day was so cold. With the skill of a Kuranko story-teller, Sewa exploited the comic possibilities of the situation. "You are really sweating. But the heating is off, and it is really cold in here. Are you well? You are the only person sweating in the whole store. Maybe you are sick. Do you need a doctor? Do you need medicines?" Realizing he was trapped, the man was perspiring not only because of the extra layers of garments he was wearing—five pullovers and two overcoats—but from fear. The Nigerian store manager arrived on the scene, and Sewa explained how he had observed this customer gain an extraordinary amount of weight since entering the store. As the store manager prepared to call the police, the shoplifter fell to his knees and started to cry. He implored Sewa not to turn him in. He was an illegal immigrant. He would be deported. It would be the end of him; it would be a death sentence. Sewa told the man to stand up and stop crying. He then walked to the store manager's office, explained the shoplifter's plight, and prevailed on the store manager not to call the police. The call was not made, and the Congolese man was allowed to leave the store, still wearing the stolen clothes, vowing he would never return, not even to Wandsworth.

If sympathy for others in a situation similar to one's own is one consequence of hardship, preoccupation with one's own plight is, paradoxically, another. Suffering, like physical pain, narrows the scope of what one can take in, what one can deal with. One sees the world solely from the standpoint of one's own struggles. Accordingly, one identifies readily with those who share one's own hardships while tending to see others as aliens if not adversaries. Hence the dependency, gratitude, and idealization focused on those who offer support, salvation, and sympathy, and the vilification of those that vex and humiliate—dem people.

Within days of leaving London I was on my way to the United States and a new job at Harvard. Inevitably, I experienced something of the disorientation and despair that Sewa had described to me so vividly, though, in retrospect, I would remember it as ludicrous and absurd. Minutes after arriving in Boston, I was told in no uncertain terms by an immigration officer that my old Green Card should have been turned in to the U.S. authorities when it expired seven years ago; my failure to do this constituted "a problem, a serious problem." I protested that I *had* relinquished my card in Copenhagen when I interviewed for my new Green Card. Why then, had I not signed a document to this effect, so that immigration in the United States could see that I had indeed given up the old card? As my wife and children watched with growing concern and bewilderment, I was instructed to follow the officer downstairs to passport control where, after a long wait, I was interviewed by another officer, even more officious than the first, who lectured me on the importance of rules and regulations and on how they existed for a reason. Irregularities simply could not be ignored. I was then grilled on why I insisted on saying that I had not signed any document in Copenhagen when I turned in my expired card and was asked repeatedly if and when I had visited the United States during the past eight years and for what reason. Finally, I was told I would be "let off with a caution" and "given a year." "So in a year's time I reapply for my Green Card?" I asked fecklessly, hoping to give the impression of complete respect for, and abject dependency on, the officer's greater knowledge. It was uncanny, I thought, as I rejoined my family, how instinctively one seeks to appease the powers that be, avoiding any remark or action that might appear to question their authority or challenge their power. And I thought of Sewa's tactics for avoiding the police and slipping invisibly through the net that, in his eyes, was ceaselessly trawling for those who were not *en règle*.

I also found myself pondering the difference between what Charles Bukowski calls "ordinary madness"—those myriad miseries and mystifications of existence that vex but do not destroy us—and those experiences that so overwhelm us that we completely lose our hold on life.

It is, of course, misguided to assert that certain experiences of separation and loss are *in their very nature* more unbearable than others. Much depends on an individual's inner resources or on what his or her external environment offers by way of support and care. Much also depends on a person's previous experience of loss, and the values that have been instilled in him or her. In Sierra Leone, suffering is seen as an unavoidable part of life. Though one imagines a better life, a fairer lot, one is taught to stoically accept the inevitability of hardship. What matters most is how one endures it. Sewa possessed this kind of fortitude and patience, and he had known loss. But he was totally un-

Bukowski—ordinary madness

prepared for the bureaucratization of everyday life in Europe, the impersonality of its cities, the nonnegotiability of one's relationship with the law, and the very different ethos governing relationships between men and women. This was what exasperated him and fed his paranoia, for it is generally true that when the world refuses our efforts to interact with it on social and reciprocal terms it becomes, in our imaginations, a locus of minatory power. During Kuranko initiations, for example, the heightened fear of witchcraft undoubtedly arises from people's loss of control over the fate of their children and from anxieties over whether or not their sons or daughters will successfully survive the grueling ordeals to which they must submit. Something similar occurs with migrants and refugees. One readily falls prey to fears that forces, named or unknown, are conspiring against one when, in reality, it is simply one's powerlessness and estrangement that produces this erosion of self-confidence, this pervasive sense of shame, persecution, and smallness. The foci of Sewa's anxieties were, of course, the police and black English gangs. As in comparable situations, the paranoid preoccupation itself generates the effects attributed to external agents.[5] Thus the greater the amount of intellectual labor expended on the minatory object, the more vulnerable, trapped, worthless, and unreal one feels oneself to be. This process is directly analogous to Marx's concept of alienation (*Entäusserung*):

> The worker puts his life into the object; but now his life no longer belongs to him but to the object. Hence, the greater this activity, the greater is the worker's lack of objects. Whatever the product of his labour is, he is not. Therefore the greater this product, the less is he himself. The *alienation* of the worker in his product means not only that his labour becomes an object, an *external* existence, but that it exists *outside him*, independently, as something alien to him, and that it becomes a power on its own confronting him; it means that the life which he has conferred on the object confronts him as something hostile and alien. (1961:70; emphasis original)

What is the threshold of tolerance, the breaking point, for any individual, beyond which adversity comes to be experienced as unbearable, hope is abandoned, and he or she can no longer seize the day. This point would seem to be determined, first, by the sheer weight of the world—its unresponsiveness to one's presence or one's voice, and its obdurate refusal to acknowledge one's needs, let alone one's aspirations. Second, it is determined by the extent to which an individual falls prey to the thoughts, imaginings, and self-fulfilling prophecies that are born of his or her frustrated efforts to speak or act. Such, it would seem, was the fate of Mohammed who, at least in Sewa's eyes, had not only lost touch with his homeland and given up on the possibility of making a life for himself in Britain but who had allowed himself to fall into decay, losing his dignity as a man and seeking refuge in cheap booze, a victim of his own cynicism. Yet Cedric, despite the rejection and prejudice he had encountered, persevered in his search for legitimate employment and clearly felt ashamed at having to resort to underground work in order to survive. So it was neither complete success nor complete failure that characterized the lives of the Sierra Leoneans I met in London, but rather compromise—a balance struck between the gains one hoped to make for oneself and one's children and the losses one would sustain in doing so.

My old friend S. B.'s daughter Isata and her family lived in a newly built townhouse in Lee. During the afternoon I spent with her and her two young children, Munah and Kalil, we talked about the difficulty of keeping alive the dream of returning home to live while meeting the demands of the life one had chosen to live abroad. Isata had a well-paying position in one of London's most prestigious private banking houses and commuted to the city every weekday, leaving her children in the care of a live-in help, Fodiya, who also hailed from Freetown. Despite success in her job (she was the first black woman to be employed in the bank), Isata spoke of the emptiness of the lives of many of her colleagues, most of who were single and spent their earnings in restaurants and bars, or on holidays abroad. She missed the social vitality of Freetown, the daily encounters with family and friends, the ebullient greetings, the humor and eventfulness of everyday life. But then, she said, there was the poverty of Freetown, the lack of any infrastructure, the corruption in government, and the fact that things seemed to be getting worse, not better. Late that afternoon, Fodiya's brother-in-law dropped in on a quick visit. He listened closely as Isata continued to talk about the life she missed in Sierra Leone, and the bungalow she and her husband were building at Hill Station. "I don't want to be here in ten years' time," she said. "I want to be back in Freetown. And it's not because I want to go back and make a difference; it's because my heart is there. I'm Sierra Leonean. When I come home from work I change into Sierra Leonean clothes, prepare Sierra Leonean food. At home we speak Krio. I'm not British and I don't want to be. They would never accept me here anyway."

Fodiya's brother-in-law seemed unimpressed by Isata's nostalgia and declared that he had no intention of ever returning home to live. His arguments were pragmatic. Here in Britain he was making good money; back home he would be out of work. Even if he was gainfully employed, his family and friends would burden him with their demands. In Sierra Leone, moreover, he would have no pension against his old age, no health care, nothing. And he chided Isata for her sentimentality, which, he argued, would not last a day if she were living in Freetown in penury. But Isata was no idealist, and she explained that when, some years ago, her father had persuaded the Bank of Sierra Leone to offer her a senior position, she turned it down, telling the bank she simply could not support herself and her family on the salary. The bank pointed out that she would make ten times the official salary by doing favors and receiving kickbacks. Her response: she could not live that way; she could neither accept nor bring herself to participate in underhand practices.

When I met S. B.'s sons, Abu and Chelmanseh, both of whom had married English women, I heard similar stories. Though they had made lives for themselves in Britain and had well-paying jobs, they missed Sierra Leone. This was where they felt at home, and had every right to be. This was the place that had nourished and shaped them; this was irrevocably the place that defined who they really were.

Traveling back to my hotel one night on the Tube, I got to thinking how, in a cold and an inhospitable social environment, one not only withdraws into oneself but also seeks the company of one's own kind. The first-generation migrant lives a life apart, a ghettoized existence, avoiding the risk of humiliation among strangers and falling back on the familiar world of fellow expatriates. Only gradually does one expand one's circle, and then only to those in similar situations. But even as one's world becomes cosmopolitan, it remains marginal to the mainstream culture.

My train of thought was interrupted by a drunken Yorkshireman loudly lecturing a European tourist on English football teams, telling him which one he should follow and citing all manner of slurred statistics on the past performances of competing clubs. I was reminded of the previous summer in Zurich when I had watched, with a group of students from the C. R. Jung Institute, some of the final games in the UEFA European Football Championship—the Netherlands versus Latvia, and Germany versus the Czech Republic. These games had followed Italy's loss to Bulgaria the day before, a loss that had inspired bitter recriminations in the Italian press and even rumors of game fixing. An Italian Canadian in our group confessed to being deeply distressed and said he had been on medication all day. At first I thought he was joking, but as others arrived in the TV room—a Swede, a German, a Swiss, a French woman, and an American woman—and everyone began to banter about who he or she was "going for" and whose nation had been beaten, I became increasingly fascinated by the passionate nationalism that in the course of that night would find expression on the faces of thousands of German fans—stunned, pale, tearful, and open-mouthed—not knowing where to look or what to do as their defeated side wandered solemnly from the field. Two months later, when China lost to Japan in Beijing's Workers' Stadium, it was as though the traumatic events of the 1930s and 1940s were being replayed, and again my thoughts turned to this powerful and magical confluence of subjectivities—the first individual, the second national—that will bring people to life one minute—chanting, singing, shouting in unison—and the next render them bereft, ashamed, and inconsolable. People need extensions of themselves, borrowing a second self or second skin from a cause, a club, a national symbol like a flag, or enlarging their sense of self with beer, belligerence, and being in a crowd. The human imagination is, to use Freud's phrase, "polymorphous perverse." It is a migrant form of consciousness that is constantly seeking some object that will give the isolated ego a sense of greater power and presence. One will feel good about oneself on the strength of the clothes or cosmetics one puts on, the car one drives, the house one owns, the club or congregation to which one belongs, the body one builds, the food or drink one consumes, the things, families, or friends one has. If the migrant appears to put an inordinate effort into acquiring and displaying what he or she perceives to be the crucial symbolic capital of the host culture, or seems to cling to the customs of the culture left behind, it is because he or she confronts every day the experience of being drained and diminished, cut down, made to feel small, reduced to a state of what Giorgio Agamben calls "bare life." Perhaps this was the key to Sewa's nightmares. The image of his brothers' fighting him was in fact an image of the struggle within him, between two incompatible modalities of being, the first seen as retrograde and unfulfilling, the second as filled with uncertain possibilities. But this is not to say that migrants are the only ones engaged in the struggle to sustain or augment their being-in-the-world. Long before migration and education became the preferred way of enlarging one's horizons, Kuranko social imaginaries embraced, especially among the powerless, all manner of ideas as to how to gain the wherewithal denied them in their everyday existence. Although the dutiful performance of one's assigned role, the acceptance of one's lot, and the authority of the past have always been valorized, a tension nonetheless exists between what is given and what is desired. A young wife, harassed by her senior cowife or spurned by her husband; an orphan child feeling unfairly treated by his stepparents; a young man denigrated by his father or elder brother—these are, if Kuranko folktales provide any measure of the fantasy life of those hard done by, the typical situations in which the imagination seizes on the possibilities of the bush: a domain lying beyond the village where demonic "distributors of being" such as djinni, tricksters, and supernatural agents may transform the fortunes of those in despair and produce a fairer distribution of that which makes life worthwhile—recognition, status, fine clothes, wealth, or simply love.

There has been a gradual shift in the Kuranko social imaginary from the early twentieth century, when people began to entertain transformations that involved journeys beyond one's own parochial borders and an openness to a future that compromised the past. Traditional societies are so-called because they "deny history" (the phrase is Mircea Eliade's); it is the ancestral past that defines what is of value, and it is an ethic of duty that decrees that each person faithfully respect time-honored protocols. To depart from these is to take one's life into one's own hands. But as Sewa observed, though not in so many words, farming is a dead-end job; there is no future in it. The life of the farmer implies a reversion to and a repetition of time past; one reproduces life but produces nothing new. Behind Sewa's prejudice against farming was a preoccupation with creating a life that did not follow the precepts and precedents of the past, a life in which time was claimed for oneself and one's own lifetime was considered apart from the life of one's society. Such an openness to the future was both exhilarating and terrifying.

Marx observed that regardless of historical circumstances and independent of its location in the private or public realm, labor power (*Arbeitskraft*) "possesses a 'productivity' of its own, no matter how futile and non-durable its products may be" (Arendt 1958:88). Commenting on Marx's observation, Hannah Arendt writes that productivity "does not lie in any of labor's products but in the human 'power', whose strength is not exhausted when it has produced the means of its own subsistence and survival but is capable of producing a 'surplus', that is, more than is necessary for its own 'reproduction'" (1958:88). It is this critical relationship between labor action and the existential will to be that I want to explore here.

The struggle for being first makes its appearance as nebulous yearnings, vague imaginings, and wishful thinking that fasten on to no specific object or, rather, move restlessly from one object to another, much as an infant is curious about everything and anything it can touch or put in its mouth. This is the prototypical expression of what we call the imagination; it is consciousness in its most opportunistic, promiscuous, and migratory mode, or, to invoke the language of Edmund Husserl, it is intentionality in its most primordial and preconceptual form. This is the "uncertain, shadowy" existence we sometimes speak of as the private domain that has not yet been transformed "into a shape fit for public appearance" (Arendt 1958:50). This is also the domain of "intellectually diffuse" experiences or "hazy and unelaborated attitudes" that, as Claude Lévi-Strauss pointed out, are "emotionally intolerable unless they are objectified and integrated in ways that enable us to act and in forms that can be shared (1963:191–72).

There is a close affinity here with Jean-Paul Sartre's theory of the imagination. Sartre sees human intentionality as a vital if "undifferentiated" disposition of consciousness toward an external world that al-

reln bet labor action &
existential will

ways remains to some degree separate from the objects at which it aims, the persons with whom it forms attachments, or the cultural projects whereby it strives to "realise itself" (2004:30).[6] It is because the relationship between the thinking subject and the object of his or her thoughts is restive, indeterminate, and unstable that we find ourselves craving things even when satisfied with what we have, conjuring objects that do not strictly speaking exist, desiring to do things that are not socially acceptable—all while denying the reality of certain objects and experiencing the reality of others in many different ways. The space of religion may be thought of as similar to the space of dreams, a penumbral domain in which consciousness is loosed from the objects, routines, and environs to which it is conventionally tied and freed to entertain or succumb to other modes of objectification. It is a space as haunted by established models and extant memories as it is filled with the aura of imaginary possibilities.

In the West we typically theorize this transfiguring will to be in terms of deep intrapsychic impulses such as instincts, needs, and desires. In tribal societies, however, the relationship between inner and exterior worlds is not ruled solely by *human* subjectivity, which means that inert objects, including the dead, can exert influence over the living to the same extent that living subjects exert influence over them. Moreover, the relation between psyche and world is far more likely to be understood as an intersubjective relationship between self and other, and social and extrasocial space. Among the Yaka of southwest Congo, sociality is conceived as a complex interweaving that connects agnatic and uterine kin, the living and the dead, human beings and water spirits, and humans and nature. "Paradoxically," writes Devisch, "the person's center of gravity is not based in the individual and his innermost being, but essentially in the exercise of exchange and 'interanimation'. . . . More graphically, an individual's center of gravity and social identity as a person is situated at the level of the skin, with its capacities of sensorial and sexual contact, that is, at the interface (*luutu*) with others and the world" (1999:54). Where Westerners search their souls or memories and rack their brains in an effort to know who they are, traditional Africans deploy images of searching and hunting in a much more literal way. Of the social imaginary among the Yaka, Devisch describes a fabulous and "nebulous zone" of "floating forces or energies

. . . fantasies, compulsions and desire where unbridled aggression, exploitation, chance and abuse have free reign" (1999:60). He refers to this as the "imaginative unconscious" (60) because, while everyday consciousness is associated with the domestic space-time of the village, the imagination is associated with night and the forest and finds expression in the figure of a vagrant hunter or enchanted sorcerer-wanderer who "roams the depths of the forest in search of unknown and untamed forms of being and forces belonging to an extraordinary realm far beyond the domestic order" (65).[7]

A recurring ethical quandary in traditional Africa is thus to bring the wild energies and potentially destructive forces that belong to the bush safely into the space of the village since the power to combat witchcraft is itself a kind of witchcraft, the power to ward off sorcery is acquired through training as a sorcerer, the initiation of children into adulthood requires sojourns in the bush, and the vitality and viability of the village depends on making farms in the bush where capricious spirits must be appeased and the dangers of the unknown must be negotiated.

Since human sociality emerges at the intersection of free and bound energies, or wild and domesticated powers, it is useful to think of the social as "potential space" (Winnicott 1974:113–16)—a space in which human intentions, desires, or dispositions are realized in relation to many possible others, objects, and goals. What we call culture is simply the sum total of the *approved* forms and images onto which our will to be may fasten or cathect, or, to use Husserl's term, fill itself in or fulfill itself (*Erfülling*). But cultural patterns and artifacts never entirely govern, delimit, or capture the existential imperative that often attaches only temporarily to certain objects and remains mercurial, dissatisfied, and unbound. There is always a "more" and an "otherwise" to consciousness than is suggested by the particular names, objects, and persons on which it happens to fasten. As Lévi-Strauss puts it, "the mind always has more meanings available than there are objects to which to relate them," thus creating a gap between the signifying and the signified (1963:184). Thus sexual desire may find momentary expression in a fantasy built up around a particular person only for this attachment to be betrayed by another fixation. Or the frustrated desire for status in his village may lead a man to fantasize and form alliances with bush spirits or totemic animals, or to migrate across tribal and

gap bet Signifying
+ Signified

international borders in pursuit of wealth, occult powers, magical medicines, or Islamic learning. And self-styled witches may confess to an ability to assume spirit forms, transporting themselves from place to place by willpower alone, and even flying to London and back within an hour (Shaw 2002: 202). As Sartre puts it, our desire "posits an object; but this object exists only as the correlate of a certain affective consciousness: it is neither drink, nor sleep, nor anything real and all effort to define it is by nature doomed to failure. In a word the *desire* is a blind effort to possess on the representative plane what is already given to me on the affective plane" (2004:70).

We imagine, as we live, beyond our means. And it is this gap between the objects on which we fasten in our ongoing search for satisfaction, for the consummation of our being-in-the-world, and the undifferentiated yearnings that are the precondition of existence itself that marks the terrain I have attempted to explore through Sewa's story—reducing the meaning of his life neither to the external situation that bears on him nor to his own subjective yearnings. Rather, it emerges from the tension between these fields. Moreover, I have avoided speaking of him as an exemplar of the search to be part of global modernity precisely because, as I have argued, his struggle for being is not reducible to history but constitutes an expression of the human condition that everywhere entails a perplexing indeterminacy between our confused longings, imaginings, and desires, on the one hand, and the external world, on the other, and that affords us ways and means of realizing these longings and integrating them with the longings of others.

— desire is a blind effort to possess the representative plane what is already given to me on the affective plane "

In a sense nature is independent of thought.

—A. N. WHITEHEAD, *The Concept of Nature*

7 A Walk on the Wild Side

the idea of human nature revisited

It was in Switzerland—or, more precisely, on an excursion to the summit of Rigi Kulm, 5,906 feet above Lake Lucerne—that I found myself thinking about the place of nature in European Romanticism and the idea of human nature that is so intimately related to it. It was here that countless nineteenth-century visitors making the so-called grand tour spent a night in order to watch the sunrise over the Alps. An ecstatic Victor Hugo compared the scene to a monstrous ocean of gigantic waves and likened them to the petrified breath of Jehovah that had stirred on the original face of the waters of the world, while William Wordsworth's heart "leap'd up" at "the terrible majesty" (1960:280) that met his eyes on his tour of the French Alps in 1791, and in *The Prelude* confessed that the mountains revealed to him "the universal reason of mankind." By contrast, an irreverent Mark Twain described how he

(human) nature + Eup Ramewism /

and his traveling companion were so exhausted by the climb to Rigi Kulm from the lakeside town of Wäggis that for two mornings in a row they slept in and missed the fabled sunrise altogether. On the third day, they woke in darkness and hastened to the summit only to discover that the sun, which they thought was just rising, was in fact about to set (2003:143–162).[1]

Twain's tomfoolery apart, it is tempting to see the European "thirst for the Alps" (Simmel 1991:96) as a response to the political and social turmoil that had accompanied urbanization and industrialization from the late eighteenth century. Recoiling from the horrors of the French Revolution, whose ideals he had initially embraced, Wordsworth's Jacobinism and utopian communism quickly passed, via an infatuation with the rural working class, into a faith in nature. Thus, with "melancholy waste of hopes o'erthrown" and good men on every side falling off to selfishness, he wrote in *The Prelude*:

> I yet
> Despair not of our nature; but retain . . . a faith
> That fails not, in all sorrow my support,
> The blessing of my life, the gift is yours,
> Ye mountains! thine, O nature!
> (1960:32–33)

That the turn to nature implies a return to God is suggested not only in Wordsworth's images of "God and Nature communing" in the same poem but in the poetry of Gerard Manley Hopkins. In *God's Grandeur*, written over seventy years after Wordsworth's *The Prelude*, Hopkins also invokes a world despoiled: "Generations have trod, have trod, have trod; / And all is seared with trade; bleared, smeared with toil; / And wears man's smudge and shares man's smell: the soil / Is bare now, nor can foot feel, being shod" (1953:27). Yet for all this, he writes, "nature is never spent," and "there lives the dearest freshness deep down in things"—the inscape and instress of God—through which we may recover our original humanity (27).

In his 1849 essay on nature, Ralph Waldo Emerson defined nature as "essences unchanged by man" (2003:182), and he argued that every generation longs to "enjoy an original relation to the universe" (181), which is to say, a direct and sensible relationship with the natural world that allows "the knapsack of custom" to fall from one's back (1995:260) so that one becomes "part or particle of God" (2003:184). Similar ideas inform the work of Mary Shelley who—in the "wet" and "ungenial" spring of 1816, when "incessant rain often confined" her, Percy Bysshe Shelley, and their infant son William to their villa on Switzerland's Lac Léman—wrote her terrifying indictment of the presumptions of science and its mainly male advocates, observing that "the effect of any human endeavour to mock the stupendous mechanism of the Creator of the world" would be "supremely frightful" (qtd. in Hindle 1992:xvii). And like Wordsworth, Hopkins, and Emerson, she conflated nature not only with the divine but with the feminine. Nature was always a mother, or at least a "she."

Nowadays we are perhaps less inclined to polarize nature and culture, seeing the first as some pristine essence that becomes overlain or corrupted by an artificial or secondary reality that we call culture or civilization. New reproductive and genetic technologies, as well as medical advances in organ transplantation, seem to have dissolved time-honored distinctions between nature and culture and demand a new synthetic vocabulary of biosociality, hybridity, and biopower.[2] Even the line between biological kinship, based on natural or consanguineal bonds, and adoptive, assisted, fictive, and artificial kinship seems impossible to draw (Strathern 1992). Yet despite those who argue that contemporary social and technological innovations render the nature-culture dichotomy outmoded, voices continue to be raised in protest against the destruction of "natural" habitats and biodiversity, and against the "unnatural," abominable, and uncontrollable repercussions of genetic modification.

Historians of ideas have often seen these very different conceptions of nature not just as signifying postmodern and premodern worldviews but as defining different stages in human history. Thus R. G. Collingwood outlines three quite different ideas of nature, each based on a different root metaphor. The ancient Greeks compared nature to mind. Nature was "saturated and permeated by mind" (1944:3) and possessed a soul or life of its own. By contrast, the thinkers of the European Enlightenment compared nature to a machine created by God, but one requiring rational human management. From the late eighteenth century forward, the modern scientific view emerges of

no longer a nature/culture divide.
diff concepts of nature.

nature as a counterpart to history—evolving and developing over time. The trouble with Collingwood's model is that it is so deeply grounded in the modernist notion of teleology that it fails to recognize that though different epistemes may dominate public or scientific discourse in different epochs and in different societies, each exists everywhere and at all times as a potentiality that may be realized under certain conditions. Thus the Hellenistic worldview finds expression in contemporary Western notions of the earth as a living organism (the Gaia hypothesis), or in the idea that the same reciprocal and ethical relationships that inform human intersubjectivity should govern our relations with the natural world (Abraham 1997). The Enlightenment view of nature as something to be domesticated and dominated for the benefit of humanity underwrites the exploitative ethos of modern capitalism (Horkheimer and Adorno 1972).

My interest is not in the debate over whether nature is something to be manipulated and managed or something to be protected and preserved; rather, I want to explore how both these modes of relating to the natural world are ways of addressing phenomena that lie at the limits of human comprehension and control. The word *nature* is, of course, not the only word that may be used to mark the extrahuman domain.³ In medieval thought, it was the macrocosm—the great world within which the small world of human existence was embedded. For Karl Jaspers, this is the Encompassing (*das Umgreifende*)—a "subversive" term for demarcating the limits of knowledge and reawakening us to that which makes being possible but which being can never grasp through "the perspective of the conceptual" (1955:73, 60). In Aboriginal Australia it is the dreaming, the largely invisible and ambient field of ancestral essences and presences into which life passes at death and from life is drawn out in rituals of increase and rebirth. In West Africa, it is the bush, a domain of wild energies and nature spirits that anthropologists would, a generation ago, have called the supernatural. The words are less important than the phenomenological force field they cover—appearing to be *at the same time* a domain of dangerous alterity *and* a source of the vital energies without which human life and human sociality cannot be sustained. My argument is that our lived relationship with nature—whether we construe this psychologically as within us or physically as without—is, like any intersubjective relationship, profoundly ambivalent. On the one hand, genes, emotions, landscapes, and climates give us life; on the other hand, genetic mutations, ungoverned emotions, and wild nature in the form of hurricanes, tornadoes, tsunamis, volcanic eruptions, earthquakes, bushfires, and floods may destroy both lives and livelihoods.

Let me begin with two quite different ways of relating to nature (understood as that which is felt to lie at the inner or outer limits of one's physical and conceptual grasp). The first is predicated on the notion of affinity, the second on the notion of antipathy. I can best sketch what I mean by backtracking to Switzerland and the Rigi Kulm.

My excursion to Mount Rigi returned me to my native New Zealand. This was not just because the alpine scenes were so similar, the same soundless collisions of cumulus clouds over the distant peaks and cloud shadows flowing down the grassy slopes of the high valleys. It was because, as a child, I developed a deep identification with the land, so that when I thought of the world to which I was naturally heir, I did not think primarily of family or lineage, but of a quiet bend in a local river, a pine plantation, a remnant stand of native bush, a hill from which, on a clear day, I could see Mount Taranaki. These *physical* elements defined a *social* microcosm of which I felt intimately a part. Winter and summer I explored, charted, named, and absorbed this world of mine until there was not an acre I did not know by heart. This was at once my lifeworld and my self: animate, attuned, and entangled. So when I threw myself down in the long grass above Rigi Kaltbad— inhaling the odors of fescue, red clover, buttercup, and alfalfa, catching a whiff of cow dung from the half-timbered buildings at the foot of the slope, hearing the drone of a light plane rising and falling on the breeze —I was a child again, yielding to the Taranaki landscape and finding in its sights and sounds and smells the elements of a stable world to which I felt I completely belonged. It was undoubtedly this yielding or submission to the contemplation of nature that attracted many of the nineteenth-century pilgrims to Rigi Kulm. There was a strange comfort to be had from experiencing oneself in relation to the immensity of what lay before one's eyes—the accidented roof of the Alps, scalloped, serrated, snow-flecked, with its scree slopes and cirques, and the forests and pastures far below where a window glinted in the sun and you heard the syncopated clonking of cowbells. But smelling the wild-flowers, basking in the sun, or taking in the view—all images of participatory acquiescence—define only one side of the modern attitude to nature. For nature is also something to pit oneself or test oneself against, a kind of proving ground for a masculinist ethos that sees nature as something to be conquered and converted, tamed and transformed—an ethos captured in Edmund Hillary's remark to George Lowe after his ascent of Mount Everest in 1953 with Tensing Norgay: "Well, we knocked the bastard off" (Hillary 1975:162).[4]

From where I was lying I could make out on the horizon the peaks of the Eiger and Jungfrau. While many visitors had come to the Rigi to see the sunrise over these Alps, others had sought to be the first to knock them off, often at considerable risk to their lives. The Matterhorn, for example, was conquered by the English climber Edward Whymper in 1865 after six failed attempts and at the cost of the lives of seven of his climbing companions.

Two contrasted modes of relating to nature are suggested here, the first characterized by union and yielding, the second by duality and dominance. While the first suggests a willing submission to a nature that is allowed to enter and even take over one's body and soul, the second implies standing out from or standing over a nature that has been subdued or backgrounded. This is the classical panoramic or perspectival standpoint, involving a separation between subject and object, observer and observed, actor and acted on.

These contrasts apply equally to our relations with others, which is why I prefer to think of them all as intersubjective. Indeed, the copresence of *three* dimensions of relationship—the individual body, the body politic, and the body of the land—is typical of cosmologies in all human societies. Hence the classical Chinese notion of "inner and outer worlds of experience as having identical systems of physiology" (Rawson 1968: 231), Hindu and Hippocratic images of the world as a human body, the Dogon view of the earth as made up of minerals that correspond to different bodily organs—rocks being bones, small white river pebbles being toes, and a family of red clays being the blood (Calame-Griaule 1965:27–57)—and Indo-European metaphors of the foot or brow of a hill, the mouth or arm of a river, a brooding or angry sky, and family trees with branches and roots. Rather than treat these synecdochic sets as poetic forms of expression or as markers of a palaeological mode of thought, I want to show how they provide a rationale for action in contexts in which human beings come up against the limits of their capacity to comprehend and control their lifeworlds.

My first example comes from the year my wife and I spent living with an Aboriginal family in the rain forests of the southeast Cape York peninsula in Australia. Although Kuku Yalanji people do not think of nature and culture in the abstract, my suggestion that we might usefully construe nature as that which lies at the limits of our understanding and our power to act is consonant with the way Kuku Yalanji see their lifeworld. Culture (a term many Aboriginal people have now adopted) covers everything *within* one's lifeworld including land, language, kin and affines, and the ocean or rain forest ecosystems in which one lives. Although this lifeworld is divided into moieties based on an ecological distinction between rain forest dwellers (*ngalkalji*) and coastal dwellers (*jalunji*), everything and everyone in this lifeworld is thought to be intimately or affinally interconnected. That which lies outside this lifeworld, however, obeys different laws and constitutes a threat, although outsiders may be gradually accepted into one's family as affines or as friends (*jawun*). Kuku Yalanji express these social distinctions in olfactory terms. Sea people smell of salt water and sea fish; land people smell of marsupial meat; strangers have a strong odor that is quite different. "How different?" I once asked my informant Harry Shipton. "Old people said *waybala* (whites) smell like the slime of an eel," he said, "but they smell like *bama* (Aboriginals) after they bin live with us for a while." "What about me?" I asked. "You smell like bama," Harry said.

From the beginning of our fieldwork my wife and I were struck by the linkages and lines of communication that existed within the Kuku Yalanji lifeworld. Moreover, it became clear to us that knowing how to decipher these correspondences was vital to one's everyday life and livelihood.

Most afternoons and evenings we went fishing on a nearby beach or on a jetty on the Bloomfield River. Lacking the patience and ability to fish, I would sometimes drift into reverie, listening to the wind in the casuarinas, gazing at the long sweep of Weary Bay or the dark mangrove reaches of the Bloomfield. But such an aesthetic engagement

Nature as that which lies at the limits of our understanding + power to act.

with our surroundings was foreign to our hosts, who were on constant alert for the vital signs that pointed to a hidden danger, revealed a food source, or presaged some social event. People would silently scrutinize the sea or river for signs of mullet jumping, stingray basking, or schools of herring, and if we were in the rain forest, they would be on the lookout for the spoor of deadly snakes or signs of bush tucker. Before long, I lost my habit of daydreaming and became absorbed by the pregnant meanings of the environment. A frilled lizard on a palm leaf was an augury of a coming storm. A hammer bird heard in the cold months meant that mullet would be plentiful. Bean trees flowering or the wild tamarind ripening meant that scrub hen eggs could be found. The flesh of the parcel apple turning pink meant that the liver of the stingrays would also be pink, and therefore good to eat, though eating stingrays in the preceding months (October-November) would bring storms.

With the approach of the wet season, I became increasingly fascinated by the family's preoccupation with thunder and lightning. Whereas I saw storms as natural phenomena, our hosts interpreted them in social terms; they were expressions of human malevolence and of tempestuous states of mind. Thus the phrase *jarramali bajaku* (literally, "exceedingly stormy") is used of persons who lose self-control when drunk or drugged, while the term *jarramali* denotes any cyclonic or monsoonal storm, all of which may embody the ill-will of outsiders. Questions of control thus entail allusions to individual psychology, relations with others, and relations with the elements of nature.

In Aboriginal communities one is often struck by people's extraordinary tolerance of aberrant or unruly behavior, and I was sometimes reminded of my experience among the Kuranko in Sierra Leone where incorrigible individuals would draw such comments as, "He came out of the *fafei* like that" (i.e., even initiation failed to make him mend his ways); or "That is how he was made" (a danye le wo la); or "He is blameless; he was born with it" (a ka tala; a soron ta la bole). But while both Kuranko and Kulu Yalanji explain dispositions that resist socialization by invoking notions of innateness, there are practical limits to people's tolerance of antisocial behavior that, in both societies, is seen as a form of deafness to social values.

It was Christmas 1993. The heat and humidity was oppressive. Sweat dripped from my forehead onto the pages of my journal as I wrote about the tension that had built up in our camp, breaking on Boxing Day like a storm, with Sonny in a fistfight with his brother-in-law, his elder sister heaping abuse on his head, another sister throwing a couple of punches for good measure, and then the youngest sister Gladys and her husband driving off to the nearby settlement of Ayton to get away from it all. As the first thunderstorm of the wet season approached, the sky turned indigo and the wind veered and picked up. There was a rattle of dry leaves and dry leaves falling, for which Kuku Yalanji use the word *yanja*, followed by the crumpling sound of distant thunder, like heavy furniture being moved around in an upstairs room—a sound that also has its own specific ideophone, *kubun-kubun*. Painstakingly, people tracked the course of the storm, discussing where it was coming from and where it was heading, identifying its sounds, observing its effect on the foliage, comparing it with storms in the past. Indeed, the character of the impending storm was analyzed in the same way that people analyzed strangers—trying to read their intentions, second-guess their motives, identify their mood. As this discussion went on, various members of the family made forays into the bush in search of wild grape vines (*kangka*), ironwood bark (*jujabala*), and grass tree (*nganjirr*). Sonny, now sober, applied himself to the business at hand, burning knotted hanks of grass, ironwood bark, and grass tree outside our camp. As the sweet smell of the grass tree pitch (*kanunjul*) spread across the clearing, I assumed that it was meant to repel mosquitoes. But Sonny told me that the storm would smell the smoke and go away. I later asked McGinty, who was not Kuku Yalanji, if he could explain to me how burning grass tree could ward off storms. The idea seemed to both amuse and embarrass him, partly because his own people on Princess Charlotte Bay used a different method for warding off storms (a certain kind of shell), partly because he did not want to give me the impression that he was a superstitious *myal* ("bush" person). That evening, as I was helping him put up his tarpaulin and tent at the beach, he joked about the ominous rain clouds hovering over the range. "Might rain soon," he said laconically. "Better tell that storm to wait until I get my tent up."

At Gladys's house in Ayton, however, the mood was somber. Most of the family had gathered behind closed doors, huddled and anxious as the storm approached. One of the children gave my wife a clue as to why they were so fearful: "If you eat things you are not supposed to eat, a storm will come and punish you." Was lightning an agent of retributive justice, seeking out those who might have broken a food or sex taboo, or transgressed a story place? Such matters are difficult for any anthropologist to divine, for who knows what guilty secrets a person may harbor, and whether these get projected as fears of external retribution. One thing was clear, however, and that was the association of thunderstorms with vengeful outsiders.

One morning, McGinty told me that a stranger from Kowanyama had come to Wujal a few years ago. He was rumored to be a *burri-burri* man (a sorcerer), able to manipulate storms for his own nefarious purposes. That afternoon, Sonny opened up to me and explained the link between storms and affinity—a link that would make immediate sense to anthropologists long familiar with the ambivalence and uncertainty that marks relations between in-laws. As the Mae-Enga of the western Highlands of Papua New Guinea famously made this point, "We marry the people we fight" (Meggitt 1964:218). Like affines, then, thunderstorms originate *elsewhere*.

Among Kuku Yalanji, two analogous domains of relationship are posited: relations between social categories and relations between environmental elements. The key terms, and the relationships between them, may be posited thus: mother-in-law is to son-in-law as thunderstorm is to grass tree. When thunderstorms approach, it is feared that social categories which should be kept apart are coming dangerously close together: oneself and one's enemies, insiders and outsiders. This situation is compared to the infringement of the avoidance relation between mother-in-law and son-in-law, and by association any transgression of things that should be kept apart, such as people and forbidden fruits. The problem: how to drive the thunderstorm away? The solution: activate the analogies alluded to above. The practical action: grass tree logs are burned. Grass tree (as well as iron tree bark and wild grape vine) is son-in-law to the thunderstorm. The thunderstorm will smell the grass tree smoke. And just as mother-in-law will avoid her son-in-law if she smells him, so the storm will move away when it gets wind of its son-in-law, the grass tree.

This brief excursion into Kuku Yalanji ethnography enables us to see that the wild powers of what we call nature are (1) both intrapsychic and intersubjective; (2) social and physical; and (3) potentially destructive and creative. At the same time we have seen the ingenuity with which people seek to control wild nature, whether the momentary madness of a drunken and berserk individual or the passing danger of a cyclonic storm. However, control may take two quite different forms. It may entail repression and sublimation, which are strategies of avoidance, or it may entail management and mastery, which are strategies of engagement. In psychoanalytic theory these two themes are paradoxically entangled. As Géza Róheim observed, it is "in the nature of our species to master reality on a libidinal basis" (1971:105)—deferring immediate gratifications and discharging instinctual energies in noninstinctual activities and objects. For Freud, civilization is "built up upon the renunciation of instinct," which "presupposes precisely the non-satisfaction (by suppression, repression or some other means) of powerful instincts" (1961a:44). "This 'cultural frustration,'" Freud observes, "dominates the large field of social relationships between human beings . . . [and] is the cause of hostility against which all civilizations have to struggle" (44). But Freud's dictum, "where id is, let ego be," fails to acknowledge the extent to which our inner nature is not only a set of instincts to be repressed but also a source of vitality to be channeled and liberated (Marcuse 1966). In existential terms, this implies that human beings can never find complete fulfillment in slavish conformity to socially constructed, external patterns of behavior, for there must be for every individual some sense that he or she is not merely thrown into a world made by others at other times but that he or she enters into it actively and vitally as someone for whom the given world is also a means whereby his or her own particular destiny is realized. But let me return momentarily to thunder and lightning.

My theme is the paradox of power: that the same forces that threaten one's being—whether from within as libidinal energies or from without as natural elements—can, if harnessed and channeled, not only provide protection but generate and regenerate life. In the 1890s, the ethnographer W. E. Roth reported that in many parts of northern Queensland thunder and lightning were means of sorcery, but that people sometimes summoned these same forces to drive white settlers from their land (1897:168, 1903:8). I heard identical stories from Harry Shipton in

1993. Many years ago, Harry told me, a white rancher, exasperated by bama spearing his cattle, rode up to a river encampment and shot a young girl dead. Bent on revenge, the girl's father went to the rancher's place as thunder. The rancher fired shots at the thunder but his bullets passed harmlessly through the thunder's body. Then, with a single lightning bolt, the thunder speared and killed the rancher. In another of Harry's stories, a certain white man who "messed with many bama girls," getting them pregnant and causing trouble, was sought out by lightning as he was driving his tractor in a Mossman cane field. "Bang! He dead, just like that."

Among the Kuranko of northeast Sierra Leone, thunder and lightning are also means of sorcery,[5] and among the most formidable masters of this power were the warrior chiefs, Bol' Tamba Marah and his younger brother Firawaka Mamburu Marah (known as Belikoro, "Mighty Elder"), both of whom smote their enemies with lightning bolts and intimidated their own subjects in the same way.

What is fascinating here is the ambivalent and vexed relationship between secular and occult power. Ordinarily, these powers are separate and complementary, somewhat like church and state in modern Europe. Indeed, a strict distinction in Kuranko is drawn between the domain of wild powers (*suwage*) associated with magical medicines (*bese*), bush spirits (*nyenne*), and secret societies (*sumafan*) and identified with the bush (*fira*), and the domain of custom (*namui* or *bimba kan*) and law (*seriye* or *ton*) associated with secular power (*noé*) and chieftaincy (*mansaye*) and identified with human settlements (*sué*).[6] But though these domains are said to be essentially different, they are, in practice, interdependent, and each is equally vital to the Kuranko lifeworld.[7]

The Kuranko bush corresponds to nature seen as a force field that lies on the margins of human comprehension and control: a source both of the energy that sustains life—in the form of game animals, medicinal plants, and rice (the staple food crop)—and of the powers that can destroy life—in the form of witchcraft, wild animals, and intractable bush spirits. For Kuranko the paradox of power is that the locus of greatest insecurity and danger is also the place most vital to one's life and livelihood. To phrase this cybernetically, the social system —defined as a domain of nonnegotiable roles, fixed rules, ancestral

   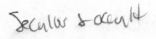 Secular & occult

values, and received wisdom—drifts toward entropy unless it perennially taps into and draws on the vital energies of the bush in the form of the fertility of its soil, its natural resources, and even the djenni loci who claim it as their own. But while Kuranko generally conceptualize the bush as an *external* domain, the term also covers *internal* powers such as the "natural gift" of intelligence, the reproductive capacity of women, the potency of men, and the disposition of magnanimity that defines personhood itself (*morgoye*). Indeed, in Kuranko myth, personhood is exemplified not by ancestors but by totemic animals that saved the lives of clan ancestors in times of danger long ago. And it is the bush that is the source of life in rituals of initiation. For while initiation is the apotheosis of sublimation, in which instinctual tendencies are brought under strict control—sexuality finding expression in marriage and childbearing, the body disciplined, the emotions cooled, speech measured, and selfishness transcended—it is also the moment at which one encounters, in cult associations, the wild powers of the djinni who, like totemic animals, are also means of imparting to ordinary human beings extraordinary powers.

The quasi human figure of the djinni embodies what one might call natural, wild, or libidinal power. All such power is ambiguous: it may work for or against one. In Kuranko terms it is hard to know whether such power will be a good cause (*sabu nyuma*) or a bad cause (*sabu yuge*). One hears plenty of anecdotes about djinni giving a wrestler strength, a dancer grace, a diviner insight, and a musician inspiration, and there are sites in every Kuranko chiefdom, associated with djinni, where the unfortunate may offer sacrifices of food in the hope that they will be helped or where the fortunate repay the djinni for help received. Several of the diviners with whom I worked had received their gifts from djinni that appeared to them in dreams during a bout of sickness, and both music and musical instruments are often said to have originally come from the bush. The great Malian musician Ali Farka Touré attributes his genius to the djinni. When he was thirteen, a series of visions and strange experiences transformed his playing, and he entered a new world that he compares with a prolonged sickness or epileptic seizure: "It's different from when you're in a normal state; you're not the person you know anymore" (Touré 1996). Despite such testimonies, the djinni are capricious, and their help often comes at a price. Sometimes, they simply withdraw their favors and disappear. Sometimes, as in European stories of selling one's soul to the devil, or Columbian stories of "baptized banknotes" (Taussig 1980), such Faustian pacts bring a sordid boon. Among the Kuranko, a djinni that has done you a favor may demand the life of one of your children or kinspeople in return. As the original inhabitants of the land, the djinni may allow human beings to make their farms on condition they make sacrificial offerings at the beginning of each farm season, but even then a djinni may cause a farmer to cut himself with a machete or injure himself with a hoe. A djinni may possess a person, driving him or her mad or causing fits of delirium. A djinni may appear in a dream in the form of a beautiful woman (succubus) or handsome man (incubus), but the sexual encounter may lead to impotence or barrenness.

What is at play here is a struggle for being that involves a struggle between what is simply given to a person—his or her role, temperament (*yugi*), or birthright—and what a person desires over and above what he or she has or who he or she is. The contrast between town and bush implies a contrast between centripetal and centrifugal forces— the first finding expression in custom and convention, the second in antinomian possibilities. Nature, in the sense in which I have been using the term, signifies a no-man's-land between the known and the unknown, necessity and desire.[8] While any social system requires dutiful conformity to ancestral protocols, social life would become empty of meaning unless each person realized in himself or herself the capacity to bring the social world into being. But this capacity draws not only on what is tried and true but also on hazardous encounters with extrasocial sources of power—bush spirits, wild places, limit experiences.

That one's being has its origin not only in one's position but in one's disposition, in one's standing within the established order of things as well as in one's relationship with forces that have not been tamed, domesticated, or socialized, is nowhere better illustrated than in the case of spirit possession, for as innumerable ethnographic studies have shown, it is by allowing oneself to be overcome, taken, infiltrated, or ridden by wild powers that one discovers the resources to go on with life in the face of quotidian hardship and oppression. Thus, in Janice Boddy's compelling account of the Zar cult in northern Arabic-speaking Muslim Sudan, we learn that humans and *zar* spirits exist in parallel but contiguous worlds, the latter "within the realm of nature" and normally invisible to humans (1989:3), much like the Kuranko djinni. Through possession, Sudanese women are taken out of their everyday lifeworlds, transcending their everyday sense of who they are and seeing the world through new eyes.

> When the drums are beating, beating, you hear nothing, you hear from far away, you feel far away. You have left the *midan*, the place of the *zar*. And you see, you have a vision. You see through the eyes of a European. Or you see through the eyes of the West African, whichever spirit it is. You see then as a European sees—you see other Europeans, radios, Pepsis, televisions, refrigerators, automobiles, a table set with food. You forget who you are, your village, your family, you know nothing from your life. You see with the eyes of the spirit until the drumming stops. (Boddy 1989:350)

As Boddy's work suggests, the world of spirits has become increasingly globalized, so that nature marks not merely the boundary between town and bush but also between local and global worlds. One also sees the widening of horizons in the changing form of witchcraft fantasies in Sierra Leone. Instead of the self-styled witch imagining that she journeys by night in some ethereal or animal shape and with her coven drains the life from some sleeping victim in another part of the country, contemporary witches imagine traveling by witch airplane across what Rosalind Shaw calls "unbounded and alluring global space" (2002:202):

> They often [describe] a prosperous city where skyscrapers adjoin houses of gold and diamonds; Mercedes-Benzes are driven down fine roads; street vendors roast "beefsticks" (kebabs) of human meat; boutiques sell stylish "witch-gowns" that transform their wearers into animal predators in the human world (no-ru); electronics stores sell tape recorders and televisions (and, more recently, VCRs and computers); and witch airports despatch witch planes—planes so fast, I was once told, that "they can fly to London and back within an hour"—to destinations all around the globe. (202)

Such flights of fancy may well appear bizarre to us—on a par with Kuku Yalanji's attempts to drive away thunderstorms by burning logs of grass tree. But human beings tend to think and act in remarkably similar ways when they come up against the limits of what they can understand or what they can control. Whenever our actions are ineffective or thwarted, and our understanding fails, we typically fall back on our own emotions, bodies, and thoughts as means of changing our *experience* of the world we cannot change. We thus move constantly between actual and imaginary modes of engagement with the world, depending on what circumstance and our own capacities allow. This kind of opportunistic switching between direct action and strategic inaction brings to mind Aristotle's distinction between active and passive agency in his *Metaphysics* (book 5, ch. 12), the first referring to a subject's action on the world that changes the latter in some way, the second referring to a subject's being subject to the actions of others—suffering, receiving, being moved or transformed by external forces.[9] Hannah Arendt speaks of this contrast between being an actor and being acted on as a difference between being a "who" and a "what" (1958:181–86).

The Coming Environmental Crisis

Widespread Western anxieties about global warming, environmental degradation, and polluting technologies have given rise to numerous forms of ecoactivism and ecophilosophy, not to mention a proliferating literature that celebrates the virtues of the natural world while decrying its desecration. Within the academy, environmental studies has become a growth industry in science and arts faculties alike.

In March 2006, one of the doyens of this field—the Japanese Canadian scientist and environmentalist David Suzuki—was awarded the Roger Tory Peterson medal from the Harvard Museum of Natural History. In an impassioned acceptance speech, Suzuki observed that we had reached "a remarkable moment in the history of life on earth" and called on his audience, as well as the developed world at large, to embrace an environmental agenda based on notions of sustainability and stewardship. In Suzuki's global conception of humanity, his invocation of our power to determine our collective fate, and his idealism—that presumes some future vantage point from which it is possible to pass judgment on our times—one sees something of the intellectual hubris that writers as different as Jean-Paul Sartre and Pierre Bourdieu have called into question. For Sartre, the bombast of intellectuals is a sign of overcompensation for their *lack* of political or social power (1983:229), an argument that echoes the idea that the Romantic infatuation with nature was a way of escaping the unmanageable mire of urban-industrial life. As for Bourdieu, his question is: "How can one avoid succumbing to this dream of omnipotence, which tends to arouse fits of bedazzled identification with great heroic roles?" How can one avoid what Schopenhauer called 'pedantic comedy'—the absurd pretension of believing that there is no limit to thought, of seeing 'an academic commentary as a political act or the critique of texts as a feat of resistance, and experience revolutions in the order of words as radical revolutions in the order of things?'" (2000:2). My own argument is somewhat more sympathetic to public intellectuals like Suzuki, though it is no less critical, since I repudiate the notion that enlightened thought operates solely from the standpoint of reason.

To those committed to saving the planet from ecological catastrophe, it might seem outrageous for an anthropologist like myself to question the rationality of their actions or of the scientific knowledge on which these actions are predicated. Still more outrageous would be the suggestion that their actions might be compared with the magical actions of, say, Kuku Yalanji attempting to ward off an impending thunderstorm by burning logs of grass tree. But the comparison *must* be made, if only on the grounds that there is, in both cases, little likelihood that the actions envisaged will *necessarily* avert the forces threatening the local or global lifeworlds in question. In other words, though human action is always subject to rationalization—in the Kuku Yalanji case, an argument that people can act on the forces of nature because those forces are essentially social and hence susceptible to human counteraction; in the Western case, an argument that people can avoid environmental disaster by using scientific evidence and democratic processes to pressure governments into making policy changes —human action is motivated primarily by an existential imperative to do *something* rather than nothing, and it is only secondarily a matter of which intellectual, cultural, or ritual *techne* makes the most sense, or is the most reasonable. Because our actions follow from a *need* to act before they follow from any conception of *how* to act, all action is to

me extent magical, which is to say that no action can be entirely
plained by reference to the models adduced in justification of it.
ccordingly, action implies an element of faith or absurdity (one acts
without being absolutely certain of the outcome) while working on the
world *obliquely*, via the actor's own subjectivity. The ritualistic or magical aspect of action involves two moves. First, the scale of the macrocosm—the locus, in my examples, of both thunderstorms and global
warming—is reduced to the scale of the microcosm, which is our most
immediate environment, the world within our reach, the world at
hand. Second, by changing our experience within this immediate
world, we conjure a sense of having made a difference to *the* world. It is
by working on our own nature, as it were—showing concern, anguish-
ing publicly, speaking out, affirming solidarity with like-minded souls
—that we transform our experience of an external nature that is, in
fact, much more resistant to comprehension and control than we are
ever likely to admit.[10]

This is precisely how Bronislaw Malinowski explains the efficacy of
Trobriand spells. Although the spells are addressed to a newly planted
garden, an ocean-going canoe, or an agricultural implement, it is the
immediate subjective effects of the spells that really matter—the ways
in which they supplement action by boosting confidence, raising spirits, increasing hope, or inducing discipline. As Malinowski observes, "it
is human nature on to which the force is directed" (1922:401).

Like Trobriand Islanders, we undoubtedly need to believe that our
actions can have real effects on the wider world, but global transformations are the product of such a multitude of causes and entail so many
unforeseen effects that the power of conscious redressive human action is far more limited than we allow. But such skepticism as to the
scope of our responsibility and agency should not be read as an argument against human action and human speech, the necessity of which
both precedes and transcends our knowledge of their consequences.
We *must* act, even if our actions only create the illusion that something
has been done, some change has been wrought, whether within or
without.

It is for this reason that I have identified nature with the borderline
between the worlds we know best and the worlds we know least, between the local spheres in which our speech and actions make a differ-

ence and the spheres that lie largely beyond our grasp, much as we wish it were otherwise. Nature is not, therefore, as Aristotle defined it, an essence,[11] either deep within or distantly without, but a threshold at which thought and language falter and mystery begins. If anything is in our nature, it is that we are fated to live betwixt and between, compelled to act, driven to understand, and bound to speak, even though we are constantly undone by what we do, confounded by what we think, and damned by what we say.

— action implies an element of faith a absurdity

⋄ it is hard to know the external world.

″ we must act even if change is an illusion

″ immed. subjective effects″

The subjectivity inherent in all observations [is] the royal road to an authentic, rather than fictitious, objectivity . . . defined in terms of what is really possible, rather than in terms of "what should be."

—GEORGE DEVEREUX, *From Anxiety to Method in the Behavioral Sciences*

8 From Anxiety to Method
a reappraisal

In the late summer of 2006 I traveled to Oxford for a conference titled "The Anthropology and Psychology of Fieldwork Experience" only to discover that the paper I had prepared for this event seemed to me, when I came to present it, embarrassingly inadequate. On returning home, I therefore set to work to redeem myself by writing another paper, bearing in mind Denis Diderot's ironic observations in *Paradoxe sur le comédien* concerning what he called *l'esprit de l'escalier* ("staircase wit")—the vexing human experience of coming up with the best response to a situation too late for it to be of any use, the mind always lagging behind life, as it were, and belatedly trying to make good its woeful inability to be on top of a situation as it actually unfolds. This existential dilemma is no doubt a product of the peculiar evolution of the human brain: the primitive limbic system enabling us to scream in

Mind always lagging behind life.

terror, flee from danger, or fight for our lives without a second thought; the more recently evolved cerebral cortex enabling us to override, deny, or feign emotions, so that we may act fearful or declare ourselves to be afraid when we feel no fear at all (Lancaster 1975:69–70). This curious duplicity is not unrelated to the subject of this chapter—the gap between the experiences of first fieldwork and the retrospective accounts one renders of that experience. Can we really revisit the past or do justice to life in language, or are we so swept away by the tide of events, so overwhelmed by the incessant demands of life, that we live in a state of absentmindedness, reflecting only when the tide is out and it is too late to really recapture the truth of what occurred? These thoughts were not unconnected with the conference, which took place in the Oakeshott Room at Lincoln College, so that as I listened to the various papers in this historic room, I was mindful of Michael Oakeshott's arguments concerning the way our thinking always unfolds in relation to the thinking of others, or the way our actions are seldom premeditated and reasoned (but rather subject to *retrospective* abridgement and rationalization), and the way that "human life is . . . a tension between pride and fear": "Each of these primary passions elucidates the character of the other, and together they define the ambivalent relationship which men enjoy with one another" (Oakeshott 1991: 119–20, 302). At the same time, particularly when papers on transference and countertransference in human relations were being read, I kept asking myself why the work of George Devereux received no mention and whether this, too, was a sign of our existential limits—a question of our inability to encompass the conditions of the possibility of our own understanding, or of a perverse forgetfulness that elides the past so that we alone may stand out from it.

My starting point is the ambivalence and anxiety I experienced when beginning fieldwork among the Kuranko in northeast Sierra Leone more than thirty-six years ago. But this initiation into anthropology also depended on the intellectual mentorship of Devereux, whose work would prove crucial to the evolution of my approach to comparative method, anthropological theorizing, and ethnographic writing. I therefore begin this chapter with a personal reminiscence of my relationship with Devereux, whose work continues to be germane to any exploration of the relationships between observer and observed in the behavioral sciences. This then sets the theoretical scene for an account of how I addressed the anxieties of first fieldwork among the Kuranko by having recourse to local techniques of dream interpretation and divination. I then proceed from questions of anxiety to matters of comparison, arguing that insights that turn out to be *personally* useful may also illuminate the *transpersonal* and *interpersonal* lifeworlds one is seeking to understand.

George Devereux

In the antipodean summer of 1973–74, thanks to an initiative by my friend Michael Young, who I had gotten to know at Cambridge a few years earlier, I spent about eight weeks in the Department of Anthropology in the Research School of Pacific Studies (RSPacS) at the Australian National University. Derek Freeman, then head of the anthropology program at RSPacS, had brought together an exceptional group of anthropologists including George Devereux, Meyer Fortes, Adam Kendon, and Peter Reynolds whose research interests encompassed biological anthropology, human ethology, kinesics, and psychoanalysis. Though these fields were all comparatively new to me, it was Devereux's work that made the most profound and enduring impression.

Like Fortes, Devereux was only a short-term visitor, and I had already been in the department for several weeks before he arrived. During those weeks, his book *From Anxiety to Method in the Behavioral Sciences* was passed around. Everyone appeared nonplussed by it, and I do not think anyone bothered to read it from cover to cover. But when the book came into my hands, I was instantly and completely enthralled. Here at last was an anthropologist who sought the universal in the particular yet did justice to the idiosyncratic and cultural contexts in which the universal is actually lived. Other thinkers possessed the same scholarly breadth and erudition as Devereux, but none, to my mind, so successfully showed how one might integrate social and psychological approaches to human reality. I felt as though Devereux was addressing and offering solutions to the very problems I had been struggling with, methodological as well as philosophical, in my own work. First was the question of reflexivity—of the reciprocal interplay of one's relationship with oneself and with others—or, as I phrased it at the time, the twofold movement that takes one out into the world of others and returns one, changed, to oneself. For Devereux, understanding this dialectical movement was imperative if anthropology was going to be truly methodical, but it had to be managed and monitored by techniques that involved the *complementary* use of psychological *and* sociological models. In other words, true reflexivity demanded scientific discipline, not artistic license or confessional impulse. Second, I found myself in complete accord with Devereux's insistence on the value of Werner Heisenberg's uncertainty principle for anthropology: interactions between observer and observed, object and instrument, are constitutive of our knowledge of all phenomena. This meant that anthropologists had to make choices of method and theory, not on the basis of an objectivist principle of representing reality, but on the basis of ethical, political, and artistic commitments to practical truths—truths that might make for a more equitable society or held out the promise of enriching rather than impoverishing our lives. Third, I was impressed by Devereux's notion that much of the experience-distant rhetoric and theoretical model building we do in anthropology may be understood on an analogy with intrapsychic defense mechanisms—subterfuges for coping with the stressful effects of fieldwork and the unsettling complexity of life. Anthropological systematizing could be placed on par with pretty much anything human beings do to bring an illusion of order to their lives: attributing causation to inanimate things, furnishing a house, making a garden, writing a book, building a nation. In other words, whatever their different epistemological values, scientific and magical reasoning provide alternative strategies for coping with the panic all human beings experience when confronted by the unresponsiveness of matter—the sheer otherness, nonhumanness, and unmanageability of many of the forces that impinge on us. Fourth, I found in Devereux's psychoanalytic arguments for the psychic unity of humankind a justification for the kind of anthropology I instinctively wanted to do: "The principle that each person is a complete specimen of Man and each society a complete specimen of Society" (1979:23). Fifth, and perhaps most momentously, I found in Devereux's focus on the politics of how ego boundaries are revised and drawn (rather than on how egos may be defined) a way around the static schemata of bounded entities—selves, social groups, tribes, cultures, nations—that dominated cultural anthropology in the 1970s.

Nothing is more sure to undermine one's social confidence than regard and respect, so when I was first introduced to the man whose work had already made such an impression on me, I was abashed and tongue-tied. I remember the day vividly. A group of us were sitting around a table in the garden at University House, eating lunch. George had only just flown in from France, and in the dazzling sunlight that filled the garden he looked etiolated, jet-lagged, and utterly out of place. I sat close to him, wanting to hear what he had to say. He was holding an unlit cigarette in a tortoise-shell holder, and his first remark was a request: Did anyone know where one could buy a Cricket lighter? His had run out of fuel. I volunteered immediately and spent the next half hour going from one kiosk to another in the city until I found a Cricket.

Years later, reflecting on this afternoon of his arrival, George would use his disoriented frame of mind—"a combination of influenza and severe jet lag"—to illustrate how consciousness continually moves between focused and diffuse extremes, between modalities of engagement and detachment:

> My total stimulability, my capacity to apprehend situations multidimensionally, was almost abolished. The moment I was able to entrust myself to my host's kindly care, I observed first an incapacity to operate in the framework of a time-span exceeding a few minutes. On talking over afterwards my behaviour while in a state of jet-lag exhaustion, my host told me that I had spoken rationally, but also that what I had said had no real continuity. I appear to have skipped from one thing to another, in response to the stimulus of the instant. My "temporal ego" had been momentarily impaired.
>
> On another level, I noted that whenever I was not the recipient of a stimulus directly addressed to me—that is, whenever I was not directly spoken to—part of my mind began to dream. Thus, I knew that I was sitting at a table and eating; I was also aware of my host's presence, but only in a remote sort of way. With my eyes open, part of my mind was periodically slipping "sideways," into a dreamlike, at least hypnagogic, state—for the first, and I hope the last, time in my life, for it was not a pleasant experience. Also, though I was able to set in motion the machin-

ery of my good upbringing, I could hear myself say "please" and "thank you" as if I were only a suitably programmed computer. At least twenty-four hours elapsed before I could once more apprehend those I met as multidimensional persons and not as mere "partial objects." So far as I know, I did nothing silly during the first twenty-four hours, but I also know that every person and thing I encountered during that period was experienced as unidimensional and non-symbolic and that successive events were apprehended as discrete: not as sequential, not as components of a temporal pattern. My time perception was not that of the historian but that of the chronicler (1979:28–29).

Despite seeing me as unidimensional and nonsymbolic, George must have divined in my eagerness to place myself at his disposal a desire for intellectual apprenticeship or affiliation. In any event, this is what happened. I accompanied him back to his third floor room in University House—realizing, as he rested awhile on each landing and complained about the stairs, that he suffered from acute emphysema. And I devoted myself to proofreading articles and running errands for him, and hearing him out as he regaled me with stories of academic politics in Paris, of the university establishment's indifference to and dismissiveness of his ideas, and of his current psychoanalytic explorations of dreams in classical Hellenic literature.

Perhaps, too, I sensed some distant kinship, born of our isolated childhoods, though the troubled circumstances of his were more political than familial. He was born in 1908 in the trilingual, tricultural town of Lugós, then part of Hungary. At the end of World War I, the town passed into Romanian hands and George's lyceé became officially Romanian. This meant that one year he was told that the Hungarians had defeated the Romanians; the next, he was taught the opposite. Experiencing a growing sense of cultural contradiction, and an abhorrence of the hypocrisy of identity politics, he found "affective sincerity in great music" and turned, for objective truth, to the study of mathematical physics at the Sorbonne in 1926. But one year before Heisenberg's breakthrough, he abandoned physics for anthropology.

I think I also identified with George's sense of marginality, of often finding himself in countries where he did not feel completely at home, of often seeming to be against the grain of what was considered important or fashionable in his field. "One of the reasons for my huge written output," he once confided to a friend, "is the fact that for all those years I had no one to talk to. So I wrote" (1979:15). And elsewhere, and for me, as it turned out, presciently: "Considering all things—even the years of actual starvation, the lifelong insecurity of employment, no retirement income . . . thirty-five years in outer limbo, I deem myself fortunate on two capital scores: I have made no compromises and I have done work that passionately interested me" (1978:402).

After Canberra, I saw George again twice, on visits my wife and I made to Paris in 1979 and 1982, and of course we corresponded frequently. One afternoon, he entertained us (more accurately, I should say, appalled and amused us) by playing one of his own compositions on his grand piano. On another he showed me some his old field notes— evidence of how much work he had still to do. But most memorable is that long-ago Austral summer when ideas seemed to materialize out of thin air, bubble up out of the earth, as from a spring, and come in dreams, when the intense, undisturbed heat of the afternoons was filled with the brittle odor of eucalypts, the screech of gallahs and parakeets, and the chug-chug-chug of water sprinklers on dark green lawns.

On the Margins

Devereux's pioneering work on the effects of countertransference in the behavioral sciences, particularly the way we readily fall back on strategies of pseudo-objectification, intellectual systematizing, selection, scotomization, and simplification in order to magically reorient ourselves in situations that seriously undermine our sense of ontological security, implies for me that the viability of any human life depends on one's sense of being able, in some small measure, to comprehend and control one's immediate circumstances. As John Bowlby (1973) and others have shown, the situations most devastating to our ontological security and sense of identity involve traumatic separation and loss. Though the prototype of all separation is separation from the mother, the bereavement reaction is a given of our biogenetic evolution and assumes the same form among all human beings. Moreover, the phylogenetically determined process of mourning, whereby one passes from anger and protest through despair and withdrawal to detachment and acceptance has an analogue in the ritual passage from separation, via marginality, to reincorporation that Arnold Van Gennep and Victor Turner showed also to be universal. Existentially speaking, separation anxiety involves a fear of losing one's hold on the world around—of being reduced to passivity, aloneness, and childlike dependency, at the mercy of forces that are unresponsive to one's needs or persons who are hostile or indifferent to one's humanity. The recovery of a sense that one can, in some way and to some extent, comprehend and control one's situation may be achieved in a variety of ways: telling stories in which we retrospectively recast ourselves as acting subjects rather than abject sufferers, having others confirm our wild guesses as to what is happening and why, seeking out familiar objects that symbolically re-store our relationship with the world we have lost, and even imagining bonds of kinship or friendship with those who have, albeit innocently, made us feel so insecure, so that we later extol their virtues out of a misplaced gratitude for their having saved our face and recognized our humanity in a place and at a time when these were imperiled (La Barre 1972:52).

Reorientations

In what follows, my focus is the liminal phase of fieldwork: the time after separation from one's familiar lifeworld but before one finds one's feet and feels at home in one's new environment.

In retrospect, three things troubled me during my first few weeks in northern Sierra Leone: the first was my dread of interrogating strangers in a language I had only a smattering of; the second was anxiety that I would never amass enough data in a year to write a PhD; the third was a deep disquiet about having brought my wife, three months pregnant, to a place so remote from emergency medical services. While this last concern found expression in a generalized sense of moral uncertainty, the first two came into focus in my dreams.

A few weeks after beginning fieldwork, I had a disturbing dream that I felt compelled to record immediately on awakening. The dream com-prised two episodes. In the first I found myself in a bare room, reminis-cent of one of the classrooms at the District Council Primary School in Kabala where I had first met Noah Marah (a teacher at the school who later became my field assistant). A corrugated iron door was opened

 liminality.

into the room and a book was passed into the room by an invisible hand or by some other invisible agency. The book hung suspended in midair for several seconds, and I identified a single word in bold type on its cover: ETHNOGRAPHY. I had the definite impression that the book contained only blank pages. In the second episode I found myself again in the same room. Again the door opened. I felt a tremendous presence sweep into the room. I felt myself lifted up bodily and, as if held in the hands or by the power of a giant, I was taken out of the room. The hands and arms of the giant exerted such pressure against my chest that I could not breathe easily. I was borne along aloft, still being squeezed. At this point I awoke in fear from the dream.

The dream obviously manifested several of my anxieties at that time: my concern that I would not prove capable of carrying out the research for a thesis or book on the Kuranko; my dependence on my field assistant who, at that time, mediated all my relationships with Kuranko people and was instructing me in the language; the mild paranoia, vulnerability, and estrangement I experienced in the villages, surrounded by people I did know and talk I did not understand.

The day after this dream I made a trip to Dankawali (a village about twenty-five miles from Kabala) where I met the brother of Alpha Kargbo II, a Kuranko elder with whom I had spent some time in Kabala during the preceding weeks. On learning that Alpha's brother, Fode, knew something of dream interpretation, I recounted my dream to him. He was puzzled, and the dream was discussed among other elders who were present. I was asked whether the giant flew up into the sky with me and whether or not he had placed me back on the ground. After I had answered these questions, Fode announced the meaning of the dream: it signified importance; it meant that if I were a Kuranko man I would be destined to become a chief. Fode added, "You will become a very important person; I do not know about you because you are a European, but for us the book means knowledge, it came to reveal knowledge." Some confusion had followed from my reference to a giant since the word cannot be translated exactly into Kuranko (and I had relied, in this conversation, on my field assistant to interpret for me). The nearest equivalent to our word *giant* is *ke yan* (literally, "long man"), which designates a tall bush spirit that sometimes allies itself with a hunter. I was told that if this bush spirit appears in a dream then it wishes to help the dreamer.

Despite Fode's caveat (that he might not be able to interpret correctly a European's dream using Kuranko hermeneutics), his elucidation of the meaning of the dream was quite consistent with orthodox Kuranko readings. Thus a book signifies knowledge; being in a strange place among strange people signifies good fortune in the near future; being in a high place signifies the imminent attainment of a prestigious position; flying like a bird signifies happiness and prosperity. Where Fode's interpretation differed from my own was not only at the level of exegesis; it was in his conviction that the dream presaged future events rather than revealed present anxieties. Nevertheless, his assurances did help me allay my anxieties, and I felt that his interpretation of my dream consisted of more than pat references to commonplace Kuranko images: a fish with scales foretelling the birth of a son; a fish without scales foretelling the birth of a daughter; being in a dark forest or a swamp signifying a conspiracy; and so forth. Fode's interpretation suggested conscious or unconscious sympathy for my situation as a stranger in his society. Indeed, from subsequent conversations with many informants I became convinced that while a great number of dream events have a standardized significance attached to them, the dream interpreter negotiates a commentary that speaks directly to the client's situation. In other words, although dream interpretation is inductive (according to the official Kuranko point of view), it probably involves unconscious and inadvertent introjections by both the analyst and the analyzed, that is, it is largely intersubjective, interpretive, and intuitive. This intuitive element in dream analysis may make it liable to abuse. On one occasion I met a man who told me that he had dreamed the previous night that a European had come and given him some money (to distribute to others) and a multicolored collarless shirt. He added that he had woken up that morning and given money to others, and therefore I owed him that amount. I knew him well enough to suspect that his "dream" was probably a ruse to extort money from me.

By turning to Kuranko oneiromancy, I not only went some way toward alleviating my anxieties about doing fieldwork; my eyes were also opened to the importance of dreams and portents in Kuranko life—a subject I researched during my fieldwork in 1969–70 and am now researching among expatriate Sierra Leoneans in London.

A similar transformation of self-centered reflections into research concerning the lifeworlds of others followed from a consultation with a

Kuranko diviner not long after I began fieldwork in the village of Firawa in late December 1969. During my first few weeks in the village, I found myself so captivated by the things I heard and saw around me that it was all too easy to believe I intuitively understood them. But understanding is never born of enchantment, any more than initiation is consummated in newness alone. Understanding comes of separation and pain. To understand is to suffer the eclipse of everything you know, all that you have, and all that you are. It is, as the Kuranko say, like the gown you put on when you are initiated. To don this gown you must first be divested of your old garb, stripped clean, and reduced to nothingness.

I would begin my days at Noah's brother Abdul's house. The porch was of mud and dung, its floor as burnished as a river stone. Sitting with my back against the wall, I could observe the comings and goings in the compound and ply Noah and Abdul with questions. Abdul was ensconced at a treadle sewing machine at the other end of the porch, putting the finishing touches to the white country-cloth gown his niece would wear for her initiation. He was a taciturn man at the best of times, and I suspected that the row of pins he held tightly between his lips was a pretext for ignoring my questions. So it was Noah who bore the brunt of my incessant curiosity as groups of strangely attired women performed before the house before receiving a dash and moving on, or groups of pubescent girls, their hair braided, beaded, and decorated with snail-shell toggles, their waists encircled with strings of beads, danced out the last days of their childhood. But behind the drumming that lasted long into the night, and the air of festivity, there were deep shadows. I was told of the neophytes' vulnerability to witches and of the dangers attending cliterodectomy. I heard of fearful encounters with bush spirits and arduous hazings. And I wondered how these young girls would feel, returning after weeks of sequestration in the bush, not to the security of their parental homes but to the uncertainties of life as newlyweds in the houses of strangers.

If I empathized with the neophytes, it was, I suppose, because I was also like a child, and because the shock of too many new experiences— a language I could not grasp, food I often found unpalatable, customs I could not understand, afflictions I could not cure—was beginning to erode my own self-confidence and make me vaguely paranoid. As the days passed, I began to miss my wife Pauline, and to worry about her.

One evening I went out to the latrine that stood in the grassland behind the house where I was staying. For a while, the silence around me was broken only by the repetitive piping of a *sulukuku* bird. Then suddenly I was startled by the presence of several Senegalese fire finches flitting above me. Aware that for Kuranko these small, crimson birds embodied the souls of children who have died in infancy, I became convinced that something was amiss in Kabala, that my wife had had a miscarriage, that her life was in peril.

That night I slept badly, and in the morning I confided my anxieties to Noah. He, too, was missing his children and wondering about his wives back in Kabala. Perhaps it was time for us to return. But I was determined to stay, at least until the initiates entered the *fafei*—the bush house where they would live for several weeks after their operations, receiving instructions from older women.

It was at this time that I consulted my first Kuranko diviner. His name was Doron Mamburu Sisay. Noah had sought his advice and allowed me to sit in on the consultation, and so, a couple of days later, without thinking too much about it, I asked if I might follow suit. "The *tubabu* (white man) wants to know if you can look at the stones for him?" Noah asked. Doron Mamburu gestured that we should go inside his house.

Stooping, I followed Noah through the low doorway into a house that smelled of stale wood smoke. Doron Mamburu dragged shut a rickety cane door whose daubing of mud had all but flaked off. He then sat and waited, his eyes becoming accustomed to the gloom, before spreading out a mat on the earthen floor and ordering me to sit down opposite him. "Why have you come?" he asked. Noah spoke for me. "He wants to find out about his wife," he said. "She is expecting a child. He is worried about her. He wants to know if all is well, if all will be well."

The diviner emptied some stones from a small monkey-skin bag and with the palm of his hand spread them across the mat. Most were river pebbles: semilucent, the color of rust, jasper, and yellow ochre. Among them were some cowrie shells, old coins, and pieces of metal. When I handed Doron Mamburu his fifty cents consultation fee, he mingled this with the other objects. "What is your wife's name?" he asked. "Pauline," I answered, pleased to have understood the question.

Doron Mamburu found difficulty with the name but did not ask for it to be repeated. In a soft voice he addressed the stones, informing them of the reason I had come. Then he gathered up a handful and began to chant. At the same time, with half-closed eyes, he rhythmically knocked the back of his cupped hand against the mat. With great deliberation he then laid out the stones, some in pairs, some singly, others in threes and fours.

"All is well," Doron Mamburu said quietly, his attention fixed on the stones. "Your wife is well. She will have a baby girl." Without a pause he proceeded to lay out a second pattern. "There is nothing untoward. The paths are clear. The birth will be easy." In order to see what sacrifice I should make, Doron Mamburu laid out the stones a third time. "Your wife must sacrifice some clothes and give them to a woman she respects. You must sacrifice two yards of white satin and give it to a man you respect. When your child is born, you must sacrifice a sheep." The diviner looked warily at me, as if wondering whether I would do as the stones suggested.

"To whom must I address the sacrifice?" I asked in English. Noah translated. "To your ancestors," Doron Mamburu said flatly. Then, seeing that I was still nonplussed, he added: "You must give those things away, do you see?" Doron Mamburu began to gather up his stones. He had been working on his farm since first light and was famished. The dull clang of a cooking pot in the yard had already distracted him, and I caught a whiff of chicken and red pepper sauce.

Reassured by the diviner's insights, I nonetheless remained skeptical. "How can the stones tell you what you told me?" I asked, again relying on Noah to translate. "They speak, just as we are speaking now," the diviner answered. "But only I can hear what they are saying. It is a gift that I was born with."

"Could I acquire that gift?" I asked.

"A person cannot tell if a bird has an egg in its nest simply by watching it in flight."

I told Noah that I did not understand.

Doron Mamburu fetched the loose sleeve of his gown up onto his shoulder and frowned. "You cannot go looking for it. Not at all. It comes to you." There was a silence. "Eat with me," Doron Mamburu said, climbing to his feet. He stowed his bag of stones between a rafter and the thatch, then wrenched the door open. The sunlight blinded me. When we were seated in the yard, Doron Mamburu's wife brought us rice and sauce in a chipped calabash. But I had more questions.

"How did you get the stones?" I asked. "And the words you say to them—surely someone taught them to you?" Doron Mamburu finished his mouthful of rice. Then, as if amused by my curiosity, he said cryptically: "If you find fruit on the ground, look to the tree." I must have looked very perplexed. Doron Mamburu continued. "In my case, I began divining a long time ago, in the days of Chief Pore Bolo. I was favored by a djinni. I saw a djinni, and the djinni told me it was going to give me some stones so that I would be able to help people."

"Where did you see the djinn?"

"In a dream. They came in a dream. There were two of them. A man and a woman. They had changed themselves into human beings and were divining with river stones. They called to me and told me their names. They said, 'We are going to favor you with a different destiny.' They showed me a certain leaf and told me I should make it into a powder and mix it with water in a calabash. Then I was to get some stones from the river and wash them in that liquid. When I woke up next morning I went at once to the Bagbe River and found that leaf and those stones. I did everything the djinni told me to do."

"Would I be able to find that leaf?"

"Eh! I cannot tell you about that."

"The djinni, then, did you see them again?"

"Yes, I see them often. Every Thursday and Friday night they appear to me in a dream. Sometimes they say to me, 'Are you still here?'"

"Do the djinni speak to you through the stones?"

"Yes," said the diviner emphatically, as if pleased that I had finally understood something of what he was telling me.

"When you address the stones, you are not speaking to the djinni?"

"No! I am speaking to the stones."

Again a frown creased Doron Mamburu's forehead. Hitching up his sleeve, he scooped a ball of rice from the calabash and slipped it deftly into his mouth. I had finished eating, but not my interrogation: "Do you ever give anything to the djinni?" Doron Mamburu swallowed the rice and washed it down with some water. "From time to time I offer them a sacrifice—of white kola nuts," he answered. I could see Doron Mamburu was tired and that Noah was exasperated by my questions and the difficulty of translating them. I got up to go. "I have eaten well," I said. "You are going?" the diviner asked. "Yes, I'm going to my house."

In those first weeks of fieldwork in Firawa, the seeds of almost all the ideas that would shape my thinking over the next thirty years were planted. I was now convinced that the justification of anthropology lay not in its potential to explain social phenomena on the basis of antecedent causes or underlying laws—evolutionary, structural, or psychological—but in its capacity to explore, in a variety of contexts, the ways in which people struggle, with whatever inner or worldly resources they possess, to manage the immediate imperatives of existence. Though worldviews differ radically from society to society and epoch to epoch, our everyday priorities, as well as our notions of what makes us quintessentially human, are remarkably similar wherever one goes. To participate in the lives of others, in another society, is to discover the crossing points where one's own experience connects with theirs— the points at which sameness subsumes difference. It may be that this savoir faire, more than abstract ideas, promises the best basis for practical coexistence in a plural world.

As for Kuranko divination, I published my account of it in 1978, four years after my auspicious meeting with George Devereux, who had encouraged me to write about the interface between my own subjectivity and the subjectivities of others. In this piece (Jackson 1978; republished 1989), I included an account of my own consultations with diviners like Doron Mamburu, as well as what I learned from extensive conversations with other diviners (some of whom used techniques other than pebbles) and with clients about why they sought the insights of diviners and why they did or did not follow the courses of action and kinds of sacrifices prescribed to avert misfortune or secure a safe outcome of a journey, an initiation, a marriage, a childbirth, a course of medical treatment, a business venture, the building of a house, or the clearing of a farm. At the time I wrote my paper the orthodox anthropological approach to divination was intellectualist in character, and under the influence of the rationality-irrationality debate. Anthropologists sought to explain how diviners maintained credibility and protected the plausibility of a diagnostic system that is so hit and miss. Arguing against this intellectualist bias, I focused on the existential situations in which clients found themselves—the vexing uncertainty, enforced passivity, and conceptual confusion into which circumstances had thrown them. I argued that in so far as I had not felt any need to embrace Kuranko beliefs about spirits in order to enter into the spirit of a divinatory séance, Kuranko probably did not have to commit absolutely to the tenets of their belief system in order to use them in coping with adversity, though reifying and ontologizing these beliefs undoubtedly invests them with the kind of power or aura without which some people might deem them inefficacious.

My focus, however, was not belief per se, but the mixed emotions, the fragmented thinking, the hallucinatory images, and wild imaginings associated with separation anxiety. I approached the phenomena in two ways. First, I explored how, in the divinatory séance, subjectivity gives ground to some form of objectification in which the problem can be grasped or handled as if its locus were outside rather than within the self. Objects (or words) are invested with the emotions that have proved refractory to conscious organization; the objects (or words) are then organized and manipulated in order to achieve a mimetic or vicarious mastery over the emotions and events they stand for. This process of externalization entails two parallel transitions: (1) The consultor surpasses the chaotic and inchoate state in which he or she finds himself and, through social action, is enabled to assume responsibility for and determine his or her own situation; (2) the consultor's situation is classified according to collective dogmas of causation and, as a consequence, the consultor's group (family, subclan, or village) is enabled to act decisively to determine its situation. The diviner's role can thus be understood as one that ritualizes the transition from inertia to activity, on the one hand, and from private experience to shared experience, on the other.

My second approach was to emphasize the instrumental or praxeological, rather than expressive or semiotic, aspects of divination. The diviner's analysis transforms uncertainty into a conditional certainty, and his instructions for an appropriate sacrifice enable the consultor to regain his or her autonomy—to act on the conditions acting on him or her. This autonomy precludes anxiety. I argued that these psychological and existential changes are immediate and positive, and that the ultimate outcome of any prognostication or sacrifice does not necessarily inspire retrospective interest in the truth or falsity of the diviner's original propositions. The reassurances that follow from and the activity enabled by the consultation entail a suspension of disbelief. This pragmatist interpretation had, I argued, the added advantage that it was consonant with Kuranko attitudes to belief. What is imperative for Kuranko is not whether a story told, a prognosis offered, or a sacrifice made will give intellectual satisfaction, but whether it will improve one's lot, enable one to act, strengthen one's bonds with others, and minimize the risks of misfortune. As William James puts it: truth is what *"happens* to an idea. It *becomes* true, is *made* true by events. Its verity *is* in fact an event, a process" (1978:97).

Borderlands

I began this chapter with Devereux's assertion that anthropological knowledge is an outcome *both* of disinterested observation *and* the observer's struggle to allay his or her anxieties and get his or her bearings in a bewilderingly new environment. But in making reflexivity essential to ethnographic method, I have perhaps ventured farther than Devereux in claiming that insights gained in the course of one's personal attempts to adjust to a strange new world may afford insights not only into that world but into the human condition itself. In this view, the hermeneutic circle encompasses *three* horizons: that of one's own world, that of the society one seeks to understand, and that of humanity. In what follows, I outline what this universalizing claim entails.

I begin with the observation that separation anxiety, whether experienced by an anthropologist embarking on fieldwork or by any human being suffering a devastating disruption of his or her lifeworld may be understood as a particular instance of boundary disruption—a sudden loss of the normal balance between inside and outside. In *Beyond the Pleasure Principle* (1989:30–35), Freud noted that all organisms, from the lowly amoeba to human beings, need to *both* absorb elements of the world beyond their boundaries *and* protect these boundaries from invasive and life-threatening forces. Filtering, monitoring, and controlling traffic across body boundaries, either through practical or through imaginative strategies, is thus crucial to the life of any organism and constitutes what Vincent Crapanzano has called Herme's dilemma. Wherever microcosm merges with macrocosm, anxiety begins, and it is at the threshold between the familiar and the foreign that ritual action, taboos, mixed emotions, and intellectual concerns are concentrated.

As I became aware of the working of this subjective dialectic between being open to the Kuranko world and protective of my own sense of self, I began to see evidence of the same dialectic in Kuranko social life. Let me explain.

A few months before I left England, NASA succeeded in putting two men on the moon. I sat up all night at my Cambridge college watching the television coverage, and by the time the two silvery gray, bulky figures of Neil Armstrong and Buzz Aldrin finally ascended the ladder to the LEM and "achieved reingress," dawn was breaking. Walking back to my flat, wearied by the clichés of the night, I warmed to the sight of the sun coming out of the mist and the noise of birds.

It so happened that when my wife and I arrived in Sierra Leone, the country was in the grip of a conjunctivitis epidemic. Locals called the eye disease Apollo, though when a second wave of the epidemic swept the country, a distinction was made between Apollo 11 and Apollo 12. "What was the connection?" I asked people. The American moon landings had disturbed the dust on the surface of the moon, I was told. Just as the sand-laden Harmattan blows south from the Sahara in the dry season, filling the air and irritating one's eyes, so this cosmic dust had brought its own discomforts and disease.

Given my curiosity, people were then eager to have me clarify some of the anomalies in the accounts they had heard of the Apollo missions. Some suspected that these accounts were untrue; no one could travel to the moon. Others (ignorant as to how far away the moon was, and believing it to be just overhead, no bigger than it appeared in the night sky) asked me to explain how a rocket large enough to hold three men could come to a standstill alongside the moon and allow the men to get out and walk about on its surface. Still others demanded to know why the Americans wanted to go to the moon in the first place; what sinister designs and global repercussions did this presage? I had already noted this same suspicion of the United States in local peoples' refusal to allow Peace Corps volunteers to photograph them. Anxieties clustered around the rumor that photos showing village women with bare breasts would be used by whites in the United States as racist propaganda, a way of arguing for the oppression of African Americans on the grounds that their origins and essence were incorrigibly primitive. In many ways these anxieties anticipated the fears of a later generation: that just as Americans had once sought to steal people's vital essence by capturing their likenesses in photographs, so foreigners were now out to steal and traffic in human body parts and vital organs.

But getting back to Apollo, the questions people in Firawa and Kabala put to me should not be read too literally. People were less interested in grasping intellectually the truth of the Apollo program than in how to resolve an old existential dilemma that it had brought to mind. This was the dilemma of how to control traffic across the borders of their own local world, such that it would be perennially revitalized by imports from the outside world—and these included magical medicines, women, and commodities like salt, cloth, kerosene, and seeds—without its integrity being endangered or undermined by foreign influences they were powerless to control. It was not that Kuranko had hitherto lived in isolation, but rather that the postindependence period had brought increasing hardship in negotiating relations with the outside world that worked to their advantage. While villagers were building roads to get access to markets, young men going south in increasing numbers to work in the diamond districts, and Muslim converts making the pilgrimage to Mecca, Kuranko were coming to see that the outside world was much larger, much more complex, and probably much less manageable than it had been for their forebears. The Apollo stories encapsulated this pervasive suspicion that the might of a foreign power of which they knew very little could cause things to happen in their own backyard without their consent, without their comprehension, and without their control.

Different people, and different peoples, have different thresholds of tolerance of otherness and unfamiliarity. Sometimes one may account for these differences biographically or historically. Just as my own susceptibility to separation anxiety reflects the circumstances of my early childhood (Jackson 2006:16), so the excessive secrecy and suspicion in rural Sierra Leone may reflect slave raiding and endemic warfare in the past (Ferme 2001; Shaw 2002). But the fear of uncertainty and loss is part and parcel of the human condition, and no human being is indifferent to the real or imagined forces that threaten his or her sense of ontological security, whether these take the form of an oppressive government, the threat of foreign invasion, viral or bacterial contamination (E.coli, SARS, or HIV-AIDS), terrorist attacks, witchcraft, the infirmities of age, or natural disasters. When I first came to live in the United States, I observed the Stars and Stripes outside many homes, the ubiquitous security systems, the preoccupation with hygiene, the ownership of firearms, the massive vehicles, and the patriotic bumper stickers invoking God's blessings only to be reminded of the white flags that Kuranko villagers hung outside their houses on the advice from diviners, or the various fetishes on lintels and farm fences or worn on the body—magical techniques for bolstering one's own sense of well-being and at the same time warning away the forces of darkness that circulated like predators beyond the perimeter of hearth and home.

We take almost all the decisive steps in our lives as
a result of slight inner adjustments of which we are
barely conscious.—W. G. SEBALD, *Austerlitz*

Despite Babel

an essay on human misunderstanding

In J. M. Coetzee's *Lives of the Animals,* the central character, Elizabeth
Costello, delivers a lecture at an American university on the subject of
animal rights. Her anxious son is in the audience, and as Elizabeth
Costello reaches the end of her lecture, he hopes she will decline to
take questions from the floor. "She ought to know," he says to himself,
"that public lectures draw kooks and crazies like flies to a corpse."
Anyone who lectures for a living will recognize this experience. No
matter how painstakingly one prepares a talk, it will draw comments
that bear no relationship to what one thought one was saying, and
attract questions that preclude any response. But lecture halls and
classrooms are not the only places in which we pass each other like
ships in the night, and if an anthropologist from Mars visited earth, he
or she would undoubtedly be struck by our extraordinary capacity for

talking past each other and for "deriving different signification from the same symbols and rituals" (Ohnuki-Tierney 2004:15–21). At the same time, our imaginary anthropologist would surely be baffled by the different meanings that attach to the same gestures in different cultures—a nod signaling negation in Greece but affirmation in England, direct eye contact conveying sincerity of interest in America but antagonism in Polynesia and Africa, touching taken as an unwanted invasion of a person's private space in some societies but in others communicating empathy. And despite the similarity of facial musculature and expressions among all humans, subtle variations are liable to cause consternation. In Europe and the United States, raised eyebrows are usually interpreted as a question or a gesture of recognition, but for Polynesian New Zealanders it may communicate acknowledgment, the equivalent of the phrase "Yes, I understand" (Metge and Kinloch 1978: 11), while in Japan such behavior between adults is considered very unseemly (Eibl-Eibesfeldt 1989:453). As for suffering, I think of Sofie Danniskiold-Samsøe's research among Shi'a Iraqi refugees in Copenhagen whose stories of existential distress are often regarded by Danish doctors and welfare bureaucrats as diagnostically irrelevant, and whose lack of physical symptoms of specific illness or post-traumatic stress disorder leads to suspicions of malingering (2006). Not only would our Martian anthropologist wonder at the mutual misunderstanding and downright misery that spring from the inherent ambiguity of everything human beings say and do in the presence of one another; he or she would also be astonished by the energy devoted to reducing this ambiguity and dealing with the fallout from never knowing exactly what others are feeling, thinking, or intending.

If our Martian strayed into a university, he or she might be amazed at the industry generated by this passion for rational, systematic, and unambiguous knowledge of others and of oneself, and he or she might wonder how human beings have managed to succeed in the Darwinian struggle for survival given their Babel of mutually incomprehensible languages, dialectics, and argots, not to mention their capacity for misreading one another's gestures and minds. But our visiting ethnographer might ask a more fundamental question: why well-educated earthlings should set such store in the idea of knowing the other, or knowing themselves, when social existence is manifestly not predicated on any theoretical understanding that can be readily put into words, any more than meaningful speech is predicated on a formal knowledge of grammar. Indeed, theories, like prejudices, would seem to be one of the principal causes of misrecognition since they tend to make the other an object whose only value is to confirm our suspicions or prove our point of view. As long as mutually congenial outcomes occur, our Martian anthropologist might argue, it does not matter whether one begins, or ends, with a clear understanding of what one is doing, an empathic understanding of the other, or even knowledge of oneself.

My interest here is in what Pierre Bourdieu, deferring to Pascal, calls scholastic fallacies (2000). The first is the assumption that identity and knowledge are stable and intrinsic properties of persons and groups. It is this fallacy that produces the spurious phenomenological question of how can one *really* understand what another is thinking, feeling, or intending?[1] The question is spurious because whatever the mindset or disposition of self or other, thoughts and feelings transpire in the inter-subjective, transitive, or potential spaces *between* us that go beyond the initial situation and cannot be explained by referring back to it (Arendt 1958; James 1976; Winnicott 1974). This is the meaning of Jean-Paul Sartre's notion of *dépassement* and Hannah Arendt's notion of natality. Despite the ineradicable effects of past experiences—some harrowing, some unremarkable—something irreducibly new is born of every human encounter, and it is the possibility of this newness that explains the perennial hope that inheres in every human relationship, countering the cynicism and despair that arise whenever we fail to get our message across, find that our meaning has been missed, or become frustrated at not being recognized for who we are. As in games of chance, so in life the possibility of a change in fortune accompanies every new throw of the dice, every new deal of the cards, every new spin of the wheel. The second scholastic fallacy is to assume that human interactions are primarily motivated by the kinds of abstract ideas and rational calculations—cultural, economic, or political—that are typically adduced retrospectively in accounting for what has transpired. In fact, every human encounter involves far more than meets the eye and, as with icebergs, what is visible is only a fraction of what lies beneath or on the periphery of consciousness. Of this extra-epistemological domain that we cannot pin down conceptually Bourdieu says that here a "logic of practice" lies at the limits of discursive reason and cannot easily be put into words (1990:86).[2]

There is a long-standing humanist assumption in anthropology, first spelled out by Bronislaw Malinowski, that our goal is "to grasp the native's point of view, his relation to life, to realise *his* vision of *his* world" (1922:25). Though we most certainly get closer to this goal by taking the time to live in "natives'" own communities and communicating with them on their own terms than if we never talked to them at all and relied solely on hearsay or other people's accounts of their experience, few anthropologists these days would claim that it is possible to see the world as another sees it, or achieve the kind of Archimedean view from afar that enables us to wholly grasp the concatenation of factors that might account for another person's behavior or his or her way of seeing the world. But despite being skeptical about the possibility of gaining a conceptual knowledge of the other, we would not want to say that this precludes the possibility of the kind of affinity and recognition that is the basis of all friendship and love. And so we arrive at an apparent paradox. Given the misrecognition, *méconnaissance*, discursive incommensurability, and sheer incredulity that inform every intersubjective and intercultural encounter, how is it that mutuality is at all possible?

Return to Kabala

Carlo Levi begins his memoir of exile in Lucania, the remote province in southern Italy where he was banished in 1935 because of his uncompromising opposition to fascism, with these words: "Many years have gone by, years of war and of what men call History. Buffeted here and there at random I have not been able to return to my peasants as I promised when I left them, and I do not know when, if ever, I can keep my promise." These lines made an unforgettable impression on me when I first read them, and during the ten years of civil war in Sierra Leone, I often found myself, like Levi, "closed in one room, in a world apart," traveling in memory to a place "hedged in by custom and sorrow, cut off from History and the State" (1982:11).

When I finally returned to Sierra Leone in January 2001, everything lay in ruins. In Kabala, saplings and long grass had grown up through the shattered masonry of houses sacked and pillaged by the RUF in November 1994, and when I went looking for familiar landmarks, I found only a ghost town. At the old post office, now boarded up, a watchman was dozing on a mat on the porch; he had no idea when postal services would resume, or whether he would ever be paid for his vigil. Further along the road I passed abandoned or derelict houses that had once been occupied by the Kabala hospital staff, and in Yogomaia I identified the gutted home of the Fula paramount chief, whose son completed a medical degree in Italy and postdoctoral studies in Germany on yellow fever before returning home to practice medicine. Even in 1970, when he treated my wife and me for malaria, Dr. Jallo complained about his lack of medical supplies, his inability to relieve the suffering around him. Where was he now? And Father Joseph, the principal of the Kabala Secondary School, presently the headquarters of the Bangladeshi UN contingent; what had become of his Herculean efforts to make a difference here? I retraced my steps to the market, mindful of the speeches, slogans ("One people, one country"), and promises I had heard from politicians at the Kabala football field the day before—upgraded roads, a reliable electricity supply, interest-free loans for farmers, dispensaries, schools, bridges. Mostly I was struck by the seeming impossibility of any change for the better. All people could do was hope, beg, petition, and endure. In a ramshackle building near the market, Abdulai Fofona showed me a letter from "the redundant workers of the Ministry of Works, Kabala" in which he and others begged the minister of works to compensate them for having had their employment terminated without pay on 1 July 1993. Although some had received back pay, the rebel destruction of Kabala in 1994 prevented others from receiving theirs. Could I intercede on their behalf?

Another young man, whose name I cannot recall, told me he was going to set up an NGO as a way of attracting foreign investment to Kabala. "What would this NGO actually do?" I asked. He did not know. He seemed to think that the acronym had some magical power to attract wealth, like the airstrips in the Melanesian bush laboriously cleared to attract European aircraft loaded with cargo.

Beset by the apparent hopelessness of these attempts to communicate with the powers that be, let alone extract some reparations or material assistance from them, I looked around for L. K. Kamara's bar, forgetting for a moment that L. K. was dead and his bar, together with the old market, long gone. It was then that I remembered Mamina Yegbe and *his* petition, *his* struggle for recognition, and the misunderstandings that seemed to dog him wherever he went.

My wife and I had arrived in Kabala at the beginning of the dry season of 1969, and though the name of the town had nothing to do with the Hebrew *qabbalah* and its esoteric traditions of cosmic union and interpretation (it means, simply, "Kabba's Place"), it had been like an augury for us and drawn us to it.

In my first few weeks in Kabala I undoubtedly cut a ridiculous figure. Linguistically inept, socially disoriented, anomalous in appearance, and preoccupied by questions the point of which no one could grasp, it was perhaps inevitable that I would end up in the company of misfits.

Mamina Yegbe was at least seventy—small, spry, and always, it seemed to me, slightly bemused. Though my field assistant Noah Marah pointed out that Mamina Yegbe had lost his marbles, and tried to dissuade me from setting too much store in what he told me, I felt at ease in the old man's company and often sought him out at the town chief's house near the Kabala market, buying him packets of tobacco in gratitude for his tolerance of my stilted Kuranko.

"The world began in Mande," Mamina Yegbe said. "But yesterday and today are not the same. Whatever sun shines, that is the sun in which you have to dry yourself." And forgetting that Sierra Leone had been an independent state since 1961, he added decisively, "We are now in the period of the white man's rule." He could remember when this period began before the Cameroon War (World War I), and recalled the names of Palmer and Captain Leigh who built the barracks at Gbankuma before the British moved to Falaba. He also described the first barracks at Kabala, built on the site of today's town market, and told me when the frontier was fixed, and when the Court Messenger Force and the Chiefdom Police were inaugurated. And he recounted how taxes were paid to District Commissioner Warren—or Warensi as he was known. Initially the hut tax was two shillings and sixpence, but it later rose to five then to nine shillings, and finally to one pound five shillings, and one pound ten shillings per head. "In those days, people were happy," Mamina Yegbe told me. "We were happy with our government. All the chiefs had their favorite music, and whenever the chiefs assembled, the *jelibas* (praise-singers) would play. Chiefs Belikoro, Konkofa, Sinkerifa—I knew them all."

At the district officer's office one morning, I was working through a stack of intelligence diaries and daybooks from the colonial period, hoping to corroborate Mamina Yegbe's recollections of local history. Around me the clerks were busy with their own bureaucratic chores, filing memoranda, moving dog-eared files from the "out" tray of one desk to the "in" tray of another, sharpening pencils, or fetching ice-cold Coca-Colas for the DO.

Before being allowed to inspect the records, I had been obliged to submit five copies of my application, all typed, signed, sealed in official envelopes, stamped, and countersigned. It did not take very long, however, before I was ruing the effort and my eyes wandered—to the whitewashed wall where two wasps were adding yet another accretion of moist red clay to their nest, and beyond the barred windows of the office where the leaves of an enormous mango tree hung limply in the heat. I closed the daybook and made to go. At that instant, two clerks deserted their desks and asked for a lift to the market.

As I switched on the ignition I caught sight of Mamina Yegbe sitting on a rock under the mango tree, smoking his Bavarian pipe with the hinged metal lid. "Do you want a lift?" I called, and gestured in the direction of the market. Mamina Yegbe clambered up into the front seat of the Land Rover, beside the clerks. As usual he was wearing an embroidered tunic and a blue silk cap with a tassel, looking like a Mandarin. He sat bolt upright with an almost smug expression on his face, holding against his chest a large manila envelope marked in capital letters ON SIERRA LEONE GOVERNMENT SERVICE. The envelope was embellished with ornate signatures and sealed in several places with red wax. It resembled a Saul Steinberg drawing.

The clerks were clearly amused by the envelope. "What's the joke?" I asked. The first clerk winked at me, then nodded toward Mamina Yegbe who was gazing straight ahead. The other clerk dodged the question by suddenly recognizing two friends sauntering along the road. "Mosquito!" he yelled. "Heh! Peacecorps!" And he hung his arm out the window of the Land Rover. A thin, gangly youth who answered to the first description, and his companion, wearing faded jeans with frayed cuffs, lifted their arms to wave, but the dust in the wake of the vehicle enveloped them.

After dropping the clerks at the market, I sought to satisfy my curiosity about the envelope. "What is it?" I asked. The old man continued to gaze straight ahead, but he raised a finger to his lips as if to enjoin silence. He then got down from the Land Rover and without a word disappeared into a crowd around the kola-nut traders.

That night I drove back into Kabala from One-Mile to buy some cold Fanta at Lansana Kamara's (L. K.) bar. The bar was a shabby and poky corner room that opened onto a veranda and the marketplace. It was furnished with several warped and dusty shelves, a battered deep freeze, and five armchairs with polystyrene foam bulging out through rents in the red vinyl upholstery. The jangling strains of a hi-life hit issued from a dilapidated record player at one end of the bar. "I really love you, Fati Fatiii . . ."

L. K. did not particularly like hi-life tunes, and whenever business was slack, he would get out his records from Guinea and, with tears welling up in his eyes, listen to the stirring refrains of praise songs from old Mali.

On the walls of L. K.'s bar were several fly-specked calendars showing beaming Africans in open-necked shirts holding aloft bottles of Vimto, Fanta, or Star beer. L. K. disdained such drinks. With a lugubrious air he poured himself another large Martell brandy and a Guinness chaser.

I bought what I wanted and was about to go when I noticed Mamina Yegbe in the corner, surrounded by a dozen boisterous youths, among them the two clerks from the DO's office. One of them made a remark that I could not catch, but it drew a burst of taunting laughter from the others, and the old man shrank back as if from a blow. I saw that Mamina Yegbe was still holding the big envelope, only now it had been ripped open, and bits of sealing wax littered the floor among the beer-bottle caps.

When the old man saw me he seemed to regain his composure, but before either of us could speak, one of the clerks confronted me with bloodshot eyes and beery breath. "He says it's from Seku Touré and Siaka Stevens!" the clerk roared. "That envelope! He says they've given him a big country in Guinea and a million pounds cash! He says he's coming to the DO tomorrow to collect it!" Everyone broke into laughter. Then they looked at me, waiting for my reaction. The clerk became angry. "He says he's going to be appointed to a high position, in the government!" he shouted, as if I had failed to understand the situation. "It's all in the letter!"

I glanced at Mamina Yegbe, who raised a finger to his lips and smiled ingenuously. I appealed to L. K. for a clue as to what was going on, but L. K. simply smoothed his knitted singlet over his enormous belly, lowered his eyes, and took another sip of brandy.

The clerk, exasperated by my stupidity, lurched over to the old man, wrenched the envelope from his grasp, and shook out its contents onto the bar. L. K. dolefully moved his glass to one side as his customers pawed at the sheaf of papers, spreading them out so that I could see what they were.

I recognized several old General Certificate of Education (GCE) examination papers, some official memoranda and letters, and a page from my own field notes. I could not think how it had come into the old man's possession. Stabbing at the papers, the clerk drew my attention to a bundle of leaflets, all advertisements for Surf washing powder. "This is the letter from the prime minister!" the clerk hooted. "Can't you see what it is?'"

I recalled a Volkswagen Kombi that had turned up outside the market a few days before. A large display packet of soap powder had been fitted to the roof rack, and a loudspeaker blared out hi-life tunes. Four or five men in sunglasses and pale blue shirts had gone about distributing leaflets and occasionally giving away sample packets of Surf. In the afternoon the vehicle, still crackling with canned music, disappeared in a cloud of dust up the road toward Falaba. "Yes, I can see what it is." I knelt down and started picking up the papers that had fallen on the floor. They were already smudged with red dirt from the clerks' shoes.

The jokers appeared embarrassed by this crazy show of sympathy for the old man. They backed out onto the porch, making halfhearted gibes and clutching their bottles of beer. L. K. stared morosely at his glass of Guinness.

"Do you want a lift home?" I asked Mamina Yegbe.

"Awa." Let's go.

I looked down the unlit street, thinking "the generator's gone again" and wanted to say this to Mamina Yegbe. I also wanted to ask the old man, now sitting in silence in the Land Rover beside me, if he still intended to present his letter to the DO and claim his fortune, but it might have seemed like another taunt. What simple faith we all place in the power of printed words, these fetishized markings on a page—the clerks, this benignly deluded old man, myself!

The headlights picked out the mosque and the grove of palms beyond it.

"I'm going back to Barawa on Friday," I said. Mamina Yegbe made no response. "I'll come and see you before I go." In the darkness the town gave forth the sounds of its invisible life: a dog yelping, shouts, a radio badly tuned, an inconsolable child crying, a motor scooter spluttering down a potholed lane, the drubbing of an initiation drum. I drew up outside the house with the broken veranda where Mamina Yegbe lived.

"Ma sogoma yo" (good night), I said as the old man got down. Mamina Yegbe stood on the roadside in the glare of the headlights. "In the old days people were happy," he said. Then he turned and drifted into the darkness.

Almost all his life, Mamina Yegbe lived under a colonial regime. He had imagined it to be like chieftaincy—a source of order and benevolent power. If the great Belikoro could conjure thunderstorms at will and slay his enemies with lightning bolts, then surely the British crown or the presidents of Sierra Leone and Guinea could pay him his due and make good what he was owed. The clerks in the DO's office, who so mercilessly ridiculed him, were no less in thrall to wishful thinking. Indeed, it was the maddeningly elusive nature of fortune in the postcolonial world that compelled them to perform their derision of Mamina Yegbe so publicly. And what of today? What had changed? People had now picked up the jargon of democracy and development, of human rights, post-traumatic stress disorder, of truth and reconciliation. This was the lingo of the new colonizers, the language one needed to speak in order to find work with the various NGOs that were rebuilding the country. In the course of conversation with me, my friend Mats Utas described an ex-combatant called Alvin who had formed an NGO with 235 other ex-RUF youth. Alvin was the director or, in his words, the "commander" of this outfit with the catchy name and acronym. Other officials were listed on a stamp-embellished page as chief security officer, suicide commander, and friendly force commander, and all were interested, Alvin told Mats, in working on "trauma healing" and the three Rs—rehabilitation, reintegration, and reconciliation. It is not my intention to scoff at these mimetic responses to the invasion of a new colonial culture whose "civilizing mission" is to end corruption and bring democracy to Africa. It is, rather, to highlight the paradox and plight of people who are socially and educationally excluded from the very world whose language and culture they struggle to master in order to improve their lot. And though many of the foreign NGOs in countries like Sierra Leone have even less conversancy with local culture than young Sierra Leoneans have with the West, their position of greater power prevents them from having to come to terms with their ignorance. But as with the clerks who mocked Mamina Yegbe, their own indigent understanding is displaced onto others, and they remain blind to the absurdity of their own pro-liferating paperwork, their detailed reports, and their buzzwords like *partnership, participation*, and *empowerment*, none of which were im-proving the lot of ordinary Sierra Leoneans or connected to the issues with which the villagers were concerned.

But perhaps this is not the best way of framing the question of intercultural understanding, for though Mamina Yegbe was, in my eyes, not simply mistaken in his beliefs but a little mad, our marginality brought us together. While he, an old man, had outlived the historical period in which he had had a place, I was on the outer edge of another culture in which I was still to find my feet. In their naivety, their narrow horizons, their wild speculations, and their desperate hope, Mamina Yegbe's millenarian dreams bore comparison with the fugitive and childlike understanding I possessed at that time of the Kuranko world.

We are so used to construing understanding as a meeting of two minds, an intellectual empathy or compatibility between separate selves, that we often overlook the extent to which human affinities reflect forms of mutual recognition that are difficult to put into words or pin down. When Hans-Georg Gadamer writes that "every finite situation has its limitation" and that our particular "vantage-points" delimit our range of vision and our "horizons" (1989:302), this does not mean that the limits of *thought* are where we cease thinking; rather, they are thresholds where we have recourse to modes of understanding that reach beyond language and reason, and it is on these thresholds that our prejudices give way to alternative ways of seeing ourselves and the world—a place, as it were, where horizons fuse (388).[3] Even when an anthropologist cannot comprehend or morally accept what an informant takes to be true, he or she may nonetheless feel a profound sympathy or sense of identification with the other.

This was certainly true of my friendship with Saran Salia Sanoh, who I met through his nephew, Noah Marah, during the dry season of 1969–70, even though Noah had told me about his uncle, who was a powerful medicine master (*besetigi*), before our visit to Firawa.

Though now elderly, unmarried, and living alone, Saran Salia had been appointed leader of the young men (*keminetigi*) by the Barawa chief Tala Sewa Marah, and he invariably had several uninitiated boys living under his roof, protecting them from the forces of witchcraft and sorcery to which children are particularly vulnerable. But despite his formidable reputation, he was frail, and he came to see me at Noah's brother's house one morning complaining of sharp pains in his arm and shoulder. The reason was obvious; his right hand was swollen with septicaemia. Among the few medicines I had brought with me from Cambridge was a supply of penicillin. I gave the old man two tablets and instructed him to swallow them with water, one now and one in the evening. Then twice a day for the following week, I tracked him down and ensured that he took his pills. To my great relief the swelling subsided and his pain went away, leaving me to wonder whether he, for all his expertise in magical medicines, would see me now in a new light and agree to talk to me, with Noah's mediation, about his life as a medicine master.

Although Saran Salia recognized my interest, nine years would pass before he opened up to me. When I brought my wife Pauline and our nine-year-old daughter Heidi to live in Firawa in early 1979, Saran Salia insisted that we occupy his house. And so, after resurfacing the walls with white clay, installing mat ceilings and some borrowed sticks of furniture, we moved in and Saran Salia moved out. But hardly a day passed that he did not come to our porch for cups of tea and idle talk, or simply to sit in our hammock and doze through the heat of the day.

I can see him now, standing in the compound and looking at me. His hair is grizzled, his few remaining teeth are kola stained, and he is holding his stave across the back of his shoulders, his hands hanging loose at either end. With his shoulder blades drawn back, his head is forced forward, so that when he peers at me it is as if we share some secret. I can only guess his age, but when he speaks, his face becomes animated as though the events and emotions he recalls in such detail have returned him to a previous incarnation. Our first conversations were about his early life.

> From my birth, I was in the hands of my elders. Year after year, we made our farms, until I donned the clothes of manhood. My parents favored me. I was eating sweetly [I was well looked after]. And when my parents died, my elder brother Malfore Sano looked after me, and I was eating sweetly there as well. After he died, I chased after Kome [a powerful djinni]. I drew the Kome rope for twenty-eight years, until my brother's son, the Alhaji, told me, "Leave it!" And so my hand left it. Then Chief Sena Lai of Bandakarafaia made me his messenger [*worli*]. I was sweet there, and when he died, his younger brother Damba Lai made me his messenger. I lived sweetly there until he died. Then this child of mine, the Alhaji, called me to Firawa. He said, "You can live sweetly here." So he made a farm for me, cooked rice for me, and up until today there has been no hardship on my head. Even when my wives died, the Alhaji and his brother Lahai built this house for me and said, "Father, live here; you don't have to farm anymore; you're unable to work, so live here and rest. Let us feed you; you are old; live sweet." So things are good. And as for you [meaning me], you like me, and I like you. You like my children, and my children like you. If you have come to ask me to tell you all I know from my childhood up to now, that is what I will do.

Though Saran Salia voiced no complaints about his childhood, the deaths of his parents not long after his initiation marked a tragic turning point in his life, leaving him fearful and uncertain. One morning, our conversation turned to his childhood fears—of the djinni, of witches, of the masters of the *korte* medicines (associated with one of the men's cult associations) and of the dead. Saran Salia told me that initiation involved the mastering of such fears and, by extension, mastering one's emotions—a matter of acquiring fortitude (*yuse gbele*; literally, "a hard heart"), bravery (*kerenteye*), self-confidence (*kalai nyerela*; literally, "belief self in"), and new understanding (*hankili kura*). But becoming master of the Kome cult involved more than self-control; it meant becoming an object of fear oneself. As a boy, Saran Salia had been fascinated by Kome. He both feared it and felt it was "something out of the ordinary."

During his initiation, he was impressed by the gifts the *Kometigi* (Kome master) received and the power he commanded. "When I first saw it, I wanted to be it," he said. "As Kometigi, everyone fears you, but you fear no one because you have been immunized against all the harmful medicines."

Saran Salia's decision to become Kometigi was precipitated by the breakup of his first marriage. "The time I decided was when they took a certain woman away from me by force [i.e., another man ran away with his first wife with the connivance of her father]. That man taunted me. 'Show me that your iron can cut my iron!' he said to me. 'If you are a man, then do what you will!' I said, 'Me?' There and then I took up the Kome rope. You understand? Whoever sees Kome dies!"

Shortly after, Saran Salia's errant wife, her lover, and her father died. Though I pressed him on the matter, Saran Salia would neither admit nor deny that he had deliberately used his power as Kometigi or his knowledge of magical medicines to kill them. But he did use a cryptic phrase that I would return to time and time again in the years that followed, "There are many ways that birds fly in the sky."

Over the next few days, Saran Salia spoke to me at length about his three-year apprenticeship in Guinea, in the course of which he acquired a comprehensive knowledge of curative, prophylactic, and lethal medicines. He explained why he had forsworn the use of such lethal medicines as korte and refused to place his knowledge at the disposal of clients wishing to avenge slights or redress injustices through sorcery. Not only could I understand the logic of Kuranko medicine; I admired Saran Salia's decision to use his skills to cure and protect, not to kill.

We were talking one morning about the power one possessed as Kometigi when Saran Salia confided that he was no longer free to practice medicine. Much to his chagrin, his classificatory sons had invoked Islamic law and had obliged him to renounce his old practices as a precondition for them taking care of him in his old age. "But even now," he said, "when the xylophones and flutes play the music of the Kome and sing its songs, I long to dance." And Saran Salia began chanting in a quavering voice: "Sembe, sembe, sembe le, Kome la, eh Kome wo; n'de min i le nyonto ken yen" (Kome has great power; its equal has never been seen).

Sensing that now the time had finally come, I broached the question I had wanted to ask Saran Salia ten years ago, when I first came to Firawa. "What is Kome?" Saran Salia's voice became a hoarse whisper. "Kome does not come from the bush. I am Kome.[4] I dress myself up. It is me they dress up. If our eyes met when I was like that you would fall to the ground in fear. But I am old now. I cannot do it any more." Saran Salia went on to explain how he acquired these special powers during his apprenticeship with a medicine master called Yamisa from the town of Sigiri in Mali.

> If you are to draw the Kome rope you must first wash yourself thoroughly. You go downstream, and your teacher [karamorgo] goes upstream. He changes himself into a snake. It comes toward you through the water [with his forearm and bent wrist, Saran Salia showed me how it swam with its head above the surface]. It wraps around you. After it has wrapped around you, your teacher comes and tells you to leave it. He then takes some leaves and the head of a person who has been dead for seven days. He places the leaves and the head in a fire he has lit in a hole in the ground. You sit in the smoke. The smoke fumigates [literally, "steams"] you. It immunizes you [literally, "you imbibe the steam"] against all harmful medicines. If anyone tries to fight you, he will die.

I later discovered that it is actually the gown that is fumigated and thereby acquires the power to retaliate against an assailant. But the wearer of the gown is always in control. "If flies settle on me, they die," Saran Salia explained. "If a person slaps me, he will die. But if I go like this [Saran Salia slapped his thigh, signifying that he, and not the gown, was retaliating], the gown will cool and the assailant will not die.

I was bewildered. I found it hard to picture the events that Saran Salia had described and was not sure I would want to witness them even if invited to. But Saran Salia's willingness to share this knowledge with me created a covenant between us and bound us in a kind of conspiracy, for this was far from common knowledge. Perhaps he did not expect me to understand. After all, Kuranko were as aware of *tubabu* (European) skepticism as they were of Muslim dogmatism. This is why I think that Saran Salia opened up to me out of respect and affection, not because he thought I would accept or approve what he had to say. It was something given in exchange for the regard I had shown him, on par with his allowing my family to live in his house. But this liking was also born, I think, of the fact that I recognized him as the person he was in his own eyes. Badgered by his classificatory sons into giving up his lifelong roles as besetigi and Kometigi, he nonetheless could, in my company, find at least the semblance of respect that his own kinsmen had withheld from him, despite their attention to his physical needs.

That there were limits to our capacity for comprehending each other's worldviews was made very clear the following day in a conversation that began with Noah asking his uncle to fumigate a gown for him.

"You will provide the cloth?" Saran Salia asked. "Yes, I will bring it to you today." Then Saran Salia looked at me. "If you want it, I will also do it for you, and you can take it with you when you go back to your own country." "But could I become a Kometigi and use the korte medicines?" I asked half jokingly.

"That is impossible. You could not take the medicines to your own country. Besides, you are not used to the Kome. If you saw it, you would shit your pants in fright!" "If you have that fear deep down," Noah explained, "korte will act. But if you don't believe it, it won't act on you. If you have the fear in you, 'Oh they're going to shoot me with this korte,' you will die then. But you must have that fear of it."

And so the line was drawn. This was not my habitus. I could not enter it through an act of intellectual effort alone. Just as Noah had said, certain things are possible only when you are a part of a community that shares the same belief in their possibility, just as many actions are efficacious only when supported by faith in their efficacy. This faith is not something one can acquire or feign; it comes from being raised in a particular culture, an outcome not of formal instruction but of mimetic learning and osmosis.

We encounter other cultures as we encounter other persons, both in terms of the ideas with which we conventionally frame our understanding of reality and in terms of experiences that confound, contradict, or cannot easily be contained within the frame. This helps explain why one can be drawn to, and even feel a deep affinity for, someone whose political or religious opinions one does not share, and why friendship universally transgresses the boundaries of gender, age, ethnicity, and belief. This is also why the assumption that we may arrive at mutual understanding through intercultural or intellectual *dialogue* is deeply flawed, since worldviews tend to support particular standpoints even when pretending to embrace universal principles. Fortunately, the grounds of our common humanity lie beyond belief, transcending the *doxa* whose reified forms entrap us in a sense of being uniquely right or righteous. These grounds include human capacities for communication, recognition, and fellowship that do not depend on speech and conceptual thought. Moreover, what is striking about human interaction is that while it is seemingly dyadic, it invariably involves a third party, a shared goal, a common cause, whose presence is often shadowy or unspoken. Empathy or fellow feeling is greatest, then, not when two people mirror each other, but when both are bound together in relation to something shared—parents joined in raising their children, villagers engaged in cooperative labor, neighbors sitting together in amicable silence and solidarity. Kuranko speak of sociality as a matter of moving together, moving as one. And perhaps the most powerful expression of this capacity for transcending age, gender, ethnic, and ideological differences is the capacity for love and friendship, which, in Kuranko, is covered by the word, *dienye*, the same word Saran Salia used in describing his liking for me. Not only are love and friendship (*dien'morgoye* or *kentiye*) free of the *social* duties and obligations that characterize kinship and affinity; such relationships reflect *natural* dispositions, fortuitous meetings, and free choices. As such, friendships cross class and category lines, and they even transcend culture.

"To be in a relationship with someone," writes Robert Orsi, "is not necessarily to understand him or her; but the relationship, which arises always on a particular social field and is invariably inflected by needs, desires, and feelings, conscious and not, that draw on both parties' histories and experiences, becomes the context for understanding" (2005:6). But how could one possibly unravel and reveal all the biographical and cultural experiences, all the inflected needs and emotions, that defined the "context for understanding" my relationships with Saran Salia and Mamina Yegbe? And is it not the impossibility of comprehending this complicated background that inclines us to speak of love and friendship as mysterious, inexplicable, and even miraculous? This is, I think, what Maurice Merleau-Ponty meant when he wrote, echoing Edmund Husserl's notion of the "natural knowledge that begins with experience [*Erfahrung*]" (Husserl 1931:45), that "we must learn to find communication between one consciousness and another in one and the same world" (Merleau-Ponty 1962:353). "In reality," Merleau-Ponty writes, "the other is not shut up inside my perspective of the world, because this perspective itself has no definite limits, because it slips spontaneously into the other's, and because both are brought together in the one single world in which we all participate as anonymous subjects of perception" (353).

But what precisely was this world that belonged neither to me nor to Saran Salia alone? Partly it consisted in a sense of having undergone similar travails, the sort of experience that Sue Monk Kidd is alluding to when she writes, in *The Secret Life of Bees*, of "the wounded places down inside people that sought each other out, that bred a kind of love between them" (2002:184). Partly, too, it was a conspiratorial sense of being privy to experiences not universally shared and, in the case of Saran Salia's classificatory sons, actively censured. Perhaps every intimate relationship participates in this tacit agreement that what transpires within the relationship belongs to it and should not be made public. That Kuranko regard adultery as "darkening" or "spoiling" relationships in the public sphere is a reflection of the way adultery transgresses this unspoken line between what belongs within the house and what belongs to the village—between what should be "concealed" (*duguro*) and what should be "open" (*kenema*). Like divulging the secrets of the men's or women's cults, adultery betrays the covenant that sets private relationships apart from the more inclusive public sphere.

But living together itself creates a form of understanding, irrespective of what is said or unsaid, what is done or not done, or even whether there is affection or not. Often, I just sat and whiled away the time with Saran Salia. He would grate kola on a tobacco tin lid that he had pierced with a nail. I would boil water and make tea. But that was all. For I had learned that sociality may be consummated in silence and can do without words, just as every writer learns that it is sometimes more effective to show than to tell.

living together

Birth marks the beginning of my own existence
in time; but the givenness of birth suggests that
my existence is not quite my own, that my time is
already bound up with the time of the Other.

—LISA GUENTHER, *The Gift of the Other: Levinas
and the Politics of Reproduction*

10 On Birth, Death, and Rebirth

My flight from Singapore landed in Auckland not long after daybreak.
After collecting my bags and passing through immigration and customs, I took a taxi to my sister's address in Mount Eden. Following her
e-mailed instructions, I found the front door key in a hebe bush near the
mailbox and let myself into the house. A day and a night ago I had been
in the dank winter dark of Copenhagen, but in Auckland sunlight filled
the living room, and I could see as far as the Waitakere ranges, white
cumulus clouds above them like puppets in a Balinese shadow play. All
night on the plane, I had slept fitfully, my mind clogged with a Sargasso
of floating memories and disconnected images—from when I lived in
New Zealand or first went to Sierra Leone. Now, walking out into the
new morning, I was once again swept back into the past, experiencing

the agoraphobia that Auckland's single-storied suburbs always induces in me, the weatherboard houses and mown lawns overwhelmed by an isthmus sky. In the suburban streets, pohutukawas, jacarandas, cabbage trees, and privet hedges were in flower. The air was heavy with the peppery, spermy odor of pollen and shrill with the brouhaha of birds piping, whistling, and warbling around me. All this intensified the oppressive familiarity of the neighborhood from which I nevertheless felt quite estranged. This feeling deepened as I approached the house where my parents had lived until their deaths almost ten years ago, the trees they had planted now felled, the lot returned to concrete paths and bare lawns, and the characterless house now sitting in the middle of this desolate space looking like a dog kennel. Occasionally someone would drive down the street in a car, emerge from a driveway, or an elderly person would pass me without a glance, lugging a shopping bag. But mostly the place was deserted, its life confined behind curtained windows and locked doors.

For several days I was haunted by the past. Or perhaps I should say I was haunted by its unreality. Though stirred to scribble poems about the harsh marine light, the smells that assailed my nostrils, the deafening birdsong, the white clouds, or the old photographs and family letters that my sisters kindly copied for me, I found myself struggling like a diver in the depths, desperate to surface and breathe fresh air, to embrace something new. Auckland belonged to another life, a previous reincarnation—or to someone else. And I marveled at times, walking along Dominion Road, at how confused and lost this other me had felt forty-five years ago, riding home on the late-night bus, his head full of poems of unrequited love and the longing to get away. Back then, I had my whole life ahead of me. Now I was entering my *troisième âge*. In another twenty years, perhaps, I could well be like my mother who, in her early eighties, began a journal in which she set down reminiscences of her childhood and youth in the Taranaki town where she was raised. She told me at the time, "At my age you don't have a lot to look forward to, so you look back." At what age, I asked myself, does one cease to have a future? At what age is rebirth no longer possible? I suppose a lot depends on what the world offers you. In Sierra Leone I had met young men who felt that the world offered them very little. Some of my contemporaries, recently retired, found themselves at a loose end and

complained about the things they had dreamed of doing and had not done, while others, following in the footsteps of John Milton's "uncouth swain," were moving on to fresh fields and pastures new. The repercussions of being born to particular parents, in a particular place, at a particular time, and what it means to be born to oneself, elsewhere, and with others, perplexed and preoccupied me throughout my sojourn in Auckland.

The morning after I arrived in Auckland, an old roommate from my student days, who I had not seen for a very long time, rang to say that he had heard I was in town and would like to see me. Given the passage of so many years, I quailed at the prospect of being once more dragged back into a time that had no reality for me, but I was curious. And so we met one morning, at George's suggestion, outside one of our old watering-holes—the Queen's Ferry hotel in Vulcan Lane.

I arrived early and nervously walked up and down the lane, wondering if I would recognize George. When he finally appeared, shambling up the street toward me, I was aghast. This once fresh-faced young man was now old beyond his years—stiff-necked, hunched, unkempt, wearing an unpressed rust-colored suit, and holding a smoldering roll-your-own cigarette between his nicotine-stained fingers.

Traits that we shrug off as endearing quirks or eccentricities in a young man are all too readily read as signs of decrepitude in the old. And so, as I struggled to come to terms with George's physical transformation, I began to realize that his disconcerting pedantry and self-absorption were not symptoms of aging but simply exaggerated aspects of who he had always been. The hotel was closed, but George explained that there was now a second Queen's Ferry on Queen Street, so we crossed the road, found a table overlooking the street, and bought ourselves glasses of beer. Then, without further ado, George proceeded to unburden himself of the story of his life. "A series of missed opportunities," as he put it, "and dead ends," his "options now fast diminishing." Two failed marriages. No children. An unrewarding job in a government department that he had held for thirty years before being unceremoniously laid off. "These days they don't even give you a watch for your pains." Now, his daily routine seemed to consist of reading the morning paper, spending many hours in the pub, and in the evenings reading library books and writing letters to the editors of various journals and newspapers, chiefly about the decline of values in New Zealand political life. And he hinted darkly at a conspiracy he had uncovered, and a letter he was intending to deliver to the prime minister's residence in Mount Albert later in the day, alerting her to this hidden menace. "But things aren't too bad," he added. "Even though some evenings are rather tedious, I have plenty of time to think, and I have never been afraid of my own company. Indeed, I sometimes think that folk who have ill-considered opinions, or none at all, may not be incurious by nature, but simply have too many calls on their time from family and work to think things through carefully and logically."

Inevitably, our conversation (though the word suggests a degree of give and take, of mutuality, that did not exist) turned to reminiscences. "What ever happened to Jonathan Hunt?" "Is Wystan Curnow still teaching at the University of Auckland?" "Do you ever run into Denis Taylor?" This kind of thing. But George's interest lay less in the whereabouts or accomplishments of our peers than in the fate of his favorite pubs and old haunts, and he even ventured to suggest that we go on a tour of them. With a memory for banal detail that astonished me, he described how "Auckland had changed for the worse." He seemed to take it as a personal slight that so many of the buildings in which he had flatted as a student had been demolished, though was happy to tell me that Pembridge, the state-owned apartment block in Symonds Street where he found an apartment for four pounds a week after our flat at 23 Fairview Road, Mount Eden, fell apart, was still standing. But sadly, the Kiwi hotel had been razed to the ground and a *marae* (courtyard, meeting house) built on the site. The Grand no longer existed, nor the Central, nor the Globe. And George recalled the precise dates on which these calamities had occurred.

I felt guilty at my lack of interest in George's stories, my lack of sympathy for his fixation on the past, and my unwillingness to allow him to take my photograph. (He had wanted to do this within minutes of our meeting, explaining that if he did not do it then and there, he would undoubtedly forget, his resolution now "don't put off until tomorrow what you can do today.") But like the Wedding Guest detained by the Ancient Mariner, I was desperate to get away, to get shut of this depressing history in which George was mired, and so I announced that

I had another appointment at midday (though it was actually at two) and made to go.

It was then that he met my eyes for the first time, and asked after me. He particularly wanted to know about my daughter Heidi. I told him she was thirty-four, lived in Sydney, was a practicing artist, and taught art at a secondary school. I also mentioned that I had two younger children from my second marriage. "I regret not having grandchildren," George said. I told George about a Danish guy who, finding himself in his late sixties without children or grandchildren, advertised in the papers, offering his services as a granddad. He received hundreds of responses. "Maybe you could do the same," I said.

As I trudged up Victoria Street toward Albert Park where the red filigree of flowering pohutukawas littered the paths, I wondered whether we all, sooner or later, feel the need to render some kind of account of ourselves, divine some pattern in our lives, and imagine that everything somehow "adds up." As if, in that poignant line of Joyce Johnson's, "time were like a passage of music [that] you could keep going back to it till you got it right" (1983:237). But in George's case his recollections seemed pointless and pervaded by a sense of contingency, with George himself cast as a baffled drifter who only realizes what is happening after the event. One of his anecdotes weighed on my mind, and when I had found a quiet place under the trees, I took out my notebook and wrote it down before I forgot it:

When Lucy and I split up on November 7, 1970, I moved into a squat in Freeman's Bay. I lived there for fifteen years. It was an old warehouse. It cost me nothing. My room was on the top floor. The rain came in, but to repair the roof I would have had to climb out onto it, which was quite dangerous. So I lived with the rain. After I'd been there for a few years and people had come and gone on the lower floors, I began to suspect that no one knew I was there. Indeed, I was seldom home. After work each day I went to the pub. I had fish and chips for dinner. Got home late. Left early in the morning. On census night the other squatters forgot clean about me, so when I tried to vote in the next election I found to my dismay that I had not been registered. Officially, I did not exist.

It struck me that where most people's imaginative lives are oriented toward the future—the prospect of a fortunate meeting, a lucky break, a

Stuck in the
past

win on the lottery, a vacation, a better job, or even a favorite T V show—
George's mind was consumed by the past, which he had suffered in
complete passivity, a labyrinth in which his mind wandered endlessly,
without seeking an exit. He appeared to me as someone who had never
given birth to himself, someone to whom life had simply happened.
When I had asked if he had any friends, George spoke of an "aging
hippie" he had met in the pub one time. A heavy dope smoker. They met
regularly in the pub for many months, and then the guy suddenly
disappeared. All of George's stories were like this. Nothing added up or
made much sense. Life was a series of arbitrary subtractions—a pub
demolished "for no good reason," 23 Fairview Road redesignated 35 "for
some reason," his prostate cancer "a bolt from the blue," his first wife
leaving him "without an explanation, without a word."

I closed my notebook and walked on through the park, past the
enormous trees with buttressed roots, the fountain, and on through
the campus to Symonds Street.

My appointment was at the business school, on the corner of Anzac
Avenue and Short Street. I thought I knew the streets near the university like the back of my hand, but I was disoriented and had to ask for
directions. A young woman was coming up Grafton Road toward me. I
asked her if she could direct me to Anzac Avenue. She pointed down
Symonds Street toward the harbor. It was in that direction, a couple of
blocks after the High Court. She was walking that way herself and
could show me. She spoke with a North American accent, and I asked if
she was from the United States or Canada. "Canada," she said. "Are you
studying here?" I asked. "No, I teach at the university." I felt foolish. To
someone in their twenties, anyone over forty is old; to someone in their
sixties, anyone younger than forty is young. "What do you teach?" I
ventured to ask as we strolled along, hopeful that my sincerity would
atone for my gaffe. "Philosophy," she said. "What kind of philosophy?" I
asked. I was beginning to think I should stop bothering her; I now had a
fair idea where the business school was and should simply cross the
road and make my way there alone. "Twentieth Century French and
German," the young woman said. Astonished, I told her that I was an
avid reader of Walter Benjamin's essays, and had, only two months
before, on the anniversary of his death, followed his ghostly trail across
the Pyrenees. I then asked which philosophers she had a particular

interest in. "Levinas," she said and explained that she was writing a book about birth, time, and ethics. When she mentioned that it included a critique of Hannah Arendt's concept of natality, I was flabbergasted. The chain of coincidences was too improbable. In Harvard Yard such an encounter might be expected. But Auckland, New Zealand? This was not the Auckland I remembered.

This exchange was so bizarre that it quickly eclipsed all sense of where I was, with whom I was, and the meeting I had to attend in quarter of an hour. Without hesitating, I asked the young woman how she reconciled Arendt's apparent attribution of agency to people—our capacity for initiating the new, for breaking free from the past and creating a future—with her repeated observations that human agency is almost nonexistent and that our actions so exceed our intentions that we do not know, at any given moment, what we are doing. "Natality is not really a theory of agency," the young woman said. "Arendt is simply observing that the new arises continually in life, despite our plans, our intentions, our desires." At that moment, no one could have been more surprised by the unintended and contingent nature of new departures. But we had reached an intersection now, and the parting of the ways. As the pedestrian light changed to green, we stepped onto the crossing together.

On the other side of the road, I said, "Well, I think I go this way now, don't I?" "I'm going the same way," she said quickly. "The philosophy department is in Waterloo Quadrant. I can show you where you need to go." As we walked on, she asked me where I was from. I explained that I was in Auckland for three weeks, giving some talks at the university. She appeared to relax a little. "Are you the person giving that public lecture on quandaries of belonging?"

"Guilty as charged."

"One of my closest friends here is in anthropology. Another recent arrival. She specializes in violence."

"I've been working on violence, too. I'd like to meet her."

But most of all I wanted to know what this young woman felt about teaching continental philosophy in Auckland and living so far from home. "It can be difficult sometimes," she admitted. "Only a few people with whom one can really share one's intellectual interests. The feeling of isolation." She was amused when I told her that I had grown up in

"Chain of coincidences"

New Zealand feeling the same way, even though it was my homeland. "All through my childhood I had this fantasy that a mistake had been made and that I had been born in the wrong place at the wrong time, that another life awaited me elsewhere, and that if I was patient for long enough, I would find it."

We had now reached my destination, and she rummaged in her bag and took out her business card. *Lisa Guenther BA Bishop's Univ., PhD Toronto. Lecturer.* "It would be nice to have lunch one day, if you're free," she said. "That would be nice," I said. "I'll give you a call."

But I didn't; I got carried away by the research I was doing on Māori reactions to genetic modification, distracted by the talks I had to give and the many old friends I wanted to see.

It was not until I had returned to Copenhagen that I wrote Lisa, saying how much I had enjoyed talking to her and expressing amazement at the serendipity of our encounter and our common interests. In response, she sent me a couple of chapters from her forthcoming book.

Lisa begins her book by observing that while it is practically impossible to remember one's own birth, it is often even more impossible to accept the fact that we did not choose it, but came into existence in passivity, dependent on our parents, thrown into a world made by others at other times. While I had tended, in my early writing, to emphasize the ways we resist the overwhelming givenness of the world, gradually coming to define our own sense of who we are and often ritually renouncing that which was imposed on us in the first place without our knowledge and consent, Lisa's point of view reminded me of the positive dimensions of what is given to us, for it holds the potential of what we may become and foreshadows the ways in which we realize ourselves in intersubjective encounters with others—in conversation, in responding to the responses of others, in sharing stories. Though Hannah Arendt stresses natality solely as the advent of a new person or the making of a new beginning (1958:177–78), natality is actually double-edged since the new emerges both in the course of one's involvement with others and in one's awareness of being different from others. These two dimensions of natality—identity and difference, engagement and estrangement—find expression in quite different kinds of narrative. The first recounts who we are in relation to others, particularly those who give us life, while the second recounts who we are in our own eyes, when displaced or standing alone (see Arendt 1958:186). Of our first birth we know little except through the stories and anecdotes our parents pass on to us, introducing us to our ancestry and satisfying our curiosity about our earliest and unremembered years. Sometimes it is possible to overcome the sense of unreality that clings to our own birth by having recourse to documentary evidence. Thus Marguerite Yourcenar, researching her memoirs, describes how she was "forced"—just as if she "were trying to recreate some historical personage—to seize on stray recollections gleaned secondhand or even tenthhand; to pore over scraps of correspondence and notebook pages which somehow escaped the wastebasket (so eager are we to know the past that we wring from these poor relics more than they contain); and to burrow in registries and archives for original documents whose legal and bureaucratic jargon is devoid of all human content" (1997:4). By contrast, our second birth signals the beginning of the person we are for ourselves, and the beginning of the life we will lead "on our own initiative" (Arendt 1958:177), and it builds on memories, designs, and desires that we like to imagine are all our own—a viewpoint famously captured in Simone de Beauvoir's pronouncement in *The Second Sex* that "one is not born, but rather one becomes, a woman; no biological, psychological or economic fate determines the figure that the human female presents in society" (1953:295). But as Lisa observes in the introductory chapter of her book, we—which is to say Westerners—sometimes find it difficult to accept that we never entirely outlive ourselves (see also Barnes 1997:292), or that the past contains the germ and possibility of everything we may become (Barnes 1997:xvii–xviii). When she began writing her book, Lisa told me, she placed greatest emphasis on the first side of this aporia—"the unchosen particularity of existence," which in her case meant being born and raised in the suburbs of Winnipeg, Canada, "ardently hoping and almost believing that I had been left there by a troupe of wild-eyed gypsies who were even now on their way back to get me and take me with them." Gradually, however, her focus shifted to the critical events in her own life that marked new beginnings, new initiatives, and symbolic rebirths.

That Lisa's observations made such an impact on me was undoubtedly because I had in my own writing over many years been preoccupied by this tension between the ways in which we account for any human life in terms of what is pregiven—our culture, history, class, gender, and parentage—and what emerges in the course of an individual life from interactions and encounters with others and from contingent events.

Yourcenar's *Souvenirs pieux* emphasizes the pregiven and the pre-existent.[1] Like any other memoir, her narrative begins with the birth of an individual subject. "The being I refer to as *me* came into the world on Monday, June 8, 1903, at about eight in the morning, in Brussels" (1997:3). But after her first perfunctory paragraph, the author moves back in time, recounting her paternal and maternal family histories in such depth and detail that she is herself quickly eclipsed, and the subject of the memoir becomes, in effect, her maternal lineage. Yourcenar's avoidance of self-centredness is, of course, deliberate. By freeing the personal *voice* from the conventional autobiographical burden of tracing the development and career of a personal *identity*, she is better able to go "beyond the confines of individual history and even beyond History" and explore "the hopeless tangle of incidents and circumstances which to a greater or lesser extent shape us all" (1997:3).[2] While Yourcenar's self-effacing narrative is reminiscent of life stories in preliterate societies, where one's personal life is contingent on one's place within a lineage or close community, the autobiographical novels of Blaise Cendrars have their historical precedents in such early modern picaresques as *Robinson Crusoe*, in which the individual abandons his place of origins, wanders the world, and is reborn in another place, with another name.

Cendrars's mother was Scottish, his father Swiss. Born Frédéric-Louis Sauser in the small watchmaking city of La Chaux-de-Fonds (its other famous sons were Le Corbusier and Louis Chevrolet), he spent much of his childhood on the move. When the family returned to La Chaux-de-Fonds in 1901 and Freddy's father enrolled him in a trade school, the fifteen-year-old rebelled. Truant and restive, he ran up bills at local wineshops and kiosks, subscribed to dirty magazines, screwed around, and yearned for the exotic elsewheres he had glimpsed in Alexandria, Genoa, Naples, Brindisi, London, and Paris. Locked in his room one night by his anguished father, Freddy stole out of the house "like a sleepwalker," sick in his stomach at the thought that he would never return. Taking the first train out of Neuchâtel, he ended up in Basel. From there he picked up a train to Berlin. After traveling aimlessly around Germany for several weeks, he arrived in Pforzheim, where he fell in with a Warsaw Jew and jewelry merchant named Rogovine. Together they headed east toward Russia and the first tremors of the revolution.

For Cendrars, travel offered the possibility of another life, a chance of starting over in a place that he chose for himself. And fire is the universal image of this perennial rebirth. If the phoenix is to arise, one's previous life must be reduced to ashes. This is why Cendrars coined his name for its associations of embers, ashes, and auto-da-fé. With Friedrich Nietzsche's smoldering lines in the back of his mind—"Und alles wird mir nur zur Asche / Was ich liebe, was ich fasse" (And everything of mine turns to ashes / What I love and what I touch)—Cendrars was also aware that Blaise and *braise* were near homonyms, and the sobriquet Cendrars ironically conjoins ashes (*cendres*) and art (*ars* in Latin, as in *arson*).

So it was that Cendrars, filled with "an insatiable need for displacement and transplantation," declared that his true birthplace was the Hôtel des Étrangers at 216 rue Saint-Jacques in Paris where he lodged when he was twenty and made a complete break with the past:

> Raze my childhood to the ground
> My family and my customs
> Build a railway station there instead
> Or leave some waste ground
> To erase my origins . . .

What I find arresting about Cendrars's and Yourcenar's very different ways of telling the stories of their lives is that while he was free to symbolically repudiate his parentage, she was not, because her mother died giving birth to her. As with children given up for adoption at birth, the biological parents' abandonment of the child robs the child of the freedom to symbolically abandon and outgrow them. Instead of playing out the oedipal drama of revolt and rejection in relation to the persons who gave the child her or his initial identity and name, the child is drawn back into the past in an endless quest for the person she or he can never reject or outlive because that person "rejected" her or him and because this primal rejection has come to define her or him as someone who is fundamentally unworthy of life. Moreover, while the child grows old, the parent remains forever young. Perhaps this explains why Yourcenar's historical biographies and fictionalized autobiographies refer constantly to the past, not out of nostalgia for a golden age, but because of the tragic connection between her own birth and her mother's death, and her awareness that her own life cannot really begin until her mother's life has run its full course. When Yourcenar recounts her mother's story, she (who is old enough now to be her mother's grandmother) symbolically inverts her relationship with Fernande, her mother, and reverses the passage of time (1997:53). Speaking of Fernande, Yourcenar observes that her memoir is an effort to "recapture and recount her history" and "fills me with a sympathy for her that I have not felt heretofore. She is much like those characters, imaginary or real, that I nourish with my own substance to try to make them live, or live once again" (53). In recounting what befell her in the past, Yourcenar acts imaginatively on events she suffered in passivity, symbolically bringing her mother back to life in order that she, the author, can lay her ghost.

This compulsive replaying of the past is, of course, definitive of trauma. People who have suffered abuse as children and were deprived of any right to live life on their own terms will, as adults, repeatedly play back the situations that they suffered so passively, invading the space or exploiting the resources of others and even abusing or neglecting their own children as they attempt to reverse time and retrieve their own lost sense of agency.

Playing with Time

Not every birth or new beginning entails an *actual* death. But natality always involves a symbolic death—the sacrifice or loss of something or someone felt to be essential to the life one led and the person one was before. Birth is therefore marked by ambivalence, an ambivalence that affects male attitudes to women who, in many societies, are regarded as simultaneously a source of life and a threat to life. In traditional Māori thought, women bring children into the world of light (*te ao marama*), yet the vagina is also the source of misfortune and death (*te whare o aitua*) since it was the goddess Hine-nui-te-Po who crushed the culture hero Maui between her thighs as he sought immortality by reentering her womb. Men's ambivalence toward women extends to the land, *te whenua* (which also denotes the lining of the womb and the placenta that nourishes the fetus). Hence the saying, "He wahine, he whenua, ka ngaro te tangata" (By women and land men are destroyed). The ambiguity of birth is also a central preoccupation in West Africa. As the Bambara put it, though fire gives birth to fire (i.e., men and women reproduce their kind, and society itself is reproduced through the birth of children), fire also gives birth to ash (a metaphor for barrenness and social death). Still, ash is itself ambiguous, which is why one can blow on seemingly dead embers to start a live flame (the dead live on as ancestors, those lost to us return). It is also often true that while birth, like any gift, brings life to another, it may spell a compromise or sacrifice in one's own life, as when a mother dies in childbirth or a wayward child brings misfortune on its home. Among the Tallensi of northern Ghana, begetting (bearing) is said to be hard, a view that is charged with deep emotion and elucidated by women in terms of the pain of childbirth, the distress of losing a child, and the difficulties of raising a family. By contrast, men cite the exhausting work, heavy responsibilities, and irksome taboos that begin with a woman's pregnancy, though their tribulations really begin, they say, with the sex act itself, since ejaculation "is a giving up of something vital that is a source of strength and youth" (Fortes 1949:163). This assumption finds universal expression in the view that semen loss diminishes vigor and shortens life, as in the widely espoused Hindu view that semen is "closely associated with the idea of the soul that survives after death" (Trawick 1990:159) and that "the retention of sperm makes a man a hero and a god; its loss makes him low and animal-like" (Bharati 1976:161). By contrast, in some social imaginaries *not* to bring life into this world is considered a selfish act for which one deserves to be punished by having something vital taken away. Thus among the Senya of southern Ghana, the fact that a mother and father gave birth to a person places an obligation on that person to give birth in turn; to die without having done so invites a ritual repudiation in which the body is buried in an inverted position, hot chilies are placed in incisions on the back, and palm oil is poured into the grave (Hans Lucht 2005, personal communication).

Clearly both loss and gain, regret and hope, are felt in almost every moment of natality: a migrant leaving home hopefully to make a life in a new
country yet regretting the life he or she is leaving behind; two people
falling deeply in love but suddenly hesitating or recoiling as they sense the
imminent loss of the life they individually possessed up to that moment; a
couple on the threshold of their *troisième âge*, celebrating their freedom
from the demands of young children but also mourning the loss of the
children or the workplace that gave structure to their lives.

That every new beginning entails a loss is already presaged in the first
and formative years of a child's life, when every separation from the
mother precipitates immediate grief and every return to her side is like
a rebirth. But this oscillation in primary intersubjectivity between attachment and loss occurs to some extent every day of our lives, even if
it is only obvious during times of critical transition.

In the following pages I want to explore the *existential* repercussions
of the images of birth, death, and rebirth that make their appearance at
such critical moments. In other words, I want to explore the ways in
which birth and death are seldom simply suffered passively as events
that befall us, beyond our awareness and will, but as events that contain
the potentiality of rebirth, in which we act on the circumstances that
we were initially powerless to control. This transformation from being
acted on to acting is often articulated through metaphors of physical
balance and motility. Thus any traumatic rupture of a situation in
which we feel ontologically secure is spoken of as in terms of being
thrown off balance, of losing one's footing, of being brought low or
immobilized, while the recovery of the power to act is said to be a
matter of getting back on one's feet, getting over it, and moving on. It is
therefore not surprising that any transition from passivity to activity
typically involves a change in our experience of bodily being-in-time.

Time and Action

In his classic monograph on the Nuer, E. E. Evans-Pritchard contrasts
"ecological" with "structural" time—respectively, "reflections of their
relations to environment" and "reflections of their relations to one
another in the social structure" (1940:94). For Nuer, time is never abstract; it reflects the everyday pastoral, social, political, and ritual *ac-*

tivities that preoccupy them. Accordingly, the *experience* of time is never constant. Because life in dry-season camps is fairly uneventful and activities fairly routine, time appears to pass more slowly than during the rains (102–3). Though Nuer ecology and social structure may be unfamiliar to us, their experience of time is familiar enough. Time drags when we are doing menial work in which we exercise no choice; time flies when we have a lot to do and little time in which to do it, or are acting on our own initiative. Moreover, the time of childhood has a very different experiential value from the time of old age. Though Evans-Pritchard makes only scant mention of these dimensions of lived or phenomenal time, it is from this standpoint that I want to explore the symbolic meaning of birth, death, and rebirth.

Of time, or what we call time, Pierre Bourdieu observes:

[It] is really experienced only when the quasi-automatic coincidence between expectations and chances, *illusio* and *lusiones,* expectations and the world which is there to fulfil them is broken. We then feel directly the breaking of the tacit collusion between the course of the world—astronomical movements (such as the cycle of the seasons) or biological processes (such as ageing) or social processes (such as family life cycles) or bureaucratic careers), *over which we have less than full power or no power at all*—and the internal movements which relate to them (*illusio*). (2000: 208–9; emphasis added)

Every life crisis involves, in some sense, a crisis of agency. And as Bourdieu notes, this involves both a deepened awareness of time and a ritualized transformation of the natural passage of time.

When giving birth or attending a birth, one experiences time as compressed or condensed—as if nothing existed outside the moment in which this woman labors, this place where it is happening. One harbors one's resources, concentrates one's effort, focuses one's consciousness, and is intolerant of distractions. The everyday world seems a long way away. In these respects, confinement bears comparison with the experience of being with a loved one who is dying, or being in a traumatic accident. Time seems to hang fire, annulled by the overwhelming presence of this one painful event. But experiences of birth and death have something else in common: they are devastating to one's sense of autonomy. A woman giving birth is in the grip of powerful forces she cannot readily bring under control. Drained of energy, maddened by her inability to master her pain, she can only yield to the demonic imperative of this other life that is tearing her apart as it forces its way into the world. Similarly, those near death and those who wait and watch them dying are defeated by their helplessness in the face of something they cannot prevent. Perhaps this is why, at such times, we are mystified or outraged that the outside world is still going about its business, keeping to schedules and timetables, indifferent to our struggle for life, oblivious to our pain. And yet, within moments of a birth or a death we begin, often despite ourselves, to reclaim the autonomy we momentarily lost, returning to the world, the dazzling daylight, the mundane activities we had momentarily lost sight of. And in the stories we recount, whether to ourselves or to others, about what we suffered in passivity or silence, we recapture our sense of being able, if not to determine the way things were, at least to decide the meaning that is to be ascribed to them.

Consider the following poem that I wrote not long after the birth of my daughter Heidi in Freetown in 1970:

To My Daughter

When you were born it was easy to ignore
that I was your father;
you did not resemble me
nor behave as I do now.

As I waited outside the hospital five years ago
I thought of those desert people for whom
children are spirit ancestors
come from a sacred site
where they subsist on flowers and dew,
visible only in dreams.

Yet these men of the desert do not deny
the child is theirs
who is born to them
by magic or fortuity,
and I have followed their reasoning
and become your father.

Despite my initial experience of this birth as something wholly contingent—my daughter a stranger, everything simply happening *to* me (my wife in pain, I myself powerless to help her, the midwives and doctors telling me to leave the delivery room)—I reimagine the situation as one I decide on, declaring that I will become her father.

Here is another poem, by Donald Hall, about the birth of his son. Again, the birth suddenly and dramatically changes the way the world appears to the poet. At the same time that he is granted a kind of immortality through his son, his own decline and death are presaged, if not hastened by his son's entry into the world.

My Son My Executioner

My son, my executioner,
  I take you in my arms,
Quiet and small and just astir
  And whom my body warms.

Sweet death, small son, our instrument
  Of immortality,
Your cries and hungers document
  Our bodily decay.
We twenty-five and twenty-two
  Who seemed to live forever,
Observe enduring life in you
  And start to die together.

Consider initiatory birth. Just as every biological beginning contains the seeds of both life and loss, the symbolic rebirth of initiation involves both regeneration and death. That is to say, the precondition of coming to adulthood is the repudiation of the sexually amorphous and behaviorally undisciplined time of childhood, signified in many African societies as a taint that must be purified and exorcised through the surgical removal of the foreskin or clitoris, as well as ordeals that inculcate control over the body, the senses, and speech. Moreover, initiations are typically staged in the extrasocial space of the bush—a domain of regenerative and wild power—while the passage from passivity to activity (in which the neophytes are initially *subject to* various ordeals, instructions, revelations, and operations before returning to the town as adult subjects) is enacted as a symbolic reversal of the temporal order of the world.

In male initiation rites, the passage of human life from birth to death is typically played backward.[3] When neophytes are symbolically killed and reborn, a "natural" course of events gives way to a culturally contrived sequence that creates the impression that men have mastery over life and death. This vicarious midwifery implies that men possess the power of women to bear children and influence the destiny of their sons—a conceit that in certain New Guinea societies is bolstered by the doctrine that women's breast milk comes from male semen, and that male neophytes must ingest the life-giving semen of older men in order to be "born again" and to grow strong (Godelier 1986:51–57; Herdt 1981).[4] Whatever the psychological and social reasons behind such beliefs, they have the effect of making men the measure of all things. Rather than living passively as creatures of nature, men act purposefully and concertedly as creators of culture. In this scenario, the appearance of agency is tied to a ritualized reversal of time, for while the child's original birth set him on a course toward death, initiatory rebirth sets the young adult on a course toward elderhood and ancestorhood, both of which are associated with time past. Thus the transformation from being acted on to being an actor runs parallel to a transformation that implicitly denies the future and conceives of adult life as a movement toward an abiding past. In Aboriginal Australia this is the *jukurrpa*, the dreaming. In Africa it is the realm of the ancestors, for by symbolically "facing" them, one "turns one's back" on the future (Zahan 1979:45).

The most powerful narrative expressions of the link between existential power and temporality are oedipal myths. In the course of mundane social time it is inevitable that a child will grow up to be an adult, a girl will marry, and a son will replace his father. But the decline and death of the father is sometimes thought to be organically linked to the rising power of the firstborn son, as among the Tallensi who aver that an "inborn antagonism" exists between the *Yin* (individual destiny) of a father and the Yin of his eldest son. "When the son is still young his *Yin* is weak, but as he grows older his *Yin* grows more powerful and wants to make him master of his own affairs. The son's *Yin* wants to destroy the father's *Yin*; but the father's *Yin* desires the father to live and be well and remain master of the house" (Fortes 1949:227). In oedipal myths throughout the world, the father uses political or magical means to hinder the development or birth of his son, or the son inhibits his own development, with the effect that the passage of time is apparently arrested. Thus the father retains power and attains a kind of immortality. But this arrest of time can only ever be momentary and illusory, and when the son is finally born or comes of age, the father inevitably dies, often at the hands of the child whose life he has tried to deny in order to prolong his own. With the father's displacement and the son's assumption of power, time passes again. Complementary myths involve prevented marriages. A daughter locked away in a tower, or a father imposing impossible tasks on her suitors, has the effect of annulling time—often objectified in images of immobilization, petrification, or cataleptic sleep. When the girl is finally married, or kisses her suitor, time resumes, as in the stories of Briar Rose and Snow White (Jackson 2002:191, 226).

First Contact

My argument has been that human strategies, both ritual and narrative, for manipulating the experience of time have their origin in an existential imperative, namely, the need to feel that one is as much an acting subject as one who is acted on. Michel Foucault calls this "governmentality"—the power *relations* entailed by the fact that action involves the *interaction* of human subjects, and by the fact that every action draws out reciprocal reactions (1983:220–21). This struggle for being through doing is never more imperative than at those critical junctures in human lives at which old certainties are called into question, familiar routines are destroyed, and basic ontological attachments are sundered. But such crises of separation and loss occur not only within the lives of individuals but also within the histories of societies. As Arendt observes (1963:36–37), rebellion and political revolution are both grounded in the idea of rebirth and often take the form of violent devourings, eradications, and purgings of elements considered incompatible with the new order to be born from the ashes of the old.

One of the most dramatic ruptures with the past is the crisis of first contact. At such times, an entire society suffers the loss of certainty and is driven to question its position in space and time. In Bob Connolly's and Robin Anderson's film, *First Contact*, for instance, one is struck by the expressions of extreme grief on the faces of these New Guinea Highlanders, recoiling from the first Europeans they have ever seen— stunned into speechlessness by their firepower and their otherworldly presence, and even more deeply dismayed by the sudden loss of everything they had taken for granted, including their notions of geography and their assumptions about the sources of power and knowledge. So profound is this initial shock of seeing the outsiders that people defecate on themselves in terror, weeping and wailing, throwing themselves to the ground, or colliding with one another as they struggle to keep a safe distance from the strangers. "I was so terrified, I could not think properly, and I cried uncontrollably," recalled one man (Kirupano Eza'e of Seigu village in the eastern Highlands). Yet curiosity quickly overcame fear as people sought to place these strangers in their scheme of things. Were they enemies, the dead come back to life, or avenging spirits? To say that these Highlanders had abruptly entered historical time would be to perpetuate the popular fallacy of peoples outside history, arrested in the Stone Age, their societies unchanged for centuries. But this traumatic grief had everything to do with their being-in-time, for in having their eyes opened to the world of European power, they lost their own sense of control over their world—the myths that recounted their origins and affirmed their destinies, the reasons they had for being. A new age is born, and the old order, like a body exposed to an alien disease, begins to wane. Yet the world on which one now opens one's eyes is not without possibilities. The strangers have possessions and powers that one desires, and knowledge without which one will be at their mercy.

The narratives and rituals that emerge with first contact are vital means whereby people reimagine and reconfigure received ideas of where they stand in space and time and thereby recover a sense of their own capacity to know and act on the world in which they now find themselves.

Among the Tangu of the Madang District of northern New Guinea, traditional narratives about human origins were considered timeless because they concerned the eternal moral dilemmas that pervade human existence (Burridge 1969:201), such as where one draws the line between those realms in which reciprocity does and does not obtain.

Tangu encounters and experiences with Europeans broached a series of critical questions concerning the place of reciprocity in interactions between these two worlds, and a primal myth was reworked to explain why whites possessed greater wealth and power than blacks. The myth recounts how a woman warns her family against killing a particular fish, the *ramatzka*. When her youngest son ignores her and kills the fish, the earth trembles and the sea rises up, inundating deep valleys and dividing younger from elder brother. In the revised version of the myth, the younger brother (Tuman) becomes the ancestor of the blacks, and a loser, while his elder brother (Ambwerk), the ancestor of the whites, gets all the luck. As a Tangu informant put it, "Ambwerk had paper. Tuman had yams and other tubers. Now, if it had been the other way about (if Ambwerk, not Tuman, had shot the *ramatzka*) you white skinned people would have yams, and we black skinned people would have paper and all the other good things" (Burridge 1960:164–67). The dilemma of "how to persuade white men [associated with Tuman in the primal myth] into those reciprocal relations which Tangu regard as appropriate to community life" (407) gives rise not only to narratives that explain the historical origins of the problem but to rituals that seek to redress and remaster the situation by symbolically reversing time. Speaking of Bush Kaliai cargo cults in New Britain, Andrew Lattas aptly observes that people sought to regain "control over their future" (1998:149). In new narratives and rites, they "reread the past to give it a future, and they reread the future (that they were shown by Europeans) to give it a past *that was their own*" (267; emphasis added). In Tangu, a similar remodeling of tradition occurred in the cargo rites initiated by a millenarian leader known as Mambu who himself embodied the "new man" and the new bicultural social order: "After a communal meal in which the traditional sectionalisms of the community played no part, an individual, a man or a woman, took position in the centre of a circle of chanting villagers, with the intention that he or she should fall into a trance, be revived by massaging the mouth, and then utter a message—not in Tangu but in some other language. The themes of a symbolic death and rebirth are clear" (408).

What is compelling about these ritual strategies for regaining the initiative and accessing the cargo of Europeans is that one must first play normal sequences of events backward, returning "to the precosmogonic world from which current social differences had emerged" (Lattas 1998:xli). Like neophytes undergoing symbolic rebirth in initiation rites, cargo cultists must first abnegate control, making dream journeys to the land of the dead, slavishly imitating European routines and habits, falling into trance, and in some instances abandoning garden work and instead building airstrips in the bush where they will wait for a cargo plane to land and inaugurate the new age.

Clearly, we are dealing here with magical action that belongs to the time of daydreams, fantasies, rituals, and narratives. *Real* rebirth is impossible. The cargo is an illusion. Reciprocity with Europeans in a global economy is a pipe dream. But what drives magical action is not simply a desire to change the world but a desire to change *one's experience of one's relationship with that world.* By means of a simulacrum of the real world—an airplane built of sticks, a telegraph line made of lianas, a rifle made of wood—one is able to act in ways that break the impasse of passivity and confusion, thus generating hope, bolstering confidence, and creating an illusion that restores one's reasons for being.

I argued earlier that every life crisis involves a death and a birth—the simultaneous loss of something that gave ontological security and the possibility of a new beginning. But the terms *death* and *birth* must be understood existentially as metaphors for the experiential difference between being a subject who can act confidently on the world on the assumption that she or he knows what she or he is doing and an object who simply suffers the actions of others, not knowing what she or he might do. If one defines agency as rational action that has objectively measurable effects in the real world, then the reworking of traditional stories or the visiting the land of the dead or the falling into trance may well be construed as forms of madness—which is precisely how many European colonists characterized the mimetic practices of Melanesian cargo cultists. But the notion of agency also covers actions whose effects are felt inwardly rather than manifest outwardly, and it encompasses modes of silent contemplation, world renunciation, fatalism, and withdrawal. That the symbolic rebirth of initiation obeys a poetic logic, and entails actions that we would call mistaken or magical, should not blind us to the ways in which the *effects* of this logic and the *consequences* of this action are to be measured in relation to a person's changed *experience* of his or her relation to the world—the extent to which it encourages the belief that a person makes the world to the same extent that it makes him or her.

Can I honestly say that such a transformation occurred in me during my weeks in Auckland? That in returning to the past I was able to find a way of being more sure of my future, of feeling less regret for the life I might have led in New Zealand had I not exchanged it for a life elsewhere? Asking these questions three months after leaving New Zealand, I search through my notebooks from that time for an answer. One thing that strikes me immediately is the many poems I wrote during those early summer days as I walked through the suburbs as if in a trance. Almost all these poems recall a city in which, as a young man, I struggled to find my path but which I knew I would have to leave if I was to be the person I wanted to become. In revisiting my past I therefore reaffirmed this early conviction that my life lay elsewhere, and that the images of New Zealand that sustained me wherever I went had less to do with any original identity than with a creative impulse to explore other possibilities of being in places far from my own. Sometimes, however, one goes abroad in order to realize that one's real life is in the place one left. This was the experience of a young Māori woman I met in Auckland who had gone to Canada to study for a PhD. In North America, Marama encountered the indigenous rights movement for the first time, and during a conference at a Native American university in the United States, she became suddenly aware that time had slowed down, that people were doing things at the same pace as on a marae in Aotearoa/New Zealand, and with the same mindfulness and care. Marama felt that this care consisted of respect for the ancestral customs of that place, the ancestral presence there, the *kawa* (protocols) governing what one should and should not say or do. But it also consisted of the care with which relations with others were mediated by gifts and greetings, with respect and concern, that is *aroha*. Marama's PhD project had been an ethnographic study of the Saint Lawrence River; now she realized that it was her own river, the Waikato, that she wanted to explore, and that her own *whanau* (the extended kin group or family into which she was born, including her ancestors) grounded her sense of who she was and where and what she wanted to be.

Perhaps these are simply the stories we tell ourselves, like the cargo narratives of Melanesia, to make life more bearable, to conjure the illusion that we know what we are doing and where we are going—ways in which we take time out to draw breath, to take stock, the better to revise our course or initiate a new beginning. Perhaps if I, like George, were out of work, living in isolation, and ailing, I would tell a very different story, one resembling the story he told me. Of only one thing am I sure: we are never born once, but over and over, and every new beginning entails the inevitable loss of something we hesitate to let go. There is no reconciling these contradictory impulses—to cling to what we have and what we know, to yield to the moment and embrace the new. And yet, I remind myself, I met George and Lisa in the same place and at the same time, and they were not then symbols of past and future, but part of the present, the ever recurring present, which is where one truly lives.

What good are your roots if you can't take them with you?—GERTRUDE STEIN

11 Quandaries of Belonging
home thoughts from abroad

One of the more sobering experiences of returning to one's homeland after many years away is the overwhelming sense of how much things have changed in one's absence, and the inevitable, accompanying realization that one has also changed just as much. Fortunately, such disconcerting reflections are offset by encounters with old friends with whom one picks up exactly where one left off, as though nothing had really changed. Such was the day in January 2003 that I spent with my friend Vincent O'Sullivan in the Wairapapa, a region that the legendary Hau-nui-a-Nanaia named at the end of an epic journey in pursuit of his runaway wife, Wairaka, when he glimpsed from the ridge of the Rimutakas the glint of sunlight on the waters of the lake. I suppose I was also searching for something, something that had gotten away from me and without which my life felt tenuous and unresolved. Was it nostalgia for the place in which I had lived my most formative years? Not exactly, because it was not the past I repined for. If anything, I wanted to live in two places at once—New Zealand and Elsewhere—much as some men want both a wife and mistress. But despite the bumper sticker injunction, "think globally/act locally," it is simply not possible to *live* both locally and globally. We cannot be somewhere and everywhere at the same time, though we can, I imagine, think of ourselves as being someone and everyone at the same time. In what follows, I offer some thoughts on these paradoxes and propositions.

Vincent had just published his biography of John Mulgan, and it had inspired me to reread *Report on Experience.* In this book, which Mulgan referred to as only a "draft and outline of a book I'd like to write" (O'Sullivan 2003:330), Mulgan speaks of New Zealand in ways that were immediately familiar to me, having just flown in from Sydney on a gusty, rain-swept day, the sea cutting up rough beneath our wings, and wooden houses clustered together on the hills like lost sheep. Mulgan says that we New Zealanders—which is to say Pākehā New Zealanders —have always been too few and far between to have had the confidence needed to make the country truly and deeply our own. And so we are restive and live as strangers, he says, and go abroad, *looking not for adventure but for satisfaction.* When he took his own life in Cairo in April 1945, only twelve days before the peace, Mulgan seems to have felt that it would be as impossible for him to find satisfaction in the New Zealand of his youth as it would be to find it in the Oxford he had known before the war. In no-man's-land, oppressed by the contradictions of his war experiences in Greece, where every successful partisan raid had meant immediate German reprisals against the very villagers who had sheltered and befriended his men, and where, even as he wrote his last messages, a brutal civil war, abetted by England, was tearing Greece apart, he chose oblivion. As Mulgan's fate suggests, the question of where one belongs is clearly, and painfully, related to the question of whom one is beholden to. As with his friends and contemporaries Jim Bertram, Geoffrey Cox, Ian Milner, and Jack Bennett, Mulgan found it not enough to be a New Zealander; one was inescapably part of a wider world in which one had to take a stand, in which one was obliged to act. Vincent observes of these men of Mulgan's generation: "The sense of contending pressures could generate a peculiar

Paradox of local/global Simultaneity.

malaise of its own. As Thomas Norrington, an Englishman who knew and worked closely with several of them, concluded in retrospect, there seemed an innate melancholy in the New Zealanders he knew" (2003:115).

It was, however, in an ebullient and irreverent mood that Vincent and I shared reminiscences, sitting at a table in the shade of some fruit trees with Vincent's wife Helen and his son Dominic. It was very hot. The hills were like loaves of bread, dusted with flour, the sky deep cobalt with curious tufts of unmoving cloud, as if painted by a hyperrealist. Vincent and I were piecing together details of a weekend in late 1965 when he and his first wife, Tui, drove up from Wellington with Les and Mary Cleveland, and stayed with me in the Wairarapa. I was teaching at Kurunui College at the time and toward the end of that year had rented a schoolhouse in Featherstone so that my girlfriend, who was completing her finals at Victoria University of Wellington, could join me for the summer. I recounted to Vincent, Helen, and Dominic, how in order to get this house, I had had to pretend to have just gotten married; the result was an embarrassing ceremony in the staff room one morning, at which I was presented with "his" and "hers" bath towels and toiletries and given the loan of a car so that my new "wife" and I could explore the Wairarapa. I remembered us drinking ouzo at Morrison's Bush hotel; Vincent remembered us in the pub at Lake Ferry one day, and a trip to the Pinnacles.

No, for me it is not so much the gap between now and then that is where longing begins, but the gap between here and elsewhere. It was this gap that bothered Vincent as much as me, and led us to draw comparisons between ourselves and men like Mulgan and Dan Davin. The impossibility of keeping the home fires burning at the same time as one kindled and tended a fire in another hemisphere. "What is so living and graspable and immediately there in front of you," Vincent writes in his exquisite essay on longing; "and what is quite as real but you will never touch—the Seven Swans of Glendalough or whatever the other stories are that you hear; and that place the grown-ups talked of, the enchanted distance where they were young, that you so desperately want to know as well. That gap where for many of us longing begins" (2003:16).

What is the nature of this sense of belonging to "one dear perpetual place," this sense of *turangawaewae* that binds one to one's native soil, no matter how many other places one has worked and lived, experienced joy and sorrow, formed lasting friendships, and also come to call home? And how is it possible to reconcile this craving for anchorage, for a rock, a center, and the equally imperative longing to get away, to uproot oneself, to venture beyond the narrow horizons of the world in which one was raised and stake everything on another life elsewhere? Perhaps the problem is that we all too often see home and the world as horns of a dilemma and think we have to make a choice between polar opposites. When my friend Te Pakaka Tawhai died, his family from Tuparoa on the East Cape assumed he would be buried on his home *marae*, while his Pākehā wife insisted he be buried in the Manawatu where she, Paka, and their children had made their home. After much wrangling and bitterness, Mason Durie persuaded the families to allow Paka to be buried at Aorangi in the northern Wairarapa, midway between their irreconcilable worlds. And then there was Yorkie—Mrs. York—with whom I boarded during my year at Kuranui College. One day she said she would be happy to drive me anywhere I would like to go in the vicinity of Greytown. I asked if she would take me to Papawai marae, where, in the early 1860s, Hoani Te Whatahoro recorded from the *tohunga* (priestly expert) Nepia Pohuhu the Ngati Kahungunu traditions and genealogies that would form the basis of Percy Smith's conjectural history of the settlement of Aotearoa. Though I said nothing of my specific interest in Papawai, Yorkie seemed taken aback by my request, as if there were far better places to go sightseeing than a Māori *pa* (village), but she dutifully drove me there, and I strolled around the *urupa* (burial ground) with her, making small talk as we went along. But when I stopped in front of the monument and attempted to translate aloud the Māori inscriptions on the marble, it was all too much for her, and she astonished me by providing a fluent, if exasperated, translation before suggesting we return to Greytown for tea and cake. Yorkie was Māori. She never acknowledged it, and I never broached the subject with her. But she, too, was caught between Scylla and Charybdis. In the provincial town in which she lived, you had to be one thing or the other, and given the stigma that attached to being Māori, she had chosen to pass for Pākehā.

Is it possible to escape the double binds into which identity thinking leads us? Is it possible to move from either-or to both-and? Like globalization, biculturalism is a compelling idea. But living it is another matter.

That day in the Wairarapa, talking with Vincent and Helen over a risotto and chardonnay at Martinborough, then driving home through a landscape of olives and vineyards—themselves reminders of how foreign the familiar could become, and how familiar the foreign—as well as over the next few days in Wellington, meeting other old friends and wandering around the city I so loved, I was brought back to these questions of roots and horizons, as though every conversation, every event, was feeding an inner monologue and pressing for some kind of resolution.

First were the experiences of growing up in a rural backwater and longing to move away—so much so that one seized on whatever evidence came to hand of the mysterious elsewhere where one imagined one might come into one's own. Allan Thomas provides a telling example in his book on music in the small Taranaki town of Hawera in 1946, the final page proofs of which he was reading during the week I stayed with him and his wife, Jennifer Shennan, in Wellington. When Margaret Buist first heard Gustav Mahler's *Songs of a Wayfarer* on a gramophone record, she resolved to enter the song in the competitions, determined, as she put it, to "show these Hawera people." "I learnt the German from the record," she recalls. "Maurice Clare played the accompaniment for me. Well, the judge placed me first but she said in her comments that she'd like to talk to me because she'd also been learning German and hers seemed different to mine!" (Thomas 2004:90).

I liked this anecdote not only because it captured the tension between one's experience of the everyday, parochial world in which one lives and the remote, metropolitan world of which one can only dream but because of Buist's poignant candor and comic self-deprecation, for at the very moment she encounters this outside world, with all its magic and promise, she is brought up against the cultural, financial, and linguistic limitations that will prevent her from ever entering fully into it. But perhaps an awkward and unconsummated relationship with the metropolitan world is more comfortable than knowing it in depth. And here I think of my father, who—apart from a couple of years in the Australian outback when he was a boy, his mother having decreed that the family needed to be closer to a potential inheritance—lived in New

Zealand all his life and never expressed any desire to journey elsewhere. And yet the outside world impinged on him, as it impinged on Buist, for he was a radio ham and spent long hours in his shack calling into the ether, "This is ZL2PL calling. This is ZL2PL. Do you read me? Come in if you read me. Over . . . ," and receiving responses from places as far away as California, Canada, Britain, South Africa, and Tanganyika. Call signs were exchanged, as well as wavelengths, frequencies, contact dates and times, and sometimes some trivial domestic detail was added to the technical remarks on the QSL (quality of transmission) card he would mail, presumably to be pinned on the wall of another shack, exactly like his, tens of thousands of miles away.

But when I was a boy, eavesdropping on these cryptic messages through the sizzle and surge of ghostly oceans, the paradox never occurred to me that though my father made contact with all these exotic places, his exchanges were as minimal as they were banal. Quality of transmission was an ironic thing; he could just as well have been calling his Radio Club pals across town.

This is not to suggest that journeys have to be to the four corners of the world, for the journey to the corner store is, for some, tantamount to climbing Everest. Dublin, for Bloom, was as challenging as the Eastern Mediterranean was for Odysseus. Nor is it to imply that people who are happiest when they are close to home are insecure or unfulfilled, that Penelope was not capable of undertaking her husband's voyages. No. It is simply to suggest that those who never venture out into the world will tend to feel more insecure in their relation to that world than those who have risked getting to know it firsthand. And while the voyager will, over time, abandon the idea of a fixed identity and take on attributes of all the places he or she has lived, the homebody will cling to the idea that there is no place like home—and worry it to death. For the idea of identity is the defining preoccupation of those who want a settled worldview and whose attitude to the world is defensive. Identity is a Manichaean idea; a matter of either-or, rather than both-and. It therefore generates nonnegotiable symbolic oppositions between self and other, the first invariably good and true, the second evil and false, the first to be defended, the second to be expunged. In this Tolkienesque world people live under continual siege, imagining themselves menaced by foreign entities whose names are legion: witches; the Yel-

low Peril; blacks; Jews; communists; terrorists; foreigners; asylum seekers. While the voyager seeks to broaden her or his horizons, opening
herself or himself up to the outside world, the homebody builds walls
and fences, making forays out into the world only to do battle with the
minatory other, but always hoping to return home to a hero's welcome,
holding high the trophy won, the sense of unique identity safeguarded
and reaffirmed. To be sure, the homebody sometimes ventures abroad
as a tourist, but with a well-defined itinerary, the company of like-
minded friends, and plenty of places to provide home comforts so that
she or he need have no fear of encountering in the other that side of
herself or himself that she or he has never explored. By contrast, the
voyager is like the insignificant pine, *Pinus insignia*, or the Monterey
Pine, the *macrocarpa*, which, when transplanted from their original
habitats in North America took root in New Zealand and grew like
weeds, as if to show that even God had misjudged the ability of a native
not only to flourish in a foreign place but to make that place its own.

What is anthropology but a systematic implementation of this impulse to open up dialogue with others, to call into question the parochial view that one's own world is *the* world, and all others a diminished
version or demonic corruption of it? What but a way of making a
science of the age-old Odyssean impulse to wander off the beaten
track, to encounter the strange, and to see whether, beyond the fears
and fantasies of the homebodies, there is something one may call common ground or common humanity? What but a realization of Novalis's
Romantic vision of being at home everywhere?

For a long time, Europeans assumed that they alone were discover-
ers. Whether pursuing the Enlightenment ideal of discovering new
knowledge, or furthering imperial ambitions to discover new lands,
Europeans saw themselves as the heirs of their dethroned God, the sole
beings capable of creating anything new. All other societies were, they
believed, inhabited by beings whose lack of reason doomed them to the
perpetual recapitulation of primordial ways of life—they were as set in
their ways as they were isolated in their tribal territories. If we did not
know how well this erroneous view served European interests, we
might be astonished at how long it has persisted in the face of abundant
evidence of the vast movements of human populations from time immemorial: Bantu cultivators filling the African continent in the space

of a thousand years, Basque fishermen sailing to the four corners of the Atlantic in search of cod, Viking adventurers seeking plunder and glory, Polynesian voyagers braving new latitudes in their search for new lands. Indeed, it is hard to think of any human society that has lived in splendid isolation, and even harder to sustain the view that *they* have closed systems while we have open minds. On the contrary, networks of exchange and trade connected far-flung peoples long before the term *globalization* was invented, so that the languages of West Africa have long borne the imprint of Islam and Arabic, the source of medieval Europe's gold were the mines of ancient Mali, cowry shells from the Maldives have been the currency of West Africa since the fourteenth century, and the staple crops of East Asia—rice, bananas, yams —were the source of West Africa's own neolithic revolution.

I think there is a direct parallel to be drawn between this interdependency of widely scattered societies and the interdependency of persons. Both relationships, are, I argue in my book *Minima Ethnographica*, refractions of the same concern: the relationship between the one and the many.

In Central Australia, where I did fieldwork during the 1990s, the dreaming tracks that traverse the desert are "open systems" that cross linguistic, tribal, and ecological borders. Raiding and abduction were once as common as intermarriages, which were, significantly enough, negotiated during the course of initiation ceremonies at locations where the lands of one tribe overlapped the lands of another. Spearheads, wild tobacco, and artifacts were traded far afield, as were language, ceremony, and custom. A Warlpiri myth condenses these facts into a single narrative. Two dogs traveled from the west and camped at a place just north of Warlala, where there is a red escarpment above a plain of spinifex and blue mallee on which I stood one afternoon in 1993, listening to Zack Jackamarra recount this particular section of the two dogs' journey, this chapter of the story. At Ngarnka, well to the west, the male dog had abducted another dog's wife. Camped near Warlala, he "sang" up mist and smoke to confuse his pursuers. In the morning, the fleeing pair moved west along a dried river course, stopping at Warlala where the male dog scratched a hole in the ground and shat. From there to Yulpawarnu the dogs walked on clumps of spinifex in order to leave no tracks. After crossing the Tanami desert, the dogs reached Alekarenge (literally, "belonging to the dogs"), where they encountered "many, many other dogs" from Kayeteje, Warramunga, and other tribal areas. There, they settled down and lived with all the others.

Like most myths, the Warlpiri narrative is allegorical. Its surface features belie its hidden depths. Though set in the past and recounted in the past tense, the meaning of the myth is consummated in time present. Though the story concerns two dogs, it is really about human beings. And their identity is born of difference. As Joe Jangala observes at the end of his version of the narrative: "In the beginning, they were all dogs, not just one but many. As this story has shown, this is how they became all one family, one people."

This vision of human plurality—of us being both similar and different, rather than essentially one thing or the other—is not some idealization; it reflects a fundamental human necessity and a paradox: that life itself requires an openness to others and traffic across the borderlines that nominally separate us.

In 1950, the Australian anthropologist Kenneth Read was on a patrol in an area of the Eastern Highlands of New Guinea in which people had never before seen a white man. One morning, as Read and his companions were breaking camp, a young boy from the village approached them. Using gestures, he made it clear that he wanted to return with the strangers to the place they had come from. The boy was perhaps thirteen or fourteen. He spoke no language but his own. Yet he was prepared to throw in his lot with these outsiders and undertake a journey Read describes as "immeasurably greater than the distance involved, virtually a transition from one world to another." Even though the terrors of the unknown were mitigated by a kind of visionary opportunism—since, to have any hope of becoming a leader in one's natal village, a man had to brave the hazards of the outside world and seek out the power and wealth said to exist only in alien lands—this "leap through time," Read notes, "took a measure of courage and a degree of foresight almost impossible to comprehend" (1965:58–61). Did the boy, Susuro, whose new name was an affectionate diminutive of his adopted village, ever succeed in his aspirations? Thirty years after leaving the so-called High Valley, Read went back. Old acquaintances told him that Susuro had remained in Susuroka for several years, growing to manhood there and working from time to time in a nearby

human plurality - Similar & diff

not of speak.

township. He then returned home. Of Susuro's subsequent fate, all Read could learn was that he was dead, killed by sorcery among his own people (Read 1986:114).

Despite Susuro's sad end, the human impulse to journey beyond the horizons of one's own known world, the same impulse that drew Read to anthropology, is universal. The very existence and well-being of us who think of ourselves as kith and kin depends on some kind of rapprochement with those we regard as other, even as our negation. "The wife is fetched from among the daughters of strangers," say the Sukuma-Nyamwezi of western Tanzania (Brandström 1990:179). "We marry the people we fight," declare the Mae-Enga of the western Highlands of Papua New Guinea (Meggitt 1964:218).

Paradoxically, those who can do me most harm are the very people who can do me most good, for the things of greatest power and value always lie beyond one's ken, outside one's own circle, or in the hands of others. René Girard called this mimetic desire (1965), in recognition of the fact that our desires do not flow simply or freely from within us, but from our desire to imitate the other, possessing what he or she has, or dispossessing him or her of what he or she has in order to be alike. But even when we do not see mimetic desire at work, we see that a basic social imperative is to work out a modus vivendi with the other, turning a potential threat to one's life and livelihood into an actual boon. This not only underlies the forms of human hospitality: it is a precondition of all exchange.

This is why, for the Kuranko, the village must open itself up continually to the bush—the world that is the symbolic opposite of the moral community of human beings. In Kuranko myth, everything from xylophones and initiation drums to magical medicines and the staples of life come from the bush. Just as hunters venture into the bush at night, braving real and imagined dangers in their search for life-sustaining food, farmers must clear-cut the forest in order to plant the grain that is the staff of life, and wives must be brought into the lineage from elsewhere. Moreover, trade with the outside world is as imperative now as it was when the Scottish explorer Alexander Gordon Laing passed through Kuranko country in 1825 in search of the source of the Niger and was invited to help "open up a good road to the sea" so that villagers could exchange camwood, kola, gum copal, and rice for salt and cloth.

But the necessity of ties with the outside world is not simply economic. Secular power (chieftaincy) has always struggled to strike a balance with the "wild" powers of the djinni, just as the old struggle to draw on the vital yet potentially delinquent energies of the young, and men struggle to control young wives who, they fear, will damage the integrity of the very group to which, ideally, they should bring new life.

Vitality always exists beyond, at the edge. In that place most remote from where I am. Though the wilderness is fraught with danger, it is also the source of regenerative life. If gods and ancestors are foci of ambivalent feelings, provoking anxiety if they become too distant or too familiar, this is also true of exotic and distant places. For insular Europe, the sea and the sea voyage were for centuries the prevailing metaphors for this hunger for self-realization and riches in the beyond. For Africa, the paradigmatic example is still the Zande oracle (*benge*). At the time when the great English anthropologist E. Evans Evans-Pritchard lived among them, benge had to be sought in arduous two-hundred-kilometer journeys beyond Zandeland, journeys to the Bomokandi River in the Belgian Congo that were subject to strict taboos and frontier controls. When asked why they did not cultivate the poison creeper in their own country and so save themselves the trouble of gathering it under such dangerous and difficult conditions, Zande informants expressed "disapproval" of the question, alleging that a kinsman would die if this were done. "We may suppose," observed Evans-Pritchard, "that the mystical potency of the poison is derived partly from its scarcity and the pains that must be expended in procuring it" (1937:271). But the power of the alien lies in the illusion of its essential otherness, not simply in its scarcity. As in medieval philosophy, *alteritas* connotes not only otherness but the possibility of transcendence. That which is furthest from my grasp and control is that which poses the greatest existential threat to my being. By making that foreign thing my own, by assimilating it to myself, by incorporating it within my being, by bringing it under my control, I disarm its menace. But more significant, the symbolic blood, sweat, and tears that go into the taming of the alien object are felt to now imbue the object with value. Accordingly, *its* power objectifies *my* power over it. That which was alien now stands to augment rather than threaten me. Let us now consider this phenomenology of value in more depth.

- greatest existential threat comes from lack of grasp or control.

I have argued that neither home nor the world can be assigned fixed values. Each is always regarded ambivalently. Though there is no place like home, familiarity breeds contempt, distance lends enchantment, and the grass is always greener on the other side. But even when the world represents the possibility of greater fortune or rebirth, it remains a place of peril and uncertainty.

What makes the difference between a place, person, or object being assigned a positive or negative value is the degree to which it is felt to be within our control and subject to our own choosing. This existential hypothesis runs right through my work. Except in the extreme cases that Erich Fromm calls totalitarian and masochist personalities, most human beings neither want to rule the world absolutely nor want to abnegate completely their part in determining how the world will be governed. Generally speaking, human beings seek to strike a balance between being actors and being acted on, so that—in spite of being aware that eternity is infinite and human life finite, that the cosmos is great and the human world small, and that nothing anyone says or does can immunize him or her from the contingencies of history, the tyranny of circumstance, the accidents of fate, and the finality of death— every human being needs some modicum of choice, craves some degree of understanding, demands some say, and expects some sense of control over the course of his or her own life. In this view, the worst that can befall a human being is to become a mere creature of circumstance, subject to the whims and will of a powerful other whose ways can neither be comprehended nor controlled.

Let me go back, for a moment, to the Wairarapa, and my year teaching at Kurunui College. Sam Mead, the principal, was also the brother of the All Black rugby player Colin Mead. Grant Batty, a future All Black, was in my third form class, as was the future writer and critic Martin Edmond. And Martin's mother, Lauris, who I never actually met at that time, would become one of New Zealand's best-regarded poets. I, too, was working at being a writer. Every day after school, except Fridays when I hitchhiked to Wellington to spend the weekend with my girlfriend, I hastened back to Yorkie's where I was translating various writings of Blaise Cendrars and trying to write about my experiences in the Congo the previous year. During much of that year—and, tragically, for many years since—rebel insurgencies made travel in the interior unsafe, and I spent a lot of my time in Léopoldville working with youngsters who had lost their parents and been displaced from their homes in the secessionist wars that followed Congolese independence in 1961. Though often homesick, I knew I could return to New Zealand whenever I wished. But for the orphans I worked among, or for Joshua Nkomo's Zimbabwe African People's Union freedom fighters, awaiting the call to return to Southern Rhodesia and join the battle against colonial rule, who I used to hang out with at the Palace Hotel, there was no freedom to move; only a long wait for things to improve, or a window of opportunity to open. This is the difference between being an expatriate and being an exile—this freedom to return to the place you call home and claim your birthright there, recognized as a kinsperson and not a stranger. I suppose that when I visited Papawai with Yorkie and recalled the meetings of the Māori parliament that took place there in the 1890s, I was also mindful of the losses of land and livelihood that were then eroding the soul of the *tangata whenua* ("people of the land") of Aotearoa New Zealand.

To be exiled is not merely to be driven from and estranged from one's homeland; it is to be forced on a journey into the world, a journey made against one's will, to places not of one's own choosing. But ethnography shows us that people respond to this situation in very different ways. While it is experienced by some as social death and engenders prolonged grief, including idealizations of the homeland as a paradise lost, deep embitterment toward those who have taken one's birthright away, and the sustained, brooding contemplation of how one can, through civil action or violent confrontation, make good one's losses, others experience it as a painful rebirth, accepting the irreversibility of the situation into which they have been unjustly cast, but building a new future out of what they can retain from the past and what they can gain from the new world in which they have been thrown. If the first involves a fixation on the past, the second is a decisive orientation toward the future. If the first is centered on the idea of an original home as foundational, the only place one can exist with dignity and have a say, the second is centered on the world as a place of possibility.

Consider, for example, Liisa Malkki's ethnographic research among Hutu refugees in rural western Tanzania. Malkki worked in two "accidental communities"—the first a Hutu refugee camp known as Mishamo, the second the Tanzanian township of Kigoma on Lake Tanganyika, where many other Hutu had settled. Malkki was immediately struck by the differences between the Hutu in these two communities. While the "town refugees" sought ways "of assimilating and manipulating multiple identities—identities derived or 'borrowed' from the social context of the township" (1995:36)—that engendered a cosmopolitan, creolized sense of self that celebrated its adaptiveness and "impurity" (37), the camp refugees defined themselves as a nation in exile, recollecting "traces and afterlives" (Malkki 1997:93) in order to nurture their dream of returning to a homeland where they truly belonged. In Mishamo camp, Hutu worked tirelessly on a collective narrative that, like biblical epics, rationalized the essential moral difference between Hutu and Tutsi as a Manichaean contrast between good and evil. Cosmological in scale, these mythico-histories reimagined the crucial events whereby Hutu had lost their homelands and envisaged how this loss might be redressed or avenged. According to the mythic version of events, Hutu were the original and autochthonous inhabitants of Rwanda, but the Tutsi, migrating from the north at a later date, had usurped Hutu power through stealth and trickery. This involved a negation of reciprocity. The Hutu allowed the Tutsi pastoralists to graze their cattle on their land. In return, the Tutsi gave dung to the Hutu to make their fruit trees grow, milk to make their children stronger, and cows. But before long, the Hutu were beholden to the Tutsi and obliged to work for them. Thus Hutu (which in folk etymologies means "servant" or "slave") lost their autonomy. Though they regained it for a while under Belgian rule, independence restored Tutsi fortunes. They blocked Hutu advancements through education, and in 1972, determined to tip the demographic and social balance further in their own favor, Tutsi massacred Hutu and forced tens of thousands into exile. The Hutu rationalization for righting these wrongs touched on familiar themes: First, the notion of first settlement, of historical precedence, as giving primary rights in a place. Second, the notion of what Malkki calls "romantic autochthony" (1995). Hutu were autochthonous—they were born of and belonged to the earth; Tutsi came from the sky. Third, images of chicanery, theft, and trickery. Hutu were conned by Tutsi. From this derived the fourth theme: Hutu were morally and spiritually superior to Tutsi, who were morally untrustworthy, power-hungry,

"multiple identities"

individualistic, and materialistic. All these assumptions found expression in bodily stereotypes of self and other: Hutu were stocky, solidly built workers, while Tutsi were tall, lazy, and physically weak. If Tutsi married Hutu, they weakened and impoverished the Hutu stock.

The implication of Malkki's work is that when people are isolated from others they tend to develop simplistic and fundamentalist notions about those others that readily colonize their minds and lead, in some cases, to violent, even genocidal, actions. But when people are obliged to coexist in the same place, on roughly the same terms, they tend to see themselves and others as variations on a single human theme, different but not demonically or dangerously other.

Sometimes we become so fixated on our own perspective that we fail to see that everyone else has a perspective too, and that no one has any special claim to the truth. All we can do is to see what consequences follow from believing a viewpoint to be true, to see what general good or harm is entailed by it.

In closing, I would like to refer to Caroline Daley's *Leisure and Pleasure: Reshaping and Revealing the New Zealand Body, 1900–1960*. In the introduction to her history of how the modern body was revealed, shaped, and marketed between 1900 and 1960, Daley cautions us from thinking that our own histories are unique. "We have become so accustomed to history books telling national stories that we often forget to place those tales in their international contexts," she begins. "If New Zealand historians were less intent on trying to crack the code of New Zealand's uniqueness, and not so obsessed with quests for national identity, they might notice that many of the supposedly particular characteristics of this society are really not so particular after all" (2003: 3–4). These remarks are equally pertinent for anthropology, which has so often described what is different about human kinship systems, modes of inheritance and succession, beliefs and rituals—inventing arcane vocabularies for distinguishing them—that it has created the impression that every local moral world is a world unto itself, a bounded and insular entity, possessing its own essence, its own identity, even its own nature. But what defines the human condition is that everyone is both identical and different—that underlying our manifest diversity are identical structures of experience that betray the effects of millions of years of shared evolution, not to mention the historical movements of people, ideas, stories, and commodities that had globalized us for aeons before the term was coined. As long as we regard ourselves as isolated and unique we risk throwing up stereotypes of the other that bear no relation to reality. And yet, paradoxically, we can only reach an understanding of what is held in common by entering deeply into another local moral world, living in it, speaking its language, sustaining a conversation with it over time.

In the years that followed the end of civil war in Sierra Leone, I revisited the country that had long been my home away from home and wrote about my experiences. One thing that struck me in working and talking with displaced Kuranko villagers was the absence of vengefulness, the stoic acceptance of loss as a precondition for creating a new life, for moving on. Although Western governments have obliged Sierra Leone to undergo a truth and reconciliation process—with alleged war criminals arraigned before a special court, and the endless recounting of terrible stories—everyone I spoke to in the Freetown refugee camps saw no point in raking over old coals. Enjoined to recount the past in order to have a future, these people saw it as more expedient to forget it in order to build something new. What follows may be a trivial comparison perhaps, but it is one that comes to mind: Billy Collins's poem about walking in the woods one day without a pen, and nothing to write on anyway, but suddenly finding the lines of a poem in his head:

> Six or eight exhalations,
> the braided rope of the syntax,
> the jazz of the timing,
> with the little insight at the end
> wagging like the short tail
> of a perfectly obedient spaniel,
> sitting by the door (2000:132)

Lines he lost because the call of the clear morning in the woods was greater than the call to return home to write. No regrets. Which is why I like to imagine that the little insight at the end might have had something to do with letting go and with opening oneself up to new possibilities, of seeing the world not as one thing, or one place, that has primary value, but as something of many possibilities, many places, all potentially as illuminating as the next, so that there is in going out into the world not a loss of one's natal home, but a creative transformation of one's relationship with it.

I wrote these lines in Denmark within weeks of returning from the antipodes, wanting to collect my thoughts while they were still fresh and to keep alive a sense of the summer. Every morning, after finishing a stint of writing, I would walk to the Café Europa on Amagertorv for an espresso and to read the *Herald Tribune*. I sat at the same steel table every morning, black-and-white photos on the nearby wall keeping me company: Bertolt Brecht, Alexander Dubček, Astrid Lindgren, Jean-Paul Sartre, and Coco Chanel. After reading the newspaper and finishing my coffee, or jotting down some notes I might incorporate into my essay, I would stroll back to my office along Gammel Strand, the old street that runs beside the canal and where, until about forty years ago, clinker-built fishing boats would come in from the harbor to unload hampers of cod and skate. Near Hojbro—High Bridge—there is a statue of one of the white-bonneted fishwives who used to sit together along the quay, cleaning and selling fish. And there are still fish restaurants on the strand, where one can sit outdoors in summer, within sight of the flea markets that attract both locals and tourists, and a stone's throw from the copper-roofed Christiansborg Castle that is now the Danish House of Parliament. Walking these cobbled streets, with the facades of eighteenth-century houses to my left and the canal to my right, I felt elated and at home. Who was to say that this was not my place, and that others who had come to this city as refugees and migrants could not also refer to their experiences of belonging here as grounds on which to claim a form of experiential citizenship? And who, moreover, could claim that our citizenship of our countries of origin was compromised or invalidated by our feelings for Europe or other places where we had made our lives, albeit as designated strangers?

There is fairly widespread usage of the concept of
culture, in which the spiritual world is lifted out of
its context, making culture a (false) collective noun
and attributing (false) universality to it. This . . .
concept of culture . . . plays off the spiritual world
against the material world by holding up culture
as the realm of authentic values and self-contained
ends in opposition to the world of social utility and
means.—HERBERT MARCUSE, *Negations*

12 A Critique
of Colonial Reason

Of all the questions that have weighed on the minds of human beings,
the question of identity and difference is surely among the most refractory. It simply does not seem possible for us to live with the paradox of
plurality—that while we are all members of the same species, sharing
similar capacities for speech, sociality, and conceptual thought, no two
individuals are exactly the same, either in appearance or ability. The
matter is further clouded and complicated by the question of cultural
difference, for while many people need to feel part of a bounded culture
with a unique character, history suggests that the boundaries between
cultures have constantly been transgressed, blurred, and redrawn, so
that the idea of separating entire populations on the basis of singular
and unvarying traits is at best a fiction and at worst an invitation to

violence. In fact, the differences and disagreements *within* any population are as great as the differences *between* populations, and unique traits never cluster in such numbers as to warrant the ascription of significant discontinuities to the relations between individuals, nations, or cultures (by this reckoning, race is a complete misnomer). Moreover, there is probably no society on earth whose worldview is so insular that it does not contain at least the germ of the notion of a universal humanity. Despite differences based on language, heritage, and interests, there exists the potentiality for strangers to be accommodated, for enmities to be overcome, and for cultural barriers to be transcended.

Yet we persist, in both popular and academic thought, in emphasizing what divides us, not what we have in common. All too readily we fall into the trap of assuming that the category words with which we discursively differentiate ourselves from others are more than consoling illusions that provide us with a sense of stable identity in an unstable and multiplex world; of believing they are markers and reminders of real and ineradicable differences historically, divinely, or culturally given. Following Theodor Adorno, I want to challenge this kind of identity thinking, not simply on the grounds that it is politically dangerous and ethically flawed but on the *empirical* grounds that it does not represent the way in which human beings actually live their everyday lives. Indeed, if the way we thought determined the way we live, we would be lost, for our lives would be locked into the verbal cages to which we consign ourselves and others according to the precept "to each his own." Thankfully, life confounds and overflows the definitions we impose on it in the name of reason or administrative control, and it is this excess of meaning, this tendency of life to deny our attempts to bind it with words and ideas that redeems us.

The Antinomy of Reason and Unreason

We are nowadays so accustomed to speaking of the world as deeply divided—nations, cities, houses, and even personalities divided within and among themselves—that we seldom stop to reflect on the implications of such glib distinctions as modern versus premodern, north versus south, Christendom versus Islam, first versus third world, haves versus have-nots. So habitual are these ways of reducing lifeworlds to worldviews and life to language that we are blind to the ways in which they reinforce the inequalities they are meant to bring to our attention. For in assuming that science, rationality, and democracy are necessary conditions for economic growth, human freedom, and greater equality, and that superstition, tradition, illiteracy, and autocracy are inimical to progress, we perpetuate a view of ourselves as morally as well as materially superior to "them," describing them mostly in terms of what they want or need or lack, as if their lifeways were not only an impediment to progress but a curse, like the mark of Cain. From this it is a short step to assuming that their historic failure to become as successful as we are is a sign of some social or intellectual deficiency that can only be made good by our enlightened interventions—helping them develop our preferred model of government, introducing them to our notion of human rights, teaching them our scientific techniques of healing, and bringing to them our systems of schooling. Entrapped by the very terms with which we have come to characterize "our" relations with "them," we perpetuate the idea of the civilizing mission that was the pretext for colonialism.

Of all the binary oppositions we deploy none is more insidious than the one that draws a contrast between reason and religion, the latter being, as Émile Durkheim put it, "a sort of speculation upon that which evades science or distinct thought in general," a matter of the things that "surpass the limits of our knowledge" (1915:24). To this distinction between science and superstition, "the world of the mysterious, of the unknowable, of the un-understandable" (24), we graft on another, readily identifying what Durkheim called "the crudest religions" (48) with simple societies and the "higher" religions with complex ones. Thus, despite the fact that Western secular thought is steeped in Judeo-Christian traditions, we like to think (like Max Weber in *The Protestant Ethic and the Spirit of Capitalism*) that "our" religious traditions are compatible with scientific progress, while non-Western religions are defined by the irrational forces of fanaticism, fatalism, emotionalism, and quietism. My argument is therefore not only against the false dichotomy of reason and unreason, but against the way these terms have been used to distinguish between two different kinds of society, and two classes of humanity, conventionally labeled civilized and savage, or

reason/religion

Weber ~ that our relig traditions are compatible w/ science

modern and premodern. This language game, in which reason is assigned to oneself and unreason to the other (though we are careful nowadays to euphemize unreason as cosmology, myth, religion,
folklore, cultural values, traditionalism, fundamentalism, or spirituality) is a strategy for denying coevalness (Fabian 1983) and, when applied to entire societies, has no empirical justification. All human
beings think and act rationally *and* irrationally, depending on circumstance, and to consider oneself intrinsically or wholly reasonable is
itself a form of irrationalism.

Colonial India

In his *Elementary Aspects of Peasant Insurgency in Colonial India*,
Ranajit Guha writes of the "sense of identity" that was imposed on the
peasant

> by those who had power over him by virtue of their class, caste and official
> standing. It was they who made him aware of his place in society as a
> measure of his distance from themselves—a distance expressed in dif-
> ferentials of wealth, status and culture. In other words, he learnt to recog-
> nize himself not by the properties and attributes of his own social being
> but by a diminution, if not negation, of those of his superiors (1983a:18).

Although this submission to the powers that be was frequently mediated by Indian notions of devotion, deference, duty, and spiritual commitment, the discriminatory framework of colonialism pervaded the
subaltern imaginary in both conformity and revolt, *as if people were
bound to react to domination in the very terms with which this domination had been effected.* Even though Guha argues that peasant insurgency was political in character, it was consistently described by the
colonial authorities in terms of forces that lay outside the pale of reason
and political consciousness. In particular, the phenomenon was natu-
ralized through imagery that likened revolt to an earthquake, a wildfire,
the outbreak of a thunderstorm, or the spread of a disease (1983b:2).
Because the colonizer believed that his power was an exercise of enlightened reason, peasant power could only be understood as an expression of mindless passion. And while the power of reason associated
with colonial rule was inscribed in laws laid down by enlightened men,

the power of unreason associated with the subaltern masses was seen to be blindly driven by religious passions, instincts, custom, or criminality. Enlightened rule was thus conceived as a form of domestication that would tame the unruly lives and landscapes of the unenlightened.

Guha is insistent that though peasant rebellion took the form of destruction by wrecking and burning, this was not because the insurgent was naturally given to mindless violence. But rather than argue that this violence was an expression of an incipient political consciousness, arising from the exclusion of Indians from the colonial administration that controlled their destiny, I would like to point out that violence was a product of the very stereotypes that the oppressor imposed on the oppressed. Frustrated in his attempts to reason with his oppressor, the rebel becomes the ungovernable creature that he has been made to be, expressing through *deliberate* acts of public violence the madness that in the colonial imaginary comes naturally to him.

At the same time as the colonized are depicted as debased human beings, associated with backwardness and emotionality, the conscience of the oppressor is pricked by the knowledge that this debasement is in large measure a product of colonization itself. As such, it might appear only reasonable that a human being would protest his or her degradation. But rather than attribute to the colonized masses the capacity for reasoned action, the well-meaning colonizer distances himself from those he has degraded by characterizing their power as "charismatic" or "spiritual" or (more recently) promulgating myths of primitive ecological wisdom that idealize their harmonious relationship with nature and condemn European economic activity as environmentally destructive (Milton 1996:109). But despite the desire to recognize in the other some trace of common humanity, the discursive strategy of offering the oppressed the compensatory notions of a greater closeness to God or to nature effectively reinforces the political order that excludes the colonized from the sphere of *political* power.

The same distorting lens and double standard that led Westerners to assume that Indian peasants were outside the pale of reason produced the conviction that Indian traditions could not be truly scientific and that Indian thought was prevalently mythico-religious in character. Despite the fact that Sanskrit and Pali "have a larger atheistic and agnostic literature than exists in any other classical tradition" (Sen

2005: 202–6), Indian writings on nonreligious themes, including mathematics, grammar, epistemology, economics, and natural science have been largely ignored in the West. Indeed, so effective was this colonial exoticizing of India that many Indians have embraced Western stereotypes and have become willing participants in the neo-Vedanta project of defining India as a homeland of spirituality, the antithesis of the materialistic decadence of the West.[1] Speaking of Swami Dayanand Saraswati (1824–83) and Swami Vivekananda (1863–1902), two of the most redoubtable of these late-nineteenth-century revisionist thinkers, Ashis Nandy notes how deeply their ideas "fitted the dominant structure of colonial thought, as well as the ideology of some Western Orientalists" (1988:24): "[They] tried to Christianize Hinduism, particularly the dominant Hindu concept of the desirable person. In doing so, they identified the West with power and hegemony, which in turn they identified with a superior civilization. Then they tried to 'list' the differences between the West and India and attributed the former's superiority to these differences" (24–25).

At worst, this process of remaking oneself in the image of the colonizer entails defining oneself through negation: Hindus had lost the original Aryan qualities they once shared with Westerners, but they could recover their spiritual and ascetic heritage through an imitation of Christian traditions. But by buying into the myths of ancient wisdom, spiritual identity, harmony with nature, and instinctual musicality, the colonized could only deepen and perpetuate the inequalities of colonial rule that were founded on the spurious distinction between religion and reason.

Antipodean Instances

In turning now to the colonization of Aotearoa New Zealand in the early nineteenth century, I want to explore the ways in which discursive strategies that denigrated or spiritualized Māori both reinforced Pākehā assumptions of racial difference and shaped the ways in which Māori resisted those assumptions.

While most nineteenth-century Europeans denigrated Māori as creatures of nature, living depraved, sinful, undeveloped lives, and prone to violence and cannibalism, some saw them as deeply religious, with beliefs, myths, and superstitions that constituted genuine cosmologies. In the thought of Thomas Kendall, who came to New Zealand as a Calvinist missionary in 1814 but who by 1827 had lost his soul to the heathen that he had come to "improve" and convert, these two strains are both in contention (Binney 1968). Thus Kendall's contempt for native beliefs coexisted uncomfortably with a profound intellectual curiosity about the Māori worldview, just as his desire to keep himself socially separate from Māori was compromised by a need for their company (Binney 1968:76–77). In Kendall's struggle to reconcile a view of Māori and Pākehā as radically different with an anthropological relativism that recognized historical and human continuities between them, we may discern one side of the tragedy that is colonialism. Since the colonizer cannot abandon the idea of the other as inferior without calling into question his right to have power over him, he has recourse to a compromise. He will deny reason and secular power to the colonized, but will recognize the latter's humanity by seeing him as potentially a spiritual equal. For the colonized, a similar dilemma emerges. By entering into contracts and treaties with a materially and militarily more powerful polity, his autonomy, sovereignty, and identity are undermined. But through spiritual power he imagines that he will make good whatever political losses he has suffered. Gradually, these stereotypes will come to constitute a "second colonization" (Nandy 1988:xi) in which *both* Māori and Pākehā unwittingly collude.

Let us review the early period of culture contact. In the decade before 1820, Māori relations with Europeans were motivated by economic and political interests. Missionaries were tolerated not because Māori had much interest in Christianity, but because they sought new opportunities for trade and the acquisition of muskets (Binney 1968:30). In the late 1820s all this changed. Where only a few years before, flax and potatoes had been traded for weapons, reading matter was now the commodity in greatest demand.

But was it Christian notions of salvation from sin and spiritual rebirth to which Māori were drawn, or a desire to safeguard or salvage their dwindling political and economic power? By the early 1820s Māori in Northland had diversified their agriculture to include pig breeding, as well as imported crops such as turnips, parsnips, carrots, cabbages, and peas (Cruise 1957:116; Martin 1845:280), and by 1830

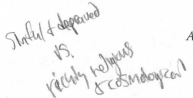
Sinful + depraved
vs.
racially religious + cosmological

most chiefs had Europeans living among them and mediating trade relations with the outside world (Polack 1840, vol. 1:172). But profits from sales of flax, potatoes, and other crops had been used, with disastrous results, to acquire muskets, gunpowder, and iron tools. Musket warfare decimated defenseless southern tribes, epidemic illness led to dramatic population decline, pigs ravaged gardens, the tapu system of prohibitions for controlling food production and conserving resources was undermined by the market economy, and villagers often starved or worked themselves to exhaustion in an effort to produce goods for Europeans (Hargreaves 1963:103; Wright 1959:65–77). It was against this background that Māori turned their attentions from traders to missionaries, as if the Bible held the secret to European power. Significantly, slaves were among the first to convert, and they became the principle evangelists, catechists, and teachers (Markham 1963:66; Taylor 1868:13; Williams 1935:233; Wright 1959:160–61; Yate 1835:240). But one suspects that Māori were not so much seeking individual salvation as the means to regain their health, social integrity, honor, and power. It was literacy, rather than Christian teachings per se, that held the promise of this restoration. Māori spoke to the explorer Colenso of being sick for lack of books ("E mate ana matou i te pukapuka kore") and of needing books to use as guns to shoot evil spirits or as compasses with which to reset their course (Bagnall and Petersen 1948: 50). By 1845 there was at least one New Testament for every two Māoris in New Zealand, but any hope Māori may have placed in these texts as magical or practical solutions to their problems was already waning. Religious instruction had made no difference to their lot, and though some Europeans were advocating that Māori be taught English so they could acquire the kind of knowledge most relevant to their needs (Polack 1838:100), and many Māori were making the same demands (Parr 1963:216), the missionary counterargument was that this would only make Māori vulnerable to the profane subculture of illiterate whalers and sealers. More to the point, perhaps, the missionaries were well aware that such a move would free Māori from their dependency on the missions. As for Māori, they undoubtedly had already seen that illiterate Pākehā were succeeding where they were failing, and that missionaries were selfishly and competitively interested in saving Māori souls, rather than being dedicated to the protection of Māori interests, as if the injustices in this life could be redeemed in the next. Te Pakaka Tawhai puts this succinctly: "While the Christian God pro-vides Māoridom with its first Redeemer, he appears mostly to ignore needs at the temporal and profane level, leaving this domain to the ancestral gods who continue to cater for those needs" (1996:11).

When large-scale colonization got under way in the 1840s, there was widespread Māori repudiation of literacy and mission-based Chris-tianity, yet in attempting to control and comprehend the forces work-ing against them and bring unity to tribes still bent on settling old scores, Māori had recourse to many of the ideas they had assimilated from their oppressors. At *runanga*, or meetings, where only a decade before catechisms were recited and instruction in literacy was eagerly received, questions of unification and the recovery of lost mana were now vigorously discussed. A form of theocratic rule, modeled on the English monarchy, was widely debated, and the voices of new religious leaders, called *tohunga* or *wairuarua*, were heard. At a meeting with Māori in 1856, the missionary Thomas Grace poured scorn on the "absurd pretensions of the Wairuarua" only to be told, "When the missionaries came we consented to them because we thought they were a law of life to the body. When the Wesleyans came we consented to them because we thought their worship was a law of life for the body. Afterwards, when the Romanists came, we consented unto them be-cause we thought they, too, had a law of life for the body. For the same reason we now listen to the Wairuarua" (Grace 1928:60).[2] Christian teachings were also repudiated if they conflicted with Māori notions of identity, including the imperatives of revenge for insults suffered and the upholding of the mana of one's land. Thus John White relates that "no less than ten of the Rev. M. Brown's Native Congregation at Tau-ranga left him, returning their books to him, and saying, 'We must fight to defend ourselves. . . . If we may not fight, we will no longer be missionaries'" (1887:157).

Critique of Religion

As many writers have observed, the Māori orientation to the cosmos is relational (Durie 2001:x; Tawhai 1996:14). The world is made up of networks, conceived genealogically (*whakapapa*), that connect not

relational networks
genealogy

only people but people and their land, their ancestors, and their valued objects (*taonga*) in terms of the principle of reciprocal exchange (*utu*). But all these relationships are prone to grow cold, weaken, and die unless continually renewed by the energy and actions that breathe life back into them—gift exchanges, greetings, acts of compassion and conviviality (*aroha*), and respect for the tapu that determines correct conduct between different entities, both social and natural. Both the life essence of any life form or the mana of any person is in a constant state of flux, waxing and waning according to the individual capacities of an actor and the forces of circumstance.

Like any catastrophe, colonization ruptured the network of relationships that constituted the Māori lifeworld, reducing people's capacity to act effectively in relation to the circumstances that overwhelmed them. In the period 1840–1901, the Māori population fell from 100,000 to 45,549, and Māori land was reduced from 66 million acres to 3 million acres. In a prevailing image of the times, people became slaves or exiles, lacking power, influence, or presence. It is in this passivity, defeat, and shame that accompanied the loss of land, livelihoods, and health, as well as the loss of the means to act against colonial power, that we may begin to approach the history of Māori consciousness over the past 150 years.

But is it more useful to construe present-day social inequalities in New Zealand between Māori and Pākehā as a legacy of colonialism or to simply see them as *humanly* intolerable? Should claims for social justice be made on the basis of ethnic identity and historical wrongs or on the basis of manifest need? There is no doubting the statistical evidence of inequality in Aotearoa New Zealand; Māori are educationally and medically much worse off than New Zealanders of European descent, and far more of their young people are in prison. Many Māori explain these facts as a direct effect of colonization, regarding everything from European schooling to drugs, alcohol, and fast food as destructive of their cultural and life essence (*mauri*). For them the New Zealand state is a bad breast, associated with materialism, indifference, and double-dealing, and they take refuge in the belief that the recovery of their spiritual heritage through speaking their language, repossessing their stolen lands, and separating themselves from European mores is the only way they can heal and reempower themselves. Yet this very language of resistance is born of the colonial encounter, every bit as much as the nineteenth-century and early twentieth-century Pākehā fantasies of Māori dying out or becoming fully assimilated into European society. These views are defenses against seeing oneself as the other, and reinforce, in Māori and Pākehā minds alike, notions of mutual difference at the expense of notions of common humanity.

Such assumptions always depend on the power of words to delude us into thinking that different names signify different realities. Thus nineteenth scholars of Māori society persistently spoke of Māori lore rather than law, of Māori religion and cosmology rather than science, and of Māori tradition and myth rather than history. But inscribed in these nominal distinctions is a more entrenched myth: that the European scholar possesses reason while the Māori—for all his or her spirituality, knowledge, and tradition—does not. So profoundly have these discursive markers entered our consciousness that they continue to be the terms on which "we" talk about "them," and both Māori and Pākehā deny their coevalness.

In the 1920s, the ethnographer Elsdon Best observed that Māori possess a "mythopoeic nature," and that "true to his . . . ever-present human desire to know the origin and meaning of everything [he] has evolved a cosmogonic scheme" (1954:10). In 1965, the scholar J. C. Laughton asserted in a similar vein that the "central feature in Māoritanga is the religious nature of the Māori. The whole ancient Māori life turned upon the poles of religion [and] community life . . . was built around 'the concept of the divine'" (1965:435). But is there any empirical justification for this reification of spirituality, or is it a projection of a Eurocentric worldview that habitually separates spirituality from science and religion from reason?

What we do know is that the nineteenth-century scholars on whom we rely for accounts of the "Māori as he was" wanted to construct abstract and systematic models of Māori *thought* rather than see knowledge, as Māori did, as a potentiality and resource with which social relations were produced and reproduced. As for Māori practical and scientific knowledge of medicinal plants, ocean navigation, kumara storage, flax cultivation, and agriculture, this would remain unacknowledged until researchers in the 1960s turned their attention to it. The emphasis was on belief, not knowledge. Rather than investigate *korero*

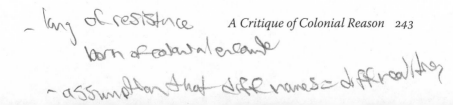

A Critique of Colonial Reason 243

tahito (ancestral explanations) in the form in which they appeared in the course of events such as *hui* (social gatherings) and *tangi* (funerals), scholars like George Grey and John White compiled collections of contextless information from key informants, all of whom were mission-educated and literate men, and doubtlessly disposed to present their knowledge in ways that met the expectations of the scholar-collector or satisfied their own need to show that they, too, had a religious system or philosophy that bore comparison to the religion and philosophy of the Pākehā. But, writes Sir Apirana Ngata, "neither Grey, nor any of the men who helped him to make his collection" sought to "discover the authorship, the history and the background of the cryptic expressions and allusions contained in these compositions" (1959:xxxi). Moreover, in the works of scholars like Grey, Edward Shortland, Thomas Gudgeon, William Colenso, White, and Edward Tregear, the crucial Māori concepts of mana, tapu, and mauri are defined without reference to the contexts in which they were used, so giving the impression that they constituted a belief system that answered peoples' need to comprehend the world, rather than control or manage it. But the evidence points to a people whose aesthetic and spiritual ideas were thoroughly integrated with the practical business of agriculture, politics, and communal life. The "dissociation of sensibilities," whereby spirituality becomes an unworldly cult of inwardness concerned with the fate of the soul, and the sacred contrasted with the secular, is a seventeenth-century European development and does not accord with what we know of pre-European Māori society. But we may hypothesize that as the Māori economy was destroyed by colonization and political resistance to invasion failed, Māori increasingly had recourse to occult ways of recovering mana and surviving as a people. Indeed, spiritualized notions of Māori culture, of Māoritanga and *tikanga* Māori, suggest the enduring hold of reified forms of self-definition that had their origins in the discursive conventions of colonialism, particularly the split between reason and unreason.[3]

Comparable observations have been made of the contemporary Museum of New Zealand, Te Papa Tongarewa, which projects a bicultural ideology based on enforced contrasts between Māori spirituality and Pākehā materialism (Goldsmith 2003). Margaret Jolly perceptively notes how Te Papa plays down the sacred in Pākehā cultural history, by contrast with the Māori exhibits, which "create a strong sense of seriousness, calm and spirituality" (2001:445)—something that may be seen as an expression of liberal Pākehā guilt since, in extolling Māori spiritual superiority and pandering to the stereotype of crass Western materialism, Pākehā seek to compensate Māori for their political powerlessness without actually changing the status quo (see also Brown 2002:293).

There is an implicit collusion here between Māori and Pākehā, both of whom all too often depict Western culture as bereft of spirituality and romanticize Māori culture as a domain of authentic values (Brown 1989). In recent years, however, many New Zealanders of European descent have repudiated this ritualized self-deprecation, while Māori intellectuals have bemoaned the fact that among Pākehā "there is little recognition that the Māori world is anything other than a cultural object noted for its spirituality and its music" (Jackson 2001). To construct Māori rights on the basis of spirituality and aesthetic presence rather than rationality is to introduce a double standard into discussions of social justice, pitting "cultural values" against sound scientific understanding. The effect is to force Māori into making claims for social justice in terms that are deemed, by the dominant culture, to be inimical to economic development and the national good. In as much as these priorities express the neoliberal philosophy of global capitalism, Māori are marginalized both locally *and* internationally, their place in global culture defined solely in terms of their identity as bearers of an ancient heritage. Thus the bind in which many indigenous intellectuals find themselves in the cosmopolitan world: recognized and respected only as custodians of non-Western lifeways, tribal values, and a spirituality that the West has allegedly lost. Indigenous people are thus doomed to define themselves, and be defined, in terms of their radical otherness rather than their common humanity.

Such has been the case in dialogues between Pākehā scientists and Māori activists over the introduction to Aotearoa New Zealand of biogenetic technologies. Debates have centered on Māori resistance to the Human Genome Project ("an insidious expression of genetic capitalism"), on proposed amendments to euthanasia laws ("yet another technology of genocide"), on genetic engineering (GE) techniques for the biocontrol of noxious weeds and possums, on GE techniques of livestock breeding, and on the bioprospecting of native flora and fauna. Mindful of New Zealand's bicultural constitution, the Labour government that came to power in 1999 saw that any radical division between Māori and non-Māori over the uses of gene technology would have serious consequences for the economic and cultural future of the nation. The Royal Commission on Genetic Modification was therefore established in May-June 2000 to receive submissions, convene meetings, and organize workshops that would explore the issues. A considerable body of material now exists on the Royal Commission Web site that provides insights into the cultural and political dimensions of the ongoing debate. While many Pākehā see biocontrol as a practical solution to an environmental problem, Māori argue that transferring genetic material across species boundaries constitutes a dangerous, unprecedented, and irreversible intervention in the natural order of things for, like mixing waters from different catchments or sources, moving genetic material from one species (a virus or parasite) to another (the possum) outrages tikanga Māori (the Māori way of doing things), disrupts the whakapapa (genealogy) and mauri (life essence) of those species, destroys a primordial balance between Ranginui (sky/father) and Papatuanuku (earth/mother), and by infringing these tapus threatens the world with illness and degradation (see Parliamentary Commissioner for the Environment 2000:25–27).

When the Royal Commission completed its work, lip service was paid to respecting the Māori point of view, but politically it was ignored, the unspoken assumption being that European "science" and Māori "values" could not be placed on the same epistemological footing. The Māori lawyer Moana Jackson concludes a trenchant critique of this double standard, and the way it deployed value-laden terms to suggest an opposition between allegedly superior and inferior ways of reasoning, by pointing out that epistemology is not the issue; the issue is the political one of recognizing that the Māori viewpoint is not an intellectual conceit but a matter of existential survival: "For the issue is not just about the potential and unknown risks of GE but also the nature of the constitutional relationship that the Treaty sought to establish between our people and the Crown. On a matter that holds so many risks for what Māori submitters called the 'ira tangata,' it is not enough that we be heard with 'exquisite politeness' and then marginalised. Our mokopuna [grandchildren] demand more" (Jackson 2001).

Presently, Māori are fighting for custodial (kaitiakitanga) rights over the foreshore and seabed on the basis of the 1840 Treaty of Waitangi.[4] In 2003, seeking to allay Pākehā anxieties that they would be banished from their beloved beaches if Māori custodial rights were confirmed, the government created a new public domain for "people of New Zealand title," coining the term *ancestral connection* to help Māori identify their rights to take *hangi* (earth oven) stones or protect burial sites. This is reminiscent of the Aboriginal Land Rights Act (Northern Territory, Australia) of 1976, in which "the critical criterion of traditional ownership . . . is that traditional Aboriginal owners must have a primary spiritual responsibility for rites and land" (Maurice 1988:92), a responsibility that implied an actual and ongoing relationship with land that people had lost to pastoralists or been driven from. Understandably, many Aborigines felt that the original injustice of losing their land to white settlers was compounded by the new injustice of having to prove their relationship to this land. As one man expressed it in a conversation with me, "The land was taken from us in a day; why can't it be returned in a day?" With regard to the seabed and foreshore controversy in New Zealand, Māori argued that they should not be blamed for losing contact with their land and that the invention of the phrase *ancestral connection* implied that *rangatiratanga* (chieftainship) rights granted under the Treaty of Waitangi were now being disregarded and Māori interests made secondary to a so-called national interest, which could only mean the interest of the more numerous Pākehā. Like the notion of spiritual connection, ancestral connection implied a double standard in which Māori "values"—a euphemism for prerational or premodern beliefs—were contrasted with the rational scientific knowledge allegedly more in the *national* interest. Whether or not Māori believe that their feelings about their land imply a radically different worldview, they are driven to prosecute their claims for their land and for social justice in terms of a discursive framework biased toward the nonsecular and based on lore rather than law, religion rather than reason. In other words, Māori intellectuals are caught in a bind. By arguing the case for social justice in the language of traditional, ancestral, cultural, or spiritual values, they risk perpetuating the epistemic split between unreason and reason that has always diminished such claims in European eyes. Yet by not invoking their own worldview, they risk abandoning the symbolic system that underpins their sense of having a distinct identity

istory. But rather than think of one's unique identity—ethnic or
onal—as being in conflict with one's identity as a human being
ong other human beings, it is important to give both modes of
entification their due. Judgment then consists of knowing when to be
true to oneself or one's own kind, privileging one's particular worldview
over others, and when to be true to the humanity one shares with all
others, regardless of their ethnic, historical, or social identity.[5] Let me
give an example of how pluralism is never simply an epistemological
matter (a question of knowing who you are), but a practical judgment (a
question of knowing what is most relevant given the situation at hand).

General statements about "the" Māori worldview are not hard to
come by. According to such statements, the entire cosmos comprises a
network of relations of kinship and alliance that includes all beings and
all things—people, plants, animals, and the elements. The primal parents of this plethora of forms, each of which possesses its own tikanga
or natural function, were Ranginui and Papatuanuku, sky and earth.
These days, many Māori intellectuals will not only draw hard and fast
distinctions between indigenous and nonindigenous worldviews but
will also argue that conflicts over the meaning of land tenure and land
rights are grounded in differences between spiritual and material attitudes toward nature. In the words of one notable Māori scholar, "Māori
people do not see themselves as separate from nature, humanity, and
the natural world, being direct descendants of Earth Mother. Thus, the
resources of the earth do not belong to humankind; rather, humans
belong to the earth. While humans as well as animals, birds, fish, and
trees can harvest the bounty of Mother Earth's resources, they do not
own them. Instead, humans have 'user rights'" (Henare n.d.:202).

A year after the introduction of GE technology to New Zealand in
2003, I met Manuka Henare in Auckland and asked him how many
Māori, in his view, embraced the "traditional" belief about not intermingling the genes of different species. I took care to explain that I was
not calling these beliefs into question; rather, I was curious to know to
what extent these beliefs were politically and situationally, rather than
culturally, motivated. Did people hold these beliefs to be true because
they simply could not comprehend the world in any other terms, or did
they espouse these beliefs for the sense of solidarity and common cause
they provided in the face of a dominant Eurocentric and supposedly
scientific worldview that they felt they did not own or understand?[6]

political & situational
culturally motivated

pluralism as practical judgment
- knowing what is relevant to situation

Manuka made two points. First, he observed that relatively few Māori are radically opposed to genetic engineering on a priori cultural or cosmological grounds. However, most will speak against it, saying no at first, because they are wary of being railroaded into giving their assent to something that may prove later to be to their detriment. People are conservative and cautious, Manuka said, because Pākehā have ridden roughshod over their intellectual and cultural property rights in the past; their inclination is therefore to go slow, to wait and see how things work out, how the land lies, before rushing into anything.

Manuka's second point was that Māori attitudes to genetic engineering depended on context. He described to me a Māori gathering at which he asked people to raise their hands if they were diabetic and using insulin. As he had expected, a large number of people raised their hands. He then asked how many people were against genetic engineering. All of them were. Manuka then told his audience that insulin was produced through genetic engineering. How many people, he now asked, would continue using insulin? All said they would. If it was a life-and-death issue, Manuka said, one would set aside one's ideological objections to genetic engineering.

This kind of pragmatism struck a chord in me, for I had long been critical of the view that the way human beings live their everyday lives is wholly determined by the views they espouse or the beliefs they hold. In my view, it is facile to claim that our worldviews so deeply penetrate and permeate our consciousness that our actions can be explained simply by reference to them. The immense variability in commitment to doctrine is strong evidence that doctrine does not determine experience in any straightforward way. Moreover, beliefs are more commonly post facto rationalizations than a priori determinants of action. And human beings are motivated by many imperatives apart from belief, even though they cannot always say what these imperatives are. That is to say that our existential *situations*, individual *biographies*, and political *interests* also find expression in the ideas we draw on, the symbols we use, and the beliefs we become known by. Consider, for instance, the furor that followed the publication in the Danish newspaper *Jyllands-Posten* on 30 September 2005 of twelve cartoons lampooning the prophet Muhammad. On February 13, 2006, in the same week that Danish embassies in Damascus and Beirut were sacked and burned, *Time* magazine headlined its coverage of the story "When Cultures Collide" and spoke of a "deepening divide between Islam and the West" (47–49). But attempting to grasp the complex events that led up to and followed the publication of these cartoons in terms of *intercultural* conflict is both simplistic and dangerous, for a vast array of factors found expression in the discursive terms that came to the fore in this case—Islam, the West, free speech, blasphemy. Although these terms are definite and denotative, the factors that flowed into them are infinite and connotative—and include everything from individual grievances and dissatisfactions to a shared sense of powerlessness and religious outrage. A theory of the imagination is demanded here, for what is often an amorphous sense of malaise will opportunistically latch onto any event, story, or image that offers, if only for a moment, the possibility of explaining in a nutshell what feels wrong in one's life, as well as offering a chance to both express that knowledge and redress the injustice. The tragic irony is, however, that the language we use in trying to grasp our private dreams and discontent takes on a life and logic of its own, becoming an inseparable part of who we imagine we are, governing our consciousness and precluding the possibility of seeing things in any other way. This is what Jean-François Lyotard calls the *differend*: the manifold experiences and events that are silenced or occluded by any dominant discourse (1988). Because it is difficult to vary a point of view to which one has become attached as the truest, most parsimonious, or most expedient way of accounting for one's being-in-the-world, it is imperative that we seek to recapture and remember the wealth of experience that is funneled into our preferred images, that finds expression in our simplistic terms, or is cathected onto the objects we consider sacrosanct. This is why I have argued that strong opinions and beliefs are screens as much as sources, contrivances as much as causes. And though at any one time the screen obscures what lies behind it, screens shift as the scene changes. This is not just because human consciousness is continually switching from one thing to another, foregrounding very different beliefs in different contexts; it is because there are always several worldviews impinging on our consciousness and available for use. Opportunistic borrowing rather than slavish adherence is typical, not atypical, of practical religion. As the Labour MP John Tamihere put it in his maiden speech to the New Zealand parliament in 2000, representing urban Māori who do not define Māoriness in terms of traditional modes of kinship grouping, ancestral land, and language: "There is no exclusive Māori way forward. Moreover, under conditions of social change, ideologies will come to serve new interests. Thus "traditional" Māori thought is more often invoked by contemporary Māori to express political grievances than to legitimate ancestral practices. And the very essence of traditional concepts is thus compromised. Ethnography gives us glimpses into a pre-European Māori way of thinking that was contrapuntal and dynamic: life was a perpetual interplay between the countervailing forces of *tupu* (the unfolding or growth potential of every life-form) and *mate* (the process of weakening, sickening, or diminishing). Nothing was static or fixed in this lifeworld; everything was seen as waxing or waning, struggling toward union or separation, tensed between growing and withering away. In such a dynamic cosmos, identity was unstable and fluid, which helps explain why Māori were so open to new technologies of growth and empowerment (muskets, literacy, new plants and animals) in the early years of contact, and so ready to repudiate imported ideas when their negative repercussions became apparent. Whatever augmented life was seized on; whatever diminished life was spurned: "Mauri tu mauri ora, mauri noho mauri mate" (an active spirit means life, an inactive spirit leads to death). By contrast, contemporary Māori thought is often essentialist, definitive, and exclusive, and terms like *mauri, mana,* and *tikanga* are used in their intransitive rather than transitive aspects.[7]

Rather than see worldviews or master narratives as descriptions of actual experience, I suggest we see them as a repertoire of *possible* ways of understanding and acting on one's circumstances. In effect, they are drawn on and actualized opportunistically and in multiple ways in relation to the everyday situations in which people find themselves. Though commonly reified and treated as though they were natural or God-given, doctrines and cosmologies do not orchestrate practice as much as provide people with post facto ways of evaluating, legitimating, and rationalizing what they have done—and giving themselves reasons, beyond their own inclinations, for doing what they want to do. It is consoling to think that our actions are reasonable or that they follow ancestral protocols, but the truth is that we invoke abstract notions like reason, scripture, or tradition to enforce and validate pre-

traditional invoked to express political

⊗ worldviews or master narrating as are of many possibilities ferred modes of being, not because we are intrinsically reasonable, ethical, or traditional but because, like all human beings, we seek to vindicate, valorize, and authorize our actions in terms of some authority greater than our own. This does not necessarily mean that we live in bad faith, invoking ideology to justify actions that are self-interested or explain our inability to act on our own initiative; it simply means that it is probably impossible for any human being to live a meaningful life without reference to some body of ideas taken to be both external and shared. But there is a trap, nonetheless, in confusing stratagems for rationalizing one's behavior with models for explaining it.

My argument, then, is that we should see appeals to the past in the light of people's lives in the present. Whether our history is the cause of our present social ills can never be ascertained. There are simply too many variables at play to work out the chains of cause and effect, if indeed the notion of causation is valid. Yet in constantly deploying master narratives in which social inequalities and injustices in the here and now are explained as direct effects of traumatic events in the past, and by fostering the belief that justice may be served by reversing time and restoring some original dispensation, we risk creating the very divisions such narratives and beliefs purport to explain.

In an address to the New Zealand Psychological Society on 29 August 2000, the associate Māori affairs minister Tariana Turia spoke of Māori violence, self-loathing, ill health, and feelings of helplessness and despair as symptoms of post-traumatic stress disorder. Comparing colonial oppression to the Holocaust, Turia argued that Māori internalize negative stereotypes, integrating them into their psyche and soul, as in vernacular uses of the word *Māori* to connote something second rate or broken down. Many Pākehā New Zealanders were outraged by Turia's comparison between colonialism and the Holocaust and the implication that they perpetuated negative stereotypes of Māori and were somehow responsible for Māori suffering. My own view was that Turia was correct in her observations about negative stereotypes and the self-abnegating effects these have on young Māori, but I could not agree that invoking the colonial past will help us explain or change the structures of inequality in New Zealand society. The master narrative of victimage—like the master narratives of firstness, of slavery, and of dispossession—are rhetorically useful ways of expressing grievances and clearing the air, but if repeated like mantras, they take on a life of their own, creating a culture of complaint and a performative mode of self-pity and abjection that effectively closes off the possibility of any other way of apprehending one's situation or creating a viable future. It is fallacious to claim that narratives constructed after an event remain faithful to the nature of that event, or that collective memory preserves the past as perfectly as kauri gum preserves an entrapped insect. Narratives of historic loss are best seen as ways in which we give public expression and authority to our present sense of social suffering—a generalized malaise that cannot, however, be reduced to any defining event, any one cause. Perhaps this is why the so-called Māori renaissance in the late twentieth century—with its promotion of Māori language, culture, and spirituality—has had no effect on reducing the socioeconomic inequality between Māori and Pākehā (Sissons 1994:100, 105). Indeed, one Māori scholar has even gone so far as to say that the politics of culture has been "an unmitigated disaster for the vast majority of working-class Māori" (Poata-Smith 1996:110). But what troubles me most about cultural narratives based on fundamentalist assumptions, sweeping generalizations, and a conflation of biography with history is that they prevent us from having the kinds of conversations among ourselves that search for common ground and move from defining what is mine or yours to what is ours.

In the 1970s, I taught in a New Zealand university department that combined programs in social anthropology and Māori studies. One of my colleagues and closest friends during these years was Te Pakaka Tawhai, and during two successive summers my family and I stayed with Te Pakaka's family on their East Coast farm.

One memorable afternoon, Te Pakaka and his brother Joe drove me to the isolated settlement of Reporoa to see the carved house, Te Auau. We stopped for a while on a high ridge. The hills were bare except for stands of cabbage trees and an occasional dark grove of karaka. Cloud shadow and wind combed the long grass. Far below the shoulder of the hill, breakers like braided ropes were unraveling on a long white beach. The road wound down into a hollow in the hills, where the meeting house was cradled as in the palm of an upturned hand.

Paka and Joe explained to me that unlike most meeting houses, Te

a trouble w/ cultural narratives + generalz.

Auau had not been conceived as the body of an ancestor. Carved figures with out-thrust tongues and glaring eyes did not defy the visitor. The flax *whariki* mats on the floor, woven from flax and kiekie, were gold in color, or patterned with charcoal, lilac, and pink. Dyed in pastel hues, the decorative *tukutuku* panels on the walls were reminiscent, in Te Pakaka's words, "of a fading rainbow." The spirit of the house was one of welcoming and warmth.

But Te Pakaka wasn't going to let me romanticize Te Auau. Life, he explained, was a constant struggle between progression and regression (see Tawhai 1978:16). In this struggle between the processes of tupu (unfolding, growing, strengthening) and mate (weakening, dwindling, dying), an individual or a kin group will seek whatever will augment rather than diminish its being. Sometimes this will demand being welcoming and open to the outside world; sometimes it will demand closure and opposition. Hence the saying, "Ko Tu ki te awatea, ko Tahu ki te po."[8] Carved houses enshrine both a particularistic ethos, centered on identifications with specific ancestors, and horizons that are open to the wider world.

Te Pakaka's account of Uepohatu Hall is illuminating in this respect. Built in 1942, the hall was named for one of the renowned chiefs of Ngati Porou, a direct descendant of Maui, the ancestral discoverer of Aotearoa. The building was the inspiration of Sir Apirana Ngata who supervised its construction at a time when the Māori Battalion was suffering calamitous reversals in the North African desert. No family in Ngati Porou was spared the anguish of loss. To help share the grief and reaffirm the value of life, Ngata brought people together in night schools to receive instruction in whakapapa (genealogy) and to recover the waning arts of carving, weaving, and poetry. To give material form to this spiritual renaissance, Ngata proposed that a great hall be built as a permanent memorial to all who had fought for freedom in the two world wars. But for succeeding generations, Uepohatu Hall would become not only a memorial to warrior ancestors but a place pervaded by the spirit of those who built it.

In the summer of 1945, Te Pakaka and other boys from Manutahi Primary School were sent to help work on the hall. Te Pakaka stoked fires for cooking *paua* (abalone), helped the tukutuku frame makers, and fetched and carried for Ngata himself. Sometimes Ngata would summon Te Pakaka to work with him on the woven tukutuku panels. Te Pakaka would take a seat on the reverse side of the tukutuku frame, pulling the dyed flax threads through the slats while the great man regaled the awestruck boy with stories of his artistic forebears or instructed him in *waiata* (song, chant). Te Pakaka was aware that he was involved in something momentous and would never forget a single detail of that long hot summer: the stipend he was paid that enabled him to shoe his horse Dan; the breathless trips to the local shop for Ngata's tobacco; the way the great man ate half slices of bread heaped with marmalade at tea breaks and afterward smoked his bent and foul-smelling pipe before laying it aside and returning to work on his translation of the Bible.

Te Pakaka once told me that Uepohatu was one of the few places that brought Māori and European traditions together without compromising either. The interior of the hall is carved and decorated in the style of other Māori meeting houses, but the outside is unembellished and resembles an ordinary European community hall. Within the body of the hall, biblical motifs are juxtaposed with images of the rivers, mountains, and shoreline that sustained the soldiers far from home. And in its dedication to Uepohatu, the hall harks back to Maui who, using his grandmother's lower jaw as a fishhook and clotted blood from his own nose as bait, hauled up the North Island (Te Ika a Maui), with Hikurangi emerging first from the waters—a place of salvation and newborn life. As Te Pakaka expressed it, Uepohatu "embraces to itself the mana of all the peoples of New Zealand," its purpose "to concentrate the mana of all New Zealanders under the one roof."

This was also the source of Te Pakaka's charisma and strength: his ability to steer a course between two cultures, to strike a balance between two traditions without sacrificing the integrity of either. Here was a man who was a master of the *taiaha* (longstaff weapon), yet he practiced karate with equal passion. Here was a man who could greet my interpretations of Māori myth with generosity, even when I lost the plot. When we stayed on the coast, I would help out with the shearing. One afternoon, after hours of backbreaking work in a shearing shed in the Waiapu Valley, Paka told me the story of a pregnant woman who, craving *kai moana* (seafood), ignored a tapu and, night after night, crept down to the coast to gather shellfish. One morning, as she retraced her steps upriver to her own *kainga* (village), the sunrise found her out and she was turned to stone. There she is today, in the middle of the river, arrested forever, her kits filled with the illicit seafood. The story inspired a poem that I showed to Paka, hoping I had not taken too many liberties with what he had told me. He smiled. I had got it a bit wrong, but I had made something compelling of what I had heard. What mattered was life—life that produced life. In Te Pakaka's view, "ancient explanations" and ancestral wisdom (*korero tahito*) were invaluable not because they held the key to understanding every epoch or every existential quandary that human beings face, but because they were flexible and adaptable, able "to accommodate the capacity of the narrator to render them more relevant to the issues of the day" (Tawhai 1996:14).

Te Pakaka died in 1988. So I cannot ask him if we still do justice to life when "the issues of the day" seem to admit of no ultimate resolution and we turn to observing the human traffic along the great river of life, with all its eddies, countercurrents, rapids, falls, and stretches of dead water, noting those unpredictable moments when, as in certain Taoist paintings, one catches a glimpse of a solitary person in a boat between the high walls of a gorge, struggling to bring his craft under control with a single oar—moments when our individual lives for all their courage or insignificance become one with the life that precedes and outlasts it: the life we variously call history, tradition, genealogy, or destiny. "life"

Notes

Preface *theme and variations*

1. As Robert Orsi observes, we both make the world and are unmade by it, and terms like *empowerment, agency,* and *transcendence* place too much emphasis on the heroic subject and play down the ways in which we suffer that which is given and which we cannot change. To recognize limitations, constraints, and suffering, Orsi suggests "replacing the meaning-making subject with a more tragic figure whose engagements with the world, within particular circumstances of power, proceed through media that may embody meanings against him or her" (2005:170).

2. This conversation took place as we were strolling along Sankt Hans street, only a stone's throw from my apartment. A few weeks later I was amazed to discover, thanks to my friend Hans Lucht, also an ardent admirer of Hamsun's writing, that after returning from the United States in the fall of 1888, Hamsun rented a cheap room under the roof at 18 Sankt Hans Gade, where he began writing *Hunger.* He lived on rye bread without butter or cold

cuts, and was often without food at all for several days at a time, during which he chewed match sticks to stave off hunger. On receiving this information, I hastened to Sankt Hans street, determined to find the very spot where, according to my clear recollection, I had spoken to Steve about Hamsun. It was only after finding the spot that I looked at the numbers on the houses. I was standing directly in front of number 18! This was, I later discovered, the very building in which Hamsun had lived.

3. Noah's comments bear an uncanny similarity to Aesop's fable of the eagle and the fox. Despite an agreement to live together amicably in the same neighborhood, the eagle kills the fox's cubs: The fox being "a land animal (*chersaia*), could never hope to pursue a winged bird. She had no option but to content herself, in her powerlessness and feebleness, with cursing her enemy from afar" (Aesop 1998:3). Time passes, and the eagle, still looking for an easy way of getting food, seizes some burning entrails from a sacrificial altar. The eagle's nest catches fire, the eaglets fall from the nest, and the fox devours them.

4. Amartya Sen has recently pointed out that the "exaggerated focus on religiosity" by Western observers of India has led to a neglect or denial of scientific, secular, and skeptical traditions that date back to the second millennium BCE, such as the Lokayata tradition of skepticism, and the Carvaka system (Sen 2005: 21–25). One might also mention the skeptical strain in Nagarjuna's doctrine of emptiness (Burton 1999:19–43), though Hajime Nakamura calls Sanjaya "the first skeptic in India" (1986:162).

5. Lest it seem that dilemma tales are mere casuistry, one might note the impossible choices that often confront Africans who lack sufficient resources to survive. A particularly dramatic and poignant example is the use of antiretroviral (ARV) medicines to combat AIDS. Even though the cost of ARVs in Uganda has fallen considerably ($500 per month in 2000 to $28 in 2003), families and individuals face dreadful decisions as to who will be treated: "People have to prioritize their resources: Do you pay ARV medicine for a sister forever and give up paying school fees for your child? . . . Many people prefer to keep silent about such painful decisions, and just let things take their course, as if there was no decision to make" (Whyte et al. 2004:21).

6. Derrida speaks of this tradition as logocentrism or the "epoch of the logos." It assumes a universal logic and rationality, based on Western philosophical models, and "a fixed, foundational principle which can be uniquely named . . . whether it be 'being' or 'God'" (Moran 2000:448).

1. The UN high commissioner for refugees estimates that between 1994 and 2004 more than five thousand asylum seekers have drowned in the Mediterranean.

2. Benjamin's famous *Theses on the Philosophy of History* were written during this winter of 1939–40: reflections, he noted in a letter to Gretel Adorno, that were part of his "methodological preparation" for the sequel to the Baudelaire book and not intended for publication.

3. According to Henny Gurland, they were joined at some stage by "Birmann, her sister Frau Lipmann, and the Freund woman [Grete Freund] from Das Tagebuch" (Scholem 1982:225).

4. Arendt writes that the problem was not that the refugees' transit visas were invalid, but that (1) the Spanish border had been closed that very day; and (2) that the border office did not honor visas made out in Marseilles (1973:169).

5. Benjamin was not the only émigré to take his own life during those dark times. Ernst Weiss, the Czech novelist, took poison in his room in Paris when the Germans entered the city, as did Irmgard Keun, a German novelist. Walter Hasenclever, the German playwright, took an overdose of Veronal in the concentration camp at Les Milles, and Karl Einstein, the art critic and specialist on Negro sculpture, hanged himself at the Spanish frontier when he found he could not get across (Fry 1945:31).

6. See Benjamin's commentary on Bertolt Brecht's poem "Legend of the Origin of the Book Tao Te Ching on Lao Tzu's Way into Exile" (1983:70–74), which itself references section 78 of the *Tao Te Ching*: "In the world there is nothing more submissive and weak than water. Yet for attacking that which is hard and strong nothing can surpass it. This is because nothing can take its place" (Lao Tzu 1963:140).

7. After interrogating the detainees, they designated the pro-Nazis "dangerous" and ensured that the others were given clearances.

8. Arendt escaped with Fittko but chose to make her own way to Montauban, where she had friends with whom she could stay, and where, astonishingly, her husband Heinrich Blücher (who had been interned in northern France) found her.

9. See Benjamin's "On the 'Legend of the Origin of the . . . Tao Te Ching,'" first published in the *Schweizer Zeitung am Sonntag*, 23 April 1939.

10. In *Pascalian Meditations*, Pierre Boudieu confides, "I have never really felt justified in existing as an intellectual; and I have always tried . . . to exorcise everything in my thinking that might be linked to that status, such

as philosophical intellectualism. I do not like the intellectual in myself" (2000:7).

11. As Martin Jay reminds us, Benjamin never overcame, or wanted to forget, his traumatic loss of his closest friend, Friedrich (Fritz) Heinle, who killed himself in protest at the war in 1914, or the terrible specter of the industrialized war itself (2003:11−24).

2 of time and the river: the interface of history and human lives

1. Aristotle's distinction, in the *Nicomachean Ethics*, is as follows: "Production (poesis) has an end other than itself, but action (praxis) does not" (1983:153).

2. Thus Maja Povrzanovic's telling observation that during the Yugoslavian war, the "grammar" of nationalism figured significantly in the discourse of international commentators and national leaders far from the front lines, but for the "forgotten majority" of civilians, life was a struggle "to defend not primarily their 'national territory' but the right to continue their lives in terms of gender, occupation, class, and place of residence and not be reduced to their national identities" (2000:154).

3. The (Phalange) Christian militia fighting against the Palestinian Liberation Organization (PLO) in 1975−76, which precipitated civil war in Lebanon, was simply another violent expression of this desire to purge the "enemy within."

4. Under the postmandate so-called National Pact (*al-Mithaq al-Watani*), public offices in Lebanon are distributed among the major religions and sects. Thus the president of the republic is always a Maronite Christian, the premier a Sunni Muslim, the speaker of Parliament a Shi'a Muslim, and so on.

5. Natural disasters may also be likened to war. In the wake of the Asian tsunami of December 2004, Anders Johansson, a Swedish writer and former foreign correspondent, wrote, "This was a war situation without a declaration of war. Nobody could be prepared for that, even with the best preparations" (qtd. in Cowell 2005:5). Asian villagers accustomed to great hardship, and whose worldviews teach the acceptance of suffering, may find disasters easier to bear than people who have grown up in a safe, prosperous, and stable world, taught to expect cradle-to-grave security as a natural due. Thus Swedes and Danes may have been less able than others to come to terms with their devastating losses in the Asian tsunami.

6. Who would have predicted that seventeen months after these public gatherings Lebanon would once more be plunged into a humanitarian crisis as Israeli warplanes laid waste to suburbs, towns, and ports, maiming and

killing innocent civilians on the pretext that Hezbollah was a terrorist organization that had to be destroyed if Israel was to exist.

3 imagining the powers that be: society versus the state revisited

1. Many of these points were echoed in another piece in the *Independent* in November 2004 in which Sahr Joseph Komba accused the president of being a "false prophet" who had disappointed his people and showed no signs of care or concern for the poor (Komba 2004).

2. I borrow the term *social imaginary* from Charles Taylor to denote not just the ways in which people theorize social reality "in a disengaged mode" but the ways in which they imagine their social existence in images, anec-dotes, and stories concerned with "how they fit together with others, how things go on between them and their fellows, the expectations that are nor-mally met, and the deeper normative notions and images that underlie these expectations" (2004:23). I am, however, skeptical of the view that the forms of human imagining are entirely determined by sociocultural conditions, and I agree with Jean-Paul Sartre (1940) that the imagination is but one expression of the human striving for presence in relation to others and the world. Inchoate, amorphous, and volatile, this will to exist fastens or focuses opportunistically on various objects—some actually at hand, some absent, some wholly fantastic—in its search to objectify or consummate itself in the world. But unlike reality testing, imagining always goes beyond what the world actually is or what any person can actually be.

3. In the course of an interview with Valarie Kaur in July 2005, a Japanese American man (the Reverend Saburo Masada from Fresno, California) drew a comparison between the experience of being interned with his family dur-ing the Second World War and childhood abuse. "Incest is where an inno-cent child is violated and abused by someone the child looks up to, loves and respects. That means the mother or father. When that abuse happens, the child still loves the parent, but they're being abused. How do you deal with that? I think that is partly the reason that Japanese Americans are only now—sixty, forty years later—talking about it, because it was such a traumatic experience to be abused by our government we loved and cared about. A child can't hate the parents, and I can't hate the government. This is my country! And yet, I'm going to have to express some very negative feelings about this country. Our country needs help, like abusing parents need a lot of help. These leaders need to face up to the crime they are committing even today [a reference to the post-9/11 attacks on Arab and Sikh Americans]" (Kaur, personal communication).

4. Michael Herzfeld observes that state-inspired simulations of familial relations, as well as popular images of family life, project forms of intimacy that may not exist in social practice or experience: "Cultural intimacy is not the same as the public representations of domestic intimacy; it is the antithesis of the latter. True cultural intimacy is rarely acknowledged by state actors" (2004:329).

5. Ghassan Hage has written perceptively on the homely imagery of national belonging: "All the qualities that are valued in the homeland are those that are normally (that is, within patriarchal discourse) associated with mothering: protection, warmth, emotional and nutritional security" (1996:473). Home, nation, and family "are seen to provide their inhabitants with virtually the same thing: familiarity and security" (468).

6. According to local traditions, Moré Musa Kargbo ruled during the period of the Sofa invasion of northern Sierra Leone. He was a staunch ally of the Yalunka chief of Falaba and helped repulse the Sofas (led by Samori Turé's son) at Falaba. Moré Musa was subsequently appointed chief of Dankawali by the English who had helped the Kuranko and Yalunka resistance to the Sofas with arms and ammunition. However, the captains Blanding, Palmer, and Farné (?) may not have actually visited this area until around 1914 when the British established barracks at Gbankuma and Falaba.

7. This Kuranko tale is reminiscent of a recurring theme in South American myth of the *bicho enfolhado*, in which Fox deceives Jaguar by smearing himself with honey (Lévi-Strauss 1973a:112) and which involves a complex structure of culinary symbols. The culinary triangle of boiled/roasted/rotted marks out a semantic field in which the contrast between the boiled, peeled, and buried yam and the roasted, charred, and putrescent hyena is mediated by "sweet" foodstuffs that are eaten raw. Consumed in their natural state, honey and rice flour are also cultural products, the former collected from man-made oblong, woven beehives, the latter prepared by pounding rice in similarly oblong but wooden mortars. The sweet, raw substances thus mediate a transformation in the story from an unjust situation to a situation in which the injustice is redressed. See Jackson 1982:120–22 for an extended structural analysis.

8. Andrew Shryock has recently emphasized this gestaltlike switching and interplay between background and foreground in his characterization of the dialectic between private and public frames of reference as "off stage/on display" (2004), and Michael Herzfeld has written at length on the interface between dominant and demotic discourses, deploying the term *cultural intimacy* to capture the ironic counterpoint between projected and mediatized cultural images and the lived experiences of cultural life (1997).

9. Alfred Schutz further distinguishes the world of our predecessors (*Vor-welt*) and the world of our successors (*Folgewelt*), defining the Mitwelt as the world of our contemporaries (1972:207–14).

4   *on the work of human hands*

1. "By contrast, mine operators were reportedly promised a 400,000 yuan bonus if they could raise output by 4000,000 tonnes in the last two months of the year. They could afford at least three deaths and still come out with a profit" (Watts 2005:2).

2. No one, unless he or she is mad, sees the extrahuman world as permanently and intrinsically animate. Among the Ojibwa, for example, there is an implicit category distinction in the language between animate and inanimate. But while stone, thunder, and objects such as kettles and pipes are grammatically animate and Ojibwa sometimes speak of stones as if they were persons, this does not mean that Ojibwa are animists "in the sense that they *dogmatically* attribute living souls to inanimate objects such as stone"; rather they recognize "*potentialities* for animation in certain classes of objects under certain circumstances. The Ojibwa do not perceive stones, in general, as animate, any more than we do" (Hallowell 1958:65; emphasis added).

3. Following Elizabeth Povinelli, in her 1993 ethnographic study of labor and work among the Belyuen of the Cox Peninsula in northwest Australia, I prefer to speak of labor-action in order to avoid the Eurocentric assumption that labor implies economic labor; to emphasize that labor is a form of action and vice versa; and to show that the analysis of labor relations affords insights into *all* forms of human interaction: ritual, religious, social, political, and economic.

4. The Kuranko word *wale* signifies both work and any form of dutiful action such as raising a child, ruling a chiefdom, or performing a hereditary task.

5. In many Aboriginal societies sacred sites or story places are said to recognize the sweat smell of those who bear a kinship relationship to them. Illness or misfortune may come to those who trespass on a sacred site but whose body odor cannot be unrecognized (Jackson 1998:181–83; Marett 2005:61–62; Povinelli 1993:31).

6. This touches on a complementary theme: Under what conditions does a person become a thing? The same intersubjective logic whereby things take on the properties of persons explains why, when human actions are morally wrong or relationships in breach of convention (as in incest), images of immobilization and physical weakening are common tropes—the malefactor turned to stone or wasting away.

7. Warlpiri will speak of a deceased person as someone who has been lost, or as *kumanjayi*, a word for a person whose name has been put out of circulation for a generation and whose living traces have been erased from the ground.

5 *storytelling events, violence, and the appearance of the past*

1. Rosalind Shaw's superb ethnographic work among the Temne shows how the present and past "mutually configure" each other, and how the habitus of the slave trade produced "oblique" effects and "practical memories" in contemporary cultural preoccupations with secrecy, suspicion, danger, theft, and witchcraft (1997, 2002, 2003). Mariane Ferme argues, in a similarly nonreductive vein, that we should be alert to "the importance of understanding history not only as a site of causal explanations but also as a source of particular forms—symbolic, linguistic, practical—that social actors deploy to rework the social fabric in response to contingent events. These new social and cultural forms are the effect of a dialogical mediation between the present historical situation and a past repertoire of ideas with which social actors critically engage" (2001:227).

2. Kenya Fina Mara and Tina Kuyate were both married to the late Diang chief Magba Koroma II, Tina being *baramusu* (senior wife) and Kenya Fina *gberinya* (second-married, junior wife).

3. The Senegalese fire finch (*tintingburuwe*) habitually flits and nests around houses, and it is this association with domestic space that may explain why the souls of dead infants are said to inhabit the fire finch while awaiting possible reincarnation, for a small child does not enter the public domain for some time after its birth.

4. This circumlocution conveys the idea that women prepare the best food for their lovers.

5. The Seli is the largest river draining the southern area of Kuranko country. In referring to a local river, the locus of the story ceases to be mythical and is suddenly brought closer to home.

6. *Bal'fole*, lit. "xylophone-hitter," by implication a praise-singer, a *jeleba*.

7. The Kuranko phrase "ko manni a nyorgo manni" literally means "something happened, its partner [i.e., the same thing, its counterpart] also happened.'"

8. Throughout the telling of this story, Keti Ferenke acted as a kind of second to Kenya Fina, and at this point—responding to Kenya Fina's own aside—he interrupted the story to remind everyone of an incident that had taken place in Kondembaia a few days before. A man had quarreled with

another man and inflicted a minor wound with a knife. Wary and afraid of the offender, people had kept their distance from him.

9. *Kemine gbana*—an unmarried young man, an idler, a drifter. Here the term is used as a synonym for a commoner, someone of inconsequential status.

10. *Hake* is sometimes translated as "sin," though the word covers a multitude of motives—hatred, ill-will, malice, envy—and distracts from the principle of retributive justice that lies behind it. In Kuranko thought, intersubjective relationships are governed by reciprocity, so that if a person offends, wrongs, or injures another person without justification, the offence calls for payback (*tasare*). This compensatory action may be effected through several means. It may follow a court hearing, in which case the offender must indemnify the person to whom injury has been caused. It may follow a verbal apology, in which the offender begs forgiveness. It may, if recourse to legal means or the workings of individual conscience are unavailing, lead the injured party to take matters into his or her own hands and seek sorcery as a form of revenge. Alternatively, if the injured party feels that no worldy agency can secure redress, he or she may be inclined to leave matters in the hands of God. In a previous discussion of hake (Jackson 1982:29–30), I speak of automatic redress, in which an unprovoked and unjustified offence will boomerang back against the offender, particularly if the victim is protected by magical medicines. In conversations with Kuranko informants in January-February 2002, however, such redress was thought to require divine agency. As Noah put it, "People feel that God is just and omnipotent. One way or another He'll avenge the crime or wrongdoing."

6 *migrant imaginaries: with sewa koroma in southeast london*

1. When I saw Sewa in London a year later, and we discussed this dream again, Sewa spoke of a certain younger brother who had spread a story alleging that Sewa had received special powers from his father, which is why he enjoyed greater good fortune than his brothers. This, Sewa told me, was the source of the dream image of his brothers' resentment and aggressive stance toward him.

2. Lest one seem to be attributing paranoid obsessions to Africans that are presumably absent among Europeans, it is worth noting that questions of trust and transparency pervade the ethical and epistemological discourse of the West, and that the "deceptive order of ordinary appearances" is a recurring and endemic issue of everyday life in *all* societies. What Henri Ellenberger calls "the unmasking trend" (1970:537) in European history, characterized by "the systematic search for deception and self-deception and the

uncovering of underlying truth," may be traced back to the seventeenth-century moralists. In anthropology, a similar view informs both British empiricism and French structural anthropology, hence the remarks by Claude Lévi-Strauss that "the nature of truth is already indicated by the care it takes to remain elusive"; and "to reach reality one has first to reject experience" (1973b:57–58). In other words, anthropologists take as little at face value as the people they study.

3. Nigerians referred to Peckham as "Little Lagos."

4. Sewa separated from his girlfriend Stephanie because of fears that her jealous ex-boyfriend, who was half Jamaican and half English, might stab him or have one of his gang do so: "You have to be very careful of that mixed race; they are dangerous, they could do anything."

5. In his study of the "cultures of secrecy" associated with cargo cults in Papua–New Guinea, Andrew Lattas perceptively observes that a preoccupation with realizing "new identities and new forms of sociality" that would emancipate the imagination and give scope for greater autonomy actually *increase* paranoid fears that others, notably whites, are tricksters and deceivers determined to keep power and wealth to themselves (1998:xxii, 45–49).

6. I find Georg Groddeck's notion of the "it" helpful here—the nebulous, preobjective, and amorphous life force that precedes specific symbolic or cultural expressions of identity, so that we may say not only "I live" but "I am being lived" and, methodologically, set greater store by abstaining from immediate interpretation than by rushing to judgment (1977:132–57). The same tension between "I" and "it" is found in Zen practice, where the absence of will and striving allows action to occur of its own accord, in its own time, in its own way (Herrigel 1972:73–86).

7. A similar conception of spirit beings (*maroi*) is found among the Belyuen aboriginals of the Cox Peninsular in northwest Australia. Like the imaginative unconscious, which is forever in search of objective expression, the maroi are associated with patrilineal forebears and are said to search for parents in whom they can become embodied beings and try to "catch" people hunting, camping, and traveling through the countryside (Povinelli 1993: 140). Among the Tupian Urubu of Amazonia, it is the father's soul that in nightly dreams or daydreams moves about as a ghostly wanderer "looking for some material object in which to embody itself" (Huxley 1963:185).

7 *a walk on the wild side: the idea of human nature revisited*

1. Fourteen years after Twain's misadventure, Georg Simmel would publish his own devastating critique of the alpine experience, seeing it as an

expression of capitalism's infatuation with private property—an egotistical and hedonistic pursuit of subjective experience disguising itself as a desire to build character or acquire moral virtue (Simmel 1991:96).

2. In a compelling paper that documents a Suyá man's experiences of receiving a kidney transplant in Brazil, Nancy Scheper-Hughes and Mariana Leal Ferreira show that Suyá notions of the shamanic transmigration of souls enabled Dombá to come to terms with the biomedical transmigration of organs (2003:132), suggesting a surprisingly "fluid and open-ended" conception of "reality, nature, human/animal, and self/other relations" (131). Even kinship identity, for the Suyá, is remarkably fluid since it is based less on descent than on the sharing of intimate bodily substances including milk, semen, blood, urine, sweat, spit, pus, vaginal secretions, and feces (146).

3. This way of construing nature echoes the sixteenth-century sense of nature as "all matter that exists in the world without the intervention of human agency or activity," by contrast with culture, "which commonly refers to human activity, products, and accomplishments" (Bennett, Grossberg, and Morris 2005:236). Yet rather than define nature and culture as designating extrahuman and human realms, my focus is the space between that which can and cannot be controlled, and I treat the ways in which this relationship is named as a secondary matter.

4. Hillary's attitude toward the Himalaya region would change dramatically as he devoted his energies to raising funds and working for the Sherpas, building twenty-seven schools, two hospitals, and twelve medical clinics, plus numerous bridges and airfields, as well as rebuilding monasteries and reforesting valleys and slopes in the Mustang, Khumbu, and Pokhara regions. And it is also important to emphasize that in practice mountaineers are just as likely to have "flow experiences" as mystics, as evidenced in this comment by a rock climber: "You are so involved in what you are doing [that] you aren't thinking of something else; you are totally involved in what you are doing. . . . Your energy is flowing very smoothly. You feel relaxed, comfortable, and energetic" (qtd. in Csikszentmihalyi 1990:53).

5. *Sangbalmatigi* (literally, "thunder master").

6. Suwage connotes both witchcraft and antiwitchcraft powers—an indication of the ambiguity surrounding the domain of extrasocial forces.

7. A direct analogy is with the public spheres of men and women (*ke dugu* and *musu dugu*), for while these are strictly separated, they, too, are functionally complementary.

8. Among the Bambara the term *sako*, which connotes social necessity, translates as "death matter," while the complementary term *dunko*, connoting inward personal desire, translates as "depth matter" (Cissé 1973:148–49;

Kassim Kone, personal communication), while among the Dogon the domain of imperfection and disorder, associated with Yourougou, the pale fox, lies outside the domain of reason and social order associated with Nommo (Calame-Griaule 1965).

9. "Potency" is the usual translation of Aristotle's term for "a source of movement or change" (Aristotle 1941:765).

10. A good example of this invitation to *react*, even if one cannot *act*, is the headline of *Time* magazine's special report on global warming in its 3 April 2006 issue: "Be Worried. Be *Very* Worried. Climate Change Isn't Some Vague Future Problem—It's Already Damaging the Planet at an Alarming Pace."

11. Compare this to the Arabic word for nature, *tabi'ah* (literally, "that which is stamped or impressed [with a quality]"), which, like the Greek *physis* and Latin *natura*, refers to innate tendencies in beings.

9 *despite babel: an essay on human misunderstanding*

1. As Kuranko observe, "Morgo te do ka ban" (A person can never be fully understood); "n'de ma konto lon" (I don't know the inside story); "n'de sa bu'ro" (I don't know what's in the belly).

2. Althought Bourdieu speaks of the ethnographic interview as informed by "a sort of *intellectual love*" and being "a sort of *spiritual exercise*, aiming to obtain, through *forgetfulness of self*, a true *transformation of the view* we take of others in the ordinary circumstances of life" (1996:24), his commitment remains to a way of knowing the other via "the social conditions of which she is the product" (21).

3. I am indebted to Francis Clooney for pointing out to me the relevance of Gadamer's notion of horizon to my argument, and for his edifying work on the fusion of horizons in Vedic texts (2004).

4. The force of this simple declaration should not be underestimated. Uninitiated people and women believe that Kome is a "bush thing" (*fira ro fan*) like animals and djinni, certainly not a person.

10 *on birth, death, and rebirth*

1. The book was translated as *Dear Departed* (1997).

2. Elsewhere, she has noted: "It is *very important* that the reader *not* get the impression that the author is greatly or personally interested about her origins, since the whole quest is more sociological and historical than personal" (qtd. in Beaver 1992:13).

3. Among the Jalé in the highlands of West New Guinea, the emerging

neophyte, his body greased, is pushed out of the narrow entrance of a men's house by an elder in an act of symbolic parturition and rebirth, before being nursed and fed by his agnates (Koch 1974:408–409). Curing rites also often have recourse to birth imagery and notions of symbolic reversal. In the Ndembu Nkula cult, for instance, which treats women experiencing menstrual disorders, frigidity or barrenness, the male healer (circumcised and therefore "pure") is regarded as a "spiritual midwife who pulls the afflicted client backward from a special hut in an explicit imitation of the act of delivering a child" (Turner 1967:140–41). Among the Yaka of southwest Zaire, curing rites also invoke "the primal womb, the uterus of the world" in bringing an afflicted person back to a state of full generative vigor (Devisch 1993:ch. 7; Devisch 1999: 136–37).

4. The Lega of Central Africa go as far as saying that women are "compensated" for being excluded from male initiation and not knowing the secrets of circumcision by being given exclusive knowledge of the secrets of childbirth (Biebuyck 1973:50).

12 a critique of colonial reason

1. Agehananda Bharati refers to this participation as "the pizza effect" (1976:183). Ashis Nandy (1988) perceptively points out that in so far as political domination is homologous with sexual and patriarchal modes of domination, the colonized are symbolically feminized and infantilized, and all women seen as weak and irrational creatures prey to their emotions or spiritual sensibilities.

2. One of the first of the prophets was the mission-educated evangelist Papahurihia, who had a large following in Northland between 1834 and 1840. Knowledgeable in both Judeo-Christian and Māori traditions, Papahurihia had also picked up, in the course of his travels, skills of ventriloquism and hypnotism, and he used these in communicating with the dead (Gudgeon 1907:75). Papahurihia was, however, only one of many new *tohunga* (prophetic leaders) using séances and other spiritualist techniques to control and comprehend the forces that were now colonizing Māori lands and lives. As such he was a precursor of charismatic figures like Te Kooti Arikirangi (who founded the Ringatu faith in 1868), Te Whiti-o-Rongomai (who led passive resistance to Pākehā settlement in Taranaki in the 1870s), Rua Kenana Hepetipa, the "New Messiah," Te Mihaia Hou (who created the community of Maungapohatu in 1906), and Ratana (who proclaimed himself *mangai*, the mouthpiece of God, in 1918 and promoted a pan-Māori ideology that transcended tribal differences.

3. The term *Māori* is itself a product of culture contact. Before the arrival of Europeans, the peoples indigenous to the islands that Dutch explorers had named Zeelandia Nova comprised many named *iwi* (tribes) and *hapu* (subtribes). But in comparing themselves with Europeans, who were radically different and culturally anomalous, people came to see themselves as relatively alike and normal (*Māori*).

4. *Kaitiaki* is from the verb *tiaki* (to guard, protect, keep, watch for, wait for) and implies the responsibility of *tangata whenua* (people of the land) for the preservation and vitality of all things in their domain. Kaitiakitanga entails *rangatiratanga*, recognized in the Treaty of Waitangi as the inalienable right of Māori to determine the sustainability of the environment of Aotearoa New Zealand.

5. In Hannah Arendt's view, judgment is impeded by the habit of referring constantly to the past. To make a "genuine experience of the present possible" and to judge things anew, we must learn to bracket the historical matrix in which past judgments, and the unexamined assumptions these imply, are contained (2005:101).

6. See Mita Ririnui, chair of the Labour Māori Caucus in 2001, who pointed out that to "interfere with another life-form is disrespectful and another form of cultural arrogance" (cited by Pockley 2001).

7. Roger Neich has remarked on this transformation in Māori carved art during the course of the nineteenth century. Under the influence of Christian and European culture, a powerfully connotational style became progressively informed by identity thinking: "Carvers made their meeting house carvings more and more denotational by using mnemonic devices, adding distinguishing attributes, illustrating famous incidents and adding printed name labels to carvings" (1983:250).

8. The literal translation is "Tu in the daytime, Tahu in the evening." Tu is the god of war, and his spirit Mauri Tu governs the space in front of a meeting house where visitors are met with aggressive displays; *tahu* (to light) symbolizes "the milder and quieter reception within the lighted house at night" (Hiroa 1966:373).

References

Abraham, David. 1997. *The Spell of the Sensuous: Perception and Language in a More-Than-Human-World*. New York: Vintage.

Ackerley, C. J., and S. E. Gontarski. 2004. *The Grove Companion to Samuel Beckett: A Reader's Guide to His Works, Life, and Thought*. New York: Grove.

Adorno, Theodor W. 1973. *Negative Dialectics*. Trans. E. B. Ashton. New York: Continuum.

———. 1978. *Minima Moralia: Reflections from Damaged Life*. Trans. E. F. N. Jephcott. London: Verso.

———. 1981. *Prisms*. Trans. Samuel and Shierry Weber. Cambridge: MIT Press.

Aesop. 1998. *The Complete Fables of Aesop*. Trans. Olivia Temple and Robert Temple. Harmondsworth, UK: Penguin.

Akhmatova, Anna. 1974. *Poems*. Trans. Stanley Kunitz and Max Hayward. London: Collins and Harvill.

Arendt, Hannah. 1958. *The Human Condition*. Chicago: The University of Chicago Press.

——. 1963. *On Revolution*. New York: Viking.

——. 1969. "Reflections on Violence." *New York Review of Books*, 27 February, 24–26.

——. 1970. *On Violence*. New York: Harcourt Brace.

——. 1973. *Men in Dark Times*. Harmondsworth, UK: Penguin.

——. 1977. *Between Past and Future: Eight Exercises in Political Thought*. Harmondsworth, UK: Penguin.

——. 1978. *The Jew as Pariah: Jewish Identity and Politics in the Modern Age*. Ed. Ron. H. Feldman. New York: Grove.

——. 1982. *Lectures on Kant's Political Philosophy*. Ed. Roland Beiner. Chicago: University of Chicago Press.

——. 2000. "Labor, Work, Action." In *The Portable Hannah Arendt*, ed. Peter Baehr, 167–81. New York: Penguin.

——. 2005. *The Promise of Politics*. Ed. Jerome Kohn. New York: Schocken.

Aristotle. 1941. *The Basic Works of Aristotle*. Ed. Richard McKeon. New York: Random House.

——. 1983. *The Nicomachean Ethics*. Trans. David Ross. Oxford: Oxford University Press.

Bagnall, A. G., and C. Petersen. 1948. *William Colenso*. Wellington: A. H. Reed.

Bakhtin, M. M. 1993. *Toward a Philosophy of the Act*. Trans. Vadim Liapunov. Austin: University of Texas Press.

Barnes, Hazel. 1997. *The Story I Tell Myself: A Venture in Existential Autobiography*. Chicago: University of Chicago Press.

Bascom, William R. 1973. "A Yoruba Master Carver: Duga of Meko." In *The Traditional Artist in African Societies*, ed. Warren L. d'Azevedo, 62–78. Bloomington: Indiana University Press.

——. 1975. *African Dilemma Tales*. The Hague: Mouton.

Basso, Keith H. 1996. "Wisdom Sits in Places: Notes on a Western Apache Landscape." In *Senses of Place*, ed. Steven Feld and Basso, 53–89. Santa Fe: School of American Research Press.

Beauvoir, Simone de. 1953. *The Second Sex*. Trans. H. M. Parshley, New York: Knopf.

Beaver, Harold. 1992. "Remembering the World She Never Knew." *New York Times Book Review*, 1 March 1992, 13.

Beckett, Samuel. 1958. *The Unnameable*. New York: Grove.

——. 1987. *Proust. Three Dialogues: Samuel Beckett and Georges Duthuit*. London: John Calder.

Benjamin, Walter. 1969. *Illuminations: Essays and Reflections*. Ed. Hannah Arendt. Trans. Harry Zohn. New York: Schocken.

———. 1983. *Understanding Brecht*. Trans. Anna Bostock. London: Verso.

———. 1998. *The Origin of German Tragic Drama*. Trans. John Osborne. London: Verso.

Bennett, Tony, Lawrence Grossberg, and Meaghan Morris. 2005. *New Keywords: A Revised Vocabulary of Culture and Society*. Oxford: Blackwell.

Benoit, Hubert. 1984. *The Supreme Doctrine: Psychological Encounters in Zen Thought*. New York: Inner Traditions International.

Berry, Jack. 1961. *Spoken Art in West Africa: An Inaugural Lecture Delivered on 8 December, 1960*. London: School of Oriental and African Studies, University of London.

Best, Elsdon. 1954. *Some Aspects of Maori Myth and Religion*. Wellington: R. E. Owen.

Bharati, Agehananda. 1976. *The Light at the Center: Context and Pretext of Modern Mysticism*. Santa Barbara: Ross-Erikson.

Biebuyck, Daniel. 1973. *Lega Culture: Art, Initiation, and Moral Philosophy among a Central African People*. Berkeley: University of California Press.

Binney, Judith. 1968. *The Legacy of Guilt: A Life of Thomas Kendall*. Auckland: Oxford University Press.

Bird, Charles S., with Mamadou Koita and Bourama Soumaoro. 1974. *The Songs of Seydou Camara*. Vol. 1, *Kambili*. Bloomington: African Studies Program, Indiana University Press.

Boddy, Janice. 1989. *Wombs and Alien Spirits: Women, Men, and the Zar Cult in Northern Sudan*. Madison: University of Wisconsin Press.

Borges, Jorge Luis. 1970. *Labyrinths: Selected Stories and Other Writings*. Ed. Donald A. Yates and James E. Irby. Harmondsworth, UK: Penguin.

Bourdieu, Pierre, 1990. *The Logic of Practice*. Trans. Richard Nice. Stanford, Calif.: Stanford University Press.

———. 1996. "Understanding." *Theory, Culture and Society* 13 (2): 17–37.

———. 2000. *Pascalian Meditations*. Trans. Richard Nice. Cambridge: Polity.

Bowlby, John. 1973. *Attachment and Loss*. Vol. 2, *Separation: Anxiety and Anger*. Harmondsworth, UK: Penguin.

Brandström, Per. 1990. "Seeds and Soil: The Quest for Life and the Domestication of Fertility in Sukuma-Nyamwezi Thought and Reality." In *The Creative Communion: African Folk Models of Fertility and the Regeneration of Life*, ed. Anita Jacobson-Widding and Walter van Beek. 167–86. Uppsala, Sweden: Academiae Upsaliensis.

Brodersen, Momme. 1996. *Walter Benjamin: A Biography*. Trans. Malcolm Green and Ingrida Ligers. London: Verso.

Brown, Maria. 2002. "Representing the Body of a Nation: The Art Exhibitions of New Zealand's National Museum." *Third Text* 16 (3): 285–94.

Brown, Ruth. 1989. "Maori Spirituality as a Pakeha Construct." *Meanjin* 48 (2): 252–58.

Burridge, Kenelm. 1960. *Mambu: A Melanesian Millennium*. London: Methuen.

——. 1969. *Tangu Traditions: A Study of the Way of Life, Mythology, and Developing Experience of a New Guinea People*. Oxford: Clarendon.

Burton, David. 1999. *Emptiness Appraised: A Critical Study of Nagarjuna's Philosophy*. Richmond, UK: Curzon.

Calame-Griaule, G. 1965. *Ethnologie et Langage: La parole chez les Dogon*. Paris: Gallimard.

Camus, Albert. 1955. *The Myth of Sisyphus*. Trans. Justin O'Brien. London: Hamish Hamilton.

Chabal, Patrick, and Jean-Pascal Daloz. 1999. *Africa Works: Disorder as a Political Instrument*. Bloomington: Indiana University Press.

Cissé, Youssouf. 1973. "Signes Graphiques, Représentations, Concepts et Tests Relatifs à la Personne chez les Malinke et les Bambara du Mali." In *La Notion de Personne en Afrique Noire, Paris 11–17 Octobre, 1971*, ed. Colloque international sur la notion de personne en Afrique noire, 131–79. Paris: Éditions du Centre National du Recherche Scientifique.

Clastres, Pierre. 1977. *Society against the State: Essays in Political Anthropology*. Trans. Robert Hurley. Oxford: Blackwell.

Clooney, Francis. 2004. "A Fusion of Horizons: H.-G. Gadamer and the Meditation on Fullness (*Chandogya 7*)." In *Horizonte des Horizontbegriffs: Hermeneutische, phänomenologische und interkulturelle Studien*, ed. Ralf Elm, 285–308. Berlin: Academia Verlag.

Collier, M. J. 2004. "Is the President of Sierra Leone Listening to the Cries of His People?" *Independent*, 28 May 28.

Collingwood, R. G. 1944. *The Idea of Nature*. Westport, Conn.: Greenwood.

Collins, Billy. 2000. *Taking off Emily Dickinson's Clothes: Selected Poems*. London: Picador.

Connolly, Bob, and Robin Anderson. 1987. *First Contact*. New York: Viking.

Costa, R. H. 1972. *Malcolm Lowry*. New York: Twayne.

Cowell, Alan. 2005. "For Swedes, 'No Experience at All.'" *International Herald Tribune*, 7 January.

Crapanzano, Vincent. 1992. *Hermes' Dilemma and Hamlet's Desire: On the Epistemology of Interpretation*. Cambridge, Mass.: Harvard University Press.

Cruise, Richard Alexander. 1957. *Journal of a Ten Months' Residence in New Zealand, 1820*. Ed. A. G. Bagnall. Christchurch, New Zealand: Pegasus.

Csikszentmihalyi, Mihaly. 1990. *Flow: The Psychology of Optimal Experience*. New York: Harper and Row.

Daley, Caroline. 2003. *Leisure and Pleasure: Reshaping and Revealing the New Zealand Body, 1900–1960*. Auckland: Auckland University Press.

Dannekiold-Samsøe, Sofie. 2006. *The Moral Economy of Suffering: Social Exchange Among Iraqi Refugees in the Danish Welfare State*. Ph.D. thesis, Institute of Anthropology, University of Copenhagen.

D'Azevedo, Warren L. 1973. "Mask Makers and Myth in Western Liberia." In *Primitive Art and Society*, ed. Anthony Forge, 126–50. London: Oxford University Press.

Deluz, Ariane. 1979. "George Devereux: A Portrait." In *Fantasy and Symbol: Studies in Anthropological Interpretation*, ed. R. H. Hook, 11–18. London: Academic Press.

Derrida, Jacques. 1993. *Aporias*. Trans. Thomas Dutoit. Stanford, Calif.: Stanford University Press.

———. 1994. *Given Time: 1, Counterfeit Money*. Trans. Peggy Kamuf. Chicago: University of Chicago Press.

Devereux, George. 1968. *From Anxiety to Method in the Behavioral Sciences*. The Hague: Mouton.

———. 1978. "The Works of George Devereux." In *The Making of Psychological Anthropology*, ed. G. D. Spindler, 361–406. Berkeley: University of California Press.

———. 1979. "Fantasy and Symbol as Dimensions of Reality." In *Fantasy and Symbol: Studies in Anthropological Interpretation*, ed. R. H. Hook, 19–31. London: Academic Press.

———. 1980. "A Sociological Theory of Schizophrenia." In *Basic Problems of Ethnopsychiatry*, 185–213. Trans. Basia Miller Gulati and Devereux. Chicago: University of Chicago Press.

Devisch, René. 1993. *Weaving the Threads of Life: The Khita Gyn-Eco-Logical Healing Cult among the Yaka*. Chicago: University of Chicago Press.

———. 1995. "Frenzy, Violence and Ethical Renewal in Kinshasa." *Public Culture* 7 (3): 593–629.

———. 1999. "Sorcery and Fetish." In *The Law of the Lifegivers: The Domestication of Desire*, by Devisch and Claude Brodeur, 57–91. Amsterdam: Harwood.

Dummett, Michael. 1978. *Truth and Other Enigmas*. London: Duckworth.

Dumoulin, Heinrich. 1994. *Zen Buddhism: A History*. Vol. 1, *India and China*. Trans. James W. Heisig and Paul Knitter. New York: Macmillan.

Durie, Mason. *Mauri Ora: The Dynamics of Maori Health*. Oxford: Oxford University Press.

Durkheim, Émile. 1915. *The Elementary Forms of the Religious Life: A Study in Religious Sociology.* Trans. Joseph Ward. London: Allen and Unwin.

Eibl-Eibesfeldt, Irenäus. 1989. *Human Ethology.* New York: Aldine de Gruyter.

Eliot, T.S. 1959. "Burnt Norton," from *The Four Quartets.* London: Faber.

Ellenberger, Henri F. 1970. *The Discovery of the Unconscious: The History and Evolution of Dynamic Psychiatry.* New York: Basic Books.

Emerson, Ralph Waldo. 1995. *Essays and Poems.* London: J. M. Dent.

———. 2003. *Selected Writings.* Ed. William H. Gilman. New York: Signet.

The Epic of Gilgamesh: A New Translation, Analogues, Criticism. 2001. Ed. and trans. Benjamin R. Foster. New York: Norton.

Erlanger, Steven. 2004. "Palestinian Victims of a Palestinian Bomber." *International Herald Tribune,* August 20.

Evans-Pritchard, E. Evans. 1937. *Witchcraft, Oracles and Magic among the Azande.* Oxford: Clarendon.

———. 1940. *The Nuer: A Description of the Modes of Livelihood and Political Institutions of a Nilotic People.* Oxford: Clarendon.

Fabian, Johannes. 1983. *Time and the Other: How Anthropology Makes Its Object.* New York: Columbia University Press.

Feld, Steven. 1982. *Sound and Sentiment: Birds, Weeping, Poetics, and Song in Kaluli Expression.* Philadelphia: University of Pennsylvania Press.

———. 1984. "Sound Structure as Social Structure." *Ethnomusicology* 28 (3): 383–409.

———. 1996. "Waterfalls of Song: An Acoustemology of Place Resounding in Bosavi, Papua New Guinea." In *Senses of Place,* ed. Feld and Keith H. Basso, 91–135. Santa Fe: School of American Research Press.

———. 2001. Liner notes to *Bosavi: Rainforest Music from Papua New Guinea.* Smithsonian Folkways Recordings SFW CD 4087.

———. 2004. Liner notes to *The Time of the Bells.* VoxLox 204.

Ferme, Mariane. 2001. *The Underneath of Things: Violence, History, and the Everyday in Sierra Leone.* Berkeley: University of California Press.

Finkelstein, Norman G. 2000. *The Holocaust Industry: Reflections on the Exploitation of Jewish Suffering.* London: Verso.

Fittko, Lisa. 1991. *Escape through the Pyrenees.* Trans. David Koblick. Evanston, Ill.: Northwestern University Press.

Fortes, Meyer. 1949. *The Web of Kinship among the Tallensi.* London: Oxford University Press.

Fortune, Christopher, ed. 2002. *The Sándor Ferenczi–Georg Groddeck Correspondence, 1921–1933.* Trans. Jeannie Cohen, Elisabeth Petersdorff, and Norber Ruebsaat. London: Open Gate Press.

Foucault, Michel. 1972. *The Archaeology of Knowledge.* Trans. A. M. Sheridan Smith. London: Tavistock.

———. 1983. "Afterword: The Subject and Power." In *Michel Foucault: Beyond Structuralism and Hermeneutics,* by Hubert L. Dreyfus and Paul Rabinow, 208–26. 2nd ed. Chicago: University of Chicago Press.

Freud, Sigmund. 1961a. *Civilization and Its Discontents.* Trans. James Strachey. New York: Norton.

———. 1961b. *Totem and Taboo: Some Points of Agreement between the Mental Lives of Savages and Neurotics.* Trans. James Strachey. London: Routledge and Kegan Paul.

———. 1989. *Beyond the Pleasure Principle.* Trans. James Strachey. New York: Norton.

Fromm, Erich. 1950. *Man For Himself: An Inquiry Into the Psychology of Ethics.* London: Routledge and Kegan Paul.

Fry, Varian. 1945. *Surrender on Demand.* New York: Random House.

Gadamer, Hans-Georg. 1989. *Truth and Method.* 2nd rev. ed. Trans. rev. Joel Weinsheimer and Donald G. Marshall. New York: Crossroad.

Girard, René. 1965. *Deceit, Desire and the Novel: Self and Other in Literary Structure.* Baltimore: Johns Hopkins University Press.

Glassie, Henry. 1993. *Turkish Traditional Art Today.* Bloomington: Indiana University Press.

Godelier, Maurice. 1986. *The Making of Great Men: Male Domination and Power among the New Guinea Baruya.* Cambridge: Cambridge University Press.

Goldsmith, Michael. 2003. "'Our Place' in New Zealand Culture: How the Museum of New Zealand Constructs Biculturalism." *Ethnologies Comparées,* no. 6.

Grace, Thomas Samuel. 1928. *A Pioneer Missionary among the Maoris, 1850–1879: Being Letters and Journals of Thomas Samuel Grace.* Ed. S. J. Brittan, G. F., C. W., and A. V. Grace. Palmerston North, New Zealand: G. H. Bennett.

Gramsci, Antonio. 1971. *Selections from the Prison Notebooks.* Trans. Q. Hoare and G. N. Smith. New York: International Publishers.

Graves, Robert. 1965. "The Cool Web," from *Collected Poems 1965.* London: Cassell.

———. *The Greek Myths.* Vol. 1. Harmondsworth, UK: Penguin.

Groddeck, Georg. 1977 *The Meaning of Illness: Selected Psychoanalytic Writings.* Trans. Gertrud Mander. London: Hogarth Press.

Gudgeon, Thomas W. 1907. "The Tohunga Maori." *Journal of the Polynesian Society* 16 (62): 63–91.

Guenther, Lisa. 2006. *The Gift of the Other: Levinas and the Politics of Repro-duction*. Albany: State University of New York Press.

Guha, Ranajit. 1983a. *Elementary Aspects of Peasant Insurgency in Colonial India*. Delhi: Oxford University Press.

———. 1983b. "The Prose of Counter-insurgency." In *Subaltern Studies 2: Writings on South Asian History and Society*, ed. Guha, 1–42. Delhi: Oxford University Press.

Habermas, Jürgen. 1989. *The Structural Transformation of the Public Sphere: An Inquiry into a Category of Bourgeois Society*. Trans. T. Burger and F. Lawrence. Cambridge: MIT Press.

Hage, Ghassan. 1996. "The Spatial Imaginary of National Practices: Dwell-ing-Domesticating/Being-Exterminating." *Environment and Planning D: Society and Space*, no. 14:463–85.

———. 1999. *White Nation: Fantasies of White Supremacy in a Multicultural Society*. Sydney: Pluto.

———. 2004. "Identity Fetishism: Capitalism and White Self-racialisation." In *Racialisation: Studies in Theory and Practice*, ed. John Solomos and Ka-rim Murji, 185–205. Oxford: Oxford University Press.

Hallowell, A. Irving. 1958. "Ojibwa Metaphysics of Being and the Perception of Persons." In *Person Perception and Interpersonal Behavior*, ed. Renato Taguiri and Luigi Petrullo, 63–85. Stanford, Calif.: Stanford University Press.

Hamnet, Ian. 1967. "Ambiguity, Classification and Change: The Function of Riddles." *Man* 2(3): 381–93.

Hargreaves, R. P. 1963. "Changing Maori Agriculture in Pre-Waitangi New Zealand." *Journal of the Polynesian Society* 72 (2): 101–17.

Henare, Manuka. n.d. "*Tapu, Mana, Mauri, Hau, Wairua*: A Māori Philoso-phy of Vitalism and Cosmos." Unpublished manuscript.

Herdt, Gilbert H. 1981. *Guardians of the Flutes: Idioms of Masculinity*. New York: McGraw-Hill.

Herrigel, Eugen. 1972. *Zen in the Art of Archery*. Trans. R. F. C. Hull. London: Routledge and Kegan Paul.

Herzfeld, Michael. 1997. *Cultural Intimacy: Social Poetics in the Nation-State*. New York: Routledge.

———. 2004. "Intimating Culture: Local Contexts and International Power." In *Off Stage/On Display: Intimacy and Ethnography in the Age of Public Culture*, ed. Andrew Shryock, 317–35. Stanford, Calif.: Stanford Univer-sity Press.

Hillary, Edmund. 1975. *Nothing Venture, Nothing Win*. New York: Coward, McCann and Geoghegan.

Hindle, Maurice. 1992. Introduction to *Frankenstein*, by Mary Shelley, vii–xliii. Harmondsworth, UK: Penguin.

Hiroa, Te Rangi [Peter Buck]. 1966. *The Coming of the Maori*. 2nd ed. Wellington: Whitcombe and Tombs.

Hopkins, Gerard Manley. 1953. *Poems and Prose: A Selection*. Harmondsworth, UK: Penguin.

Horkheimer, Max, and Theodor Adorno. 1972. *Dialectic of Enlightenment*. Trans. J. Cumming. New York: Herder and Herder.

Husserl, Edmund. 1931. *Ideas: General Introduction to Pure Phenomenology*. Trans. W. R. Boyce Gibson. New York: Macmillan.

Huxley, Francis. 1963. *Affable Savages*. London: Rupert Hart-Davis.

Illich, Ivan. 1973. *Tools for Conviviality*. London: Calder and Boyars.

Jackson, Michael. 1978. "An Approach to Kuranko Divination." *Human Relations* 31 (2):117–38.

———. 1982. *Allegories of the Wilderness: Ethics and Ambiguity in Kuranko Narratives*. Bloomington: Indiana University Press.

———. 1989. *Paths toward a Clearing: Radical Empiricism and Ethnographic Inquiry*. Bloomington: Indiana University Press.

———. 1998. *Minima Ethnographica: Intersubjectivity and the Anthropological Project*. Chicago: University of Chicago Press.

———. 2002. *The Politics of Storytelling: Violence, Transgression and Intersubjectivity*. Copenhagen: Museum Tusculanum Press.

———. 2003. "The Politics of Reconciliation: Reflections on the Postwar in Sierra Leone." In *Being There: New Perspectives on Phenomenology and the Analysis of Culture*, ed. Jonas Frykman and Nils Gilje, 95–105. Lund, Sweden: Nordic Academic Press.

———. 2004. *In Sierra Leone*. Durham, N.C.: Duke University Press.

———. 2005. *Existential Anthropology: Events, Exigencies, and Effects*. Oxford: Berghahn.

———. 2006. *The Accidental Anthropologist: A Memoir*. Dunedin, New Zealand: Longacre.

Jackson, Moana. 2001. "An Exquisite Politeness: The Royal Commission on Genetic Modification and the Redefining of the Treaty of Waitangi." Web document, printouts on file with author.

James, William. 1904. "A World of Pure Experience," *Journal of Psychology, and Scientific Methods* 1: 533–543, 561–570.

———. 1976. *Essays in Radical Empiricism*. Cambridge: Harvard University Press.

———. 1978. *Pragmatism*. Cambridge: Harvard University Press.

Jaspers, Karl. 1955. *Reason and Existenz: Five Lectures*. Trans. William Earle. New York: Noonday.

——. 1967. *Philosophical Faith and Revelation.* Trans. E. B. Ashton. New York: Harper and Row.

——. 1985. *Psychologie der Weltanschauungen.* Munchen: Piper.

Jay, Martin. 2003. *Refractions of Violence.* London: Routledge.

Johnson, Emily D. n.d. "A Sense of Time in the Fife Coalfields." Electronic document, www.princeton.edu/stcweb/html/pope01essay.html (accessed 25 October 2006).

Johnson, Joyce. 1983. *Minor Characters: A Beat Memoir.* London: Virago.

Jolly, Margaret. 2001. "On the Edge? Deserts, Oceans, Islands." *Contemporary Pacific* 13 (2): 417–66.

Keats, John. 1958. *The Letters of John Keats, 1814–1821.* Vol. 1. Ed. H. E. Rollins. Cambridge: Cambridge University Press.

Kidd, Sue Monk. 2002. *The Secret Life of Bees.* New York: Viking.

Kimmelman, Michael. 2004. "Art: The Memories; Postwar Japan/Mon Amour." *New York Times,* 26 December.

Klein, Melanie. 1989. *Narrative of a Child Analysis.* London: Virago.

Knox, Thomas W. 1878. *The Underground World: A Mirror of Life below the Surface.* San Francisco: J. M. Rising.

Koch, Klaus-Friedrich. 1974. "Sociogenic and Psychogenic Models in Anthropology: The Functions of Jalé Initiation." *Man,* n.s., 9 (3): 397–422.

Kofman, Sarah. 1988. "Beyond Aporia." Trans. David Macey. In *Post-structuralist Classics,* ed. Andrew Benjamin, 7–44. London: Routledge.

Komba, Sahr Joseph. 2004. "Kabbah Has Disappointed Sierra Leoneans." *Independent,* 1 November.

Kurkiala, Mikael. 2003. "Interpreting Honour Killings: The Story of Fadime Sahindal (1975–2002) in the Swedish Press." *Anthropology Today* 19 (1): 6–7.

La Barre, Weston. 1972. *The Ghost Dance: Origins of Religion.* New York: Dell.

Lakhoff, George, and Mark Johnson. 1980. *Metaphors We Live By.* Chicago: University of Chicago Press.

Lancaster, Jane B. 1975. *Primate Behavior and the Emergence of Human Culture.* New York: Holt, Rinehart and Winston.

Lao Tzu. 1963. *Tao Te Ching.* Trans. D. C. Lau. Harmondsworth, UK: Penguin.

Larreta, Enrique-Rodriguez. 2002. "'Gold Is Illusion': The Garimpeiros of Tapajos Valley in the Brazilian Amazonia." Stockholm Studies in Social Anthropology 50. Stockholm: Department of Social Anthropology, Stockholm University.

Lattas, Andrew. 1998. *Cultures of Secrecy: Reinventing Race in Bush Kaliai Cargo Cults.* Madison: University of Wisconsin Press.

Laughton, J. C. 1965. "Report." In *Proceedings of the General Assembly of the Presbyterian Church*. Wellington.

Leitch, Alison. 1996. "The Life of Marble: The Experience and Meaning of Work in the Marble Quarries of Carrara." *Australian Journal of Anthropology* 7 (3): 235–57.

Levi, Carlo. 1982. *Christ Stopped at Eboli*. New York: Norton.

Levi, Primo. 1989. *The Drowned and the Saved*. Trans. Raymond Rosenthal. New York: Vintage.

Lévi-Strauss, Claude. 1963. *Structural Anthropology*. Trans. Claire Jacobson and Brooke Grundfest Schoepf. New York: Basic Books.

——. 1973a. *From Honey to Ashes*. Trans. John Weightman and Doreen Weightman. London: Jonathan Cape.

——. 1973b. *Tristes Tropiques*. Trans. John Weightman and Doreen Weightman. London: Jonathan Cape.

Lowry, Malcolm. 1969. *Hear Us O Lord from Heaven Thy Dwelling Place* and *Lunar Caustic*. Harmondsworth, UK: Penguin.

Lugwani. 2005. Web document, printouts on file with author.

Lyotard, Jean-François. 1998. *The Differend: Phrases in Dispute*. Trans. Georges van den Abbeele.

MacLeod, Robert. 1958. "The Phenomenological Approach to Social Psychology." In *Person Perception and Interpersonal Behavior*, ed. Renato Taguiri and Luigi Petrullo, 33–53. Stanford, Calif.: Stanford University Press.

MacPherson, C. B. 1962. *The Political Theory of Possessive Individualism: The Family, Property and Social Transition*. Cambridge: Cambridge University Press.

Makdisi, Jean Said. 1990. *Beirut Fragments: A War Memoir*. New York: Persea.

Malinowski, Bronislaw. 1922. *Argonauts of the Western Pacific*. London: Routledge and Kegan Paul.

Malkki, Liisa. 1995. *Purity and Exile: Violence, Memory, and National Cosmology among Hutu Refugees in Tanzania*. Chicago: University of Chicago Press.

——. 1997. "News and Culture: Transitory Phenomenon and the Fieldwork Tradition." In *Anthropological Locations: Boundaries and Grounds of a Field Science*, ed. Akhil Gupta and James Ferguson, 86–101. Berkeley: University of California Press.

Mamet, David. 2005. "Obituary: Arthur Miller." *New York Times*. 13 February.

Marcuse, Herbert. 1966. *Eros and Civilization: A Philosophical Inquiry into Freud*. Boston: Beacon.

—. 1988. *Negations: Essays in Critical Theory*. Trans. Jeremy J. Shapiro. London: Free Association Books.

Marett, Allan. 2005. *Songs, Dreamings, Ghosts: The Wangga of North Australia*. Middletown: Conn.: Wesleyan University Press.

Markham, Edward. 1963. *New Zealand; or, Recollections of It*. Ed. E. H. McCormick. Wellington: R. E. Owen.

Martin, S. M. D. 1845. *New Zealand: In a Series of Letters*. London.

Marx, Karl. 1906. *Capital: A Critique of Political Economy*. Trans. Samuel Moore and Edward Aveling. New York: Modern Library.

—. 1934. *The Eighteenth Brumaire of Louis Bonaparte*. Moscow: Progress Publishers.

—. 1961. *Economic and Philosophic Manuscripts of 1844*. Moscow: Foreign Languages Publishing House.

—. 1964. *Pre-capitalist Economic Formations*. Trans. Jack Cohen. London: Lawrence and Wishart.

Marx, Karl, and Frederick Engels. 1976. "The German Ideology." Trans. C. Dutt. In *Karl Marx, Frederick Engels: Collected Works*, 5:19–608. Moscow: Progressive Publishers.

Maurice, Mr. Justice. 1988. *Jila (Chilla Well) Warlpiri Land Claim*. Canberra: Australian Government Publishing Service.

McNaughton, Patrick R. 1988. *The Mande Blacksmiths: Knowledge, Power, and Art in West Africa*. Bloomington: Indiana University Press.

Meggitt, Mervyn. 1964. "Male-Female Relationships in the Highlands of Australian New Guinea." *American Anthropologist* 66 (4): 204–24.

Merleau-Ponty, Maurice. 1962. *Phenomenology of Perception*. Trans. Colin Smith. London: Routledge and Kegan Paul.

Messenger, John C. 1973. "The Role of the Carver in Anang Society." In *The Traditional Artist in African Societies*, ed. Warren L. d'Azevedo, 101–27. Bloomington: Indiana University Press.

Metge, Joan, and Patricia Kinloch. 1978. *Talking Past Each Other: Problems of Cross-cultural Communication*. Wellington: Victoria University Press.

Miller, Henry. 1961. *The Cosmological Eye*. New York: New Directions.

Milton, Kay. 1996. *Environmentalism and Cultural Theory: Exploring the Role of Anthropology in Environmental Discourse*. London: Routledge.

Montaigne, Michel de. 2004. *The Essays: A Selection*. Trans. M. A. Screech. Harmondsworth, UK: Penguin.

Moran, Dermot. 2000. *Introduction to Phenomenology*. London: Routledge.

Nakamura, Hajime. 1986. *A Comparative History of Ideas*. Rev. ed. London: KPI.

Nandy, Ashis. 1988. *The Intimate Enemy: Loss and Recovery of Self under Colonialism*. Delhi: Oxford University Press.

Nash, June. 1979. *We Eat the Mines and the Mines Eat Us: Dependency and Exploitation in Bolivian Tin Mines*. New York: Columbia University Press.

Neich, Roger. 1983. "The Veil of Orthodoxy: Rotorua Maori Woodcarving in Changing Context." In *Art and Artists in Oceania*, ed. S. Mead and B. Kernot. Palmerston North, New Zealand: Dunmore.

Ngata, Apirana. 1959. *Nga Moteatea*. Wellington: A. H. and A. W. Reed.

Oakeshott, Michael. 1933. *Experience and Its Modes*. Cambridge: Cambridge University Press.

———. 1991. *Rationalism in Politics and Other Essays*. New, exp. ed. Indianapolis: Liberty Press.

Ohnuki-Tierney, Emiko. 2004. "Betrayal by Idealism and Aesthetics: Special Attack Force (Kamikaze) Pilots and Their Intellectual Trajectories (Part 1)." *Anthropology Today* 20 (2): 15–21.

O'Nell, Theresa DeLeane. 1998. *Disciplined Hearts: History, Identity, and Depression in an American Indian Community*. Berkeley: University of California Press.

Onians, R. B. 1951. *The Origins of European Thought*. New York: Arno.

Orsi, Robert. 1996. *Thank You, St. Jude: Women's Devotion to the Patron Saint of Hopeless Causes*. New Haven: Yale University Press.

———. 2005. *Between Heaven and Earth: The Religious Worlds People Make and the Scholars Who Study Them*. Princeton: Princeton University Press.

Orwell, George. 1962. *The Road to Wigan Pier*. Harmondsworth, UK: Penguin.

O'Sullivan, Vincent. 2003. *On Longing*. Wellington: Four Winds Press.

Özyürek, Esra. 2004. "Wedded to the Republic: Public Intellectuals and Intimacy-Oriented Publics in Turkey." In *Off Stage/On Display: Intimacy and Ethnography in the Age of Public Culture*, ed. Andrew Shryock, 101–30. Stanford, Calif.: Stanford University Press.

Parliamentary Commissioner for the Environment. 2000. *"Caught in the Headlights": New Zealanders' Reflections on Possums, Control Options and Genetic Engineering*. Wellington: Office of the Parliamentary Commissioner for the Environment.

Parr, C. J. 1963. "Maori Literacy 1843–1867." *Journal of the Polynesian Society* 72 (3): 211–34.

Piaget, Jean. 1973. *The Child's Conception of the World*. Trans. Joan Tomlinson and Andrew Tomlinson. Frogmore, U.K.: Paladin.

Poata-Smith, Evan S. Te Ahu. 1996. "He Pokeke Uenuku i Tu Ai: The Evolution of Contemporary Maori Protest." In *Nga Patai: Racism and Ethnic Relations in Aotearoa/New Zealand*, ed. Paul Spoonley, David Pearson and Cluny Macpherson, 97–116. Palmerston North, New Zealand: Dunmore.

Pockley, Peter. 2001. "New Zealand Says Yes to GM Trials." Web document, printouts on file with author.

Polack, J. S. 1840. *Manners and Customs of the New Zealanders.* 2 vols. London: James Madden and Hatchard and Son.

———. 1938. *New Zealand: Being a Narrative of Travels and Adventures during a Residence in That Country between the Years 1831 and 1837.* 2 vols. London: Richard Bentley.

Povinelli, Elizabeth A. 1993. *Labor's Lot: The Power, History, and Culture of Aboriginal Action.* Chicago: University of Chicago Press.

Povrzanović, Maja. 2000. "The Imposed and the Imagined as Encountered by Croatian War Ethnographers." *Current Anthropology* 41 (2): 151–62.

Rasmussen, Knud. 1929. *Intellectual Culture of the Iglulik Eskimos.* Vol. 1 of *Intellectual Culture of the Hudson Bay Eskimos.* Copenhagen: Gyldendalske.

Rawson, P. 1968. *Erotic Art of the East.* London: Weidenfeld and Nicolson.

Read, Kenneth. 1965. *The High Valley.* New York: Scribner.

———. 1986. *Return to the High Valley.* Berkeley: University of California Press.

Redmond, Anthony. 2001. "Places that Move." In *Emplaced Myth: Space, Narrative, and Knowledge in Aboriginal Australia and Papua New Guinea,* ed. Alan Rumsey and James Weiner, 120–38. Honolulu: University of Hawaii Press.

Ricoeur, Paul. 1992. *Oneself as Another.* Trans. Kathleen Blamey. Chicago: University of Chicago Press.

Róheim, Géza. 1971. *The Origin and Function of Culture.* New York: Doubleday.

Ronan, C., ed. 1978. *The Shorter Science and Civilization in China.* Vol. 1 (abridgement of Joseph Needham's original text). Cambridge: Cambridge University Press.

Roth, W. E. 1897. *Ethnological Studies among the North-West-Central Queensland Aborigines.* Brisbane: Edmund Gregory.

———. 1903. "Superstition, Magic, and Medicine." In *North Queensland Ethnography: Bulletin No. 5,* 3–42. Brisbane: George Arthur Vaughan.

Said, Edward. 2000. Commencement address, American University of Beirut.

Salmond, Anne. 2000. "Maori and Modernity: Ruatara's Dying." In *Signifying Identities: Anthropological Perspectives on Boundaries and Contested Values,* ed. Anthony P. Cohen, 37–58. London: Routledge.

Sampson, Steven. 2003. "From Reconciliation to Coexistence." *Public Culture* 15 (1): 179–84.

Santayana, George. 1953. *The Life of Reason; or, The Phases of Human Progress.* New York: Scribner.

Sartre, Jean-Paul. 1940. *L'Imaginaire: Psychologie-phénoménologique de l'imagination.* Paris: Gallimard.

———. 1969. "Itinerary of a Thought." *New Left Review,* no. 58:43–66.

———. 1983. *Between Existentialism and Marxism.* Trans. John Matthews. London: Verso.

———. 2004. *The Imaginary: A Phenomenological Psychology of the Imagination.* Trans. Jonathan Webber. Rev. Arlette Elkaïm Sartre. London: Routledge.

Scheper-Hughes, Nancy, and Mariana Leal Ferreira. 2003. "Dombá's Spirit Kidney: Transplant Medicine and Suyá Indian Cosmology." *Folk,* no. 45: 125–57.

Scholem, Gershom. 1982. *Walter Benjamin: The Story of a Friendship.* London: Faber and Faber.

Schutz, Alfred. 1972. *The Phenomenology of the Social World.* Trans. George Walsh and Frederick Lehnert. London: Heinemann.

Sebald, W. G. 2001. *Austerlitz.* London: Hamish Hamilton.

Sen, Amartya. 2005. *The Argumentative Indian: Writings on Indian History, Culture and Identity.* New York: Farrar, Straus and Giroux.

Sextus Empiricus. 1996. *The Skeptic Way: Sextus Empiricus's "Outlines of Pyrrhonism."* Trans. Benson Mates. New York: Oxford University Press.

Shaw, Rosalind. 1997. "The Production of Witchcraft/Witchcraft as Production: Memory, Modernity, and the Slave Trade in Sierra Leone." *American Ethnologist* 24 (4): 856–76.

———. 2002. *Memories of the Slave Trade: Ritual and the Historical Imagination in Sierra Leone.* Chicago: University of Chicago Press.

———. 2003. "Robert Kaplan and 'Juju Journalism' in Sierra Leone's Rebel War: The Primitivizing of an African Conflict." In *Magic and Modernity: Interfaces of Revelation and Concealment,* ed. Birgit Meyer and Peter Pels, 81–102. Stanford, Calif.: Stanford University Press.

Shryock, Andrew. 2004. "Other Conscious/Self Aware: First Thoughts on Cultural Intimacy and Mass Mediation." Introduction to *Off Stage/On Display: Intimacy and Ethnography in the Age of Public Culture,* ed. Shryock, 3–28. Stanford, Calif.: Stanford University Press.

Simmel, Georg. 1991. "The Alpine Journey." *Theory, Culture and Society* 8 (3): 95–98.

Singer, Isaac Bashevis. 1976. "Knut Hamsun: Artist of Scepticism." Introduction to *Hunger,* by Knut Hamsun, 5–11. London: Picador.

Sissons, Jeffrey. 2004. "Maori Tribalism and Post-settler Nationhood in New Zealand." *Oceania*, no. 75:19–31.

Steiner, George. 1998. Introduction to *The Origin of German Tragic Drama*, by Walter Benjamin, 7–24. London: Verso.

Sterne, Laurence. 1980. *The Life and Times of Tristram Shandy, Gentleman*. New York: W. W. Norton.

Strathern, Marilyn. 1992. *After Nature: English Kinship in the Late Twentieth Century*. Cambridge: Cambridge University Press.

Tamihere, John. 2000. Maiden speech to Parliament. Electronic document, *www.scoop.co.nz* (accessed 27 August 2003).

Taussig, Michael. 1980. *The Devil and Commodity Fetishism in South America*. Chapel Hill: University of North Carolina Press.

Tawhai, Te Pakaka. 1978. "He Tipuna Wharenui o te Rohe o Uepohatu." MA thesis, Massey University, Palmerston North, New Zealand.

——. 1996. "Aotearoa's Spiritual Heritage." In *Religions of New Zealanders*, 2nd ed., ed. Peter Donovan, 11–19. Palmerston North, New Zealand: Dunmore Press.

Taylor, Charles. 2004. *Modern Social Imaginaries*. Durham, N.C.: Duke University Press.

Taylor, Richard. 1868. *The Past and the Present; or, New Zealand with Its Prospects for the Future*. Wanganui, New Zealand: William Macintosh and Henry Ireson Jones.

Thomas, Allan. 2004. *Music Is Where You Find It: Music in the Town of Hawera, 1946; An Historical Ethnography*. Wellington: Music Books New Zealand.

Thomas, Louis-Vincent. 1958–59. *Les Diola: Essai d'analyse Fonctionelle sur une Population de Basse-Casamance*. Paris: Institut Française d'Afrique Noire.

Touré, Ali Farka. 1996. Sleeve notes to *Radio Mali*. World Circuit CD WC8 044.

Trawick, Margaret. 1990. *Notes on Love in a Tamil Family*. Berkeley: University of California Press.

Turner, Victor. 1967. *The Forest of Symbols: Aspects of Ndembu Ritual*. Ithaca, N.Y.: Cornell University Press.

Twain, Mark. 2003. *A Tramp Abroad*. New York: Modern Library.

Tylor, E. B. 1891. *Primitive Culture: Researches into the Development of Mythology, Philosophy, Religion, Art, and Custom*. 3rd ed. 2 vols. London: J. Murray.

Watts, Jonathan. 2005. "Blood and Coal: The Human Cost of Cheap Chinese Goods." *Guardian*, 14 March.

Weber, Max. 1978. *Economy and Society: An Outline of Interpretive Sociology*, ed. Guenther Roth and Claus Wittich. Berkeley: University of California Press.

Weiner, James. 1991. *The Empty Place: Poetry, Space, and Being among the Foi of Papua New Guinea*. Bloomington: Indiana University Press.

Werfel, Alma Mahler. 1959. *And the Bridge Is Love*. London: Hutchinson.

White, John. 1887. *The Ancient History of the Maori, His Mythology and Traditions*. 2 vols. Wellington: G. Didsbury.

Whitehead, Alfred North. [1920] 1971. *The Concept of Nature*. Cambridge: Cambridge University Press.

Whyte, S. R., et al. 2004. "Treating AIDS: Dilemmas of Unequal Access in Uganda." *Journal of Social Aspects of HIV/AIDS Research Alliance* 1 (1): 14–26.

Wikan, Uni. 2002. *Generous Betrayal: Politics of Culture in the New Europe*. Chicago: University of Chicago Press.

Williams, Herbert W. 1935. "The Reaction of the Maori to the Impact of Civilization." *Journal of the Polynesian Society* 44 (4):216–43.

Winnicott, D. W. 1974. *Playing and Reality*. Harmondsworth, UK: Penguin.

Wordsworth, William. 1960. *The Prelude; or, Growth of a Poet's Mind*. London: Oxford University Press.

Wright, Harrison M. 1959. *New Zealand, 1769–1840: Early Years of Western Contact*. Cambridge: Harvard University Press.

Yate, William. 1835. *An Account of New Zealand*. London: R. B. Seeley and W. Burnside.

Young, Michael. 2004. "United by Its Divisions: The Paradox of Lebanon." *International Herald Tribune*, August 28–29.

Yourcenar, Marguerite. 1997. *Dear Departed: A Memoir*. Trans. Maria Louise Ascher. London: Virago.

Zahan, Dominique. 1979. *The Religion, Spirituality, and Thought of Traditional Africa*. Trans. Kate Ezra Martin and Lawrence M. Martin. Chicago: University of Chicago Press.

Index

Malinowski, Bronislaw: on ethnographic method, 177; on Trobriand spells, 152

Malkki, Liisa, 228–230

Mamet, David: on Arthur Miller, xxv

Maori (Aotearoa/New Zealand), 74–75; and colonialism, 238–253; cosmological beliefs of, 241–242, 248; and genetic engineering, 245–249; and *hau*, 73; and literacy, 239–241; and missionization, 240–241; and myths of birth and death, 203–204; parliament, 228; renaissance, 253; and spirituality, 238–253

Mara, Kenya Fina, 84–94, 264 n.2

Marah, Noah, 18, 48–51, 161–167; on concept of *hake*, 94–95; on moral systems, xviii–xix

Marah, S. B., 58, 103, 118

Marcuse, Herbert, 145, 233

Marginality, 159–161

Marx, Karl, xxvii, 23, 82; on alienation, 126; on phenomenology of labor, 71, 72, 131

Méconnaisance, 177. *See also* Misunderstanding

Memory, and invocation, 81

Merleau-Ponty, Maurice, 190–191

Mining: coal (China), 65–66, 263 n.1; coal (Fifeshire), 78–79; copper (Sweden), 61–65; diamond (Sierra Leone), 102; gold (Brazil), 66–67; marble (Carrara, Tuscany), 68–69; salt (Poland), 65; tin (Bolivia), 67–68

Misunderstanding, 174–177

Montaigne, Michel D.: and skepticism, xxi

Mulgan, John, 217–218

Munch, Edvard, xv–xvi

Nandy, Ashis, 238–239, 269 n.1

Nash, June, 67–68

Nature: Arabic word for, 268 n.11; as borderline phenomena, 148, 152–153; Enlightenment view of, 137; Romantic conception of, 135, 237; as feminine, 137; and God, 136–137; Hellenistic concept of, 137; versus culture, 137, 267 n.3

Ngarinyin (Australia), 69–70

Ngata, Apirana, 254–255

Nuer (Sudan), 205–206

Oakeshott, Michael, 155; on conversation, x; on time, 80

Oedipal myth, 209–210

O'Nell, Theresa DeLeane, 97

Orsi, Robert, 57, 190, 257 n.1

Orwell, George, 61–62

O'Sullivan, Vincent, 216–220

Piaget, Jean: on animism, 70, 71

Plurality, xvii, 28–29, 224, 233–234

Poetic thinking, xii–xiii; and didacticism, xiii; and intersubjectivity, xii; and the rebus, xii; and rhetoric, xiii

Power: paradox of, 57–60, 145–148, 225–226; pastoral, 57; powers that be, 40–60, 178; wild, 147

Praxis: and *poesis*, 23–26, 260 n.1

Psychic unity: of humankind, 157

Pyrrhonism, xv, xxi. *See also* Skepticism

Radical empiricism, xvii, xxv. *See also* James, William

Rasmussen, Knud: on Iglulik Eskimo, xxii–xxiv

Read, Kenneth, 224–225

Michael Jackson

is Distinguished Visiting Professor in World Religions at Harvard Divinity
School. He is the author of several books including *In Sierra Leone* (2004)
and *At Home in the World* (1995).

Library of Congress Cataloging-in-Publication Data
Jackson, Michael, 1940–
Excursions / Michael Jackson.
p. cm.
Includes bibliographical references and index.
ISBN 978-0-8223-4054-6 (cloth : alk. paper)
ISBN 978-0-8223-4075-1 (pbk. : alk. paper)
1. Philosophy, Modern—20th century. 2. Intellectual life—20th century.
I. Title.
B804.J151   2007
128—dc22   2007016096

210 - governmentality Foucault

221 - identity as manichaean
    - either or

222 - Anth - as systematic implementation of
    of the impulse to open up dialogues w/ others

230 - identical structures of experience

234 - identity + category words as illusions
    unrepresentative of 'cultures'

248 @ situational v. culturally motivated)

249 - pragmatism

253 - trouble w/ generalizations.

important pages

25 - agency & praxis, Foucault & Arendt

look up antinomian   p. 54

62 - lifeworlds - munares in situ ?

70 - gap bet percept & concept.

57 - the 3 welts

77 - Stones, connectas

81 phenomenolog. past

84 - evoking Buthlih

100 - mortality vs. habitus

131 - labor action & existential will

175. - paradox of power

150 - direct action & strategic murder

⊗ 176 - Scholastic Fallacies Bourdieu
                dépassemen & mortality.

198 - chan of coincidences

200-203 - discussion of mortality.

205 - evans-pritchard Nuer